The Book of God

HE BOOK OF GOD.

𝔗𝔥𝔢 𝔄𝔭𝔬𝔠𝔞𝔩𝔶𝔭𝔰𝔢
of
𝔄𝔡𝔞𝔪=𝔒𝔞𝔫𝔫𝔢𝔰.

BY

E. V. KENEALY, LL.D., Q.C.

אורה אתכם ביד־אל
אשר עם־שרי לא אכחד

I will teach you by the hand of God ;
That which is with the ALMIGHTY ONES will I not conceal.

JOB XXVII., II., 10.

LONDON:
REEVES & TURNER, 238, STRAND.

LONDON,
PRINTED BY S AND J BRAWN, 13, PRINCES ST, LITTLE QUIEN-ST, W.C.

CONTENTS.

CONTENTS.

THE APOCALYPSE.

In the Name of the God of Truth,

The Lord of Light—the Lord of the Universe ;
Who framed the Kosmos of innumerable spheres ;
From whom cometh all that is beautiful :
The Creator and the Sovereign Ruler,
The Father and the Judge ;
The Eternal Fire who is alone in the Orb of Circles ;—
Who first gave form to the Elements,
The stars, the firmament, the shining planets,
The sun and comets, rapid in their wandering flight ;
The lightnings which are his quick sceptre ;
The whirlwinds, the luminous expanse ;—
Who fabricated the earths in choirs innumerable,
And made them to be the habitation of life :
And from the essential energy of the material and imma-
    terial,
Made spirits manifest in soul and body.
In His Name—the Name of the Most High God,
I deliver unto the Earth this Book ;
That it may be an Everlasting Testament through Time
    everlasting
Of the whole duty of Man

This is the Book of Light .
This is the Book of the Children of Heaven .
Which God hath graven in fire
On the stupendous pillars of the Universe.
Let no man approach unto it.
Whose soul is not pure ·

Let no man touch it with his hand,
Who hath a thought of sin within his heart.
Let no man gainsay its words—
They are the Words of Truth the most Ancient.
There is but One only God—
This is His Book :
There is but One only Heaven— ·
This is its law.
The Heavens and the Earths inhabited by spirits,
The myriad-folded hearts of men ;—
Behold, they shall bear witness unto its verity.
In the face of death and desolation.
O Sons of men ! know this—
That in this book which now I hold,
The law of Truth is opened :
The Light of Heaven is unveiled.
Like the Everlasting Universe of the Lord of Beauty,
It comprehendeth all.
It is the First and the Last
Of things recorded.

O God ! give unto thy sons.
The brightness of thy Spirit .
That they may read, know, and understand
O God ! give unto thy sons
The illumination of thy Wisdom ,
That they may believe thine heavenly precepts.
From all evil guard us, O God !
That our intellects may be calm and holy,
While meditating on thy Holy Word.

THE LIFTING OF THE VEIL.

———◇———

In the name of the Most Holy One.

I stood in spirit before the Thrones of God,
I moved in light before the Supreme ;
His brows were lost amid the infinite,
His feet were resting on the sun.
The Heavens were before Him like a carpet spread ;
And He was clothed in the flame of lightnings .
Darkness and mysterious Silence,
Were round, and over, and before the Lord
He was alone in light—
Alone in a far off sphere
Alone—alone, and no created essence
Shared the mystery of darkness with the Supreme.
And all the Powers, and all the Princes,

B

And all the blessèd Spirits of the Universe ;
And all the mighty Energies and Essences ;
Were before the Thrones of God.
And they hymned to Him in the measure of the stars ;
And in the ever-moving radiance of the globe of elements;
They rejoiced in the splendours of His essence ;
In the emanating loveliness of the Lord.
And a Voice came forth from the place,
A Voice from the place wherein the Thrones were ;
A Voice of deep thunder and eternal melody ;
Bright as lightning, softly-sweet as if a flute breathed.
It was the Voice of God himself,
I knew it—and my spirit knew it in the spirit :
The everlasting Voice of the Father, and the King,
Who speaks, and the Universe is still.
And the Voice said : Son of Man !
And I answered, Behold, I am here ;
And the Voice said, I am the Lord thy God who made
      thee,
And breathed my flame into thy breast.
I sent thee upon the earth to preach to earth,
The words of Truth and Light and Wisdom ;
To develop ancient holiness ;
To reveal the things that I made manifest —
I bore thee on the lightnings of the sun,
Where the morning walks in glory ;
I wafted thee on the wings of cherubim
Where the stars set in the evening hour ,
I lifted up the Veils of Mystery,
Opening unto thine eye many secrets

And placed my thunders in thine hand of fire,
To smite the fanes of superstition.
And now, answer thou me and say,
Whether thou hast fulfilled thy solemn work?
Whether thou hast cast down one stone
From the gloomy fabrics of the universe?
Then the Voice ceased, and there was silence;
A silence that pierced my soul;
An awful stillness came upon my spirit;
I stood abashed, and downcast and afraid.
And in a little while the Voice again spake,
Saying unto me, Son of Man!
And I answered, Behold I am here:
And the Voice said, Answer thou me.
And I fell down prostrate before the Thrones;
The coldness of death smote me, through and through.
And the awe of that mysterious Silence
Froze the spirit within my soul.
Meaner than a worm, am I, O Holy One;
An abject sinner loaded with his sins,
I have strayed in clouds of darkness;
I have walked in vanity and death;
I have wandered away from the straight path
In which I should have paced with Thee,
And, formed out of dust and clouds and ashes,
I have followed after dust and ashes, and decay
Earth and the things of Earth, O Lord!
Have led my spirit from Thee;
I have been deaf to the Voice of God,
Which spake within my troubled soul.

Upon that which is perishable, did I fix mine heart ;
Upon that which passes away for ever ;
But upon Thee, the Eternal and the Everlasting King,
Little did I repose my wandering thought.
Yet now, O Lord, and now will I awaken,
And now will I pour out my voice ;
Depart thou, from me, O my foolishness !
Henceforth I am the servant of the Most High.
And while I spake, I remained prostrate,
For the mystery of God was upon me like a mountain ,
A deep and all-subduing Awe ;
The shadow of a death-like swoon
And there was a sound of music in the Heavens,
A soft and sacred harmony ;
And the Powers in the far-off distance,
Hymned sweetly upon golden instruments :
And a light like that of the purple ruby,
Descended slowly above my head ,
Covering me over as if with a crown of splendours,
Like a rainbow arching the ocean.
And as I lay I heard a trumpet sound
A wild and solitary blast ;
Then my spirit shook,
As if a thunderbolt had riven it in twain
A whirlpool of light snatched me upward ;
A flashing vortex of quivering flame ,
And all the brightness of the universe
Surrounded me with glittering colours
God himself, the Infinite, the All-Powerful.
Lifted me among the fiery substance of the stars ,

THE LIFTING OF THE VEIL.

I saw the sun in his grandeur ;
The planetary choirs danced around him.
The morning with its varied tints of beauty,
Illuminated the golden arches ;
And the seven pure rivers of the Celestial
Flowed and sparkled in sunny light.
I saw in them, the Author of Nature,
The divine resplendent God of Heaven ;
Whose presence is as the warmth of vernal summer ;
Who is the Tree of Life growing in Paradise.
As the moon accompanies the traveller
In his lonely walk in the midnight hour ;
She cheers him with her soft light ;
She seems to glide in beauty by his side :
Yet is she still unmoved and far away,
Throned in the depths of the firmament ;
Even so did God lead me,
Upward and on into the broad heavens
I saw Him not, but yet I knew Him ;
I beheld not His majestic Image :
He was far away in His Own Sphere ;
The Central Glory of the Divine Presence.
Like the shifting beauty of the heaven
Whose face is varied with new splendour ;
Purple and white, and rose and silver ;
The deep intense also of night's starry fires ;—
Even so is the ever-flashing face of God
As it moved before me in a glimpse ;
Yet was it but as a fleeting dream,
Wherein He glittered, yet concealed himself.

And as I was borne along in fire,
I saw a splendid Angel of the Sun ;
He poured forth his voice,
And this was the burden of his speech.
Hail thou who art PARASU RAMA,
In the golden plains of beauty ;
The chosen child of lightning and of truth ,
Long have I looked for thine arrival.
Hail thou who art IMAUM MAHIDI,
Fiery-cinctured by the Word of Heaven :
Long have I looked forth from the mountains,
To behold the sunlight of thine advent.
Now ascendest thou,
Unto the Pillars of God whereon the Universe is sus-
    pended,
Enveloped in the dark lightnings,
And in the quickly rolling thunders of his flame.
To the silent Waters from whose deep Abysses
These lofty Pillars rise ;
Darkness broods above their awful bosoms ;
And many a great Spirit guides their far-extended strength;
And into the Mountains from whose recesses
These ocean waters flow :
And into the Winds in whose embrace they rest,
Smaller than the motes in a sunbeam.
And into the still, the solemn Whirlwind,
From whose least breath these Winds are born ;
The Whirlwind whose place is afar off,
In the arms of the all-sustaining God.
These Pillars are called the True ;

And these Waters are called the Ancient;
And these Mountains are called the Strong;
And these Winds are called the Everlasting;—
Therein shalt thou be made a witness of the Truth,
And of the Sacred Light, which is the breath of God:
Therein shall the Mysteries of the Universe
Be uncurtained before thy rapt gaze.

Then the lightnings flashed,
And the thunders answered the lightnings;
And the Angel of the Sun departed;
And I wended onward in my flight.
I saw the stars which no eye on earth beholds,
Glittering in their golden zones of light;
Beautiful they were, and of rapid dance;
Inconceivable, and to be paralleled only by the thought.
The magnitude of their dark circles
Was beyond all the imagination of man;
The seven-rayed spheres of solar light were there,
But only God could span their mighty orbits.
Like walls of glittering gold and beryl,
The firmament extended itself in the far distance;
And veiled in deepest night and flame and star,
I saw the everlasting seat of God's splendour.
Folded in beams of light were the Spirits of Heaven,
Beautiful as flowers resting in the sunshine;
There was no revolution of day or night,
But the perpetual glory of God illuminated all.
Hear me, O ye Spheres of Beauty,
Hearken unto me, O ye Children of Paradise,

And thou, O Time, everlasting image of Eternity,
And thou, O Earth, bow down thine ears ;
For now was opened unto me the boundless majesty,
The vast stupendous nature of the Universe ,
The fiery splendour of the heavens and the suns that roll
    for ever,
The far-extended earths, and oceanic globes.
In light—in fire—in mist—in flame,
I moved, as floating on the sunbeams,
Breathless in seraphic trance ;
The coursers of the morning bare me.
What gleam—what glory bursts afar ?
What Splendour couching in the sun ?
She rose—she smiled—she stood unveiled—
I looked—and I beheld All.

DEFINITIONS, ETC.

APOCALYPSE—a Revelation; an uplifting of the Veil, which separates the Invisible from the Visible.

ARK, a mystic name for the Holy Spirit. Parkhurst in his Greek Lexicon, though he has entirely omitted it in the Hebrew, where it ought to be found, says "Ἀρχη in this application answers to the Hebrew ראשית *rasit*, or Wisdom; and what word could be so proper as that which in the language of the Western world was unknown, but which had the meaning of the emblem of the female generative power, the Arg or Arca, in which the germ of all nature was supposed to float or brood on the great abyss, during the interval which took place after every mundane cycle?" This was the vessel or symbolic boat-shaped ark or cup, which we find everywhere in the Sacred Mysteries under different names in Greece, Egypt, India, Judæa, &c., and on whose misunderstood symbolism, Faber has raised one of the most extraordinary structures of erudition and folly that the world has ever seen—I mean his literal interpretation of the Arkite mythos in Genesis. The navi-form Argha of the Mysteries alluded solely under an expressive type to the Holy Spirit—the Queen of Heaven; the Great Mother of all existences; and from her the *nave* in our churches and in all the ancient temples was denominated, that nave being one of the most sacred parts of the fane. For the sake of the unlearned, I add that nave comes from the Latin word *navis*, a ship. Thus the Holy Spirit was the Ship of Life which bore over the vast Ocean of the Infinite, the germs of all being: and God was the ruling Force And the Moon in her crescent or boat-like shape thus became one of the emblems of the Holy Spirit. The crescent which every true Islâmite wears, and the same symbol throughout Hindostan, alludes to the Holy Spirit, who was an essential part of the true

B 3

Arabic faith as preached by Mohammed, though by his followers
it has been wholly ignored. The mystic word ALM, which that
Great Prophet prefixed to many chapters of the Korân, and
which no commentator has ever been able to explain, alludes to
her, the *Alm* or Immaculate Virgin of the Supreme Heavens. It
signifies also AL, God, and M. 600, which covertly refers to a
secret cycle of the most high importance, which the reader
will find explained in this work. Timæus, the Locrian,
alluding to the Holy Spirit under her mystical name of *Arka*,
calls her 'Αρχὰ των ἀρίστων, or the *Principle of best things.*
The word *arcane* or *secret* is derived from this, and covertly
alludes also to its symbolic meaning. To no one is the *Arcane*
exhibited, says the *Codex Nazaræus*, (a volume of great antiquity),
except to the Most Great and Most High, who alone knows and
doth discern all things   Pausanias relates that Æsculapius, which
was a symbolic name for the Messiah, was called Archagetas, which
he translates *the primæval divinity,* but wrongly, for it means,
born of the Archa. What the Greek sage called το αρχαιον
χαος, alluded mystically and mysteriously to this ark, for
χαος and χαως, was αω, and σαω, *I save,* with the X or sacred
cross at the beginning; and this X was also the Greek monogram
for 600.   Jablonski says ; Ιω, *Ioh, Ægyptus* LUNAM *significat,
neque habent illi in communi sermonis usu, aliud nomen quo Lunam
designent præter Io*   Io in the Egyptian signifies the Moon, &c.
Eustathius declares that Io signifies the Moon in the dialect of
the Arg-ians.   In Cambodia, this Divine Spirit is adored as the
Soul of the Universe, under the name of ON-AO, and the chief
temple of the empire is erected in her honour   *Cunctorum dicas
supremum numen Iao,* says Macrobius, citing the oracle of Apollo
Clarius, I. *Saturnal.* Throughout the Apocalypse God and the
Holy Spirit are called AO. The pillar and the circle IO allude
mystically to this, and constitute 10, the perfect number. *Arka*
in Javanese, according to Sir S. Raffles, means the Sun   In connection with this he mentions a celebrated sacred poem which
they have called *Kûn da,* or *Kûn-dina*—this he declines giving
It is probably like the Song of Solomon, or the Geeta-Govinda.
This poem he says is also called *Pepa-Kam .* this is Pi-Akm, *The
Wisdom,* it also means *The Father and the Goddess of Love.* The
whole alludes to the Sacred Spirit of Heaven.

AVATAR—a descent of the Messiah-Angel in his due cycle:
sometimes, but improperly called a Theopany.

BEAUTY—the Beautiful : the perfection to which every Existence should aspire.

BETH בַּיִת A house: thus Elisa-beth is the house of Elisa. In some countries pronounced Bat, Bad, Abad. Baal-bec is supposed to have been really named Baal-beth. In the Welsh, Bett-Ys, is the Place of Fire. As Aleph, the first letter of the Hebrews meant the God of Fire, so Beth, the second letter, meant his House; and AB meant All.

BIRTH—the re-appearance of a Spirit in some new form, within our circle of existence. Death, its disappearance and palingenesis into another circle, after an interval in *Hades* or the Invisible.

BLOOD—a symbolic name for Truth, true Religion.

BODY—a material covering, or means of manifestation, for those orders of existence whose nature confines them to material spheres. Angels and Spirits consist of two natures, spirit and soul. Men consist of spirit, soul and body: the lower existences consist only of soul and body. Man is inferior to Spirits and Angels because he has a body: but is superior to all below him, for they are without spirit.

CHERUBIM כְּרוּבִים—Oxen, that is, heavenly beings, bright with solar splendours; creatures lustrous as the sun himself Three orders of them are mentioned in the Apocalypse: the highest with eight wings, the next in rank with six, the lowest with four wings. They are mentioned in Genesis iii 24, attended by *a flaming fire turning upon itself*, which is the true version.

DAY OF JUDGMENT—the period after death, when the animating principle assumes its new condition of being.

DEATH—is any change from one condition of existence to another. It is the same as birth. The animating principle dies as to one mode of manifesting its power, and is born anew in some other. Spirits and Souls have existed from an immemorial time; and every new birth is but a new manifestation of an animating principle which has been in action for millions of years, and has transmigrated through innumerable orders of life When the animating principle passes out of any form it goes into some other form as nearly as possible in harmony with its true nature. Thus a man may remain a man for ever. no better and no worse.

ESSENCE—the vital and immortal energy in things. It is distinguished from the visible or the corporeal.

ETERNITY—is that which never has had beginning and never will have end. It is the state of God alone, and is peculiarly connected with the Supreme.

EVERLASTING—is that which has had beginning, but never will have an end. It is the attribute of the Holy Spirit, and of all spirit-existences.

FINAL DAY—the end of the *Kalpa*, or allotted period during which a sphere like the earth undergoes not change or revolution.

GOD—the Almighty and Supreme Father, sometimes applied to the Holy Spirit, but not correctly, for She is only His regent or representative · sometimes in a lower sense to a divine nature, as a god.

GODS—all divine natures that exist below God, and the Holy Spirit.

HEAVEN—the place in which God actually manifests his presence to the Spirits who inhabit it. HELL—every place in which that presence is not actually beheld. Thus this earth is in reality a Hell, because God is not manifested there ; and it would be absolutely a place of misery if the Sun and Light, which are shadows of the presence of God, did not shine upon it. God manifests his Presence in various gradations of splendour, according to the sphere on which he shines; according to the knowledge and virtue in each sphere, so is His Light. Irrationality and utter darkness constitute the lowest hell : a chaos of confused and frantic existence, never blest with a ray of light.

IMMORTALITY—is an attribute of souls ; as health and vigour are of bodies : it is that enduring principle of life which we see in all living things.

INFINITY—as to place, is the co-relative of Eternity as to duration. As the latter has neither beginning nor ending, so also Infinity has no limit. God may therefore be truly defined as the Eternal-Infinite.

LAPSE—is the fall of one of the high Spirit-existences into a lower condition of an existence of the same nature, as where a celestial lapses into a sub-celestial. RISE—is the opposite of this, as where a Celestial ascends to the condition of a Supra-Celestial.

LOGOS—is a word with three meanings. First the Holy Spirit, the first Word that God spake, and consequently the first of his created Essences. Second, the Universe, which He next formed Third, the Messenger from God to Man, who proclaims the celestial Word or Revelation.

M—a letter peculiarly sacred in all languages and all religions : it is a symbol of waves or waters Ⰼ. M final, in the Eastern languages, means 600 It is the monogram of Maya, Maia, Mary, Minerva, Mercury, Manu (the anagram of πνευμα, or Pneuma, Numa), Messias, Μητις, or *Divine Wisdom* Mimra, *the Word*, Matrix, Mater, Mamma, Mas (*the Male*) Mihr (commonly called *Mithras*) the Monad, Mystery , and an immense variety of words which bear those refined and subtle meanings familiar to every student in theology. All letters are mystic : this is pre-eminently so.

MESSIAH—a Messenger of God · a divinely-sent Spirit who preaches Truth to mortals. The Saviour, because he announces tidings of salvation, and points out the way that leads to Light. A man in all respects while he sojourns on earth not exempt from human error, except in his teachings, which are infallible

METASOMATOSIS—is the transmigration from one body into another; as where the nature of a murderous human being passes into the manifestation of a hyena ; or the nature of an elephant ascends into the manifestation of a Man.

METEMPSYCHOSIS—is the transmigration of a spirit-existence into a lower order of life, to which its desires incline it. It then becomes connected with soul.

MYSTERY—a holy but ineffable truth, to be pondered upon in the mind, rather than communicated in words.

MYTHOLOGY—a representation of sacred truths, under the guise of Fable, Symbol, or Parable.

PALINGENESIS—regeneration, or new birth ; the first condition of an existence in an altered form of life. It applies equally to metasomatosis and metempsychosis.

PAN—the All, used indiscriminately in ancient Mythology to signify God, and the all-pervading Spirit. As sylvan Pan, it means the Messiah , or Messenger of God. This word consists of *three* letters, which is a mystical allusion

PARADISE—a Garden in Heaven, to which Celestial Spirits, on their ascent from the terrestrial sphere, are *first* admitted. Paradise is thus described in the Brahmin theology. Round about the Mountain stand seven ladders, by which you ascend a spacious plain in the middle whereof is a bell of silver, and a square table surrounded with nine precious stones of beautiful colours. Upon the table lies a Silver Rose, called *Tamara Pua*, which contains the images of two Women as bright and fair as a pearl ; but these two are only One, though appearing as if distinct according to the medium, celestial or terrestrial, through which they are viewed In the first aspect she is called Briga Siri, the Lady of the Mouth: in the other Tara-Siri the Lady of the Tongue—or the Spirit of Tongues. In the centre of this Silver Rose, God, has his permanent residence.

REVELATION—an inspired doctrine received from God by one of the Messiah-angels, and by him published to mankind

SATAN—a symbolic name for that which is vicious an allegorical personification of moral evil. Not a being—but a symbol.

SAN—Son, Azan, Azon, As-On, the Fiery Sun, Gr. $Z\eta\nu$. Hesychius says that the Sun was called Saos the Saviour by the Babylonians. He was called Zauan by the Sidonians. In India Hercules was called Ador-San, the Lord of Light He was adored in Temples called Zaanim. Princes in Greece were styled Zanides, or sons of Zan. Places peculiarly sacred were called San-Sanna. It is the first syllable of Sanctus. The Etruscan name for Italy was Au-soni-ya Some of the ancients taught that the soul and spirit were divine emanations from the Sun. hence Macrobius tells us that they called the spirit, Zoan—a living thing. Zion is another form of this. Za implies greatness Zan har in the Madagascar language means God ; Har is the Hindu Heri, or Sovereign. Sin, Sen, a cycle Sol-Sin, a year. Punico-Maltese, Sena, a year. Snin, the seasons. Irish, Soinn. Heb. and Chald , Sena, a year.

SERAPHIM—שְׂרָפִים Fiery Winged Serpents , that is Archangels of the most transcendent glory , flame like in splendour and majesty, which live in the presence of the Serpent of Eternity—GOD. The word Cherub also meant Serpent. It is a compound word, formed of כר kr. circle, and אוב aub. serpent—a Serpent in a Circle.

SHEKINAH—a mystic word, often typified as a Rose, a floral wreath, a Lotus, an Egg, or any oval emblem, a Dove, a Boat, the Ocean, the Moon, a Virgin, a wheel, a nimbus of splendours, a golden crown, &c. God, when He meditates on Divine Beauty, is said to be One : but when He creates to be Bi-Une. The Syrians symbolized this communion by their image of Ad-Ad, the Sun-Father, shooting down his splendid rays towards the Earth, while she sent forth rays of splendour upward that met and mingled with his beams This word has an affinity to the Indian Yoni Calli, is the Hindu name of the Holy Spirit In the Mexican language it means the House, or Tabernacle of God

SHM, Shem, שם—the Sun. This is the Mexican god Chemin.

As a name of the Sun, says Parkhurst, it came to denote the Trinity. It also means *to place in order with great care*, and *to make waste and utterly desolate:* herein exhibiting the Generator and the Destroyer. It meant also an *Onion*, On-Ion, from the regular disposition of the involucra, or integuments, thus symbolizing the Universe. An onion was considered to be αιων των αιωνων· and the word Oannes bare a mystical allusion to this, in its signification of the divine Messenger, who appeared in his cycles or ages. Shamen, Shemesh שמש, שמן, are words relating to the heavens and the Sun. Baal Shamen is Lord of the Heaven. Shema-El, the heavenly brightness of God; by the Greeks changed into Semele; the mother of Bacchus, which was a Messianic name. Assyria was called Shems and Shams, because of the sun-worship prevalent there. The Ethiopians pronounced the word Zam and Tzam. Sons of Shem means Sons of Heaven, a name appropriated of old by the true believers in God's unity. In India *Suna* is god of the sky : *Saon* of Samothrace, is son of Zeus· he is the Saviour. *Iasion* is son of Jupiter, or God. *Azon* or the Sun, in Hebrew, Vedic Suna, Gothic Sunna, German Sonne, Spartan Asana, Greek Zan, Assyrian San, Hebrew Shanah, Sion, Zion, Shanskrit Ahan or Day, Shan in Tartar and Chinese, Sun and Son in English, are all cognate words expressing the same idea.

SON OF MAN—a title given to the Divine Messenger or Incarnation, who, if he were not born of a mortal, could not live or move in a terrestial sphere. He is called also a king of men.

SOUL—an animating essence, which includes all existences from man downwards, to the least one which has life. It is of the same nature as the Spirit, although inferior to it, for the Spirit is an actual portion of the Fire of God. The Spirit never can die ; but it is possible for the soul by long continued conjunction with body to reduce itself finally to a mere point in life. To prevent this, God has imbued it with an aspiring energy which ever lifts it from the clay to its original Fire-fountain.

SPHERE—an inhabited orb like the earth.

SPIRIT—An immortal essence and energy which includes all existences from man upwards through the manifold degrees that lead to the Supreme. Its lowest development is in human beings In seven high orders of beings it exists without soul; in the three lowest orders with soul Josephus, *Antiq. Jud* lib. i, cap. i, sect. 2, thus speaks of the soul given by God to man : Και πνευμα ενηκεν αυτω και ψυχήν. He placed in him a spirit and a soul. See *post*, page 189.

SUPRA-CELESTIAL--the home of God and the Holy Spirit. CELESTIAL—the permanent home of Spirits next in order. SUB-CELESTIAL—the angelic spheres. TERRESTIAL—the spheres of matter.

THE HOLY SPIRIT—the second Great Being of the Universe : the Great Mother, Nature: called also Providence ; *Perem-Atma ; Anima Mundi* : the Queen of Heaven.

THE WORLD—the same as the Universe : called also the Kosmos from its beauty and order.

TRINITY—the three Essences which constitute the All of existence : one in quality ; innumerable in development God is like a Tree which out of one sap produces all the fruits and flowers in the Universe He is in all ; all are in him.

TSAR and Zar—צר a rock. As temples were erected on rocks these eminences were called Sar-On, from the Deity, in whose honour they were built. The term Sar was always used as a mark of high honour. Thus God is called the rock of refuge, the rock of salvation : and Jesus addressing Peter, says, On this rock I will build my church. (*Matt.* xvi , 18) In compound words it denotes respect, as *Sar*-danapalus ; Nebuchadonnezar. High groves, or rather hills, with woods of antient oak, were named Tsaron, because they were sacred to On Lilius Gyraldus calls Saron, the God of the Sea Diana was named Saronia and Sar-Ait · and in the religious feasts called Saronia Sacra, Orus, the Messiah, was said to have been born. Diodorus Siculus speaking of the Druids of Gaul, styles them'philosophers, theologians, men held in supreme honour, whom they designated Saronides. Oaks were called by the same name. Æsar ، and Kaisar are from this root

VIRTUE—the condition of that existence, which employs all its time in the acquisition of knowledge and the diffusion of good among others, from the mere delight which it finds in both.

WINE—a symbolic name for truth, and true religion.

𝔗𝔥𝔢 𝔅𝔬𝔬𝔨 𝔬𝔣 𝔊𝔬𝔡.

BOOK I.

1. In the SACRED APOCALYPSE, which here follows, certain great and leading principles of the primeval the-ology, are alluded to, which require to be explained. They belong to a system of heavenly polity, or the religious government of God over man, in which the most pro-found wisdom, and the most universal benevolence were alike displayed. It is not intended that any other than a very cursory sketch of these principles shall be given in this Essay : to expound them at length, and with the copiousness of elucidation which they might receive from history and mythology, profane as well as sacred, would fill volumes, and they would even then have failed to be illustrated by all the light which they deserve. Those who are interested in such subjects will be assisted in working them out for themselves by the hints herein offered, and the authorities herein cited. Those who have

not time to do so, will probably rest content with the brief notices that are presented in the following pages. May the Sacred Light illuminate all who read them.

2. The student who devotes himself to themes of this high nature, will do well to bear in mind, the words of one, who was well capable of raising his sublime intellect to the most exalted purposes, but who was so misled by worldly shows that he sacrificed God and Heaven to the merest phantoms, and reaped what all such sowers reap, a life of sorrow, disappointment, and disgrace. Holy mysteries, says Lord Bacon, must be studied with this caution, that the mind for its module be dilated to *the amplitude of the mysteries*, and not the mysteries be straightened and girt into the narrow compass of the mind. And if this Essay be studied with this august spirit, I believe that every man who masters it will recognise its truths, with the most supreme advantage to himself, both in this life, and the more important life that is to follow.

3. It was the belief of ancient men, that God (AB) (1) was the Parent of all peoples, and that He felt the most tender love and paternal sympathy for the various races that He had formed : they held also that for their more effectual knowledge of Him, and of the way that led to Him, God gave Revelations, which contained the Laws, the Maxims, and the Truths, which practically adopted in their lives on earth, would ensure to all a state of future happiness in heaven. They believed that God was One Supreme and Splendid Being; eternal in nature; spiritual in essence; wise, pure, beneficent, and just; that He pervaded all places, and extended through all Infinity; but that the Thrones of his magnificence, were

more especially exalted in the supercelestial regions of Divine Light, to which none but the most wise and hallowed Spirits could ascend : and that a great portion of the ineffable felicity of the All-Father, consisted in the innocent enjoyments of the virtuous and loving creations on whom He had bestowed existence.

4. The Hindu sages, who from the most early period, have promulgated ideas of the Supreme Creator far more sublime than any to which Europe has been accustomed, acknowledged and developed this truth in their proverbial phrase—*One Brahm without a second;* and the Greek philosophers who borrowed whatever was good in their science from the East, while they did all they could to poison it by an infusion of their own shallow speculations, adapted the Hindu axiom into their language under the form of Ἑν το Παν—*The One who is All :*—a divine creed which modern religionists entirely ignore : but which is nevertheless the one great actual fact in the Universe.

5. God, though One, the ancients did not suppose, as modern ascetics do, to be alone in solitary and morose magnificence. They did not make of Him a monk, or a gloomy anchorite secluded in the inaccessible silence of the spheres. Albeit none could share with HIM, the glory and surpassing majesty of the supreme heaven, they declared nevertheless that He was perpetually surrounded by other gods of light, beauty, purity, and divineness : immortal in their essence, for it emanated from the Most High; but all proceeding in fiery stream from Him; and all alike dependent upon His laws, as they were encompassed by His love. Chief among these—pre-eminent in wisdom, loveliness, and all that is essentially celestial and most

pure, they held one Divine Nature to be ; and this Nature they called the Spirit of God—the Dove, the Holy and Divine Spirit of love the most divine.

6. The golden fancy of the Past exhausted itself in describing the matchless glory of this exalted Being. She was the Virgin-Spirit of most ineffable loveliness ; the Logos, the Protogonos : the *Mimra-Daya* מימרא יד׳, or Word of God, by whose intermediate agency the whole spiritual and material Universe, was developed, fashioned, beautified and preserved. She was the Astræan Maid of purest light, clothed in the sun, and mantled in the shining stars : the moon and silver spheres of heaven were beneath her feet : she was crowned with all the brightness, majesty, and knowledge, that her Celestial Essence merited or required. She was the Minokhired and Mayu-Khratû, or Divine Intelligence of the Zoroastrian and the Zend. She was the *Shekinah* שכינה, of the Jew, in whose shining, central, circumambient flower-like glory, God was wont to manifest His presence when He created : she was the Eros or Divine Love which impregnated by heaven, produces all things. Under the congenial symbol of the *Dove* (2), she became the national ensign of the greatest empires ; on whose coins she was at one time imaged as that bird of love, standing on a globe (the Universe) with pinions closed, and with a glory of sunbeams round the head ; at another, sitting on the sphere with wings displayed, as if she brooded over it, while the blaze of sunbeams spread behind the whole, until they terminated in a shining starry circle. The Spirit of God, says the Talmud (*Chagiga*), hovered over the waters like a Dove which spreads her wings over her young ; and her benignant energy was thus symbolized.

In China she is represented as Kûnwyn, the dove-like Goddess of Mercy, riding on a dolphin in a *troubled sea,* distributing acts of grace, and exhibiting her power to save. *Kûn* is a mystic word, and has the meaning of Shekinah ; the exquisite and celestial Rose of Beauty joined on to the prolific stem. She was the zodiacal sign Virgo, who bare an ear of corn, emblematic of her productive powers, and a lovely babe, her offspring or Incarnation : she was Venus Urania or Heavenly Beauty, whose every look and thought were hallowed in the all-hallowing light of the Supreme Lord. She was Vesta symbolized by Fire, the electric or magnetic flame which is the Life diffused throughout the Universe : and was defined by one of the early theologues to be the Celestial Soul, *the Fountain and Source of all other souls ;* the best and the most wise ; the producing Power who obeys the will of the great Creator, God, and promptly executes His bidding. She was the *Ceres Mammosa,* or all-fruitful ; and like Isis, which in the Old Egyptian means *The Antient,* as her husband Osiris means the All-Seeing, the Almighty-One, she was denominated and adored as *Altrix nostra* ; the nurse of man, and indeed of all existences. *I called upon God,* says Solomon (vii. 7), *and the Spirit of Wisdom came to me. I preferred her before sceptres and thrones, and esteemed riches nothing in comparison of her : neither compared I unto her any precious stone, because all gold in respect of her is as a little sand : and silver shall be counted as clay before her. I loved her above health and beauty, and chose to have her instead of light ; for the light that cometh from her never goeth out. All good things together came to me with her, and innumerable riches in her hand. * * For she is a treasure unto* *men that never faileth; which they that use become the friends of God, being commended for the gifts that come from learning. * * Wisdom, the mother of all things, taught me; for in her is an understanding spirit, holy, one only, manifold, subtil, lively, clear, undefiled, plain, not subject to hurt, loving the thing that is good, quick, which cannot be letted, ready to do good, kind to man, stedfast, sure, free from care, having all power, overseeing all things, and going through all understanding, pure and most subtil spirits. For Wisdom is more moving than any motion: she passeth and goeth through all things by reason of her pureness. For she is the breath of the power of God, and a pure influence flowing from the glory of the Almighty: therefore can no defiled thing fall into her. For she is the brightness of the Everlasting Light, the unspotted mirrour of the power of God, and the Image of his goodness. And being but one, she can do all things: and remaining in herself, she maketh all things new: and in all ages entering into holy souls, she maketh them friends of God, and prophets. For God loveth none, but him that dwelleth with Wisdom. For she is more beautiful than the sun, and above all the order of the stars: being compared with the light, she is found before it. For after this cometh night: but vice shall not prevail against Wisdom.* The Universe, says an early writer, hath a Ruler set over it; the Logos or Word: the fabricating Spirit which is its Queen: *this is the First Power after the* ONE: ungenerated, incomprehensible, inclining and dependent on Him, and ruling over all things which *He* created; the faultless genuine Emanation of the All-perfect. So in the Indian Purana shown by Mr. Halhed to Mr. Maurice, the Spirit whose essence is eternal, one and self existent, is represented as in the first place giving birth to a certain pure æthereal LIGHT—a *Light* not perceptible to the elementary sense, but extracted from the all-comprehensive essence of his own perfections. *Hist. of Hindostan*, i. 64. There is, says Pindar in his sixth Nemæan Ode, one kind both of divine beings and of men; and both draw breath from the same *Mother*. The Platonist Apuleius (*Metam.* xi.), introduces her thus sublimely describing herself; and there can be no doubt that when he was initiated into the Greater Mysteries, he was taught the truths which I now reveal. Behold, Lucius, I, moved by thy prayers, am present with thee; I, who am Nature, the Parent of all things, the Queen of all the elements, the primordial progeny of the Eternal, the Supreme of Divinities, the sovereign of the spirits of the dead, the first of the celestials, and the uniform resemblance of gods and goddesses. I who rule by my nod the luminous summits of the heavens, the salubrious breezes of the sea, and the mournful silences of the realms beneath; and whose one divinity the whole orb of the earth venerates under a manifold form, by different rites, and a variety of appellations. Hence the primogenial Phrygians call me Pessinuntia, the mother of the gods; the Attic Aborigines, Cecropian Minerva; the floating Cyprians, Paphian Venus; the arrow-bearing Cretans, Diana Dictynna; the three-tongued Sicilians, Stygian Proserpine; and the Eleusinians, the ancient goddess Ceres. Some also call me Juno, others Bellona, others Hecate, and others Rhamnusia. And those who are illuminated by the incipient rays of that divinity, the sun, when he rises, the Ethiopian, the Arii, and Egyptians skilled in ancient learning, worshipping me by ceremonies perfectly appropriate, call me by my true name, Queen Isis.

7. Virgil when he conducts his hero to the Elysian Fields, and faintly limns the secret of the Mysteries, alludes to this sublime doctrine, making a distinction only visible to the nice observer, between the Holy Spirit, and her Lord and Father, God.

Principio cœlum ac terras, camposque liquentes
Lucentemque globum lunæ, Titaniaque astra
SPIRITUS intus alit ; totamque infusa per artus
MENS agitat molem, et magno se corpore miscet ;
Inde hominum pecudumque genus, &c.—*Æn.* vi.

"First, then, the *Divine Spirit* within sustains the heavens, the earth, and watery plains, the moon's enlightened orb, and shining stars ; and the *Eternal Mind,* diffused through all the parts of nature, actuates the whole stupendous frame and mingles with the vast body of the universe. Thence proceed the race of men and beasts, the vital principles of the flying kind, and the monsters which the ocean breeds under its smooth crystal plain." And this was no other than the doctrine of the old world universally.

8. The people of Laos have a fair poetical fable, symbolic of the creation, which beautifully reveals a hidden truth. They say that both Heaven and Earth have been from everlasting, only that the former was never subject to any change, but that the earth (the created spheres of life), has undergone a variety of revolutions. After the latest, which was one by waters, a most holy mandarin (God) descended from the highest of the celestial circles, and with one stroke of his scymetar, cut in two a certain lotos-flower which floated on the surface of the waves, and from that flower sprang up a most lovely Virgin, with whom the Mandarin fell in love : but her inflexible modesty rendered all his addresses fruitless

nnd ineffectual. The Mandarin was too exalted in justice to put any constraint upon this surpassing Virgin ; but he placed himself before her, and admired her fragrant beauty from morning to evening, gazing upon her with all the starry tenderness of love; and by the miraculous force of his glances, she became the most joyful mother of a numerous offspring, and yet continued a pure Virgin. When the children (all existing spirits), grew up, the Mandarin considered himself as under an obligation of making some provision for them, and for that purpose created that beautiful variety of beings, which now replenishes the earthly spheres ; and having accomplished this he ascended into heaven, his own and primal circle.

9. The Hebrew priests, who did not themselves originate anything, but who were copyists, or rather plagiarists, of the theosophical knowledge of the nations from whom they emigrated, or among whom they dwelled, have handed down to us a picture of this Heavenly and most Glorious Being, whom they called Wisdom, because she was the Virgin-Pallas from the brain of God. *By Wisdom, God formed the heaven and the earth;* is the opening verse of *Genesis;* and it was to Wisdom, as the primary emanation from the Supreme Boodh or Father, that some of those fine fragments of Oriental divinity which they have incorporated with their writings, especially refer. *And thy counsel who hath known, except thou give Wisdom, and send thy Holy Spirit from above,* Solomon, ix. 17. *For thine incorruptible Spirit is in all things. Let all creatures serve Thee,* says the Hebrew author of the Book of *Judith,* (xiv. 14), *for* THOU *didst speak and they were made.* THOU *didst send forth thy* SPIRIT, *and it created them.* She is faintly imaged also in the remnant of a

faint tradition of the Mighty Spirit Metathronos, who in the Talmud is said to share the Throne of God. (*Bereshith Rabba.*) But the whole mythos has been completely destroyed by the Hebrew Rabbis. Yet we read in Ecclesiastes xii., Remember thy *Creators*;—and in Isaiah, xliv. 2, Thus saith the Lord, thy *Redeemers*. And in Gen. i. 26, God said (to the Holy Spirit) let us make man in our image, after our likeness; so Aleim (3) (the Powers), ´created man in their own image; in the image of Aleim created he them; *male* and *female* created he them. This, say the Paulites, proves a Trinity in unity, —but was the Trinity male and female? In the so-called *Proverbs of Solomon*, (which are indeed no more his than they are Solon's), we find her thus described;—

Happy is the man who findeth Wisdom; and the man who getteth an understanding of her; for to know her is better than the merchandize of silver, and to gain her than fine gold. She is more precious than rubies [the magnet]; *and all the things thou canst desire are not to be compared to her. Length of days is in her right hand; and in her left riches and honour. Her ways are ways of pleasantness, and all her paths are peace. She is a* TREE OF LIFE *to them that lay hold of her; and happy is every one who keepeth her. The Lord by Wisdom hath founded the earth; by her knowledge did he establish the heavens; by her intelligence the depths are broken up and the clouds drop down dew.* In another chapter this Divine Being is introduced as thus describing herself. *I Wisdom dwell with prudence, and find out knowledge of wise inventions. Counsel is mine, and sound reason, I am understanding; I have strength. By me kings reign, and princes decree justice. By me princes rule, and nobles, yea, and even all the judges of the earth. I love them who love me, and those who seek me early shall find me. Riches and honour are with me; yea, everlasting riches and righteousness. My fruit is better than gold, yea, than fine gold; and my revenue than choice silver. I lead in the way of righteousness, in the midst of the paths of judgment; that I may cause those that love me to inherit substance; and I will fill their treasures. The Lord possessed me in the beginning of his way, before his works of old. I was set up from everlasting, from the beginning, or ever the earth was. When there were no depths, I was brought forth; when there were no fountains abounding with water. Before the mountains were settled, before the hills was I brought forth : while as yet he had not made the earth, nor the fields, nor the highest part of the dust of the world. When he prepared the heavens, I was there : when he set the compass upon the face of the depth : when he established the clouds above : when he strengthened the fountains of the deep : when he gave to the sea his decree, that the waters should not pass his commandment : when he appointed the foundations of the earth : then I was by him, as one brought up with him: and I was daily his delight, rejoicing always before him; rejoicing in the habitable part of his earth ; and my delights were with the sons of men. Now therefore hearken unto me, O ye children; for blessed are they that keep my ways. Hear instruction, and be wise, and refuse it not. Blessed is the man that heareth me, watching daily at my gates, waiting at the posts of my doors. For whoso findeth me findeth life, and shall obtain favour of the Lord. But he that sinneth against me wrongeth his own soul . all they that hate me love death.*

10. There is in truth no part of primeval religion wherever we can find its traces on the vast earth, in which this Sacred Spirit does not figure prominently : the central figure beaming with splendours. She was Juno, the wife of God, or the Celestial Majesty of Heaven : she was called Issa or Ish-l-Aum, which means the Virgin of God, from whence the name of Asia itself came ; and the religion of the Arabs from the most ancient ages was called Islâm. She is the Indian Lakshmi with the infant Incarnation on her bosom ; and Lakshmi Narayan, or the Holy Spirit of the Naros, who bears the Messiah in her lap. She was Al-Ma, and Aum-Ma, the Pure, the God-Mother ; because through her we all appeared. She was the Magna Mater, and Sibylla, symbolized over the whole earth by the crescent silver moon, the lunette-shaped boat, the flowing sea, the mystical rose, the winged cup, (4) the ear of corn, the horn of plenty, the water lily (or Nymphæa), the honey-breathing hive, the sea-shell ; and a variety of emblems all typical of her peculiar and transcendant properties. She appears on almost all the medals and sculptures of the Past, either emblematically, or as a beautiful Virgin, robed and crowned, and flashing loveliness and light (5)

11. But of all pure and shining images to which the nations of old were used to compare her, there was none more frequent than the Rainbow ; and in the ancient mystical theology, the word is scarcely ever used, without bearing secret relation to the Divine and Virgin Spirit of God. Thus Iris (or rainbow) was designated from the very beginning, the Messenger of the Gods ; signifying by a bold figure that the Holy Spirit whom Iris represented, was the medium of the appointed Messengers, to

whom his Revelations came. When the hour approached
in which the destined mother on earth, of the Messiah, was
to conceive him, she perceived the fragrance of celestial
lilies, and was enveloped in a heavenly Rainbow ; feeling
a sweet influence like a sunbeam, pervade her inmost
essence : and when the virtuous spirit of man emancipa-
ted from earth, sought that paradise-garden to which all
its best and noblest aspirations tended to uplift it, it was
borne into the sphere of happiness on a Bridge of Rain-
bows, shining more magnificently than all the other constellated lights and meteoric flashes of the Universe.
There was a beautiful recondite meaning in comparing to
a Rainbow, the form of this Holy Spirit, whom philosophers call Nature, Providence, &c., but Christians most
irrationally designate the Holy Ghost ; a false version of
the word *Geist* in Luther's German translation of the
Bible. It is, as if she said, I am all the splendid colours
of the Rainbow (that is all the divine and varied beauty
of the Universe), concentrated into One , and yet they
are nothing but my simple, sunlike, and uniform brightness, variously refracted and represented. In the Saïtic
temple she was the veiled mysterious Isis, spangled all
over with starry brilliancy : while near her was inscribed
in words as noble, solemn and sublime as were her own
immortal attributes, that mystic inscription, for the con-
cluding line of which we are indebted to the platonic
sage Porphyry ; for Plutarch either did not know, or
dared not venture to transcribe the whole.

I am All that is : I am All that hath been ;
I am All that will for ever be :
And my Veil no mortal hath drawn aside.
The fruit that I brought forth was the Sun. (6)

And these two sublime Beings, the Creator and the Created, the Lord of all, and the Genitrix of all, were the ruling Essences that breathed into the Past, that calm, august, and moral grandeur which we are accustomed to associate with its sacred roll of sages and ascetics, and which so long retained primeval men in a purity of life and sublimity of thought, to which modern days present no parallel.

12. God having thus determined to create, and having begun with the Spirit, who henceforward bare his name, desired further to develope himself in various splendid and immortal forms. These forms infused into the Spirit of God, were by her emaned in the shape of Spirits or angelic beings, of the most supreme grandeur, only one degree removed from herself ; for *She* came direct from God, and was therefore transcendently lovely and could not err; but *they* proceeding from her were removed one degree more distant, and were consequently subject in some sort to imperfectness. Thus the whole Infinite became filled with Spirits ; all after the First and Second, equally wise, lovely and powerful ; all clothed in sun-like light, and brightened with immaculate purity. Thus also the Universe began to consist of three : 1. God ; 2. The Spirit of God ; 3. Spirits. But these three were absolutely one in essence, though not in form. As the sun is an aggregate of particles of light; as the Ocean is an aggregate of particles of water ; and the sun and the particles are one, and the sea and the drops are one ; so God, the Spirit of God, and all other Spirits throughout the unbounded Universe, were absolutely one, though in three-fold form, and were One in Three, and Three in One. Hence the primeval dogma of a Trinity, which as ex-

plained in modern times, is inexplicable, absurd, and even ludicrous ; but as thus simplified is truth, wisdom, and beauty as it were in one.

13. This absolute identity, or *one-ness* of God with all existence, and all existences with God, is divinely illustrated by Jesus, the ninth Messiah of Heaven, in one of his most striking parables, the true Pantheistic meaning of which has wholly escaped the biblical commentators : or which, if it should have been made manifest to them, they purposely and craftily conceal from those whom they profess to teach the truths of heaven. *When the Son of Man shall come in his glory*, says Jesus, *and all the holy angels with him, then shall he sit upon the throne of his glory : and before him shall be gathered all nations : and he shall separate them one from another, as a shepherd separateth his sheep from the goats: and he shall set the sheep indeed on his right hand, but the goats on the left. Then shall the King say unto them on his right hand, Come, ye blessed of my Father, inherit the kingdom prepared for you from the foundation of the world : for I was an hungered, and ye gave me meat : I was thirsty, and ye gave me drink . I was a stranger, and ye took me in : naked, and ye clothed me : I was sick, and ye visited me: I was in prison, and ye came unto me. Then shall the righteous answer him, saying, Master, when did we see thee, an hungred, and fed thee ? or thirsty, and gave thee drink? When did we see thee a stranger, and took thee in ? or naked, and clothed thee ? Or when did we see thee sick, or in prison, and came unto thee ? And the King shall answer and say unto them, Amen, I say unto you, Inasmuch as ye have done it unto one of the least of these my brethren, ye have done it unto me. Then shall he*

say also unto them on the left hand, Depart from me, ye cursed, into everlasting fire, prepared for the devil and his angels. for I was an hungred, and ye gave me no meat : I was thirsty, and ye gave me no drink: I was a stranger, and ye took me not in : naked, and ye clothed me not : sick, and in prison, and ye visited me not. Then shall they also answer him, saying, Master, when saw we thee an hungred, or athirst, or a stranger, or naked, or sick, or in prison, and did not minister unto thee ? Then shall he answer them, saying, Amen, I say unto you, Inasmuch as ye did it not to one of the least of these, ye did it not to me. And these shall go away into everlasting punishment: but the righteous into life everlasting.—MATTHEW xxv. 31.

This creed,—although it shines upon the thought, so exquisitely clear and true, that the wonder is how people have remained ignorant of it, and why they prefer their ignorance to that august and everlasting knowledge which is as it were in their footpath, waiting only recognition,—is absolutely lost to Europe and its Churches. And yet was ever any so well adapted to fill even the most inconsiderate with solemn feelings ? How consolatory to think in the spirit of that sacred similitude which Jesus used, that every good and holy act which we do on earth to our fellow creatures, is done absolutely not merely to them, but to God *who receives it in them;* but how dreadful also is it to be assured, and to know moreover that the assurance is beyond all doubt, that every evil act which we do unto any is, in effect done as it were, individually or personally against the very God of Heaven whose representative he is : and that he who in the slightest degree wrongs, maltreats, or deceives another, injures, insults, and tells a lie to the Supreme Ad-Ad (7), who lives visibly even in the least of those creatures, to whom He has transferred a portion of His glorious being. The murderer who destroys life, murders God who is in that very life : the robber who thieves from his fellow mortal, robs not him only, but the Divine Being, of whom he is a living portion : and the man who by fraud or violence, or false pretence, seduces a young virgin from her purity, is as guilty as if it were the Being of Life and Beauty and Innocence whom he misled and deceived ; for in her soul she is an actual part and image, and consubstantial portion of the Splendid Light that shines supreme throughout the Worlds.

14. The religion here developed, though mystical, and perhaps recondite, at the first glance to the ignorant and carnal-minded, was beautiful in the extreme ; and the source of its beauty is to be traced to its truth; for to declare its absolute and perfect truth is the object of this Volume. God is eternal ; but Spirit and Matter have been created, and are only everlasting. It follows from this, that there was a time when there was neither Spirit nor Matter. At that time God was One and Alone, for there existed nothing else. But when God resolved to develope his majesty in a form, which, though separate, was nevertheless as much a part of himself as a sunbeam belongs to the sun, he made that development first in a Spirit of the most divine loveliness, wisdom and power, that it was possible for the Supreme Being to emane. And God said, Let there be LIGHT, and there was LIGHT. (*Gen.* i., 3.) This spirit is not eternal, for God made it : it is an everlasting Splendour. This Spirit is not infinite, for only God is infinite ; but it is universal,

which is the very nearest approach to infinity that the mind can conceive. This Spirit is not all-powerful, but it possesses every exquisite quality that God can transfer from his own essence, into that supremely pure essence which the most resembles His own; and which is only one degree removed from the majesty of the One. This great Essence, as I have before said, is called the Spirit of God; an universal and an everlasting Spirit, and was the second great Power that began to exist, when God developed beauty out of himself. And through the me-dium of that Power it was, that all that now is, came into Being. All that exists, says *Sohar*, all that the Ancient has formed, can only have existence by reason of a Male and a Female.

15. A self-existent, uncreated, eternal Being, the original Source of all creatures, and of all worlds, and of all the gods who made and governed them, lies therefore at the basis of all the ancient theosophy, although our priests do all that they can to mystify or conceal the fact. In the Hindu system this Uncreated and Eternal Being is named Brahm (8) the Formless, that is, the original Great or Mighty One, the all-pervader; and this Power is sometimes designated Para-Brahm, as indicating the superlative of all Dominion and Magnificence. The real doctrine of the whole Indian scripture, says Colebrooke, (*As Res.* viii., 468), and higher authority cannot be cited, is *the Unity of the Deity in whom the Universe is comprehended:* and this Unity is but another name for His universality. The Ancient of the ancient, says *Sohar*, has a form and has no form. He assumed a Form when he called the Universe into being: and the rabbinical writer here drew undoubtedly from Indian sources. Among the

ancient Persians and Medes the name of God was
Zervan-Akerene, or Uncreated Time, or the Infinite
One, as appears in the Zand-a-Vesta: the Egyptians
called him Athou, or Athyr, that is *Ancient Darkness*:
the Chinese designated him T'AO and AO, that is
the Three-One. According to these systems, this original source of life, considered as undeveloped, and as
existing in and by himself, had as yet no proper *per
sonality*. He was the One of the Greek philosophers,
or the Monad, that is, the abstract principle of Unity;
but not One in the concrete sense, and as distinguished from two or more taken in a concrete sense. In
order, however, that a development of this Original might
be made, a Pothos, or *desire*, called by the Hindus, *viraj*,
was ascribed to him, the tendency of which was towards
development, emanation, or creation. God, the original
source of all things, has developed himself: the creation,
rational and irrational, therefore exists. In the develop-
ments which the Godhead has made, his personality, so
to speak, has become perceptible to the rational beings
whom He has created; and all things, and all beings,
as Jesus says, are, as it were, a mirror of Him. And, in
complete consonance with the Triune-All, before alluded
to, and its general knowledge among the primeval men,
we find that the leading nations of antiquity, with whose
theosophy we are in anywise acquainted, have represented
the development of God as threefold, or tripartite; as the
Tri-mourti, or the Tri-vamz. Thus, in the Hindu system
of theology, from Brahm, the original source, proceed,
when He developes himself, Brahm-*ma*, the Producer,
Vishnu, the Preserver, Shiva, the destroyer, and renewer. These are the three forms in which Brahm re-

appears, and it is in these only that worship is paid to the original Divine Being, who is considered as developing himself in all. The Ved begins and concludes with the three peculiar and mysterious epithets of God , *Ong, Tut, Sut,* equivalent to the *Magnus Divus, Ultor,* and *Genitor* of the ancient *Zeus.* Among the Buddhists, Buddh*ash,* the Developer, Dharm*ash,* the developed, and Sanggh*ash,* the hosts, who issue from the development, constitute the three great existences of the Universe, as formed by Boodh, the First. God, says Lao-Tseu, the great Messiah of the Chinese, is, by his nature, One ; but the First has produced a second, the second a third, and these three are all things. In vain may your senses enquire concerning all three : your *reason* only can affirm anything respecting them , and this will tell you that these are only One. Orpheus called this Triad, Aitheros, Phanes, Chaos, (God, the Spirit, and that which was of both, but imperfect) ; Pythagoras, the Monad, Duad, and Triad ; and Plato, the Infinite, the Bounded, and that which is compounded of the two others. The *Father,* says Zaratusht, perfected all things, and delivered them to the *Second Mind,* whom the nations of men call the first,—implying that they did so in ignorance ;—but all things, he adds, are the progeny of *One Fire.* This Second was called Rhea, the fountain of the immortal and divine ; for first receiving the Power of All things in her ineffable embraces, she pours running generation into everything ; her hairs (all spirits, souls, and existences) are ever-growing beams of light that terminate in the merest point ; that is, she produces archangels, or the highest, and other existences thence downward unto the very lowest living images of the Eternal Life, whom she embraces, and who is God. Lord Kingsborough, in his magnificent work on the Mexican Antiquities (p. 410) gives the name of their Trinity as Om-Equeturicki and Ur-Ao-Zoriso, signifying the Blessed : Ur-upo, the Holy Spirit : Urus-Ana, their offspring. Their Hermes, or heavenly Messenger, was Omid-euchtli, the very name prefigured by one of the Hebrew priests. One, say the Chaldee Oracles, which are certainly a reflex of a religious belief, whose date is lost in far antiquity, has produced a Second, which dwells with it. From this proceeds a Third, which shines through the whole Universe. The Phœnician theology assigns to the Universe a *triplex principium*,—Belus, Urania, and Adonis, or Heaven, Earth, and Love, which unites the two. The primeval Arabs called it Al-Lat, Al-Uzzah, and Manah, or the Goddesses. The Magian division was Oromasd, Ahriman, and Mihr ; the Egyptian Amoun-Ras, Muth, and Chous, which subsequently grew into Osiris, Isis, and Orus, (אור *aur*, fire). When He exerts his creative energy he is Amoun (God) ; when He displays his skill in perfecting and harmoniously arranging he is named Ptha (9) (the Holy Spirit) ; and when he dispenses blessings He is termed Osiris, the Father of the Messenger. So Jamblichus relates : and albeit not exactly correct, the reader will see how it accords with the Truth revealed in this volume. The Kalmuck Triad was Tarni, Megonizan, Bourchan : the Siamese Phut-Ang (God), Tham-Ang (Word of God), and Tauk-Ang (Imitator of God) . the Samothracian, Axieros (or the Almighty), Axiokerses-Axiokersa (God in union with the Holy Spirit, the Great Fecundator, the Great Fecundatrix), and Casmilus, or he who stands before the face of Deity. The old German was Perkunos, in honour of whom his votaries kept a fire of oak-wood always burning; Pikolos, and Pothrimpos; the Tartar, Artagon, Schiego-Tengon, and Tangara: the Peruvian, Apomti, Charunti, and Intiquao-qui: the ancient Swedish, Odin, Thor, and Frigga. The Scandinavians called the three divisions Har, Jafnar, and Thride, and sometimes Othin, Vile, and Ve: the Irish, Kriosan, (10) Biosena, and Shiva: the Tyrians, Monimus, Azoz, and Ares: the Greeks and Romans, Jupiter, Neptune, Pluto: and the Canaanites, Baal-Spalisha, or self-triplicated Baal. And the like correspondences have been found among the Indians of South America in their Otkon, Messou, and Atahauta; and in the West African Islands and other places; all demonstrating, not only an identity of religion, but even of family from a remote era. The freest wits among the Pagans, says Cudworth, (*Preface to the Intellectual System*), and the best philosophers, who had nothing of superstition to determine them in that way, were so far from being shy of such an hypothesis (the Triune Nature of the All) as that they were even fond thereof. And that the Pagans had indeed such a cabbala among them (which some perhaps will yet hardly believe, notwithstanding all that we have said), might be further convinced from that memorable relation in Plutarch, of Thespesius Solensis, (*Libro de his qui serò a Numine puniuntur, tom.* 2); who, after he had been looked upon as dead for three days, reviving, affirmed amongst other things, which he thought he saw, or heard in the meantime, in his ecstacy, this, of *Three Gods in the form of a triangle pouring in streams into one another.* This triangle, or pyramid, which I shall explain by and bye, is represented in the most ancient coins of Thibet; it is of a blue colour, to denote its celestial nature, and has sometimes in its centre the Tamara, or lotos flower ; sometimes a circle, the emblem of God : it is occasionally also delineated with three lunettes, and three asterisms, all of which typify the Holy Spirit.

16. The material Universe, however, did not yet exist; the All was constituted of celestial worlds only, and these were filled with Spirits of Life, which shone around the One, the Universal Life, from whom all existence came, and without whom there could be none. In the very beginning, as has been shewn, God made all spirits after the Second, equal in beauty, in light, in intelligence, and purity. He surrounded his Thrones in Heaven by those dazzling beings. They were as great and splendid as the brightest stars that now fill the material Kosmos. But their will was free. God would not be surrounded by machines, which *should* be virtuous because they were fashioned to be so, and could not be otherwise because made as if to order ;—which like a clock, or clockwork mice, might be wound up to do a certain thing, and could do only that certain thing : moving like automata, but as their fabricator designed, without any independent power, or free volition of their own. It is obvious that the Supreme Father could not be encircled by toys of this kind. His felicity must be participated in by free Spirits capable of such participation : he could not share it with slaves or pieces of mechanism. But this freedom which was an absolute *necessity* to the happiness of the whole Universe of Spirits, became in course of time a source of calamity to some. It was not possible even for the Supreme Father to do what was impossible, although modern religionists always assume that He can and that He does. He could not at the same moment

make them free to will, and *not* free to will. As God
cannot make that which is white, black, while it is yet
white; or cause that fact not to have happened, which
has actually already happened; or form a diamond without the diamond properties of splendour ; so he could not
restrain a Spirit who had full liberty of will, from the
fullest exercise of that free will, without at the same
moment restraining that which was given to be unrestrained.   And as the will was free, and the intellect was
great, and the desires of those splendid Spirits were large,
vast, and soaring, these three combined, produced inclinations, which, as they could not be gratified by limited
natures, and ended therefore in disappointment, hatred,
or envy, disqualified their owners for the paradise-sphere,
where only love and happiness exist.

17. An illustration of this will make it probably more
clear than mere description.   Let us suppose a Spirit as
large and splendid, as lovely with refulgent light as the
star Venus : let us suppose this radiant creature before
the throne of God : let us suppose that from a perpetual
contemplation of the Beatific Beauty it becomes discon-
tented with its own condition, and wishes to be God ;
or to be as holy, wise, infinite, and powerful as the
Almighty Lord and Father.   This very wish, which
would appear natural, is in reality evil : for all discontent
and envy of another are evil.   But such a wish as this
cannot be gratified.   This glorious but ambitious spirit
cannot be God : it becomes unhappy : it grows gloomy :
it is no longer fitted for a heavenly sphere, where only
blessedness and love can live.   What is to become of it ?
It has absolutely done no evil ; but it has unfortunately
made itself unfit for heaven.   God does not detrude it

into darkness. He is too beneficent to plunge it into a fiery hell, for merely exercising that fiee will which He himself made free. He removes it to another region : lower indeed in splendour of light than that which it had first occupied, but still a region of magnificence. It was once celestial; it is now infra-celestial. If it purifies itself in the latter from that evil thought, and grows thoroughly convinced of its folly, while it sincerely repents its ingratitude and disloyalty to the Father who created it, God says, It is my law that you shall re-ascend. But if instead of doing so, it hardens itself in its discontent, or accuses God of injustice, or cries out against Him that He made it capable of error, it must be obvious that this is sinking into a still lower deep of sinfulness, and that even for the sub-celestial it is too impure. It cannot any longer live there, any more than men can live in pure ether; for no spirit can abide in any sphere for which its qualities are unsuited. And as the sub-celestial, though far inferior to the celestial, is nevertheless of a heavenly nature, a spirit that is not in accordance with it cannot dwell there. Thus it descends into a terrestrial sphere and assumes a terrestrial form, suited to the nature of its dwelling-place; and there also an opportunity is offered for its self-purification. This, in brief, is the origin of the terrestrial worlds, and the races that are now upon them. The last were all once pure Spirits before the Thrones of God, and the terrestrial spheres and all matter were made only when spirits fell from heaven.

18. But in what way is this self-purification to be brought about if man on earth receives no glimpses of the Divine? He is surrounded wholly by material things; he can soar indeed in fancy to the spheres; he can trans-

port his thoughts aloft, and float among the beaming stars, but after all his lot is miserable. He contemplates the heavenly arch : he sees the sun sink behind golden mountains of resplendent brightness, or the moon rise a pure silver orb out of deep and purple glens, while the stars shine with living lustre ; and all above him fills him with this thought : Why cannot I mount and leave this wretched place of low and mean pursuits, for yonder swiftly rolling spheres of brightness, peace, and purity ? God knew this, and therefore God in his wisdom made a Law, that *Revelations* of himself to man should be from time to time given, as the exigencies of man required. The first races he illuminated by the means of divine patriarchs, ancients, or Boodhoos : but as years revolved, certain Men or Messiahs, of a grander order, and more extensive views, were sent on earth, who were the Messengers of God to man. These were emanations from the Holy Spirit of God : they came out of her as the rainbow is the child of the Sun. They were not archangels or gods despatched from the paradise-circles upon a special errand to mortals ; for this would contradict two laws of God, which like all divine laws are immutable and perfect. First, it would be unjust in God to send a pure and sinless archangel out of his own sphere of happiness, into a sphere of wretchedness and suffering, such as the earth of mortals is ; and this consequently could not be done by God. The common notion of the sects who call themselves "saints," that God is All-powerful, and can do what He pleases, is founded on modern foolishness, and would have been considered by the ancients to be dread blasphemy. This is the notion of a savage despot, whose caprice is his law ; but it is not consistent with the sublime nature of the Father. God cannot do as he pleases in the popular acceptation of the term. He could not send a perfectly just man into a state of everlasting misery : if He did so, He would not be a God at all. If he did any thing wrong, or unjust, or foolish, or inconsistent with his divine and exquisite perfectness, He could not be God. It is obvious therefore that as God cannot commit injustice, the general supposition adopted from the Jews, that He can be unjust if it so pleases Him, or capricious, or wayward, or revengeful, or false, because He so chooses, is repugnant to all true conceptions of the Divine Being, and is indeed nothing but the most dark impiety.

19. Secondly, God could not do so because He would have to break one of the material laws which He has made : and as all God's laws are perfect, it follows that if He broke the perfect, He would act inconsistently with himself—which it is obvious God cannot do. It is a law that a bird cannot live under water ; that a fish cannot live on the land ; that an animal cannot live in fire ; that a man cannot live in ether. If therefore God were to send a divine angel out of one of his ethereal spheres to be His Messenger, he would have to violate this Law which He has made ; and compel that angel to exist in a sphere for which by nature he was not constituted. It is equally clear that God would not do this. Therefore God by the medium of the Holy Spirit, permits certain beings of a special order, to assume the nature of Men, and to descend on earth ; and these convey to mortals the Revelations with which they are charged. Hence they are called Sons of God ; but in reality they are not more so than other beings, because every Existence is a Son of God

inasmuch as it is from God alone that it draws the vital essence in which it subsists. And these special beings when they come on earth are called Incarnations.

20. The whole ancient world, the remains of all primeval religion, the temples, towers, obelisks, frescoes, the mouldering ruins of palaces, of gates and pillars, are filled with traces of these celestial Messengers. They are the Twelve Angels of this revealed Apocalypse; they are the twelve *Tien Hoang* or Heavenly Men of Fohi, with human faces and dragon bodies. (11) The Chinese call Fohi himself a *Kûntzè*, which signifies Shepherd, and All-Teacher. Twelve are the *Æsers* to be worshipped, says the Edda; and as Odin's surname was Asa; and as he was Godam, Gaudama, and Boodh from Asiatic Tartary, this doctrine like that of the twelve pagan gods is thus traced up to the very earliest æras of revelation. (12). The Goths were originally Scyths; from them they inherit the wandering Celtic propensity; all the old northern scalds and historians agree that their ancestors came from the high North-east, and brought the religion of that country with them; which was in fact the primeval religion. These Twelve Messiahs, of whom I have just spoken, are the Twelve *Imaums* or Sacred Priests of ancient Arabia, in commemoration of whom Jesus sent forth Twelve Apostles. And after twelve days, says the *Codex Nazaræus*, the Holy Spirit brought forth Twelve Figures, mutually unlike, mutually like, and each had a winnowing fan in the hollow of his hand. These fans the reader will see in the Egyptian frescoes and carvings which are thousands of years old: and though the *Codex Nazaræus* is not genuine as a whole, it contains passages that belong to almost the primal books. So the Egyptians (one of

whose mystic names for their Messiah, was Ramses Mia-
mûn), said that Osiris (God) had enclosed in the Egg from
which the world was originally produced, *twelve* white
pyramidal figures to denote the infinite number of blessings which he intended to shower down upon men ; but
that Typhon, his brother, the author of evil, having
opened this Egg, introduced twelve black pyramids, the
causes of all the miseries with which the earth is overrun : thus drawing a beautiful distinction between the
true religion as preached by the Twelve, and the false
caricatures of it which the priests set up.   They are
alluded to also in the Mim-Ra of the Chaldæans, or Ray
of the Holy Spirit who is mantled in the Sun.   By the
Burmese the Incarnation is called *Loghea*, or the doctrine ;
which the Greeks not inaptly changed into *Logos* or message of God ; and on which Christian writers have made
the most absurd and monstrous guesses ; and by the
later Arabs, he is called *Resoul*, or *the Sent*.   In the
Brahmin theology these Messengers were designated *Brah-
madicas* (preachers of God), and *Narasinhas*, or lions of
the Holy Spirit, as Jesus also was designated the lion of
the tribe of Jid, or Juda.   The Egyptians, among other
titles, called the Incarnation *Andro-Sphynx*, and *Sarabbas*
or God's Abbot; symbolizing him by the winged lion,
and the golden serpent coming out of the mystic coffer or
ark ; and by the first Iranians he was revered as an *Ha-
zarah*, a mystic title of the highest honour; and from
which indeed we have the Hebrew name of Azariah, or
God is my comforter.   The Japanese call him Gi-won, and
Goso-Tennoo, or the Ox-headed Prince of Heaven : the
ox being typical of the Sun or God, from whom he is sent.
He is the long-expected Parasu-Rama, and Mahidi of

Indian and Arabian theology; and the So-Shiôsh or Saviour king, and Baggava-Matteio of the Boodh, or wisdom-born religion. The people of Laos in the East Indies, call their Messiah, Xaca; and believe that the religion which he established, after having lasted a certain cycle, shall give way to another which shall be founded or renovated by a new Xaca, who shall arise and demolish the old temples, break down their sacred images, and burn their scriptures, after which he shall promulgate new laws, and a pure form of worship. This is the doctrine of the Apocalypse, and it appears to refer in a striking manner to the advent of the Tenth and Eleventh Messengers of Truth. So the Hottentots say that Gounja Ticqvoa (the God of Gods), sometimes descends, and becomes visible to men, in appearance, shape, and dress the finest among mortals. Jupiter was called Καταιβατης, or the Descender, because the Messiah descends from heaven; and Epiphanes, or the Appearer, the very word which is used for the Epiphany of the Ninth Messenger. The Incarnations thus were called in the Mysteries of Greece, Θεοι αδελφοι, or the *Brother-gods*, though the populace could not tell wherefore. This unity between them was signified by the Romans, when they called them *Consentes*, as it were *consentientes*, or having one mind. And the Greeks who borrowed everything divine from the religions of almost all people, not only so designated the various Messiahs, as all emanating from one Parent, but they symbolized him also under various names. Now he is Bal-Kiun or the Lord Kiun (the Kûntzè of Fohi), which, by a transposition of the vowels (a common custom in ancient times), became Bul-Khan, or Vul-Khan, the Lord of Fire, the Child of the Sun.

Hephæstos was the Greek form for Ashta-Abba, or Father-Fire; and Zeus his sire (God), was said to have hurled him like a star from heaven to earth, which signifies his divine mission from above. In ancient paintings he wore a *blue* hat to indicate his celestial origin. Throughout the whole of the primal theology, when it was yet comparatively pure in form, he is represented as a son of God or Jah-son, who was to quit his heavenly abode and to live among men, to be their Teacher, Saviour, Prince. They gave him different names according to his different functions. Hence Philo Judæus calls the Incarnation, Αρχαγγελος πολυωνυμος, the Archangel of *many names*. And the old Roman, or rather Etruscan oath, *me dius fidius*, by the son of God, was in allusion to the Naronic Messenger. Sometimes he is Apollo the god of prophecy, fighting against the serpent Python; or Sampson, sprung from a miraculous conception and slaying thousands of the wicked; sometimes he is Hercules (13) destroying monsters and giants, and purging the earth of all its crimes and enormities; one, while he is Hermes, son of Maïa, or the Messenger of God, flying about every where to execute His decrees, and conducting souls into the other world; and another while he is Perseus, delivering Andromeda, or human nature, from the monster that rose out of the great deep to devour her; or Elijah borne up to heaven on a chariot of fire-winged steeds. He is always some child of destiny, giving battles and gaining victories : all his acts are miracles : and success accompanies him in the most difficult undertakings. His career is one of pure beneficence, and unmitigated labour, or romantic adventure, or the most ascetic piety. The wicked are opposed to him in all places, for the wicked are the natural enemies of Truth and Beauty. (14). Frequently he succumbs and is destroyed; like Melicart he disappears in fire; like Phœnix he is self-consumed; but his heroic spirit mingles with the stars.

21. But this symbolic hero did not confine himself to mere warfare; he was Hermes the most eloquent of speakers, with "chains of gold flowing from his mouth, with which he linked together the minds of those who heard him;" he was a sweet-voiced musician, like Orpheus and Amphion; he built cities by his words; he animated stones into men; he was a conquering prince who went with armies of truth to subdue the earth. The tongue is the great instrument of knowledge and civilization: hence the Holy Spirit who inspired the Messiahs, was called the Spirit of Tongues. Lucian relates that in Gaul he saw Hercules, (one of the symbols of Messiah), represented as a little old man, whom in the language of the country, they called Ogmius, (15), drawing after him an infinite multitude of persons, who seemed most willing to follow, though led by fine and almost imperceptible chains, which were fastened at one end to *their ears,* and held at the other, not in either of Hercules's hands, which were both otherwise employed, but tied to the *tip of his tongue,* in which there was a hole on purpose, where all those chains concentered. Lucian wondering at this manner of pourtraying Hercules, was informed by a learned Druid, who stood by, that Hercules did not in Gaul, as in Greece, among the vulgar, signify Strength of Body, but rather the Force of Eloquence; which was there very beautifully displayed by the Druid in his explication of the picture that hung in the Temple. In a word all religions have him, and confess his universality:

the Christians and the Jews are the only people who strenuously maintain that he was never sent to any one except themselves (16)—all other profane wretches being unworthy of the paternal care of God. When he died or was destroyed (17), he re-ascended to heaven; he became a god, an Ancient, a Boodhoo; and reigned with the Divine Father whose message he had performed. There he was surrounded by the happy spirits whom his teaching had saved from evil; or as Plato in his Timæus expressed it, They who rightly and virtuously finished the course of life assigned to them by nature, returned to that star (Messiah) with which they were connected.

22. And here it may be well to observe that the entire structure of the Latin and Greek churches, (or Catholicism), is based on the divine system now developed; with this difference, that *they* degrade the Spirit of God from Heaven, into an earthly woman whom they call the Virgin Mary; and the heavenly Messenger, whom she emanes, and sends, Jesus, (18), they elevate from a mere Man or Spirit, to an equality, if not an identity with the Eternal Lord and Maker of all things. The Reformed Protestant systems do the same. But what is to prevent either from returning to the same Fountain head, which is developed in these pages? or what is to prevent all the nations of the earth from again embracing the One Universal Faith which their forefathers all believed?

23. It is not possible to imagine a more ennobling form of religion than this: but it was once the universal creed, embracing all mankind as if in one brotherhood. It operated the greatest wonders; it inspired resplendent deeds of heroism, virtue, and charity; deeds with which all ancient history is illuminated. The daughter dies to save

D

her father · the son sacrifices his life to preserve his parents, to emancipate his country, to make free his friend ; the wife is willing to surrender up her own existence, so that the days of her husband shall be prolonged.   Not by the august men who received these hallowed doctrines from the Messengers, were the vile rabble of divinities invented, who subsequently brought the very name of religious worship into contempt ; who polluted Olympus ; who desecrated Meru ; but by the priests and poets, who fabricated lies and legends without number, and gradually perverted religious beauty into profaneness.   Therefore was it that Plato wisely banished all such from his model republic, as common nuisances and pests ; and the almost divine Pythagoras gave currency to the tradition that Homer and Hesiod were in hell chained to brazen pillars and stung by serpents, for daring to blaspheme religion by their fables, (19). The most horrid legends were thus forged ; as they were graced by all the charms of flowing song, they obtained the widest circulation. Wickedness of every kind could point out to one of the newly-sprung divinities, and invoke its example, as an inducement to crime, or a protection from infamy ; and the robber, the assassin, the adulterer, or even worse, could hold up his head audaciously before his fellows and shield himself under the foul ægis of the Hermes, Mars, or all-sustaining Zeus of poetical creation, and popular belief.   Hence Varro, if we may believe Augustine, (*De Civil. Dei*), says, that things thus became attributed to the gods, which one would have blushed to ascribe to the most vile of men.   *Denique in hoc, omnia Diis attribuuntur, quæ non modo in hominem, sed etiam in contemptissimum hominem cadere non possunt.*   What took place·

in Greece and Europe generally, took place in India and throughout the East, and unfortunately still in a great degree subsists in those unchanging lands. A multitude of gods and goddesses was in later times imagined by the poets of those mighty regions; a great lyrist Dwa-payana, surnamed Vyasa, or the compiler, arose and col-lected a number of idolatrous hymns, which he pretended were part of the Scriptures of God; and the common people under the leadership of their priests, whose inte-rest it has ever been to keep them ignorant, credulous, and enslaved, were taught to abandon the one pure pri-meval faith which God himself had given; and to be allured by the meretricious myths of those whose very existence depended on their remaining in darkness. (20).

24. In the primal ages of mankind, when their lives extended to a greater period than at present, though not to the extent mentioned in Genesis, the teaching of truth was chiefly patriarchal. One common language prevailed everywhere. All the languages of the earth, says Mau-rice, (*History of Hindostan*, i. 49), are derived from one grand primeval alphabet, which was once general like its religion, till like that religion in its progress to remote countries and distant generations, its original simplicity and purity were debased and corrupted by mankind. For the first 200 years after the creation of mortals, God taught them by divine instincts: after this in every 100 years he set up a Teacher who kept alive his holy knowledge. Twenty-four of these appeared and taught, and they are comme-morated in the Apocalypse as the Twenty-four Ancients; when, as the race of men had now grown widely diffused, it became necessary to make an improvement, and to adopt a wider range. Of several of these Maha-Bads,

D 2

or Great Prophets, (Boodhas, or men of wisdom), we have remains, not *all* authentic, in the *Desâtir*, or Book of Regulations; a manuscript volume written in a tongue of which no other vestige subsists, and which would have been unintelligible without the assistance of a Persian translation which was found with it. This volume fell accidentally into the hands of Mûlla Firûz Bin Kaus, by whom it was translated, and given to the world in 1818.

25. The doctrines of religion hitherto promulgated had not extended beyond Asia; but the human race was now circulating far and wide. A change therefore became absolutely necessary. The first Ancients had been merely men; but a nobler order of Teachers was now to appear. One Revelation would not suffice for this wide earth : nor would the earthly patriarchs who had hitherto preached, possess a sufficiency of authority over their fellow-men. Nations were perpetually changing; colonies were perpetually going forth; language was perpetually varying; books were liable to corruption. God resolved therefore to renew his Messages; and as He always works uniformly in his least as in his greatest manifestations, it was His will to send His new representative in that which has been appropriately named the Cycle of the Sun. This is the lunisolar *Naros*, or Sibylline year; it is composed of 31 periods of 19, and one of 11 years; and is the most perfect of the astronomical cycles: and although no chronologer has mentioned it at length, it is the most ancient of all. It consists of 600 years, of 7,200 solar months, or 219,146½ days : and this same number of 219,146½ days gives years, consisting each of 365 days, 5 hours, 51 minutes, and 36 seconds, which

differs less than 3 minutes from what its length is observed to be at this day. If on the first of January at noon, a new moon took place in any part of the heaven, it would take place again exactly in 600 years, at the same moment and under the same circumstances, the sun, the stars, the planets, would all be in the same relative positions. Cassini, one of the greatest of astronomers, declares that this is the most perfect of all periods; and adds that if the ancients had such a period of 600 years, they must have known the motions of the sun and moon more accurately than they were known for many ages after the flood. It was known, however, but it was guarded as the most religious of all secrets; hidden as this very Apocalypse itself was, from all mankind, except the priests, and communicated only to a favoured few, who did not betray the confidence reposed. Yet it was covertly hinted at in the Sibylline oracles; it was the unacknowledged source from whence the Hebrew priests, who brought their sacred volumes from Egypt or the centre of India, drew predictions of a Messiah, and it was in some manner guessed at by Virgil in his celebrated fourth Eclogue, which was certainly suggested by passages in this Apocalypse. *The last period sung by the Sibylline prophetess is now arrived, and the grand series of ages, that series which recurs again and again in the course of one mundane revolution, begins afresh. Now the Virgin Astræa returns from heaven, and the primæval reign of Saturn recommences. Now a new race descends from the celestial realms of holiness. Do, thou, Lucina, smile propitious on the birth of a Boy who will bring to a close the present age of iron, and introduce throughout the whole world a new age of gold. Then shall the herds no longer dread the fury of the lion, nor shall the poison of the serpent any longer be formidable: every venomous animal and every deleterious plant shall perish together. The fields shall be yellow with corn; the grapes shall hang in ruddy clusters from the bramble, and honey shall distil spontaneously from the rugged oak. The universal globe shall enjoy the blessings of peace, secure under the mild sway of its new and divine sovereign.* Nor can I doubt that the master of Plato alluded to it in the following, though if he had been initiated, he could not have been ignorant. Socrates, endeavouring to satisfy the mind of Alcibiades on the subject of acceptable worship, says, ἀναγκᾶιον οὖν ἐστι περιμένειν ἕως ἄν τις μαθη ὡς δεῖ πρὸς θεοὺς καὶ πρὸς ἀνθρώπους διακεῖσθαι. It is therefore necessary to wait till some One may teach us how it behoves us to conduct ourselves both towards the gods and men. To which Alcibiades makes answer: πότε ουν παρέσται ὁ χρόνος οὗτος ω Σώκρατες; καὶ τίς ὁ παιδεύσων, ἥδιστα γὰρ ἄν μοι δοκῶ ἰδεῖν τοῦτον τὸν ἄνθρωπον τίς ἐστιν; when shall that time arrive, O Socrates? and who shall that Teacher be? for most eagerly do I wish to see such a man.—*Alcibiades.* But as Socrates had not been initiated, and knew not the Naros, he could give no answer.

26. Upon the *necessity* of Revelations from God to Man, in order to declare not only his Laws, but to confer upon his creatures some knowledge of the Celestial, I suppose no one can entertain a rational doubt. The united voice of all nations seems to recognize it as a sacred truth: there are few, even among the most barbarous, who have not claimed for themselves the priesthood and the messages of divine Prophets, who were commissioned to raise them from the depths of ignorance, and to bless them

with the light and arts of civilization. That persons have aiisen, who falsely laid claim to the Messianic character, and daringly announced themselves to be the messengers of Heaven, in no way weakens the assurance of this hallowed calling; it only demonstrates still more potently the necessity which the human mind feels for an authentic apocalypse of the hidden Past and Future : and shews that for want of the living presence of the true Apostles, the soul of man yearns for that which is tangible and visible ; and will too frequently accept it as holy, without requiring the best proofs of that holiness. Man cannot indeed subsist without some Revelation of the ordinances and puiposes of the Most High ; and we may be certain that this desire has not been implanted in him except for wise ends, and that God would not perpetually balk the august curiosity which He has inspired ; and to confine this Revelation to only one people, and to hide it from almost all others, would not, and indeed could not be consistent with the character of the King and Father of mankind. (21). We may be certain, therefore, that if God ever sent a Revelation, he sent it to all men. But as this would be an impossibility, if it were confined to only one place, and time, it follows that He must send many Revelations, if he willed that the whole world should be partakers of the knowledge which was needed. And as it would not be consistent with the dignity of His Apostle, that a number of similar apostles should at the same time co-exist and preach, it follows from this that his Apostles would appear at intervals, and in different countries, and would preach in different languages, and in different types and figures, according to the genius of the people to whom each was sent. The dialect that

would suit a Chinese, or a Greek, or Roman, would fall
without effect upon the soul of an Indian or an Iranian;
the subtile and sublime mysticism that would captivate
the Egyptian or the Arab intellect, would be utterly lost
upon the dull Hebrew, or the carnal European, whose
coarser mind is unable to comprehend those ideas which
to an Oriental fancy are the impersonation of all that is
beautiful. As the Revelation therefore must be given
to all, and as this could only be effected by sending
men to all the people, whose importance seemed to justify
the special interposition of the All-Ruler, it was necessary that Messiahs should appear in Scythia, China, India,
Arabia, Irân; in fact, wherever there was one vast and
common centre from which the teachings of the Holy
One could be most generally disseminated. Hence also,
as they could not all appear at the same æra, they would
be sent successively, that is at certain fixed periods; as we
see the seasons of the year, as we see the tides, as we see
the lunations, as we see the growth of trees : in a word
all the visible operations of the Divine, which are always
regular in times and modes. For this purpose the period
of 600 years seemed to God to be the best; the interval
being not too long for the teachings of the preceding
Messenger to be forgotten ; nor too short to prevent their
having due influence on mankind; and as during this
time also a cyclic revolution took place in heaven, it
seemed consistent that He should give that cycle as a
sign infallible to man when he should expect the advent
of the new Messiah.

27. This sublime provision requires no elaborate argument from any, to make manifest its wisdom or its beauty.
When it is once confessed that God interferes in the

government of the worlds which He has formed, and that
He benevolently desires the happiness of His creatures,
all the rest must follow; namely, that the only course
consistent with that interference is a Revelation of himself, universally delivered, and miraculously preserved.
If it were given by only one man to one people, it never
could be universal. An old and haughty nation like the
Chinese, for instance, would never be persuaded that all
their ancestors, so wise, so pure, so excellent, were utterly
excluded from all the active interference of heaven; and
that it was never exercised until thousands of years had
passed away, and millions of men had lived and died,
when it was at length put forward as it were by accident,
for a wandering horde of exiles out of Egypt, or in a
paltry district like Judæa, which is but a little larger than
Wales. (22). As the sun and moon, therefore, *renew* their
course mysteriously in heaven at the end of every 600 years,
God resolved that this period should be the cycle of his
Messiahs, and should constitute the interval during
which they were each destined successively to re-appear.
It was called in the primitive ages the Naros, from *Nara,*
which was a mystic name for the Virgin Spirit of God;
whence she is called in one of the Hindu books Narayana, which is translated the Mover on the waters, though
it has another secret meaning which I cannot reveal; and
by Amosis it is said, "the Spirit of God brooded like a
dove over the face of the waters." The Dove that is fabled
to have descended on Jesus was the Holy Spirit thus symbolized; and note that Homer calls Iris a Dove (23). Jesus
was the Ninth Messenger of God, and appeared in the Ninth
Cycle; and Juvenal, who knew nothing either of him or of
the Naros, says in his XIII Sat., v. 28, *Nona ætas agitur, &c.,*

D 3

"Now is the ninth cycle or age," which it undoubtedly was; but in what way, was an entire secret to him, and indeed, to all others except the deeply mystic and initiated. The Naros, the Apocalypse, and in later and corrupt ages, when the priests invented the horrible tenet of a blood-mediation, a human sacrifice, were the three great secrets of the Ancient Mysteries; and circumcision, which was a primary rite among the novices, was adopted as a masonic symbol, by means of which the brethren were enabled to recognize and assist each other, in whatever part of the world they might be; while by those without, (the exoteric, the profane), it was a sign which from its peculiar nature was secure from all discovery. Pythagoras called it his golden thigh; Abaris called it his golden arrow: both meant the same thing. Jesus himself, (who as a Messiah, of course knew of the Naros), when he predicted to his disciples the Epiphany of his successor, (the tenth Messenger), clearly alluded to it, but in a way which none but the initiated could understand. There shall be *signs*, he said, in the Sun and in the Moon, and in the Stars; and then also shall appear the *sign* of the Son of Man in Heaven. (*Luke* xxi. 25,) which was as precise and certain an allusion to the lunisolar cycle as could possibly be made without revealing the secret to mankind. (24). Job (xxviii. 32) also covertly alludes to the Naros in a passage which has been most artfully disguised in the Vulgate version. "Canst thou bring forth *Mazzaroth* in his season, or canst thou guide *Arcturus* with his sons?" A more false and disingenuous translation it is not possible to conceive. The real version is, Canst thou bring forth the Twelve in their season; or, Canst thou guide Ash (עַיִשׁ, the Holy Spirit) with her sons? (or, more literally her flock), mean-, ing Thou canst, &c., &c. And as this sacred drama was written by Amosis, one of the Twelve Messiahs of God, the importance of such an allusion by him will be at once perceived; nor is the weight to be attached to it the less, because of the secret and mysterious way in which its sense is guarded.

28. The period of six hundred years, says Bailly, a period which was indeed preserved but misunderstood at Babylon, will supply me with another argument. It is evident they preserved it, since it is cited by Berosus, one of their historians: it is as evident they did not understand it, since they made no use of it for the regulation of time. It should seem that they took no notice of it in their books of astronomy, inasmuch as Hipparchus, who examined the Chaldæan periods of motion in the stars, makes no mention of *this*. Hence we necessarily conclude that it was not the result of their own labours. It was therefore transported among them : and those two facts, the knowledge of the period of six hundred years, and the return of comets, belonged to astronomy in an improved state, *previous and foreign to the Chaldæans*.

29. A variety of circumstances all apparently slight, but nevertheless significant, shew the importance of the number 6, and the word Naros in ancient tradition. Adam is said in Genesis to have been formed on the sixth day. So we are told that Noah was six hundred years old when the flood of waters was upon the earth. *Gen* vii. 6. This mystically means that the cycle of the Naros was come. In the Hebrew Chaldee, the name and quality of the Divine Spirit Narah-Yona are preserved. נערה Naarah, a Virgin, and Naaray נערי, Child of the

Lord. Ner נר means Light, from the Arabic *nur*, to give light. Nahr (נהר) in Hebrew and Arabic is a *River*, and נריה Neriyyah is Lamp of the Lord. The Hindus preserve the tradition in the name *Narad*, whom they believe to be a great Prophet, who is for ever wandering about the earth, giving good counsel. (25.) A very distinguished son of Brahma, (the Holy Spirit), named Narad, (says Jones), whose actions are the subject of a Purana, bears a strong resemblance to Hermes, or Mercury. He was a wise legislator, great in arts and in arms, an eloquent Messenger of the gods, either to one another, or to favoured mortals, and a musician of exquisite skill. His invention of the Vina, or Indian lute, is thus described in the poem entitled *Mogha*. Narad sat watching from time to time his large Vina, which by the impulse of the breeze yielded notes that pierced successively the regions of his ear, and proceeded by musical intervals. *As. Res.* i. 264. Hermes, as the classical reader recollects, invented the lyre also, and Phœbus always carried one. Skanda, which with the Hindus is a symbolic name for the Messenger, is called Shanmatura (six-mothered), and Shandanana (six-faced). Both allude to the Naros of six centuries. So the Japanese Incarnation is seated on a lotos flower, with *six* beautiful infants round his head, which form a crown or circle of rays. The druids also paid great veneration to the number six. As to what remains, says Mayo, vol. ii. p. 239, respecting the superstitions of the Druids, I know not what was the foundation of the religious respect which they had for the number six; but it is certain they preferred it to all other numbers. It was the sixth day of the moon that they performed their principal ceremonies of religion, and that

they began the year. They went six in number to gather
the misseltoe; and in monuments now extant, we often
find six of these priests together. In the old pictures of
the Annunciation, the Angel Gabriel is always painted
with a bunch of lilies, which he is offering to the Virgin
Mary. This is but the ancient myth of Juno's conception of one of the divinities. Juno, surprised that Zeus
should produce Minerva from his head, went to Oceanus
to ask his advice, whether she could have a child without
her husband's concurrence. She was tired on her journey, and sat down at the door of the goddess Flora, who,
understanding the occasion of her journey, desired her to
be of good heart, for she had in her garden a flower, and
if she did only touch it with the tips of her fingers, the
smell of it would make her conceive a son presently. So
Juno was carried into the garden, and the flower shewn
to her; she touched it and conceived. The flower was
called *Nerio* or *Nerione*, (the Naros). Nereus in Hesiod
is called " the truth-speaking." I doubt if Hesiod really
knew what the Naros meant, but the allusion is
curious. In Burgundy was found a statue of a young
man with short hair, wearing a short cloak like
Apollo Belvedere; in his right hand a bunch of grapes;
in the left some other fruits which time had defaced.
It was inscribed *Deo Bemilucio VI.* The numerals have
puzzled all the antiquaries; but the young man was an
image of the Incarnation, and the six indicated the Naros.

30. In the Vishnu Purana, the Naros is thus alluded
to: When the practices taught by the Vedas and the
institutes of law shall have nearly ceased, and the close
of the Kali age shall be nigh, a portion of that Divine
Being who exists of his own spiritual nature in the charac-

ter of Brahmah, and who is the beginning and the end, and who comprehends all things, shall descend upon the earth. By his irresistible might he will destroy all whose minds are devoted to iniquity: He will then re-establish righteousness on earth; and the minds of those who live shall be awakened and shall be as pellucid as crystal. The men who are thus changed by virtue of that peculiar time shall be as the seeds of human beings, and shall give birth to a race who shall follow the laws of the age of purity. As it is said, *When the sun and moon and the lunar asterism Tishya and the planet Jupiter are in one mansion, the Age of Purity shall return.*

31. The Hindus would readily admit the truth of our gospel, says a very learned writer long resident among them, but they contend that it is perfectly consistent with their own Sastras. The Deity, they say, has appeared many times in many parts of this world and of all worlds, for the salvation of his creatures: and though we adore Him in one appearance and they in others, yet we adore they say, the same God; to whom our several worships though different in form, are equally acceptable if they be sincere in substance. *As. Res.* i. 274. And this it will be seen is precisely the doctrine taught in the Apocalypse, which is now for the first time rescued from obscurity and foolishness. In the Hindu theology, it should be noted that Messiahs are not specially appointed by God to be sent to the earths of mortals; as the Christians preach that Jesus was, and so was destined by the All-Father to a death of agony: but their mission is accomplished in this wise. When the cycle approaches in which the Incarnation of a new Messenger is to take place, one of the divine angels who commiserates the condition of

mankind voluntarily offers himself as an ambassador; he is willing to descend from the glorious happy spheres, and to take upon himself the burden and the wretchedness of humanity, for the sake of the vast amount of good which the teaching of the Messenger usually accomplishes; his desire is granted, and he is clothed in flesh: he descends: he preaches: he suffers and dies, and reascends into the splendour of the empyrean. It is on this, as will be seen, the Christian mythos is founded; but the Hindu form of the truth is infinitely more beautiful than that which the half rabbinical, half pagan notion of God himself incarnate, has diffused through Europe. The Hindu form is also that which is developed in the Apocalypse; for there proclamation is made in Heaven for one who will volunteer to open the Book, that is, to diffuse its teachings; and it is answered voluntarily by one of the happy Spirits, symbolized as a lion-like Lamb, and who is himself in this a type of the various Messengers who follow. I need not add, that this explication of the Messianic mission is the only true one. Nor did it belong solely to the Orient. God, says Socrates in Plato, (*Symposium*), mixeth not with man, but by the mediation of this Daimon or Blessed Spirit, by whom all communion and conference betwixt the gods and men is maintained. This also was the popular belief in the days of Jesus. The *gods* in the likeness of *men* have come down to us —*Acts* xiv. 11.

32. This voluntary offering and self-sacrifice of the Messiah Angel, was compared from the early ages to a martyrdom—for he abandoned for a period the blissfulness of heaven, and took upon himself the tribulations of humanity. Hence it was likened to an impalement on a rock like that of Prometheus, and to a crucifix like that

of the Buddha of Nepaul, and Jesus of Nazareth : the mythologies of all nations are full of allusions to it as a death, a shedding of blood, and it is more than once alluded to under that figure in the Apocalypse.

33. The Mussulmans, says Sir W. Jones, (*Gods of Greece, &c.*), are already a sort of heterodox Christians : they are Christians, if Locke reasons justly, because they firmly believe the immaculate conception, divine character, and miracles of the Messiah : but they are heterodox in denying vehemently his character of *Son*, and his equality as *God*, with the Father, of whose unity and attributes they entertain and express the most awful ideas ; while they consider our doctrines as perfect blasphemy, and insist that our copies of the Scriptures have been corrupted both by Jews and Christians. It is not unusual among the poets of Persia and Turkey, to allude, even in their profane and unchaste compositions, to the miraculous power of Issa's (Jesus) breath, which could give health to the infirm, and restore the dead to life. These allusions are intended seriously. I have read in some Travels, of a Turk who was bastinadoed almost to death for uttering disrespectful words against the Messiah ; although he might with impunity have cruelly abused the followers of that divine personage. And when their poets speak of him, let their allusions be ever so silly or indecorous, they speak of him, according to the learned critic Revicksky, in the same manner that they would do of Mohammed himself.—*Spec. Poes. Pers.*, 97. Comparing this behaviour of the Mohammedans with that of our own to the heavenly-inspired Prophet of Arabia, we should be filled with shame, had not the odious bigotry and intolerance with which the priests have filled the Paulite-

Christian mind, obliterated all notions of truth, justice, or enquiry in matters of religion.

34. The apocryphal Esdras (as he is called, though I do not believe him to be a less genuine writer than some of those who have been admitted into the Canon), gives us in full the Hebrew belief of the Messiah. Paulite writers say that this alludes to Jesus; but no Jew would so write of the despised Galilean. And this Hebrew article of faith was only a reflex of that which came from China and Hindostan. *I Esdras saw upon the Mount Sion a great people, whom I could not number, and they all praised the Lord with songs. And in the midst of them there was a young Man of a high stature, taller than all the rest, and upon every one of their heads he set crowns, and was more exalted; which I marvelled at greatly. So I asked the angel, and said, Sir, what are these? He answered and said unto me, These be they that have put off the mortal clothing, and put on the immortal, and have confessed the name of God; now are they crowned, and receive palms. Then said I unto the angel, What young person is it that crowneth them, and giveth them palms in their hands? So he answered and said unto me, It is the Son of God, whom they have confessed in the world. Then began I greatly to commend them that stood so stiffly for the name of the Lord. Then the Angel said unto me, Go thy way, and tell my people what manner of things, and how great wonders of the Lord thy God thou hast seen.*

35. It appears, says Colonel Wilford, (*As. Res.* x. 27), that long before Christ, a renovation of the universe was expected all over the world, with a saviour, a king of peace and justice. This expectation is frequently mentioned in the Puranas; the earth is often complaining that

she is ready to sink back into Pátála, under the accumu-
lated load of the iniquities of mankind : the gods also
complain of the oppression of the giants. Vishnu comforts
the earth and the gods, assuring them that a Saviour
would come to redress their grievances, and put an end to
the tyranny of the Daityas or Demons; that for this purpose
he would be incarnated in the house of a shepherd, and
brought up among shepherds. The followers of Buddha
unanimously declare that his incarnation in the womb of
a Virgin was foretold several thousand years before it came
to pass. Not only the Jews, but the Romans on the authority of the Sibylline books, and the decision of the Sacred
College of the Etrurian augurs, the sole depositaries in
Rome of primeval religious knowledge, were all of opinion that this momentous event was at hand. All these
facts prove the knowledge of the Naros, and of the
avatar of the Ninth Messiah in the days predicted in the
Apocalypse : and on no other hypothesis indeed can they
be explained, unless on one which has a series of miracles
for its basis. While this sheet is passing through the
press, a work has appeared, (*Travels in Egypt and Syria,
by S. S. Hill*), in which the author details a conversation
between himself and a Mohammedan ; which shows how
strongly this belief of a renewal of revelations has entered into the Oriental mind. According to this speaker
the world is on the eve of another religious revolution—
We are now, said he, just what the Jews were at the
advent of the Messiah, and what the Christians were at
the coming of Mohammed ; and *until a new dispensation
be given we shall grow worse and worse; but this will
come.* As the Gospel succeeded the Pentateuch, and the
Koran the Gospel, so sure will *another and purer dispen-*

sation explain the three that have preceded it, and establish a law adapted to extend at least to all those of the three faiths which owe their existence to revelation, and perhaps to the whole human race. The dispensation through Jesus, the Son of Mary, was like that through Moses, and given to spread, and the means to that end were adopted. When the Messiah appeared, the Jewish religion had expired in spirit, and the world was overrun with wickedness. The Romans, who then governed, were to be converted by words and reason. But as you know from your Scriptures that these were not always the means used by the legislators and prophets of the Jews, you must acknowledge that God permits the acts of mankind to march by steps, unchecked by his will and unforeseen by themselves; and what means He will employ in the event of his again addressing himself to the human race it is impossible to foresee. This of course was all new to Mr. Hill.

36. A glorious picture of Divine Polity is thus developed before our eyes, in which the Heavenly Father is represented, seated on his Thrones and sending forth among mankind Messengers of His sacred truth, which is thus dispersed throughout the whole length and breadth of the world. We know what innumerable atheists and infidels (26), have been made in Europe by the exclusively bigoted views of the Celestial government, which have tainted even Christianity itself; views which are the natural consequence of that gradual and almost imperceptible influence which the rabbinical writings and precepts had over the early Fathers; many of whom were also converts from Judaism, and like modern Protestants believed in Paul and his fancies rather than in the divine Jesus; and as these rabbis were at all times the most narrow-

minded of theologians, it can scarcely be a matter of surprise, that they debased all that they touched to the very
lowest standard of nonsensical' Talmudism. They were
in fact Hebrews only in the name : of the great principles
of Osarsiph or Amosis, who was one of the greatest scholars of his age, if not the very greatest, they had no ade-
quate conception : they had about the same idea of his
genius, as the miserable believers in Johanna Southcott
had of the Holy Spirit of Heaven; or the unhappy followers of Joe Smith possess, of the grandeur, moral worth,
and elevating influences of true religion. By demanding
therefore as an article of belief, the soul-debasing creed,
that God was so partial in his administrative office, as to
leave the great bulk of mankind in dense ignorance,
while he enlighted but a few, who to say the least, were
never pre-eminently distinguished above their fellows by
their superiority in virtue : the Western Churches created
so much disgust, that among those who had seriously considered the subject, and who had taught their souls by
daily meditation, that God, if He existed at all, was Universal in all things, a belief in their dogmas became impossible ; and from doubt and infidelity the way is short
and easy into an absolute disbelief in God himself. And
as falsehood must always produce evil, we see the same
result happening at present all over Europe, where men
are rushing into positive atheism, because they think they
must either do this, or believe in a series of legends to
which the lies of Paganism are far superior, whether we
regard them for their poetic colouring, or for the species
of moral which is often conveyed under the guise of
grossness itself. (27). He, however, who shall behold God,
as He is made manifest in this Apocalypse, and by the light'

which the Naros and the Messengers throw over all past events, will run no risk of sinking into atheism; but on the contrary, will find his soul and reason alike enlarged, and his conceptions of the Divine Being raised from the most petty, to the most sublime, majestic, and comprehensive degree of which the human understanding is capable. He will see God, as it were by his own mouth, teaching the early races of men; he will see Him commissioning Messenger after Messenger into regions the most distant from each other, but at intervals as fixed and regular as the revolutions of the stars themselves; he will see that these Messengers have in their æras established and re-established the One Primeval Religion, and have perpetually renewed its beauty, covered over it as it were with the slime and corruption of priestliness; he will see that God has ever preserved all over the world the grand and leading outlines of a belief in Himself; and that the lies, the superstitions, the low and debasing ideas of things spiritual, which have converted the very Holy of Holies into an abomination of desolation, have been the life-long work of the sacerdotal order: who are for ever adding creeds, articles, and legends to the simple preachings of the Inspired Apostles of the Lord. In what part of the genuine Law of Amosis are the Jews taught to expiate their sins by the sacrifice of a cock? Yet we know that they do so sacrifice, and that they do so hold.(28). In what sermon, parable or speech of Jesus, is he found saying that Tom, Dick, or Harry, can change a wafer into his body and blood, and that that wafer will ensure them heaven? Yet we know that all the priests of Rome pretend that they can do so. In what discourse did the Son of Mary ever declare that God predestined John to ever-

lasting flame, and Will to everlasting paradise (29), though
John was a good man in all relations of life, and Will was
a thief, a murderer, and perjurer? yet we know that this
is the belief of millions of men, and that with Calvin's
subtleties they can support it by arguments drawn from
Paul, and such like wretched casuists. And the observations on this head that apply to Judaism and Christianity,
apply to every form of religion in the world, which has
been taken out of the hands of sages, and fallen into the
clutch of priests.

37. That during so many thousand years this mystic
Cycle, of such wide-diffused importance, which was known
to so many, should have remained unknown to the whole
world, and be only now brought prominently forward,
would strike any one as a most curious fact; but it will
not be wondered at by those who know the watchful
jealousy, with which the priesthood kept the knowledge
even of letters from the common people. To pry into
science, or to divulge it, without initiation into their
Mysteries, was likened by the Hebrews to eating of the
fruit of the Tree of Knowledge, which entailed death as a
punishment: and for aught we know, had it ever been
attempted, the priests would not have hesitated to murder
their betrayer. It was for divulging the secrets of the
gods, that Tantalus was fabled to have been plunged into
hell; and the guardian of the Sibylline Books was liable
to the penalty of death if he revealed aught that they
contained. In the temples were Sigalions, or images of
Harpocrates, with his finger on his lips, to indicate religious secrecy and silence; and they had two species of
disciples, the esoteric, or brethren to whom they explained
everything: the exoteric, or multitude to whom they

spake in riddles, and whom they left in ignorance, as they do still. In a niche of the Temple of Isis, at Pompeii, was found a marble statue of a female with her forefinger on her lip. I give the following passage from Varro, which shows that a statue of this kind was always seen in temples of Isis. *Quoniam in omnibus templis ubi Isis et Serapis colebatur, erat etiam simulacrum quod digito labiis impresso, admonere videbatur ut silentia fierent.* In all the temples where Isis and Serapis were worshipped, there was also an image, which with the finger impressed on the lips or *labia*, seemed to admonish that silence should be maintained. But had not this junction of the forefinger with the lip, another and a mystic meaning also, which alluded to the very mystery that was to be kept secret? and did it not symbolize the Shekinah or Yoni of Heaven, the Sacred Spirit who is the Mother of all existences?

38. The Genesis which is ascribed to Amosis, is itself in parts profoundly enigmatic. Taken to the letter, says the learned Maimonides, this work gives the most absurd and extravagant ideas of the Divinity. Whosoever shall find the true sense of it, *ought to take care not to divulge it.* This is a maxim which all our Rabbis impose on us; and above all respecting the true meaning of the work of the six days. If a person should discover the hidden secret of it, either by himself, or by the aid of another, then he ought to be discreetly silent; or if he speak of it, he ought to speak of it obscurely, and in an enigmatical manner, as I do myself, leaving the rest to be guessed, by those who can understand me. Herodotus, who as a Greek, could have no terror of the priests of Egypt, unless, indeed,

he was initiated into their Mysteries, thus speaks,
when excusing himself for not informing his readers
of the secret reasons why the Egyptians revered the
images of animals. If I should take upon me to give
the reasons of this opinion, he says, I must enter into
a long discourse of divine things, which I avoid with
all possible care, having hitherto said nothing of that
kind, unless in a transitory manner, and compelled by
the force of necessity. (Lib. ii.) In our schools, says
Rabbi Abondana, Natural Philosophy is to be learned
from the first chapter of Genesis, upon which account it
is called the study of the Work of Creation; which being
encumbered with great difficulties, is not wont to be
publicly explained, but only in *private* to the party that
desires it. As for Metaphysics, neither is this study to
be otherwise attained to; it being grounded upon the first
chapter of Ezekiel, which is looked upon as no less difficult, and therefore not to be explained but with the like
caution. (*Polity of the Jews*). In the Book of Sohar it is
said; Alas for the man who thinks that the Law contains nothing but what appears on its surface; for if that
were true there would be men in our day who could
excel it. But the Law assumed a body; for if angels are
obliged, when they descend into this world to assume a
body in order that they may subsist in the world, and it
be able to receive them; how much more necessary was it
that the Law, which created them, and which was the
instrument by which the world was created, should be invested with a body in order that it might be adapted to
the comprehension of man. That body is a history, in
which, if any man think there is not a soul, let him have
no part in the life to come. And so strictly was this

esoteric knowledge guarded, that even Jesus himself, the purest of human beings, ordered his disciples not to "throw their pearls before swine;" that is, to disclose nothing but to those who were enrolled.

39. It was for the esoteric order, therefore, and for the truly wise, that the Greater Mysteries, of which all ancient history is full, were first invented; and to them in these Mysteries this Apocalypse was for the first time communicated, though even from these the secret of the Naros was in a great measure withheld. Accordingly we know that the most splendid and dazzling figures were scenically represented; figures calculated to fill with delight and wonder; a series of illuminated paintings passed before the eye, vivid with all the glory of art; thunders rolled, and lightnings flashed; fiery meteors were beheld; the whole past, present and future were unveiled, and the initiated brother never could forget the magnificent spectacle on which his eyes had feasted, and in which his ear and mind were alike charmed by the melodies and songs that breathed into his soul, secrets guarded from the whole community. The mystagogue, habited like the Demiourgos, and moving in a cloud of luminous glory, sang a divine hymn, of which the following fragment will convey no unfair idea as to the sublime nature of the whole. *I will declare a secret to the initiated, but let the doors be wholly shut against the profane* (30). . . *Suffer not the prepossessions of your mind to deprive you of that happy life, which the knowledge of these mysterious truths will procure you; but look on the Divine Nature; incessantly contemplate it, and govern well the mind and heart. Go on in the right way and see the* ONE GOVERNOR OF THE UNIVERSE. *He is One and of him-*

E

self alone; and to that One all things owe their being. He operates through all, was never seen by mortal eyes; but does himself see everything. In the most Holy Mysteries of those who are made perfect, says Proclus in *Plat. Repub.*, p. 380, the gods exhibit many forms of themselves, and appear in a variety of shapes; and sometimes indeed, an *unfigured light of themselves*, is held forth to the view, sometimes *this light is figured according to a human form, and sometimes it proceeds into a different shape.* This doctrine, too, of divine appearances in the Mysteries, is confirmed by Plotinus, *Ennead* i. lib. 6, p. 55. and *Ennead* 9, lib. 6, p. 700; and Aristides tells us that in the shows of the Mysteries innumerable generations of men and women appeared to the Initiated. If the reader, when he shall have perused this Apocalypse, and contemplated it as a whole, will but form to his mind's eye an image of what it must have been, when scenically represented, or recited as an Oratorio, amid music, light and song; with all those dazzling appurtenances of matchless art, vivid colour and magnificent decoration, with all those awful alternations of the deepest shadow and the most brilliant torrents of lustre, for which the dramatic pictures of the ancients were eminently distinguished, he will understand clearly to what Proclus, Plotinus, and Aristides allude, when they speak of the things of multiform shape and species, "and the innumerable generations" which passed before the eye; and will be convinced that the sublime symbols and chain of prophecies herein contained, and no others, were the many-shining splendours that were flashed across the vision of those whom the priests thought worthy of initiation, and who consequently regarded that initiation ever after as the most wondrous incident in their whole existence. Among the many excellent things, writes Cicero, which the Greeks have taught the Romans, are the Mysteries. Well indeed are they called initiations; since they introduce us to the *first principles* of Wisdom and enable us to live more happily and to die with better hope. No person, remarks Payne Knight, could be perfect who had not been initiated into them. They were divided into two stages or degrees; the first or lesser of which was a kind of holy purification, to prepare the mind for the divine truths which were to be revealed to it in the second or greater. From one to five years of probation were required between them, and at the end, the initiate, on being found worthy, was admitted into the inmost recesses of the Temple, and made acquainted with the first principles of religion,—the knowledge of the God of Nature, the First, the Supreme, the Intellectual; by whom men had been reclaimed from rudeness and barbarism to elegance and refinement; and been taught not only to live with more comfort, but to die with better hopes. When Greece lost her liberty, the periods of probation were dispensed with in favour of her acknowledged sovereigns; but nevertheless, so sacred and awful was this subject, that even in the lowest stage of her servitude and depression, the Emperor Nero did not dare to compel the priests to initiate him, on account of the murder of his mother. To divulge anything thus learnt, was everywhere considered as the extreme of wickedness and impiety, and at Athens was punished with death.

40. The beginning of Callimachus's Hymn to Apollo, (the Messiah), plainly shews that he was revealed and beheld in the Mysteries: he was the Ach-Arez (31).

t. 2

See how the laurel's hallowed branches wave !
Hark ; sounds tumultuous shake the trembling cave !
Far, ye profane ! far off !—*with beauteous feet*
Bright Phœbus comes, and thunders at the gate.
See ! the glad sign the Delian palm hath given ;
Sudden it bends, and hovering in the heaven,
Soft sings the swan, with melody divine ;
Burst ope, ye bars ! ye gates, your heads decline—
Decline your heads ! ye sacred doors expand !
He comes ! the god of light ! the god's at hand.
Begin the song, and tread the sacred ground,
In mystic dance symphonious to the sound.
Begin, young men : Apollo's eyes endure
None but the good, the perfect, and the pure.
Who view the god are great ; but abject they
From whom he turns his favouring eyes away.
All piercing god ! in every place confessed ;
We will prepare, behold thee, and be blessed.

41. There is a curious fragment of one of the Welsh
Druids or priests of Boodh, which alludes to this secret,
under the name of Awen, in words that to me are perfectly
clear. I cite it, with one or two alterations, from Davies's
Celtic Researches. I am Taliesin. I will record a true string,
which shall remain to the end as a pattern to Elphin (the
Spirit.) A royal tribute of gold, duly counted, may be abhorred, because perjury and treachery are odious. I seek not to
procure advantage by undermining the laws of our song.
*No one shall discover the secret which is committed to me
by a brother ;* a man of wisdom, eminently skilled in the
studies of the Sywedydd (the god Siva.) Concerning the
bird of judgment (or Phœnix) ; concerning the fire of

judgment; *concerning the changes of the Teacher of Man;* and concerning men well versed in divine lore. It is the mystery of the God who has appreciated the desert of the transgression of Bardism, which he gave, together with its secret, the *Awen* (32), not to be divulged. And seven score personifications pertain to the *Awen*—in the *deep* which is void of wrath; in the deep where extreme indignation dwells—in the deep beneath the elements—and in the sky above the elements. There is one who knows that state of pensive meditation which is better than cheerfulness. I know the laws of the endowments of the *Awen*, when they stream forth, concerning the secrets of the understanding; concerning the blessed Gods; concerning an inoffensive course of life; concerning the ages of deliverance; concerning that which beseems princes and the duration of their bliss; and concerning the analysis of things on the face of the earth.

Few would be found to say that this passage from Taliesin is not enigmatic in the highest degree; fewer would allege that it does not embody a secret of the most profound importance. Those who study this volume will be convinced that the only secret to which it *could* refer is that which is here alluded to.

42. A remarkable example of the sacred secrecy common to all priests in those days, is to be found in the second book of Esdras, which is itself one of the Apocryphal, or hidden volumes, to which the laity are prohibited to resort for doctrinal teaching. It appears from this that the whole Law of the Jewish people had been burnt by their conquerors, and that not a single copy could be discovered. Esdras, therefore, was divinely appointed to bring forth anew by a species of inspired transcription from the

oracles of heaven, wherever he could hear them, the lost sacred writings. *These words,* says Esdras, *Thou shalt declare, and these thou shalt hide * * * For Thy Law is burnt, therefore no man knoweth the things that are done of Thee, or the works that shall begin. But if I have found grace before Thee, send the Holy Spirit into me, and I shall write all that hath been done in the world since the beginning, which were written in thy Law, that men may find thy path, and that they which live in the latter days may live. And he answered me saying, Go thy way : gather the people together, and say unto them that they seek thee not for forty days. But look thou, prepare thee many box trees, and take with thee Sared, Dabria, Selemia, Ecanus, and Asiel ; these five which are ready to write swiftly. And come hither, and I shall light a candle of understanding in thine heart, which shall not be put out till the things be performed which thou shalt begin to write. And when thou hast done, some things shalt thou publish, and some things shalt thou shew secretly to the wise. To-morrow, this hour shalt thou begin to write * * * And the next day, behold a Voice called me, saying, Esdras, open thy mouth and drink that which I give thee to drink. Then opened I my mouth, and behold He reached me a full cup, which was full as it were with water, but the colour of it was like fire. And I took it and drank : and when I had drank of it, my heart uttered wisdom, and knowledge grew in my breast, for my spirit strengthened my memory. And my mouth was opened and shut no more. The Highest gave understanding unto my five companions, and they wrote the wonderful visions of the night that were revealed, and which they knew not : and they sat forty days, and they wrote in the day, and at night they brake bread. As for me, I spake in the day, and I held not my tongue by night. In forty* *days they wrote two hundred and four chapters. And it came to pass that when forty days were fulfilled, that the Highest spake, saying, The first that thou hast written publish openly, that the worthy and unworthy may read it. But keep the seventy last that thou mayst deliver them only to such as be wise among the people. For in them is the spring of understanding, the fountain of wisdom, and the stream of knowledge. And I did so* (33). More authentic authority as to the custom among divines in this matter, cannot be resorted to, than that of this learned priest; and what he did, and even boasts that he did, was in accordance with all sacerdotal usage and tradition. (34).

43. And as the Rabbins borrowed nearly all things from the Heathen philosophers, so they followed their method of concealing them from the people, by wrapping them up in fables, allegories, and dark sayings. We read in the treatise *Halichot Olam,* that the teachers among the Israelites had little schedules or scrolls of parchment, in which they set down all the traditions, sentences, decisions, statutes, and mysteries, which they learned from their masters, and that they called them *volumes of the secret things.* Jesus declares that the Scribes and Pharisees had the key of knowledge; but rebuked them for having taken it away from the people, and shut up the kingdom of heaven against men; not going in themselves, nor suffering them that are entering to go in. (*Matt.* xxiii., 13; *Luke* xi., 52.) Philo, speaking of the Essenes, whom he also calls Therapeutæ, says,—Reading the Holy Scriptures, they apply to Philosophy, making use of allegories handed down to them by their ancestors, for they believe that under the plainest words are contained mysteries. (*De Vit. Contemplat.,* p. 893.) Woe to the man, say the

Kabbalists, who avers that the Doctrine delivers common stories and daily words. For if this were so, then we also in our time could compose a Doctrine in daily words which would deserve far more praise. If it delivered usual words we should only have to follow the lawgivers of the earth, among whom we find far loftier words, to be able to compose a Doctrine. Therefore we must believe that every word of the Doctrine contains in it a loftier sense *and a higher mystery*. The narratives of the Doctrine are its cloak. Woe to him who takes the covering for the Doctrine itself. The simple look only at the garment, that is, upon the narratives of the Doctrine : more they know not. The instructed (the initiated), however, see not merely the cloak, but what the cloak covers.—*The Sohar*. It adds : Every word hides in itself a lofty meaning : every narrative contains more than the event, which it seems to recite. This holy and lofty doctrine is the true Doctrine. What man of sense, asks Origen, will agree with the statement that on the first, second, and third days in which the *evening* is named, the *morning* was without Sun, Moon, and Stars, and the first day without a heaven ? What man is found such an idiot as to suppose that God planted trees in Paradise, in Eden, like a husbandman, &c. ? I believe that every man must hold these things for *images* under which a *hidden sense* lies concealed.

44. Nothing, says Father Simon, in his *Critical History of the Old Testament*, can more clearly demonstrate the genius of the Jews, than the words of Aristæus, wherein he says that certain persons going about the translating the scriptures, have been prevented by being punished by God : one Theopompus having been so bold as to insert in

· his history, part of the Law not well translated, became dis‑
tracted. And he farther adds that the same Theopompus,
during some little interval of his madness, having prayed
to God to let him know the cause of his disease, *God told
him in a dream that all that had happened to him was because
he had gone about the publishing of sacred things, which
ought to be concealed;* at last he was cured after he had
desisted from what he had gone about. There is in the
same place another story concerning Theodectus, a tra‑
gical poet *who was struck blind, because he had·been so
rash as to insert in one of his plays something of the Law
of Moses* . but having afterwards acknowledged his fault,
and asked pardon of God, he recovered his sight. If we
compare these miracles with those related in the Talmud,
upon account of the Chaldæan paraphrase of Jonathan
upon the Prophets, we shall easily find out the rise of all
these pretended wonders. According to the testimony of
the Jewish doctors, there was a voice heard from heaven,
which asked Jonathan, *who he was that durst reveal the
secrets of God by publishing of them to men;* and they say
that Jonathan was hindered by that voice from translating
the other books of the Bible.—*Book 2, chap.* 2.

45. It will probably be asked why was this secret of
the Naros guarded so suspiciously ? The reason is on the
surface. Had it been made known to the world, that
God at the end of every six hundred years, sent forth a
Messenger, let us for a moment consider what would be
the condition of mankind when the Sacred Cycle recom‑
menced. Thousands of fanatics or impostors would arise,
every one of whom would lay claim to the mystic charac‑
ter·of the promised Messiah. Great kings, unscrupulous
soldiers, might assert their title to it by the sword, and

use it as a pretext for conquest and subjugation. Men of vast ambition and towering intellect would usurp the name, would mislead mankind, and wrap the earth in turmoil. The four quarters of the world would produce, and would be the prey of such persons: there would be no peace, nor any security perhaps for centuries; nay the followers of such individuals would probably survive for ages, and the most terrible religious struggles might be protracted to the end of time. It was absolutely necessary therefore, and indeed it was commanded by God himself, that the Cycle should not be made known; though He never ordered salutary knowledge to be locked up: now, indeed, it may be revealed, for the Twelfth Cycle is completed, and a new era of light will prevent the uprising of any without the very seal of heaven itself. Those who had the heavenly book well knew, that when the destined Messenger himself arrived, he, the bearer of the seal and of the celestial key, by a divine instinct would know who he was, and would proclaim his advent to mortals; while if the mystery were known, or hinted abroad, or the period of his epiphany discovered, he would be assailed on all sides by rivals; might be cut off by assassins before his course was completed; and perhaps even his voice and the voice of heaven speaking through him, would themselves be lost in the surrounding tumult of kings, priests (35), philosophers or knaves, contending for that diadem of truth, which he alone was ordained to wear.

46. A cogent proof that *something* had been divulged is furnished by ancient historians. The mystic word as I have shewn was Naros. It implied that which perpetually lived; which could not die: which did but disappear to be renewed in greater, or at least equal, splendour. A

shadowy form of this name was given to a Roman emperor; and accordingly, we find Suetonius, in his life of Nero,
penning the following passage :—It was early in his life
predicted by astrologers to Nero, that it would be his
fortune to be at last forsaken by all the world, which
occasioned that famous saying of his : "An artist may
live in any country," designed to insinuate some sort of
an excuse for his practice in the musical art; since it was
entertaining to him, now he was a prince, and would be
necessary for him when reduced to a private fortune. Yet
some of the astrologers promised him after his forlorn
condition, the government of the East, and some expressly the kingdom of Jerusalem; but the most part of
them flattered him with assurances of his being restored
to his fortune [*Sec.* 40]. These seem plainly to be the
elements of a report respecting Nero, which was spread
wide and far through the Roman empire : and so deeply
seated was the conviction of its truth in the common
people, that even after his death, notwithstanding the
general joy at Rome, there were some, says Suetonius,
who for a long time adorned his tomb with spring and
summer flowers : at another they set up robed images of
him in the Rostrum; and at another time they published
edicts as if he were still living, and would shortly re-
appear to the dire misfortune of his enemies. This report
had penetrated even to the uttermost bounds of the Roman
empire. Vologesis, King of the Parthians, adds Suetonius, ambassadors being sent to the senate for the sake of
renewing an alliance, earnestly besought that the memory
of Nero might be cherished. Finally, twenty years after
this, when I was a youth, there arose a person of uncertain origin who boasted that he was Nero; and so attrac-

tive was his name among the Parthians, that he was aided by them with much zeal, and finally was given up with great reluctance. The expectation therefore that Nero was to reappear and renew his former fortune, was plainly cherished by this most distant people. This account is the more to be relied on, inasmuch as Suetonius was himself contemporary with the occurrences which he relates; and evidently had no conception of the secret source of all these rumours.

Tacitus has given us several hints respecting the same phenomenon. Thus (*Hist.* ii. 8) he says:—About the same time [A U C. 823.] Achaia or Asia were terrified without any good reason, as if Nero were coming; reports being various respecting his death; and many on this account imagining and believing that he was still alive. This was three years after the emperor's death; and it shows how strongly the notion that what the soothsayers had predicted, respecting Nero would come to pass, had taken hold of the public mind, and how extensively rumours of such a nature concerning him had been spread abroad and believed. Dio Chrysostom (*Orat. de Pulchritud.* p. 371) says:—Those around Nero left him as it were to destroy himself: for even to the present time this is not certain : even now *all still desire him to live*, and most suppose that he is alive. Dio was a contemporary of Vespasian, and the above words must have been written long after Nero's death. We see n them evidence that in the provinces abroad, public opinion was divided ; a part supposing Nero to be dead, yet wishing that he were alive ; while others believed that he was not dead at all, but had escaped the blows of the assassins Dio Cassius relates that, in the time of Otho,

who succeeded Galba, a person made his appearance at
Rome who gave himself out for Nero ; and in the reign
of Titus, a pseudo-Nero made his appearance in Asia
Minor and gained a party there : afterwards he went to
the Euphrates, and there greatly increased the number
of his followers ; and finally he resorted to the King of
the Parthians, who received him with favour, and made
arrangements to attack the Romans. This was ten years
before the other pseudo-Nero, mentioned by Suetonius.
Within this small number of years therefore we have two
phenomenas of this kind in Parthia, and two in Asia
Minor. These, in addition to the like occurrences at
Rome, shew that a deep persuasion in respect to Nero's
reappearance, must have existed in the minds of the
community at large, in order to render it even possible
for impostors to play such a part with even the shadow of
success.

Lactantius, in his treatise, *De morte Persecutorum*, c. 2,
recognizes the existence of the belief in his day. Cast
down from the lofty eminence of his empire, he says,
and rolled from its height, the impotent tyrant (Nero)
suddenly disappeared. Thence some silly persons suppose
him to have been conveyed away and kept alive : according to the words of the Sibyl, in the same manner they
think Nero will come. Down to the close of the third
century, traces of the belief may still be found. Thus,
Sulpicius Severus, the ecclesiastical historian of that
period, says [*Hist. Sac.* ii. 28] : Nero, the basest of all
men, was worthy of being the first persecutor. I know not
whether he may be the last, since it is the opinion of
many that he is yet to come. Augustine, in his work,
De Civit. Dei, xx. 19, says : Others suppose that he was

not actually slain, but had only withdrawn himself that he might seem to be dead ; and that he was concealed while living in the vigour of his age, and when he was supposed to be extinct, until in his time he would be revealed and restored to his kingdom.

If it be asked, what is the meaning of all this, the answer is obvious. By some means a knowledge of the mystic name, given to Nero, had crept out; those who knew the matter but imperfectly, supposed that the Naros was a man that could never die, but was to be invested with imperial power; they did *not* know that the Naros was only a cycle, and that it was indeed true of the Man of that cycle, but of no other man. Having therefore but this flimsy knowledge, they confounded Nero, the Naros, and the Messiah all together , and thus originated a report which even to the present moment has baffled the sagacity of all scholiasts, commentators, and enquirers, but which after this revelation can no longer appear doubtful to any.

47. Another proof may be cited to shew that the Naros was in some way known, though its secret was not actually communicated.   I allude to the allegory which made *Truth the daughter of Time*, or, as Plutarch says, of Saturn taken for Time. Pindar, however, says, that Zeus was her father ; and they feigned that she was the mother of Virtue : both of which fables signified that in the lapse of Time all Truth would be developed by the Messengers. And the way in which they typified her, was no less profound or elegant. Philostratus represents Truth as a young Virgin, clad in a robe whose whiteness resembled that of snow. Hippocrates, in one of his Letters, gives likewise her Portrait. Represent to yourself, says he, a

fine woman of a proper stature, modestly dressed, with
a thousand attractive charms, the lustre of her eyes, especially, resembling that of the Stars, and you will have
the just idea of this divinity. Lactantius has left us a
saying of Democritus, that Truth lay hid in the bottom of
a well; so difficult it is to come at the discovery of it.
But if the Holy Spirit be, as she is, the great Fountain
of Truth, and if Democritus knew this, as I doubt not he
did, for he was probably initiated, the saying will have a
deeper and more beautiful meaning: as it is out of this
Celestial *Fountain*, or Well, that the Messenger of Truth
comes. The Persian priest, Giamasp, who lived in the sixth
century before the Christian era, wrote a book containing
*Judgments on the grand conjunctions of the Planets, and
on the events produced by them.* And he predicted that
at a certain period Jesus and Mohammed would appear;
and that the religion of the Magi would perish. *Hyde
de Rel. Vet. Pers.*, 385. And it was a knowledge of this
prophecy which brought Magi to Jerusalem at the birth
of Jesus. From this it is evident that Giamasp knew of
the Naros, and he probably also had read the prophecies
of the Apocalypse.

48. But though the priests concealed the Apocalypse,
they resorted to it for myths in which they faintly
imaged many of its mighty revelations. The first inventors
of the Greek mythos of Apollo, (who, as I have said, is a
personification of the Messiah), if not themselves initiated
priests, must have had this very Apocalypse before them.
One feature cannot be mistaken. I mean the Red Dragon (36). Helios (from *El.* God), or Phoibos-Apollo (the
light of life, "the light of the world"), arises out of the
golden-winged cup (Sacred Spirit). He is the sun-god, the

Light-born, λυκηγενης, because he is born in the cycle of
the sun.   He is like Jesus, a divine shepherd with flocks
of long-wooled sheep at Tænaron, and other places.   His
head is surrounded with rays.   He has children by the
Nymph *Neæra*, or Newness, a clear allusion to the Naros.
He plays his lyre at the banquet of the gods, for truth is
the music of heaven.   At the moment of his birth he
called for his bow (language), and said he would declare to
men the will of Zeus (God).   He is born in a floating star
island called Asteria, (the earth which floats in the air).
His mother is attacked by Python (the Red Dragon), before
she brings him forth.   He is called the pure, (αγνος,
Agnus Dei, the Indian Agni) ; in the primal mythos he
is exempt from all sensual love.   He is taught divination
by Pan (the All)   He went from heaven to give laws to the
Hyperboreans (the first people).   He is called Pæan, from
his healing power.   He raises the dead, &c., &c.   To the
same passage may be traced also the legends of the Wars
of the Giants, the rebellion of the Angels, with which all
the ancient mythology is filled ; and on which indeed it
may be said to have been constructed.   But the wise
ancients themselves knew better than the moderns in this
respect ; and were not so ignorant of God as to believe in
a Devil.   With them the true interpretation of the passages did not warrant a belief in the existence of any such
odious being in Heaven.   And they judged well.   There
is no Dragon, there is no War, there is no Tempter, there
is no Evil Being in the paradise spheres of God ; such
excrescences were inconsistent with the happiness, the
peace, and the beauty that are the law of that divine
region.   But in Heaven, as in all other places where created
living essences exist, the will, as I have shewn before,

is free; and where the will is free it is always liable to error. The angel spirits of the celestial are not and never were exempt from fallibility. God alone is Infallible and Incorruptible, and these attributes are part of his constitution. They cannot be given to any other existences: they belong to the Uncreated, who is God; and are incapable of being possessed by created, finite beings however high they may be placed in the order of life. Hence even the purest spirits are subject to a lapse from paradise into a lower sphere, under the temptation of their own thoughts. When this happens, it is figuratively said there is war in heaven: when they lapse lower, they are said to be cast upon the earths; when an impure thought has rendered them unworthy to stand in the presence of God, they are no longer Angels, but Dragons. That this lapse of spirits happened ages ago is certain; it was revealed in the text to the Messenger, to make manifest that what had happened in heaven must also be expected on earth, when the Holy One went forth to preach truth: and so indeed it has always been. This is its sole and its true meaning. The vulgar notion of a Devil or an Evil Being of immense power, has indeed been founded upon it, and it is still carefully fostered by the priests to keep the rabble enslaved by fear; but the existence of such a Being, if it were not impossible, which it is, is wholly inconsistent with the nature, the benevolence and the paternal character of God. Sharistani, an Arab follower of Zaratusht, the fifth Messenger of God, well describes the meaning of the fable. The first Sages, he says, did not look upon the Two Principles as co-eternal, but believed that the Light of God was Eternal, and that the Darkness was produced in time; and the origin of evil they account for in this manner : Light can produce nothing but light, and can never be the origin of evil ; how then was the evil produced, since there was nothing co-equal or like the Light in its production ? Light, say they, produced several Beings, all of them spiritual, luminous, and powerful. But a great one, whose name was Ahrimân, had an *evil thought*, contrary to the Light. He doubted, and by that doubt he became dark. Hence arose all the evils, the dissensions, the malice, and everything else that is of a contrary nature to the Light. These two make war upon one another,— that is, good and evil are perpetually opposed ; a very different idea from the European notion of Satan, with tail and horns, and saucer eyes, whom God sends forth to tempt mankind into the commission of every species of sin, that He may see whether they may be able to resist or not. The whole thing is indeed figurative ; there is no Tempter, as I have declared ; nor does God lead any into temptation. They who say so make him the Parent of all evil, and would do well to ponder on the beautiful oriental apologue : *Marok rashly said that all evil came from God ; but when he reflected on the wickedness of his speech, he imposed silence on himself, and opened not his lips for seven years.*

49. That the Naros, the Messenger, and this Apocalypse, were known to all the primeval priests, though they were guarded with the most jealous eye from the public, the slightest examination of the medals, the sculptures, or the antiquities of the Past, will satisfy any one that looks at them, with a mind instructed in the truths which I have here made known. The vast symbolic sculptures of Persepolis and Nemroud, some of which are now in the

British Museum, could have been, and were, inspired alone by the sublime figures of the Apocalypse. By the Brahmins, foremost of all the ancient priests in sacred learning, the Naros was symbolized under the form of a man six-headed (the centuries), riding on a peacock, the emblem of the starry firmament, and who was called Cartikeya, and sometimes Skanda : his robe was richly spangled, indicating thereby an astronomical secret. A star of six rays, a cross, a crown of six points, a circle, a ring, a wreath of flowers or a rosary, is a frequent emblem ; and wherever either of these is found, it may be regarded as a positive sign of the Naros. The Naros is still commemorated in India on May-day (the Hooli-feast), the day of Maïa, the Virgin of Heaven, that is מים, *Mayim*, or Waters from on high, and it is called the Naurutz festival ; though even the most learned Brahmins of the present age know, or profess to know, nothing of the object that is intended to be honoured. In the Neuruz of Irân, which was a holiday instituted by one of their most ancient patriarchs, Djemshed, and which takes place at the beginning of the year, they present each other with eggs. In Barbary the Jewish mourners at funerals eat eggs, thereby symbolizing their present belief in the resurrection of the dead ; and on Easter day the Oriental Christians present each other with eggs adorned with painting and gilding. The Russians of Narva eat painted eggs at their funeral feasts, which are held among tombs. All these eggs typify the new creation, and the new order of things ; and particularly the renovated birth which occurs in the Naronic Cycle. The Druids, who were Boodhist priests, wore around their necks an egg-formed jewel cased in gold to commemorate the same event. The pillars

Joachim and Boaz had around each of their capitals 100 pomegranates, (1 *Kings* vii. 20 ; 2 *Chron.* iii. 16, 17). This fruit was selected for two reasons : first, as a common emblem of the yoni ; secondly, on account of its star-like flower, with *six* leaves or rays at the top of the fruit : so that as the Water Lily in ancient representations is always a symbol of the Spirit of God, or of the Messiah, who proceeds out of waters, so is the pomegranate of the Naros or mystical six. A hundred pomegranates consequently represent 600, or the Magnus Annus. The Mexican and Egyptian antiquities cluster all over with these symbols : and, indeed, throughout the whole world are found the unmistakeable signs of this One, Universal and Primeval Faith founded by God himself; revealed in this Apocalypse ; miraculously preserved and renewed by the successive Messengers ; and with a paternal solicitude for all mankind without reserve, which is the blessed characteristic of the All-Father : and now finally promulgated to the public in these pages.

50. These wonderful mysteries were in the primeval theology concealed universally under symbols : we, who know, can read them at the present moment in nearly all the sacred reliques of the Past. This symbolic language was designed for an universal mode of communication among the priests, and to make them known to each other, like the mark of circumcision in the most distant regions ; so that if a priest from the farthest plains of Scythia came into Atlantis, or Africa, or England, he could, by entering a temple on which the sacred symbols were cut or painted, at once secure a home and hospitality from any of the fraternity whom he found there, simply by explaining the knowledge which he possessed. The sacerdotal order

themselves, to whom the Sacred Cycle was known, as the
passing six hundred years drew to a close, always looked
forward to the appearance of the new Messiah, who was
to be the Star, the Phœnix, the Homai or the Fong-Whang
(37), of the six hundred years that were to come; and
who was to inaugurate the most important changes, moral
as well as physical, over the face of the whole earth.
Hence the great number of Oriental and Jewish prophecies relating to Cyrus, which some Christian writers
ignorantly, and many who are not Christians, falsely,
apply to Jesus: hence the distinct promise of Amosis
himself : *I will raise them up a Prophet like unto thee,
and will put my words in his mouth, and he shall speak
unto them, all that I shall command him.*—DEUT. xviii.
81 : hence the remarkable lines of Virgil applied by that
base flatterer to a mere human being, Marcellus ; hence
also the distinct assurance of Jesus, that he would send
One after him, which was fulfilled in Mohammed, or the
Renowned, the Periclyte, which later writers changed
into Paraclete. The theologians pretend that this was
fulfilled by the *tongues of fire* (Acts ii.); but this is wholly
absurd, as Jesus evidently alluded to a Man. The very universality of these symbols, however, endangered the secret ;
and it became absolutely impossible but that some vague
knowledge of the Naros, and its Messenger, should creep
out. They who saw every day in the temples and on the
altars, certain types to which the wise and pious paid the
most profound veneration ; who were themselves not
worthy to be initiated, but who had active brains and prying intellects, and whose pursuit after the Unknown was
probably stimulated by the knowledge that it was ever
intended to be kept unknown at least from them, would

scarcely fail to pick up here and there a few stray
beams of light to guide them in their darkness. Hence
arose the notion of Genii and Daimones, whose assistance the Supreme God made use of in the government
of the earth, and in the due administration of the affairs
of men ; and whom he at times sent forth among mankind, for their education and protection. Hence also
their numerous legends of gods speaking to mankind ;
hence the mysterious hint in old theogonies of the marriage
of Earth with Heaven. But as they were unacquainted
with the exact cycles, and as the priests rather encouraged than dispelled their dreams, which were founded
after all but on fancy; it came to pass that whenever
they saw any one greater than the rest of men in power,
wisdom, strength, or excellence, they supposed him to be
a Genius of this sort, and to have come from heaven
and after death they paid him divine honours. Thus the
heavenly hierarchy became gradually filled with the names
of dead conquerors and bravos, whom the mere multitude
blindly worshipped, supposing them to have been blessed
Daimones ; and whose deeds they typified under the most
fantastic and romantic legends, until the Poets and Priests
whose lives depended on fable and falsehood, respectively
stepped in, and corrupted their entire system of theology.
But all their speculations ended eventually in disappointment; however they might peer, they could discover
nothing ; the secret of the Naros was still a secret ; impenetrable as the veil of Isis herself. The Apocalypse
that follows shews it forth for the first time to the world,
in the most clear, convincing, and conclusive manner.

NOTES TO BOOK I.

———

Note 1 (p. 18.)—Ab אָב. Father: Parent: and pronounced broadly, Aub, a Serpent. As a Persian termination, it means River. Nilab, the river Nile; Panjab, the Five Rivers; Danaub. and River, Ocean, Sea, Waters, all symbolically mean the Holy Spirit. *Angl.* Abbot, Baba, Papa. *Lat.* av-us. an ancestor. *Irish.* Ab, a Lord; Ab-har, a Canoe. There is something very curious, says Higgins, *Anacalypsis*, i 725, in the word אָב *ab.* or אָבה *abe.* The root is said to be אָבה *abe* with a mutable or omissible ה *e;* that is, it may be either אָב *ab* or אָבה *abe:* it may have either a masculine or feminine termination. This seems odd enough for the word *father:* but it is still more odd that it *always* adopts a *feminine* termination for its plural; always אָבוֹת *abut* (abbot) or אָבת *abt,* but never ם' *im.* Here the secret doctrine shows itself. So Baal in Greek has always the feminine article prefixed, Jer. ii. 18, 28, xi 13, xix. 5, &c., &c., and sometimes Baalim the plural has τας βααλιμ, 1 Sam. vii. 4. As A, the first letter, stood for Ox, (Aleph, a symbol of the Sun, and the Sun was a type of God), A stood for God; and B represented Beth, his House or Shekinah. Both had the force of A B, or A and B united; and so united they meant Parent. See Beth, in the Definitions. *Abner* אָבנר is Father of Light—a name applied to God, as Lord of the Naros. Apis, Bra-Ap-Is, was God the Father—or Pri-Apis. *Ab* was an emblem of the Triune All. A = 1. B = 2. = 3 Bra, means Creator. *Abiri,* אָבירי and *Abirim,* אָבירים the Mighty Ones: the same as the Cabiri, or Messengers of Justice, to whom the Druid temple of Abury, in Wiltshire, was raised. *Span.* Cobra. *Gr.* Οφις. Aub also means a Beam, a Cloud. From hence, says Vallancey, the Irish *Ob-air* an observer of any kind, and *abar* to relate: also Abaras a manifestation, a Poem, a work of meditation and study: whence Abaris the Hyperborean. I wish to impress on the reader, the necessity of patient and careful study of the various radical words, which he will find in this book; I have not inserted one without a purpose. They will convince him of the absolute truth and one-ness of all the analogies in names, symbols, and things to which this Volume refers ; and he will find it no unpleasing pursuit, guided by these suggestions, to find others for himself.

Note 2 (p. 20).—The house of our *Dove-like religion* (says Tertullian, with a covert allusion to the real mystery of Christianity, which was well understood until it was destroyed by the Church of Rome)is simple, built on high, and in open view ; respecting *the Light* as the figure of the *Holy Spirit*, and the East, as the representation of the Anointed Messiah.

Note 3 (p 26) —Al אֵל God, and אַיִל *Ail*, a Ram, having nearly the same sound, gave occasion to a good deal of ancient symbolism. A very curious dissertation upon the name *Aleim* אֱלֹהִים, occurs in Parkhurst's Hebrew Lexicon, where, deriving it from אָלָה *Alhe*, a denouncing of a curse, that learned author defines it to be "a name usually given in the Hebrew Scriptures to the ever-blessed Trinity, by which they represent themselves as under the obligation of an *oath* to perform certain conditions, and as having denounced a curse on all, *men and devils* who do not conform to them." The absurdity of this can scarcely be surpassed ; and yet by how many thousands is it not implicitly credited? Al. El. אֵל God. Cham-El אֵל חָם, the Most High God Greek Ἥλιος, the Sun. Lat., *Ala.*, a wing, *alo*, I nourish: *ille*, He, the prominent One. Arabic, Alla. Gr., Al-ala, a feminine Deity, Κλυθ' Αλαλα. *Plut. de amore fraterno*, 483. With the *l* doubled *all*, אַלַל, it means Nothing. Alma Venus is *Al*, אֵל, and *Ma*, מָא, the God Mother, the Olma עַלְמָא of the Phœnicians, and the *Olme* or *Virgin*, עַלְמָה of the Hebrews. *Ahl*, הַאֵל, a tabernacle, a tent: hence the words αυλη, *aula*, a hall: symbolically God, who is the Universal Protector. Angl. the All. Al is an Arabic prefix : and is to be found in Al-Achor, an idol of the Sun : the pronoun *ille* of the Romans, and the *Le* and *La* of the French are similar. *Halo*, I breathe: Lal, לַל, means to turn round, one turn of the globe. Laila, לֵילָה, (Arab, *lıel*) darkness The Persians call the glory of the Supreme Being *jellah Alla*, the Glory of God : and say one ray of this divine glory reduced Mount Pharan in Arabia into dust, and dissolved into water the *heyuela al auely*. In the Mayan, *Kinal*, or Fire of God, is a Serpent : and *Khin* is the Sun.

Note 4 (p. 28).—This cup or patera was always used in sacrifices. It was the lotus or rose symbol of the Holy Spirit from whom all being came : and as the ancients believed that all being should return back to her, they received in a patera, the blood of the sacrificed victim ; this was in accordance with the tenet that the *life* was in the blood, *Gen.* ix. 4. Pater-a was a mystic feminine of Pater—the Father; it indicates a lotus-shaped cup, or matrix, a *Shekinah.* This patera is a cognate of Pater Patricius: the Roman patres wore a lunar or crescent-shaped shoe, *calceos patricios,* by which they signified their high descent from, and future sojourn in the Moon or Holy Spirit. The chief of the Sacred College was called Pater Patratus by contraction for Pateratus, and from bearing the sacred patera : so the Father and the Holy Spirit are symbolized in the word Patri-Archa.

Note 5 (p. 28).—Hence the vow of Arrius Babinus mentioned by Montfaucon : *To thee, Goddess Isis, who art One and all things Arrius Babinus makes this vow.*

Note 6 (p 29).—This proves that it was not the common Minerva, as the Paulites pretend, for *she* did not bring forth the Sun. The Sun really meant the Messiah, or Incarnation of the Sun.

Note 7 (p. 33).—Ad-ad, הָדַד, the Deity of the Syrians : it signifies King of Kings : *he* who is essentially The One. It is found in a compound form Ad-Aur, אָדר ; and Ad-On, אָדן ; and Adonai, אָדני. Bryant says it is the same as Πρωτος, the First : hence Proteus, a name for the Holy Spirit, from the variety of her forms *Ad,* אד, is an Element. Adonis is the Sun. Irish, *ad* is water, and in the Armorican, *ad-a* is to seed. עָדָה *Adah* in Hebrew is beauty. Welsh, Adon, a Lord. Hebr. Adun אָדון, a Lord. Joined on to *Di,* ךִ, it signifies Quantity. From this root the Celts had their De, Di, Te, Dia, the only appellation by which God was known to those who spoke the Gaelic of Britain and Ireland. And so the Gauls in Cæsar's time asserted that they were all descended, *ab Dite patre,* from father Di or Dis. (*Comm.* vi. 16). Hence also the Greek, Δις Διος ; whence Latin, Deus, dius. Hence Δηω compounded with Μητηρ, Demeter or Ceres, whom Orpheus calls *seminal, heap-giving, delighting in the barn floor, affording the green fruits,* and also *Mother of all,* and *all-bestowing.*

Note 8 (p. 34).—Is not Brahm the Hebrew בָרא, Bra (Creator), and Om (God), Bra-Om, softened into Brahm, or Bram ?

Note 9 (p 37).—Ptha is the Ordainer, who did all things in truth and wisdom. She is the same as Water, which Thales called the *Principle* of all things, and God is the Spirit who has formed the Universe from this humid Principle. Synesius, full of this ancient theology, alludes to the mystic union ; and says, *The father, mother, male and female art thou.* This principle is hinted at in

F

the radical *Ain*, עִין, a pure Virgin, a Fountain ; a name also for the Holy Spirit. Thus Ænon near the fords of Jordan, meant Fountain of the Sun : hence John baptized in it, or immersed in the Holy-Spirit which was the Fountain, or feminine counterpart of the Sun, namely the Moon, *John* iii. 23. Ath-Ain became Athena or God's Fountain. At other times the name was reversed, and became An-Ait; a goddess worshipped throughout Asia : and by the Hebrew tribe of Naphthali, *Josh.* xix. 38, at Beth Anath, or the House of An-Ait. From this place they had their name Beth Ani. Bal-Ain were wells sacred to the Sun . hence the Greek βαλανεια, and the Roman *balnea*. so also *Balænæ*, large fishes, which were sacred symbols. Ouranos is the same as Our-Ain, the Fountain of Orus : and Anna Perenna was the Everlasting Fountain, or the Holy Spirit. Ur-Ania was the Fountain of Fire or God. This was Egeria, the inspiring Deity of Numa, an anagram for Amún. Egeria est, quæ præbet *aquas,* Dea grata, says Ovid. עֲנָק, henak, is a torque or necklace ; hence *annus*, a year, and *annulus,* a circlet or ring. Aonach (pronounced Enoch) in Irish signifies a cycle of the sun, an anniversary : and we are told in *Gen.* v. 23, that all the days of Enoch were 365. In the Polynesian group of islands, *hina,* from this radical Ain, means a perfect Virgin. Note also, that as On represented God, so Ain represented His Divine and Virgin Spirit.

Note 10 (p 38).—This was the name at a period comparatively modern—that is before Christianity—their more ancient manner of invocation being *Ain treidhe Dia ainm Tau-lac, Fan, Mollac,* or Ain, triple God, whose name is Tau lac, Fan, Mollac. This third person was the Destroyer, which the Hebrews afterwards changed into Moloch, מֶלֶךְ, *melk,* the Great, the Prince. The Orphic *Phanes,* was the Irish *Fan,* and the Greek *Pan* (with a digamma), which in the Coptic is *Pheneh,* or the Everlasting, according to Jablonski. In the same language it meant the *Phœnix,* which reproduced itself at the end of every 600 years from its own ashes. It has been questioned whether Phanes is not פְּנֵי יְהִוה, *Pheni Ieue ;* the faces of Jehovah. And the Mysians called Bacchus *Phanacem* or the *Phœnix.*

Note 11 (p 44).—The original name of the Seventh Messenger Moses, or Amosis, was Osarsiph, which is Sar Iph, and Sar-Iphis, meaning Son of the Serpent.

Note 12 (p. 44).—Eden, עֶדֶן, more properly Odin (as the Hebrew scholar sees), means delight ; and the Halls of Odin, meant the Paradise of delight. As I have frequently had occasion to cite

Hebrew words and their meanings, I wish it to be noted here that I quote from Hebrew, not that I at all suppose it to be the primeval language, but that all the words which I *do* cite from it, belong absolutely to the first language spoken among mankind; in the same manner as there are numerous monosyllabic words in our own dialect which belong to the same ancient tongue. Sir W. Jones asserts as a fact that the oldest discoverable languages of Persia were Chaldaic and Shanscreet . and that the Hebrew, the Chaldaic, the Syriac, and the Ethiopian tongues, are in his opinion only dialects of the old Arabic. When Homer distinguishes between the language of Gods and men, as in *Ilias*, xiv. 289, 290, 291, he means by the first the primeval language to which I here allude.

Note 13 (p. 47).—Hercules is Alcides, that is Al-s-ida, lion of Jid or God : he was called Astrochyton, or the star-clothed. Children of Israel means children of the Prince of God, that is the Messiah of God. Amosis is also called a prince or captain of God. Melchart is either *Melec Kartha*, קרתא מלך, King of the City, or ערץ מלך, *Melec Aretz*, the Mighty King, or the King of the Earth, which the Messiah is.

Note 14 (p. 48).—Whosoever gazes on the Divine Beauty like Jesus, or Actæon who saw Diana naked, is torn in pieces by dogs—a fine but melancholy truth.

Note 15 (p. 48).—This word Ogmius is pure Celtic, and signifies the secret of letters : the Irish hieratic language was called Ogham (pronounced Oum), which is the same as the Boodhist and the Brahmin Aum, and the Magian and Mexican Hom, or ineffable name of God. This last, the Greeks changed into A.OM.AΩ, or Alpha and Omega. Hermes and Hercules, were sometimes blended by sculptors into the same figure, and it was called Hermheracles. Hermes in the old Egyptian, means Interpreter, that is the Messiah was the Interpreter or had the key to the language of Heaven. Janus, which was an Etruscan name for a Messiah, was represented with *leys*.

Note 16 (p. 49). — There is no other name under heaven, given among men whereby we must be saved, says the compiler of *Acts* iv. 12 : and this narrow, confined, and exclusive system is supposed to be the policy of the Universal Father. Christ, says Bishop Pearson, is the Supreme, Almighty, and Eternal God,—a blasphemy which it almost shocks one to transcribe. Nothing can more clearly manifest that the Messiahs are not infallible in merely secular matters, than the choice of Judas Iscariot by Jesus. So the Jewish articles of belief, 8 and 9 : " I believe with a perfect faith that all the Law which at this day is found in our hands, was delivered by God himself to our master Moses (God's peace be with him). I believe with a perfect faith that the same law is *never to be changed, nor any other to be given us of God,* whose name be blessed." The old prediction given to Saturn, the Father, that one of his sons would deprive him of his kingdom, is verified every day in the worship paid to Jesus in place of Him who made him.

Note 17 (p. 49).—Xenagoras relates that Sicily being reduced by famine, the people consulted the Oracle of the Palici, and were answered that if they sacrificed a certain hero, whom authors do not name, the famine would cease, which accordingly happened. The notion that a Messiah would expiate the people's crimes, was curiously illustrated in the Palilian sacrifices, where purifications were performed with the smoke of *horses'* blood, and with the ashes of a *calf,* that had been taken out of an immolated *cow*—thus uniting in one the three emblems of the Sun (God), the Moon (the Holy Spirit), and the Messiah, their child and representative. Thus we find Buddha saying, *Let all the sins that have been committed in this world fall on me, that the world may be delivered:* (MAX MULLER, *Ancient Sanskrit Literature,* 80), which pagan false doctrine is the doctrine of the Paulites with reference to their Atonement or Redemption.

Note 18 (p. 49).—The harlot of Jericho was a progenetrix of Jesus, *Matt.* i. 5. *Salmon virum justum Booz de Raab meretrice genuit.* ST. JEROME, *Proem in Hoseam* [cited, ii. *Nimrod,* 198] I mention this, not to reflect on that Divine Messenger—as it is of little moment through whom in the body he was descended—but to show how absurdly the orthodox base their faith on the sacred purity of the genealogical line of Jesus. To obviate any inconvenience from the character of Rahab, an attempt has been made by the rigidly righteous to show that she was only an *innkeeper,* who perhaps kept a house of accommodation, but this has signally failed. The Seventy, says Parkhurst, in all these passages render it πορνη, and the Vulgate, *meretrix,* a harlot, and in like manner Rahab is called πορνη by St. Paul, *Heb.* xi. 31, and by St. James ii. 25. And indeed nothing more may be intended by the epithet *harlot,* but that she had *formerly* been so ! ! See Joshua ii. 1.

Note 19 (p. 50).—Milton has in like manner degraded both Judaic and Christian divinity by the representations he has given of the Garden of Eden, hell, devils, Heaven, &c. ; representations, which from their much-vaunted poetic skill, have brought down the minds of his countrymen to the very lowest, basest, and most irreverend notions of the Supreme Government of God, of His dealings with his creatures, and of the Future Life. These fables read at an early period, and recommended constantly to perusal by a species of parson-critics, whose knowledge is in reality but gross ignorance, become amalgamated with the mind itself, like a belief in ghosts, demons, &c., and work great evils: so that if Pythagoras were now alive, he would have certainly added to the chained in Tartarus, the wretched shade of John Milton.

Note 20 (p. 51).—The remarks of Philo-Byblius are applicable here. The Greeks, says he, who in refinement of genius excelled all other nations, appropriated every ancient history to themselves, exaggerated and embellished them, aiming at nothing but to amuse by their narratives: and hence they have turned these same histories into a quite new shape. Hence it is that Hesiod and the other Cyclic poets have forged Theogonies, Gigantomachies, Titanomachies, and other pieces, by which they have in a manner stifled the truth. Our ears, accustomed from infancy to their fictions, prepossessed with opinions that have been in vogue for several ages, retain the vain impression of these fables as a sacred deposit. And because time has insensibly rivetted these idle tales in our imagination, they have now got such fast hold thereof, that it is extremely difficult to dislodge them. Hence, it comes to pass, that even Truth, when it is discovered to men, appears to have the air of Falsehood; while fabulous narratives, be they ever so absurd, pass for the most authentic facts. Nevertheless the wise treated these Milesian myths as they deserved.

Note 21 (p. 55). — And his (the Messiah's) goings forth have been from of old, מִי טִי עֵילָם, from the days of antiquity; *not his eternal generation from the Father*, says Parkhurst, as this word has been tortured to signify, but his going forth to action, his proceedings or acts for the benefit of his people, and the destruction of his enemies. Even from the perverted Hebrew tracts, the Rabbins have not wholly banished allusions to the avatars of these Messiahs. The Song of Amosis reminds the Israelites of the days of old, the years of many generations in which ὅτε διεμεριζει ὁ Ὑψιστος ἐθνη ἐστησεν ὁρια ἐθνων κατα ἀριθμον ἀγγελων Θεου—when the Most High divided the nations, he fixed their boundaries according to the number of the *Messengers* of God; which the common version impudently renders the children of Israel, *Deut.* xxxii. 8. This accords with what I have said (ante p. 56) as to God sending his Messengers to all the central or principal empires on the earth. They are again alluded to in the ladder which Jacob beheld in vision, with *Messengers of God ascending and descending on it*, Gen. xxviii. Nor is it without deep significance that in the Chinese language, Logha, or Logos, means Six, in allusion to the Naros in which he appears; and that in the same language Shiloh means the Sun, which we know was a symbol of the Messenger. Bell's *Travels in Asia*. This word occurs Hebraically שׁילה, (Shiloh), Gen. xlix. 10, but it is admitted that it has no meaning whatever in that language. It is the Chinese word copied from the Scripture of Fo-hi, and brought from India by the Jewish priests, who evidently knew that it meant the Messiah, *"for unto him shall the gatherings of the people be"* And the occurrence of this Chinese word in the Jewish scripture is pregnant with meaning, and historical interest. The word is not to be found in the Septuagint! In the Book which bears the name of Joshua, Auses or Jesus, the Cabiric Messenger or Messiah of War, is mentioned. I cite it, not that the book is at all genuine, but as a record of the Hebrew belief, which was also that of the Gentile world generally. *And it came to pass when Joshua was by Jericho, that he lifted up his eyes, and looked, and behold there stood a Man over against him, with his sword drawn in his hand; and Joshua went unto him, and said unto him, Art thou for us, or for our adversaries? And he said, Nay, but as Captain of the Lord's host, am I now come. And Joshua fell on his face to the earth, and said unto him, What saith my Lord unto his servant? And the Captain of the Lord's host said unto Joshua, Loose thy shoe from off thy feet, for the place whereon thou standest is holy,* Josh. v, 13.

Note 22 (p. 57).—Its precise size may be gathered from Templeman's *Survey of the Globe*, where he allows to Wales 7011 square English miles, and to Judæa 7600

Note 23 (p 57).—The divine birth of the Messenger was thus symbolized by the Scythians, according to Diodorus Siculus. They deduced their origin from Scythes, who was the son of a Virgin sprung from the earth, that is, whose origin they did not know. They said she was half woman and half serpent, and that God fell in love with her, and that Scythes was the child of this union.

Note 24 (p. 58).—Phanes, the God of Fire, Pan, Van, Phennische, Phœnix, all are typical of the 600 years.

Note 25 (p 60)—Neri, according to Luke, was one of the progenitors of Jesus—it means *my light*.

Note 26 (p. 67).—This is the case with Mr. L , says Dr. Priestley, a most excellent man, who is now reading my sermons on the evidences of revelation; and I hope to good purpose. He, like thousands of others, told me that he was so much disgusted with the doctrines of the Church of England, especially the Trinity, that he considered the whole business as an imposition without further inquiry.—*Memoirs of Theophilus Lindsay*, 381.

Note 27 (p. 68).—Mark i. 23; Luke viii 1-2; Matt xii. 22; Mark v The Old Testament is scarcely better. I call upon the Theist, says Sir William Drummond, who has contemplated the Universe as the work of Intelligence, to consider whether the Old Testament, if literally interpreted, presents him with such exalted notions of the Deity, as natural religion is itself capable of inspiring. It is monstrous to be told, if the sense be taken literally, that the Infinite Mind shewed its *back parts* to Moses. —*Œdipus Judaicus*, p. xiii.

Note 28 (p. 69.)—The day previous to the day of expiation, the more self-righteous Jews provide a fowl, but it must be a cock, which they send to an inferior Rabbi to be slain. After it is slain, the person whose property it is, takes the fowl by the legs, and with uplifted hands, swings it nine times over their heads, and at the same time prays to God that the sins he has been guilty of during the year may enter into the fowl. When I followed the Jewish customs I was very tenacious myself in having a fowl slain; in so doing I thought I was justified.—*Ceremonies of the Jews*, by Hyam Isaacs, p. 54. The Rev. Mr. Herbert (*Nimrod*) in his learned Miscellany, speaks of the Hebrew offering mentioned in *Leviticus* xvi., 7, 8, 9, 10, as a sacrifice of one goat to God, and of the other to the Devil, yet it is upon this the Atonement is based. Thousands can perceive the absurdity of the cock and goat, who do not, however, reflect that they probably hold equal absurdities as points of faith. We want a Lucian to open their eyes to the folly of these atonements. Hurd mentions another form of this insanity and blasphemy among the Hebrews. The father of every family made choice of a white cock, and every woman of a hen : but such as were pregnant took both a cock and a hen. With these fowls they struck their heads twice ; and at each blow the father of the family said, Let this cock stand in my room; *he shall atone for my sins :* he shall die, but I shall live. This being done, the necks of the fowls were twisted round, and then their throats were cut. Surely there never was a readier mode invented to make smooth for sinners the road to hell, than this fearful one of an Atonement. Yet it is innocence itself, when compared with the Jewish sacrifice of men. The reason of this absurd custom, says Kingsborough's *Mexican Antiquities*, vi., 209, was derived from the Hebrew word Gebher, which signifies a man, and in the Talmud a cock. That Gebher should suffer for their transgressions they could not doubt, because the Talmud declares it, but as it appeared to some of their Rabbis unreasonable to suppose that the anger of God could be appeased by a human sacrifice, they took this word in its other signification of a cock, and accordingly made expiation for their sins by the blood of that bird. On the summit of Kedar Nauth, in the Himalaya, Cali is supposed to have her residence. One among the numerous proceedings of her votaries is to scramble as high up the mountain as they can attain, taking with them a goat for an offering (a scapegoat); the animal is turned loose, with a knife tied round his neck; and the belief is that the goddess will find the victim and immolate it with her own hand, thereby redeeming the sacrificers from all their load of sin. Upon the tenth day of the month, says Sir Isaac Newton in his *Observations on the Apocalypse* (p 310), a young bullock was offered for a sin-offering for the High Priest, and a goat for a sin-offering for the people: and lots were cast upon two goats to determine which of them should be God's lot for the sin-offering; and the other goat was called Azazel, the scape-goat. The high Priest, in his linen garments, took a censer full of burning coals of fire from the altar, his hand being full of sweet incense beaten small; and went into the most holy place within the veil, and put the incense upon the fire, and sprinkled the blood of the bullock with his finger upon the mercy seat, and before the mercy seat seven times: and then he killed the goat which fell to God's lot, for a sin-offering for the people, and brought his blood within the veil, and sprinkled it also seven times upon the mercy seat and before the mercy seat. Then he went out to the altar, and sprinkled it also seven times with the blood of the bullock, and as often with the blood of the goat. After this he laid both his hands on the head of the live goat, and confessed over him all the iniquities of the children of Israel, and all their transgressions in all their sins, putting them upon the head of the goat, and sent him away into the wilderness by the hands of a fit man, and the goat bore upon him all their iniquities into a land not inhabited. *Levit.* iv. & xvi. While the High Priest was doing these things in the most holy place, and at the altar, the people continued at their devotion quietly, and in silence. Then the High Priest went into the holy place, put off his linen garments, and put on other garments, then came out, and sent the bullock and the goat of the sin-offering to be burnt without the camp, with fire taken in a censer fiom the altar; and as the people returned home from the Temple they said to one another, God seal you to a good new year! In the great Temple of Samorin, the priest cuts the throat of a cock with a silver knife dipped in the blood of a hen, and holds the cock with a knife over a chafing dish, in the middle of the altar. This altar is pompously illuminated by wax tapers, and at the close of the sacrifice the priest takes a handful of corn and walks backward from the altar, keeping his eyes stedfastly fixed upon it. When he comes to the middle of the chapel, he throws the corn over his head, and in this way the sins of all the people who are present, and take part in this eucharistical ceremony, are supposed to be atoned for. So the Brahmins teach their followers that if a dying person takes hold of a cow by the tail, and the priest puts a little water into his hand, and *receives a small sum of money*, then when he comes to cross the dreadful fiery river, which separates the earth from eternity, the cow will, by his laying hold of her tail, carry him safely over. The people of the Phillippine Islands have an atonement of their own, which is just as good as any other. After a concert of vocal and instrumental music, two old women step forward and pay the most devout homage to the Sun. This act of adoration being over, they dress themselves in pontifical vestments, and bind a ribbon round their heads in such a manner that they appear to have two horns growing out of their foreheads. In the meantime they hold something in their hands resembling a girdle, and thus arrayed they dance and play upon a kind of rural pipe, say their prayers, and pronounce some particular words with their eyes fixed on the Sun. During this act of devotion the hog that is to be sacrificed is bound fast to a stake, and they all dance around him. A flaggon of wine is next brought to one of the old women, who pours a cup full of it on the hog, performing at the same time some ceremonies suitable to the solemnity of the occasion. She then stabs the hog, and lets him bleed to death; they wash their musical pipes in the blood of the victim, and dipping one of their fingers into it, mark the foreheads of the men with a bloody cross. The carcase is then washed before a slow fire, and the priestesses cut it in small pieces, and distribute it; and all who partake thereof are cleansed from sin. it has been washed away in the blood of the Hog. Into such horrible excesses did the Paulite doctrine of a blood atonement lead, that three considerable sects at least of those who professed to be his followers, made an Eucharistical cake of flour, and the blood of an infant a year old, which was punctured all over until enough had been got to temper the composition. If the infant died it was called a blessed Martyr; but if it survived it was destined for the priesthood. These and similar horrors prepared the Romans to carry out the proscription of Nero against the Paulite Christians, who had, by their dread superstitions, made the whole Gentile world their bitterest foes. And it can hardly be doubted that like the Jews, ancient and present, they crucified children at their nocturnal orgies, as was charged against them by hosts of accusers. There is a shocking anecdote of this soul-destroying superstition among the South Sea Islanders, in the *Quarterly Review*, Aug., 1809 This chief, it says, who went to the god of the English for healing, did not in the meantime neglect his own; and when his disease became desperate he resolved upon a desperate remedy. It is the dreadful belief of these islanders that if a human victim be offered in vicarious sacrifice for the sick, his life and strength will pass into the patient : the nearer the relative who suffers the more acceptable is the atonement to the Odooa supposed to be and this wretched old chief clinging with cowardly selfishness to life sent for his younger son, Colelallo, to have him strangled. The youth was told he was to have his little finger cut off—a common form of propitiatory sacrifice; but as soon as he came into his father's presence he was seized. Then, comprehending their intention, he bade them use no force, and he would submit to his father's will, &c., &c. Antiochus Epiphanes when he conquered the Jews, and entered the inmost recesses of their Temple, found a man whom they had kidnapped, and were feeding daintily that they might sacrifice him to God, to atone for their sins. The same bloody reason was advanced by their priest Caiaphas, as one of those for which they ought to murder Jesus. *Now Caiaphas was he, which gave counsel to the Jews, that it was now expedient that one man should die for the people*, John xviii. 14.

Note 29 (p. 70).—This awful doctrine is contained in the XVII Article of the Church of England. "Predestination to life is the everlasting purpose of God, whereby (before the foundations of the world were laid) he hath constantly decreed by his counsel secret to us, to deliver from curse and damnation *those whom he hath chosen in Christ out of mankind*, &c., &c." Those whom he hath *not* chosen of course go into both curse and damnation.   •

Note 30 (p. 73).—Saint Chrysostom says, When we celebrate the' Mysteries, we send away those who are *not* initiated, and shut the doors, ·a deacon exclaiming, Far from hence, ye profane! close the doors. The Mysteries are about to begin. Things holy for the saints ; *hence all dogs.*—See *Apocalypse* xxii. 15, for a remarkable confirmation of the fact that the Apocalypse was indeed the ritual of the Mysteries. And in this passage doubtless originated the oriental hatred of dogs, which subsists to the present day The Turks, says Busquebius, reckon a dog an unclean and filthy creature, and therefore drive them from their houses. *Dog of a Jew, Dog of a Christian*, are Arabic terms of contempt It is curious to note the folly of even Cicero on this subject, when he professes to treat of it.—ii. *De Nat. Deor.* c. 20. Cicero, Macrobius, and Plutarch, all exhibit the most profound ignorance of the secret of ancient religion. The Greek and Latin mythologists knew *nothing* of the real pontifical creed.

Note 31 (p. 75).—Ag, Og, Ac, Oc, Onc, Ong, (*Agom*, אֹגָם a pool, Ocean; Greek, Ω Κεανος, Ω Γην, (Hesych), Gothic, Oggur. God and the Sun were adored by the Arabs, under the name of Al-Ach-Aur. The Shepherd-Kings were Uc-Chusi, signifying the Royal Cuthites. It is found in Babylonish names, as Ochus, Belochus, and in Egyptian, as Ach-Arez, mighty sun ; Ach-En-Che-rez ; Ach-Aur Ach-Oris. Bag, in Irish, is a circle and a cycle ; in Shanscreet it is the same. *Bagha* in the Shanscreet also means the *Sun*, and the *Yoni ;* Bagha-vad-Geeta, is Song of the Holy Spirit. Bag-d-Ad is the sun-like House or Tabernacle of God. Osiris may have been a form of Uch Sihor. The Sun was styled El-Uc-Or, which· the Greeks changed to Lycoreus. Latona, Apollo's mother, was transformed into a wolf—that is, was transfigured into Light, like Jesus on the Mount, for the wolf was but a sacred type of the sun. And as a star (which is a sun) conducted the Magi to the manger of the infant Messiah, so the Hirpi, who were worhippers of fire, that is Truth, were conducted to their settlement in Campania by a wolf—that is by a Priest of the Sun.—*Strabo.* v. Aca, Oice, Oige, Uige, in Irish, water ; *aqua*, Cann-Oice, the star Oice, sometimes written for Cann-Ob, whence Canobus in the Constellation Argo. Chaldee עָרֶן, Org, Arg; Ethiopic, *houg*, the sea, or a lake. Jupiter was called Lucetius by the Etruscans: and the Greeks made of the root λυχνος, a lamp, and a host of cognate words. Nag, in Irish, is Star, whence *Maiddin Nag*, the matin or morning star, is literally the Chaldee and Syriac נַג, *nag* and נֵגָא, *naga*, light, spendour. Venus, the star of love (Buxtorf,) מְדִנָה (*medinah*), Medina, the Orient, from דָנַח *denah*, to arise ; and hence the Irish Maiddin, morning, because of the sun's position. The Sacred Poem which passes under the name of Lycophron, is in reality the *Manifestation of Light*. Groves were called lucus, as being consecrated to the god . only scholiasts can derive the word *a non lucendo*. Cioros, which was Uch-Ur, was a Greek name for the Sun : it is nearly the same as Orus. Hesychius says, Curis was Adonis. Apollo was called Kyrræus Kyrene, the daughter of God, was really Kyrain, the Fountain of the Sun. Hesychius tells us that ωγην anciently meant the Ocean, which is evidently derived from the Phœnician הוג Og, or encompassing. From Uc-Ait the Greeks formed Hecatus (Apollo) and Hecate. In the Mysteries, Ceres was called Aχ θεια (*Ach theia*) or the great Goddess pre-eminently. The reader will have noticed the "beautiful feet" mentioned in the Hymn. Beautiful feet were an ancient symbol of the Messiah. Thetis (the Holy Spirit) was silver-footed, and the divine Achilleus, was ποδαρκης, which contains an allusion to his swiftness and to the Arc. The Hindu city, Narayanu Pura resplendent like a hundred million suns, wherein is the fire that shall consume the world, is "the place of *the most excellent feet*." The Grand Lama of the Boodhists is saluted as "the most excellent feet," and the Emperor of Ava as "the golden feet." The common word *patam* ending the names of Indian cities appears to mean "feet ;" the British Museum contains a gigantic gilded foot of Buddha, the sole of which is divided into compartments, and covered with mystical figures. So we read in the Jewish tract, *How beautiful upon the mountains, are the feet of him who bringeth good tidings, who publisheth peace , who bringeth good tidings of good ; who publisheth salvation* [that is a Messenger], Is lii. 7. So in the Apocalypse, we read, *And his feet were like smelting brass when it burneth brightly in a furnace of fire*. Hence Hercules, which I have already shewn, was a name for the Messiah, was known by his *foot*—Ex pede Hercules. And oracles were given from a sacred patera or seat, called a *tripod*—the three signifying the All, and the beautiful feet their celestial character. So it was by the gliding motion that the gods and goddesses of old mythology were always known. The Menu-Taur, and the Bulls of Colchis, solar emblems, that is types of the Messiahs, had *brazen feet*, and breathed celestial fires from their nostrils,

Note 32 (p. 77)·—Is not this the און *Aven* or *Aun*, the Sun, indicating that the Naros was the secret of the Sun? And have we not it also in the Gothic, *Rona*, a Mystery, *a counsel whose soul is secrecy*? This is the Naros transposed. *Awen*, in the Cymric, is *a River*, like Nara, as before mentioned. אן, Aun, the Sun must not be confounded with עַם, Om, God; the latter was the Supreme Lord. The former was the Holy Spirit of God, and sometimes the Divine Messenger, symbolized as usual by the Sun. This Aun in time grew to signify heaven, and when pronounced according to the Masoretic punctuation, Aven, it is nothing more than our English haven (rest) and heaven. Faber, speaking of the calves of Jeroboam, says, *that they were in their use and application designed to be the images of the two sacred Bulls, which were living representations of Osiris (God) and Isis (the Holy Spirit).* Potipherah was a high priest of On, or Aun, and there was a magnificent Heliopolis, or City of the Sun in most of the great ancient empires Babel-On is an instance. On, Un, An, says Drummond, in the ancient oriental languages, signified the Sun; Ona, Una, Ana, the Moon. Ana, in Shanscreet means Mother. Hence the Hebrew Hosanna, and the Latin *Anna Perenna.*

Note 33 (p. 79).—This suggestion of the supernatural was of course caught at and improved by the Papists. When the Council of Nice was convened to decide what books of the Jews were and were not canonical, we are informed that the bishops there assembled were by a very extraordinary miracle convinced which were inspired and which were apocryphal books after this manner. Having put all the books that laid claim to inspiration under the communion table in a church, they prayed to God that those which were not apocryphal might be found above or upon the table, and those which were apocryphal might be found under, and accordingly as they prayed it came to pass!!

Note 34 (p. 79).—The later Jews, says Cunæus (*de Rep. Ebr.* iii. 4) were so incensed and grieved that the Bible was translated into Greek at the request of Ptolemy Philadelphus, that they had a public fast for it on the eighth day of Theuth. Whence it is easy to see what care or desire such men, who could bear so much malice and hatred to any men whatever, would have to instruct and reform the heathens, when their sole desire and business was to prevent their coming to the knowledge of anything right and good.

Note 35 (p 82).—The falsehood of *priests* when they wish to decry a creed opposed to their own is without parallel. Thus Rabbi Solomon Jarchi, describing the worship of Baal-Peor, says; *Eo quod distendebant coram illo foramen podicis, et stercus offerebant.* As if anyone but a Rabbi could allege that this was meant for worship, and anyone but an idiot could believe it. We shall soon hear it said that those reverend clergymen who administered the Eucharist to

the donkey at Oxford simply did it in commemoration of the
Last Supper One of the venerated fathers of the Church,
Jerom, whom Rome has made a saint, invents a nearly similar
tale In his Commentary on Isaiah, lib. **xi**, he says ; Taceam de
formidoloso et horribili cepe, et *crepitu ventris inflati quæ Pelu-
siaca religio est !*

Note 36 (p. 87).—This is the Titan Porphyrion (the Scarlet),
who waged war with God, and was bound down in the infernal.

Note 37 (p. 93).—This was the Heavenly Eagle of Fohi : Ababil
among the Arabs had the same mystic signification. By the ancient
Irish the Holy Spirit was adored as Chri-Om-Ruach—the Spirit of
the Sun-God, *Om ;* and in the temples erected to Her, she was surrounded by twelve gods, who were the twelve Incarnations. Her
image was of pure gold—theirs was of silver Ham. Om. הם
Heat, Fire, Black; Latin, Amo. The Japanese Supreme God, is
called Camî, Shanscr , Cama, the god of love Cham, Chemmis,
Chammia, a name of Diana, all come from these roots. אם Am,
a mother and *Am,* says Festus, præpositio loquelaris significat
circum The ancients said *am urbem,* for *circum urbem,* and the
like. Mamma, *Amo,* I love, Aum, and Om, God, is Om-n-Is, the
All. Amir, אמיר a branch: hence Arabic, *Emir,* or branch
from the Lord of all. The word Om is always prefixed in pronouncing the words which represent the superior seven worlds, as if
to show that these seven worlds are manifestations of the power
signified by that word. In an old Purana we read ; All the rites
ordained in the Vedas, the sacrifices to the Fire, and all other
solemn purifications shall pass away : but that which shall never
pass away is the word OM, for it is the symbol of the Lord of all
things. This Hindu word, will be found in the celebrated
Greek noun $O\mu\phi\eta$, which signifies a Divine Voice; an answer
given by the Deity to him who consults. $\Phi\eta$ or $\phi\iota$ is the root of
$\phi a\omega$, I speak, and I shine. In the Hebrew, *phe* פה or *phi,* פי
is a noun in regimine, and means an opening, a mouth, a measure
of capacity. Thus the literal meaning will be the mouth, or the
opening of Om. This is not far from the Divine Voice of the
Greek. Hesychius and Suidas interpret the word $o\mu\phi$, to be the
sacred voice, the holy sound : and hence comes $o\mu\phi a\lambda os$, a navel,
which was a name given to Delphi. But Delphi has the same
meaning as Yoni. $O\mu\phi a\lambda os$, or phallus means the generative
power of Om. Bacchus was called Om-Esta, and Om-Adios, or
the holy son of Om Om also means a circle, or cycle ; hence
am-bire, ambages, circum. In the Irish Iom, Uim, Aim, is a
cycle, a period, the globe of the earth Arabic *Aem* is years.

NOTE UPON ON.

On, Eon, Aun, אוֹן. The Sun. Copt. On. אלוֹן Al-On the oak—the Sungod. עָן On is sheep: Al Quzwini says it is the star *Agnâm.* Helio-Polis was the City of On. Hence Ham, who was worshipped as the Sun, got the name of Am-On, and was styled Baal-Hammon. El was sometimes joined, and it became El-On; other peoples went farther, and added Ab-El-Eon, which is Pater Summus Sol. Vossius thinks that this is the original of Apollo. It was sometimes made Ab-Ad-On. Ani אָנִי is a ship, and the Sun was the Ship of the Heavens. Am On, אמוֹן also means an Artificer, Artifex Mundi. Amnis, a river, is derived from it. *Labitur et labetur in omne volubilis œvum.* Still glides along, and will for ever glide. The inhabitants of Heliopolis worshipped the God Gennæus in the form of a Lion—a lion of the sun. Was this God the same as Janus? Strabo calls the temple of Jupiter Ammon, Ιερον Ομανου : but is not this Ham הָם and Om, and Aun? It was from a priest of On, Oenuphis, that Pythagoras learned the true system of the heavenly bodies moving round the Sun in unceasing motion. But how comes On to mean the generative principle? It is a part of Yoni: it is Ω-ον, the egg, the Mundane Egg. It is the neuter of the Greek pronoun ὁς, meaning existence, which always carried along with it the idea of destruction, and necessarily of reproduction, that is the Generative Principle: and I-ον is the On of I, and I, the Jod, is ten, the perfect number, the number of the Ten Spheres, or orders of existence. The Kal On, or Beautiful of the Platonists, was the Hindu Holy Spirit Cali, and On, blended together, and thus constituting all that was Divine. The On-I-On, on account of the similarity of its coats to the planetary spheres, and as a type of the everlasting renewal of ages, was called, from being sacred to the Father of Ages, αιωνων, onion. Heaven, says Boethius on Porphyry, is referred to the most ancient *Ophion,* who has no beginning. But this Ophion is the same as the Orphic Dragon, and it is οφ-ιον, the Serpent and the Yoni, or On himself in the Shekinah, when he is creative. It was a mystic name for the Apocalypse. Elion enters into the construction of many words thought to be Greek, as Pygmalion, which is פּוּג מֵע לִיוֹן *rest from the Most High God.* Pygmalion, like Prometheus, was a sculptor, and Venus (the Holy Spirit) animated one of his statues, as Minerva did those of Prometheus, with celestial fire. Another cognate of this radical is Iin, יִן, Wine; Gr., οινος; Lat., Vinum; Ital. and Span., Vino;

Fr., Vin; Celt, Gwin; Cimbr., Vien; Gothic, Vein; Old Germ., Uain; Danish, Vien; Dutch, Wün, Saxon, Fin; and Engl., Wine and Vine.   But this *wine* has a mystical relation to יונה Yoneh, the Dove, the Holy Spirit, which, as Parkhurst says, is used in a *passive* sense, while the Creator Lord is the *active* power.   Wine, therefore, and the Holy Spirit, are in reality but one word or root in the primitive language; hence Truth, her essence, is spiritually called *wine*, and sometimes blood, for wine is the blood of the grape; and hence also the remarkable part which wine plays in the Old Testament and the New.   A careful consideration of these two curious synonyms will help the reader through many difficulties in theology.   We find another cognate also in Canaan, כנען anciently pronounced Cnaan.   Sanco-niatho says that Isiris was the brother to Cna.   Hence Canaan means Sun-worshipper.   *Kin* כין is Nature, the Mother and Directress of all.   Hence the Kann, or Diana of the Etruscans, and the Kiûn, כיון or round cross cakes, in honour of the Queen of Heaven.   Juno was named Kiun.   Apollo Cunnius conveys the same idea; hence κυνειν προσκυνειν, προσκυνησις, adoration.   Diodorus Siculus calls the Sun-God of Egypt, Kan; and Colonel Tod has remarked that the Lotus is equally sacred to the Egyptian deity, Kan, and the Hindu goddess Kaniya, or Venus, as well as to Crishna or Apollo.   The Canaanites built temples to *Herm*, הרם the Projector.   Professor Wilson speaks of a Pandæan dynasty of kings, ending with Guna Pandya.   This is identical with the Pand-ion of Greece, and the Apollo Cunnius, or Γυνη.   In the Hebrew *gn*, גן is Garden, and so metaphorically a Woman.   Hence Paradise, the Garden of Delight.   The Greek word ευνη a bed, and the English word *honey*, are forms of this word: it also signifies an *anchor* a mystical sacred symbol ⚲ of the Triune All.   Ken, כהן or Cohen, means Priest: hence Khan, and King, impersonations of power and wisdom.   In early times the Priest was usually the Prince.   *Rex Anius, rex idem hominum, Phœbique sacerdos* —Æneis iii, 80.   We find it compounded with Athoth, as Can-Athoth, Can-Osiris, Can-Ophis.   The Egyptian Hercules was called Côn.   Genesis calls God Konah, קנה xiv, 19.   Urchan and Orchan were names of the God of Fire.   Cuno-Belinus, the Apollo of Britain, was male and female   Chan, Chon, Chen, כהן A priest; and from the union of the regal, with the sacerdotal character, Tart., Khan, Germ., Koning; Angl King, Queen; Chandra, the Moon in Shanscreet; Cann in Irish is the Moon; Gr, μηχανη; Lat., machina, machina mundi, *Lucr.*, v. 97. *Chn* and *Aph* are found in Cneph, of which Plutarch says that it meant the All-Good, without beginning, without end. This is the Irish *Cnaimh*, or *Cnaiv*, the Great winged One. The Phœnicians had the same idea. *Zus hu Asphira* (says Sanconiathon) *acranitha meni arits chuia*. Jupiter is a feigned sphere : from it is produced a Serpent, *Asphira hu chial d'Alha dilh la strura ula shulma*. The Sphere shews the divine nature to be without beginning or end. Last of all is the affinity with this radical of Yuneh, Yoneh, Juneh, Jonah, יוֹנָה a Dove. Shanscr. Yoni. Vocula hœc Indica valet *natura muliebris*. Brachmanni fingunt τo *Yoni* interdiluvium formam columbæ induisse. Abiyonah אֲבִיּוֹנָה mentioned once only in the O. T. (*Eccles.* xii.. 5), and there translated *desire*, really means the father of the Yoni. In the Maya language, one of the most ancient of which there is any record, *yecunah* means love.

NOTE UPON ASA.

Asa, אסא Physician. Ees and Is always had relation to Light and Fire Pers, Azur, fire ; Aziz, lightning, which is the same as Isis. Ceres was called Azazia, and by the Ionians, Az-E-sia : this became Hesus, Zesus, and Jesus. Jezabel, so called from Aza-Bel, for all the Sidonian names are compounds of sacred terms. El-Ees became -Elysium. As-El became the Etruscan Sol. Ash אש is fire; Εστια Vesta ; Lat, asso, to roast; Engl., ashes ; άλς the sea; Eesel, a title of Mithras. The Asœ was a Scandinavian title for the Gods. The As Soors are Indian deities The Arabic Az and Azar implies a high degree of excellence and power Azoz was one of the Syrian Trimurti. Eeswar is a Hindu divinity. Ais, Eis, Ois, Easc, a cycle: whence Eas, Easc, the Moon (Irish), Ais-beis, Ois-beis, an epicycle, Aision, a crown, are evidently of Chaldæan origin. Chaldee עיזק hizak, annulus. Egyptian, *Oeish*, a period, a round of time, whence Isis, the cyclic moon. Egyptian, *Ioch*, the moon. Syr, *Asan*, a crown ; hence the Persian Magi were called *Ostanes*, or doctors, that is, learned in cycles (Suidas). Ish יש and Ishis ישיש, very old or ancient, whence Isis, and *Ice*, or water in a state of purity and solidity. Ishing, the Chinese Husheng, Isho ישע salvation, and the Saviour: also the Cup of Salvation. But how came this word into China ? It is a primitive radical. With this radical also are connected An-ait; An ais means a Fountain of Fire. This is Esta and Vesta ; virgins consecrated

themselves to Hestia, *Lat.* Æstas, Æstus, Aestuo : hence also the
Gaulish Mars, Esus, Æsus, Hesus, Hesar and Cæsar. Zaz, Zazil,
Mayan, light and lightning. Niebuhr speaks of some very
ancient Latin coins called *ases*, without inscriptions, which have
the head of a young man on one side wearing a Phrygian
bonnet, and on the reverse a wheel *with six spokes*. This is the
revolving cycle of 600, and the bonnet, or mitre, signifies that
it was sacred. In the Etruscan, Æsar meant God and the
Sun. Bacchus was called IHΣ. In the Gothic, As, Aes, Aesus
is the name of Odin. *Izar* is יָצַר, *iasar*, he formed. Oz-Uz
is *exceeding strong ·* and the Syriac Az-Az-Os, and the Arabic
Az-Eez, excellent, precious. In the Arabic Az, and Azar,
always implies excellence and superiority In the Hindustanee,
God is called Eashoor, Esur, Iswur ; in the Shanscreet, Eswara ;
in the Arabic Usar, the All-beholding God. In Egyptian it is
Oshiris. In the Irish the Messiah is called Iosa, and Esa ; in
the Arabic, Issa. In the language of the Yezeedis, Yezdan
means God. God, says Bochart, was called Al-On by the
Carthagenians, but the Etruscans gave him the name of Æsar.
This word is of Syrian and Phœnician origin. Asar, or Asara,
was one of the Gods adored by the idolatrous Jews · and the
name of this idol was derived from אֲשֵׁרָה *Ashra*, which
signifies a grove. Hence Rabbi Kimchi tells us—every wooden
idol was barbarously called Ashra. In another place he says,
*Et fuit Asaræ domus et locus et expositio ejus est, quod mu-
lieres ibi sedentes, solicitè quærebant et expectabant Asaram*
—that is, waited for a Redeemer, a Messiah. The old Egyptian word for a Bull was ⲀⲤⲒ *Asi.* In Coptic ⲂⲀⲤⲒ
bahsi, signifies a cow, and ⳘⲀⲤⲒ *masn*, a bull; but *m*, is only the
usual and ancient prefix. This bull is the Solar splendour.
Aesar was the name also of one of the ancient Irish gods ; the literal
meaning of the word is " to kindle a fire " In the Hebrew אִזָא
aza, means *to illuminate*. אֵשָׁא *asha*, is Fire. In the Shanscreet, *Osch*, or *Asch*, is Fire, or Heat ; and the Egyptian word
Osiris, has been by Schelling thought to be compounded of the
two primitives אִישׁ *aish* אסר *asr*, or a Fire-Enchanter.
Aesar, in the old Etruscan, meant a God. The *Aeswar* or *Iswara*
of the Hindus is analogous. In the Baghavad-Geeta we read ;
Aeswar resides in every mortal being, and puts in movement,
by his supernatural powers, all things which mount on the wheel
of time As Fire was supposed to be the first Principle it was
also supposed, by a peculiar refinement, to be the destroyer,

whence arose the idea of the Creator and Destroyer being identified The primitive Fire was supposed to have an insatiable appetite for devouring. Maximus of Tyre relates that the ancient Persians threw into the fire combustible matters, crying, *Devour, O Lord!* In the Irish language *easam*, or *asam*, signifies to *make*, or *create*. It would not be difficult to shew the universality of these analogies and allusions.

NOTE UPON CAR

Car, Cur, Chri, Cor, Sar, Sir. שער חרה צהר. The Sun; Zend, Khoro; Hur, Ahuro; Shanscr., Surya; Gr., Σειρος, Σειριος. The Druidical *Crios* is the Sun. חר *Kar*, a hole through which white light appears. Kur כר Lambs. Koresh, כרש Cyrus, the Sun; Gr. Κυριος, a lord. The Lord's anointed. —*Isaiah* xlv., 1. Cor, the heart. Gael, coir, genitive choir, a space of ground enclosed on all sides. Gor is a circle Proserpine was called pre-eminently Korè, the Virgin daughter Ceres, Χρηστος, the Mild, the Evangelist, and Χρηστης, the Prophet, are forms of this root; it subsequently became Χριστος, the Anointed, the surname given to Jesus. Χρης, is a good Genius, one who confers benefits. Chrishna, is the Indian Messiah. Hrsh חרש is the solar fire. Vulcan, and Jupiter also, was called Chry-sa-Or Creas, Creasna, Cheres, Creeshna, Cur, Cores, and Kuros, says Alwood, all mean the Sun. It is from the Ceres, or Χρης, that the Christians have got their custom of burning candles before their crucifixes and images, and of carrying them in their processions. Ceres was called *Tædifera. Quos cum Tædiferâ nunc habet ille Deâ* —*Ov.* Fast. iii. And, *Et per Tædiferæ mystica sacra Deæ.*—*Ov.* Epist. ii., 42. Axio-Kersa, a name of Ceres, comes from this root. Pythagoras's School of Wisdom was held at Creston. The ancient Romans, copying the Etruscans, celebrated a feast called Charistia, on a day sacred to Concord and the Loves, and in love and harmony they finished the old year, and began the new. A similar feast was in use among the Celtic Druids. Hence the Eu-Charist. In Hebrew, the feast was called *qum*, קום, from which comes Communion. Fr. Chretien, a Christian: Crete, a holy island. In India, Lakshmi is called Chri. Keren, קרן, a horn, or emblem of power; in Japanese the Phœnix, Gr. κερας. Gerenios, applied to Nestor, is an Ammonian title, and signifies a princely and venerable person. The Egyptian Crane, for its great services, was held in high estimation, being sacred to the God of Light, Ab-Is, אב אש, or, as the Greeks expressed it, Ibis—hence its name. Apollo was named Craneus and Carneus, which was no other than Cereneus, the Lord of light, and his festival was styled Carnea. The priest of Cybele, in Phrygia was styled Carnas. Cuaran, Curuinne, Cru-inne (Irish), a cycle, sphere, globe; Chald. כרן caran; Arabic, Krun, a sphere. Quære—If Chronus does not derive from this word · as Saturn (a name of the Sun) does from the Satharn (cycle) of the Druids?

Note upon Argha.

The reader of this Volume, and of such as may follow, must bear religiously in mind, that the words Argha, Lotus, Shekinah, Theocrasia, Yuneh, &c, are symbolical : they are not things but ideas, which, without these terms would be unintelligible. I feel obliged to state this, because there are malignant, sensual, and guilty spirits, who out of Truth and Purity themselves extract the very opposite. The poverty of all languages forces those who use them, to adopt phrases which are felt to be inadequate to the idea intended. Thus, when the Hindu uses the word Lotus, he does not mean the flower simply; but some Transcendent Presence with the fragrance and beauty of a thousand heavens mingled into one : he designates this for brevity's sake by the most beautiful flower in his beautiful land. So the Hebrew by the word Shekinah means a *blaze of glory;* and with this, God is said to be surrounded when He creates. But these divine ideas may be tortured by the wicked into a gross or physical meaning; and from this I wish to guard all my readers. God is not a man, nor does He do as a man. Nevertheless we are obliged to speak of Him as the Male Principle. Bishop Warburton alluding to this, calls it *magnum et pavendum mysterium,* a great and fearful mystery, and it is so. Let no man therefore presume to profane it, or put upon my words constructions which I abhor. In the heaven worlds all is purity, of the purest nature; and he who thinks or would teach otherwise, is unable to comprehend what Beauty is.

The Book of God.

—•◦•—

BOOK II.

1. That men possessed of such supreme intelligence, as the ancients, drawn from the very highest and purest sources, should have accomplished great works on earth, and exercised a transcendent influence over their fellows, seems but naturally to follow, and they certainly succeeded in accomplishing both. They sent forth colonies all over the world, and over these colonies they placed priests to whom they imparted their science; they established an Universal Church with a hierarchy like that of Tibet, Benares, or Rome; traces of which even now are as universally discovered; so much so that it may be said with truth, that nearly all existing creeds are but off-shoots and modifications of that pure primeval monotheism, which God himself founded through their instrumentality, and which He has preserved to the present moment by the medium of His Messengers. So widely

was their dominion diffused that in Europe alone, the French Institute in 1804, found that there were 127 towns, which had anciently been in part at least Cyclopean, that is, reared by the Gnostic priests, or Cyclopes, the sons of the Cycle : who were fabled to be one-eyed, (1) because they were pure Monotheists ; and to be the sons of Vulcan, because he, as has been shewn, was a name and symbol of the Fire-Messenger. They possessed powers of machinery to which modern skill is unequal ; though modern vanity has excused itself by saying that these were the works of "hundred-handed Giants." (2.) The Druidical circles, cromleachs, cairns, altars (called in Wales, *Minnu-geyr*, or seats of Mah-Nuh) Tolmen, Towers, Salsette, Elephanta, Elora, Carnak, &c., are the work of these gigantic engineers (3). They used neither mortar nor cement, nor steel, nor iron to cut the stones with ; and yet they were so artificially wrought that in many places the joints are hardly seen, though many of the stones, as in Peru, are 38 feet long, 18 feet broad, and 6 feet thick, and in the wall of the fortress of Cusco, there are stones of a still greater size. (*Acosta*, vi. 14) The well of Syene made 5400 years ago, when that spot was exactly under the tropic, which it has now ceased to be, was also one of their works of wonder. It was so constructed, that at noon, at the precise moment of the summer solstice, the entire disk of the sun was seen reflected on its surface—a work which the united skill of all the astronomers in Europe, would not now be able to effect.

2. By what means, asks Maurice, was it possible for such ponderous stones, as, for instance, those that crown the summit of the grand portal of Chilambrum, forty feet long and five broad, to be raised to the altitude of 122

feet, but by the aid of geometry joined to mechanics? From what other source has it arisen that the amazing colossal carved work and images in Salsette and Elephanta, are executed according to the rules of such just proportion, as they are represented to be by Mr. Hunter and others, and that such lofty columns richly adorned with mythological sculptures are seen elevated, to a vast height in every province of Hindostan? *Hist. of Hindostan,* i. 489. One of these astonishing structures still in part exists in our own land. Mr. Waltire, says Higgins, thought this temple (Stonehenge) had been constructed for several uses : that it was peculiarly well contrived for the performance of secret rites which were practised in early times—as, if a person stood without, he could not see anything that was done in the centre, provided the entrance were closed, as it might be very effectually by three persons standing before it. If a person stood on the large stone or altar, within the inner curve, which is a parabola and not an ellipse, he might be heard when speaking by all within the temple. Another use for which he thought this structure had been erected was that of making astronomical observations on the heavenly bodies. By careful observations made on the spot, Mr. W., found that the barrows or tumuli surrounding this temple accurately represented the situation and magnitude of the fixed stars, forming a correct and complete planisphere, [or orrery]. Eight hundred only can be seen by the unassisted eye, but he thought he traced fifteen hundred, the smaller representing stars too minute to be observed without some instrument similar to a telescope ; and that there are some other proofs of the occupiers of this structure having possessed something answering to our reflecting telescope. He thought he could prove that *other barrows registered all the eclipses* which had taken place within a certain number of years; that the trilithons are registers of the transits of Mercury and Venus; the meridian line had then been even with the avenue or approach by the grand entrance and the altar stone within the innermost curve, but which is now removed seventy-five degrees from it. *Celtic Druids*, xviii. (4).

3. How early the Chaldæans began to cultivate astronomy is recorded by Porphyry from Aristotle, who relates that when Alexander was in Babylon, Calisthenes on enquiring of the Chaldæan Priests of Bel, found that they had a series of astronomical observations, extending back for a period of 1903 years, written, or rather engraved on tiles or bricks. But we advance far beyond all this, says Bailly, in his *Histoire de l'Astronomie Ancienne*, sect. xiii, and think it by no means improbable, that the most celebrated discovery of our own time, namely, *the true measurement of the earth*, was ascertained in those far remote ages. A very strong proof leads us to this opinion. Aristotle (*De Cœlo.* lib. ii.) relates that in his time, mathematicians reckoned a degree at 1111 stades, and the circumference of the earth at 400,000. The learned are agreed that by these stades was not meant either the Greek or Alexandrine stadium: the lesser of which would give a measurement nearly double that of the real circumference of our globe. I have ascertained the true value of the stadium to which Aristotle alludes, and I find it to be as near as possible to the degree of our own æra, namely 57066 toises: an approximation remarkably singular if it belong to those primal ages. How know we to what point of perfection, Astronomy was then carried?

We can only gather our ideas from detached and fragmentary facts : but the whole, the combination of those fact has escaped us, and it is this which constitutes true know ledge. The vantage ground on which we stand at present, in composing a history of Astronomy, is the large collection of scientific facts which we now have, and the power of weighing probabilities, or assimilations to those facts, when evidences fail us. This measurement, is not therefore the work of those Greeks who preceded Aristotle : this we may be assured of for a strange, but, nevertheless, true reason, *because it is exact.* The Chinese and Chaldæans made but a rough guess at the true measurement. To whom then are we to attribute it, but to an unknown ancient people ? But how could this people remain unknown, if they had been cotemporaneous with the Indians and Chaldæans ; or how is it that their renown in philosophy and science has not come down to our own times ? It can in no way be accounted for but by supposing them to be before both the Indians and Chaldæans. And the measurement spoken of by Aristotle must have either reached him from the Orient through Callisthenes, together with the records of the Babylonian Observatory, or it must have come to him through some Chaldæan medium : and this nation which knew of it so accurately, must have derived it from some elder people [the Atlanteans] which eclipsed all others in science. To which observation may be added the following fact ;—that the septennial cycle or the week, the days of which were dedicated to the planets by the Chinese, the Indians, the Ethiopians, the ancient and modern Europeans, *not in any order regulated by the distance, or the size, or the brilliancy of them, but arbitrarily,* are a further proof of one uniform

G

system of religious astronomy, prevailing at one time among a most powerful people : and the possession of a scientific knowledge also of the order of the heavens, which modern ages are always claiming for themselves, but as we have seen, without any good reason. This ancient lost people were the people of the great island-continent Atlantis, which was destroyed by a deluge ; and in which the pontifical empire of Enoch, the second Messenger of God, and the first and greatest of astronomers, was established, and where it long flourished. From them came all the ancient astronomical knowledge (5).

4. In Siberia, says Bailly, under the 50th degree, and between longitude 80 to 130, are found the vestiges of a civilized people ; the ruins of many cities once flourishing ; manuscripts on silver paper, in characters of Chinese ink, in gold and silver ; pyramids which are tombstones for the dead, and inscriptions in a language that is unknown : figures of men and animals, in gold, in silver and in bronze. The human figures bear a remarkable resemblance to the gods of India. M. D'Anville remarks that Serica, the town called *Sera Metropolis*, was the residence of kings who had governed a people by whom the sciences had been cultivated ; and who are mentioned in Chinese history under the name of Hoei-he (*Geographie ancienne*, ii. 326). Serica is in fact that part of Tartary in which Selingiskoi is found. I have remarked that in this locality, Indian idols have been discovered · the Indians themselves have a tradition, of which they do not know the true meaning. This tradition, which embraces the exact knowledge of the movement of the stars, coupled with that of the period of 180 years, which has never, been used by any other people than the Tartars, seems to

demonstrate that the latter people departing from the North of Asia carried with them traditions of which they did not really know the exact bearing or sense. It was in this region that the twenty-four Boodhoos or Ancients promulgated their doctrines, and prepared mankind for the advent of the First Messenger : but it was not in this region, but in the lost Atlantis, that astronomical science reached its culminating excellence.

5. One of the most remarkable of modern scientific instruments, the orrery, appears to have been a very old invention. Landseer, in his *Sabæan Researches,* has shewn that the word אֲשֵׁירָה *Ashre,* rendered *Groves,* in our translation of the Old Testament, means a kind of orrery, or armillary machine made for purposes of divination : and supposes them probably to have been about the height of a man, with small balls branching off curvedly from the sustaining rod or axis : and referring to 2 *Kings* xxi., he says : The Sabæan *Ashre* appears to have been erected within the precincts of the Temple, where the altars also were built; but besides these perhaps immoveable armillary machines, which for the purpose of divination, Manasseh had constructed in the courts of the Temple, he had also a small copy, or graven image of the *Ashre* within —doubtless to assist in the celebration of those Sabæan rites, which were performed during his idolatrous reign, and which are described by Ezekiel. For there can be no reasonable doubt, that the idolatries which this writer saw on the banks of the Chebar, were those with which the Temple at Jerusalem had really been polluted. It is certain that the word translated " groves," cannot always be interpreted to mean *a grove of trees :* since we read of *setting up groves under every green tree* (2 *Kings* xvii: 8),

nor always strictly designated *an image,* for we also read that the people *made them molten images, and made a grove, and worshipped all the host of heaven, and used divination* (v. 16). See also *Judges* vi. 25, 2 *Kings* xxiii. 4. Hence Selden supposes the term was used for the images worshipped in the groves, especially Ashtarte or Venus. I have no doubt that the *Ashre* were orreries, and that for purposes of astrology they were always used in the Temples, and groves, near the images of the gods. These images were either molten, or were trees themselves. Dr. Gloster Ridley says: Trees were the original temples of the gods: they were also the symbols or images of them: and their several attributes were expressed by several trees which were perpetually appropriated to their respective deities, and called by their names: and therefore addressed and appealed to, as if they had themselves the attributes and powers of their Prototypes, to hear the covenants made in their presence and to punish the violators of them. We are told in the Chinese annals that the Emperor Yu, son of Shun, who reigned in the 23d century before Jesus, invented a great sphere of gold, set with jewels, exhibiting the earth and revolving planets, as far as their revolutions were at that time known. On this sphere the planets were represented by jewels that corresponded to them in colour; and this doubtless was an orrery.

6. In the study of the history of mankind, says Humboldt, *Researches,* i. 147, as in that of the immensity of languages spread over the face of the globe, it would be losing ourselves in a labyrinth of conjectures were we not to assign a common origin to so many races and so many different tongues. The roots of the Shanscrit found in

tho Persian tongue, the great number of roots of the Persian, and even of the Pahlavi, which we discover in the tongues of Germanic origin, give us a right to consider the Shanscrit, the Pahlavi, or the ancient language of the Medes, the Persians, and the Germans, as derived from one and the same source. It would no doubt be absurd to suppose the migration of Egyptian colonies. wherever pyramidal monuments and symbolical paintings are found: *but how can we avoid being struck with the traces of resemblance offered by the vast picture of manners, of arts, of language and traditions, which exist at present. among nations at the most remote distances from each. other ?* Why should we hesitate to point out wherever they occur, the analogies of construction in languages, of style in monuments, and of fictions in cosmogonies, although we may be unable to decide what were the secret. causes of those resemblances, while no historical fact carries us back to the epocha of the communications which existed between the inhabitants of different climates ? * * * Kalm relates in his Travels in America, that Mr. Verandrier had discovered in 1746, in the savannahs of Canada, nine hundred leagues west of Montreal, a. stone tablet fixed in a sculptured pillar and on which were strokes that were taken for a Tartarian inscription. Several Jesuits at Quebec assured the Swedish traveller that they had examined this tablet, which the Chevalier Beauharnois, then governor of Canada, had sent to M. de Maurepas, in France. We cannot but deeply regret having no further knowledge of a monument so interesting to the history of man. * * * The Anglo-American antiquaries have made known an inscription which is supposed to be Phœnician, and which is engraved on the rocks of Dighton, in Narraganset Bay, twelve leagues south of Boston. Drawings of this inscription have been repeatedly published from the end of the 17th century down to the present time by Danforth, Mather, Greenwood, and Sewell. The natives who inhabited these countries, at the time of the first European settlements, possessed an ancient tradition, according to which *strangers in wooden houses* had sailed up Taunton river, formerly called Assoonet. These strangers after having conquered the red men engraved marks on the rocks, which are now covered by the waters of the river. Count de Gebelin does not hesitate, with the learned Dr. Stiles, to regard these marks as a Carthaginian inscription. * * * In the voyage made by M. Bonpland and myself to ascertain the communication between the rivers Orinoco and Amazon, we were told of an inscription, which it was asserted was found in the chain of granite mountains, that in the seventh degree of latitude extends from the Indian village of Uruana as far as the western banks of the Caura. A missionary, Ramon Bueno, a Franciscan monk, having accidentally entered a cavern formed by the separation of some ledges of rocks, beheld in the middle of the cave a large block of granite, on which he saw what he believed to be characters formed into various groups, and ranged on the same line. The missionary gave me a copy of part of those characters. Some resemblance to the Phœnician alphabet may be discovered in them ; but I much doubt whether the good monk, who seemed to be but little interested, had copied it carefully. It is remarkable that in this savage and desert country, where P. Bueno found letters engraven in granite, are a great number of rocks, which at considerable heights are covered with figures of animals, representations of the sun, moon, and stars, and other hieroglyphical signs. The natives relate that their ancestors in the time of the *Great Waters,* came in canoes to the tops of these mountains, and that the stones were then in so plastic a state, that men could trace marks on them with their fingers. *This tradition indicates a tribe in a different and inferior state of civilization from that of those who preceded them, discovering an absolute ignorance of the use of the chisel and every other mechanical tool.*

7. Payne Knight in his *Letters to Sir W. Hamilton* (p. 87), thus speaks of the temples which exist in Egypt, and more particularly those very curious ones in the island of Philæ, on the borders of Ethiopia, which are probably the most ancient monuments of high art now extant, at least if we except the neighbouring temples of Thebes (6). Both were certainly built when that city was the seat of wealth and empire, which it was even to a proverb during the Trojan war. (*Il.* ix., 381.) How long it had then been so we can form no conjecture, but that it soon after declined, there can be little doubt ; for when the Greeks, in the reign of Psammetichus (generally computed to have been about 530 years after the siege of Troy), first became personally acquainted with the interior parts of that country, Memphis had been for many ages its capital, and Thebes was in a manner deserted. Homer makes Achilles speak of its immense wealth and grandeur as a matter generally known and acknowledged ; so that it must have been of long established fame even in that remote age. We may therefore fairly conclude that the greatest part of the superb edifices now remaining were executed, or at

least begun, before that time, many of them being such as could not have been finished, but in a long term of years, even if we suppose the wealth and power of the ancient kings of Egypt to have equalled that of the greatest of the Roman emperors. The finishing of Trajan's column in three years has been justly thought a very extraordinary effort, for there must have been at least 300 good sculptors employed upon it; and yet in the neighbourhood of Thebes we find whole temples of enormous magnitude covered with figures carved in the hard and brittle granite of the Libyan mountains, instead of the soft marbles of Paros and Carrara. Travellers, who have visited that country, have given us but imperfect accounts of the manner in which they are finished; but if one may judge by those upon the obelisk of Rameses, now lying in fragments at Rome, they are infinitely more laboured than those of Trajan's column. An eminent sculptor, with whom I examined that obelisk, was decidedly of opinion that they must have been *finished in the manner of gems* with a graving tool, it being impossible for a chisel to cut red granite with so much neatness and precision (7.) The age of Rameses is uncertain, but the generality of modern chronologers suppose that he was the same person as Sesostris, and reigned at Thebes about 1,500 years before the Christian era, and about 300 before the siege of Troy. Their dates are however merely conjectural, when applied to events of this remote antiquity. The Egyptian priests of the Augustan age had a tradition which they pretended to confirm by records written in hieroglyphics, that their country had once possessed the dominion of all Asia and Ethiopia, which their king, Ramses, or Rameses, had conquered. (*Tacit.*

Annal, ii, 60.) Though this account may be exaggerated, there can be no doubt, from the buildings still remaining, but that they were once at the head of a great empire ; for all historians agree that they abhorred navigation, had no seaport, and never enjoyed the benefits of foreign commerce, without which Egypt could have no means of acquiring a sufficient quantity of superfluous wealth to erect such expensive monuments unless from tributary provinces, especially if all the lower part of it was an uncultivated bog, as Herodotus, with great appearance of probability, tells us it anciently was. Yet Homer, who appears to have known all that could be known in his age, and transmitted to posterity all that he knew, seems to have heard nothing of their empire and conquests. These were obliterated and forgotten by the rise of new empires ; but the renown of their ancient wealth still continued, and afforded a familiar object of comparison, as that of the Mogul does at this day, though he is become one of the poorest sovereigns in the world. But as far as these Egyptian remains lead us into unknown ages, the symbols they contain appear not to have been invented in that country, but to have been copied from those of *some other people still anterior,* who dwelt on the other side of the Erythræan ocean. One of the most obvious of them is the hooded Snake, *which is a reptile peculiar to the south-eastern parts of Asia,* but which I found represented with great accuracy upon the obelisk of Rameses, and have also observed frequently repeated on the Isiac Table and other symbolic works of the Egyptians. It is also distinguishable among the sculptures on the sacred caverns of the Island of Elephanta, and appears frequently added as a characteristic symbol to many of the idols of the

modern Hindus. Among the Egyptians, as before observed, the Cow was the symbol of Venus, the Goddess of
Love, and the passive generative power of nature. On
the capitals of one of the Temples at Philæ we still find
the head of this Goddess represented as of a mixed form ;
the horns and ears of the cow being joined to the beautiful features of a Woman in the prime of life, such as the
Greeks attributed to that Venus, whom they worshipped
as the Mother of the prolific God of Love, Cupid, who
was the personification of animal desire, or concupiscence,
as the Orphic Love, the Father of Gods and Men, was of
universal attraction. The Greeks who represented the
Mother under the form of a beautiful Woman, naturally
represented the son under the form of a beautiful Boy ;
but a people who represented the Mother under the form
of a cow, would as naturally represent the Son under the
form of a calf. This seems to be the case with the Hindus
as well as with the Egyptians.

8. The same learned writer refers to two curious facts,
as establishing not only the antiquity of the human race
to an extent greater than is vulgarly supposed, but also
their wonderful skill in mechanics. Thrace, he says, was
certainly inhabited by a civilized nation at *some remote
period*, for when Philip of Macedon opened the gold
mines of that country, he found that they had been worked
before with great expense and ingenuity by a people well
versed in mechanics, *of whom no memorials whatever were
then extant.* Of these probably was Orpheus, as well as
Thamyris, both of whose poems, Plato says, could be read
with pleasure in his time. * * * * The Cow is in
almost all the Hindu pagodas, but the Bull is revered
with superior solemnity and devotion. At Tanjour is a

monument of their piety to him, which even the inflexible perseverance and habitual industry of the natives of that country could scarcely have erected without greater knowledge in practical mechanics than they now possess. It is a statue of a Bull lying down, hewn with great accuracy out of a single piece of hard granite, which has been conveyed by land from the distance of a hundred miles, although *its weight in its present reduced state must be at least a hundred tons.* PAYNE KNIGHT. *Letter to Sir W. Hamilton, 4to, London,* 1786; *in the Private Case* (21b) *at the British Museum.*

9. The allusions therefore to high art which are to be found in the Apocalypse will strike no one with surprise. In the 3000 years which had passed previous to the epiphany of the First Messenger, (I purposely exclude the additional 200; see *ante,* p. 51), civilization had grown rapidly, and had advanced into states which are popularly called *savage.* It can hardly be doubted, says the compiler of Lord Kingsborough's *Mexican Antiquities,* vi., 15, that the Mexicans were acquainted with many scientifical instruments of strange invention as compared with our own : whether the *telescope* may not have been of the number is uncertain : but the thirteenth plate of M. Dupaix's *Monuments,* which represents a man holding something of a similar nature to his eye, affords reason for believing that they knew how to improve the powers of vision. For proof, says Parkhurst, that the *circulation of the blood* was known to other ancients besides Plato, particularly to Hippocrates, I refer to the learned Dutens' *Enquiry, &c.,* part iii., ch. iii. That the Chaldæans and Egyptians were better skilled than the Greeks in the severer sciences, says Sir W. Drummond (*Anti-*

quities of Zodiac, 34), may be inferred from the occasional,
I might say, the frequent admissions of the Greeks themselves. It may be inferred from the fact that the most
distinguished philosophers of Greece went to Memphis,
and even to Babylon, to study geometry and astronomy;
and lastly and principally it may be inferred from those
fragments of science gathered in part by Thales, Pythagoras, and Democritus, which seemed once to have belonged to a mighty system. *The difficulty is perhaps to
decide when, where, and by whom this system was originally
constructed.* The fact, however, is certain, that at some
remote period there were mathematicians and astronomers
who knew that the Sun is in the centre of the planetary
system, and that the earth, itself a planet, revolves round
the central fire: who calculated, or like ourselves,
attempted to calculate, the return of comets, and who
knew that these bodies move in elliptic orbits immensely
elongated, having the Sun in one of their foci: who indicated the number of solar years contained in the great
cycle, by multiplying a period (variously called in the
Zend, in the Shanscrit, and the Chinese, *ven, van,* and
phen), of 180 years by another period of 144 years: who
reckoned the Sun's distance from the Earth by a measurement equal to 800,000,000 of Olympic stadia, and who
must therefore have taken the parallax of that luminary
by a method not only much more perfect than that said
to have been invented by Hipparchus, but little inferior
in exactness to that now in use among the moderns: who
could scarcely have made a mere guess, when they fixed
the moon's distance from its primary planet at 59 semi-
diameters of the Earth: who had measured the circumference of our globe with so much exactness that their

calculation only differed by a few feet from that made by our modern geometricians : who held that the Moon and other planets were worlds like our own, and that the Moon was diversified by mountains and valleys, and seas : who asserted that there was yet a planet which revolved round the Sun beyond the orbit of Saturn : who reckoned the planets to be sixteen in number, and who calculated the length of the tropical year within three minutes of the true time : nor, indeed, were they wrong at all, if a tradition mentioned by Plutarch be correct. All the authorities for these assertions are stated in my Essay on the Science of the Egyptians and Chaldæans ; and, therefore, I think it unnecessary to repeat them here. In the same Essay, chapters 1 and 9, I have shewn that it may be considered as almost certain that the use of the telescope and microscope must have been known to the ancient astronomers of Egypt and the East, and in chapter 9, I have cited a Greek author, who distinctly describes these instruments; but in countries where knowledge was in the hands only of a few, who carefully concealed their discoveries from the public, it may be easily imagined that little was known to the people of the art of assisting the powers of vision by the aid of glasses. It may be said that the fragments which we have collected here are widely scattered. This I admit ; but as we infer the existence of the poet from *disjecta membra,* so we infer the existence of the system from the disjointed parts and the scattered remains. If in crossing the desert you find the spring of a watch in one place, an index in another, and pieces of a broken dial-plate in a third, you will scarcely doubt that somebody in the desert must have had a whole watch.

10. When we look for monuments of ancient science, he adds (*Antiquities of Zodiac*, 51), whether in India, or Bactria, or in Chaldæa, or in Egypt, we find remnants which seem to have belonged to one common system. Among other examples the zodiac may be cited. We find all the Oriental nations, with the exception, indeed, of the Chaldæans, agreeing in the division of the zodiac into 12 signs. It would seem from this circumstance that *they had followed some common model*, the more especially as all the emblems in the Egyptian, Indian, and Arabian zodiacs are nearly, if not exactly similar. To whom then shall we attribute the invention of the zodiac if not to the *common ancestors* of the nations we have named? And that these common ancestors were those to whom the Apocalypse was revealed, and that upon its express revelation nearly all the pure primeval forms of religion were modelled, and eventually disseminated over the earth, is a conclusion to which all must come who will enter upon the study of that work as it is here developed.

11. Characters, says Humboldt (*Researches* i. 145) are found in Ethiopia, which have an astonishing resemblance with those of the ancient Shanscrit, and particularly with the inscriptions in the Caves of Canara, *the construction of which preceded all the known periods of Indian history.* The arts appear to have flourished at Meroe, and Axoum, one of the most ancient cities of Ethiopia, *before Egypt rose from a state of barbarism.* Sir William Jones believed that he had traced the same people in the Ethiopians of Meroe, the first Egyptians, and the Hindus. Yet it is almost certain that the Abyssinians, whom we must not confound with the Autochthones of Ethiopia, were an

Arabian tribe, and according to the observation of M. Langles, the same hamyaritic characters which we discern in the *east of Africa,* still decorated in the 14th century of the vulgar era, *the gates of the City of Samarcand.* Some connexion, therefore undoubtedly existed between Habesch, or ancient Ethiopia, and the elevated plain of Central Asia.

12. An amazing similarity of construction has been remarked between the Mexican taocallis and the Temple of Bel, at Babylon. Zoega was particularly struck by the analogy, though he had been able to procure only very incomplete descriptions of the group of the pyramids of Taotihuacan. (*Zoega de Orig. Obelisc,* 380.) According to Herodotus, who visited Babylon, and saw the Temple of Bel, this pyramidal monument had eight stories. It was a stadium high, and the breadth of its base was equal to its height. The outer wall which surrounded it was two stadia square. The pyramid was built of brick and asphaltum. A temple was erected on its top, and another at its base. In the Mexican taocallis, as in the Temple of Bel, the lower temple was distinguished from the temple on the platform of the pyramid; and as the Chaldæans made their observations from the top of the temple, so did the Mexican priests observe the rising and setting of the stars. The whole of these American works resemble those which are daily discovered in the eastern part of Asia Among the hieroglyphical ornaments of the pyramid, we distinguish heads of *crocodiles spouting water,* and figures of men sitting cross-legged in Asiatic fashion. As the structure is placed in a plain, says Humboldt, (*Researches* i. 111,) elevated more than 1300 metres above the level of the ocean, and since croco-

diles haunt only the rivers which are near the coast, it seems strange that the architect instead of imitating plants and animals belonging to mountainous countries, should have employed in their reliefs, with extreme industry, the gigantic productions of the torrid zone. Had Humboldt known that the Crocodile was a symbol of God, and Water of the Holy Spirit, and that the emanation of the water here alluded to the birth of the Holy Spirit, he would not have made this remark. Yet he might have found, if he had sought, that among the inhabitants of the Ombite-nome, God was worshipped under the form of this creature; and in the remaining sculptures of the Temple of Ombos, the highest honours of divinity are appropriated to a figure with the head of a Crocodile. (*Description de l'Egypte*, i. *pl.* 43.) How came they then to represent the same idea in regions so far apart?

13. In May, 1830, there was read at the Asiatic Society, a paper from the pen of Colonel Tod, on a gold ring of Hindu fabrication found at Montrose, in Scotland. The ring, the subject of this Essay, was in the possession of the Countess of Cassilis, and was dug up on the fort hill, near Montrose. The ring bears the miniature Lingam and Yoni, of Hindu adoration: round and over which is wreathed the Serpent; on either side is the Sacred Bull, with the hump on the shoulder, which caused the whole design to be mistaken for the arms of Mar, supported by the winged *wiverns*, or griffins, under which supposition it was purchased by Miss Erskine, of Dun, from whom it came into the possession of its present owner, who having shewn it to Col. Fitzclarence, that gentleman obtained permission to submit the relic to the inspection of Col. Tod. After suggesting the reasons

which occur at first sight of the ring, for pronouncing it
to be of Hindu origin, the author urged the similarity of
religion once prevailing among all the tribes who peopled
Europe from the East, as well as in India and Egypt; in
proof of which he adduced the existence of exactly the
same symbols as those upon the ring in the ruins of Pompeii, of Pæstum, and of Cortona, as well as in various
parts of France. The remainder of the paper was principally occupied with the arguments for ascribing a
common origin to the Indo-Scythic martial races of India,
and the early colonists of Europe. These symbols, it will
be seen, were those by which the Great Father and the
Great Mother were typified in the Mysteries; which still
exist throughout the greater part of the oriental world;
which Jesus alluded to when he made *Love* the foundation of his religion; which the early Christians celebrated
in their *Agapæ* or love-feasts, held in caverns at night,
like the Eleusinian and Cabiric rites, though the priests
of course have assigned other and different reasons for
these assemblies.

14. There is not, says Max Muller, (*Ancient Sanskrit
Literature*, 13,) an English jury nowadays which, after
examining the hoary documents of language, would reject
the claim of a common descent and a legitimate relation-
ship between Hindu, Greek, and Teuton. Many words
still live in India and in England that have witnessed
the first separation of the Northern and Southern Aryans,
and these are witnesses, not to be shaken on cross examination. The terms for God, for house, for father, mother,
son, daughter, for dog and cow, for heart and tears, for
axe and tree, identical in all the Indo-European idioms,
are like the watch-words of soldiers. We challenge the

seeming stranger, and whether he answer with the lips of
a Greek, a German, or an Indian, we may recognize him
as one of ourselves.   Though the historian may shake his
head, though the physiologist may doubt, and the poet
scorn the idea, all must yield before the facts furnished
by language.   There was a time when the ancestors of
the Celts, the Germans, the Slavonians, the Greeks, and
Italians, the Persians and Hindus, were living within
the same fences, separate from the ancestors of the Semitic and Turanian races.   General Vallancey, says Davies,
(*Celt. Res.* 224,) has proved that Irish has a certain degree
of connection with Chaldaic, Arabic, Persian, Coptic, and
Phœnician.   From these premises, and from other data, he
infers that in the Irish we are to acknowledge emigrants
from India to the coast of Arabia, Egypt, and Phœnicia,
and from the latter country by sea through Spain to the
British Islands.   The Irish language appears to have
arrived at maturity amongst the *Japetidæ* while they
were yet in contact with Aramean families, and formed a
powerful tribe in Asia Minor and in Thrace.   It may,
therefore, in particular instances, have more similitude or
analogy to the Arabic dialects, than what appears in those
branches of the Celtic that were matured in the west of
Europe.   Those who used this language consisted partly
of Titans, of Celto-Scythians, or of those Japetidæ, who
assisted in building the city of Babel.   Irish, or a congenial dialect once prevailed in Thrace, and was diffused
from thence all the way to the islands of Britain, whilst
at the same time it branched off to the Italian side of the
Alps.

15. Some granitic rocks, says Humboldt, (*Researches* i,
177), which rise on the savannahs of Guiana, between the

Cassiquiare and the Conorichite, are covered with figures of tigers, crocodiles, and other characters, which may be regarded as symbolical. Similar figures are found 400 leagues to the north and the west, on the banks of the Orinoco, near Eucaramada, and Caicara: on the borders of the river Cauca, near Timba between Cali and Jelima: and even on the elevated plain of the Cordilleras, in the Paramo of Guanacas. The natives of these regions are *unacquainted with the use of metallic tools, and all concur in asserting that these characters already existed when their ancestors arrived in those countries.* Is it to a single nation trained to industry and skilled in sculpture, such as the Toltecks, the Aztecks, and the tribes that emigrated from Aztlan that these marks of remote civilization are owing? In what region must we place the seat of this culture? Is it to the north of the river Gila, on the elevated plain of Mexico? or in the southern hemisphere, or those lofty plains of Tiahuanacu *which the Incas themselves found covered with ruins of majestic greatness,* and which may be considered as the Himalaya and Thibet of South America? These problems are not to be solved in the present state of our knowledge.

16. It is excellently remarked by Wilford, says Faber (*Pag. Idol.* i. 60), that *one and the same code both of theology and of fabulous history* (8), has been received through a range or belt about forty degrees broad, across the old continent, in a ·south-east and north-west direction, from the eastern shores of the Malayan peninsula to the western extremity of the British isles: that through this immense region, the same original religious notions re-appear in various places, under various modifications as might be expected; and that there is not a greater difference be_

tween the tenets and worship of the Hindus and Greeks, than exists between those of the churches of Rome and Geneva. Immense as such a territorial range may be, the preceding observation is yet too limited. It applies with equal propriety *to the whole habitable globe:* for the arbitrary rites and opinions of every pagan nation bear so close a resemblance to each other, that *such a coincidence can only have been produced by their having all had a common origin.* Barbarism itself has not been able to efface the strong primeval impression. Vestiges of the ancient general system may be traced in the recently discovered islands of the great Pacific Ocean : and when the American world was first opened to the hardy adventurers of Europe, its inhabitants from north to south venerated, with kindred ceremonies and kindred notions, the gods of Egypt and Hindostan, of Greece, of Italy, of Phœnicia and Britain. * * * This enterprising people, were known by various names. They were called *Scuths, Chusas, Chasas, Cisseans, Cosseans, Coths, Ghauts,* and *Goths,* from their great ancestor *Cush,* whose name they pronounced *Cusha, Chusa, Ghoda, Chasa, Chasya,* or *Cassius.* They were styled *Palli, Bali, Bhils, Philistim, Palistim, Bolgs,* or *Belgæ,* from their occupation ; for the term denotes *Shepherds.* And they were partially denominated *Phanakim* or *Phœnicians* and *Huc-Sos* or shepherd-kings, from their claiming to be a royal race : *Sacas, Sagas, Sacasenas, Sachim, Suchim, Saxe,* or *Saxons,* from the god *Saca,* or *Sacya; Budins* or *Wudins* from their god *Buddha* or *Woden; Teuts* or *Teutons* from their god *Teut* or *Taut;* and *Germans* or *Sarmans* from their god *Sarman* or *Saman* and his minis- ters the Samaneans or Sarmaneans, or Germaneans, as they are indifferently called, according to a varied pronunciation of the same word. * * * The evidence indeed for the remote antiquity of Buddhism rests upon exactly the same foundation as that for the remote antiquity of Brahmanism. There is scarcely a country in which we do not find both systems more or less blended together, and Buddha as much as Siva or Osiris, under his various names of Buddha, Saca, Taut, Teut, Thoth, Bod, Wod, Hermaya, Hermes, or Mercolis has been worshipped from Japan in the East, to Ireland in the West. (i. 88). All these facts tend to prove the uniform system of theology established by the 24 Ancients, and renovated by the Messengers of the Cycle (9).

17. The same author (Faber) in his second chapter has collected proofs that all the religions of the earth were at first One, and emanated from one centre. He gives remarkable evidence of this, by citing some tenets of a striking character, in which they all agreed. I summarize here from that chapter, some of the extracts which he has made from reliable sources, of the grounds on which his proofs are based; and I have added to them certain selections by myself. They are singularly interesting; and they are truly appropriate in this place; for the reader will find that they embody in some measure, portions of the teaching of this Apocalypse; and as their antiquity extends even into the very morning of the ages, it will be at once seen that they *could* not have been gleaned from a work said to be written not quite 1800 years ago—while no one will assert that the pretended John of Patmos extracted from Chinese or Indian sources, the doctrines which *he* puts forth in his Revelation.

18. It is well known, says Holwell (*Interesting Histori-*

cal Events, i. 3), that at the capture of Calcutta, A.D.
1756, I lost many curious Gentoo manuscripts, and among
them two very correct and valuable copies of the *Gentoo
Shastah.* They were procured by me with so much trouble
and expense, that even the commissioners of restitution,
though not at all disposed to favour me, allowed me 2,000
Madras rupees in recompense for this particular loss : but
the most irreparable damage I suffered under this head of
grievances was a translation I made of a considerable part
of the Shastah which had cost me eighteen months' hard
labour. As that work opened upon me, I distinctly saw that
*the Mythology as well as the Cosmogony of the Egyptians,
Greeks, and Romans, were borrowed from the doctrines of
the Brahmins contained in this book, even to the copying
their exteriors of worship, and the distribution of their idols,
though grossly mutilated and adulterated.*

19. The various systems of Pagan idolatry, says Faber,
in his preface, in different parts of the world, correspond
so closely both in their evident purport, and in numerous
points of arbitrary resemblance, that they cannot have
been struck out independently in the several countries
where they have been established, but must *all have originated from some common source.* But if they all originated from a common source, then either one nation must
have communicated its peculiar theology to every other
people in the way of peaceful and voluntary imitation :
or that same nation must have communicated it to every
other people through the medium of conquest and violence:
or lastly, all nations must in the infancy of the world
have been assembled together in a single region, and in a
single community, must at that period, and in that state
of society have agreed to adopt the theology in question,

and must thence as from a common centre, have carried it to all quarters of the globe. These are the only three modes in which the universal accordance of the Gentiles in their religious speculations can possibly be accounted for. But as the incredibility of the first, and as the equal incredibility and impossibility of the second, may be shewn without much difficulty, the third alone remains to be adopted. Now this third mode, both perfectly harmonizes with the general purport of heathen idolatry, and minutely accords with an historical fact which is declared to us on the very highest authority. An examination of the theology of the Gentiles forces us to conclude that all mankind were once assembled together in a single community, and that they afterwards spread themselves in detached bodies over the face of the whole earth. From this assertion I do not very materially dissent. Faber uses it to connect it with some maniacal nonsense suggested by Bryant, about the mythos of Babel, the Noachian deluge, helio-arkism, the miraculous confusion of tongues, and I know not how many other fables. The real truth of it, however, consists in this, that although polytheism was the earliest, though not the first, form of religion, it gradually infused itself into the sublime system of Theism, which the Ancients and the first Messiah of God preached; and the two becoming imperceptibly blended, the result is seen in the general uniformity of which Faber speaks.

20 The Hindu sages view their principal God as triplicating himself, and as thus sustaining under his three grand forms, the characters of the Creator, the Preserver, and the Destroyer. They do not however use the term Creator in the scriptural sense of the word, as denoting

one who causes something to exist out of nonentity, but
rather as one *who gives regular form and activity to crude
pre-existing materials.* The creative power disposes such
materials into definite shape and thus fashions a world : the
preserving power upholds the world when it *is* fashioned ;
and the destroying power reduces it at length to its consti-
tuent elements, sometimes by a deluge of water, and at other
times by a deluge of fire. Everything is then absorbed
into the unity of the Great Father, and this mysterious
Being during the period that elapses between each two
mundane systems, reposes on the surface of the mighty
deep, floating securely either in a wonderful egg (Sphere),
or in the calix of the lotus, (the Shekinah), or on a
naviform leaf, or on a huge Serpent coiled up in the form
of a boat, or in a sacred ship denominated *Argha,* of
which the other vehicles are consequently symbols. To
destroy, however is but to create afresh ; for destruction
affects form alone : it reaches not to substance. Hence
when the Great Father has slept a whole year of the
Creator,* the space which ever intervenes between world
and world, he awakes from his slumber and produces a
new order of things. Out of the chaotic materials of the
prior world, another world is fashioned : the Preserver
again supports it—the Destroyer again dissolves it, and as
it was preceded by a world, so in due time it is likewise
succeeded by one. This alternate destruction and reproduction is thought to be repeated again and again, so that
in the lapse of countless ages, an enormous number of
successive worlds is believed to have existed. * * Brahm
is introduced in different parts of the Geeta, saying : *I*

---

* The Apocalypse alludes to this, and calls it "*silence in*
Heaven for half-an-hour."

am of all things transient the beginning, the middle, and the end ; the whole world was spread abroad by me in my invisible form. At the end of the period Kalp, all things return into my primordial source, and at the beginning of another Kalp I emane them all again. I am the under-standing of the wise, the glory of the proud, the strength of the strong. I am the eternal seed of all nature. I am the father and mother of this world, the grandsire and the pre-server. I am death and immortality. I am entity and nonentity. I am never failing and wise. I am all-grasping death. I am the resurrection. The great Brahma's is my womb, in it I (GOD) *place my fœtus ; and from it is the production of all nature. The great Brahma's is the womb of all those various forms which are conceived in every natural womb, and I am the being that soweth the seed.** All things in short are in a state of perpetual solution and reproduction. *The earth is perishable,* say the Hindu bards, in one of their funeral hymns; *the ocean, the gods themselves pass away. How should not that bubble, mortal man, meet destruction? All that is low must finally perish · all that is elevated, must ultimately fall: all compounded bodies must end in dissolution : life must be concluded with death.* Brahm the Great Father is *that whence all beings are produced : that by which they live when born, that towards which they tend, and that unto which they pass.*

21. In the theological Works of Hermes Trismegistus (Thoth, the Sixth Messiah,) which contain an account of the old Mizraimic philosophy (10), it is laid down, that *nothing in the world perishes, and that death is not the*

---

* Compare with this the exclamation of *Wisdom* cited in page 26, and the identity of her and Brahma will be apparent.

destruction, but only the change and translation of things.
Agreeably to this maxim it is further taught, that *when
the world becomes degenerate, then that Lord and Father,
the Supreme God, and the only governor beholding the
manners and deeds of men, by his will, which is his benig-
nity, always resisting vice and restoring things from
their degeneracy, will either wash away the malignity
of the world by water, or else consume it by fire,
and then restore it to its ancient form again.* In the
celebrated answer given by the oracle of Sarapis to
Nicocreon, King of Cyprus, who sent messengers to enquire what Divinity he ought to adore under that name,
the priest said. *My divinity shall be described in the
words I now utter. The canopy of heaven is my head;
the sea is my belly: the earth my feet, my eyes are in the
ethereal region, and mine eye is the resplendent and far-
shining lamp of the Sun.* The prevalence of such an opinion
among the Egyptians, respecting the Pantheism of the Universe, and the successive destructions of the world, by inundation and conflagration, is mentioned also by Julius Fir-
micus, and it is eminently set forth in the curious dialogue
between Solon and the Egyptian priests as recorded by
Plato. Solon, we are told, wishing rather to learn the
sentiments of the Egyptians, then to declare his own, put
many questions to one of their priests on various points
of antiquity. Thus, from a desire to reduce Chronology
to some degree of certainty, he asked respecting the age
of Phoroneus, esteemed the first of men, and Niobe, and
Pyrrha and Deucalion after the flood, and other matters
which enter so largely into the mythological genealogies
of the Greeks To this the priest replied; O, Solon, Solon,
you Greeks are always children, nor is there an old man.

among you. Having no ancient traditions, nor any acquaintance with chronology, you are as yet in a state of intellectual infancy. The true origin of such mutilated fables as you possess is this. There have been and shall again be in the course of many revolving ages, numerous destructions of the human race : the greatest of them by fire and water, but others in an almost endless succession at shorter intervals. (*Plato, Tim.* 22—23.) This is exactly the Hindu theory, and every discovery of geology shews that it is true. The same doctrine is mentioned also by Origen. They hold, says he, a succession from age to age of many conflagrations and many inundations, and esteem the flood of Deucalion as an event but of yesterday. Indeed to such as are disposed to listen to their speculations, they teach that the world was never produced, but has existed from all eternity : and he adds that the wisest among the Egyptians had communicated their theory of successive conflagrations and inundations to his opponent Celsus (*Orig. adv. Cels.* i.). According to these there was originally a boundless darkness on the Great Abyss, but Water and an Ethereal Spirit acted by divine power on Chaos. Then sprang forth holy *Light ;* then all the gods made an orderly distribution of things out of seminative nature. So Sanconiathon, speaking of the Holy Spirit, calls her the Air shining with ethereal light, by whose fiery influence on the sea and earth, winds were begotten, and clouds, and great defluxions of water. The Hermetic books are full of the same allusions. The great god [it should be Goddess] of the Egyptians, though clothed with the attributes of the Deity, was no more the Supreme Being, than the Great God of the Hindus. He [She] is described as being the Soul of the World, and as

H 2

partaking of the nature of both sexes precisely in the same manner as that Siva-Ardha-Nari, who floated in the ship Argha (11), on the surface of the waters. From this their common parent all souls are derived. He [She] is ever pregnant and ever productive. Death is nothing more than a change of body, and a passing from visibility into invisibility. Every day some part of the world passes into this invisibility. It does not utterly perish, but only disappears from our sight, being either translated into some other place, or changed into some other form. In a similar manner animals are dissolved by death, not that they may be utterly destroyed, but that in due season they might be made again. As for the world, which is the body of the Great Father, it makes all things out of itself, and it perpetually renews all things. In the whole Universe nothing utterly perishes. Itself is unchangeable : its parts only admit of alteration. Yet of these, subject as they are to mutation, none utterly perishes, or is absolutely destroyed ; for what is incorruptible cannot be corrupted, and what is a part of the Great God cannot be annihilated.

22. The Iranians held the same doctrines respecting a succession of worlds that the Hindus had adopted : and the conclusion is rendered more probable, both from the common Gothic or Celtic descent of the Indo Scythæ, and the military and sacerdotal castes of the Persians ; and from the circumstance of the primeval Babylonian empire comprehending within its limits that part of Irân, which still bears the name of *Chusistan*. There is a tenet of the ancient Magi, preserved by Theopompus, which is so nearly allied to the doctrine in question that there can be little doubt of its having been maintained by

them. It was their belief that men would live again in another state of existence and become immortal; nor are we to suppose that this means simply their belief of a resurrection in the modern sense of the word; for it was additionally their opinion, that the things which now are, would for ever continue to be designated by the names of their possessors. There is some degree of obscurity in this statement; but since the doctrine held by the Hindus is precisely that which renders it perfectly intelligible, I am inclined to believe that it has been regularly deduced from that doctrine.

23. The mystic philosophy of the Chinese Book, *Yeking*, bears a close resemblance to that of the Pythagoreans. Eight Koua, or symbols, each composed of three lines, hieroglyphically express certain general things, on which the nativity and corruption of all particular things are allowed to depend. Of these the first represents the heaven, the second the earth, the third, lightning, the fourth, mountains, the fifth, fire, the sixth, clouds, the seventh, water, and · the eighth, wind. From these variously combined the perpetual variety of nature originates. Now the Pythagoreans expressly held the doctrine of a succession of worlds, and a transmigration of each, and taught much respecting the potency of numbers, and a perpetual destruction and reproduction of the Universe. If then, the theology of the Chinese, which similarly treats of generation and destruction, resemble that of the Pythagoreans, it must have inculcated the tenet of a succession of worlds. The substance of what they teach would seem indeed to be this, that destruction and reproduction in perpetual vicissitude, spring from the numbers three and eight, with which every new world commences.

24. In supposing such to be the doctrine contained in the Book *Yeking*, one is the more confirmed by the circumstance of Buddhism prevailing so generally in China; the worship of Buddha has been the religion of the Chinese from the very commencement of the empire. Now the doctrine of a succession of worlds is held no less decidedly by the Buddhists than by the Brahmins: nor is it set forth with greater precision in any country than in that of the Burmese, who are both determined Buddhists and near neighbours of the Chinese. The Universe is called by them *Loghas* (Logos), which signifies successive destruction and reproduction: because it is conceived that the Universe after it has been destroyed either by fire, water, or wind, is again of itself restored to its ancient form. They say that the age of man has not always been the same with what it is at present, and that it will not continue to be the same; but that it is lengthened or shortened according to the general merit or demerit of men's actions. After the first inhabitants, their children and grandchildren had gradually and successively shorter lives, in proportion as they became less virtuous; (12) and this gradual decrease continued until men came to live ten years only; the duration of the life of men in their greatest state of wickedness. The children of these, considering the cause of their parent's short life, and dedicating themselves more to the practice of virtue, had their lives gradually lengthened. Now this successive decrement in the duration of the life of man, followed by an increase, must take place 64 times after the reproduction of a world before that world will be again destroyed. In the present world eleven of these changes have taken place; nor will it be destroyed until it has passed through

fifty-three more changes. The Burma writings allege three remote causes for the destruction of a world— luxury, anger, and ignorance. From these, by the power of fate, arise the physical or proximate causes, namely, fire, water, and wind. When luxury prevails, the world is consumed by fire : when anger prevails, it is destroyed by water ; and when ignorance prevails it is dispersed by wind. The Burmas do not suppose that a world is destroyed, and a new one instantaneously regenerated ; but that the destruction takes up the space of an Assenchiekat, that the reproduction takes up another, and that a third intervenes between the end of the old world, and the beginning of the new. At the end of each of the 64 changes in the life of man which take place during the existence of every world, an almost total destruction befalls the human race. *After the greater part have perished, a heavy rain falls, and sweeps away into the rivers unburied bodies and filth.* Then follows a shower of flowers and sandal wood to purify the earth ; and all kinds of garments fall from above. *The scanty remains of men who had escaped from destruction now creep out from caverns and hiding places, and repenting of their sins henceforth enjoy longer lives.* A thousand years before the destruction of a world a certain Nat (13), descends from the superior abodes. His hair is dishevelled, his countenance mournful, and his garments black. He passes every where through the public ways and streets with piteous voice, announcing to mankind the approaching dissolution. When it is to happen by fire, as soon as the Nat has ceased to admonish men, a heavy rain falls from heaven, fills all the lakes, causes torrents, and produces an abundant crop. Mankind now filled with hope sow seed more plentifully : but this is the last rain : not a drop falls for a hundred thousand years, and plants with every vegetating thing perish. Then die all animals ; and passing on to the state of Nat, are from thence transferred to the abodes *Zian* (14) or Arupa. The Nat of the sun or moon, having now become Zian, *these luminaries are darkened and vanish.* In their stead two suns arise, which are not Nat. The one always succeeds to the other, rising when it sets, so that there is no night : and the heat consequently becomes so intense, *that all the lakes and torrents are dried up, and not the smallest vestige remains upon the surface of the earth.* After a long interval, a *third* sun arises : *then are dried up the greatest rivers.* A *fourth* sun succeeds, and two being now constantly above the horizon, even *the seven great lakes or oceans disappear.* A *fifth* sun arises and *dries up the sea.* A *sixth* sun rends asunder this and the other 1,010,000 earths, while from the rents are *emitted smoke and fire.* Finally, after a very long interval, a *seventh* sun appears, by which Mienmo, (the Burman centrical mount Meru), and all the inhabitants of the Nat are consumed ; and as in a lamp, when the wick and oil are exhausted, the flame goes out, so when everything in this and the other 1,010,000 worlds is consumed, the fire of its own accord will die away. Such is the manner in which the Kosmos is destroyed by fire (15). (*As. Res.* vol. vi. p. 174-249) Similar to this is the apocalyptic theology of Siam, or more properly Sian and Zian, its real name. The figure of the world according to their doctrine is eternal : but the world which we see is not, for whatever we see therein lives in their opinion, and must die : and at the *same* time there will spring up other beings of the same kind, another heaven, another earth, and other stars : and this is the ground of what they say, that they have seen nature decay and revive again several times. (LOUBERE's *Siam*, p. 119.) Adair, in his *History of the American Indians*, relates a conversation with one of their priests, when he spoke of the dreadful day in which *Lôak Ishto-hoollo*, would send *Phutchick Keeraah Ishtò*, the great blazing star, *Yahkanè eeklénna Loak loáchàchè*, to burn up half the earth with fire ; *Pherimmi Aiúbe* from the north'to the south ; *hassé oobèa perà*, toward the setting of the sun, *according to the ancient true speech that Ishto-hoollo Aba spoke to his beloved Loáche*, p. 89. From whence but the Apocalypse could all these analogies have come ?

25. When the Goths who were a branch of the Chasas, or Chusas, or Indo-Scuths, emigrated from the East and invaded the Roman empire, they brought with them the Buddhic theology of their ancestors : and as a part of it they have preserved with a considerable degree of accuracy the doctrine of a succession of worlds. According to the Scaldic philosophers, a world luminous, glowing, not to be dwelt in by strangers, existed before all things. This world is named *Muspelsheim.* There black Surtur * holds his empire. A flaming sword shines in his hand. He shall come at the end of all things : he shall vanquish every god : he shall give up the Universe a prey to the flames. Next in order to Muspelsheim, the abode of Surtur, was created another world, which commences with a man and his three sons, born from a mysterious *Cow.* At the close of the present system, that is in the

---

* This God is described to be black, because He was the God of the primeval Black Nation : and also because He is hidden in impenetralle darkness.

Maha-Pralaya of the Hindus, all will be involved in destruction. The great ship *Naglefara* shall be set afloat;
the mighty serpent vomits forth floods of poison; the
Black Deity and his Genii invade the perishing Universe;
and the power of dissolution wraps the whole earth
in fire and flame. But to destroy in one form is only to
reproduce in another. *There will arise out of the sea, a*
new earth most lovely and delightful: covered it will be
with verdure and pleasant fields: there the grain shall
spring forth and grow of itself without cultivation. Vidar
and Vale shall also survive, because neither the flood,
nor the black conflagration shall do them any harm.
They shall dwell in the plains of Ida, (the Hindu Ida-
vratta) where was formerly the residence of the gods.
The sons of Thor, Modè and Manè repair thither: thither
come Balder and Hoder from the mansions of the dead·
They sit down and converse together: they recall to mind
the sufferings which they had formerly undergone. Nor
do the gods alone tenant the renovated universe: while
the fire devours all things, two persons of the human
race, the one male and the other female lie concealed under
a hill. These feed on the dew and propagate so abundantly
that the earth is soon peopled with a new race of mortals.
The sun also, at once a Female and the brilliant monarch
of Fire, before it is devoured by the wolf Fenrir shall
have brought forth a daughter as lovely and resplendent
as herself, who shall go in the track formerly trodden by
her mother. Everything in short shall be renovated,
and the destruction of one world shall only be the har-
binger to the creation of another (16).

26. The opinions of the Goths respecting alternate
destruction and reproduction are so well summed up by

Mr. Mallet, that I cannot refrain from giving his statement at some length. The philosophers of the North, he
says, considered nature as in a state of perpetual labour
and warfare. Her strength was thus continually wasting
away by little and little, and her approaching dissolution
could not but become every day more perceptible. At last
a confusion of the seasons, with a long and preternatural
winter, was to be the final mark of her decay. The moral
world is to be no less disturbed and troubled than the
natural. The voice of dying nature will be no longer
heard by man. Her sensations being weakened, and, as
it were, totally extinct, shall leave the heart a prey to
cruel and inhuman passions. *Then will all the malevolent
and hostile powers whom the gods have hitherto with much
difficulty confined, burst their chains and fill the Universe
with discord and confusion.* (*See* APOCALYPSE, section
48) The host of heroes from Valhalla shall in vain
attempt to support the gods; for though the latter
will destroy their enemies, they will nevertheless fall
along with them. That is, in other words, in that
great day, all the inferior divinities, whether good or
bad, shall fall in one great conflict back again into the
bosom of the Grand Divinity, from whom all things have
proceeded, as *emanations of his essence,* and who will
survive all things. After this, *the world becomes a prey to
flames,* which are however destined rather to purify than
destroy it, since it afterwards makes its appearance again,
*more lovely, more pleasant, and more fruitful than before.
In this new earth which is to succeed that which we inhabit,*
there are to be again subaltern divinities to govern it, and
men to people it This in general is what the Edda means
to tell us. Although the circumstances of the relation are

darkly and allegorically delivered, yet they are not detailed so obscurely, but that one easily sees it was the idea of the northern philosphers, that the world was to be renovated, and spring forth again, more perfect and beautiful.

27. Mallet, says Faber, speaks somewhat too exclusively of its being the opinion of the Goths that the present world would be destroyed by fire. In reality they have blended together the two notions of a destruction by *fire*, and a destruction by *water*, each of which is indifferently called by the Hindus, a *Pralaya*, or Flood. This will be evident to any one who examines either the preceding extract from the Edda, or the more ancient Voluspa, where it treats of the same subject. In both mention is made, not only of devastating fire, but likewise of a wonderful ship being set afloat on the swelling ocean ; and we are further taught that the new earth is to arise out of the sea. *The giant Rymer*, says Voluspa, *arrives from the East, carried in a chariot; the ocean swells; the Great Serpent rolls himself furiously in the waters, and lifteth up the sea.* The Eagle screams, and tears the dead bodies with his horrid beak. (APOCALYPSE, section 34.) *The vessel of the gods is set afloat ; the vessel comes from the east; the host of evil genii arrives by sea. Loki is their pilot and director. Their furious squadron advances, escorted by the wolf Fenrir. Loki appears with them. The Black Prince of the genii issues forth from the south surrounded with flames ; the swords of the gods beam forth rays like the sun. The rocks are shaken and fall to pieces.*

---

* See APOCAL., section 56. This is the dracontine Typhon of Egypt, who is expressly said by Plutarch to be a personification of the Deluge.

(APOCALYPSE, section 57.) *The female giants wander about weeping. Men tread in crowds the path of death. The heaven is split asunder; the sun is darkened; the sea overwhelms the earth; the shining stars vanish out of heaven; the fire furiously rages; the ages draw to an end; the ascending flame licks the vault of heaven* (APOCALYPSE, section 57.) Here the agents of destruction are both fire and water; and while the whole world is convulsed we are presented with an image of the ship of the gods floating on the surface of the agitated ocean. This agrees with the periodical voyage of the Indian Menu : but the Goths in the course of their progress westward, from their original settlements in Cashgar and Bokhara, have deviated somewhat from the genuine tradition, though they have no t altogether lost it. The Voluspa proceeds like the Edda, to describe the production of a new woild out of the ruins of its predecessor, in a manner which exactly corresponds with the rising of the present world out of the waters. *Then we see emerge from the bosom of the waves an earth clothed with a most lovely verdure. The floods retire; the eagle soars wheresoever he lists, and seizes his fishy prey : on the tops of the mountains, Balder and his brother, the warrior gods, return to inhabit the ruined palaces of Odin. The gods assemble in the fields of Ida : they discourse together concerning the heavenly palaces, whose ruins are before them : they recollect their former conversations and the ancient discourses of Odin.*

28. It is observed by Mallet, that the doctrine of the Gothic philosophers is precisely the same as that espoused by the Stoics, and as a proof he adduces several passages fiom the writings of Seneca. The observation is just; but the doctrine in question was by no means peculiar to

the Stoics. It was held also by the philosophers of other schools. The principle which they laid down universally, as being indisputable, and which formed the basis of all their subsequent reasoning, was the eternity of matter. This was declared by them to be at once uncreated, and incapable of annihilation. There was among the heathen philosophers, says Bayle, a great variety of opinions about the origin of the world, and the nature of the element or elements, of which they pretended particular bodies to have been formed. Some maintained that water was the principal of all things. Others gave that pre-eminence to air; others to fire; others to homogeneal parts; but they all agreed in this—that the matter of the world was un-produced. They never disputed among themselves upon the question, *whether anything was made out of nothing?* they all agreed that *that* was impossible. But though the eternity of crude matter was thus maintained, a frequent change of figure in that matter was fully acknowledged. Matter itself, they taught, is indeed eternal; but in addition to the changes of form which we daily witness, it successively undergoes at the end of certain vast periods, mutilations which are equivalent *to the destruction of one mundane system, and to the production of another from its ruins.* This point is argued by the philosopher Sallust. Drawing a distinction between substance and form, he allows the corruptibility of the latter, but denies that of the former. (*De Diis et Mund.,* C. viii., xvii) In a similar manner, Timæus, the Locrian, though he admits the creation, or rather the generation of the world by a Deity—(for he represents it as being the offspring of his god)—yet he acknowledges nothing more than a produc-tion out of already existing materials. (*De Anim. Mund,*

p. 545.) Precisely the same language is held by Ocellus Lucanus (*de Univ.*, C. i., ii.) ; and accordingly it is on this identical principle that he undertakes to answer those writers who made the history of Greece commence with Inachus. That epoch, says he, was no real beginning, but only a change ; for as Greece had been in a state of barbarism before the days of Inachus, so will it again relapse into a similar state at some future period—a singular prophecy, which we now see realized. At the same time he intimates the existence of certain physical, as well as moral revolutions. The different parts of the earth are liable to corruption and change, sometimes in consequence of a deluge produced by the sea, and sometimes by the more silent operation of dissipating winds or undermining waters ; meanwhile the substance of the earth itself is incapable of corruption. Such also is the doctrine of Macrobius. (*In Somn. Scip.* ii., 10.) Nothing can be properly said to perish throughout the whole world. Those things which seem to be destroyed, only change their appearance. The world itself remains, though the human race has often been almost totally swept away either by inundation or conflagration. In this tenet, with some smaller varieties, the Stoics, the Epicureans, and the Platonists were all agreed.

29. In the same way the devouring Jupiter of the Stoics swallows up at the close of each world the whole host of hero-gods ; and as it was the universal doctrine of those philosophers that during the intervals of the successive conflagrations by which the mundane system is destroyed, that god retires into himself and converses with his own thoughts ; so at the end of each interval he produces a new frame of nature, together with a new

family of inferior divinities out of his own substance. Such speculations are plainly the same as those of the Indian school. The devouring Jupiter occupies the place of Siva, or Maha-Cali, or the Destroying power; and his solitary abstraction during every intervening period is palpably no other than the profound solitary meditation of the creative Brahm, while he floats inactive on the surface of the chaotic abyss. The world, says Seneca, being melted, and having re-entered into the bosom of Jupiter, this god continues for some time totally concentered in himself, and remains concealed, as it were, wholly immersed in the contemplation of his own ideas. Afterwards we see a new world spring from him, perfect in all its parts. Animals are produced anew. An innocent race of men is formed under more favourable auspices, in order to people this earth—the worthy abode of virtue. In short, the whole face of nature becomes more pleasing and lovely. (*Epist.* 9, and *Quæst Nat.* iii., c. *ult.*) And again, speaking of a mundane dissolution, as involving the destruction or death of all, he teaches us, that when the laws of nature shall be buried in ruin, and the last day of the world shall come, the southern pole shall crush, as it falls, all the regions of Africa, and the north pole shall overwhelm all the countries beneath its axis. *The affrighted Sun shall be deprived of its light;* the palace of heaven falling to decay shall produce at once both life and death, and some kind of dissolution shall equally seize upon all the deities who thus shall return into their original chaos. (*Herc. Æt.,* 1102.)

30. The opinions of the ancient Druids have not come down to us with so much precision as might have been desired; yet there remains sufficient proof that they

agreed with all the other primeval peoples in these particular points of doctrine: and that like the other
Oriental priests, they anticipated geological discoveries
by several thousand years. They were in fact themselves
an order of Eastern priests located in Britain, adoring
Buddwas, and symbolizing him as the Mighty Serpent.
Dr. Borlase, says the author of *Celtic Researches*, p. 119,
has demonstrated the general and close analogy of the
Druids to the Magi of Persia. It almost constituted
identity. They scarcely differed in their name, for Pliny
calls the Druids the Magi of the Gauls and Britains.
The most able author of the *Indian Antiquities* marks,
with a deep and sound learning, the same affinity between
the Druids and Brahmins of India. It may be extended
to the Chaldæans and the Orphic priesthood of Thrace, as
well as to many others. As this resemblance of character has been justly deemed both too perfect and general
to be resolved into accidental coincidence, it has been the
ingenious labour of many learned men to ascertain the
several means by which the institutions, opinions, and
customs of the Eastern world have been imported into
the West of Europe.

31. Cæsar assures us that the Druids held the soul to
be imperishable, and that after death it passed from one
body to another. Lucan explains that they taught that
the same *spirit* would animate a new body, not here, but
in a different world. Hence, like the Hindus, they must
have maintained the tenet of a succession of worlds.
Diodorus says that they declared that the souls of men,
after certain determinate periods, would pass into other
bodies; and, according to Valerius Maximus, so fully
were the Gauls impressed with the idea that they should

animate new vehicles hereafter in a renovated world, that they were wont to lend money on condition of its being repaid them when they should again become incarnate,—an amount of faith which one might vainly hope to find among the most devout Christians. Agreeably to these notions, they burned, on the funeral pile of the deceased, whatever he had best loved, whether servants, or animals, or valuable treasure, so that their original owner might continue to possess them in his new world,—a devotedness in which they stand in curious contrast to our own times, for we sacredly keep all these possessions to ourselves, thus reconciling our faith with our interest in a manner peculiarly agreeable (17).

32. And as in Wales and England, Mona and Scotland, we find corresponding features of one system, so, also, we may recognise them in the sister country. In Ireland, on the first of November, the autumnal equinox, the time when the Sun was in Taurus, it was usual to extinguish all the fires, except the sacred fires of the Druids. Dr. Hyde, the Orientalist, says that the Gebirs of Persia do the same, and he adds that the Jews, when they were in captivity, adopted the same rite. This identity between Ireland and Persia is only one of the multitudinous facts that establish one origin, one language, and one religion, in the remotest ages. Strabo says that there was an Island near to Britannia in which Ceres and Proserpine were worshipped with the same rites as in Samothrace (lib. iv.), and this Island was Sacred Ierna. I had not been a week landed in Ireland from Gibralter, says Vallancey, where I had studied Hebrew and Chaldaic under Jews of various countries and denominations, when I heard a peasant girl say to a boor

standing by her, *Feach an Maddin Nag* (Behold the Morning Star), pointing to the planet Venus, the *Maddina Nag* of the Chaldæan. Shortly after, being benighted with a party in the mountains of the western parts of the county of Cork, we lost the path, when an aged cottager undertook to be our guide. It was a fine starry night. In our way the peasant, pointing to the constellation Orion, said that it was *Caomai*, or the Armed King, and he described the three upright stars to be his spear and sceptre; and the three horizontal stars, he said, were his sword-belt. I could not doubt of this being the *Chimah*, כימה of Job, which the learned Costard asserts to be the constellation Orion. Job xxxviii. 31. *Chimah*, it should be added, means *a warrior armed with a coat of mail.*

33. They who are acquainted with day and night, says the Geeta, know that the day of Brahm is a thousand revolutions of the Yugs, and that his night extendeth for a thousand more : as on the coming of that day all things proceed from invisibility to visibility, so, on the approach of that night, they are all dissolved in that which is called invisible : even the Universe itself having existed is again *dissolved :* and now again on the approach of Brahm's day, by the same overruling force it is re-produced. Who that reads this, is not startled by its similarity to 2 *Peter* iii. : *There shall come in the last days scoffers, walking after their own lusts, and saying, Where is the promise of his coming? for since the fathers fell asleep, all things continue as they were from the beginning of the creation. For this they are willingly ignorant of, that by the Word of God the heavens were of old, and the earth standing out of the water and in the water : Whereby*

*the world that then was, being overflowed with water,
perished: but the heavens and the earth, which are now, by
the same Word are kept in store, reserved unto the fire against
the day of judgment and perdition of ungodly men. But,
beloved, be not ignorant of this one thing, that one day is
with the Lord as a thousand years, and a thousand years
as one day. The Lord is not slack concerning his promise,
as some men count slackness: but is longsuffering to us-
ward, not willing that any should perish, but that all should
come to repentance. But the day of the Lord will come as a
thief in the night; in the which the heavens shall pass away
with a great noise, and the elements shall melt with fervent
heat, the earth also and the works that are therein shall be
burned up Seeing then that all these things shall be dissolved, what manner of persons ought ye to be in all
holy conversation and godliness? Looking for and hasting unto the coming of the day of God, wherein the
heavens being on fire shall be dissolved, and the elements
shall melt with fervent heat? Nevertheless we, according
to his promise, look for new heavens and a new earth,
wherein dwelleth righteousness.* But did Peter get all this
from the Geeta? Undoubtedly not. Where then did
he get it from? Not from the Apocalyse of Ioan, which
did not appear until many years after Peter's death, but
from the original Apocalypse, which must have been communicated to him by the Ninth Messenger. From that
Sacred Volume also was derived the following passage,
which we find in the *Vishnu Purana*, p. 633. At the end
of a thousand periods of four ages, it says, the earth is for
the most part exhausted. A vital dearth then ensues, which
lasts a hundred years, and in consequence of the failure of
food all beings become languid and inanimate, and at last

entirely perish. The Eternal then assumes the character of the Destroyer, and descends to reunite all his creatures with himself. He enters into *the seven rays of the sun*, drinks up all the waters of the globe, and causes all moisture whatever in living bodies or in the soil to evaporate, thus drying up the whole earth. Thus fed through his intervention with abundant moisture, *the seven solar rays dilate to seven suns*, whose radiance glows above, below, and on every side, and sets the three worlds and Patala in a blaze. The three worlds consumed by these suns become rugged and deformed throughout the whole extent of their mountains, rivers, and seas : and the earth bare of verdure, and destitute of moisture, alone remains, resembling in appearance the back of a tortoise. The Destroyer of all things who is the Flame of Time, becomes the scorching breath of the Serpent, and thereby reduces Patala to ashes. The great Fire, when it has burnt all the divisions of Patala, proceeds to the earth and consumes it also. A vast whirlpool of eddying flame then spreads to the region of the atmosphere, and the sphere of spirits, and thus wraps them in ruin. The three spheres shew like a frying-pan amidst the surrounding flames, that prey upon all moveable or stationary things. The Eternal having consumed the whole world, breathes forth heavy clouds ; and these resembling vast elephants in bulk, overspread the sky, roaring and darting lightnings. Some are as black as the blue lotus ; some are as white as the water-lily : some are dusky like smoke, and some are yellow : some are of a dun colour like that of an ass : some like ashes sprinkled on the forehead : some are deep blue as the lapis lazuli : some azure like the sapphire : some are white as the conch or the jasmine, and some are black as the collyrium : some are of bright red like the lady-bird : some are of the fierceness of red arsenick, and some are like the wing of the painted jay. Such are these massy clouds in hue ; in form some resemble towns, some mountains, some are like houses and hovels, and some are like columns Mighty in size and loud in thunder they fill all space.' Showering down torrents of water, these clouds quench the dreadful fires which involve the three worlds, and then they rain uninterruptedly for a hundred years, and deluge the whole world. Pouring down in drops as large as dice, these rains overspread the earth, and fill the middle region and inundate heaven. The world is now enveloped in darkness, and all things animate or inanimate having perished, the clouds continue to pour down their waters for more than a hundred years.

34. It is the mystery of our holy language, says Rabbi Bechai, that a serpent is called *Seraph*, as an Angel is called Seraph : and in accordance with this supposed mystery, adds Faber, it has been imagined that Satan tempted Eve under the form of one of those resplendent Winged Serpents which are denominated Seraphim , and that he succeeded the more easily because the angelic Seraphim were wont to appear to our first parents under the precise form assumed by the seducer ! *Pag. Idol.* i. 448. But how came the following passage into a writer of the 6th century, who was not a Jew ? A quick gliding train of radiant *Seraphim*, says Taliesin, the Pagan bard of Wales, in due order, mysterious and pure, shall deliver Elphin—*i.e.* (Al-phi, the Voice or Word of God)—

> *Aches ffysgiolin*
> *O blan Seraphin,*
> *Dogyn, dwfn, diwerin,*
> *Dyllyngein Elphin.*

35. Where did this Pagan priest get the Seraphim, if not from the old Apocalypse ? It is not in the work of John. These Seraphim are the fiery splendid Serpents of Heaven (a symbolical name), which in the *Geeta* are described thus : There is a fair and stately mountain, and its name is Meru, a most exalted mass of glory, reflecting the sunny rays from the splendid surface of its golden horns. It is clothed in gold, and is the venerated haunt of gods and heavenly choristers. It is beyond imagination beautiful, it is not to be reached by sinful man, and it is guarded by *Serpents.* Many celestial medicinal plants adorn its sides, and it stands piercing the heavens with its aspiring summit : a mighty mountain inaccessible even to the human thought : *it is adorned with trees and pleasant rivers,* and resounds with the delightful songs of various birds. Thus finding in Wales and Hindustan the same picture-sentiments, shall we err in tracing them to one source, and what other can that be but the Apocalypse ? the primary fountain from which all the creeds on earth at one time flowed in pure and silver stream.

36. So also in the Sibylline Oracles, we are told ; And when this shall come to an end, the day of the Almighty decreed in the beginning shall come upon good men. The productive earth shall yield its boundless store of best fruit for mortals, of wheat, wine and oil. Then will He give from above the delicious drink of sweet honey and trees, and the fruit of fruit trees, and fat sheep and oxen, and the lambs of sheep, and the kids of goats, and he will make the sweet fountains to burst forth with white milk. The cities, moreover, shall be full of good things, and the fields shall be rich ;

there shall be no more sword on the earth, nor alarm
of war, nor shall the earth any more be shaken with
heavy groans. There shall be no war, nor drought upon
the earth, nor famine, nor hail threatening the fruits.
There shall beside this be great peace through all the
world, and one king shall be the friend of another
until the end of the age : and a common law for all the
earth shall the Eternal in the Starry Heaven make perfect for men; for He only is God, and there is no other.
He will also burn with fire the cruel rage of men.
Earnestly intent in your hearts upon my opinions, avoid
sinful worship : serve the Living One : keep yourself
from adultery and forbidden intercourse with males,
nourish your own children, and do not destroy them.
For the Eternal will be angry with those who commit
such sins. Then will he set up a perpetual kingdom
over all men, when He gives his holy law to the pious :
to all has He promised to open the earth and the gates of
the world of the blessed every kind of joy : also perpetual
wisdom, and endless gladness. From all the earth shall
they bring frankincense and gifts to the House of God :
nor shall there be any other house where consultation
shall be made by men of a future age, but that which
God has given to faithful men of reverence. And all
the paths of the field, and the rough shores and the lofty
mountains, and the raging waves of the ocean, shall be
safely travelled over and sailed upon in those days. The
abundance of the good shall extend over the earth. The
prophets of the great God shall take away the sword,
for they shall be the judges and the just kings of
mortals. Riches shall be lawfully acquired among men.
The dominion and the judgment of the great God .

shall be the same [*i.e.*, both shall be universal]. The wolves and the bears shall eat grass together on the mountains, and the leopards shall feed with the kids. The bears shall dwell in the same herd with the calves, and the carnivorous lion shall eat straw at the stall like the ox, and children, the very babes, shall lead them in bonds : even the maimed shall be a terror on earth to the beasts, and dragons shall repose by the side of infants, nor shall they harm them. The hand of God shall be on them (18). See *ante*, page 53, 54. The Sibylline Prophetess was a secret name for the Spirit of God.

37. In the Polynesian mythology, though it comes under the questionable shape of a missionary's volume, the Supreme God To-Ivi, existed from eternity. After innumerable years had passed away, he cast his shell as birds do their feathers, or serpents their skins—thus his splendid form was ever renewed. In the highest heavens he dwelled alone. He first created Hina, (from עִין, a Fountain), who is also called his daughter. Countless ages passed, and with her aid He made the heavens ; and after them all existences in ten orders. In the same work (Ellis's *Polynesian Researches*, i. 312), we read of the Incarnation, and of the Virgin of earth who is his mortal mother. Oro, says the legend, desired a wife from the daughters of men (19). Tufarapainuu and Tufarapairai searched through the whole of the islands from Tahiti to Borabora, but saw no one whom they supposed fit to become the spouse of Oro, till they came to Borabora. Here they found Vairaumati. When they beheld her. they said, This is the excellent woman. Returning to the skies they informed Oro, and represented her as a *Vahina purotu aiai*, a Virgin possessed of all loveliness. The

I

God fixed the *Rainbow* in the heavens, one end of it resting in the valley, near her residence, and the other penetrating the skies, and thus he sought the home of his beloved. When he emerged from the vapour which like a
cloud had encircled the Rainbow, he discovered the dwelling of Vairaumati, the fair mistress of the cottage, who
became his wife. Every evening he descended on the
rainbow, and returned by the same pathway on the following morning to the heavens. His wife bore a son
whom he called Hoa-t-Abu-iterai, the *Sacred to the
Heavens*. This son became a powerful ruler among men.
It may fairly be asked how these poor savages acquired
a tradition of this recondite nature;—of an incarnate
King and Messiah, and of a Rainbow as a divine medium,
if not from the Apocalypse, and the universal system of
religion which was founded upon it?

38. Taliesin thus mystically alludes to the confusion
prevailing among mankind at the close of the cycle, and
its dispersion by the *Rainbow-like Holy Spirit*. I saw a
fierce conflict in the vale of Beaver, *on the day of the Sun*,
at the hour of dawn, between the birds of wrath (wicked
men) and Gwydion (the son of God). On the day of God,
they securely went to Mona to demand a sudden shower
of the sorcerers; but the Goddess of the Silver Wheel, of
auspicious mien, the Dawn of serenity, the greatest re-
strainer of sadness, speedily throws round the hall, the
Stream (the emanation) of the *Rainbow ;* a stream which
scares away violence from the earth, and causes to subside
the bane of its former state around the circle of the globe.
The books of the Ruler of the Mount record no falsehood (the Book of God). The Chair of the Preserver
remains here; and till the doom shall it continue. In

the "day of God," here mentioned, it would seem that Taliesin has actually quoted the Apocalypse, where it is called κυριακῇ ἡμερα, "the day of the Lord."

39. By the Mexicans, the Holy Spirit, was worshipped under the name of Cihuacohuatl, or the *Serpent-Woman :* and also as Tonacacihua, or *woman of our flesh :* she was the companion of God, Tonacateuctli. The Mexicans considered her as the mother of the human race [all beings], and after the God of the *Celestial Paradise,* Om-Eteuctli, she held the first rank among the divinities of Anahuac : we see her always represented with a great Serpent. Humboldt *Researches,* i. 195. Purchas, in his *Pilgrimage,* says that they believed the world to have been made by gods ; but professing themselves ignorant of the precise mode in which it was formed, they imagined that since the creation, four suns had successively appeared, and disappeared ; and they maintained that that which we now behold is the fifth. The first Sun perished by a deluge of water, and with it all living creatures : the second *fell from heaven* at a period when there were many giants in the country, and by the fall everything that had life was again destroyed. The third was consumed by fire. And the fourth was dissipated by a tempest of wind. It is impossible not to see the striking resemblance between this system, and that of the Burmese ; and not to be struck by the similarity which it bears to the Egyptian tradition, mentioned by Herodotus, namely that *the Sun had four times deviated from his* regular course, having twice risen in the west, and twice set in the east (*lib.* ii. c. 142). And all these mythologies bear the most curious correspondence to the Apocalypse. Another fact may be cited to prove this ; and it is one of those singular demon-

strations which almost admits of no dispute.   It must be premised that although in the primeval Mexican paintings they had pictures of a *horse*, the animal itself was un-known to them : but they knew from their sacred writings of the descent from heaven of him who was to come on a white horse, and *heavenly armies followed after him on white horses*.   When, therefore, the Spaniards landed, and with their cavalry marched into the country, the Mexicans believing this to be the very Avatar predicted in the Apocalypse, willingly submitted ; and this accounts for the rapidity with which Spain achieved the conquest of that gallant people.   But the Mexicans had been isolated from the rest of the globe since the fearful Atlantean Deluge : it follows therefore that they must have had the Apocalypse before that catastrophe ; and though the Book itself may have been lost or concealed, its mighty images were represented in their temples.

. 40. Ovid represents Pythagoras as adducing the story of the Phœnix by way of exemplifying the perpetual destruction and reproduction of the world ; and in point of application there is reason to believe that the mythos originated from this very doctrine.   The poet's account of it is nearly the same with that given by Herodotus.   The historian informs us that the Egyptians have a sacred bird called the *Phœnix*, which he never saw except in a picture.   Its form according to the delineation of it, was that of an eagle ; and its wings were of the blended colour of gold and ruby.   It was wont to make its appearance only once at the end of 600 years, and *that* upon the death of the parent bird.   The Heliopolitans asserted that whenever that event took place, it came from Arabia to the Temple of the Sun, bearing the dead body of its parent inclosed in a ball of myrrh, which it prepared in the following manner. First it made a ball shaped like an egg of such a size as it found itself by trial able to carry. Next it hollowed out the ball and introduced the body of the dead bird into the excavation. Lastly, it closed the aperture with myrrh, and the ball being thus made of the same weight as it originally was, it carried it to the Temple of the Sun at Heliopolis (ii. 73). In several of these particulars Ovid agrees with Herodotus : but he adds to them some others not specified by the Greek historian. He tells us that the Phœnix possessed the power of self-reproduction, which peculiarity fitted it to be the type of the world. When its long life of six centuries was drawing to a close, it prepared for itself an aromatic nest in the branches of an oak, or on the summit of a palm tree (20). Its work being finished, it placed itself upon it, and ended its life in the midst of sweet odours. From the body of the deceased bird soon sprang a young Phœnix destined to live through the same long period as its parent had done before it. With pious care it still hovered near the nest which had given it birth ; and as soon as its strength was equal to the task, it bore away that which had equally been its own cradle and the tomb of its parent and deposited it before the gates of the Temple of the Sun (*Met.* xv. 392). Nonnus extends the life of the Phœnix to a *thousand years*, and alludes to the familiar story which, however, is mentioned neither by Herodotus nor Ovid, of the parent bird burning itself upon the odoriferous pile which it had carefully prepared, and of a young Phœnix springing to life from the ashes of its sire (*Dyon.* xl. 375). This doctrine of the renewal of the world held by the ancient philosophers has received a

great accession of probability from the astronomical discoveries of La Place, who has demonstrated that certain
motions of the planetary bodies which appeared to Newton to be irregular, and to portend at some future period
the destruction of the solar system, are all periodical;
and that after certain immensely elongated cycles are
finished, everything returns again to its former situation.
The ancient philosophers of the East had a knowledge of
this doctrine, the general nature of which they might
have acquired by reasoning similar to the above, or by
the same means by which they acquired a knowledge of
the Naros, that is through the Apocalypse.

41. One of the characters, attributed to the Great
Year, says Boulanger, was the Phœnix, an *apocalyptical*
dogma, enveloped in an allegory, become by its fable unintelligible. In the Chaldee, as well as in the Coptic
Phenische makes up the cycle—600.

Ph.	פ	80		Φ	500
E	ה	5		N	50
N	נ	50		N	50
N	נ	50			———
I	י	10			600
K	ק	100			———
Sh.	ש	300			
E	ה	5			
		———			
		600			

The Chaldæans had another name for the Phœnix, viz.,
כלע, *clo.* (*Buxtorf*) : and these letters used as numerals
make up the same number : Caph final=500 ; Lamed=
30 ; Oin=70.=600, whence, perhaps, the Coli Yug of

the Brahmins. The mythos, though an enigma to Boulanger, explains itself in the doctrine of one world rising
out of the ruins of another at certain stated immense
periods, and one Messiah following another in the same
manner. And the Christian fathers were wont to employ
it as a symbol of the resurrection, when the microcosm
man will issue forth in renovated beauty from the decayed
ruins of his former self. Herodotus, as we have seen,
mentions that the Phœnix was one of the sacred birds, or
hieroglyphics of the Egyptians, and it is a curious circumstance that we find nations the most remote from each
other well acquainted with this symbol. The ancient
Irish ascribed a longevity of *six centuries* to their Phœnix,
and considered *the production of the young bird as a
restoration to life of the old one.* At the same time they
remarkably explain the mythos by declaring this hieroglyphical bird *to mean only a celestial cycle.* By the
Japanese the Phœnix is called *Kirin*, and by the Turks
Kerkes. According to the latter it lives a thousand years.
When the thousand years are past it gathers pieces of
wood in its bill, and kindling a flame is consumed in the
fire and becomes ashes. Then, by the command of the
Almighty, the Air (the Holy Spirit) restores these ashes
to life; and it again lives a thousand years, and so on to
the day of judgment. (21.) The Phœnix is also very
plainly the same as the *Simorgh* of Persian romance; and
the account which is given us of this last bird yet more
decisively establishes the opinion that the death and re-
vival of the Phœnix exhibit the successive destruction and
reproduction of the world, which many believed to be
effected by the agency of a fiery deluge. When the
Simorgh was asked her age, she informed Caherman that

this world is very ancient, for it has been already seven times replenished, with beings different from man, and seven times depopulated : that the age of the human race in which we now are, is to endure seven thousand years, and that she herself had seen twelve of these revolutions, and knew not how many more she had to see. (*Orient Collect.* ii., 119.) The *Simorgh* is in reality the same as the winged *Singh* of the Hindus, and the *Sphinx* of the Egyptians. It is said that the former will appear at the end of the world, and that such will be the size of this monstrous lion-bird, that as soon as he is born he will prey upon an elephant, which will shrink into absolute insignificance compared to the bulk of its mighty devourer. From these the Rabbins have borrowed their mythos of an enormous Bird, sometimes standing on the earth, and sometimes walking in the ocean, the waters of which reach no higher than its legs, while its head props the sky ; and with the symbol, they have also adopted the doctrine to which it relates. They teach that there are to be seven successive renewals of the globe ; that each reproduced system will last seven thousand years ; and that the total duration of the Universe will be 49,000 years. This opinion, which involves the doctrine of the pre-existence of each renewed creature, they may either have learned during their Babylonian captivity, or it may have been part of the primeval religion which their priests had preserved from remote times. The disciples of Jesus enquired of him whether a blind man had been born blind in consequence of his own sin, or that of his parents. Now it is obvious that no sin of *his* could have been deemed the cause of a blindness, which was coeval with his birth, unless it had been committed *before* his birth ; but it could not have been committed *before* his birth unless he had lived in some prior state—that is, in some other world. This question therefore necessarily implies that they had the doctrine of the pre-existence of souls; nor did Jesus at all reprove them for it, or intimate that they were mistaken. On the contrary, his reply would go to show that he himself also professed the same belief. *Jesus answered, it was not because this man sinned, nor his parents, but that the works of God should be made manifest in him*—which reason is evidently an interpolation, for God never makes manifest his works or his wisdom by inflicting misery on a human creature. The same tenet appears to be inculcated in the *Book of Wisdom* viii., 19, 20. *For I was a witty child, and had a good spirit—yea, rather being good, I came into a body undefiled.* But if his goodness was the cause of his being thus born, he must have lived in the judgment of the writer previous to his birth into the present world. And they proved its truth by two passages in their books. The first is in *Deuteronomy* xxix., 14, 15. *Neither with you only do I make this covenant and this oath. But with him that standeth here with us this day before the Lord our God, and also with him that is not here with us this day.* Whence they argued that since the covenant was made with generations unborn as well as born, the former must then have been actually in existence, though they had not as yet been born into this world. They also adduced a passage from Jeremiah (i., 5), in which God declares to the prophet that *before he had formed him in the womb he knew him*, or, as they translate it, *had endowed him with wisdom :* whence they argued that if Jeremiah possessed wisdom before his birth, he must have existed antecedently to it. So also we read in *Psalm* xc. *Lord, thou hast been our dwelling place in all generations, before the mountains were brought forth, or even the earth and the world were made;*—which shows the belief in an existence before any part of the material universe was brought into action: an existence in the bosom of the Holy Spirit of the Heavens.

42. It is curious, and may not be uninteresting to trace the word Phœnix to its root, and to take a glance at its cognates. The radical from which it is derived is Aph אף, Heat. Aptha, Apha, Pthas, Ptha, an Amonian name for God, and Fire, and Vulcan. There was a Temple of Venus Aphacitis, near Mount Libanus. Zozimus says that near the temple was a large *lake*, made by art, in shape like a *star*. About the building, and in the neighbouring ground, there at times appeared a *fire* of a globular figure which burned like a lamp. It generally shewed itself at times when a celebration was to be held; and he adds that even in his time it was frequently seen. Diana was called Apha and Aphœa. Dyctinna, which was a surname also for both Minerva and Diana, was called Aphœa. Mars was called Aphœus. Aphetor was what the ancient Dorians expressed to be Apha-Tor, a fire tower, or phallic tower, or Prutaneum. This in aftertimes was changed to Prætorium, and the chief persons who officiated were called Prætores or priests of fire; hence they were called Aphetæ; and every Prætor had a brazier of live coals carried before him as a badge of his office. This Ptha, which denoted Thoth or Hermes, was T and R united, thus, ♀. This was the *crux ansata*, and was often formed as a *Key*; which was the foundation of the numerous allusions to

the Keys of Heaven, of Hell, and of Death. It was in all the ancient temples, as an emblem of the Naros and the Resurrection : all the Egyptian gods bore it in their hands. Sometimes it was figured thus, ♀, a circle surmounting a cross. This is the Linga and Yoni of India united. Pthas, in Greek numerals, is equal to 600. The deity Pthas presided in the Kingdom of Omptha—the cycle of Aum. Luther took for his coat-of-arms a Cross rising out of a Rose—this was a mystic symbol—the Linga rising out of the Yoni, as we see in the Indian carvings. This root, pronounced broadly is Oph, a serpent; and was variously pronounced Ope, Oupis, Opis, Ops, and by Cicero, Upis. It was an emblem of the Sun, and of time everlasting. The Egyptian Opas was the same as Osiris. Ob and Aub are but variations. The basilisk, or royal Serpent, was named Oubus—a prophetic deity, whose sayings were oracular. All the mythologic legends of Serpents have reference to the God adored under this symbol. His pillar, cone-shaped, was called Ab-addir, or Splendid Father. Cecrops introduced Serpent worship into Greece at a very early period. Callimachus calls Diana, Dupis. As a compound it makes Cnuphis, and Cneph, and Caneph. Ops was esteemed the goddess of fire and riches; it was a title given to Cybele, Rhœa, Vesta, Terra, Juno; but all these were one. The Tsabii worshipped Beltha, which was Bel and Ptha, God and the Holy Spirit.

43. Vallancey, copying from an old Irish glossary, thus writes : The Phœnix is a bird about the size of an Eagle, and when *restored to life*, lives 600 years, or 600 turns of Baal, the sun; and there is but one of the species in the world, and she makes her nest with combustible spices;

and when the sun sets them on fire, she fans the flame
with her wings, and burns herself; and out of the ashes
arises a small embryo, which becomes another Phœnix.
Una est quæ reparat seque ipsa reseminat Ales, Assyrii
Phœnica vocant. (*Met.* xv. 392.) Pluchè derives the
name from the Phœnician word *phanag,* to be in delight
and abundance; but it is more rational to draw it
from *phanah,* pronounced *phanach,* which signifies to
return: and this agrees better with the story of the
Phœnix, which might be expressed by *ophen,* a wheel, or
rather by *phonech,* that which returns or turns round.
In Irish, *phainic* is a circle or ring: hence it signifies an
Eagle or any great bird that flies in circles, as those birds
do; whence the Egyptian *pheneh,* cyclum, periodum,
ævum. The word also signifies a *Raven,* whence the
raven became sacred in Eastern countries, and in the
Mithraic Mysteries.

44. All these varied features of one common creed
among every people on the earth, are so remarkable that
it is impossible to withhold assent from the fact: while
the mythos of the Phœnix is so striking a representative
of the Messenger who is ever connected with the Temple
or Tabernacle of the Sun, and who always re-appears on
the expiration of the Cycle, that I think no one can
doubt that it bears the double type of the destruction
and reproduction of worlds, and the aphanism and new
Epiphany of the Sacred Herald of the Most High. And
I believe, on fair examination, it will be made manifest
to the mind that almost every great characteristic of this
ancient and primeval creed, has flowed directly from the
language of the Apocalypse, and from no other book that
now exists on earth. Nor can the similarity between

them and it, and each other, be accounted for on any other hypothesis. This truth will appear absolutely demonstrated beyond all cavil, if the reader will compare certain peculiar incidents in the Ancient Mysteries with what I have already pointed out, as articles of faith, and with those parts of the Apocalypse itself, to which those incidents bear relation.

45. Biblical writers, like Faber, who study to support a system, not to discover or preach Truth, are in the habit of pretending, upon these facts, that the whole ancient world was wrapped in idolatrous darkness, and that it worshipped a multiplicity of deities. That the populace were grossly ignorant then, as they are now, may be conceded; and that the herd of priests encouraged them in that ignorance is as true of those distant ages as it is of the present; but who would seek the truths of Christianity in some ranting chapel in the remote provinces ? who would not rather search after them in the acknowledged guides and leaders of the church ? This the biblicals do not do; but they extract from mythologists like Hesiod, and fabulists like Ovid, and dotards like Varro, Plutarch, and Diodorus, *their* notions of ancient religion, and then exclaim, Thus lost in superstition were all the peoples of the past! whereas these writers knew absolutely nothing of the Truth, which was revealed only to the initiated in the Greater Mysteries; or, if they did, they could not venture to disclose it. And the biblicals talk perpetually of ancient polytheism, as they do now of the polytheism of India, when they know that monotheism was the creed which all the sages promulgated; and that this Triune-All, of which I have spoken, was essentially distinct from the least recognition

of any Power but the One. How utterly reduced to silence these writers were, when Rammohun Roy pointed out, that with equal reason, Christianity itself might be accused of idolatrous teaching as the pagan system, is well remembered by those who have taken interest in such investigations. The editor, says that acute reasoner, alluding to one of those blatant missionaries to India, who by preaching Paulism, disgrace Christianity, denies positively the charge of admitting three Gods, though he is in the practice of worshipping God the Father, God the Son, and God the Holy Ghost. I could wish to know what he would say when a Hindu also would deny Polytheism on the same principle, that if three persons be admitted to make One God, and those that adore them be esteemed as worshippers of One God, what objection could he advance justly to the *oneness* of three hundred and thirty-three millions of persons in the Deity, and to their worship in different emblems; for oneness of three or of thirty millions of separate persons is equally impossible according to human experience, and equally supportable by mystery alone? This argument of course was not answered, nor could it be; and yet we find these tractarians still pretending and declaring that idolatry is the national religion of the East, when they would act more fairly if they contented themselves with saying that, like our Paulite atonement, it is the national superstition, which it unquestionably is. But though this be so, the founders of the religion were not in fault; no founder ever preached idolatry; his successors in the priesthood are they who have done it all; and every European who holds the vulgar doctrine of the Trinity is as much a polytheist as the ignorant inhabitant of the East; for the recognised definition of that mystery, "three *persons* in one God," if it have any meaning at all, means "three *gods* in one God," and is as near polytheism as can well be. Yet so great is the power of words in deceiving the fallible mind of man, that he who would avert his belief immediately from the latter definition, unhesitatingly adopts the former, which, as I have shewn, differs in no way whatever from it, in its real and essential interpretation.

NOTES TO BOOK II.

Note 1 (p. 118).—The Cyclopes were called one-eyed, for another reason also, because they invented the telescope. Vulcan their father was a fabricator, as Jesus was said to be a carpenter, and the son of a carpenter, which only meant the *Artifex Mundi*. All these things may appear to be, and they are, riddles, but the theological student knows that religion has always been wrapped up in them. Thus Saturn devouring his children, means God absorbing all things into himself; and raising the dead, restoring the blind to sight and the mad to reason, simply means to purify the souls of the ignorant, who are in reality, blind, irrational, and in a state of death.

Note 2 (p. 118).—Syene, says Strabo, stands immediately under the tropic; a well is sunk here, which marks the summer solstice, and the day on which it happens is known, when the style of the sundial casts no shade at noon. At that instant the vertical sun darts his rays to the bottom of the well, *and his entire image is described upon the water (lib. xvii.)* Who could have conceived, says Maurice, that one of the most difficult processes in the whole science of chemistry, that of reducing to powder, and rendering potable the golden calf, could have been known at so early a period as when Moses led out of Egypt into the desert the children of Israel? *Hist. of Hindostan*, i., 483. The Pharos built by Sostrates of Cnidus, contained several stories, and was surrounded by galleries supported on marble columns. This miraculous tower as Cæsar calls it, was near 400 feet high: on its summit was a vast mirror of polished steel, so disposed as to present the image of distant vessels before they were visible to the eye. It was destroyed, as Abulfeda relates, by the Christians, and it may be questioned whether such a work could now be constructed. Can it be wondered that with all these facts before him, Whitehurst felt himself compelled to acknowledge from what the fathers of human science have delivered down to posterity, concerning the chaotic state of things, and the universal fluid in which the earthly particles were suspended, that the

Newtonian doctrines respecting gravity, fluidity, and centrifugal force were known in remotest antiquity, though afterwards forgotten and lost, till revived by our great mathematician. (*Inquiry* page 18.)

Note 3 (p. 118).—From the Buddhistic title for the Messiah, namely Saca comes Saca-sa; hence Saxon and Scythian. The universal affinity of all these Cyclopean structures, is curiously shewn in the Travels of Mr. Walters in the Pundua Hills, printed in the *Asiatic Journal* for 1829, p. 322. As he advanced still further, it says, Mr. W. saw some most magnificent scenery, which we regret that our limits will not admit of particular reference to. What is very singular, however, is his falling in with gigantic stone monuments and door-ways, *that strongly reminded him of Stonehenge.* These upright stones and stone doors are monuments to the memory of departed rajahs and chiefs. The first gateway of stone he passed (formed of three single slabs) was twelve feet high, and he conjectures that *some of these monumental stones weigh thirty tons.* These stupendous monuments are found near all the villages on the hills. The Cosseah monuments are numerous, and of large size, about Nunclow. The circular and square stones, supported by stones placed on end, *are extremely similar to the* '*cromlechs' found in Cornwall and Wales;* doubtless those ancient monuments were appropriated to the same purpose, the reception of the ashes of deceased chiefs enclosed in urns. If this was the case, how singular it is that the customs of nations, in the same stage of society indeed, but situated at such an immeasurable distance from each other, should be found so exactly to coincide ! If any doubt exists as to the purpose for which the monuments in Britain were erected, is it not dissipated by observation as to the *actual use* of similar monuments in this country at this day ? I did not observe that any of the upright stones were placed in *circles* like those of Stonehenge, but generally in lines. So we read that on the shores of Oceanus, stood a stone called Gigonian, so vast that no force could move it, but at the touch of Asphodel it would move. *Ptol. Heph. ap. Phot.* lib. 3. This was a rocking stone, such as we have in Cornwall : and the Asphodel was the Druidic art. The worship of Baal or Bel, as they called the Sun, was spread to the north and the west, by the merchants and mariners of Tsidon, Tyre, and Carthage. Vossius has traced the worship of Belenus or Belen, evidently the same as Balen, to Aquileia on the Adriatic, to Noricum, a southern province of Germany, and to Armorica in Gaul. The name of Beli or Bali seems to have been equally known to the Goths and Celts. If the Goths according to the Edda do not give a distinguished place to Beli in their mythology, it is easy to discern in the name of Balder, the Hyperborean Apollo, the elementary words which compose it, and which are clearly Baal Adur, the brilliant lord, or the lord of fire. The name of Beli was familiar to the ancient Britons, (see DAVIS's *Mythology of the Druids*,) and the descendants of the Celts of Scotland often speak of Bel without suspecting its Chaldæan origin. Beltain is nothing else than the ancient god of the east, בל אי׳תן Bel-itan, or Bel the mighty, the name which according to Ctesias the Babylonians gave to Bel, and which he writes Βελιτανης.

Note 4 (p. 120).—Near the city of Benares in India, are the astronomical instruments, cut out of the solid rock of a mountain, which in former times were used for making the observations just now alluded to, which Sir W. Jones and the priests say were only back-reckonings. The Brahmins of the present day, it is said, do not know the use of them: they are of great size, and tradition states them to be of the most remote antiquity. Maurice observes that circular stone monuments were intended as durable symbols of astronomical cycles, by a race, who not having, or *politically forbidding* the use of letters, had no other permanent method of instructing their disciples, or handing down their knowledge to posterity. The number of stones at Stonehenge was originally 600, to commemorate the six centuries. Of the lily which Gabriel in all the old Annunciation paintings, presents to the Virgin, Parkhurst says, "Its *six-leaved* flower contains within it seven apices or chives; i.e., *six* single headed ones, and one triple-headed One in the midst." Now what does this symbolize? The six leaves and the six chives are the Naros: and the triple-headed central Chive, is the Messiah, whom the Celestial Messenger thus brings to the Sacred Virgin. See *ante*, p. 61. So the Muses were said to speak Θεων οτι λειριοεσσι, with the *lilied* Voice of the Gods *Theog.* 41; *Iliad*, iii. 152. The arrow or javelin-headed writing found in Assyria and Babylonia, is an imitation of the spear-head or liliaceous writing of the primitive Assyrians, if it be not the same. So language was called "a flight of arrows:" and the first Messiah in the Apocalypse is seen with a bow. In conformity with the six centuries of the Naros, the globe was at first divided into 60 degrees, which subsequently multiplied by 6, became 360, at which it now remains: the hour also was divided into 60 minutes, of 60 seconds each: the Tartars and Chinese had a period of 60 days, and the Asiatics generally a cycle of 60 years: the Roman lustrum of 5 years represented this when multiplied by 12 : and the Babylonian great year was 3600, being the Naros multiplied by 6 : a more remarkable proof of all things flowing from one common centre and fountain, can hardly be conceived ! The Tartar cycle called .Van was 180 years or three sixties : which multiplied by 12 times 12=144, makes 25920 years, the exact period of the revolution of the heavens.

Note 5 (page 122).—Genesis makes the increase of the waters of the Deluge, continue for 150 days (viii 3), that is five months of 30 days each—a clear proof that in the time of the writer whenever it was, the year was thought to consist of only 360 days, that is 30 × 12   The Septuagint speaks of tke 27th day of the month, as that on which the waters ceased to flow (viii. 4) : in which it differs from the Hebrew, Chaldee, Samaritan, Arabic, and Syriac Books of Genesis, which all assign that incident to the 17th day. As the Apocalypse, xii. 6, speaks of a year of 360 days, three years and a half = 1260 days, it thereby *conclusively* establishes itself by the best of all evidence, namely internal evidence, to be entitled to an antiquity ascending to a period almost primeval ; and I would not deny the same character to that particular portion of Genesis, above cited, did it not shew by internal evidence also that it had been corrupted by the Talmudists.

Note 6 (page 127).—Dr. Huntington, in his *Account of the Porphyry Pillars in Egypt*, tells us that the hieroglyphic characters wherewith they are engraven, are probably the aboriginal Egyptian letters, long become obsolete ; and they resemble the Chinese characters, each whereof represents a word, or rather an entire sentence ; besides they seem to be written the same way, namely from top to bottom.

Note 7 (page 128).—In *Exod.* xxviii. Moses is commanded to take two onyx stones, and grave upon them the names of the children of Israel ; *with the work of an engraver in stone like the engravings of a signet, shalt thou engrave the two stones with the names of the children of Israel.*   In the same chapter is a direction to engrave twelve stones with the names of the children of Israel, according to their names, like the engravings of a signet.   In these passages we have a constant reference to a well-known art of engraving names upon signets ; and these engravings cannot be regarded as cyphers, or mere hieroglyphical symbols ; for (in v. 36) we find another command to make a plate of pure gold, and grave upon it like the engravings of a signet, *Holiness to the Lord* קדש ליהוה Kodesch Layhova.   From this emblem of sanctity, Hermes the Messenger was always represented with the *caduceus*, a word

evidently kindred with *kodesch.* There is a degree in masonry called
" a Chapter of the Grand Inspector of Lodges, or Grand Elected
Knights of Kadosh," who seem to have borrowed their title and
functions as Inspectors from those of the Egyptian Mercury. The
badge borne by Mercury appears to be alluded to by the manner
of answering the question " Are you Kadosh ?" upon which the
person questioned places his hand upon his forehead and says,
" Yes, I am " The sacred words are Nekam Adonai ; which probably have the same signification as the words engraved on the
plate worn by the Jewish high-priest, Adonai or Adonis, meaning
Lord. The mitre worn by the high-priest 'of masonry, in the
royal arch degree is surrounded with the words Holiness to the
Lord.

Note 8 (page 139).—The Peruvians of quality, says More (*Explanation of Grand Mystery,* 86), and those too of mean sort, would
sacrifice their *first born* to redeem their own life, when the priest
pronounced they were mortally sick ; and Picart has a plate in
which a representation is given of a scene in Florida, where the
first-born child, if a male, was sacrificed to the Sun. And as the
King of Moab when in distress, took his first-born son that should
have reigned in his stead, and offered him for a burnt offering (2
Kings iii. 27) so Hacon, King of Norway, offered his son in sacrifice
to obtain of Odin, the victory over his enemy Harald. Aune,
King of Sweden devoted to Odin the blood of his nine sons to
prevail on that god to prolong his life ; and the ancient history of
the North abounds in similar examples.—*Mallet's Northern Antiquities,* i. 134.

Note 9 (page 141).—AL (God), AUM (God), BRA (the Creator), are
three sacred names with which all the ancient theology is filled :
the *Alhambra* in Grenada commemorates them. Aum was changed
by the Greeks into Aun, and On, the Sun—it meant the Self-
Existent. In the *Kabala* the First Cause (God) is named *A in*
(Nothing, Not anything). This is the formless Brahm of the Hindus. From this Ain or *On,* came *O-On* the Mundane Egg, or
Sphere, which God is represented in old paintings and sculptures,
as discharging or emaning from his mouth : and from this O-On,
came *Zo-On,* or living creature which the Mundane Sphere or the
Universe is. Plato in the Timæus calls God, $Z\omega ov$: and Aristotle
(*Metaphysic,* xiv. 8), says, $\phi a\mu\epsilon v$ $\delta\epsilon$ τov $\Theta\epsilon ov$ $\epsilon\iota v a\iota$ $Z\omega ov$ $\dot{a}\iota\delta\iota ov$,
$a\rho\iota\sigma\tau ov$—we say that God is the *Living One,* the venerable, the
most excellent.

Note 10 (page 145).—Cudworth, says Faber, *Pag. Idol.* i. 121,
seems to me rightly to conclude on the authority of Jamblichus,

that the *Trismegistic Books really contain the Hermaic opinions.* His argument is now much strengthened by the circumstance of the same theory respecting the world being found to prevail throughout the East. It was long a favourite axiom with the priests that everything which did not coincide with *their* notions of the Future was a forgery or a fable. But this seems to be now reluctantly abandoned.

Note 11 (page 148).—One of the Shanscreet emblems, says Wilford, is named *Argha*, which means a cup, dish, vessel in which flowers and fruit are offered to the Deity: but this cup or dish must always be shaped like a *boat* or *ship;* and hence Iswara has the title of Arga-nautha, or the Lord of the boat shaped vessel. The *name* is preserved by the Laplanders, who call the Holy Spirit, Virchu (Virgo) Archa. And as the Spirit comes from God, and the soul from the Holy Spirit, so their double nature enters into the composition of man. This is alluded to in *Gen.* ii. 7, where we read that Ieue Aleim breathed into ha-Adam's nostrils, the breath of *lives, hayim* חיים in the plural. This, as usual, is disguised in the English version. Job alludes to this, xxxiii, 4: *The Spirit of God hath made me ; and the breath of the Almighty hath given me life;* as if the Two had taken counsel together ; (*let us make man in our image, after our likeness,* Gen. i. 26,) and given him, the soul and spirit of which he consists, *Wisdom,* xvi. 14; *Hebrews,* iv. 12. It is more than probable, says Maurice, that the secret and mystic sense of the word Aleim (plural) was known to the Rabbins, and preserved among the most venerated arcana of their cabalistic doctrines in every period of their existence as a nation ; and though it might not be prudent to reveal that mystic sense to a wavering and infatuated people, who were for ever relapsing into polytheism, yet that the doctrine of the world, created, regulated, and governed by three sovereign hypostases, made a part of the creed of the ancient synagogue, there can be no stronger evidence than their devout and rapturous expressions concerning the *Three Great Sephiroth,* or Celestial Enumerations, *Hist. of Hindostan,* i 72. But the Three Sephiroth had nothing to do with the Aleim properly considered : the Aleim meant God and the Holy Spirit : the Sephiroth meant God, the Holy Spirit, and all Existences—the Trinity.

Note 12 (page 150).—This is the rabbinical theory, as developed in Genesis, where there is a gradual shortening of human life from the supposed days of the first people.

Note 13 (page 151).—Nat or Nauth signifies Lord, and is used in composition with the names of the Gods, much in the same man-

ner as the Canaanites used Baal, which is a word of the same import. Thus we have Jagan-Nath, Suman-Nauth or Somnauth,
and the like. In the Apocalypse we have this Nauth descending
and binding Satan for *a thousand years*. In the Kingdom of As-
sam, when any person is taken sick, a priest is sent for, who
breathes upon the patient, and repeats several prayers over him.
So Jesus breathed on his disciples, *John*, xx. 22. How comes this
analogy ?

Note 14 (page 152).—*An, Ana, Aine, Onn* (Irish), a cycle, seasons :
hence Lu-an the Moon, the An or cycle of L, ל = 30. Bel-ain a
year, the cycle of Belus. Ain-leog, a swallow, a cyclic or revo-
lutionary bird. Ain-naomhagh, the celestial bird, the Phœnix, and
perhaps the fabulous bird of the Brahmins, the Auny. Onn as
applied to the cycle of the sun, signifies the sun-fire, &c. Ægypt.
Oein, and Hon the Sun ; כהן און Cohen or Ken On, Priest of the
Sun ; in Irish, Conach Oin; Persian, Ayinè, seasons, revolutions ;
Chald. עין hon, time, honan עינן, to observe the times, whence
the Irish Anius, an astrologer, astronomer, &c. The Druidical
temples named Ana-mor, were composed of 48 stones, denoting
the number of the old constellations, with a Kebla of 9 stones
near the circumference, or the inside, to represent the sun in its
progress through the signs. Ao, Ion, Io, Iao, and O, says Sir W.
Drummond, were the same word originally, though pronounced
differently by different nations. This is the root of the Latin
Janus, Jovis, and Jupiter, which is Iao-pater, and Ieu-pater,
corrupted into Jupiter. It seems likewise that both Ion and Ianus
were the same with Zan, On, or Oannes, that *imago biceps* which
returned to the sea with the setting sun; and which was worshipped as a solar symbol, or an Incarnation, by the Cretans, Egyptians, Phœnicians, and Babylonians. All the greater gods enume-
rated by Ennius were Asiatic before they were Italian, and a curious
proof that they were so is furnished by one of the etymologies of
Jupiter, which we are told is not derived from *Juvo* and *Pater*,
but from the Shanscreet word *jû*, æther, heaven, and *pitri*, father
(Jupitri), which explains the reason of the title having been applied as well to the firmament as to the Deity. Hence Ennius
wrote ; Aspice hoc sublime candens quem invocant omnes Jovem.
Mystically it was used by the Etruscans in *rings*, or oviform presents which they made, and which bore the initials A.O. *amico
optimo*. The reader will see the importance of A.O. when he
comes to the Apocalypse.

Note 15 (page 152).—The reader cannot fail to perceive that
the whole of this theory is founded on the Apocalypse, sec-

tions 55, 56, 57. Yet who can believe that the Burmese borrowed it from the mutilated Greek-Hebrew copy? It is evidently taken from the true primeval Apocalypse and no other.

Note 16 (page 154).—Edda, fab. ii., iii., iv., xxxii., xxxiii. Bishop Percy supposes that there is some defect or ambiguity in the original, because the Sun in the same sentence is spoken of as both masculine 'and feminine : a mode of phraseology carefully preserved both in the French translation of Mallet, and the Latin one of Goranson. There may be an ambiguity, but there is no defect. This very ambiguity indeed which perfectly accords with the opinion entertained by the ancients respecting the two sexed character of the Divinity whom they venerated in the Sun, is the best proof of the genuineness of the ancient verses referred to as an authority by the compiler of the Edda : and I greatly doubt whether the Bishop's attempt to remedy this supposed erroneous reading by using the word *parent* rather than *mother*, has not completely marred the intentional mysticism of the writer. The version of Mallet is . *Le Roi brillant du feu engendrera une fille unique, avant que d'etre englouti par le loup ; cette fille suivra les traces de sa mere, apres la mort des dieux.* That of Goranson : *Unicam filiam genuit, rubicundissimus ille rex, antequam eum Fenris devoraverit , quæ cursura est, mortuis diis, viam maternam.* Such language exactly describes the solar Siva in his double character of *Ardha-Nari ;* and ought to be scrupulously retained, as exhibiting a faithful picture of the theological notions which the Goths brought with them from the East

Note 17 (page 162).—The Roman Lar in fact was the same as the Brabin of the Tonquinese. When a man comes into possession of any tenement, he entertains this household deity in a small hut or apartment prepared for his reception. He is solemnly invited by beat of drum, and presented with agreeable perfumes, and a variety of dishes. After having been thus entertained he is expected to protect their houses' from fire, lightning, thunder, wind, rain, or any thing by which they or their inhabitants may be injured. This mode of attaining the favour of heaven was certainly more innocent than that practised by the Athenians and Massilians, who sacrificed a man annually for the welfare of the state. They loaded him with the most dreadful curses ; they prayed that the wrath of the gods might fall upon his devoted head, and thus be diverted from the rest of the citizens; and they solemnly called upon him to become their *ransom*, their *salvation*, and their *redemption ;* life for life, and body for body ; after this they cast him into the sea, as an offering to Neptune.—*Faber, Pag.*

Idol, i. 476. As a friend of mine, who has seen my note in a former page, doubts whether the general public will accept the statement of a converted Jew, and says that the Jews will assuredly deny its truth, as they deny their crucifixion of children, (than which no fact is better established) I subjoin an authority that *cannot* be disputed with any hope of success : I mean Buxtorf. The account which he gives, is as follows : Each father of a family begins the ceremony by stepping forth into the midst of the assembly with a cock in his hands, and by repeating certain appropriate texts of scripture. Then he thrice strikes the cock against his head, and at each blow exclaims : *May this cock be accepted in exchange for me ; may he succeed to my place, may he be an expiation for me. On this cock, death shall be inflicted, but to me and to all Israel there shall be a fortunate life. Amen.* Afterwards placing his hands upon the victim he slays him. Then drawing the skin tight around the neck, he mentally confesses that he himself was worthy of strangulation, but that he substituted, and offered the cock in his own room. Next he cuts its throat with a knife, silently reflecting that he was thus worthy of being slain with the sword. Next he violently dashes the carcase on the ground to denote that he was worthy of being stoned to death. Lastly he roasts it with fire to intimate that he deserved the punishment of burning. And thus by these several actions the idea was conveyed that the cock underwent four sorts of death in the place of the Jews, being accepted as their representative and substitute. *Buxtorf, Synag. Judaic,* p. 509. See *Chambers's Journal,* Sept. 14, 1861. The Jews wrote to the editor complaining of the article as a libel ; but the author of it verified every fact by actual records, and the Jews dropped the subject.

Note 18 (page 169).—See section 7 of the Apocalypse, for the *Song of the Angels,* on which those Sibylline passages were founded. The Jews transferred this to the writings of one of their priests ; but I have brought it back to the original.

Note 19 (page 169).—Ar. Aur. Or אוּר FIRE, whence from its brightness, Lat , *aurum,* gold ; Gr., πῦρ, fire ; Angl , burn · Lat., uro, ardeo ; *Hari,* the Hindoo Lord of Light · hence ara, oro, hora, ἱερον. Zeus was called Κωμυρος, or Cham-Ur. See Lycophron. As a first syllable it generally indicates a *sacred* word, as Argha, Ari-ya, Ar-canus, Ur-anus, Urim and Thummim ; so *Armon,* הרמון a pomegranate tree, from רמון *rimmon,* a pomegranate. Arka in Javanese means the Sun. אל אור Al Or, God of light. From this word comes Alorus, Al-Horus, Aηρ, Aër, air, aërial, year.

also Hρ, the dawn, and Aurora, Uri-El, a Fire-Angel of God. *Arabot* ערבות the ninth heaven, is called by the Rabbis, the supreme sphere, *ubi Deus thronum habet gloriosissimum.* אלף אור Alph-Aor, leader of light, Orus. To express Fire or Light, the ancients said at first Ur, then an Aleph was added at the beginning of the word to pronounce it more softly, and that made *Aur.* Others have added the letter N, and have pronounced it *Nur.* The Greeks have put a labial letter at the beginning, whence they have made it *Pur.* Orion, is Aur-Ion, the Dove of Fire—a name for the Cabiric Messenger : though he destroys, it is in love and humanity to the rest of the world. Orion is described by Palœphatus as hunting with Diana—this is a Messiah.

Note 20 (page 173) —The Spirit of Wisdom or the Tree of Life, whose Golden Bough, or Messiah, conducts the soul to the Elysian Fields, was thus described by Virgil in his 6th book.

> A mighty Tree that bears a Golden Bough
> Grows in a vale surrounded with a grove
> And sacred to the *Queen* of Stygian Jove
> Her nether world no mortals can behold
> Till from the bole they strip the blooming gold.
> The mighty Queen requires this gift alone,
> And claims the shining wonder for her own.
> *One plucked away, another Branch you see*
> *Shoot forth in gold, and glitter through the Tree.*
> Go then : with care erect thy searching eyes
> And in proud triumph seize the glorious prize.
> Thy purposed journey if the Fates allow,
> Free to thy touch shall bend the costly Bough,
> If not, the Tree will mortal strength disdain
> And steel shall hew the glittering Branch in vain

Note 21 (page 175).—We see a Phœnix, says Montfaucon, represented upon a Medal of Constantine the Younger, on the top of a craggy rock, all radiant, with this inscription, *Felix temporum reparatio,* the happy restoration of the times ; which is agreeable to the opinion of the ancients, that the Phœnix renewed itself ! ! There is no reference as the reader sees to renewing *itself,* but renewing *times*—a very great difference But thus it is that ecclesiastical writers translate, paraphrase, and change, relying on the insuperable ignorance of their readers.

NOTE UPON BAL.

Bal, Bel, Bol, Baal בעל. Lord, Sun ; Irish, Bealtinne ; Fires in honour of Belus. It is often compounded with other terms, as

Bel-Adon, Bel Orus, Bel-On, from which came the Bellona of the
Romans: Baal-Samin, Baal-Athis. Nimrod, i. 299, suggests that
the *Tower* of Belus, and the hanging *Gardens* of Babylon, intimated the mystic union; the Garden was the Female Principle
herself, under a venerated symbol the Tower on the other hand,
symbolized the masculine energy; the phallos. Some even say
that from Bel (God in his Cabiric character) comes *Bellum* war.
Bala, is one of the names of Boodh: in Ireland the various places to
which Bal or Baali is prefixed, such as Baltimore, Ballinasloe, &c,
were Boodhist villages. The Hindoos have Bala-Rama. Like the
word Al, though a masculine noun it makes its plural in the feminine *Bolim*, בְּעֵלִים. The Pelasgi, who used B. and P. indiscriminately, formed from this Πελω, I am. also Belinus. It no
doubt hence entered into the formation of Apollo; A-Bol, Bali, and
Palistan, and Balistan, a name for Thibet, the City of God, come
from this root: also the Bull, the symbol of the Sun. The word
for the Sun is in Hebrew *Sur:* in Chaldee *Tur*. In the Hebrew
this would be TR, the same as Taurus. This is T = 400. R. 200 =
600. Bala-Deva in India is represented with a plough share in his
left hand, a symbol of the procreative or generative power; and
in his right hand a club like that of Alcides, typical of strength.
The *Bulla* which the Roman children carried around their necks,
as an amulet, was succeeded by the Papal *agnus dei*, with the same
object the Pontifical Bull comes from this root. The temple of
Bel at Ba-Bel-On, as described by Herodotus, was pyramidal. Hera,
says Hitzig, was the counterpart and wife of Zeus-Bal, and was
symbolised as the Moon. Baaltis and Bualtis was a Tsabœan name
for the Queen of Heaven, Bol-Berith, בְּעַל בְּרִית. Sometimes
she was called Anna-Berith, which the Greeks changed into the
nymph Anobret who conceived by Zeus. God the purifier was the
same as the Ζευς Καθαρσιος of the Greeks. In the Philippine
Islands, the whole of their religious ritual consists in songs and
hymns which parents teach their children to learn by heart They
call the Supreme Being, Boodh-Ala, and Abba, which of course
gives occasion to missionaries to declare that they are descended
from the Jews, the word Abba in Hebrew and Syriac signifying
Father and Parent. But most of the Asiatic nations apply this
title to the Supreme Creator.

NOTE UPON DI.

Di, Dio, Ti, Du, Dus, Thu. Thus, GOD; Shans, Dew, Deo, Deva;
Lat., Deus, Divus; Gr, Θεος: Celt., Du, Dia, Deu. This was
the common name for the Deity. Thus Dis and Dus, added to Arez,

one of the names of the solar god, signified the God Sol. Dı is דּי dius. It is probably old Etruscan. B D. and B T. are found in almost every country to be sacred letters, and to refer to the Supreme. In Shanscreet Di-Jana is goddess Jana, as Di-One and Di-Ana is goddess Ana, the Yoni. In the Arabic Du and Dsu signify Lord: transposed the Hebrew Dii דּיי is Jid, which also was a divine name. Hence also Ida, a holy mountain. Lord Kingsborough shews that Dios was a name for God in South America. Ceres was called Δηω. Ti-mor in Irish is God, the Great Circle. The Gypsies call God, *Dewla*. Ti, Tidh (Irish) a great cycle. Ti-greine the ecliptic, or circle of the sun. Dra, Drach, Draoch, Dur (Irish) a wheel, circle, cycle, period. Duir-teach, the round cell of a Druid; a temple, cell, church. The temples of the Druids were all circular: hence Drochad the arch of a bridge: Reall Draoch the cyclic planet, the Sun, Moon; whence the Druidical circular Temple named Rolldrich, near Chipping Norton in Oxfordshire. Chald., *dor*, דּור a circle, Arab. *Dur*, circumambulation. General Vallancey, (*Collectanea* iu. 503,) says; Welsh *Drud*, a Druid, i.e. the absolver or remitter of sins: so the Irish Drui, a Druid, most certainly is from the Persian *daru*, good and holy man. Ouseley (*Collect. Orient.* iv. 302,) says. In the Arabic, *deri* means a wise man, which in Persian is *daru*, whence English Druid. The Vates or Prophets, the last order of Druids, were called Baidh (Boodh) Faith, Phaithoir. This Baid is the Chaldæan Bada בְּדָא *bda-prædicavit*, בְּדִּים *badım dıvinatores*. The Irish Phaithoir is the Hebrew פָּתַר *ptr.*, to solve an ænigma.

NOTE UPON PHI.

Pi, Ph, Pa, Pu, the; Phi פִּי A mouth, an oracle: *he* (Aaron) *shall be to thee instead of a mouth*, Exod iv, 16. With this in composition is found the particle Al. Phæthon was an ancient title of the Sun, a compound of Phi-Aith-On. Bacchus was called Phi-Anac by the Mysians, rendered by the poets, Phanac and Phanaces. Hanes was a title of the same Deity, equally reverenced of old, and compounded Ph' Hanes: it signified the Fountain of Light. From it was derived Phanes of Egypt, and Fanum, a temple, Eu-hanes, and Oannes. The antient name of Latian Zeus, was P'Ur, by length of time changed to Puer. He was the Deity of Fire, and his ministers were styled Pueri; and because many of them were handsome youths selected to that office, Puer came at length to signify any young person. *Purim* was divination by fire-lots. It was of Chaldaic

ı 2

original, and was brought from Babylonia into Italy. It is mentioned in Esther iii. 7. They cast Pur before Haman, that he might know the success of his purposes against the Jews. D'El Phi (Delphi) means the Voice of God. The ancient form of the Greek *Phi* ☽ had a mystic signification. The Phœnician *Alpha* means a Bull. According to the theology of the Greeks, says Proclus, in his commentary on Plato's Parmenides, even Jupiter and Dionusus are styled Boys and young persons. The people of Amphissa perform a ceremony, says Pausanias, in honour of persons styled *Anactes Paides* or Royal Children ; but who these Anactes Paides were is matter of great uncertainty. Byrant endeavours to explain the difficulty by putting the particle P, before Ades, but this only ends in nonsense. The true explanation is that the Royal children were the Incarnations, of whom neither Proclus nor Pausanias knew anything. I do not believe that either of them was fully initiated.

The Book of God.

———•◦•———

BOOK III.

1. The characteristic qualities of the various Messengers of God, their attributes, and modes of dealing with mankind, as developed in the Apocalypse, and regarded by the ancients, do not differ very materially from the views practically adopted by the moderns, and sanctioned by common sense, and all notions of political justice. As mildness, mercy, and compassion are essential features of the Father, we find that the great majority of his divinely commissioned Incarnations were essentially distinguished by these qualities, and appeared simply in the benign light of Teachers, seeking to raise mankind to heaven by wisdom, truth, and charity; but as unerring justice, and the most utter disunion between the Divine and evil are also vital essences of the Supremely Pure, so it is seen that three out of His Twelve Angels were permitted to assume the part of Judges, whose errand was to overwhelm the guilty with deserved though long delayed retribution. The first order are the Messianic Messen-

gers; the second are the Cabiric. It *may*, and I have no doubt, will be said, that this view of God is utterly false, as it represents Him in the light of a *persecutor* for opinion, and would justify the enormities of the Inquisition, the execution of Fisher, and the burning of Servetus. I am bound to meet this argument, and I will do so. In the first place, it is not true that what God permits He consequently commands. He permits murders, rapes, and robberies every day, but can in no wise be said to order them to be committed. (1.) In the second place it is not true that what God foreknows he necessarily destines. God foreknows, and every living man foreknows, that the wicked will do wickedness, that ships will sink, and houses will burn, that thieves will rob, and murderers will slay; but that this prescience makes either God, or you and me, to ordain those sins or calamities, or that our knowing them beforehand necessarily makes us either to cause or to sanction them, seems to me too manifestly erroneous to be refuted. I know indeed that this is the commonly received opinion, but it is evidently false. God foreknows that a murderer at a certain hour will take a life, just as *I* know that according to the almost unerring doctrine of chances, some individual man to-morrow will undoubtedly slay some other man in some part of the earth. But am I causer of that crime? It may be said I am if I *can* prevent and do not. The answer is, I am not *bound* to prevent by force, nor should I be justified in slaying the man who is about to sin. Those who think otherwise make God the cause of all crime, for he undoubtedly could prevent it by suddenly striking dead or paralysing the arm of the criminal, or by forcing him to change his evil thought, and yet He does not. But he could only do this by *perpetually*, and without one moment's interval, interfering with all human action, and by making all his creatures slaves, by depriving them of free will, by systematically changing them from active thinking beings into lifeless puppets, which *could* not stir until He pulled the strings; in other words, by reducing creation and all its living splendours into a piece of mechanism, worked, as it were, by wires and pulleys. It is on the whole better that some men should be killed, than that this glorious Universe of millions and millions of stars, and innumerable millions of millions of animated beings, should be wholly deprived of free and soaring thought, individual action, grand and lofty emotion vivified by love, by charity, by benevolence; and should be transformed into a dead machine, peopled with automata or marionettes, incapable of doing aught but lying dormant until God moved them: which should speak with his speech, think with his sentiments, and be incapacitated from generating out of themselves any thing godlike or beautiful; which should be like the dull clay that of itself produces not, but waits until the seed is sown, and can even then give nothing forth but what was primarily contained within that very seed. An universe so constituted might gratify a curiosity collector, or appear precious in the eyes of a savage; but after the first wonder were over, it would cease to please. It would be wholly unworthy of the Divine Creator, and would be a source of misery to every thinking creature in it, who, if he were constantly constrained in thought and action, would curse rather than bless the Author of his existence. It is palpable, therefore, that God could not, and ought not to make such a creation; and we know He

did not ; for the veriest slave is in his thoughts as free
the greatest monarch, and the will of the smallest insect
is as practically unrestrained as that of the loftiest angel.

2. Having thus established that what God foreknows
or permits, He does not consequently command, I relieve
the believer at once in His divine attributes from being
asked to associate Him with all the particular thoughts
or things which to the judgment of the Messengers
seemed necessary at the time, and which to the judgment
of posterity may seem open to reproach. I have already
stated that these Messengers are not infallible ; they *could*
not be so, for God alone possesses that attribute. They
are left as free to think and do as all other beings ; they
will be judged by these their thoughts and deeds like all
other beings. On them alone rests the responsibility of
all their acts, not on God, who did not command, though
He indeed foresaw. If Amosis extirpated idolatry by the
sword ; if Mohammed, for the most dreadful of abominations that the mind can conceive, substituted by violence
a sublime creed and a system of purity ; if Chengiz-Khan,
like a destroying angel, swept before his armies thousands
of the wicked, who in the eyes of all thinking men perpetrated crimes every day of the deepest dye, and on their
ruins raised a temple to monotheism—for these things, if
they were wrong, they must each one render an account
to Heaven. God did not say to them : Ye shall kill all
who disbelieve : but He left them free to do exactly as they
thought expedient under all the circumstances surrounding their actual position. God indeed foresaw, and permitted it to be revealed in the Apocalypse, that they
would do these things, just as he foresaw and revealed in
the same divine work that Lao-Tseu and Jesus would be

slain; but what sane man ever argued that God was answerable, because he so foresaw, or that the Chinese and Jews were not guilty of a ruthless murder because that very murder had been revealed? If the cruel Jews must answer for the murder of Jesus, although it was foreshown, so must the three Messengers answer for *their* acts, although they were predicted. No distinction can be made, or will be made; the simple difference will be that the Jews condemned an innocent man, and the Messengers destroyed only the guiltiest of wretches; the Jews crucified for the most base of purposes; the Messengers adjudged for the most sublime of all: the ruin of idolatry, the substitution for it of God. The Jews did nothing beautiful, or good, or pure, which in the eyes of One who weighed them in the balance, might possibly to some extent diminish their weight of crime. The Messengers, on the contrary, devoted their whole lives and thoughts to the propagation of a system of Theism, or belief in One God, which has mainly held the bulk of mankind from idol-worship—has diffused among them august ideas; has inspired them with the most exalted sentiments of the present and future; has been, as it were, the salt of the earth, that alone preserved purity upon it, and has saved it from being changed into that living hell which the priests of evil have sought to make it, and which they always *did* make it, wherever they possessed an undisputed sway.

3. In thus reasoning it will be seen that I have voluntarily taken the strongest ground against myself. I may be said to have, to some extent, conceded that those three Messengers persecuted, or did wrong, for the sake of religion; and may be probably accused of the old

K 3

Jesuit notion that the end justifies the means. I wish, however, to set myself right. I do *not* admit that either of these Incarnations did evil, or was wrong in the course he took; on the contrary, I hold that each was perfectly right. I do *not* admit that he persecuted for religion; on the contrary, I aver that it was his duty as a Messenger to destroy disbelief. I do *not* assert that the end justifies the use of bad means; on the contrary, I am of opinion that the means used were just, and that the end was great and godlike. Upon *what* do I base these opinions? I assume it as conceded that they were Messengers of God. No Christian can deny Amosis to be so: no Eastern Theist can refuse the title to Mohammed and Chengiz-Khan. I will confine myself to the first; because if what I advance be true of him, it must be true also of the others. Amosis was divinely appointed to re-establish a system of monotheism. God himself gave him this command. It is a fair deduction that God did so, because he was the only creature then existent who seemed most capable of carrying out the design of God,—he was the lion-lamb come down in human form to open the Book. To succeed in this he must have possessed all the qualities necessary for it; judgment, knowledge, intrepidity, stedfastness, self-denial, holiness; and history tells us that he *did* possess them. Here, then, is a man pre-eminently possessed of all these virtues, who has an end in view, about the divinity of which no man can doubt; for it is the propagation of true religion, as it is revealed by the very tongue of God himself. The chances consequently are as ten hundred thousand to one, that he will do nothing but what is absolutely right and requisite: and if he does do anything which to men appears questionable, the chances are in the same ratio, that these men judge mistakingly; for no one among them can possess the same means of forming an opinion as *he* had, and no one among them is possessed of the same splendid qualities, that, as I have shewn, are essentially inherent in his missionary character. When therefore I hear it proclaimed by this Messenger, that he will cut off a tribe of infidels by the sword, I regard him not as a priest, but as a judge, who, having well weighed all the circumstances, is deliberately convinced that they deserve death; that their removal is a public necessity, and so proceeds to execute his judgment. Who can say that they do not deserve death? Who can say that they are not a moral pestilence fraught with ruin? No man has the same means of knowing that Amosis had. He says so, and what he says, I believe. If he was wrong, God will make him answer for it, but upon what pretence can any man declare that he *was* wrong, without denying his divine priesthood, his ennobling qualities, his opportunities of forming the best opinion, and his inflexible adherence to true justice? It may be said this punishment is persecution for opinion, and God is not a persecutor; and persecution is wicked, and Amosis, being a persecutor, is wicked also. No Christian, indeed, can say this, for to do so were to deny Jesus, who confessed Amosis to be the Messenger of God, and who himself said; *Think not that I am come to send peace on earth; I come not to send peace but a sword.* (Matt. x. 34.) And again; *Ye shall hear of wars, and rumours of wars : see that ye be not troubled; for all these things must come to pass, but the end is not yet : for nation shall rise against nation, and kingdom against kingdom, and there shall be famines and pestilences, and earthquakes in divers places: all these* *are the beginnings of sorrows* (Matt. xxiv. 6—8): passages which suggest that Jesus himself at times mistook his own æra, and confounded the ninth cycle with that fierce and warlike one, which under his successor, Ahmed, was to follow. Those, however, who deny Christianity and Judaism may use the argument above stated. The answer is, all punishment is persecution for opinion: and all punishment is therefore wrong, if what you allege be true. Thieves have a strong opinion that they are ill-used men : that they cannot get work, or that if they do get it, they are under-paid ; that property is unfairly distributed : that the rich are their lawful enemies ; that it is unjust in the extreme that one man should possess thousands while they starve ; that idleness is more agreeable than labour ; and acting on these opinions and a variety of analagous ones which might be advanced, they plunder their neighbours, and are punished ; but did any man ever seriously maintain that they were objects of persecution ? Murderers have an opinion that revenge is sweet, and they kill men under the influence of that sentiment ; but who ever held that they were ill-used victims and entitled to our sympathy as objects of persecution, against whom the sword should not be drawn ? Idolators are of opinion that it is praiseworthy to slay their first-born as blood-sacrifices to God ; that it is holy to pass their innocent children into the burning fires of Moloch, and so to destroy them ; that it is a blessed thing to prostitute their wives and daughters to the service of the idol or the priest, so that the price of their debauchery goes into the treasury of the church ; that Mendesian worship (whose horrors I cannot further allude to, but

which every scholar will understand) is an intimate communion with the Divine Being, and that in the blood of
a murdered or crucified man all their sins are washed
away; and if such fearful crimes be punished by extermination, will any say that the Messenger herein is not
the faithful minister and servant of the Most High Judge
himself, who uses him to sweep this plague-spot from the
earth? or who will dare to allege that the punishment of
robbery is legal, but that the condemnation of these
wretches is unjust? Methinks I hear it said, this exon-
erates the Inquisition? By no means. And for these
reasons: the Inquisition was not founded and presided
over by a divinely-appointed Messenger of God, but by
corrupt and evil-minded priests; and the Inquisition did
not punish for these crimes, but for mere *opinion*, not
practically carried out. I have no right as a Judge to
destroy a man who merely *thinks* Mendesian worship is
divine; but the moment I find a man or a community of
men who practise this and similar atrocities every day as
part of their religion, or who live in crime because they
hold that the Lamb has saved them from perdition, God
and man will acquit me for destroying them off the face of
the earth; and this was the exact thing which these
three Cabiric Messengers of Judgment did, and which
I maintain they were perfectly right in doing.

4. To repress, to subdue, to destroy wickedness and the
wicked by the sword, if necessary, is a right acknowledged
by the whole earth; and if it were not so, the earth
could not be inhabited. Were there no terror for the
evil but in the promised judgments of a future life, the
evil would combine together, and annihilate the good
from the face of the globe; law would perish; justice,

truth, and mercy would not exist; the fair sphere of nature would be overrun and desolated by the licentious and the cruel; and their instant annihilation by the Supreme King would become a work, not only of necessity, but of benevolence. But fortunately for mankind, the destroying power of justice is conceded: it is agreed that criminals may be cut off. I do not justify the wars of Napoleon, or of such conquerors. I do not say that the Crusades were lawful. The first were for selfish aggrandizement by the ruin of others; the second were waged for an unhallowed Church: but when I see the divine Minister of God, who appears in the divine cycle, and when I see that his main object in unsheathing the sword, is to root out the churches of abomination, and the communities who live in the daily practice of crimes that appertain only to an infernal pandemonium, can the slightest doubt exist in my mind that justice demands their destruction; or that that the Minister who prepares and compasses it, only carries out the decree of God himself, and judicially rules that they are unfit to live, or to pollute the earth by their odious superstitions? (2.) A contrary opinion cannot be maintained without practically admitting that God punishes no crime, and that everybody may do exactly as he pleases. If Amosis was not justified in destroying those who lived like demons, who were monsters of blood, licentiousness, and the most unnatural lusts, by what title can any law repress crime? and by what title are assassins hanged? It may be said that Amosis was a stranger; he was not the judge over these men; and that he had no right to interfere with them. If Amosis were a mere man, this might be urged; and his conduct was a breach, perhaps, of international law. But Amosis was something more than man. He was the accredited Messenger of Heaven: he had a divine mission to extirpate idolatry ; he treated its upholders as all civilized states at the present day treat pirates, namely as the general foes of God and man, and without inquiring curiously into international law, they hang and destroy them wherever found. Nobody doubts that they act properly : to do otherwise were tacitly to support crime. Amosis did no more, but he did so by a higher title than either kings or states. If the latter are right, *he* must perforce be right also, for none can show a charter so supreme as his. It may be said, Why did he not leave them to God ? If all criminals are to be left to God, and not restrained by man, how long would nations last ? how long would peace or happiness exist ? or property be secure ? or life be safe ? or modesty be protected ? Those who argue in this way, wilfully shut their eyes to the legitimate consequences of their arguments.

5. It may be asked, why did God appoint these beings to be His Messengers, when he knew that they would inevitably destroy ? why did He not select all his Incarnations from among mere teachers ? and must He not be taken to sanction these and their acts, when He might have sent others of a different stamp ? It might be answered to this, why does God permit any thing at all to happen that is not consonant with perpetual peace and universal blissfulness ? Why does He permit hurricanes, lightnings, thunders, or volcanic eruptions that hurl unoffending people into ruin ? These forces of nature though apparently hurtful, are nevertheless fraught as we know with benevolent operation. The lightnings, hurricanes, and thunders clear the atmosphere overcharged

with dangerous exhalations : the volcano is the outlet of those subterranean fires which tend to fructify the earth for man. The Messenger of God armed with his sword and sceptre, gives lessons to mankind that a course of crime cannot be persisted in, without attracting certain punishment, and that that punishment will come upon them like fire from heaven. We know the atheist argument against future retribution ; and many have confessed that it is not easily combatted. God does not punish the evil on this earth, they say : what reason have we to suppose that He punishes them anywhere else? `The career of these Messengers is a conclusive answer to such an argument. God might if he pleased have commissioned all his Messengers with mercy alone, but in such a case He would have seemed voluntarily to relinquish *one* of his sovereign attributes, that of the Judge, and to have manifested himself only in another, that of Teacher. I do not see why He should do this. I do not know why God should not come forth and judge the guilty. I have never heard a good reason given why He should not arise as King.

6. But let no man from this my teaching, dare to arrogate to himself, the power to destroy. That power belongs exclusively to the Messenger, and to no other. In the Seven Thunders, appended to the Apocalypse, this distinction is palpably shewn ; for while the Three Cabiric Avataras, are said to go forth with the sword of God, three mere terrestrial Conquerors, Cyrus, Cæsar, Napoleon, are seen descending to the pit of fire and blood, which is alone their appropriate dwelling place. *Behold*, says some Hebrew priest, the *name of the Lord cometh from afar: his wrath burneth and is heavy to bear : his lips are filled with*

indignation, and his tongue as a devouring fire. His breath
as a torrent overflowing even to the midst of the neck, to destroy
·*the nations unto nothing, and the bridle of error that was in*
the jaws of the people. (Is. xxx. 27). I can understand the
wicked crying out against Him, or His Messenger, when He
thus developes himself; but the wicked would prefer not
to be punished either here or hereafter ; and they cannot
be supposed to look very favourably upon their punisher.
But I cannot understand why good men should find fault
with God, because the vicious do not escape. It is in
vain for them to speak of God's mercifulness. This mercifulness means no more than this, that He will give to
every man the fullest possible reward for his least possible
excellence; but though He does this, if He wavered, if
He were unjust, if He weakly pardoned murderers and
thieves, and allowed them into Paradise to associate with
the purest angels, the very stones thereof would cry out
against Him. These benevolent people who think that
He must forgive everything, do not know him and cannot
appreciate His ineffable justice : nay, they unconsciously
commit impiety against Him when they ask that He shall
pardon crime, rampant and unrepentant, in deference to
their kindly gentleness and compassion. God does not do
so ; and in fact, God *cannot* do so, without abdicating his
seat of justice and ceasing to be God.

7. This theory may not be popular, nor suit the maud-
lin sentiments of hypocritical professors, who pretend
that everything is love, that God is the paternal deity,
and that He is all mildness and compassion. But the
whole world and every man and woman in it must confess the existence of a fierce avenging Nemesis, which
smites every man the moment he violates one of the phy-

sical laws : and the same Power is present to inflict a blow when he tramples on the moral institutes. From this, the dearest child of his flock is snatched away ; from that, empire, in its most coveted hour ; from another, all that his heart yearned for, is suddenly made his, and he dies almost the moment he possesses it. The story of Niobe is not a fable. Whosoever unduly exults in aught that he has, will most assuredly be smitten by the arrows of the Sun ; and will live to weep over ruins. It is not for me to justify the existence of this dread Power—sufficient for the present page is it, that we all feel, confess, and fear its force. And this being so, how utterly childish it is to deny that God sends forth punishing Ministers, avenging Messiahs (3), even as he sends the devastating elements to purge the sky and earth of their corruptions. He, and He alone is Judge where, and when, and how He shall punish : if He does it here, He will not do it elsewhere also : if He reserves his day of wrath for another life, He will not exterminate as well in this. But that his minister Nemesis is perpetually present, and walks through every household, is as certain as that the sun shines, and that man suffers.

8. To those who will not at present accept my words, I commend the language of the Ninth Messenger, who in his parable expresses exactly the same truth. *The ground of a certain rich man, he says, brought forth plentifully : and he thought within himself saying, What shall I do because I have no room where to bestow my friuts ? And he said, This will I do : I will pull down my barns and build greater ; and there will I bestow all my fruits and my goods. And I will say to my soul, Soul, thou hast much goods laid up for many years ; take thine ease*

*eat, drink and be merry. But God said unto him, Thou
fool this night thy soul shall be required of thee; then
whose shall those things be which thou hast provided?*
Luke xii. 16.

9. Yes! let it be proclaimed that the Eternal Lord of
Light and Truth, is a Judge more terrible than all the
lords and kings of earth; that He arises in his thunders
and goes forth to execute his edict on the guilty; that
there is no man living, or that ever lived, or that ever
shall live, who can defy His Laws with impunity, or
bribe Him into mercy by repentant words;—by tears
from the eyes, or sorrows on the lip, or even in the
heart. The most dreadful of sinners may indeed mould
himself into an archangelic brightness; but until he do
so by a long series of deeds that practically annul and
atone for the past, he cannot hope for mercy. The most
bitter sobs of penitence that were ever breathed are
useless; *deeds alone prevail with God;* and by deeds
alone, can be unbarred the golden gates that give to
man admission into Paradise. If the living spirit be
evil when it leaves the earth, though all the priests of
earth combined their prayers for its salvation, it cannot
ever mount to God: an impassable zone of fire separates
the guilty soul from souls that are all pure, and from the
sphere of Him who is transcendent Purity. It is as effectually kept back from the impenetrable heaven, as the
body of man is kept down upon the earth when it longs
to soar into the sun: it could no more exist or pass into
the celestial region than it can now ascend through intervening space, and grasp the nearest star. The Laws of
God exclude it from him; He knows it, nay He sees it
not; it is millions of miles away from Him; though he

be everywhere, yet its evil essence cannot come within his influence; and by no efforts can it ever reach Him, until it has purified itself from past sin, by along unselfish series of heroic acts in the service of its fellows.

10. That the views are true which in the foregoing and following pages are rather hinted at, than developed, the common sense of mankind will in time enable them to feel, though at the present moment they may appear in advance of the age, and may probably startle the mere many who are always led by those whom they have been taught to follow, but whom they should in reality despise. It remains to be seen whether even now, there are not enough among the enlightened and the well-disposed, to give them practical shape. The time is ripe for an Universal Church, which should be pre-eminently the church of all. Our old cathedrals are deserted, our churches and meeting-houses are in the possession of pew-owners, who rule the congregations with an iron rod; the rich support the minister, but the rich have little or no abiding faith, while the great multitude of the people, are without shepherds that sympathize, or heads that guide them into true knowledge. So long as any one existing creed is taught that it alone possesses truth, and that all others are the slaves of error or ignorance—so long as Europeans are divided from Asiatics, and the West practically believes that the East is worshipping the devil, a line of demarcation will exist among mankind, which will perpetually operate to keep them enemies or strangers. But when the world believes that God has revealed his truth to the whole world, and not to any little hole and corner that may be found in it; that every religion that exists is in reality but a branch of the One Religion; that Mohammed was inspired

as well as Moses, and Fohi sent as truly as was Jesus, then will begin that æra of universal brotherhood to which so many sublime thinkers have looked forward with hope; and the true millennium of peace and faith be felt over the globe. Will not the good aid in the formation of this happy period. Will they not come forward and lay the foundation of this Universal Church? Happy they who may respond. They shall be hailed by future ages as the true Apostles of the Creed of Heaven; and by God himself they will be regarded as the corner-stones on which the glorious Fabric of the ONE TRUE FAITH was first supported in this latter age. They shall have Thrones and Crowns of Light in Heaven, who shall have aided to diffuse God's light on earth.

NOTES TO BOOK III.

NOTE 1 (page 198).—The fore-knowledge by God of things that are to happen, must not be wrested as any argument for predestination. A very acute writer asks: Does God's infallible knowledge of the Past and his certain knowledge of the Present, prove him to be the agent in all past and present crimes: also whether the knowledge any one may have of another's past actions, or of those he is about to commit, makes *him* the author of his neighbour's doings? or what connection there is, or possibly can be, between knowing a thing and causing a thing?

Note 2 (page 206).—While I write this, we hear that the King of Dahomey and his priests are preparing another sacrifice of 2000 human beings to their infernal deities. If France or England were to send an expedition which would sweep the upholders of this system from the earth, would not the whole world applaud; and would any but the most diseased brain find fault with them for the persecution?

Note 3 (page 210).—The Three Cabiri were types of the three Avenging Messiahs of God: and this would in part explain the human sacrifices which were offered to propitiate them. Cabiri from *Cabr* כבר *multitude*, denotes the large armies and followings that were with these three Mighty Ones: "heavenly armies followed after them." In the Arabic, *al. Gibbar*, means the Mighty, the Giant. See Dr. Hyde's ed. of Ulug Beg. p. 45.

The Book of God.

---·◇·---

BOOK IV.

1. The Apocalypse that follows differs so materially in
form from that which has so long usurped the name, that
it may possibly be expected, I should render some account
of the mode in which it has been constructed, or the
principles on which I have interfered with that, which for
so many centuries has been accepted, at least by many, as
the inspired work of some inspired writer. My answer
is simply this: He who does not recognize in my construction of it, an unity, a chain of fulfilled events, a
divine system, materially different from the unconnected
rhapsody which has been so long palmed off upon the
world, would not be persuaded though I were to work a
miracle before him, or an Angel from God were to descend
visibly and shout it in his ear. All I ask is that one
may be compared with the other; that they may be
placed side by side, and fairly examined. That which
is of heaven will then be confessed. That which is
not so, must naturally be condemned. But before this is

done, let the staunch adherent for the common form,
enquire for himself, what satisfactory evidence has he that
the work which bears the name of John—whoever he was
—is at all authentic? (1.) Does he know that some of the
greatest of the biblical critics have wholly rejected it as
spurious? as negativing in its vulgar shape every aspect
of a divine origin? and have pronounced it to be the manifest forgery of some Jewish convert to Christianity, in an
age when it was thought, as even Mosheim acknowledges,
that pious frauds and lies in furtherance of Paulism—or
pseudo-Christianity—were the most acceptable service that
could be rendered to God? (2.) The banishment of John
to Patmos, says Eichorn, must be *a mere matter of imagination*; for otherwise the author, by mingling historical
and unhistorical [*i.e.* unreal] circumstances, has presented
us with a hermaphrodite fiction which no critical taste
can justify. And a matter of fiction it may be: for real
history nowhere says that John was banished to Patmos:
and what ecclesiastical tradition says respecting this, has
no other source than the Apocalypse, interpreted in an
unpoetical manner, which has substituted fact in the place
of fiction.—*Introduction to the New Testament*, 1810.

2. In New Testament criticism, says De Wette, *nothing
stands so firm*, as that the Apostle John, if he be the
writer of the Gospel and the first Epistle, did *not* write
the Apocalypse: or if the latter be his work, that he is
not the author of the former. So Ewald: That the Apocalypse was not written by the same author who composed the Gospel and the epistles, is clear as the light of
the sun. So Lücke: Either all criticism of the New
Testament canon is but idle sport, or the result, viz., that
the author of John's Gospel and first Epistle *cannot be*

the author of the Apocalypse stands immovably fast. A still later writer, Credner, speaks with no less confidence : Between the author of the Apocalypse and the Apostle John, there exists a diversity so deeply pervading, that even to the mere supposition that the Gospel and first Epistle, were the production of the same mind, when it had attained to higher spiritual progress, which at an earlier period could have composed the Apocalypse, no place can be given ; *since it would be altogether unnatural and inadmissible.* Moses Stuart, from whom I cite these authorities adds : Those who are well acquainted with the critical writings of such men as De Wette, Bleeke, Ewald, Credner, Schott, Lücke, and Neander, must doubtless know that they cannot have united in denying the *apostolical* origin of the Apocalypse, from any common sympathy in theological views ; nor from any favouritism on the part of some of them towards neology (*page* 286). * * * A Dionysius, a Eusebius, a Luther, a Schott a Neander, and a Lücke, he continues, not to mention others, have doubted ; and against these the accusation of contempt, or of undervaluing the sacred books in general could not well be brought (*page* 287). It appears from a fragment of Papias (he adds, *page* 290), that there was a John of some note in Asia Minor, who was a πρεσβυτερος, (a presbyter), and a μαθητης Κυριου (a learner of the Master) : and a contemporary in part with John the Apostle. Dionysius of Alexandria, and after him, Eusebius, and since him not a few others, have thought it *not improbable* that the Apocalypse might be ascribed to John the Presbyter. May not the John mentioned in the Apocalypse, then be intended to designate this individual and the book itself be no forgery, although not written by the

L

apostle, but a work from the hand of one who has given his true name? The *possibility* of this cannot well be denied. Yet a little after he says, Could a man that was capable of writing the Apocalypse, and who felt free to address the leading churches of hither Asia, as the author of the Apocalypse has done, remain in obscurity, and scarcely be thought of, or any where mentioned? Things of such a nature are not wont to take place in such a way. On the very face of the whole matter therefore, it is an improbability that the second John wrote the Apocalypse. One might as well think of attributing Virgil's Æneis to a Codrus, or Paradise Lost to Sir Richard Blackmore. Eusebius, however, who perhaps had better opportunities of hearing how matters stood in those remote days, was not so certain as Stuart. The statement of those is true, he says, who assert that there were two of the same name in Asia; that there were also two tombs in Ephesus, and that both are called John's, even to this day, which it is particularly necessary to observe. *For it is probable that the second, if it be not allowed that it was the first, saw the Revelation ascribed to John.*—Ec. Hist. iii. 39.

3. The language of the book, says De Wette, is entirely different from that of the fourth gospel, and the three epistles of John the Apostle. It is characterized by strong Hebraisms and ruggedness, by negligences of expression, and grammatical inaccuracies, while it exhibits the absence of pure Greek words, and of the apostle's favourite expressions. The style is unlike that which appears in the gospel and epistles. In the latter there is calm deep feeling : in the Apocalypse a lively creative power of 'fancy.' In connection with this, the mode of representing

objects and images is artificial and Jewish. On the contrary, John, the son of Zebedee, was an illiterate man in the Jewish sense of that epithet : a man whose mental habits and education were Greek rather than Jewish, and who, in consequence of this character, makes little, or no use of the Old Testament or of Hebrew learning. Dionysius of Alexandria, in the third century, ascribed the Book to John the Presbyter, not to John the Apostle. (EUSEB., *Hist. Eccles.*, vii., 25.) Some who were before us, he says, have utterly rejected and confuted this book, criticising every chapter, shewing it to be throughout unintelligible and inconsistent, adding, moreover, that *the inscription is false*, forasmuch as it is not John's ; nor is it a Revelation which is hidden under so obscure and thick a veil of ignorance ; and that not only no apostle, but not so much as any holy or ecclesiastical man was the author of this writing ; but that Cerinthus, founder of the heresy, called after him Cerinthian, the better to recommend his own forgery, prefixed to it an honourable name. For this, they say, was one of his particular notions, that the Kingdom of Christ should be earthly, consisting of those things which he himself, a carnal and a sensual man, most admired—the pleasures of the belly and of concupiscence, that is, of eating and drinking, and marriage ; and for the more decent procurement of these, feastings and sacrifices, and slaughter of victims. * * * But who the author was is uncertain, for he has not said, as in the gospel often, that he is " the disciple whom the Lord loved ;" nor that he is he " who leaned on his breast ;" nor the brother of James ; nor that he is one of them who heard and saw the Lord ; (3) whereas he would have mentioned some of these things if he had intended

plainly to discover himself. * * * * And, in short,
throughout the gospel and epistle, it is easy to observe one
and the same character. But the Revelation is quite different and foreign from these; without any affinity or resemblance, not. having so much as a syllable in common
with them. Nor does the Epistle (for I do not here insist
on the Gospel) mention or give any hint of the Revelation, or the Revelation of the Epistle. And yet Paul in
his Epistles has made some mention of his Revelations,
though he never wrote them in a separate book. Besides
it is easy to observe the difference of the style of the
Gospel and the Epistle from that of the Revelation, for
they are not only written correctly according to the propriety of the Greek tongue, but with great elegance of
phrase and argument, and the whole contexture of the
discourse. So far are they from all barbarism or solecism,
or idiotism of language, that nothing of the kind is to be
found in them, for he, as it seems, had each of these gifts,
the Lord having bestowed upon him both these—knowledge and eloquence. As to the other, I will not deny
that he saw the Revelation, or that he had received the
gift of knowledge and prophecy. But I do not perceive
in him an accurate acquaintance with the Greek language; on the contrary, he uses barbarous idioms and
some solecisms, which it is necessary that I should now
show particularly, for I do not write by way of ridicule.
Let none think so. I simply intend to represent in a
critical manner the difference of these pieces.

4. Luther thus speaks of it : In this book of the Revelation of St. John I leave it to every man to judge for
himself; I will bind no man to my fancy or opinion. I
say only what I feel. Not one thing only fails in this

book, so that I hold it neither for apostolical nor prophetical. First, and chiefly, the apostles do not prophecy in visions, but in clear plain words, as St. Peter, St. Paul, and Christ in the gospel do; it is moreover the apostle's duty, to speak of Christ and his actions in a simple way, not in figures and visions. Also no prophet of the Old Testament, much less of the New, has so treated throughout his whole book of nothing but visions; so that I put it almost in the same rank with the fourth book of Esdras, and cannot any way find that it was dictated by the Holy Ghost. Besides, I think it too much that in his own book, more than in any other of the holy books which are of much more importance, he commands and threatens that if any man shall take away from the words of this book, God shall take away his part out of the book of life; and, moreover, declares that he who keepeth the words of this book shall be blessed, though no one is able to understand what they are, much less to keep them; also there are much nobler books, the words of which we have to keep. In former times, likewise, many of the fathers suspected this book, though St. Jerome talks in high words, and says it is above all praise, and that there is much mystery therein. My spirit can make nothing out of this book; and I have reason enough not to esteem it highly, since Christ is not taught in it, which an Apostle, above all things, is bound to do. As he says (*Acts* i.) *Ye shall be my witnesses.* But let every man think of it as his spirit prompts him. My spirit cannot adapt itself to this production; and this is reason enough why I should not esteem it very highly.

5. Luther's doubts did not confine themselves wholly to the Apocalypse; he extended them to the Epistle to

the Hebrews, which all scholars have long since given up as the work of Paul, and that also of James, and of Jude; and he printed them merely as an appendix to his version of the New Testament, and without number or page. This arrangement, by which these four books were excluded from the canon, was continued in the Lutheran editions of the Bible, down *to the beginning of the 17th century.* In some cases they were even printed with the title of Apocrypha. The strict followers of Luther for a long time, and in fact even down to the middle of the 17th century, refrained from appealing to them as canonical. In the second quarter of the 16th century the leading and most influential persons concerned with the reformation in Switzerland adopted views respecting the Apocalypse much like those of Luther. At the conference between the Romanists and Reformers at Berne, in 1528, Zuingle refused to admit *proof texts* from the Apocalypse, " because it was not a biblical book," *i. e.* not a canonical one. (*Werke,* ii, *Abth.* i., 1. 169.) In this he was joined by Œcolampadius and Bucer, who were present, none of them regarding the Apocalypse as authoritative. And this state of things would probably have continued to the present time had not some anonymous writer soon after that period published a *Commentarius,* which proved that the Pope was Antichrist, and the Scarlet Whore; and this at once established its canonicity with all well regulated Protestants; and as a canonical work against Popery it has still held its ground.

6. Having examined, says Michaelis, the evidence for and against the Apocalypse, I must now propose the question, How is it possible that this book, if really written by St. John the apostle, should have either been

wholly unknown, or considered as a work of doubtful
authority, in the very earliest ages of Christianity? The
other apostolical epistles are addressed only to single communities or churches; but the Apocalypse, according to
its own contents, was expressly ordered by Christ himself,
in a command to St. John the Apostle, to be sent to
seven churches; and not only these seven churches were
in that part of Asia Minor where Christianity was in the
most flourishing situation, but among them was Ephesus,
where St. John spent the latter part of his life; and consequently where every work of St. John must have been
perfectly well known. If St. John, then, had actually
sent the Apocalypse to these seven churches, and that too,
not as a private epistle, but as a Revelation made to him
by Jesus Christ, one should suppose that its authenticity
could not be doubted, especially at a time when there were
the best means of obtaining information. We cannot say
that the book was kept secret, or was concealed in the
archives, lest the prophecies against Rome should draw a
persecution on the Christians, for secrecy is contrary to
the tenor of the book, and the author of it enjoins that
it should be both read and heard. Though the figurative language of the Apocalypse, continues Michaelis,
when compared with the simple style of St. John's gospel,
cannot be alleged as an argument that the two books
were written by different authors, since the same author,
when animated by a spirit of prophecy, will write in a
different manner from that in which he had written as an
historian; yet there is a certain character in the language of the Apocalypse which is hardly to be reconciled
with the manner which is visible in St. John's gospel.
Throughout almost the whole of the Apocalypse, we find

the author an imitator of the ancient prophets [the converse of this is nearer the truth, for it was they who
imitated him]; from whom he borrows his images, and
renders them more beautiful than they were in the
originals : but St. John's gospel has a soft and gentle
character peculiar to itself, so as to exhibit no trace of
imitation. Further, the author of the Apocalypse (whom,
from the title of the book I will call John the Divine, in
contradistinction to John the Apostle), has not borrowed
his imagery merely from the canonical books of the Old
Testament, for he has taken a great part of it from the
Jewish antiquities, and the theology of the Rabbins, so
that his work has almost a cabalistic appearance. And
he not only seems himself to be intimately acquainted
with these subjects, but to presuppose the same intimacy
in his readers, and to have written for those only who
were initiated into the abstrusest doctrines which were
taught in the schools of the Rabbins; nor does it ever
once occur to him that what he says may appear foreign
or obscure. But John the Apostle seems to have been
well aware that not all his readers had this kind of
knowledge ; for he has frequently explained circumstances
relative to the city of Jerusalem, and the customs of the
Jews, with more historical perspicuity than we find even
in the other evangelists.

7. Lucke, who generally writes, says Stuart (p. 297),
in a spirit of moderation and candour, has, as we
have seen above, expressed a most unqualified negative upon the question of the *apostolic* origin of the
Apocalypse. The same author has, however, admitted
fully that no valid claims can be made out for the
second John at Ephesus. He gives up even all pre

tences to conjecture who the author was. His general conclusion is that John the Apostle *may* have had the visions related in the Apocalypse : that he *probably* spoke of them in the circle of the Asiatic churches ; that some gifted man there heard him, and undertook to write them down : that in so doing he has mingled his own conceptions with those of John : that the apostle, when he saw the writing (for he allows that he *probably must* have seen it), finding that it did not substantially disagree with his own doctrinal views, or with those of Paul, suffered it to circulate without remark, at least, without opposition ; and that all this *might* happen, because, as he avers, the primitive Christians were much more concerned about the matter of a writing, viz, whether it was truly Christian or not, than they were respecting the author of it. He acknowledges, with much candour, that he has no *data* on which to build all this ; but he thinks that some such *supposition* is necessary, in order to reconcile the apparent difficulties that exist as to the composition of the book in question. Erasmus, in the first edition of his Greek Testament, has inserted in his Remarks on the Apocalypse some intimations of doubt among the Greek churches of ancient times respecting it, as testified by Jerome. Erasmus himself thinks it strange that the writer of the Apocalypse so often mentions his own name, contrary to the usage of John. Paul, he significantly suggests, relates his visions (2 *Cor.* xii.) with great modesty. Besides, the title of the book is Ιωαννης θεολογος, Ioan the Divine, or the theologue. The difference of style, he further suggests, is also great between Ioan's gospel and the Apocalypse. All this, he says, makes him doubt about the *apostolic*

L. 3

origin of the book; "unless indeed the general consent of the Christian world should be in favour of it, or especially the *authority* of the Church defend it, if indeed the Church should determine in its favour." So Erasmus was much in the same plight with Eusebius: critical arguments seemed to invite him one way, and the voice of the Church another. He then goes on to relate the doubts of Dionysius of Alexandria, of Eusebius, of Caius the Roman Presbyter, &c.; and he concludes with naming several of the fathers who were its strenuous defenders, but who were strong Chiliasts (Millennarians). All this is merely a masked battery for assault. Finally he comes out with the conclusion, that the book being made up of visions and allegories, cannot be so profitable as some others; and in order to soften down this, he suggests that even among precious jewels, one kind of gold may be much more pure and valuable than another. Such reflections show in reality his secret doubts: they show also how timid he was in venturing to say anything which would call in question the established opinions of the Romish Church.

8. The arguments of Dionysius, a disciple of Origen, and an eminently learned Bishop of Alexandria, in the third century, are contained in an extract from a treatise of Dionysius, in the seventh book of Eusebius's *Ecclesiastical History*. They are thus abridged by Dr. Lardner: Dionysius' objections are five in number. 1. That the evangelist John had not named himself either in his gospel or in his catholic epistle: but the writer of the Revelation names himself more than once. 2. That though the writer of the Revelation calls himself John, he has not shown us that he is the apostle of that name.

3. That the Revelation doth not mention the catholic
epistle, nor that epistle the Revelation. 4. That there is
a great agreement in sentiment, expression, and manner
between St. John's epistle and gospel, but the Revelation
is quite different in all these respects, without any resemblance or similitude. 5. That the Greek of the gospel
and of the epistle is pure and correct, but that of the
Revelation has barbarisms and solecisms. These, it will
be seen, have been much amplified by other ecclesiastical
critics; and it is not without significance that in so far
distant an age such doubts should have been generally
spread by writers who, in all other respects, were devoted
adherents of the so-called Christian system. And it is
absurd to suppose that, if John were really the author of
the Apocalypse, so many eminent divines would in almost
his own age stand up and deny it before men.

9. We are told by Michaelis, that Amphilochus, who
was bishop of Iconium about the year 370, says in his
metrical catalogue of canonical books, Some ascribe the
Apocalypse to St. John, *but most persons consider it
spurious.* In fact it was almost universally condemned
as such by the members of the Greek church, at the end
of the fourth century. Hence Jerome, in his epistle to
Dardanus, says that the Greek church rejected the
Apocalypse with the same freedom as the Latin church
rejected the Epistle to the Hebrews; and Junilius, an
African bishop, of the sixth century, says, *cæterum de
Johannis Apocalypsi apud Orientales admodum dubitatur.*
The authority of the Apocalypse, therefore, instead of
gaining, lost ground among the Greeks: and Lardner
acknowledges, not only that the two celebrated Greek
commentators, Chrysostom in the fourth, and Theophy-

lact in the eleventh century, have not quoted it in a
single instance ; but that Nicephorus, patriarch of Constantinople, about the year 806, expressly rejected it.
He continues thus : That the style of the Apocalypse
is very unlike that of any other book in the New Testament is a fact which no man who understands Greek, and
is capable of judging impartially, will deny. Nor is this
difference of such a kind only that we might ascribe it to
the peculiarity of the subject, and say that the same
author when he wrote in the character of a prophet
would use different modes of expression from those which
he had adopted as an historian ; whence might be explained the contrast between the simple, unadorned style
of St. John's gospel and the rich figurative language of
the Apocalypse. *But when the rules of the Greek grammar are accurately observed in St. John's gospel, and are
frequently violated in the Apocalypse,* we have a difference
which cannot be ascribed to the dissimilitude of the
subject ; for the same author who wrote correctly as an
historian, would not be guilty of solecisms even in writing
prophecies.

10. The Apocalypse is said to have been written A. J. C.
95. As Ioan the disciple was a cotemporary of Jesus,
there is no reason for supposing that he was not born at
or about the same time, so that he would be upwards of
ninety when he wrote it. When Jesus died as some say
A. J. C. 33, as other and better authorities, A. J. C. 57,
there were only 120 converts in all to Christianity, (*Acts*
i. 15) ; yet we are asked to believe that some years after,
there were seven bishops in seven flourishing churches, in
seven chief cities of Asia : and that they all recognized a
right in Ioan to be their guide and patriarch ; he then

being without any crime, an exile in a desert island, where he could get no materials for writing, and from which under the vigilant guardianship of Roman soldiers, he could have no means of transmitting his pastoral epistles, to those for whom God especially designed them. All this is as incredible as transubstantiation.

11. The 85th of the *Apostolic Canons*, which are supposed to belong to the 4th century, does not mention the Apocalypse among the apostolic writings. In the *Constitutions* also, which probably originated in Syria and the adjacent regions, there is no notice of the book. It has been inferred from the circumstance of the Apocalypse being wanting in the Peshito, that it did not belong to the canon of the Syrian church. It has also been thought that the theologians of the Antiochenian school, among whom are Chrysostom, Theodoret, and Theodore of Mopsuestia, omitted it out of the catalogue of canonical writings. It appears also to have been rejected by the theological school of Nisibis, which may be regarded as a continuation of the Antiochenian. Junilius does not mention it in his list of prophetic writings. Cyril of Jerusalem has omitted it in his *Catecheses;* as also Gregory of Nazianzen ; and the 60th canon of the Laodicean synod. Amphilochus of Iconium, says that some regarded it as a divine production, but that others rejected it. Eusebius's testimony respecting the Asiatics, is that some rejected the Apocalypse, while others placed it among the acknowledged. Euthalius when dividing part of the New Testament stichometrically, says nothing whatever of the book, and Cosmas Indicopleustes excludes it from the list of the canonical. In like manner Nicephorus, patriarch of Constantinople in the ninth century, appears

to have placed it among the unacknowledged. His name-sake Nicephorus Callistus quotes from Dionysius as follows. Some of these who have preceded us, *have destroyed and restored again the book itself,* and correcting it through every chapter, *have brought it into that condition that it cannot be recognised,* and it seems to be conposed without any reasonable design. And they report that it bears a false inscription. He adds, without adopting the opinion of Dionysius, that it had been composed by Cerinthus; but this though an error, does not weaken the force of the fact mentioned by that author, that the book had been *mutilated* by its possessors. We shall find however in another place, a statement made by this historian, quite at variance with the fact of the Apocalypse being the work of any writer after Jesus.

12. One word, says Stuart, on the idea of an impostor's having composed this book—for more than a word is not needed. If there be any book in all the Scriptures, which bears unequivocal marks of a most serious and earnest state of mind, the Apocalypse must be regarded as such a book by every impartial and feeling reader. A deeper tone of earnestness never pervaded any writing. What could an *impostor* have in view by composing such a book? How could he expect the Asiatic Christians to receive it? How could he suppose that John would not at once overthrow its credit? Was it fame that the impostor courted? How could he obtain it where detection of his imposture was certain? Was it personal honour or gain that he sought for? How could he obtain either so long as he kept himself concealed and was unknown? In fact the allegation of imposture may be made, for it has been, by heated and indiscreet disputants, but

it is not deserving of any special notice. The importance of this remark is obvious; for if it be conceded that John was not the writer, it is of great consequence to believe that it was written by some real man; and with some real, grave, and holy object in view; and this I think cannot well be doubted by any.

13. The language of Irenæus, has been cited as a proof of the Christian origin of the Apocalypse—but it in truth proves nothing of the kind. He simply says that the Apocalypse—that is, a copy of the Apocalypse—was seen some time before the period in which he wrote. Οὐδὲ γὰρ πρὸ πολλοῦ χρόνου ἑωράθη [ἡ Ἀποκαλυψις] ἀλλά σχεδὸν ἐπι τῆς ἡμετερας γενεας, προς τῷ τελει τῆς Δομετιανου αρχης, that is : The Apocalypse was seen not long ago, but almost in our generation, near the end of Domitian's reign. These words are cited by Eusebius, *Hist. Eccl.* iii. 18 , but they cannot 'mean the *Revelation* itself; for a Revelation is not seen—a Revelation is seen, shewn, and heard. They allude no doubt to the Book in which it was described. And this would lead to the surmise that Irenæus did not then know of any existent copies. The *oldest* traces, says Olshausen, of the existence of the entire New Testament as a *completely finished collection*, are first found 300 years after the times of the Apostles. The especial reason why so much time elapsed before this body of writings was exactly compiled is, that the individual Books thereof which naturally existed earlier than the collection, were in circulation, at first partly separate, partly in smaller collections. But this latter clause, I must add, is mere assertion without *real* historical proof.

14. With these facts and opinions before us it is melancholy to read in *Doyly and Mant's Bible* the words fol-

lowing: The testimonies in favour of the Book of Revelation being a genuine work of St. John the Evangelist,
are *very full and satisfactory*. , It is more charitable to
suppose that these reverend doctors were ignorant, than
that they deceived—though it is very common with
writers of that class to presume immoderately on the profound ignorance of their readers. In another place they
say that "it was called the Revelation of *Saint* John the
Divine," which it never was; but this assertion is like
many others which they have made. Lee, in his book on
Prophecy, 237, was too candid for these editors. It is
true, he says, tradition makes Patmos the place of John's
exile under Domitian, but this seems to have no better
authority than that of *conjecture.* And certainly conjecture, or rather fancy has been very busy with this John.
Tertullian relates that Domitian having commanded him
to be thrown into boiling oil, was so enraged at finding
him come out unhurt, that he exiled him to Patmos. As
nobody can believe the first portion of the narrative, it
makes one suspect the second also; and yet the testimony
of writers of this class is cited every day in proof of historical facts. It is not without *some* significance, that the
copy of the Apocalypse which Bruce brought with him
from Abyssinia, ascribed its authorship to Ioan, Bishop
of Constantinia, but who *he* was nobody seems to know.
(*Travels* ii , 407.)

15. When the reader has got thus far, he will probably
hesitate before he gives unlimited credence to all that he
has hitherto heard with reference to John, to the boiling oil,
to Patmos, &c. ; and when he thus hesitates, all I ask him
to do is to compare. It has not unfrequently been charged
against this book, says Stuart, that it is altogether *unique;*

that the genius of the whole New Testament stands in opposition to it, or at least is as widely distinct from it as possible. This is perfectly true, and the reason that it is true is this—that the real Apocalypse was given to the priests and to man, thousands of years before either the New Testament or the Old. No wonder therefore that it savours of a different age, a different nation, and a different order of thought, and that it should be as widely distinct from it in all material respects as one book can be from another. The fact is, this is the very Apocalypse of Adam himself which is mentioned in Epiphanius (*Hæres* xxxi., 8), and which was then in the possession of the Gnostics, or Buddhists, of the first century; though by that writer it was supposed to have subsequently perished; and many copies of it certainly *were* destroyed in all quarters by the priests and monks, who, while they have carefully exterminated thousands of the most sublime works ever dictated by heaven to the philosophers of old, have piously preserved Catullus, Petronius, Martial, and the other degraded singers of the stews. The Manichæans used it, and called it the *Book of Perfection.* I feel certain also that it was one of the Hidden Volumes of the Essenes, which were revealed only to him who swore to preserve *the books and the names of the Messengers.*—Josephus' *Wars, Book* ii, c. 7. It passed subsequently under the names of Abraham, Moses, Elijah, Elias, (4) Zephaniah, Zechariah, Hystaspes, Peter, Paul, Cerinthus, St. Thomas, Cæcilius, Stephen the Martyr, and probably of others; which means no more than this, that some of those persons possessed or distributed copies of it, with additions and interpolations of their own, among their followers, by whom it was then ignorantly assigned to the person so distributing, and who in reality was only a copyist of it, as I profess to be   That a genuine transcript and translation of the original, probably in Syriac or Chaldee, was in the hands of the person who assigned it to John, is by no means certain; but if it were, he must, when changing it into so-called Greek, have mutilated and transposed it designedly, as Nicephorus reports, for some purpose known only to himself. (5.)

16. Assuming then that it may be taken as an historical fact that the Apocalypse was long anterior to John, by whom else than Adam, if we so call the first Messenger, shall we say that it was written? I have already spoken of internal evidence, *ante* page 187, that is the evidence furnished by the book itself, irrespective of all others; and this evidence exhibiting further a connected series and subject of the most important matters that can affect mankind, beginning almost at the beginning, and going down to the end, appears to me to be exceedingly powerful. We have not, as in the common version, the whole history of the earth ignored, until the days of the supposed John; but we have a syllabus of the entire history of the human race, beautifully connected, and limned, as it were, in outline, by the hand of God himself. A careful examination of the Apocalypse will more positively demonstrate this than any argument whatever. This being conceded, the Book must be divine; and if divine, to whom was it given by its Heavenly Inspirer? If it be true, and who can doubt it? that God ever gave a Revelation, He must have given it when it was needed, that is, by the early dwellers of the earth; and if it be true that He has inspired a series of Celestial Messengers, He un-

doubtedly bestowed this on the first, for there is no other extant, with such genuine marks of antiquity.

17. That there were Præadamites no rational person will presume now to deny; to do so, would be to ignore the facts of history, and the discoveries of geologists, which conclusively show that the race of mankind has been upon the earth many centuries before chronology will at all fit into the popular æra of Adam. But as there is a certain class of persons who believe nothing that is not proved to be in the Jewish books, it is easy to shew that the writer of Genesis himself declares that there were Præadamites; the wonder is that people have not seen this long before. It is a favourite theory with Biblical logicians that the second chapter of Genesis, beginning with verse 4, and containing an account of the formation of Adam, is not a continuation of chapter I., but a *recapitulation* of it in other words. Than this nothing can be more absurd. Giving the compiler of the Genesis tracts credit for even the lowest amount of literary skill, he would hardly commit a blunder of this nature. Nor can any reasonable excuse be offered, why, having given *one* account in chapter I., ending at chapter II., verse 3, of the formation of man, he should immediately after give another and a different version. The truth is he does not do so; he was not so grossly ignorant and unskilful as his Biblical apologists pretend him to be. In chapter I., verses 26—29, we have a history of the Præadamite races as God made them, men and women, with dominion over the animals, that is a nomadic tribe of hunters and shepherds; such is the obvious meaning of the writer's language. After that, as time advances, and agriculture becomes needful, a new ordinance is made, for a race that would till the ground;

which we know that hunters (like the Red race), and shepherds (like the Tartars and Arabs), never can be brought to do. A new leader of men is needed, and he is sent. This is Adam. The earth is made ready for the advent of an agricultural people, by the mist that waters the whole face of the ground. And this leader is to be the first Messenger to whom a Law is revealed. *And Ieue Aleim* (God and the Holy Spirit), *formed a man, of the dust of the ground* (symbolical of his teaching agriculture, not *man* as the English version most falsely puts it ;) *and this man became an inspired creature.* This translation, as may be seen by any one who studies even Parkhurst, though he was no Orientalist, sub voce נפש (*nephesh*), is quite as true to the genius of the Hebrew language as that which the Vulgate gives ; and is also in accordance with the context, which the common version is not ; for the very same word *nephesh* is used for the *fish* in verses 20 and 21, chapter I. ; and for the *beast* of the earth in verse 24. And for this man God expressly makes a garden, as if to teach him, by example, the agricultural art. This and much more that follows is no doubt symbolical ; but it establishes that Adam was *not* the first of human beings, but that he came upon the earth many ages after. It may be said that this view of the æra of Adam is inconsistent with the high state of art mentioned in the Apocalypse. I at once admit the fact, but I am not bound by *all* that the Genesis writer says. For me it is enough that out of his own mouth I prove the existence of Præadamites : and I cite his testimony with no other view. I will no more admit his authority against the plain statements of the Apocalypse, and the innumerable reliques of primeval art, civilization, and splendour, with which the old world abounds, than I would for the rabbinical fables in which he is so profuse, and the evidently Jewish bigotry by which he is inspired.

18. "Cain," says Bayle, believed that all the earth was inhabited : for a man who believed that the whole race of mankind was comprised in the family of Adam could not have found a better way to avoid being killed than to absent himself from that family : and here on the contrary, Cain seems not to have feared any murderer, provided he did not leave it. He fears he shall be killed only in case he became *a vagabond and fugitive on the earth*, Gen. iv. 14. I find scarce one, who has undertaken to refute this objection of the Præadamites, otherwise than by recurring to the fecundity of Eve, and computing how many children might be born of her and her daughters in the space of one hundred years. But this, in my opinion, does not come up to the point; it supposes that Cain feared his brothers and nephews. Now, it was not them he feared ; for as I said before, if they had been the occasion of this fear, he could not have desired anything better than to be banished : nor would he have esteemed the exile to which God had condemned him, a punishment too great for him to bear. It must therefore be the inhabitants of remote countries that he feared : people unknown and no ways tied to him by any relation. God so far from undeceiving Cain about his supposition that there were men everywhere, seems to have confirmed it. He does not answer him, Thou hast no need to fear murderers in remote countries : for there is not one man there. But he encourages him by giving him a mark which would prevent any one that found him from killing him : and this manifestly supposes that Cain

might find people in every place where his steps might carry him.

19. But though Adam was not the first man, there are traditions which shew that a person under that name, real or symbolical, exercised a singular influence in his own age upon his cotemporaries. This man as I have said was the First Messiah from God · this man was the author of the Apocalypse. Traces of him may be found in many nations : but except among the Jews, who claim him for themselves alone, or those who have imbibed the fancy from the Jews, there is no tradition anywhere of his being the parent of mankind; or of his adventures with a talking serpent. This a rabbinical allegory, which exposes all who believe in it literally to contempt or ridicule.

20. I do not value the writings of Paul very much ; he has done more to destroy *true Christianity* than any writer that ever lived, but he may be taken as a witness of what the early Jews, from whom he *professed* to apostatize, believed about certain allegorical mysteries, which simple Christians are taught to confide in as actual facts. I have already cited a passage from Maimonides (*ante* p. 71), which shows the insanity of believing according to the letter. The following strange passages from Paul, shew that *he* also held similar notions about the entirely symbolic character of parts of the Old Testament. I have no doubt there are many others ; but they are hardly worth looking for, as *literal* believers may be taken to have wholly abandoned reason, and to be insensible to all proof. In 1 *Corinth,* x, we read thus : *Moreover, brethren, I would not that ye should be ignorant, how that all our fathers were under the cloud, and all passed through the*

sea : and were all baptized unto Moses in the cloud and in the sea ; and did all eat the same spiritual meat ; and did all drink the same spiritual drink : for they drank of that spiritual Rock that followed them : and that Rock was Christ. But with many of them God was not well pleased : for they were overthrown in the wilderness. This indicates a very strong doubt in the mind of the writer about the literal acceptance of much that has been vulgarly taken for reality. It does not look as if he at all regarded the pillar of cloud, or the Red Sea, in both of which the Jews were baptized unto Moses, as anything but symbolical : the same observation may apply to the spiritual meat and drink (manna and quails) (6) ; and the waters from Horeb; to neither of which does he appear to give a literal meaning ; and that the Jews of Moses's time drank of the Rock Christ seems lunacy itself. There is another passage in *Galatians* iv, equally startling and inexplicable. *For it is written, that Abraham had two sons, the one by a bondmaid, the other by a freewoman. But he who was of the bondwoman was born after the flesh ; but he of the freedwoman was by promise. Which things are an allegory ; for these are the two covenants; the one from the mount Sinai, which gendereth to bondage, which is Agar. For this Agar is mount Sinai in Arabia, and answereth to Jerusalem which now is, and is in bondage with her children. But Jerusalem which is above is free, which is the mother of us all.* Now if all this about Abraham and his two sons is *an allegory*, where shall we decide between that which is true and that which is mythical ? To decide is impossible : to let the Church decide for us against our own reason is madness. We should therefore exercise a little common sense : and reject whatever is repugnant to our own understanding, or to experience. And all these myths about ribs, and serpents, are evidently so.

21. Internal evidence is not the only evidence that the Apocalypse was written by the first Messenger, whom we may call Adam. There are not wanting historical traditions, which indeed are slight, although not worthless. The reader may give what weight to them he thinks fit: or he may give none at all, for this Essay claims higher authority than any historical proof whatever. One of the most ancient traditions of the Oriental world, and one which all the learned Arabs and Mohammedan priests hold implicitly to this present day, is, that God commanded the splendid Angel Azaz-El, to bear a Message or a Revelation to Adam, whom they call *Sefi Alla*, the chosen, the wisdom-word of God; and that Azaz-El having refused he immediately fell, and became Iblîs, which means *Despair*. As Adam was then in his human appearance, though in reality a Messiah, this disobedience of Azaz-El, who did not know that he was commissioned to a Divine Incarnation, may easily be explained; and if the tradition be accepted as true—and I know not why it should not be *so* received—it will at once explain why God lifted Adam on high in divine ecstacy, and ruled that the Revelation which he was to receive, should be actually presented to him in Vision, and not brought to him by any of the Heavenly Spirits.

22. Cedrenus and Syncellus have two curious fragments of ancient tradition, one copied from the other in nearly the same words, which assign to Adam the receipt of an Apocalypse. Τω χ ἔτει μετανοήσας ὁ Ἀδὰμ, ἔγνω δι Ἀποκαλυψεως, τὰ περὶ τῶν ἐγρηγόρων, καὶ τοῦ κατακλυσμου καὶ

τὰ περὶ μετάνοιας, καὶ τῆς θείας σαρκώσεως, καὶ τῶν περὶ
καθ' ἑκάστην ὥραν ἡμερινην καὶ νυκτερινὴν αναπεμπομένων
εὐχων τῷ Θεῷ ἐξ ὅλων των κτισμάτων διὰ Οὐριὴλ του ἐπὶ
τῆς μετανοίας αρχαγγελοῦ. In his six hundredth year,
Adam repenting of his sin, learned by an *Apocalypse* all
the things about the Watchers, and the inundation of
waters, and about repentance, and the divine Incarnation,
and the prayers presented to God by all creatures, through
every hour of the day and night, by Uriel the archangel,
of repentance.

22. Epiphanius, speaking of the Gnostics, says : They
produce other Revelations of Adam, αποκαλυψεις καὶ του
Αδαμ αλλας λεγουσιν. From these he cites a fragment,
which it will be at once seen is identical in spirit with
the words in the text ; διὸ καὶ ἐν ἀποκρυφοις ἀναγινώσκοντες,
ὅτι εἶδον δένδρον φερον δωδεκα καρπους τοῦ ἐνιαυτοῦ, και
εἶπε μοι τουτο εστι τὸ ξυλον τῆς ζωῆς· ὁ αὐτοὶ ἀλληγορουσιν
εἰς τὴν κατα μῆνα γινομενην γυναικαιαν ῥύσιν. *Propterea
in Apocryphis legunt ; vidi arborem duodecim fructus quo-
tannis ferentem, et dixit mihi, hoc est lignum vitæ. Idip-
sum de menstruis mulierum profluviis interpretantur* (7).
It seems to me very clear from this, that the Apocalypse which the Gnostics used as the Revelation of Adam,
was this very work which has so long passed under the
name of Ioannes. And the explanation of the Tree of Life
is merely a falsehood of Epiphanius : but the twelve fruits
from the Tree, are the Twelve Messengers, in commemoration of whom Herodotus relates that in the Egyptian
temples there were *twelve* golden pateræ, ii. 151. Tertullian, c. ix. *de Anima*, says : An ecstacy fell on Adam (*Gen.*
iv.), the operating influence of the *Holy Spirit of Prophecy.* Is not this the very essence of the Apocalypse as

M

here explained? and is it not clearly deducible from the passage that it was the very same Apocalypse as the Gnostics used?

23. Hottinger, (*Hist. Orient.* p. 22.), cites an Arab writer, who reports, that God delivered to Adam a book of twenty-one pages. This was the first Book direct from heaven, and written in the first language. It contained precepts, traditions, promises and denunciations on future ages, and the interpretation of certain mysteries; and exhibited the laws *and histories of the whole earth.* And in this also, the Supreme God, represented the generation of men, one after the other, and their career, and their transactions, with those also of their Kings, and all and every of the revolutions on earth. And when Adam saw these things, and what calamities should befal men, he wept with a great weeping. Then God commanded him to write them down with a pen, and he took the skins of cattle, and prepared them until they were white, and he wrote. Is there one word in this description of the revealed volume, which is not strictly applicable to this Apocalypse? and what has become of this Book, if it be not the Apocalypse?

24. An Arabian doctor, quoted by Kircher (FABRIC. *Cod. Pseud. Vet. Test.,* i, 18) says that, Adam meditating one day by the banks of a river issuing out of Paradise, on the good that he had lost, and the evils into which he had fallen, with voice, eyes, and hands elevated to God, implored some alleviation of his misery. On the third day after his prayer the Angel Raziel (the Wisdom of God) came to him, and handed him *a Book, that shone like white flame,* on which were letters traced by which he was enabled to learn and understand, all the wonderful

events *which either had been, were, or were to be,** and to perceive all things in the heavens, the earths, the waters, the abysses, and the places under the abysses; all the heavens, and the Messengers who were their ministers, their virtues, and their employments, the motion of the sun and moon and stars, and their natures and all things by which the world is regulated. If this be not a description of the Apocalypse, as here printed and interpreted, it would be hard to say what is.

25. The Jews of the Cabbala have preserved the tradition; they relate that after Adam's sin, the Book of Revelation which had been given to him in his ecstacy, *and which was full of mysteries and signs expressive of the most profound knowledge,* was taken away by the angel Raziel, by whom it had been shewn to him at first; that the patriarch then went forth and wept, and having fully repented, Raziel was again sent by God to restore the Book to Adam, *lest men might lose its wisdom and instruction;* that Adam then delivered it to Sheth, from whom it came to Enoch and Abraham, and so in succession to the most wise of every generation. Now, if this be true, and God did indeed reveal an Apocalypse to Adam, and that the wisest of the Hebrews still preserved it, how came it to be lost? Answer—it is not lost, but has been miraculously preserved, though under a false name, and in many fragments, and that it is now restored to the world in its pure and primal shape.

26. Kyssæus, a Mahommedan writer, relates that when Abraham, (a priest of Brahm), opened the chest of Adam, behold in it were the *Books of Adam;* likewise the Books of Shet or Sasan, and of Edris (Enoch), as also the characters

* The very words of the Apocalypse.

of *the prophets who were to follow.* Berosus likewise tells us that Xisuthrus (Adam) composed certain writings at the command of the Deity, which were buried in Sippara, the City of the Sun in Ba-Bel-On-Ya, and which writings were actually dug up, at a later period, and were preserved in the metropolis of Chaldæa. And it was from these writings deposited in the Temple of Belus, that Berosus took some of the outlines of his history of the præ-adamite rulers of Chaldæa. Observe here that this Sip-para comes from *Saphr*, סֵפֶר, which means a Book, a Scribe, and numbers; that it is the root of the Greek σοφος, a wise man; of the *Persian* Sofi, a sage; of the *English* Sapphire, because *blue* was the emblem of heavenly Wisdom : and a sapphire girdle was worn by the Messenger. This is mentioned in the Apocalypse. Does this furnish a reason why the work itself was secretly deposited in the Sapphire-City ?

27. There is a curious passage in Ælian, says Herbert, in *Nimrod*, where he speaks of a *Hawk* which brought to the Egyptians, *in the times of the beginning*, a Book bound in purple, containing the written ordinances of their re-ligion, for which reason the scribes and interpreters thereof used to wear hawk's wings upon their heads. Now we know that the hawk like the eagle and vulture were solar emblems : this hawk therefore means, a Child of the Sun —an Incarnation. And whenever we see in Egyptian hieroglyphics a hawk-headed creature, we may be sure that it alludes either to the Messenger himself, or one of his priests. And as the hawk, the vulture, and the eagle were all three birds of prey, they symbolized under either figure, the Cabiric Messenger, or Messiah of Justice, who bore the thunderbolt of God within his talons. And to

this Messenger express allusion is made in I. Chron. xxi. 15, II. Sam. xxiv. 16. But the Book above alluded to, was not the Book of Thoth; what other volume then could it be? I answer it was this Apocalypse, which thus got to Egypt in the primitive ages—the times of the beginning.

28. The religion of the primeval Persians, says Hyde. *Hist. Rel. Vet. Pers.* ii, was called *Millat Ibrahîm*, or the Abrahamic Religion : and he says that it was contained in a Book called *Sofhi*, or Wisdom This Revelation they believe descended from Heaven during the feast of Ramazân, and it was contained in ten books or chapters, the truth of which was denominated Pâzend, "*full of counsel, wisdom, and secret mysteries.*" It exists, or can be found, no longer ; and orthodox commentators have puzzled themselves and their readers in attempting to prove that it was given to the Jewish patriarch Abraham, as he is called, whom biblicals delight to dub the Father of all religion in the East. But Abraham is not a name —it is a title of honour. אברהם Abraham is Father of a multitude. אברם Abram, Father of elevation. It may mean in addition to numerous other explanations of which it is susceptible, the Father, (*Ab*), from the Sun, (*Ram*), a designation that would apply to any one of the Twelve Messengers. It might therefore mean Adam himself the First Messiah, and it is possible that it may have been the work mentioned by Kyssæus. And this view is confirmed by the fact, that the Book of Abraham which the Jews preserve, the *Jetsira*, or Creation, is nothing but a pure cabbalistic farrago of equal foolishness with the Talmud itself. It is assuredly not the *Sofhi*, for it is the reverse of Wisdom. Where then is the *Sofhi?*

Is it not the Apocalypse, "full of counsel, wisdom, and secret mysteries?" This hypothesis is confirmed when we recollect what Hyde further says, that Ibrahîm is synonymous with *Imaum*, or High Priest, and is the same as the Persic *Pîshvâ*, or Sovereign Pontiff. And who so eminently worthy of this honourable surname as the First Messenger, the chosen *Imaum* of God himself for this divine Revelation? Imaum is Hom-Aum, the name of the sacred Brahminical Fire.

29. One of the mythical legends related of Ibrahîm, is evidently founded on the Apocalypse, and is typical of what befals the heavenly Messenger. When it pleased God, says Abu Mohammed Mustapha, to send forth Ibrahîm, Nimrod dreamed that he saw a Star rising out of the East, which obscured the sun and moon, so that their light faded. From which being seized with great fear, he consulted his magicians, who told him that in that year a boy was to be born who would destroy himself and his kingdom. Then did Nimrod give command, that every boy who should be born in that year throughout the country, should be immediately put to death, and he gave orders also to separate the husbands from their wives, sending out the former to war, or into encampments. Then the mother of Ibrahîm fearing that her son might perish, *hid* him in a cave, and every day of his infancy was as a month; and every month was as a year; until at last he said to his mother: Lead me forth, &c. If the reader will turn to the Apocalypse, he will see that this is but a new version of the Red Dragon, the Woman and the man-child; and in conformity with the primeval symbol, we have nearly similar stories related of most of the Holy Messengers.

30. From a similar source, proceeded a curious mythos prevalent among the Tartars of the Corea. A daughter of the God Hoang-Ho, became pregnant by the action of a sunbeam. In due time she brought forth an egg, and from the egg was born a man-child. The king of the country jealous of his address, sent assassins to murder him. By these he was pursued to the bank of a river, and was on the point of falling into their hands, when he addressed a prayer to his father the Sun. Scarcely had he finished it, when *the fishes* rising to the surface of the water, formed a bridge for him, over which he passed in safety, and thus made his escape. The reader will see the importance of these allusions to the hiding and the fishes as he proceeds.

31. The Tsabæans say of Adam that when he quitted the country adjacent to India for the confines of Babel, he carried with him many wonderful things, amongst which were one *Tree*, whose branches, leaves, and flowers were all of gold, and another all of stone [emerald], and also two of the leaves of a third Tree, so verdant that the fire could not consume its leaves, and so large as to cover ten thousand men of equal stature with Adam. In this mystical way, it would appear, they mentioned this divine Apocalypse—in words which the initiated would understand, but which to the many would only be a source of ignorant wonder. A Tree, a Pillar, and a Sceptre, in ancient theology, were common names for a Book. So we are told that when Juno was married to Jupiter, she gave him a Tree that bare golden fruit a covert allusion to the Incarnation whom she produced, and to the Book which the Incarnation promulgated. Note also the Twelve Trees in the Apocalypse. *Aos*, one of the primi-

tive words, in Irish is a tree, and it signifies knowledge : so in Hebrew, עץ, *az*, or *ez*, is a Tree. When Moses sent out to search the land, he bade them try to find if there were any עץ, *az*, there; that is, any learned men, any adepts, any acquainted with the Sacred Mysteries— not if they had *wood* in the land, than which a more absurd translation could not be presented. That this is the true version is confirmed even by the Talmudists, who say that the reply was not, as the text has it, that there were Giants (an absurd answer to the supposed question put), but that there were Anakim (Enochians) men of learning in the country. So Taliesin, chief of the Welsh bards, alludes to his mystic knowledge of the Sacred Books :

> I know the intent of the *Trees*
> In the memorial of compacts.
> I know good and evil.

and again—

> I know which was decreed
> Praise or disgrace, by the intention
> Of the memorial of the *Trees*, of the Sages—
> I understand my institute.
>
> Davies' *Celt Res.*, 248.

In allusion to this also, the primeval priests had the figure of a Tree imprinted upon their bodies, and were therefore called *Dendrophori*, or tree-bearers, a symbolic reference to their possession of the secret of letters, and of this Apocalypse. By the Hindus, as Herodotus relates, it was called the Tree of Frankincense, whose fragrance was guarded by winged Serpents or Seraphim. The Golden Apple-trees of the Hesperids, guarded by a Dragon, mean the Golden Volume of the Apocalypse, which the Pontiff preserved; and Iasion's expedition in search of the Golden Fleece, or vesture of the Apocalyptic Lamb, was allusive to a search after the same concealed volume. It was likewise called the Golden Napkin, which the Great Mother Ceres gave to one of the Kings of Egypt. Charax, of Pergamus, says that Phryxus had left behind him some books written on *sheep-skin*, in letters of gold; and Dionysius Scytobrachion, of Mitylene, who flourished a little before Julius Cæsar, mentioned that the Golden Fleece, the cause of the Argonautic expedition, was a Book that taught the art of *making gold*,—that is, beautifying the world. By the Scyths it was called *The Golden Bowl that fell from Heaven;* by the Etruscans, *The Golden Ancile;* and by the Chinese, *Waters of Immortality.* It was concealed also under various other names familiar to the classical student, such as *The Arrows of Hercules;* for Hercules was a name for the Messiah, and arrows indicate language; and *The Horses of Rhesus,* for horses are solar symbols, and Rhesus was a disguise for Rhœa, the Holy Spirit (*ante*, 36). Thus it meant the sun-like emanations of the Queen of Heaven. It was called also the *Table,* and sometimes the *Tablets of the Sun.* This symbolism and concealment pervades the whole of ancient history. Helene or Selene (the Moon, S-El-Ain, the Fountain of the Most High) was a resplendent statue of the Holy Spirit, radiant with the rarest metal and jewelry, and enshrining in its breast a copy of the Apocalypse; it was stolen away by Paris, to Tro-Iah (the Tri-God) the name of a sacred city; and hence the holy war which followed. Nor is it to be wondered that so mysterious and symbolic a Book as the Apocalypse should give birth to mystery and symbolism in all things.

32. This Sacred Book of the Tsabœans, if it could be now procured, would, I doubt not, be found identical in all essentials with my Apocalypse. We find a glimpse of it in the well-known work of Maimonides, where it is called the Book of Thammuz (8), or *the Hidden one*. From that it would appear that it spoke of a Dragon or Serpent, and Tree of knowledge of good and evil. Both of these are in the Apocalypse. It may be said that they are also in the second and third chapters of Genesis. This is so—but who shall say that these were not founded on the Apocalypse, or on some Tsabæan or Indian superstition ? It is *certain* that they must be figuratively accepted; it seems equally certain that they are in a mutilated form. The Tsabæans also had other Books of Revelation called the Book *Tam Tam*, or Sam-Sam, from םם *sm*, the Sun : hence the Arabic Zem-Zem, or Well of Wisdom ; the Book *Hassearab* ; the Book of *The Messenger Hermes* ; but we know nothing of them except from Maimonides, who never sank the Jew in the philosopher. They maintained that Adam was like others, the offspring of a man and woman, though they greatly extolled him, calling him the *Prophet of the Moon :* and asserting that he taught men to worship the Moon, and composed certain works on agriculture.—*More Nevochim* (Teacher of the Perplexed) All these allusions shew that Adam was believed to have been a Messiah, and that he gave Revelations.

33. One fact suffices to shew that the common account of Adam cannot be relied upon, as having reference to any particular man, as the Hebrew doctors pretend. We are told that the Genesis Adam lived 930 years. Is it possible, that if this were so, he, the Patriarch

of the human race, as it is urged, skilled in all the varied accomplishments which by that time were known and diffused among his posterity, would have left no record in writing of his astounding experience, and of those personal communications which it is said that God himself held with him in the most eventful periods of his protracted career ? Can it be credited that God who was so continually interfering in the good government of mankind, would have prevented him ? is it not on the contrary more likely that God would have inspired him to leave this mighty memorial behind, as an authoritative guide to all posterity ? No such memorial is alluded to in Genesis; from which I think the inference is clear that the original tract relative to Adam, has, like every other part of the Hebrew writings, been sadly mutilated by the Jews. And one reason why they pretended that the First Naronic Messenger, was in reality the · Parent of the human family, and above all of the family of their patriarch Abram, was, that upon this device they might found one of their claims to universal pillage. And not content with this, they feigned that Noah, the Chinese Fohi, also was a Jew, so that in every way they might make good their demand upon the nations to surrender all to them, as being the first progenitors of men.

34. I hold, says Pererius, that Adam at the time when he conjectured the nature of all animals and birds, in the same moment committed it to writing, and that he likewise reduced their nomenclature into a commentary. For how otherwise could it have happened, that every name which Adam gave, should have continued to the time of Moses, if Adam had not at the same instant .when he called all beasts and birds by their names, com-

posed a catalogue of those names for the use of posterity ;
and that the various names of so many creatures, which
he might never again see, should not escape the memory
even of Adam himself? From all which Pererius concludes, that there were Præadamites; that Adam composed books, and that the art of writing was well known.
Ought he not to have concluded also that no reliance can
be placed on the Genesis tract which does not speak of
any such Book?

35. The Jewish sages have handed down a tradition of
two Psalms, which they declare to have been written by
Adam. I entertain no doubt that he wrote psalms; and
I have inserted two after the Apocalypse. But they are
not in the Rabbinical form, but as they were really
written. If he wrote these, why may he not have written
the Apocalypse?

36. Almost all ancient nations, says Higgins (*Anacalypsis*, ii. 147) had a tradition, that *they once possessed
Sacred Writings in a long-lost language*. The possessors
of these Writings, and this old language, must have been
the people who erected the Pyramids; the gigantic stone
circles, and the other Cyclopean buildings which are
found of such peculiar character and size all over the
world. Can these traditions be relied on? The biblicals
always argue for the Noachian deluge, on the ground of
general tradition; and I do not know why this should
not be as good a proof for me, as it is surmised to be for
them. Some people, says *Nimrod*, i. 18, are apt to argue
as if they took for granted, that there never were any
Holy Scriptures in the world before Moses wrote his for the
use of a single people. This however is a mistake. At
Athens they had a prophetic and mysterious Book, which

they called the *Testament:* to which they believed the
safety of the republic was attached. They preserved it
with so much care that among all their writers no one
ever dared to make any mention of it : and the little we
know of this subject has been collected from the famous
oration of Dinarchus against Demosthenes, whom he
accuses of having failed in the respect due to this *Ineffable
Book*, so connected with the welfare and safety of the
state. *Spineto on Hieroglyph*, p. 123. Was not this
Book the Apocalypse? I have already explained *why* it
was so carefully concealed.

37. Plato has the following allusion, which I think
intimates some knowledge of the Apocalypse. A *gift* as
it appears to me, says Socrates, (*Philebus*, 18), from gods
to men, was through *a certain Prometheus*, (a name for the
Messiah), cast down from some quarter by the Gods, along
with *a certain fire the most luminous ;* and the men of old
being better than us, and dwelling nearer to the Gods, have
handed down this story, &c. This gift, among other mystic
titles, passed in those days under the name of Ἱερος Λογος,
or *the Sacred Discourse ;* and it is mentioned by Fabricius.
(*Bib. Gr.* i. 118, 462); though the extracts which Syrianus
professes to take from it are spurious. It is referred to
by Herodotus under the name of *Divine Traditions ;*
with a declaration that he will not publish them ; and it
is in all probability the *Holy Tradition* recommended by
Orpheus to his favourite scholar, and quoted by Justin
Martyr. There is another hint of it in Plato's Republic,
x. It is proper indeed, he says, always to believe in those
Ancient and Sacred Discourses which announce to us that
the soul is immortal, and that it has judges of its conduct,
and suffers the greatest punishments when it is liberated

from the body. But what Ancient and Sacred Discourse is there, or have we any record of, that tells these things, if it be not this Secret Volume of the Mysteries?

38 Josephus in his Wars of the Jews, says: What did most elevate them in undertaking this war, was an ambiguous oracle that was found in their *Sacred Writings*, how about this time one from their country should become governor of the habitable earth. (Book vi., c. 5, s. 4.) What Sacred Writings were these? Not the traditions of the Rabbis handed down from early times, for these were not committed to writing. Were they those which Esdras was ordered not to publish? See *ante*, p. 79. Were they not the same as those which the Greeks possessed and guarded so carefully? Were they not the Apocalypse? and was not the prediction on which they relied, that contained in section 31, from which one of their own writers, Haggai, had quoted? but which they misinterpreted from their ignorance of true chronology: for the Great Messenger there predicted did not appear for 1200 years after that writer's prophecy of him?

39. Plato again, in his Phædo, treating of the immortality of the soul, tells us, that we must search out the strongest and best arguments to prove it, unless any can by a more safe and certain way, that is to say some *Divine Word* or *Tradition*, transmit it to us. Now, what this λόγος θείος or Divine Word should signify, if not the Apocalypse, it would be hard to imagine. In another place he speaks of ἐπίκτητος γνῶσις, or a *Traditionary Knowledge*; which from the peculiar mode in which alone the Apocalypse was communicated, namely, to the most perfect of the Initiated, might fairly enough allude to it. And Plutarch mentions a Παλαια Πιστις, or *Ancient*

Creed, which does not exist at present in any known Greek form, if we except the Apocalypse. Pherecyides, the master of Pythagoras, by some said to be an Assyrian, wrote a book called *Theogony*; from whence he received the name of Theologos, or the Divine. Diogenes Laertius, and Suidas, both relate of him that he had no instructor, but that he got all his knowledge from *the hidden Books of the Phœnicians*, which he possessed : and in imitation of these he himself wrote his *Theology* in symbols and ænigmas : whence also he was surnamed Σκοτινος, or the darkly-mystic. Can it be questioned that these hidden and ænigmatic writings were the Apocalypse ; and that it was communicated by him to his disciples ? We are told also that he wrote certain books upon the theology of Ophion (meaning the Serpent On, the Phœnix On, the Mouth of On, and the Serpent of the Yoni, that is the Messiah) ; and these related to his birth (that of the Man Child) ; the War in Heaven ; the Winged Tree ; and the Veil ; and these books according to Isidorus (*Cit. Clem. Alex. Strom. lib.* i., *p.* 632, *ed.* 1629), were taken from the *Prophecy of Cham*. But is not this Cham a radical and important part of the name Adam ? Origen says that Pherecydes describes the two hostile armies, the one commanded by Saturn (Satan), and the other by Ophion ; and the agreement that whichever of the two should be beaten into the waters, should remain expelled from heaven. Does not this seem like an amplification of the Apocalypse ? I may add here that the author of *Nimrod* is of opinion that this *Prophecy of Cham*, is alluded to by Lycophron in his Cassandra (another prophetic vision), in verse 508, as being the " wonderful worm-eaten seal " with which the Twins are said to have sealed Attica. This I own is rather far-fetched, but it is the opinion of very learned men : it *may* be right, and the seal may allude to the Sealed Volume which only the Messenger of God could open. But this Book of Cham, or Ophion, was also called Orion, or Indian Bird of Fire, of which Clitarchus says, that it resembled a heron in size ; red (φοινιξ) as to his legs, and withal so musical as to rival the Sirens in its music : and he adds that the Kings of India had large waggons so constructed that trees might grow in them ; and so they carried this Bird about with them, where, as Nonnus relates, *from the topmost honey-dripping branch the sweet Bird Orion, sings with a divine voice like the sagacious swan, nor does he scatter it carelessly on the breath of zephyr, while he waves his wings, but sheds it like honey into the mouths of the wise, like a certain man.* I believe also that the Apocalypse was called for the sake of disguise, *The Lamb with Two Tongues,* το διγλωσσον ἀρνιον, which Helen was said to possess, together with the Tripod of Pelops : and that the two tongues meant the exoteric, and the esoteric interpretation. Nor can any other meaning that I see be assigned to it than this. The Lamb, I need not add, was an allusion to the lion-like Lamb, or the Messenger. Bion of Smyrna called it the *Two-headed Lamb,* δισσινιον ἀρνα, *Epith. Achil.* which the Apocalyptic Messiah was.

40. So Memnon, which was a Messianic name—meaning Mim-n-On (the Six hundred of On the Sun), when dead was transformed into a Bird, incomparable, as he himself had been among men, for beauty and sagacity ; the Orion of the Indians, and Phœnix of the classical writers. Memnon was the Son of Aurora (the Morning), whose Persian name was Ho-mai, or the Bird of Paradise.

Now Phœnix was the Bird of the Morning also, and of Paradise : his dwelling was in the very East, at the Gate of Heaven, in the Land of the Spring, and in the Grove of the Sun, upon a plain of unalloyed delights, lying *twelve* cubits higher than the highest of mountains, and which alone of all the Earth, was unhurt by the Fire of Phaeton, and the Water of Deucalion. Phœnix was also the Sacred Palm Tree—a Tree of Life, or an offshoot from Her who is.

41. Reference has been made to a volume called Kirâni, which a King of Persia presented to Thoth, many thousands of years before Mohammed adopted the same title for his Korân, or the Teacher. This was a Secret and a mystic Book : the biblicals who allude to it say that it was magical. It is related of Harpocration, (that is the god of sworn taciturnity, *premens vocem, digitoque silentia suadens*), when he was travelling in Babylonia, and about four miles from a city called Seleutica, that he found three towers which had been built by Giants (or priests of Anûk), and among them *columnam cum turre magnâ*, and with a Temple to be ascended by 365 silver steps. Upon that column the Book of Kirâni was found inscribed. The author of *Nimrod* says, that this was the column which went by the name of the Pillar of Achicarus, and that the writing upon it was in a sacred character, upon the meaning of which Democritus and afterwards Theophrastus, wrote discourses ; and he adds that Ach-icarus, which means Son of the Ocean, was worshipped as a Prophet and demigod by the people of Cimmerian Bosphorus. Was this Ach-icarus the same as Ach-Adam ; and were the Kirâni Mysteries those of the Apocalypse ? The coincidences are curious A volume

of the Kirâni was found in the tomb of Priam King of Troy, with his bones. From the traditionary notices of it which exist, it must have been a most venerable record of antiquity. Some writers maintain that Kirâni is in allusion to the Queen [of Heaven] Κοιρανη, which they say it means: others interpret it simply A Collection. Salmasius thinks it has the same sense as the Arabic Korân. Mention is made of a manuscript in the library of Mr. Grelot, entitled The Golden Epitome, or the Book of the Ancient Kiranids. Is this volume no longer to be found ?—or have the priests bought and destroyed it ? To what other book that we know, could the name of *Golden Epitome* apply so well as to this Apocalypse, which is a picture in brief of the whole world's history ? It has been attributed to Thoth; it has been assigned to Zaratusht, whom some think to be Adam. No one ever seems to have seen it, though the number of guessers at its contents have been numerous.

42. Harpocration's own account of it, may be cited. When I formerly travelled, he writes, through the country of Babylon I found a city, Seleutica by name, the history whereof I have written : after that I saw another city yet, seventeen Persian miles distance from Seleutica, which Alexander of Macedon demolished. This is called little Alexandria. The third year it happened that I found an old man skilled in foreign learning, and in the Greek tongue : but he said he was a Syrian by nation, was taken captive and lived there ; and he went round the city with me, and showed me everything. And when we came to a certain place about four miles distance from the city, we saw a *pillar* with a great tower, which the inhabitants of Syria said they brought from the edifice of

Solomon, and placed it there for the health and cure of the men of that city. Looking therefore well upon it I found it was written in strange letters. The old man therefore as soon as he was asked by me, agreed to shew me, and I willingly lent an ear to him, while he discoursed and expounded the barbarous letters that were upon the pillar, in the Æolic tongue. My son, saith he, you see three towers standing here, one of which is five miles distant, another two and a half, and another four. These were built by the Giants who had a mind to climb into heaven : for this their impious madness, some of them were struck with thunder : others through the just judgment of God, knew not themselves, and the rest were cast into the Isle of Crete, into which God being angry with them, hurled them. The old man then bade me measure the greatness of the stone with a cord. Therefore measuring that which was nigh I found it two-and-thirty cubits high, and seventy-nine broad, and there were 208 steps to it. We also saw a sacred cloister, and in the middle of the cloister there was a Temple having 365 silver steps, and 60 more of gold, by which we went up to pray to God. And he told me the Mysteries of the Living God, *which I will not tell to all.* I was indeed willing to be informed of other things : but my main design was to be informed of the pillar. And the old man drawing aside a silken veil shewed strange and foreign letters engraven upon it. And because he was skilled in my tongue, I entreated and begged of him that he would candidly and without envy make plain all things to me. Now the things that were read upon the pillar were these *This is a manifold Table of the true example . always having, and knowing, and foreknowing the Immis-*

sions [Messengers] *of the Divinity.* Such was the volume which Harpocration says that he transcribed ; but the volume which now bears his name, says nothing whatever of the Immissions or Messengers of the Divinity. A copy of the true Kiráni is known to have been once in the Vatican ; but the work under that name which was published at Constantinople in 1168, under the Emperor Manoel by some anonymous monk, is the evident forgery of some fortune-telling impostor : certainly not one likely to have been graven and preserved in the manner related. Making all due allowance for embellishment, I think it can hardly be contended that there was no such volume, nor can it be denied that it bore the impress of a remote antiquity—remote enough to have been deposited in Priam's golden coffin. What has become of it perhaps the Vatican could tell, but the Vatican never speaks. The fragment of it that remains, and which I have cited, is in accordance with the Apocalypse—am I over fanciful in supposing it to be the same ? The reader will see in a subsequent page how strangely the pillar, the temple, and the mystery, correspond with an historical narrative of Nicephorus, and with a vision of Swedenborg. The sceptic will exclaim, Who minds a vision ? The sceptic does not ; but a believer in the Apocalypse cannot treat any vision with disdain.

43. The singularity of this most ancient word Kiráni, and its resemblance to the name of Mohammed's scripture, is not less to be noted than other coincidences of the same kind. The reader cannot have failed to observe the remarkable name of the Mexican Messiah, given *ante*, page 37, Omid-euchtli : he will find in the Orphic Hymns that Omadius was a primeval name for the Sacred

Incarnation. So we read in Haggai ii. 7: *And the Desire
of all nations shall come,* חמד HMD. From this root
says Parkhurst, the pretended prophet Mohammed, or
Mahomet had his name. Yet there can be no doubt that
in this place the great Arabian Messenger of God, is here
expressly foretold by Haggai, and by name: there is no
pretence even by the biblicals, that it is interpolated by
the Arabs. Did not Haggai copy the prediction from
some other volume? We shall see that he copied it from
the Apocalypse. [Section 31]. How did the name get
to Mexico.—We find it in Japan as Amida; we find it in
Greece before Homer sang. Or is it an anagram of the
Shanscreet Adim, (Amid), and was it a general name for
the Celestial Interpreter? So we find Manu is Numa;
and this read backwards is Amûn, or the Hidden, which
the Messiah is always said to be. Kir, we know, is a
radical for the Sun, and Ani, is Ain, the Fountain, the
Holy Spirit; and it entered into the word Anna-Perenna,
which was one of her titles. See *ante,* page 108, Kyrene.

44. This passage of Haggai, says Dr. Henderson, has
long been regarded as one of the principal prophecies
relative to the time of the Messiah's advent. That it was
so applied by some of the early Jewish Rabbins is undeniable. Thus in the chapter of the Jewish Sanhedrim,
entitled חלק, *Halk,* the following interpretation is
given as that of Rabbi Akiba, who flourished before the
time of Jerome. *For a little I will give the kingdom of
Israel, after our desolation, and after the kingdom, behold
I will shake heaven and earth, and* MESSIAH SHALL COME.
The rendering of the Vulgate supports the same view.
Et veniet Desideratus cunctis gentibus. See *Minor Prophets,* page 355. But the reverend Doctor throws no

light on the singularity of the circumstance ; while Archbishop Newcome, and others of the Paulite prelates and
fabricators, pretend, against the voice of all antiquity, that
the word ought to be plural ; and they propose to interpret it, riches, or treasures ! !

45 Of this name (Adam), says Parkhurst, I meet with
no trace in the Greek and Roman mythology, unless in
that of Admetus, who was so beloved by Apollo, that the
God having been banished from heaven, commenced herds-
man, and kept his flock for him. This tradition or
mythos is however one of very great significance : as the
reader who has advanced thus far will see. Adam mystically may mean Ad-M, the Father, six hundred : meaning the First one who appeared in the Naronic Cycle.
The *true* derivation of Adam אדם, however, is in the
Arabic, where it means to serve, to minister : and it is
characteristic of the Jewish conceit that when they arro-
gated to themselves alone, the title of God's chosen
people, they not only chose the first Messiah for their
progenitor, but also made him the first man. Stephanus
περι πολεων, on Adana, tells us that Saturn or Kronos,
was called Adanos ; and that this Adanos was the son of
Heaven and Earth : to which Vossius, (*de Idolat.* i. 38.),
adds ; Neither may we conceive that his memory was lost
in Asia among the Gentiles—many things prove the contrary : Adana an ancient city in Cilicia, built by the
Syracusans, was so called in memory of Adam. For it is
evident that the Grecians having no words ending in *m*, ·
for Adam read Adan ; and the termination added, Adanos,
whence the city Adana. Note, that *Adhán* in Shanscreet
means the richest land.

46. But though Vossius artfully glosses over this matter,

and Parkhurst affects ignorance of any allusion to Adam among the Gentiles, how came the latter to be silent about that remarkable character among the Rabbis, whom they name Adam Kadmon? and who is in reality the very Adam of the Apocalypse, and the propagator, if not the inventor of letters, under the Greek mythos of Kadmos. Euhemerus calls Kadmos, Phœnix, which we know was a secret name for the Messiah; and כדם *Kedem*, or the East, was another of his appellations. See *ante*, page 96, note 2. This Adam is called Adamus Primus, Occultus, the first Adam who was concealed; so the Orphic Phanes who was both the Holy Spirit, and the Messiah, was styled the hidden; and Jesus was reproved by his own relations, for concealing himself, and not manifesting his royal nature before all. *His brothers therefore said unto him: Depart hence, and go into Judæa; because thy disciples also may see the works that thou doest. For there is no man that doeth anything in secret, and he himself seeketh to be known openly: if thou do these things, shew thyself to the world. For not even did his own brothers believe in him.* John vii. 3. Jesus was chary, above all other things, of announcing his divine character to men; either, because this is a characteristic of the Messiah, or the time did not seem ripe for him to do so. Adam means strictly in Hebrew, the two natures; or as the biblicals say, it applies to both sexes; but it really alludes to the heavenly and the terrestrial combined in the celestial Messenger to man. Parkhurst also says that the name Adam may be derived from כדמרת *Cedemut*, signifying likeness of God, and between this and Kadmon there is scarcely any difference. The reader who chooses to examine this and the other analogies pointed out, thoroughly, will have little doubt resting on his mind. Kadmos, Kam, Kamillos and Kasmillos were old sacred names; Creuzer admits that the last was a Hermes, or Heavenly Messenger; Kam is the Indian Kam Diva or Cupid, who is in reality but a name for the Messiah. Thus the Cupid of the Persians, appears seated on a *Rainbow* in the front of one of the rock temples of Mihr, or the Holy Spirit; and the Cupid of the Greeks and Romans, who was also a symbol of the Incarnation, is represented either floating on the ocean in a shell, or riding on the back of a *fish*, or gliding over the Waters in a cup, the Argha of the Hindus, while he expands his sail to the zephyrs. The scholiast on Apollonius, (*Argonaut* I.,) says, curiously enough, Κασμιλος ὁ Ερμης εστιν. Casmilus is Hermes the Interpreter; which we know was a Messianic name. This Kasmilus, Bochart makes to be the same as *Chadmel* חרמאל, which means Minister of God: the difference between this and Kadmon Adam, the Indian Adim आदिम, or the First, and Adn, is so trivial, that no philologist will question their identity.

47. The scholiast on Lycophron, does not hesitate to say that Cadmus was but a name for Hermes the Heavenly Messenger: Phavorinus makes the same admission; and Nonnus, says that in his Four Books, "the prophetic hand of the first born Phanes, (query, Oannes) wrote all the wonderful things that are to be accomplished in this world"—a clear allusion to the Apocalypse. He adds that the first of these books was coeval with the first times of civilization; and that it contained all that the sceptre-bearing Oph-Ion, [Serpent-Woman, or God and the Spirit], had permitted. These are singular passages. I cite them from Bryant's Analysis; where also he inti-

mates that the Sun was styled Achad, Achon and Achor ;
and expresses his opinion that the name Cadmos is a compound of Achad-Ham (or Adam), which the Greeks have
thus altered, as they altered all foreign words. This Oph-
Ion, is the same work, as that which Pherecydes introduced among his followers. See *ante*, page 255.

48. The reader will not fail to notice the references to
cut gems which are scattered throughout the Apocalypse ;
and especially to the diamond. This gem was called
thenceforth by pre-eminence the Adamant ; *Adamas-
gemma*. There are no existing memorials from which information may be obtained, says Maurice, *History of Hindostan*, i. 478, relative to the period of the first discovery
and working of the mines in the neighbourhood of the
Adamas river, so denominated from the diamonds found
on its shores. It probably goes back to that of the foundation of the Indian empire, *if not to the remotest annals
of time.* Might he not have added that it was denominated from the first Messiah ?

49. Manetho notices a *Sacred Book* in the great Egyp-
tion Library of Osymandias ; and which was said to have
been written by Phre Suphis—or the Wise One of the
Sun. Its contents were not disclosed to any one, except
the High Pontiff. Colonel Tod, in his annals of Rajasthan, an enormous province almost unexplored, in the
most remote part of India, speaks of Jesulmer, (anagra-
matically Jerusalem, the Jews being originally Yadûs
from Yodiah or Oude,) as a place of great antiquity and
in a peculiar manner sacred among the Buddhists. Of the
vast number of MS. books in its extensive libraries, many
are of the most dark antiquity, and in a character no longer
understood by their possessors, or only by the Supreme

N

Pontiff, and his initiated librarians. There is one volume held so sacred for its contents, that it is suspended by a chain of gold in a golden casket in the Temple of Chōōnt Amōōn (Kûnt-Amûn, that is, the *Hidden Tabernacle*), in the desert, and it is only taken down to have its covering renewed, or at the inauguration of a Pontiff. It is believed that any person reading it, would be instantly struck blind. Some time ago, says Higgins, *Anacalypsis*, i. 412, the prince of the country caused it to be brought to him in order that he might read it; but his courage failed, and he sent back the Volume unopened. It bears the traditionary name of Soma-dit-ya Sooroo Acharya (the Moon-born Incarnation of the Sun), and I have no doubt that it is the Apocalypse of Adam, and it is probably written in the primeval language.

50. Nor is it in Jesulmer alone that we should expect to find a secret volume of this nature. I entertain a conviction that there are copies of it in Samarcand; but as that Great City is sealed against Europeans, years may elapse before it shall be brought to light. I once had hope that I should travel thither, and explore both it and Benares; but circumstances have not favoured me, and it is now too late to do so. The reader may surmise from the following letter written from Samarcand, and which appears in that always respectable publication the *Standard* newspaper, of January 25, 1866, what choice treasures exist in the library belonging to the Mahwee, or Temple of the Mysteries :—At length, the writer says, the dangers and privations which I underwent in travelling to this city have been amply rewarded. I have to-day for the first time been permitted to enter the sacred precincts of the Mahwee, or Temple of

Mysteries, and I have become acquainted with Seh.
Your readers can have no conception of the difficulties that
beset me on every side ; but fortune has befriended me
thus far, and I hope ere long to return to England
richly laden with the treasures of Tartar literature and
science.   At the same time, I cannot but be aware of
the chances that militate against the success of my undertaking ; and therefore I think it advisable as often
as any opportunity presents itself, to send you some
small instalment of the riches which I have amassed.
I have said that I to-day became acquainted with Seh.
He is a man fitted in every respect to elicit the utmost
admiration from all who are so fortunate as to share
his regards ; for in goodness of heart and urbanity of
manner he is as conspicuous as in philosophical attain-
ments.   I conversed with him for some hours, and he
was at the pains to make me understand the whole
arrangement of the Mahwee, over which establishment
he presides.   He also showed me the library which is
under the same roof, and which contains *such store of
rare and priceless volumes, that I know not whether I
was more pleased at the sight of so great an accession to
the civilized world's knowledge, or chagrined at the thought
of its too probable inaccessibility.*   I found there many
classical works with which we are acquainted, both ancient and modern—a fact which I regarded with sentiments of the liveliest admiration, seeing that the possession of these noble writings had apparently done
nothing to ameliorate the condition or extend the civil-
isation of Tartary.   Upon my mentioning this matter to
Seh, he smiled somewhat mournfully, and said—" My
friend, we gladly adopt whatever truth may flow in upon

us from the outer world, but we care not to emulate your
greed of gain.   Lest, therefore, our people should seek
after a condition for which they are ill-adapted, we
preserve our stores of wisdom in the Mahwee, and reveal
it but to the philosopher.   Reflect upon the state of
the masses in your civilised Europe, and tell me if you
perceive that superiority over Tartary which your words
would seem to imply.   Here, as you have doubtless observed, they who are born but to misery soon find a safe
retreat in the black night of death, where they may
securely travel to the Unknown.   In Europe would they
not be compelled to live, a burden to themselves and a reproach to their fellows?" I was struck with this answer, and
I could not but reflect that there might be more equality
of happiness amongst various nations than would   at
first sight appear, and that an increase of physical comfort in some classes of a nation might not be an unmixed
good, if necessarily accompanied by a universal accession
of mental feeling, which would render the perception of
all misery much more keen.   Amongst other notable
objects in this library I came across several works which
have for ages been a fruitful source of regret with all
scholars, such as Sanchoniathon's "History of Phœnicia,"
and Quintilian's "Treatise on the Causes of the Corruption of Eloquence."   I intend, as soon as practicable, to
furnish you with a complete list of these hitherto lost
works, but in anticipation of that purpose I must here
add that Seh exhibited to me a complete MS. of "Tacitus,"
containing the whole of that celebrated historian's 30 books.
Surely this fact alone will be sufficient to produce an expedition to Samarcand for the purpose of obtaining so
inestimable a work !

51. The Druses, says *Nimrod*, as our great traveller Mr. Pococke, was told, have a silver box closed in such a manner as not to be opened, and many of them know not what it contains. They pay a sort of worship to it; and his informant believed that it contained images of the nature of both sexes. iii. 386. His informant was wrong. The silver box contains the Apocalypse: probably with symbols of the Great Father and the Great Mother; certainly with the mention of the Two Powers—God, and the Holy Spirit. And this copy, if it could be procured, would no doubt agree in all things with mine.

52. As Adam was the first man to whom an ecstatical Vision was ever given, or who beheld the glories of heaven, (*And* God, the ALMIGHTY POWERS *caused a profound ecstacy to fall upon the Man, and he slept.* GEN. ii. 2) (9), it was therefore fabled that he dwelled in the Garden of Paradise. After he had tasted the Fruit of the Tree, he left it; that is when he got the Apocalypse, or Knowledge, ecstacy departed. Augustine, alluding to this, in his commentary on Genesis, says: That divine trance which God sent on Adam, when he dreamed a Vision in his sleep, is rightly understood to mean that it was sent to this end that his mind might participate in the angelic wisdom; and, entering into the sanctuary (Shekinah), of God, might understand the very limits of knowledge. To what can this apply but to this Apocalypse? and is not the very Shekinah of God here mentioned in a way that to those whom I have so far initiated into celestial science, must be as plain as the sun itself?

53. That a mystic meaning was intended to be conveyed by the compiler of Genesis, when he alluded to the

Garden, is clear from the words of the most learned of the Hebrew doctors. It is part of the foundations of the law, says Maimonides, to know that God may cause the sons of men to prophecy. Now prophecy can rest only on an eminently wise man, who has the power of ruling his propensities, with whom no bad imagination has any prevalence whatever in this world, but who by his knowledge is always able to overcome his bad imagination, and who, moreover, is a man of a very extensive and well-regulated mind. The man who is replete with such virtues, and whose bodily constitution too is in a perfect state, on his entering into the GARDEN (10), and on his being carried away by those great and extensive matters, if he have a correct knowledge so as to understand and comprehend them—if he continue to keep himself in holiness—if he depart from the general manner of the people who walk in the darkness of temporary things ; if he continue to be solicitous about himself, and to train his mind, so that it should not think at all of any of those perishable things, or of the vanities of time and its devices, but that it should have its thoughts constantly turned on high, and fastened to the Throne of Glory, so as to be able to comprehend those pure and holy Intelligences, and to meditate on the wisdom of the Holy One, blessed be He ! which wisdom is displayed throughout from the first Intelligence even to the centre of the earth : and if by these means he come to know His Excellency, then the Holy Spirit dwells immediately with him ; and at the time when the *Spirit* rests on him, his soul mixes with the degree of those angels that are called *Ishim* (angelic men), so that he is changed into another man.

Moreover, he himself perceives from the state of his knowledge that he is not, as he was, but that he has become exalted above the degree of other wise men.

54. And as the Holy Spirit was a Garden, so she was called the Garden of Paradise. Hence, when it disappeared from earth the early Fathers said that Paradise was in the Moon, which was but another name for that Divine Being. One of the Homeridæ calls Elysium Hermione, that is Hermes and Yoni, where the Messenger lives, star-like (*ante* p. 46), with his followers under the sway of the Holy Spirit. The gardens which Jupiter Ammon gave to the mother of Bacchus, are called in Pausanias, The Garden of Dionusos ; and Dionusos means the Soul (part of the essence) of God. And in those gardens stood a Mount Meru, resembling the horn of an Ox, and styled the Hesperian horn. It produced vines and every delicious fruit, and among others golden apples. And as all being first appeared in the North (see Apocalypse, section 4), Paradise was sometimes fabled to have been carried back thither : the Egyptians called it Saïs, and placed it there : not, says Proclus, because it is so, nor because its climate is cold, but because *it partakes of a certain peculiar emanation from God.* So Mount Meru, according to the Puranas, is a glorious habitation lying to the north of India. They sometimes mention places again to the north of Meru, and yet they continually speak of it as being the North Pole itself. The reason of these contradictions will appear from the very reason of the North being held *sacred.* Giordano Bruno thus mystically alludes to this, and calls it the North, the Great Bear, the place where the sailors (the faithful) take counsel in the devious and uncertain ways

of the sea ; towards which all those who suffer tempests lift up their hands in their distress (Ave Maris Stella, as they say in Italy); towards which the ambition of the Giants aspired (alluding to the attack made by the Dragon on the Woman. See Apocalypse, section 8): the place where the proud generation of Belus piled up the Tower of Babel (that is, introduced the worship of the Dove); where the magicians of the steel mirror (those Initiated into the Greater Mysteries) seek the oracles of Floron, one of the great princes of the Arctic spirits; where, the Cabbalists say, that Samael wished to exalt his throne in order to assimilate himself to the First High-thunderer. So the Hebrew writer : *Beautiful for situation, the joy of the whole earth, Mount Zion on the sides of the north : the city of the Great King,* Ps. xlviii. 2. And the reader is requested to examine the glowing picture of this Garden of Delight, which he will find in the last five sections of the Apocalypse, and he will find it correspond with the general description of the ancient theosophists.

55. From the most ancient times among the Hebrews it was a tradition that Adam wrote a *Book of Revelations.* In the twenty-first chapter of *Avodath Hakkodesch,* we read as follows : The theologists or divines say that the angel Rasiel was Adam's instructor or teacher. When he was in paradise (in ecstacy), this Angel brought him from heaven a Book, by means of which he conceived mighty things concerning the higher spheres, and which things had not been shewn, nor had they even been imagined by the Angels of the Most High. And the archangelic Spirits assembled before him to hear the deep and wonderful secrets which were revealed in that Book. In the Book of Sohâr, at the *Parasha Beresith,* there is

another account. When Adam was in Paradise, God sent him by the holy angel Rasiel, who is placed over the secrets (or learning) of the upper or chief Spirits, a Book containing the writing or wisdom of the superior Angels. And he, Adam, divided or digested the seventy different kinds of wisdom into a hundred and seventy discourses of the sublime science, in order to attain by means of the Book to the scripture of wisdom : and to know the fifteen hundred keys, which it was not given to the upper saints to know, and which were kept secret in that Book, until the time of Adam. When the Book was given to Adam, the higher angels assembled before him to hear and to know the contents thereof. In the same hour the holy Angel Adarniel came to him and said, *Adam ! Adam, the Glory of thy Lord was hidden : for the Archangels are not permitted to know the Glory of thy Lord : But to thee it is permitted to know all.* This Book was kept concealed by Adam till he went out of Paradise : and every day he made use of this treasure of his Lord. And he knew the sublime secrets which the archangels of God, holy and blessed be his name, knew not. But when he had transgressed, and had departed from the commandment of his Lord, the Book departed from him, and he beat on his forehead and wept. Then God made a sign to Raphael, and permitted that the Book should be again given unto Adam. And Adam neglected not to read it : and he left it to Sheth, and from one generation unto another it descended to Abraham, who by means thereof beheld the Glory of the Lord.

56. The Rabbinical writings likewise mention a certain *Staff*, which was given to Adam. This staff I take to be

the same as the Tsabæan Tree of golden leaves, and these golden leaves were the Apocalypse of revealed wonders. Rabbi Eliezer relates as follows. The staff which was created between the stars (that is, in the evening), was given to the first man in Paradise. Adam gave it to Enoch : Enoch to Noah : Noah to Shem : Shem to Abraham : Abraham to Isaac : Isaac to Jacob. Jacob carried it along with him into Egypt, and gave it to his son Joseph. When Joseph died, his household of goods were seized and carried to the palace of Pharaoh, who was well skilled in enchantments. When Pharaoh saw the staff, and read the inscription upon it, he set an esteem upon the staff, and planted it in the midst of the garden, which belonged to the house of Jethro. He only [that is Pharaoh] might view and *read* this staff. No other man ventured to come near it. But Moses, when he was come into the house of Pharaoh entered the garden of Jethro ; and seeing the staff, and *having read what was inscribed thereon,* he laid hold of it, and carried it away. When afterwards Jethro saw Moses, he said, This man will deliver Israel out of Egypt; and under this conviction he gave him his daughter Zipporah to wife. In *Medras Vijoscha* there is a different account. Here the Staff becomes a *Tree,* which puts forth almonds, that is, symbols of the Holy Spirit of God. When I was grown, says Moses, I went out to see the oppression of my brethren, and I saw an Egyptian man strike a Hebrew man—one of my brethren ; I struck him dead, and buried him in the sand. When Pharaoh heard of this he intended to take away my life ; and by his order, a sword being brought, he endeavoured to slay me with it ten times. But the Holy and Blessed God wrought a miracle, for my neck became as hard as a marble pillar, and the sword had no power over me. And then I made my escape to Jethro, who caused me to be kept seven years bound in prison. When I went out of Egypt I was forty years old. And as I stood near a well, I beheld Zipporah, Jethro's daughter. And when I had seen that she was chaste, I told her that I would marry her. Then did she acquaint me with her father's custom, saying to me : My Father tries at a certain Tree, which he has in his garden, every one who has a mind to marry one of his daughters : for, as soon as the suitor comes near the Tree, he is swallowed up. Whereupon I asked her whence that Tree was brought. And she answered me : The Holy and Blessed God gave to the first man the *Staff*, which He created in the evening of the Sabbath. The first man gave it to Enoch : Enoch to Noah : Noah to Shem : Shem to Abraham : Abraham to Isaac : and Isaac to Jacob. Jacob brought it into Egypt, and gave it to his son Joseph. After the death of Joseph, the Egyptians plundered his house, and carried his Staff to the palace of Pharaoh. Jethro was one of the greatest magicians in Egypt. He saw the Staff, and having a great fancy for it, stole it, and brought it into his house. On this Staff was cut the *Schem hamphurash*, שם, (*Name*), חם, (*Sun and Lord*), פרהש. (*Branch of Fire.*) (11.) And in it were inscribed the ten plagues [which the Holy and Blessed God suffered to come upon Egypt.] It was kept many years in my father's house, till at length he took it in his hand, and went into the garden, and put it into the ground : and when he entered the garden again, with an intent to take it away, he saw that it had sprouted, and blown, and had ripe almonds on it. He left it standing, and therewith he is accustomed to try every one who seeks a daughter of his in marriage. I have no doubt that the meaning of all this is, that Jethro had a copy of the Apocalypse, which, being one of the pontiffs of Egypt, he would necessarily possess; and knowing that the Naros was come, he presented it to every suitor of his daughter to expound its mysteries, being well assured that if it should fall into the hands of the real Messenger, he would have no real difficulty in explaining its meaning; and to him he was resolved to give his daughter. This would be in accordance with all that we know of the subtlety of the high priests of Egypt. Moses was able to expound it, for being himself one of the Branches of Fire, he knew of course of all that was prefigured, and so we find him succeeding in his marriage suit.

57. The same symbol of a Sceptre (meaning the Apocalypse), is commemorated by Pausanias. The Chæroneans, he says, venerate above all the gods, the *Sceptre* which Homer says Vulcan made for Jupiter. This sceptre *Hermes* (the Messenger) received from Jupiter, and gave it to Pelops. Pelops left it to Atreus: Atreus to Thyestes; and from Thyestes it came to Agamemnon. This sceptre, too, they denominate *the Spear;* [Hence Minerva is always represented with a Spear—in reality it is the sacred Apocalypse;] and indeed that *it contains something of a nature more divine than usual is evident from hence, that a certain splendour is seen proceeding from it.* There is not however any temple publicly raised for this *Sceptre;* but every year the person to whose care this *Sacred Sceptre* is committed, places it in a building destined for this purpose; and the people sacrifice to it every day. And it was in furtherance of all

these disguises that the Holy Book was called the Brazen Tripod of Pelops, which contained the knowledge of things past, present, and to come.

58. Although little is preserved in history of the Sibylline books, enough remains to excite our curiosity as to what they really were. The legend of their introduction to Tarquin is related thus by Niebuhr. An old woman Amalthæa (12), had offered to sell the king nine books for three hundred pieces of gold : being treated with scorn, she burned three, and then three more, and threatened to destroy the others, unless she received the same price for them which she had asked for all. The King repented him of the incredulity which had lost him the greater part of an irreplaceable treasure : the prophetess gave him the last three books and vanished. They were deposited in the Capitoline Temple in the Cell of Jupiter, and there they were preserved until the Marsic war, in a stone chest, under the guardianship of Decemviri. When the Temple was burned either intentionally or accidentally in the 173d Olympiad, they were destroyed by the fire with the other sacred offerings. Fresh copies were subsequently procured from Samos and Troy. That they were a national possession of peculiar sanctity, says Sir G. C. Lewis, (*Credibility of early Roman Hist.* i. 514,) and that their antiquity was considerable, cannot be doubted ; it is also highly probable that an account of their introduction was preserved among the pontifical records—but that the account was contemporary with the event we have no proof ; and it is to be observed that in this, as in other cases, the legend fluctuates between the two Tarquins. After they had been consumed, says Niebuhr, in the time of Sylla, the guardians of them

may have ventured to tell, what previously could not cross their lips. Whether they contained presages of coming events, or merely directions what was to be done for conciliating or appeasing the gods, is perplexing, owing to the mystery which enveloped these books from the time when Tarquinius condemned a decemvir to suffer the punishment of a parricide for blabbing. [*Dionysius,* iv. 62; *Val Max.* 1, 1. 13]. That much of this is mythical cannot be doubted; but who can deny that there is a substratum of truth at the bottom, and that these books appeared to be so valuable, that death was the punishment for any violation of secresy with respect to their contents? Varro relates that they were written on palm leaves, and partly in verses, *partly in symbolical hieroglyphics.* They were assuredly mysterious in the highest degree. It is related by Livy that in B C. 293, in consequence of the mortality caused by pestilence, the Sibylline books were consulted, and the response obtained was that Æsculapius should be brought to Rome. But Æsculapius (the Healer) was a name for the Messiah; and the meaning of this is that the Romans should avert the wrath of heaven by reverting to the true religion. Lewis, Arnold, and Niebuhr talk here about a sacred serpent and a tame snake, than which nothing can be more trifling or ridiculous, though it is quite worthy of the believers in Genesis. The latter says: It is true if these *books of fate,* by order of which more than once in seasons of perilous warfare, two Greeks and two Gauls, a man and woman of each people were buried alive, were the Sibylline books, as Plutarch conceives, then what went by that name among the Romans, can never have come from a Greek source. No one had ever asserted that they did so come. All

that has been alleged is that they were transcribed in
Greek. I myself entertain no doubt that these books
were the Apocalypse, and that they contained as here, the
secret of the Naros, else why should Tarquin sacrifice the
man who divulged them? It is true that they do not
name Æsculapius, nor prescribe a blood-atonement, but
the first was only a symbol ; and the last was common to
every form of religion then prevalent; and the Apocalypse
contains words which might be so interpreted. And if
the priests wanted a human vicarious sacrifice, they would
of course declare to the people that they took the command from their sacred hidden volume of truth, and
probably cite the passage which they misrepresented or
misunderstood.

59. These Sibylline volumes may possibly have in fact
contained the very threats that are in the vulgar book of
Revelations : and which are so evidently a sacerdotal
interpolation. *If any man shall add unto these things,*
God shall add unto him the plagues that are written in
this book : and if any man shall take away from the words
of the book of this prophecy God shall take away his part
out of the book of life, and out of the holy city, and from
the things which are written in this book. And these very
threats may have been produced by the priests to justify
the sacrifice of the man who made the public acquainted
with their contents.

60. The present things which pass under the name of
Sibylline Oracles are of course spurious. As for the
Sibylline oracles, says Cudworth, there may, as we conceive, be two extremes concerning them ; one in swallow-
ing down all that is now extant under that title, as genuine
and sincere. Whereas nothing can be more manifest

than that there is much counterfeit and suppositious stuff in this Sibylline farrago which now we have. From whence besides other instances of the like kind, it appears too evident to be denied, that some pretended Christians of former times have been for pious and religious frauds, and endeavoured to uphold the truth of Christianity by figments and forgeries of their own devising—which, as it was a thing, ignoble and unworthy in itself, and argued that those very defenders of Christianity did themselves distrust their own cause, so may it well be thought that there was a policy of the devil in it also, there being no other more effectual way than this, to render all Christianity, at least in after ages to be suspected. Insomuch that it might perhaps be questioned whether the truth and divinity of Christianity appear more in having prevailed against the open force and opposition of its professed enemies, or in not being at last smothered and oppressed by these frauds and forgeries of its seeming friends and defenders. (*Intel. Syst.* i. 463).

61. In the Book of *Joshua*, x. 13, there is a passage which rightly explained proves that the Apocalypse was known in his day, and was the Secret Book laid up in the ark. *And the sun stood still, and the moon stayed until the people had avenged themselves upon their enemies. Is not this written in the Book of Jasher?* Parkhurst, the highest Biblical authority on Hebrew, says, that this is wrongly translated, and that the version of the Seventy is the true rendering του βιβλου του ευθους, the *Book of the Right Road*, and to this purpose Josephus explains it, *Ant.*, lib. v., cap. i., s. 17, by, των ανακειμενων εν τω ιερω γραμματων, *the writings that were laid up in the sacred place.* But what were those writings? Why the Apoca-

lypse : and here is the very passage in the Apocalypse to which Joshua alludes, and on which probably he based his creed of extermination. *And I saw an Angel standing in the sun, and he cried with a loud voice, saying to all the fowls that fly in the midst of heaven, Come and gather yourselves together unto the supper of the great God. That ye may eat the flesh of Kings, &c., &c.* And the primeval theory probably was that the Sun stood still, while the battle of the heavenly Messenger continued.

62. Taliesin thus alludes to a Sacred Volume which the Druids had. A holy *Sanctuary* there is, with its productions, of the vessel of Kêd. I possessed myself of its courses which I had made my choice. *I will not disclose the progress of the law which I religiously observe. The writings of Prydain* (Hu, the Sun, also Father Adam) *are the first objects of anxious regard;* should the waves disturb their foundation, I would again, if necessary, *conceal them deep in the cell.* We may gather from this, says Davis, that the Druids had certain Ancient Writings, which they deemed more sacred by far, and of greater importance, than those songs and tales which were made public. These writings had already been concealed in times of persecution, probably during the Roman government; and they were known only to the Druids, or Bards of the highest order; for Taliesin tells us that in case of necessity he possessed the effectual means of concealing them *again.* We can only guess in general that these arcana comprehended the Sacred History, and Rituals of the Druids, and the most mysterious doctrines of the ancient priesthood. (*British Druids,* 511.) But does this correctly describe the hidden volume? and do we not see the analogy between Pri-Adain and Adanos? Hear Taliesin

himself, who in another place writes : Am I not contending for the praise of that lore, if it were regarded, which
was four times reviewed in the quadrangular inclosure?
As the first sentence was it uttered from the cauldron,
which began to be warmed by the breath of nine damsels.
Is not this the cauldron of the Ruler of the deep? What
is its quality? With the ridge of pearls round its border
it will not boil the food of a coward, who is not bound by
his sacred oath. Against him will be lifted the bright
gleaming sword; and in the hand of the sword-bearer shall
he be left; and before the entrance of the Gate of Hell
shall the horns of light be burning. The Bard here insists
upon the peculiar sanctity of the lore which he taught:
it had been four times revised in the sacred call or Ady-
tum, before it was uttered as *the first sentence,* the first revelation or fundamental doctrine of the mystical cauldron
of Ceridwen, or the Holy Spirit, the Queen of the Waters.
This cauldron had first been warmed by the breath of
Nine damsels, that is, Nine Spirits pure and beautiful as
virgins. The same cauldron communicated science, wisdom, virtue, happiness, and even immortality, but it would
not prepare the food of the coward. Observe, too, the
execration upon him who violated secrecy, and did not
keep his sacred oath not to divulge the hallowed volume;
and comparing it with the curse in the Apocalypse, as
added to it by the priests (*ante,* page 279), the similarity is so remarkable as to lead to a conclusion that
the Writings of the Sun are but another name for the
Apocalypse of him who was said to be the child of the
Sun and Moon—the inspired Messenger of Heaven.

63. My original country, says Taliesin, alluding to the
ante-terrestrial existence of all beings, is the *Land of Che-*

rubim. (See Gunn's *Nennius*, p: 41.) Can there be a plainer reference to the Apocalypse, as we now have it? More he could not say without breaking his oath or vow of secrecy; and we have already seen (*ante*, page 70), what that involved. To which this other proof may here be added, that it was for divulging the secret of the Phen, or Naros, that Phineus was blinded by Zeus; and his banquets were beset by the pestiferous Harpyes. Pitying the human race, he says (*Val. Flaccus*, iv., 479), with foolish tongue *I divulged the destinies and the counsel of Jove,* and the hidden designs about to fall suddenly on the earth, which He alone had prepared: hence this so great misfortune has fallen upon me, and I was stricken blind in the midst of my discourse.

64. Another passage may be cited to show that the volume of which Taliesin speaks, contained the Naronic cycle. I will not redeem the multitudes *with unguarded mouths* (who cannot keep a secret.) They know not on what day the *Chief* was appointed; or what hour in the serene day the *Ruler* was born; or what *Living Creature* it is which the Silver-headed Ones protect. Is not this a clear allusion to the Incarnation—the King of the Earth? The silver-headed are the Ancient of Days mentioned in the Apocalypse: and the Welsh even to the present day symbolize their expected Messiah under the name of King Arthur—a personage whose era is many centuries before their fabulous Arthur of the Round Table, with whom they confound him, and who is in reality Ar (Fire), and Thor (Thunder). That Arthur was a name for the Messiah is *proved* by the following passage in Taliesin, in a poem called *Kadair Teyrn On*—the Throne of the Sovereign On. The declaration of the luminous strain, it says, of

the unbounded *Awen*, concerning the person of two origins, of the race of Al-Adar, אל אדר (*the Glorious God*), with his divining staff (*or caduceus*), and his pervading glance, and his neighing coursers, and his regulator of Kings, and his *potent number*, aud his blushing purple, and his vaulting over the boundary, and his appropriate throne among the established train. Lo! he is brought from the firm enclosure (the firmament of Heaven), on his light-coloured bounding steeds—even the sovereign On, the Ancient, the generous Giver, the profound object of the Sage, to pronounce the blessing upon Arthur. "The person of two origins," here mentioned, taken together with all the other features of the Messenger which I have pointed out in various places, is obviously no other than one of the predicted Twelve, the lion-like Lamb. But where did the Pagan Welsh get the tradition, if not from the Apocalypse? Manifest is truth, adds Taliesin, when it shines: more manifest when it speaks, and loud it spoke when it came forth from the cauldron of Awen, ardent Goddess! Can there be a clearer allusion than this, to the Messenger who emanates from the Spirit?

65. In that strange cento, or compilation from I know not how many writers or their fragments, which passes under the name of Isaiah, there are numerous passages which belong to the true Apocalypse, and which have been incorporated with the effusions of the various Jew scribes who forged the Prophecy in the most clumsy manner. The work has only to be read *critically*, to make manifest what I mean. It should be perused also without reference to the notes, or epigraphs to the chapters. These indeed, have usually been made by the two

rival churches of Peter and Paul, the vehicle for the
most impudent falsehoods ; and so many glosses have been
foisted into the Hebrew and Greek text, and thence into
our modern versions, that a plain reader who has not
learning or time enough to investigate these may well be
deceived. And this unfortunately happens every day :
and I have no doubt that many ignorant persons will
hastily cite against me and this Apocalypse the very passages from Isaiah which I know to be false, and on the
consideration of which I have devoted years and years
of the hardest labour. In illustration of this I may
allude to that passage in the Seven Thunders, where
reference is made to the change in the earth's orbit
which undoubtedly was the cause of the great Atlantean deluge. Of this scientific phenomenon, the Jews
knew nothing : but as it was contained in one of the
most remarkable passages in the Apocalypse, the Hebrew priest, or the body of compilers, boldly seized and
transferred it to their spurious Isaiah, where it has long
puzzled the biblical commentators. So also the other
prophecies which constituted the sealed-up *Seven Thunders* of the Apocalypse, were impudently appropriated,
and by the introduction of names here and there, *forced*
to apply to Ba-Bel-On, Ethiopia, Egypt, Arabia, Persia,
and Tyre, great, powerful, and magnificent dynasties,
thousands of miles removed away from Judea, and
which had as little connection with that paltry and in-
significant province, and its proceedings, as we in England have with the land of the Mormons, or the French
empire has with some little island of unknown savages
in the remotest ocean. Yet what would be thought
of the Mormons, or the cannibals, who had prophets

by profession, who were always predicting the fall of France and her Emperor, or England and its throne? This is exactly what we are taught these Jews were doing : yet we do not laugh at them as fools or knaves. The truth is that at the period when the forged Hebrew Testament was compiled, the great dynasties above mentioned had had their day ; but the priests finding in the Apocalypse predictions in which a fate like theirs had been announced, and knowing that these predictions had been *sealed up* from the world, and only in the hands of a very few, they transferred the prophecies from the genuine Book of God, and his First Messenger, into their own wretched figments, and thus gave them an appearance of authenticity which they otherwise would not have possessed. And to a critical eye, it is as easy to discover these splendid interpolations amid their narrow-thoughted nonsense, as gold may be distinguished from brass. Let the reader compare *Isaiah* xiv., 9—23, with the two absurd chapters that follow, and he will see that they *could* not have emanated from the same pen. Other instances may be found. See chap. xxxiv., 9—15, which in verse 16 is almost admitted to be extracted from the *Book of the Lord*, that is this Apocalypse. But readers read, and they strenuously refuse either to consider or compare, and the result is, the supremacy of superstition, pontiffs in palaces, bishops on thrones, and—their own ruin.

66. But though the Jews appropriated to themselves portions of the Apocalypse, they did not then venture to publish it as a whole ; the oaths which they had taken not to divulge it operated probably on their fears, or, let us hope, their consciences. But they made extracts from

it occasionally ; and accordingly we find in their writings numerous passages which have little or no connection with the surrounding text. In this way, a considerable part of it having been divulged, the persons who gave the remainder to the world under the title of Ioannes, probably considered that they were breaking no engagement in publishing a part under a fictitious name; and as they were, perhaps, Christians—though, of this there is no proof—ecclesiastical history satisfies us that since the world began there was not a more profligate crew of forgers and liars than the first followers of Paul. From such corrupt sources, therefore, everything must be received with suspicion ; and if the sect of Christians really knew what their forefathers in the faith were, they would have very different views of religion from those which they now hold.

67. Nicephorus Callistus, *lib.* 10, cxxxiii., gives an account of an ancient manuscript found under the foundation of the Jerusalem Temple, in a nearly similar position to that in which the Sibylline Books were hidden at Rome. At the time, he says, when the foundation was laid, one of the stones to which the lowest part of the foundation was attached, was removed from its place, and discovered the mouth of a cavern which had been hollowed out of the rock. Now since they could not see to the bottom on account of its depth, the overseers of the work, wishing to be perfectly acquainted with the place, let down one of the workmen by means of a long rope into the cavern. When he came to the bottom he found himself in *water* as high as his ancles, and examining every part of the cavern, he found it to be square as far as he could ascertain by feeling. He afterwards

searched nearer the mouth of the cavern, and on examination discovered a low *pillar*, very little higher than the
water, and having placed his hand upon it, he found lying
there a *Book*, carefully folded in a piece of thin and clean
linen. This Book he secured, and signified by the rope
his wish to be drawn up. On being drawn up he produced the book, which struck the beholders with astonishment, particularly as it appeared perfectly fresh and untouched, though it had been brought out of so dark and
dismal a place. When the book was unfolded, not only
the Jews, but the Greeks also were amazed, as it declared
in large letters, even at its commencement, *In Archa
was the Word, &c.* From this it will be seen that
this Volume was the Apocalypse itself. The cavern also
was curiously symbolic, for the pillar, or Linga, in the
water, typified God and the Spirit, and the book was
the emblem of the Messenger.

68. But this is not the sole conclusion which is to be
deduced from this most important historical fact : for it
demonstrates that the Apocalypse was placed there centuries before the Christian æra, in the palmy days of
Judaism, when a theocratic priesthood had an esoteric
religion, and concealed Ineffable Volumes like those
of India, Egypt, Rome, and all the great centres of
Monotheism. It shews also that the Indian *pulleiar*
or mystic union was part of their creed. The short
preface, *In Archa was the Word, &c.*, could not have
belonged to what is now called the Gospel of John,
for this Book was deposited in this secret crypt hundreds of years before : it was in fact Enoch's introduction to the Apocalypse; and it was upon this brief
exposition of a sublime truth, that Plato founded most of

his tenets; though he could not of course refer to the Apocalypse as their source, for it was the Ineffable Volume of the Mysteries which it was death to divulge if he knew of it: and of which, if he were not Initiated, he could know nothing whatever.

69. Swedenborg, who, though he did not perceive *all* truth, nevertheless was a man who undoubtedly had many Visions from heaven, which he did not always however succeed in interpreting rightly, relates one of these manifestations, in which this incident is startlingly commemorated. That Swedenborg had no idea whatever of the exact truth, regarding the Apocalypse or its true origin, as they are revealed in this Volume, I need scarcely premise: neither does he seem to have had any knowledge of this curious passage in Nicephorus, or else I think he would have cited it. Yet we find him beholding in a Vision, a sight which could have no reference to anything else than the very thing commemorated by that historian. In departing from this place, he says, I found myself with Spirits and Angels who had passed their mortal life *in Great Tartary.* They informed me that they had *from all antiquity* possessed a *Divine Word,* which regulated their worship, and which *was entirely by correspondences* [that is symbols]. These people who worshipped Ieue only, some as an Invisible God, and some as an Invisible Power, dwelt in the spiritual world upon a plain very much elevated in the southern regions bordering upon the eastern. They allow no Christian to be among them; but if any one enter their territories, they retain him, and never suffer him to depart again. They live separate, because they possess another Word or Scripture. *Some angels then told me that Moses took from the Sacred Books*

o

*of these people, the first chapters of Genesis which treat of
the creation of the garden of Eden,* &c. While meditating
upon the Dragon, the Beast and the false Prophet, of
which the Revelations speak, an angel appeared to me
and said : Come, I will shew you into a place where you
shall see those that the Word denotes by the false prophets, and by the Beast issuing out of the earth with two
horns like a lamb, and speaking as a dragon. I followed
him and saw a great body of people, in the midst of which
were prelates, who taught that *faith alone in the merits of
Jesus Christ was sufficient to salvation;* that in order to
govern the simple, it was necessary to preach good works,
though they were not necessary to salvation. One of these
prelates invited me to enter his Temple, that I might
there see an Image which represented his faith, and that
of his adherents. I accordingly entered the Temple which
was magnificent, and in the midst of which a Woman
was represented clothed in purple, holding in her right
hand a golden crown piece, and in her left a chain of
pearls. The statue and the representation were *only
fantastic representations;* for these *infernal spirits* by
closing the interior degree and opening the exterior only,
are able at the pleasure of their imagination to represent
magnificent objects. Perceiving that they were illusions,
I prayed to the Lord. Immediately the interior of my
spirit was opened, and I saw instead of the superb Temple, a tottering house open to the weather from the top to
the bottom. In the place of the Woman-statue, an
Image was suspended having the head of a dragon, the
body of a leopard, the feet of a bear, and the mouth of a
lion ; in short it was the Beast rising out of the sea, as
described in the Apocalypse, xiii. 2. In the place of a

park *there was a marsh full of frogs*, and I was informed that under this marsh there was a great hewn stone beneath which the Word was entirely hidden. Afterwards I said to *the prelate, who was the fabricator of these illusions;* Is that your temple? Yes, replied he, it is. Immediately his interior sight was opened, like mine, and he saw what I did. How now, what do I see? cried he. I told him that it was the effect of *the celestial light, which discovers the interior quality of every thing,* and which taught him at that very moment, what faith separated from good works was. While I was speaking, a wind blowing from the east, destroyed the Temple and the Image, dried up the marsh, and *discovered the stone under which the Sacred Word was concealed.* A genial warmth like that of the spring descended from heaven : and in the place of the Temple we saw a tent, the exterior of which was very plain. I looked into the interior of it and there I saw *the foundation stone beneath which the Sacred Word was concealed,* ornamented with precious stones, the splendour of which diffusing itself over the walls of the Temple, diversified the colours of the paintings which represented cherubims. The angels perceiving me to be filled with admiration, told me that I should see still greater wonders than these. They were then permitted to open the third heaven, inhabited by the Celestial Angels who dwell in love. All on a sudden the splendour of a light of fire caused the Temple to disappear, and left nothing to be seen but the Lord himself, standing upon the foundation stone, the Lord, who was the Word such as he shewed himself, *Rev.* 1. Holiness immediately filled all the interior of the spirit of the Angels, upon which they made an effort to prostrate themselves, but

the Lord shut the passage to the light from the third
heaven, opening the passage to the light of the second,
which caused the Temple to re-appear with the tent in
the midst of it.   (13.)   That the Temple, the foundation
stone, and the Apocalypse mentioned by Nicephorus, were
here revealed in Vision to Swedenborg, seems certain;
but the man whom he mistook for Jesus, was Adam.
The passage is a most singular one : and it affords a remarkable proof of the merely biblical and therefore incorrect mode in which this great Seer occasionally interpreted
the heavenly visions.   In his vision of the Paulite prelates, and their Jezabel Church, he is however perfectly
accurate.

70. It will be seen that in the present edition I have
restored the real name of Oannes (14) to the Apocalypse,
for which that of Ioan was substituted by the papal
priests, who presented it under a modern aspect.   This
name of Oannes in the primal language meant *Divine
Messenger*, like Hermes and Meshoh.   In a fragment gar-
bled from Berosus by the ecclesiastical historian Eusebius,
from whom almost everything must be received with distrust, we have some allusion to this Incarnation : but
strangely altered.   Through its symbolism, however, truth
may be beheld.   In the *first year* there appeared out of
the Red Sea (an ocean of fire), at a place near the con-
fines of Babylonia, a certain irrational animal ($\zeta\tilde{\omega}ov$ $\alpha\phi\rho\epsilon\nu o\nu$,
which is nonsense to write of this Teacher of arts and
sciences—the word should be $\alpha\phi\theta\iota\tau o\nu$, an Immortal Living Creature : Dr. Jackson proposes to read $\zeta\omega o\nu$ $\epsilon\nu\phi\rho o\nu$,
animal sapiens), whose name was Oannes.   His body was
like that of a *fish*, but beneath his fish's head another grew;
(this also is wrong : it really means a man-headed fish like

Vishnu in the Matsyāvatāra, who when a child "*hid himself in the Moon*," Tod. *Rajasthan*, i. 601): he had also feet like a man, which proceeded from the fish's tail, and a human voice, according to the picture of him which was preserved to the time of Berosus. This animal conversed with men in the day without eating anything; he communicated the knowledge of letters, arts, and sciences : he taught men to dwell together in cities : to erect temples : to introduce laws, and instructed them in geometry : he likewise shewed them how to gather seeds and fruits, and, in short, imparted to mankind whatever was necessary and convenient for a civilized life. When the sun set, this Living Creature retired into the sea (the Holy Spirit) again, and stayed there in the night, being of the amphibious kind—that is, a being really of heaven, but fulfilling a mission among mortals. After him, there appeared several other Living Creatures (Messiahs) of the same form. This Oannes did not deliver his instructions by word of mouth only, but wrote of the *Origin of things.* Other authors have also mentioned him. Helladius calls him Oes : and agrees in general with the foregoing account : but adds that he had hands as well as the head and feet of a Man : that it was reported he was produced from the Mundane Egg (the Holy Spirit), as his name 'Ωὸν testified : and that he was in reality only a man, though clothed in the skin of a fish. Hyginus likewise writes that Euhanes, a name not very distant from Oannes (15), came out of the sea in Chaldæa, and explained astrology. All this, it need not be added, is mystical—covertly alluding to the primeval Messenger, whose name is connected with On the Sun, and αἰων τῶν αἰωνων —or Æon of Ages. He is the Indian Ar-yoon, a compound word of Ar, the Sun, and yoon, the Yoni—meaning the One who comes from the union of both : and this is the name of Aaron, and the famous Caliph Haroun, who claimed to be a heaven-descended sovereign. The word Fish is a covert disguise of his sacred origin. The whole world is filled with similar analogies. Suidas says that Æsop, secretary of Mithridates, in his Book on Helene, called Pan (a name like Phanes, sometimes of the Messenger), $i\chi\theta\upsilon\varsigma$ $\kappa\eta\tau\omega\delta\eta\varsigma$, a great, or whale-like fish. Sophocles called him a Wanderer on the Sea. The scholiast on Ajax, 695, says he was a fisherman who entangled the Giant Typhon (the Red Dragon) in his nets and caught him. Pan is Pi-An, and Pæan. In the old Irish, Ischa, which is the Eastern name of Jesus, means Fish, and the Welsh V is our single F. Our FF, is the Welsh F. Ischa with digamma is Fischa. Buddha was called Dag-Po, which was literally the fish Po, or Fish-Buddha. So the Lama of the Christians, the Pope, is not only chief of the Shepherds, but is Chief of the Fishermen, a name which he gives himself, and on this account he carries a fisherman's ring: on this account also the followers of Jesus are said to have been fishermen. Hence, when Empedocles claimed the character of a Divine Messenger, he said that his spirit had formerly sojourned in the body of the fish Hellopus. $\Theta\alpha\mu\nu\text{o}\varsigma$, τ $\text{o}\text{ι}\omega\nu\text{o}\varsigma$, $\tau\epsilon$ $\kappa\alpha\text{ι}$ $\epsilon\text{ι}\nu$ $\alpha\lambda\text{ι}$ $\epsilon\lambda\lambda\text{o}\pi\text{o}\varsigma$ $i\chi\theta\upsilon\varsigma$; a branch of olive, a bird of prey (eagle or vulture), and in the sea, a sword fish. Jesus says to Simon and Andrew, Follow me and I will make you *fishers* of men. *Mark* i. 17. The distinction between the Messianic or peace messengers, and the Cabiric or avenging messengers, is pointed out in Jeremiah xvi. 16. Behold, I will send for many *fishers*, and they shall fish them ; and after I will send forth many *hunters*, and they shall hunt them, from every mountain and from every hill, and out of the holes of the rocks. The mild and peaceful Numator, a priest of Manu, precedes Romulus the conquering king, who is again succeeded by Numa, the mild and gentle. This old mythical legend really alludes to the series of the Messengers—the Messianic and Cabiric: the fishers and the hunters. See *ante*, p. 246, as to the Persic *Pish-va*, or Sovereign Pontiff (16). Upon this mythos, I may add, all the fables of the love of Dolphins for men were founded. Enalus, the Æolian, was saved from drowning by riding on a Dolphin. Melicerta jumped into the sea to escape the rage of Athamas, and was carried by a Dolphin to Corinth. The dead body of the poet Hesiod was carried by Dolphins to the place of the Nemean games, and the life of Ar-Ion, a divine musician, was saved by a Dolphin. He was also noted, like Jesus, for his love of children. A Dolphin preserved a boy from drowning and brought him to Iassus in Caria, but pined away and died for loss of his youthful rider. Pausanias relates that he saw a Dolphin who, out of gratitude to a boy that had cured him of a wound from a fisherman, used to carry the boy upon his back. Note that in the Greek, Delphin, or Dolphin, is a mystical word. See *ante*, p. 166.

71. The Mother of this Oannes was symbolized as a Mermaid, and worshipped as Venus Atergatis—meaning the Holy Spirit. She was said to be the receptacle of all the hero-gods or Messiahs: as the Egyptian Isis comprehended within herself the first rudiments of all things. Moor's *Hindu Pantheon*, 74, 132, 134, 137. Simplicius in Aristot. *de Ans. Phys.* iv. 150. Plutarch, *de Iside*. p.

374. On one of the ancient porticoes of the Church of Notre Dame at Paris, the architect carved the Holy Spirit as a Siren with the body of a woman, and the extremities of a fish. *Banier Mythology*, bk. ii. cap. x. Fecundity was typified by the Fish. Hyginus tells us that an Egg of an immense size was reported to have fallen from heaven into the river Euphrates. While it floated in the sacred stream, Doves perched upon its exterior. Soon, however, it was rolled out to land by *fishes*, and at length it produced Venus. Ampelius relates the same story, but states that only a single dove perched upon the egg, that the Egg itself was produced by a Fish, and that in its turn it produced a Goddess kind and merciful to mortals. The fish that produced the Egg was Venus; for here again, though the Egg and Venus are really the same thing, with a blending not uncommon in ancient mythology, the Goddess appears at once the producer and the produced. These various minglings into One, of names and persons and sexes (called theocrasia), so remarkable in old mythology, intimate the Pantheism and oneness that is universal: all are One, though their manifestations, names, and qualities seem different.

72. That Hercules, who was in the whale's belly for three days, was but, like Ionah, Vishnu, Oannes, another name for the Messiah, is clear to all who have studied the subject. Herodotus tells us that he was one of the most ancient gods whom they worshipped in Egypt; in fact, he was Als-idi, or Adam the son of Jid, one of the Twelve Messengers. The Scyths had a print of his foot upon a rock like that of Buddha; it resembles the footstep of a man, and is two cubits in length, says the father of history, iv. 81. The curiosity of Herodotus was much

excited by these facts, and by what he heard of Hercules in Egypt from the priests. And being desirous, he says, of obtaining certain information from whatever source I could, I sailed to Tyre, in Phœnicia, having heard that there was there a temple dedicated to Hercules: and I saw it richly adorned with a great variety of offerings; and in it were two pillars, one of fine gold; the other of emerald stone; both shining exceedingly at night. Conversing with the priests, I enquired how long this temple had been built; they said that the temple was built at the time when Tyre was founded; and that 2300 years had elapsed since the foundation of Tyre, ii. 44. This makes it 4610 years from the present day; cotemporaneous with the founding of Persepolis. The two pillars in this ancient temple, represented God and the Holy Spirit, though Herodotus does not say so: the former being symbolized by the Golden Pillar, and the Spirit by the Pillar of Emerald, which was the type of the Rainbow. In allusion to this, the Apocalypse was sometimes called *The Table of Emerald*: and in connection with Alcides it was denominated *The Lion's Skin*, and the *Cloak of Stars*: and sometimes the *Pillars of Hercules*, a name afterwards given to a *Rock*. And this we know to have been a sacred word connected with religion. *The Lord is my rock, and my fortress: who is a rock save our God?* Ps. xviii. *Then he forsook God which made him, and lightly esteemed the rock of his salvation.* Deut. xxxii. There were others who called the Apocalypse *The Pillar of Heaven;* a name given to Atlas, who is Enoch.

73. The northern Indians, says Adair, in his chapter, *On the descent of the American Indians from the Jews,*

in the time of their rejoicings repeat Yo-ha-an, which he supposes to be a corruption of their name of God, Yo he-wah ; but which in reality preserves the traditional name of Oannes, the first born of the Sacred Yoni. In their language *Oonna* means, he is come ! a significant allusion to the Messianic teacher. According to Abydenus, Oannes was followed by *Annedotus, Enaboulus, Anementus,* and *Eneugamus,* who explained what *he* had only concisely revealed. The three first of these names are but varia-tions of the second Messenger's name, Enoch, and the last is Nu, and Manu, who is Fohi, the third Heavenly Mes-senger. Fo-hi means Fo the victim, in allusion to what I have stated, *ante* p. 63. Oannes is also the same as Sanconiathon's Protogonos, or the First-born, as he was the first heaven-sent Messenger : and his wife is said to have been Aiŏn, which is said to mean the first who found out the food which is gathered from trees—in other words she was skilled in horticulture. See *ante,* p. 236. The an-cient name for symbolic pictures was *ouen,* and the Chinese letters are called the *kou ouen.* The vehicle of all the Druid magic was a vessel called the cauldron of Ouen, Owen, or Awen, a name explained in Welsh to mean *inspiration* : and the holy city of Boodha was Ouen. Oannes, therefore, must be considered a primitive radical word, which had many meanings, but all sacred and mystic, and pronounced according to its particular signification, Yoni, Ouen, Vau-nus, Faunus, I-On, Oona, &c., &c. See *ante,* p. 76.

74. And as this first Messiah was by some said to be an husbandman, he was called Georgius, or tiller of the ground ; and this became a general name for the Incarna-

tion : hence *Saint* George and the Dragon, like the symbolic Arthur of Wales, was one of his titles. Mantuan describes him,

> Albenti sublimis equo, cui Thracia mater,
> Et pater Astur erat.

high on a white horse, whose mother was of Thrace, and whose father was Astur (a Star). The Arabs aver that he was a warrior of their own sect, and call him Deseleth Tozatzel, or the *Warrior of the White Horse;* and hold him in the highest honour. They also style him Chederles ; and they say of him that he traversed the world on horseback, and discovered the *Waters of Immortality*, of which both he and his horse drank, and from thenceforth they became invisible to human eyes. Nevertheless he rides to and fro on his immortal charger, delighting in battles, and lending his aid to the righteous cause. They further relate that Georgius attended upon Alexander when he conquered the East, and that upon such occasions he brought with him a troop of warlike spirits called Cheders, or Gaiberenleis (Cabirians.) Like most of the Incarnations his fate was sudden : he was stung to death by a dragon of the earth. This Georgius, the Phœnicians called Agruerus, the patron of husbandry : his Messianic character is shewn by his image having a bull's head. Selden, *de Diis Syr.*

75. At Naulakhi in Cashmere a tomb is shewn, where a famous ruler is said to be interred. The Mussulmans call it the tomb of Maiter Lam, that is the Lord Lama, and they say they got this name from the natives. But Lama is a primeval word that signifies the Messiah ; and it was so used by Jesus in his dying moments, when he cried out ; *Eli, Eli, Lama ozebetani,* O God ! my God, thy

Lama is forsaken. This tomb or barrow, therefore, is connected with the heavenly Messenger. The Buddhists say that it is that of Buddha Narayana, or Buddha coming out of the Waters ; and the Brahmins call him Macho-dar-Nath, or the sovereign prince from the Fish's belly. It is manifest that this fish prince is Vishnu in his fish incarnation ; Oannes and the Ionah of the Hebrews, and the Dag-On, of the Philistines. The sepulchre which contains the body of this ancient personage, is about forty cubits long; and under it is a vault of the same dimensions with a small door that out of respect is never opened. Whether this be a real tomb, or only a tradi_tionary one, in which the first Messenger is commemorated, it is impossible to prove ; but it is undoubtedly a very curious relique of the past. Of a similar character to this tomb, was that seen by Benjamin of Tudela in Alexandria. It was of marble near the sea-side, and on it were graven figures of all sorts of birds and beasts, with an inscription in characters so wholly ancient that no man could then (in the 13th century) decypher them. The length of this sepulchre was fifteen, and its width six spans. I believe it to have been a crypt for sacred concealed volumes, and that this in India was for a like purpose. That writings which were considered valuable were deposited in crypts of earth or stone, or in coffers in the ground, is manifested by the following passage in Jeremiah, xxxii. *And Jeremiah said, The word of the Lord came unto me, saying, Behold, Hanameel the son of Shallum, thine uncle shall come unto thee, saying, Buy thee my field that is Anathoth ; for the right of redemption is thine to buy it. So Hanameel mine uncle's son came to me in the court of the prison according to the word of the Lord, and said unto me, Buy my field, I pray thee, that is in Anathoth, which is in the country of Benjamin: for the right of inheritance is thine, and the redemption is thine; buy it for thyself. Then I knew that this was the word of the Lord. And I bought the field of Hanameel my uncle's son, that was in Anathoth, and weighed him the money, even seventeen shekels of silver. And I subscribed the evidence, and sealed it, and took witnesses, and weighed him the money in the balances. So I took the evidence of the purchase, both that which was sealed according to the law and custom, and that which was open: And I gave the evidence of the purchase unto Baruch the son of Neriah, the son of Maaseiah, in the sight of Hanameel mine uncle's son, and in the presence of the witnesses that subscribed the book of the purchase, before all the Jews that sat in the court of the prison. And I charged Baruch before them, saying, Thus saith the Lord of hosts, the God of Israel; Take these evidences, this evidence of the purchase, both which is sealed, and this evidence which is open, and put them in an earthen vessel, that they may continue many days.* And for aught we know, copies of the primeval Apocalypse, may still exist in some of the numerous barrows which remain in various parts of the earth.

76. Herodotus speaks of another mysterious tomb, like this, which was doubtless made with the same object. At Saïs, he says, in the sacred precinct of Minerva, behind the chapel, and joining the whole of the wall, is the Tomb of One whose name I consider it impious to divulge on such an occasion. [No wonder that the name of Adam is so rarely found in history since it was thus held impious to disclose it]. And in the enclosure stand large obelisks,

[monoliths like those at Stonehenge], and there is a *lake* near, ornamented with a stone margin formed in a *circle*. In this lake they perform by night, the representation of that person's adventures, which they call Mysteries : on these matters however, though I am accurately acquainted with the particulars of them, *1 must observe a discreet silence,* ii. 170. I ought to add that he describes the chamber as being adorned with columns made *in imitation of palm trees* : which connects it at once with the Apocalypse ; and with Phen, Phin, and Phænix.

77. The primitive inhabitants of Chile in the extreme south of America many thousand miles from New Spain, had a tradition of this stranger Messiah, declaring that in former times as they had heard their fathers say, a wonderful Man had come to that country wearing a long beard, with shoes, and a mantle such as the Indians carry on their shoulders, who performed many miracles, cured the sick with water, *caused it to rain,* and their crops and grain to grow, kindled fire at a breath, and wrought other marvels, healing at once the sick, and giving sight to the blind : and that he spoke with as much propriety and elegance in the language of their country, as if he had always resided in it, addressing them in words very sweet and new, that the Creator of the Universe resided in the highest place of heaven, and that many men and women who were resplendent as the sun dwelt with him. This is the account given by Rosales. *Mexican Antiquities,* vi. 419. The Japanese Messiah is also sometimes represented under the name of Can-On, (Priest of the Sun), and like Vishnu the lower part of his body seems to be emerging from a fish. He has four arms : his head is crowned with flowers : in one hand he holds a sceptre, in

another a flower, a ring in the third, and the fourth is closed with the arm extended. They image the Holy Spirit, seated on *twelve* cushions, (supporters, that is Messiahs), and placed on the trunk of a large tree which a tortoise supports. She is intensely black, (a symbol of immense antiquity, deep as night itself), crowned with a golden pyramid, and with bosom bare. An enormous Serpent (God) is entwined around this golden image. Tanaquil Faber speaks of a place in the Heliopolitan prefecture in Egypt, denominated Ὀνίου χωρία, the repose of Onius, and the Temple was called *Onieion* or the Temple of Onius. Has not this name a subtle relation to the title Oannes?

78. A similar tradition prevailed in Peru. We are told in the *Ceremonies and Religious Customs of all nations,* iii. 199, that a man of extraordinary shape whose name was *Khoun*, and whose body had neither bones nor muscles came *from the north* into their country; that he levelled mountains, filled up vallies, (was a Messiah), and opened himself a passage through the most inaccessible places. This Khoun formed the first inhabitants of Peru, giving them the herbs and wild fruits of the field for their sustenance. They also relate that this first founder of Peru, having been injured by some savages who inhabited the plains, changed part of the ground which before had been very fruitful into sand, and *forbade the rain to fall and dried up the plants.* But that being afterwards moved with compassion he opened the springs and *suffered the rivers to flow.* The identity of this with some of the Messianic descriptions in the Apocalypse seems plain enough. Khoun is but another form for the Chinese Kûntze for Chiun, the God mentioned in the

Old Testament, and also for Oannes, and Cohen a priest: it contains likewise the elements of Yoni, and On, and Ch or X which belong to the nomenclature of the inspired Messengers of God. In the account given, *Universal History* (vol i, p. 32—34) of the Orphic theology we read that Orpheus taught that the great God Creator, was *Phanes*, (a name taken from פבי יהוה *Pheni Ieue, faces of Jehovah*, frequently mentioned in Scripture). See Orpheus' hymn, Πρωτογ· This God according to his doctrine was represented by a threefold figure, that of an ox, a serpent, and a lion. But is not Phanes, Oannes under another form ?

79. This Oannes appears in the Nemroud sculptures. See Bonomi, *Nineveh*, 168—329. In his left hand he carries a richly decorated bag containing the Apocalypse: and his right is upraised as in the act of presenting the pine cone which was an oriental symbol of the Female Generative Power—the Holy Spirit of God. His beard has the ordinary elaborate arrangement, and on his head is the egg-shaped cap with three horns and the bull's ears all emblematic of the solar power. The head of a *fish* surmounts his other head dress, while the body of the fish falls over his shoulders, and continues down his back. The size of this majestic statue is 8 feet by 2 feet, 8 inches. A writer in the *Journal of Sacred Literature*, iii., No. 5 , New Series, comments on this figure as follows. The figure of the Chaldæan Oannes discovered in the sculptured remains of ancient Nineveh is valuable in two respects firstly in that it enables us to reunite him by name to the Mizraimite *On*, his original (the Sun). Oannes is merely the Hebrew און (Aon) with a Greek case termination : and the Hebrew form is only a tran-

script of an ancient Coptic word, which according to
Champollion signifies to *enlighten*. The primitive Aon,
therefore, was an enlightener of man to a people speaking
the primitive language out of which the Coptic sprang;
and the Jews stole the tradition, and made a Rabbinical
fable out of it which they called the Book of Jonah,
making that person like Vishnu emane from a fish.

80. In the same work (Bonomi), we find him again
represented in page 148, in a woodcut copied from the
Nemroud marbles in the British Museum. It bears the
name of Dag-On, the Fish-On, or the Fish God. The
gigantic Cherubim of the Apocalypse are also shewn in
the combination of Man, Bull, Lion, Eagle, which Layard
brought from the disentombed palace; and each of these
is, as it were, living evidence of the remote antiquity of
this divine volume. But there is one carving at Persepolis, which was founded 4600 years ago, and which demonstrates so powerfully that it was taken from the
Apocalypse (section 27), as to be almost conclusive. It
is described by Francklin in his *Tour from Bengal to
Persia*. On getting to the top of this staircase, he says,
you enter what was formerly a most magnificent hall : the
natives have given this the name of Chehul Minâr, or
Forty Pillars; and though this name is often used to express the whole of the building, it is more particularly
appropriated to this part of it. Although *a vast number
of ages* have elapsed since the foundation, fifteen of the
columns yet remain entire : they are from 70 to 80 feet
in height, and are masterly pieces of masonry : their
pedestals are curiously worked, and appear little injured
by the hand of time. The shafts are influted up to the
top, and the capitals are adorned with a profusion of fret-

work. From this hall you proceed along eastward, until you arrive at the remains of a large square building, to which you enter through a door of granite. Most of the doors and windows of this apartment are still standing: they are of black marble, and polished like a mirror. On the sides of the doors at the entrance are bas reliefs of two figures at full length: they represent a Man in the attitude of stabbing a Goat, with one hand he seizes hold of the animal by the horn, and thrusts a dagger into his belly with the other: one of the Goat's feet rests upon the breast of the Man, and the other upon his right arm. This device is common throughout the Palace, (p. 203.) The symbolic history here represented is the fall of Alexander the Great, the He-Goat with one horn; and it was for this reason, not at the suggestion of the courtezan Thais, that that conqueror destroyed this majestic building, as if he sought to efface for ever this carved prediction of his downfall: and at the same time he destroyed all the Persian sacred books, including the Apocalypse which contained the prophecy. But Nemesis preserved the memorial; as if in mockery of him, and in testification of the true Apocalypse. An engraving of this bas-relief will be found in the Ancient Universal History, vol. iv., page 57, where the figure is erroneously called a Bull; but Francklin's authority cannot be disputed; and it has been confirmed by that of Chardin and other travellers. This prophecy is commonly ascribed to Daniel, and it has been put into his book; but it was simply transferred thither from the Apocalypse. Daniel is said to have lived 2400 years ago; but the Chehul Minâr was raised 2200 years before his time, according to a native tradition, by a king, or pontiff, from Samarcand. This

He-Goat is again represented on one of the pilasters, as led captive in the train of the king, and in another he is represented as being torn in pieces by the Persic lion ; while in the first and second portal we find the Cherubim, the exact counterpart of those which have been brought to England from the Birs Nemroud. All these things have been patent for years ; yet no one has used his understanding upon them. The world has eyes to see, but it sees not. Nor is this the only record in stone which tends to show the truth of what I declare. Let the reader pause upon the following significant passage from Francklin. Underneath the above-mentioned devices, he says, there are small openings, which lead to a subterraneous passage cut out of the mountain : it is six feet in height, and four feet in breadth : the passage leads a considerable way into the rock, but it is quite dark after advancing about 30 yards, and emits a most noisome damp smell. The natives call this place the Cherk Almâs [Adamas], that is, the Talisman or Diamond of Fate : they affirm that at the end of the passage is the Talisman, and that whoever arrives thither, and *asks questions of future events,* will be answered from within : but they say that no one has ever yet been able to penetrate to the extremity of the passage, being opposed by the Demons and Genii, whom they believe to dwell there : and superstitiously imagine that all lights taken in there will go out of themselves (page 215). What was this place but the crypt like that in the Temple of the Capitol, in Jupiter's *cell,* at Rome, and the Temple at Jerusalem ; where in the first, the Apocalypse under the name of the Sibylline Books, and in the second probably under its real name, was mysteriously hidden by the pontiffs? Are we to take no note of the tradition of the place, that it contained a Talisman which held the knowledge of future events? and is not the Apocalypse that Talisman? the Talisman of Adamas, or the Diamond—the only authentic one, indeed, which the world possesses. How much is to be desired that the Shah of Persia would have this crypt examined. There might yet be found the very petroma which contained the secret Volume; as in the centre of the Pyramid was found the Chest in which in primal days it was deposited; which the ignorant call a tomb: but which was in reality the mystic coffer in which the Inspired Volumes of Heaven were laid up by the priests; and of which mystic coffer they always carried an image in their processions.

81. The ancient Mexicans, like all other primeval peoples, had a secret Holy Book called *Tao-Amoxtli*, This book, says Torquemada, the Indians declared that they had buried under ground on the arrival of the Spaniards amongst them. Brother Diego de Mercado, says the historian Torquemada, a grave father who has been definitor of this province of the holy gospel, and one of the most exemplary men and greatest doers of penance of his time, relates and authenticates this relation with his signature: that some years ago, conversing with an aged Indian of the Otomies, above seventy years old, respecting matters concerning our faith, the Indian told him that they in ancient times had been in possession of a Book which was handed down successively from father to son in the person of the eldest, who was dedicated to the safe custody of it, and to instruct others in its doctrines. Out of reverence they did not turn over the leaves with their hands,

but with a small bar, which they had made for that purpose; and which they kept along with the Book. On this ecclesiastic questioning the Indian as to the contents of that Book and its doctrines, he was unable to give him further information, but simply replied that if the Book had not been lost, he would have seen that *the doctrines which he taught and preached to them, and those which the Book contained were the same* (17); that the Book had rotted in the earth where the persons who kept it had buried it on the arrival of the Spaniards.

82. Humboldt in his *Researches*, i. 207, speaks of the *Divine Book*, Taoamoxtli which, he says, was compiled at Tula in the year 660 (a remarkable cycle), by Huematzin, and in which was contained the history of Heaven and Earth, a cosmogony, a description of the constellations, the division of time, the migrations of peoples, mythology, and moral philosophy. Was this Mexican purana, he asks, the remembrance of which has been preserved so many ages in the Azteck traditions, one of those which monkish fanaticism committed to the flames in Yucatan, and the loss of which book was so deeply lamented by Acosta, who was more learned and enlightened than his contemporaries? No doubt it was; and for the same reasons that I have already explained (18).

83. Narcissus Gilbar, a Franciscan, says Humboldt, *Researches*, i. 174, distinguished for his courage and his love of enquiry, found among some independent Indians, the Panoes, on the banks of the Ucayale, a little to the north of the mouth of the Sarayacu, bundles of paintings which in their external appearance perfectly resembled our volumes in quarto. The covering of these collections was formed of several *leaves of the palm tree,*

with a very thick pareuchyma glued together : pieces of
tolerably fine cotton formed the leaves, which were fastened by threads of the agave. When Gilbar reached
the dwellings of the Panoes, he found an old man seated
at the foot of a palm tree, and surrounded by several
young persons, to whom he was explaining the contents
of these books. The savages would not at first permit a
white man to approach the teacher, and informed the
missionary by means of Indians of Manoa, who alone
understood the language of the Panoes, *that these paintings
contained hidden things which no stranger ought to know.*
With great difficulty, N. Gilbar procured one of these
collections, which he sent to Lima for the inspection of
Padre Cisneros, the learned compiler of a periodical journal, which has been translated in Europe. Several persons of my acquaintance have seen this book of the Panoes,
every page of which was covered with paintings. There
were figures of *men and animals*, and a great number of
·isolated characters, which were deemed hieroglyphical, arranged in lines with admirable order and symmetry. The
liveliness of the colours was particularly striking : but as
no one at Lima had seen a fragment of Azteck manuscript, it was impossible to judge of the identity of the
style of paintings found at the distance of 800 leagues
from each other. Padre Cisneros wished to deposit this
book in the convent of the missions of Ocopa; but whether the person to whom it was entrusted lost it in the
passage over the Cordilleras, or whether it was taken and
sent clandestinely to Europe, it is certain that it never
reached the place of its destination. Was this manuscript
the copy of some primeval volume of the Apocalypse ?
Were the paintings of men and animals on every page

outlines of the wonderful and mysterious symbols contained in that work ? We know that Mani had a volume of this kind richly decorated with illuminations. In the early ages it was commonly believed that the sights revealed in the Apocalypse were in the nature of a majestic panorama exhibited in the heavens. The breaking of the seals, and the disclosures of what the Book contained, says Stuart (*Apocalypse*, 181), now follow in order. Is this by pictures or symbols drawn upon the pages of the book, *or by pictures in part, and partly by language ?* The latter seems the most probable. Were not the palm leaves a mystical allusion to the Phoinix, the Phœnix and the Naronic cycle ? *In foliis palmarum Sibyllam scribere Varro testatur* : as we read in Servius. *Æneis*, ii. 444. Why was a stranger hindered at first from approaching it ? Why did not the worthy Padre give some account of it in his *El Mercurio Peruano ?* Can any one believe that it was lost in the way stated ?—or that it found its way to Europe, where it was never seen ? If it were an Apocalypse, the priests in the convent would necessarily destroy it—for the *true* Apocalypse destroys the foundation of the Church of Rome, and takes away from Christianity itself, as now preached, one of its main features— its narrow-minded, bigotted, Jewish system of exclusiveness. It is melancholy to reflect what powers of evil these missionaries have had, and to survey in fancy what innumerable priceless manuscripts of old religion and mythology they have destroyed in their eagerness to support their odious creeds.

84. The tradition of a lost Book seems, indeed, to prevail universally. In Carne's *Letters from the East* (p. 188), we read as follows. The superior is a man of very digni-

fied appearance and polite manners, and seems to know the world well : he was very inquisitive about the affairs of Greece in which he took a deep interest. After breakfast he invited us to his apartment, where he produced some fruit, and a bottle of excellent white wine. He said that in their library about a century ago, was *a curious manuscript that had remained there for ages*, till the Grand Signeur sent from Constantinople to have it delivered up to him. Here the narration ends : but it must, indeed, have been a rare volume to have attracted the notice of the Sultan. In another part of the same work (p. 212), we read :—Another cause of their hatred was the Book of Might, which they, (the Arab sheiks), protested and believed the priests kept in the convent, and buried it for the greater part of the year in the earth. They said this Book had power whenever it was opened and exposed to the air, *to bring rain upon the earth*, (see Apocalypse, sect. 28), so that their hearts were made glad, and their deserts refreshed. But the priests out of the malice they bore to the Arabs, kept it in general buried deep ; in consequence they were seldom blessed with any rain.

85. To assert that all these traditions of a primeval volume are not to be relied on would be arrogant indeed. He who would do so would have but slight regard for human testimony. What are the pillars of Atlas and Sesostris ? of Seth and Thoth ? and those of the Welsh Druid Wyddon Ganhebon, " which had written upon them all the knowledge of the world ?"—what are the Seven Brazen columns of Cham and Cheiron, but so many references to such a Book ? Cham, says Postel, stole out of the Ark the Books which had belonged to Adam, and gave them to Cush his first born. In the account given by Euhe-

merus of the Island Panchaia, he mentions the Temple
of Jupiter of the Three Tribes, and in that Temple there
was a Golden Column on which Zeus himself, while he
was alive on earth (that is, while the Messenger represented him), had made inscriptions in Sacred Letters.
And, to whatsoever clime we turn, we find similar traditions. There is not a single fact in ancient history
better authenticated. With what face, then, can it be
rejected? If East and West, and North and South,
all retain the recollections of a Sacred Volume, which
was mysteriously hidden, which contained the most secret
truths of their theology, and which from all alike has
disappeared, to what other work can these characteristic
marks apply but to this Apocalypse?

86. It is not necessary to introduce here any further
historical evidence that this Apocalypse is the very work
which was given to the First Messenger, whom we may
call Adam. Those who read to the end will be convinced
for themselves; those who are not now convinced would
reject *all* evidence. I may be told that it does not necessarily follow that, because a Secret Book belonged to all
creeds, it was therefore the Apocalypse. I admit that it is
not a logical consequence; but, having *proved* that there
was a Secret Book analogous in numerous features to
the Apocalypse, and that the latter contained a *secret* of
the most vital importance, namely the Naros, it is incum-
bent upon all opponents to prove *why* the Scriptures, to
which I have alluded, were concealed and hidden, and are
still concealed and hidden; and, until this is done, my
reasoning on the matter stands without reproach.

87. It may still be urged, can it be possible that this
Book exists no where in a complete shape? I have already

P

given my reasons why I think it may be found yet in more places than one. But no one can be surprised that it should have utterly disappeared. Wars and conquests have destroyed this and innumerable other holy reliques of the Past. But its final disappearance from Europe—for I am confident that it exists in the East, and if at all in our own division of the globe, I believe it to be concealed in a certain place in the Vatican—may be accounted for by the crusade which Cæsar Augustus made against all books of a divine nature. Having usurped or glided into the mastery of the Roman world, that crafty villain sought by all means to inculcate the notion that he was a person of divine birth, and by right from heaven was the appointed king of all mankind, who was to be worshipped as a god in the numerous temples raised by his flatterers. He was perpetually promulgating, either by himself or by his parasites, new details of omens and prodigies which clearly manifested his sacred quality. His mother attending at midnight upon a religious solemnity in honour of Apollo, when the rest of the matrons retired to their homes, stayed and fell asleep in the temple. Awaking suddenly she found herself in the embraces of a Serpent, whose symbol appeared upon her person for the remainder of her life : and in ten months after Augustus was born, who was thus demonstrated to be the Son of Apollo. Before her delivery she dreamed that her bowels were expanded to the stars throughout the whole compass of earth and heaven ; his father Octavius too dreamed that a sunbeam had issued from his lady's womb. On the day of his birth, Nigidius declared that the world had got a master. The Oracle of Bacchus had promulgated the same assurance, because upon pouring wine over the altar, so prodigious a flame burst out, that it overtopped the temple, and reached up to heaven; which had never happened to any one but Alexander the Great when he sacrificed at the same altar. And the night after was seen a vision of more than mortal appearance, with thunder and sceptre, and the other habiliments of Jupiter, with a crown on, set off with rays, mounted upon a chariot decked with laurel, and drawn by *twelve* milk-white horses. While he was an infant, as Drusus relates, being laid in his cradle by his nurse, and in a low place, the next day he was not to be found; and after he had been sought for a long time, he was at last discovered upon a very high tower, lying with his face to the east. Quintus Catulus for two nights successively after his dedication of the capitol, dreamed the first night, that Jupiter out of several boys that were playing about his altar, selected one of them, into whose bosom he put the public seal of the commonwealth which he had in his hand: and the night after he saw the same boy in the bosom of Jupiter Capitolinus, whom when he ordered him to descend, the God still retained, saying that he was educated for the salvation of all. And the next day meeting Augustus, whom he had never before seen, he observed with astonishment that it was the same boy, who had appeared to him in the vision. Marcus Cicero as he was attending Julius Cæsar to the capitol, happened to mention to some of his friends a dream which he had the night before; wherein he saw a comely youth let down from heaven by a golden chain, and to whom a whip was delivered by Jupiter: and immediately upon sight of Augustus who had been sent for by his uncle Cæsar to the sacrifice, and who was as yet perfectly unknown to

most of the company, he declared that *he* was the very
boy whom he had seen in his dream.   In his retirement
at Apollonia he went along with his friend Agrippa, to
wait upon Theogenes the astrologer.   Great and wonderful things were predicted for him to Agrippa, who was
the questioner; for Octavius himself was silent; but
when at length he declared his nativity, Theogenes rose
from his seat and adored him.   And not long after he
became so confident of the goodness of his fortune that
he published *his* nativity; and struck a silver coin with
the impression of the sign Capricorn upon it, under
the influence of which he was born.   After the death of
Cæsar upon his return from Apollonia, as he was entering
the city, on a sudden in a clear and bright sky, a circle
like a *rainbow* surrounded the body of the sun; and as
he was sitting for the observation of omens in his first
consulship, twelve vultures presented themselves as they
had formerly done to Romulus.   Finally, Julius Marathus
tells us, that a few months before his birth, a prodigy
happened at Rome, by which was signified that Nature
was in travail with a King for the Roman people; and
that the senate being alarmed at it, came to a resolution
that no child born that year should be brought up; but
those amongst them whose ladies were with child, in order
to secure to themselves a prospect of that dignity, took
care that the resolution of the senate should not be entered in the registry.   All these, and a great many more
portents are related by Suetonius, and they shew the extraordinary pains which this odious knave took to establish the belief in his celestial mission.   But when he was
made Chief Pontiff, and so got possession of the Sacred
Apocalypse, which as I have shewn already passed under

the name of the Sibyl; and when also he was initiated into the Mysteries, and learned the secret of the Naronic cycle, which was revealed there, he for the first time experienced that the heaven-sent Volume demonstrated the utter falsehood of his pretensions; for the eighth cycle had not yet run its course;—the six hundred years had not expired. Stung with rage, he called in the Prophetic and Sacred Books of all the peoples whom he could command; and committed to the flames no less than two thousand—thus vainly hoping to destroy all traces of works that conclusively refuted his false pretensions to the character of a Messiah. At the same time he so mutilated those volumes which he affected to consider as alone genuine, that a perfect copy of the Apocalypse became an impossibility: and the writings of Enoch, Fohi, and Zaratusht were treated similarly. Fragments of the Apocalypse, however, existed here and there, which the Jews worked up into the writings of their pretended prophets, and which the Paulite forgers stuck together in the random manner in which they have hitherto existed. The *fatidici libri* of almost all nations being thus remorselessly destroyed, the Emperor deposited certain forged ones of his own in two gilt cases, (*forulis auratis*), under the base of the statue of Apollo in the Temple of that god on the Palatine hill, as we have seen that the Jews did also in the Temple at Jerusalem. But in the reign of Theodosius, the senate being mostly Paulites, they were no longer valued, and they were finally burnt by Stilicho under Honorius. I may add here that it was in pursuance of this scheme of Augustus that the Æneis was composed, and that its writer received from Augustus the enormous sum of £80,000. Nimrod ii., 7., thus

alludes to its political objects. These were to gild over
the usurpation of a bloody assassin with splendid fictions,
endeavouring to give it the colour of a divine right, and
the fulfilment of ancient prophecy. In the course of his
adulation, he did not scruple to insult the memory of the
murdered Tully. And as the usurper's minister was not
only a *patron* or debaucher of minds, but a debaucher of
the bodies of his fellow citizens, the pipe of Corydon was
tuned accordingly. I gladly transcribe this passage from
a most accomplished scholar, as it so thoroughly exposes
those three infamous conspirators.

88. With reference to those who complain of the obscurity of the Apocalypse, it may be fairly put to them,
whether they have indeed laboured to understand its
language. A student of astronomy may as well complain
of Newton's *Principia,* or a Greek learner of the verbal
difficulties of Lycophron, as a student of theology of the
Mysteries of Revelation. He who would understand a
work of this description should bring thought, time, and
hard exertion to its survey : he should not expect that the
sacred oracles of heaven should be as plainly manifested
as grammar rules to a beginner. The language of celestial
spirits, the visions seen by, or revealed before them, the
inspiration which such language, and such astounding
spectacles afford to the human intellect of him who is commissioned to describe them, cannot be supposed to belong
to that lower state of intelligence in which ordinary mortals live. Nor would he treat a heavenly work of this
sublime nature with fitting respect if he imagined that
every one of its holy symbols should be immediately per-
spicuous to the naked eye. But if he will devote only an
ordinary amount of research into the hidden mysteries

which the Apocalypse unveils, he will in the end see clearly the design of God, in all that has been foreshadowed; and recognize in the *universality* of the Book, the true interpretation which is divinely revealed in the following pages. The design and method of prophecies, says Daubuz, is very well expressed in that saying of Heraclitus, the Ephesian philosopher, cited out of his obscure book by Plutarch, and alluded to in Jamblichus, wherein, speaking concerning the Delphian oracle, he has made this description of it : *It neither speaks nor hides, but signifies.* That is, the Deity, in the oracle neither speaks plainly of the event, nor yet absolutely hides it from our knowledge, but sets it out in signs or symbols, which bearing analogy to the event, gives us some implicit knowledge of it beforehand : and it would be difficult indeed to discover a Volume which more singularly fulfils the condition of which Heraclitus spake, than the divine Apocalypse that follows.

89. How ardently then ought every heart to welcome the grand and glorious object with which this Volume is sent forth into the world : how eagerly ought to be received those religious truths of most remote antiquity and of the most celestial pureness; embodying the very religion and the God which our forefathers worshipped in the gigantic temples of Stonehenge and Abury ; carrying them in fraternal thought to the East and to the West, in a word, over the whole earth, and uniting them with those whose ancestors once held the same tenets, and from whom indeed we ourselves are lineally descended ; associating all the sons and daughters of men again in that Creed which once was universal, and which is alone fitted to be so, from its sublime, universal, all-comprehending

nature;—so that when they are all thus knit in one faith, all assembled before the same altar, all offering up the same prayer, all animated by the same religion, they may indeed feel and recognize their common brotherhood; and be led from thoughts of conquest or extermination, to the more genial and rational feeling of love, affinity, and benevolence. If this be a dream, it is at least one in which it is delightful to indulge; but I believe in God, and therefore I do *not* believe it to be a dream, but that it is a destined reality.

90. And here I should have referred at length, if I had space, to the figurative language in which the Apocalypse is written—a language so utterly different from that of the age in which it is vulgarly said to have been composed, and so entirely Oriental in thought and spirit that no true philologist can for a moment imagine that it was a composition emanating from the West. The biblicals are so well aware of this that they endeavour to confuse the minds of their readers, by some jargon about Hebraistic Greek, in which, relying on the ignorance that is universal, they pretend that the Apocalypse is written; but they would do better if they were at once to confess, what the most learned among them more than suspect, that the common version is a most barbarous and vile translation into vile and barbarous Greek of a work originally penned in the dialect of the farthest East, with which Hebraism has scarcely one single feature in common. I must defer, however, my observations on this head to a more favourable opportunity.

NOTES TO BOOK IV.

Note 1 (page 216).—Several apocryphal writings, says Calmet, are attributable to John, as a Book of his supposed Travels, another of his Acts used by the Encratites, Manichæans, and Priscillianists; a book concerning the death and assumption of the Virgin; a Creed supposed to have been *given by the blessed Virgin and John* to Gregory of Neocæsarea; Calmet might have added that the evidence for these is nearly as good as that for the Apocalypse. What is the meaning of: *And their dead bodies shall lie in the street of the Great City, which spiritually is called Sodom and Egypt, where also our Lord was crucified. Rev. xi. 8.* Jerusalem may have been called Sodom from its crimes, but it was never called mystically or otherwise Egypt. Was Jesus crucified in Egypt? or is it not an evident interpolation?

Note 2 (page 216).—Vogel has proved from the diversity of style in the epistles to the seven churches, from that which pervades the rest of the Apocalypse that the former comes from an entirely different hand. But of what imposture were not the first Christians capable? The theologians who piously invented Adam's riddle, as they called it, for the sake of their Redeemer, whom it pre-figured, would not hesitate to invent anything. Ὁ πατήρ μου ἐγγένησεν ἐμὲ, καγὼ ἐγγένησα τὴν μητέρα τῶν παιδίων μου, καὶ τὰ παιδία μου ἐγγένησαν τὴν μητέρα του πατρος μου. *My father* (God) *begat me, and I begat the mother of my children, and my children begat the mother of my Father.* It is, however, literally true, if Mary be the mother of God !!

Note 3 (page 219).—In chapter i. 13, John beholds in the Vision *one like unto the Son of Man.* Now, if this had been written by the beloved disciple who knew Jesus well, he would have at once boldly said, *the Son of Man*, not one like unto him, for he would have had no difficulty in recognizing in heaven, him whom he had followed and loved on earth. Observe also that there is no recognition by Jesus of the particular apostle to whom, in the agony of death, he had entrusted his mother (*John* xix. 26). Nor would

P 3

John, or any Jew, whether genuine or a convert, have fallen at the feet of an angel in *worship,* xxii. 8. Who can wonder that Michaelis felt himself compelled finally to pronounce this Book *the most difficult and most doubtful in the whole New Testament ?* After all these considerations, says an honest poor fellow, writing in Kitto's *Cyclopædia,* and the many coincidences between sentiments advanced in our book, and the New Testament, we cannot suppose that it was written in the first century by a Jewish-Christian It seems to us to have been composed *a little before Christ's appearance* by a Jew, who had studied well the Book of Daniel ! !

Note 4 (page 233).—The words, eye hath not seen, nor ear heard, neither hath it entered into the heart of man to conceive, what God hath prepared for those who love him (1 *Cor.* i. 9), are said by Origen and Jerom to be taken from the lost *Revelation of Elias.*

Note 5 (page 234).—Reference has been made by the priests to a tradition and a painting of the supposed author of the Apocalypse, which do not, either of them, bear any sign of Christianity, but indeed the reverse. Polycrates, Bishop of Ephesus, affirms that he, Ioan, wore a plate of gold on his forehead, as the oriental priests at present do , and in the picture he is drawn holding a cup with a serpent issuing out of it, from which the priests have invented an idle legend that he was condemned to drink poison. But the male figure, which has been mistaken for John, is God holding in his right the Cup or holy Spirit, out of which Life (typified by the serpent) is emaned. This Cup is the Salvation Cup of the Christians, which contains the true *wine,* of which we read that *it cheereth God and Man.* Judges ix. 13. Wine when drank in the religious festivals of the Gentiles had always a mystic signification : one portion was offered to Zeus Soter, one to Hygeia, or the Holy Spirit, one to Agathodaimon, or the Messenger—the Sacred three of all so-called paganism, but which was really the True Religion Sir W. Jones says, the orb of the Sun personified, is adored as the God Surya, whence the sect who pay him particular adoration are called Sauras. But another oriental critic has told us that Sura means both *wine* and *true wealth :* hence, in the Ramayana, it is said that the Devatas, having received the Sura, acquired the title of Suras, and the Daityas that of Asuras, from not having received it. *As. Res.* viii. 50. There is a curious mythos in Nonnus which mirrors this allusion Some time after Bacchus had discovered the use of the grape, he went and *concealed* himself in the Cave of Cybele, or stables of Rhœa, and while he was still there,

Zeus sent the Rainbow on a message to him, bidding him come forth, and teach the use of wine to all the world. Iris came, but out of deference to Rhœa spake not. Rhœa then ordered the Corybantes to give her drink from the *Goblet of the Holy Table*, of which she drank with surprise and delight, and delivered to Bacchus the commands of God with a prophecy of his future apotheosis. Homer mystically alludes to these similitudes when he says the Ocean has the *voice of wine*, calling it οινοπα ποντον, and we know that the Ocean means the Holy Spirit. He says also that wine has the *voice of fire or light*, αιθοπα Φοινον. The Brahmins declare that their sacred work called the Veda is *wine*. In that dialect of the Graic or Pelasgic tongue, which retains so many antique phrases, we find that sacred poetry or vaticination is termed Καμ-οινη (the work of wine, or Cam) and μεθυ and μεθυω are pure and analogical Greek words of the highest antiquity, of which the etymon is *after the rains*, or *After the Water*. Nimrod says that the Phrygian Gany-Medes [The Rejoicer in Wisdom], Cata-Mitus [Hanging by a thread of Destiny], Idris [the Wise], and Aquarius, or in a much older word En Och [the Source of the Waters] all mean the same person, that is Enoch the Patriarch, iii. 22. But Ganymedes was the server of wine in Heaven—that is he was a Messiah.

Note 6 (page 239).—The Jews in Arabia are so convinced that the fowls, of which the Israelites ate so largely in the desert, were only clouds of locusts ; that they laugh at our translators who have supposed that they found quails where quails never were. *Niebuhr*. But were locusts *miraculously* produced in the wilderness for *forty* years ? This would put to the blush all the other miracles.

Note 7 (page 241).—Thus the Holy Spirit is sometimes represented as a spreading Tree, and she is the ash Ydrasil of the Gothic creed, with a squirrel (or Messiah), perpetually descending and ascending the trunk. Beneath her sacred branches, in the lofty plain called Ida, the celestial gods assemble to administer justice. This is the greatest and the best of all Trees : its branches extend themselves over the whole world, and reach above the heavens. It has *three* roots widely remote from each other. The first is among the gods (the supreme heaven) ; the second among the giants in the place where the abyss formerly was (among blessed spirits) ; the third covers Nifleim or hell (the region of all existences that are not among the heavenly blessed). Under this root is the fountain Vergelmer (carnal desire), whence flow the infernal rivers: it is gnawed upon below by the mighty serpent Nidhoger, (Conscience, which is perpetually warring with concupiscence)   Under that which extends towards the land of the giants, is a Fountain in which are concealed wisdom and knowledge . he who possesses it is full of wisdom because he drinks thereof every morning *Edda Fab* vii., viii. From this Sacred Ash, the Meliæ, the first human beings were sprung. Palæphatus, *De Incredib.* c 36. The word itself, which is a primitive radical, enters into the names of the Buddhist Trivamz, *ante* page 36, and it is one of the names of the Holy Spirit, *ante* page 58. The old Greek proverb, Ἀρχή ἡμισυ Παντος, Archè is half of the All, mystically alludes to God and the Spirit. The Arabian high priests and doctors know that the Holy Spirit is an essential part of their religion, and that she is symbolized by the Crescent, to which every Islamite pays reverence ; but among the vulgar this sacred mystery is wholly unknown. It were to be wished that it were not so; for Woman can never take her right rank in the world, until she is acknowledged to be in her nature representative of the Queen of Heaven

Note 8 (page 250 .—Chamos, Thammuz, and Adonis, signify the same being, who was *concealed* and buried and then rose from the dead. Ausonius says he was the same as Ba-Chus   In the mystic theology it was a name of the Sun, and also of the Messenger, the Child of the Sun. But Adam was such a Messenger, therefore the *Book of Thammuz* would be the *Book of Adam.* Thammuz was subsequently worshipped as Adon, my Lord. But between Adn and Adm in the Shemitic, there is really no distinction. The book therefore would be the book of *Adn Ad-On,* Father On—and this furnishes an additional reason, why it may have been either this Apocalypse, or some version of it El-Am עֵיל͏ִם, Hidden time; from which word comes *Lama,* or Messiah, Yam יָם   The Sea, form parts of Ammon הַמּוֹן or Concealed, which is Tammuz, and perhaps K'mosh כְּמוֹשׁ, the Sun, Adonis. Another portion of the word is דָם, *Dam,* blood : with a formative א, it is applied to Adam and human nature, and curiously in *Num.* xxxi. 35. *And the human persons of the women that had not known man by lying with him.* This Thammuz has been pounced on by the priests, and converted into St. Thomas the Apostle, who converted all India to Christianity, and evangelized the mighty empire of Prester John ! So we hear that one of our Anglican clergymen is about to kidnap Zoroaster from his Aiyan home. One might read recently among the literary announcements of the penny critics the following paragraph. *Mr. Ernest de Bunsen is about to offer his contribution towards a reply to the great question—who was Adam? We hear that his theory,—suggested, perhaps, by a phrase of the late Baron Bunsen—is that Zoroaster was the Hebrew Adam. This suggestion is a curious one; and Mr. de Bunsen may be expected to present it ably and learnedly. Critics will be eager to know the facts from which he draws this inference.* Mr. de Bunsen is recommended to peruse the proofs herein offered, before he commits himself to so extraordinary a theory. Any identity between the *Zand a-Vesta* mythology and the Hebrew *Genesis*, is owing simply to the fact that both are founded on an older Volume of Truth; and not to the fancy of which this gentleman is made—I hope only in imagination—the literary foster-father.

Note 9 (page 269).—This the Greek calleth an ecstacy or *trance*, which the Scriptures shew to have fallen on men, when they did see Visions of God. AINSWORTH'S *Annotations*.

Note 10 (page 270)—Profound meditation on abstract and metaphysical subjects, is figuratively termed by the Rabbins, *Promenading in the Garden.* But the Garden, was also a mystical name for the Shekinah: he therefore who was in the Shekinah, or Holy Spirit, was in the Garden.

Note 11 (page 275).—The name or history of the Sun, the Branch of Fire. This clearly means the Apocalypse, in which the Sun (God) and the Shekinah, and the Messenger, each of whom may be called the Branch of Fire, are revealed. This between the brackets is an interpolation no doubt. The plagues were the Seven Vials.

Note 12 (page 277).—Amalthæa, who sold the Sibylline Books to Tarquin, bears the same name as the Nurse of Jupiter (in his Messianic character), and is Aum-Al-Thea; she is also Alma-Thea, or the Holy Spirit. Hyginus calls her Adam-Anthæa. It is strange that such analogies should exist.

Note 13 (page 292).—Yet though Swedenborg thus denounces this soul-destroying blasphemy and denominates its teachers false prophets, and children of the Beast, and though he shews their horrible transformation, yet I very much fear that most of his followers have gradually subsided into this dreadful tenet of Paul; the cause of most of the crimes of Christian Europe.

Note 14 (page 292).—The name Oannes as a symbol of an Incarnation or Messenger, is preserved in the Armoric Oan and Oanic, and in the Irish Uan, or a *Lamb*. There is a curious tradition of this name, preserved in Ethiopia; it is that of a Bird, or Phœnix named Abou Hanes, which means Father John. Bruce says it is the same as the sacred mystic Ibis of Egypt. It appears he says, on *Saint John's* day the precise time when first the fresh water of the tropical rains is known in Egypt to have mixed with the Nile, and to have made it lighter, sweeter, and more exhalea-ble in dew. *Travels*, vii. 286: that is, it appears when the blessed fruitful waters of the Nile begin to swell. Does not this symbolically allude to the patriarch Oannes? A most singular preservation of this primeval word is to be found in Tongataboo. The hair of their women remains uncut till marriage, as a token and ornament of maidenhood: it is then shorn, and by a pecu-liarity of language which implies the mystical union between husband and wife, each is thenceforth designated by the common word *Oanna*. *Quart. Rev.*, vol 3. The man-fish Oannes, is the Great Fish, Leviathan, on which according to the Rabbins, the faithful are to sup at the Day of Judgment; and he is the Fish Jesus, of which the Rev. Mr. Herbert, in *Nimrod*, iv. 26, gives this reading, Ἰησους Χριστος Θεος Ὑπατος, Σωτηρ. Jesus the Anointed, the Highest God our Saviour; which accords with the blasphemy of Bishop Pearson cited, *ante* page 99.—See Note 16, *infra*.

Note 15 (page 293).—In the birth of Beroè as given by Nonnus, we have a clear symbolical account of the emanation of the First Messenger. The sea-nymph Beroè is the root of life, the house (or Shekinah) of Venus (Beauty), God, and the Loves; the hall of Mars, the habitation of Bacchus, the firm abode of Hermes: all this means that from her issues the heaven-sent Messiah. Her birth is said to have taken place when the whole earth was washed by the Ocean; when the Star of Orchomenus rode high in the heavens; and she herself is exhibited to us as the First apparent Female, equalling the Universe in antiquity. When she is born, Eon, that is Adam appears. He is a prophet, who has been washed in the swelling floods of truth and justice. In consequence of this purification, he is restored from old age to the vigour of youth, in the same manner as a serpent at stated intervals casts its skin, and becomes young again. Approaching Beroè, he looses the Veil of Justice with which she had been swathed, and removes the mysterious covering that shrouded her—that is receives the Apocalypse, which unveils the history of mortals. This Veil is evidently the same as the Veil of Isis and the Péplos of Juno: names for the Holy Spirit. Colonel Tod relates that on visiting the sacred shrine of Eklinga in 1818, his meditations were broken by an old Rajpooht chieftain, who saluting him, invited him to enter, and adore *Baba Adam*, "Father Adam," as he termed the lingaic or phallic emblem ; *Annals of Rajasthan*, i. 516. Giafar Sadak, one of the Twelve Imaums, being asked if there had not been another Adam before the common one, made answer that there had been three before him, and that there were seventeen to follow, and being further questioned whether God would create other men after the end of this globe, he replied ; Think ye that the Kingdom of God should remain void, and his power inactive ? God is everlastingly creative. The tradition of Præ-adamites may be considered as almost general throughout the East.

Note 16 (page 295) —But what had Jesus Christ to do with a *fish ?* Why was the Saviour ΙΗΣ, which is the monogram of the Saviour Bacchus, called ΙΧΘΥΣ, the fish ? Here are the Saviour, the Cycle, and the Fish, all identified. The answer is, because they were all emblems of the Sun, or of that higher power spoken of by Martianus Capella, of which the Sun is himself the emblem ; or as Mr. Parkhurst would say, they were types of the Saviour. From this it was that the Christians called themselves in their *sacred mysteries, pisciculi*, little fishes. Ιχθυς is, acrostically, Ιησους Jesus, Χρηστος the Anointed, Θεου of God, Υιος a Son, Σωτηρ the Saviour Jesus is called a fish by Augustin, who says he found the piscity of Jesus in the word fish, "for he is a *fish* that lives in the midst of waters." This was Augustin's mode of concealing the mystery. The doctrine was probably alluded to in some way or other in the miracle of the five loaves and two fishes, (the mystic number *seven*), because Paulinus, "saw Jesus Christ in the miracle of the five loaves and and two fishes, *who is the fish of the living water.*" Prosper finds in it the sufferings of Jesus Christ, *for he is the fish dressed at his death.* Tertullian finds the Christian church in it, "So many fishes bred in the *water, and saved by one great fish.*" Jerom commending a man that desired baptism, tells him, that *like the son of a Fish*, he desires to be cast into the water Here we come to the true secret origin of baptism. Among the primitive Christians, says Calmet, the figure of a *fish* was adopted as a sign of Christianity, and it is sculptured among the inscriptions on their tombstones, as a *private* indication that the persons there interred were *Christians.* We find also engraved on gems and other stones an *anchor* (see *ante*, note, page 112), and on each side of it a *fish*, with the letters which compose the name of Jesus, inscribed around them. In these fishes we have Oannes, Vishnu, and the Syrian Dagon, all emblems of the Messiah. In the entrance of most

Roman churches is a vase full of water. This is called *Piscina*. It is true that the word may merely mean a vessel for water ; but few persons will doubt that it has a more mystical meaning, *Higgins' Anacalypsis*, i. 636. The way in which the title Ioannes got foisted on to the Apocalypse is curious. The prophet who was fabled to have been sent to the Ninivites is styled Yonas or Oannes, a title bestowed on him as the Messenger of *Yona*, the Holy Spirit. Among the Hebrews, says Hesychius, the word Ionas signifies a revealer of the word or the voice of the Most High , it also means a pigeon or dove. The translator into Greek of the Apocalypse, finding Oannes or Ionas on its title-page, changed it into the Greek synonime, which means John and a Dove. All our priests systematically ignore the all-important fact preserved by Suidas, that its original name was Θεολογια, or *Divinity*.

Note 17 (page 309) —Was this statement a pious fraud of Brother Diego? Every thing on such a subject is suspicious when coming from such a source. Or was the Book the Apocalypse, and therefore like in some respects to the creed which the brother preached? This last is the most likely supposition.

Note 18 (page 309).—Humboldt, *Researches*, i. 187, speaks of the enormous quantity of paintings, which considered as monuments of Mexican idolatry, were burnt at the beginning of the conquest by order of the bishops and missionaries.

The Book of God.

BOOK V.

1. An objection will be made against this edition of the Apocalypse, as I have before suggested, which, with many shallow persons, no doubt will be conclusive—namely, that portions of it seem to be transcripts from what is called the Old Testament. In answer to this it may be well to enquire what the Old Testament really is? I have already shewn in what manner Esdras relates that *he* compiled a version of the Old Testament [*ante*, 78] : whether it is that which now remains, and whether Judas Maccabæus, or some other Hebrew unknown to history was not its real compiler, are both matters on which some of the most distinguished scholars and divines are still at issue. Whiston, a most learned theologian, and a man of consummate honesty (too honest indeed to get promotion in the Church), has, I think, *proved* that the present Greek version of the Hebrew books is more *ancient* than

the present so-called Hebrew version, though he holds that there was another, a different and an earlier one, which was the *true* Septuagint. He furnishes a cogent argument in this, that the Greek is the version which is always cited in every part of the New Testament, and that the present Hebrew, which in many material respects, and in the parts that are quoted, is different from it, is not so cited. And he infers that the latter has been framed since the New Testament was published; as it is impossible to believe that converted Jews, as most of the early Christians and Paulites, and as the apostles and disciples were, would have cited a Greek version in preference to the Hebrew original, if *the* original existed. I do not see that any satisfactory answer has ever been given to this To a candid mind it seems unanswerable. If Jesus, and those who are called apostles, always cited the Greek and not the Hebrew (as it seems perfectly certain they did), it furnishes conclusive proof that they had the one and not the other; and, before any tribunal, it would be held to establish the one cited above any other in the world.

2. Whiston has scarcely adverted to a fact, which very greatly strengthens his position—namely, that the Jew Josephus and the Paulite Eusebius, than whom greater bigots to creed, or more rabid unscrupulous writers of what *they* call history, never lived, always seem to quote the Greek and never the present Hebrew version: a circumstance wholly inconsistent with its existence in their day. In many instances, says Butler, the Septuagint (for he assumes the present to be the true Septuagint) differs materially from the Hebrew: *the difference has not yet been accounted for on satisfactory grounds.* The ancient

fathers generally referring to it in their controversies with
the Jews, it grew out of favour with them, and some of
the Talmudists have spoken of it in the strongest terms
of reprobation. They declare that the day on which it
was made was as fatal to Israel as that of the golden calf;
that in consequence of it the earth was for three days
covered with darkness, and an annual fast on the 18th
of December was established. *Horæ Biblicæ*. But as the
Jews, says Father Simon, saw that *the Christians relied
wholly* on this translation (the Septuagint), they cried it
down; and, having before admired it as a divine work,
they now affected to look upon it as a horrid piece and
accursed of God. They forbade the Law from being writ
for the future in any other than the Hebrew-Jewish characters : and they commanded that the Hebrew text
should never be communicated to the Christians ; nay,
that they should not even be taught the Hebrew tongue.
See *ante*, page 109.

3. The discrepancies between the Hebrew and the
Greek, to which Butler refers, and which, occurring as
they do in Books on which the everlasting welfare of
those who put faith in them may vitally depend, are
necessarily of the most serious consequence, are sum-
marily accounted for by one of the canonized Fathers of
the papacy. Saint Augustine, says Simon, when he
meets with any thing in the Septuagint, which is otherwise in the Hebrew, accuses not the Jews of having
changed the text, although he believed as well as the
Fathers that the Septuagint was made by Prophets ; but
he has recourse to the Providence of God, *who permitted
these interpreters* to translate the Holy Scriptures as He
thought most fit for the Gentiles, who were to embrace

the Christian religion. This holy doctor defends by this means the Septuagint translation, and at the same time preserves the authority of the Hebrew text, which he sometimes prefers before the Septuagint : as when he examines whether in the Prophet Ionas we ought to read three days, as it is in the Hebrew text, or forty days as it is in the Septuagint, he is of opinion that we ought to follow the Hebrew in that place ! This system of falsehood which the early Christians, or rather Paulites, always supposed that God sanctioned, was carried out by themselves in their writings; and never did Payne Knight write a truer sentence than that which follows. In whatever else, he says, the early Christian writers excelled, they had no claim to excellence in either moral sincerity or critical sagacity, and none less than Eusebius, who, though his authority has lately been preferred to that of Thucydides and Xenophon, was so differently thought of by ecclesiastical writers of the immediately subsequent age, that he is one of those by whose example they justified the practice of holy lying ; or asserting that which they *knew* to be false, in support of that which they *believed* to be true And there is scarcely one of the fathers, or saints of the Papacy, of whom a similar observation may not be made (1). I wish I could believe that it was confined to those individuals ; but truth compels me to acknowledge that there are few ecclesiastical writers of any creed who do not habitually resort to falsehood, and who do not malign with the most mendacious virulence and malignity all who dissent from their dogmas.

4. The reader will not have failed to notice the remarkable admissions of Paul and Maimonides (*ante*, pp. 71 and

238), so consonant with all that has been previously said, of the figurative character of the Genesis relations. These, even as they are, have been so mutilated that they cannot be relied on; and when we bear in mind through what subtile but corrupted channels, we have what now remains of both the Old and New Testaments, the wonder is how anything of even a doubtful nature has been allowed to cotninue in them. But it seems to be the character of crime, that no matter how cautiously it guards against detection, it generally leaves marks behind it that betray. So, there are several portions of these books which show that they contained matters of which we have now no knowledge—which, indeed, have been wickedly cut out from them by the transcribers; and why these singular passages in Paul, to which I have before referred, were permitted to remain, would be strange if it were intentional; but I believe it to have been entire oversight. In the tract of Genesis which relates the quarrel between Cain and Abel, there is an an evident omission, which however has been supplied by the Targums. In several ancient Hebrew copies of Genesis, iv., there is chasm indicated thus : *And Cain said to Abel, his brother,* * * * *and it came to pass when they were in the field, &c.* The omission is supplied by the rabbis thus, in the Jerusalem Targum. And Cain said to Habel, his brother, Come, and let us go into the open country. It came to pass, therefore, when they had both gone forth into the open plain, that Cain made answer and said to Abel, his brother, There is neither Justice, nor a Judge, nor any future, nor shall a good reward be given to the Just, nor shall revenge be taken on the wicked, nor was the world created in mercy, nor is it governed in mercifulness.

Wherefore was your offering received with a blessing, and my offering not received with a blessing? Abel made answer and said to Cain, There is both Justice and a Judge, and a future time, and a gift of price for the good, and a vengeance to be taken on the bad; and the world was created in mercifulness, and it is governed in mercy also. And as it is governed according to the fruit of good works, for this reason, that as my actions are better than yours, therefore was my offering accepted with a blessing, but yours was not accepted with a blessing. And they both began to fight in the open plain. The Targum of Jonathan Ben Uziel gives another version. And Cain said to Abel, his brother, Come, let us both go into the country; and it was, when they both went into the country, Cain answered and said to Abel: As I understand the world was not made in mercy, nor is it governed according to the fruit of works, and there is a leaning to persons in the judgments that are given: For what cause was it, that your sacrifice was received, but mine was not received with a blessing? Abel answered and said to Cain, The world was made in mercy, and it is indeed governed according to the fruit of good works: and there is no leaning to persons in the righteous judgment: and moreover because the fruit of my works was better than yours, and more precious, therefore, was it that my offering was accepted with a blessing. Cain answered and said to Abel: There is neither judgment, nor judge, nor a due reward for the good, nor any punishment for the bad.' Abel answered that these all were; and for the sake of these things they contended on the face of the plain.

5. That this, or something like it, once existed in

Genesis can scarcely admit of any question : and if this
be so, we ought not so much to blame the Hebraic tracts,
for the fables which they now seem to contain, as we
ought to execrate the ecclesiastics and doctors who so
mutilated and corrupted the originals, that we are led
into doubt as to the authenticity of the whole ; when it
may be, that if we had them in their genuine state all uncertainty or scepticism would vanish. And this observation I make for those who may oppose to the doctrine put
forth in this essay, as to the authorship of the Apocalypse,
the supposed testimony of the Genesis tract, that Adam
was the first man, and Eve, his wife, the first woman. I
can only answer that no reliance is to be placed upon
that testimony, even if it existed ; and the reader, as he
proceeds, will find ample reasons to come to the same
conclusion. (2.)

6. In entering upon this discussion I can scarcely hope
that the general reader will exercise reason : he will read
and condemn without having once given himself the
trouble to reflect. Yet Bishop Marsh, Margaret Professor of Divinity in the University of Cambridge, thus
expounds the obligations of all those who have not only
subscribed to the Articles of the Church of England, but
who have devoted themselves to minister at the altar ;
and what applies to them applies to all. As our Litany
and Articles, he says, are avowedly founded on the Bible,
it is the special duty of those who are set apart for the
ministry, to compare them with the Bible, and to see that
their pretensions are well founded. But then our *interpretation* of the Bible must be conducted independently :
it must not be determined by religious system : we must
follow the example of our Reformers, who supplied the

place of tradition by *reason* and *learning*. Rosenmuller, in the first edition of his Commentary on the Old Testament, the most valuable in existence, perhaps, considered, as a critical and philological commentary on the Hebrew text, does not hesitate to pronounce the Creation, the Fall and the Deluge, as mere myths, which only idiots could believe · he describes the history of Jonah as a repetition of the mythos of Hercules swallowed by a sea-serpent : and he says that it was not written by Jonah, but by some cotemporary of Jeremiah ; while he brands the prophecy of Isaiah as being made up by one writer out of the minor works of several others. Gesenius, the Professor of Theology at Halle, maintains after Paulus, Professor at Wurtzburg, that the Pentateuch was composed long after the time of Solomon, *out of different fragments joined together ;* a conclusion in which he but followed such eminent divines as Vater, and De Wette, and Eichorn, and Astruc. Bauer, in his Introduction to the Old Testament, has a chapter on *the Myths of the Old Testament ;* and he has also published a well-known book, entitled *Hebrew Mythology of the Old and New Testament*. Bretschneider rejects even the gospel of Ioannes, as the work of a Gentile Christian of the second century ; and Eichorn pronounces the Apocalypse itself to be a mere Drama, representing the fall of Judaism and Paganism, while Semler condemned it wholly as the work of a fanatic. Hitherto England has allowed boldness of thought, and scientific criticism to belong exclusively to Germany ; but the time ·has assuredly come for this empire to throw aside the shackles which the basest of mankind have imposed on reason. Yet it is not from any natural inaptitude for these studies that the intellect of our countrymen—in my judgment the only true and real intellect in Europe—has failed to realize the most important results; but rather from that indolence and love of pleasure which the possession of wealth naturally superinduces, and that all-engrossing ardour after its further acquisition which our commercial spirit engenders. If the intellect of England were really roused to a consideration of Paulism, and the fearful wickedness and disregard of God which it produces, the creed of that wily, wicked Jew, could not endure for half a century longer; and crime would diminish to an extent hardly credible, if the evilminded were no longer assured by men of learning and ecclesiastical position, that all their sins have been atoned for by the blood of Jesus. This tenet holds out to the weak so direct an encouragement to sin, that their sinking into it seems inevitable; and it offers a positive premium to the indolent and ignorant to let reason fall asleep. The late Dr. Kitto has well described the large majority of human kind, in their dealings with the immortal spirit of life that is in them, and with the glorious awful Future. You inquire, Sir, he says, whether mankind should not be treated as children? You probably did not make the inquiry as a question for me to answer, but I take the liberty of replying to it, and saying, *Undoubtedly they should.* They are such indeed: children whom the fullgrown Christian beholds with horror and with pity, sporting on the brink of a gulf into which they must inevitably fall, unless speedy measures be taken to rescue them. And shall we not endeavour to raise them? Yes, certainly; but how shall we proceed? They are obstinate and selfwilled; they will not hearken to the warning voice, nor attend to the words of instruction. We will moralize

Q

with them. We will tell them that they are amused by toys which will quickly break in their grasp; that serpents lurk in the green sward on which they are playing, and that thorns surround the roses which they are about to pluck. We will tell them this, but it will not do. They will not believe us, till the toy is broken—till they are bitten by the serpents and the thorns have pierced their hands; and even then they will be amused by another toy, and seek another rose, till they again are pierced, deceived, and bitten, and so on continually until they sink into the gulf to rise no more. —(*Memoirs of Kitto*, 157.)

7. This indifferentism to religion, which good men, like Kitto, deplored, and which is now universal throughout Christendom, is an appalling characteristic of our times. The present age can only be paralleled by those of the Ninth and Tenth Messengers. Atheism and infidelity are among the great and rich; ignorance, contemptuous disbelief, and superstition, are the rulers of the multitude. Everything is profession, nothing is reality. Men proclaim belief with loud, sounding trumpets, but in their hearts they laugh at Revelation as a sham. It is impossible, says a most acute reasoner, to calculate the moral mischief that *mental lying* has produced in society. When a man has so far corrupted and prostituted the chastity of his mind, as to subscribe his professional belief to things he *does not believe*, he has prepared himself for the commission of every other crime. Here it may be asked, I hope without offence, do our learned priests and bishops (I speak not of the ignorant) *really* believe what they profess to venerate? No one thinks it. Bishop Colenso has publicly challenged the Bishop of Oxford to

come forward and declare what he *truly does believe;* and the Bishop, who perhaps feared he might be questioned about Jonah and his whale, has adroitly remained silent. Nearly every member of the sacerdotal order knows that none of the hierarchy regards the Thirty-nine Articles as any thing but a formula; but few of the clergy believe in them; how many of the laity despise while they affect to hold them? Among the educated a well-bred scepticism is all but general. The multitude adore money, and they ignore God. Gold and public applause are the idols of mankind. Yet they may read, if they think proper, what the Ninth Messenger thought of these, the objects of their worship. In his scornful rebuke of the Pharisees, he says: *Ye are they who justify yourselves before men; but God knoweth your hearts: for that which is highly esteemed among men, is abomination in the sight of God.* —LUKE xvi. 15. If this be so, do Christians believe it, or our purple pontiffs truly think it? They tell their flocks that the poor are the favourites of heaven, and that God will reward them for their sufferings here. What then will God do to those who, like our hierarchs, are not poor, and who do not suffer? The few and honest, who really believe, subscribe thousands to regenerate the stranger, but refuse the hundreds which would make a paradise of home. In papal countries forgiveness is offered for all crimes, on the easy condition of confessing them to a priest; in Protestant nations even confession is dispensed with; for has not the atoning blood of Jesus opened heaven to the most guilty? We cannot walk the streets, or take our seats in a railway carriage, without having thrust into our hands, by some grog-blossomed man in

black, tracts and broadsides headed with the text: The
blood of Christ cleanseth us from *all* sin (1 John i. 7);
and this tenet preached perpetually to the ignorant, and
thrust down their throats in infant-schools and meeting-
houses, produces fruits in the general infidelity, profligacy
and infanticide which are the dark iniquity of our present
days. Thus sin exists everywhere; adultery is the
fashion; seduction is universal; prostitution pollutes
every street; half our surgeons derive their income from
abortion. The West brags of its superiority to the East;
but in the latter, virtue *does* exist, and the moral excel-
lences may be found; with us there is a wide-spread
wickedness that has never been excelled since the world
began. Hypocrites in all things, we affect to look down
upon the whole world; by only one country, perhaps, we
are outdone in crime, and that is Paulite America. In
England alone 50,000 women perish annually, the victims of lust and disease; and probably twice as many
infants, carried off by abortion, poison, starvation, and
neglect. The merchant cheats, lies, and robs, for he
reads that the Jews, the chosen people of Jehovah, did the
same; and God himself, on more than one occasion,
sanctioned fraud, falsehood, and perjury. (Exodus xii.
36; Gen. xvii. 8; Gen. xxii; Gen. xxvii; 2 Kings x.
18—30.) If God did so, why may not man? and could
the Judge punish the offender for only committing the
same sin as the Judge himself had repeatedly ordered,
countenanced, or forgiven? The murderer, on the scaf-
fold, is assured by the well-fed priest that, if he is sorry
for what he has done, and professes contrition for the
gore-stained past, Jesus will wash him in his blood, and
that his spirit will ascend at once, snow-white, to heaven,

to take its place, in palaces of glory, with the purest choirs of archangelic splendour. Did not Jesus himself on the cross declare to a dying thief that he should be with him that very day in Paradise? and is not the mercy of God as infinite as himself? Who shall set a bound to it? cries the sleek parson. Thus, as God, who is all love, is to forgive every villain for his villanies, and the purest virgin is to receive no more than the most hardened harlot, the heaven of the Paulites must present a motley gathering. The most savage warfare is called hallowed; and the banners that accompany it are prayed over and blessed, because Joshua, the friend of God, exterminated all who stood in his path; and the God of Heaven is called by bishops the God of Battles when it is to Satan only, if that hellish power existed, that the name could possibly apply. Prostitution is harmless. Was not Mary Magdalene, who had seven devils (*Mark* xvi. 9), that is, who had been guilty of the seven deadly sins, the intimate friend and companion of the Apostles, and perhaps of Jesus (*Luke* x. 39, *John* xx. 11, 16); and is she not now a canonised saint? Adultery is innocent. Did not Jesus himself refuse to condemn a woman guilty of the crime, who had been taken in the very fact? and do we not see the Saviour, who pardons everybody, in every print shop, looking on her with that mercy which all adulteresses will receive? Were not Thamar (*Gen.* xxxviii. 21, *Matt.* i., 3), and Rahab, the harlots, ancestresses of Jesus himself, and was not the harlotry of the first particularly infamous, as it was with her deceased husband's own father? Bathsheba the adultress, whose husband David caused to be murdered (2 *Sam.* xi. 5; xii. 9), was also a progenitrix in the direct line; and yet from these alliances was not the immaculate Messenger of Heaven descended? nay, was he not God himself who was so born? Never, even in the worst days of Paganism, had female unchastity been more exalted, or more infamous incests been authoritatively held up as sanctioned by the Supreme. Thus every horror that can be imagined has, in consequence of these precedents, prompt and pleasant absolution. The assassin of Nabal and Uriah, notwithstanding all his crimes, continued to the last the especial favourite of the Most High; and is not John Bull quite as good as David or the dying thief, and quite as worthy of the Lord's paternal indulgence? Man is the spoiled child of God, who cannot bear to punish, and is certain to reward. His crimes are but the outbreaks of nature, which, if God the Father does not overlook, God the Son will most assuredly regard with a compassionate sympathy. He became a man, say the priests, and as he thus knows the frail nature of man, he will plead with God for every sinner, and if pleading fails, he will cry out: Have I not atoned? have I not suffered? have I not been crucified for *him*? and at this the portals of heaven open; the Most High God himself is constrained to yield, and the hideous wretch, who has committed every atrocity, and violated every law, is escorted by angels into the assembly of the just. This is Paulism,—the religion of the Protestant; but where is the Christianity that Jesus preached? It lies in the same tomb with Theism and Truth; and this Book is now sent forth among men to resuscitate all Three. It is sent forth to tell them what they will hate to hear, and what they will combine against it to its destruction for preaching, that God will not forgive any sinner who does not *himself* atone for his crimes; and that without a long career of *works* truly good and heaven-like in their nature, and a total abnegation of the odious carnal pleasures of the world, the Gates of Paradise will remain for ever closed. THIS IS THE LAW, AND THIS IS THE TRUTH SUPREME; AS TRUE AND CERTAIN AND UNCHANGEABLE AS GOD. And as all existing creeds teach otherwise, all will join against its promulgation to men. So be it; and so let it be. Nevertheless it is the most absolute verity of all verities. And I, when I shall have taught this, shall have fulfilled my duty, and shall have sounded the warning Voice of Heaven; but upon those who shall not hear it, there shall come an hour, when their conscience and their reason will proclaim it to be true; and when, though every pontiff in the land should din it into their ears that their sins are forgiven, their own sense of justice will rebel against the priestly falsehood, and they will wish, when it is too late, that they had hearkened to the cry out of the wilderness that from these pages goes upon the earth.

8. I am about to shew by facts rather than by arguments, how little reliance can be placed upon the genuineness of the Books which Europeans hold to be inspired. The value of every ancient book depends upon the character of him who gives it; and if we have received ours from the basest hands, we cannot place much reliance upon them. *Do men gather grapes of thorns, or figs of thistles?* MATT. vii. 16. The Old Testament comes from the Jews who, from the days of Joshua, had been the vilest of mankind. *Ye are of your father, the Devil,* was the indignant reproach of the Ninth Messenger to them, *and the lusts of your father ye will do. He was a murderer from the begin-*

ning. JOHN viii. 44. As they were perpetually falling away in the days even of Amosis, so they abandoned his doctrines almost to a man, after that great Judge had been assassinated by Joshua in the mountains of Nebo. During the long interval of abominations that followed, they took no care of their sacred Books. In the period of their enslavements and captivities, their distinctive character as a nation was destroyed. Of these calamities there were no less than six during the government of the Judges : 1. under Chusan Rishathaïm, King of Mesopotamia, which continued about eight years : 2. under Eglon King of Moab : 3. under the Philistines, out of which they were rescued by Shamgar : 4. under Jabin King of Hazor, from which they were delivered by Deborah and Barak : 5. under the Midianites, from which Gideon freed them : 6. under the Ammonites and Philistines during the judications of Jeptha, Ibzan, Elon, Abdon, Eli, Samson, and Samuel. Under the regal government, Tiglath Pilezer took several cities, and carried away the inhabitants, A.M. 3264 [I use the common but erroneous chronology]. Salmanezer destroyed Samaria after a siege of three years (A.M. 3283), and transported into Assyria and Media their King Hoshea, with all the most valuable population of the ten tribes [2 Kings, xvii. 6], and their places were supplied by colonies from Babelonia and Susis [2 Kings xvii. 24]. This was the end of Israel as a kingdom. An interval of more than a century followed, when Judah suffered a similar fate. Two separate deportations are narrated in the Book of Kings : others in Jeremiah and in the pretended Book of Daniel. Finally in the nineteenth year of Nebuchadnezzar, that monarch carried into penal servitude all the population except the peasants, who were the fewest and basest ; for agriculture then as now was always held in detestation by the Jews. During these changes obedience to their law and its innumerable ceremonies was no longer possible ; in fact, their religion passed from their memory altogether, and that which conquest had not accomplished their own idolatrous tendencies consummated.

9. Bishop Warburton thus speaks of the polytheism and paganism of the Jews in the days of Jeremiah and Ezekiel. The Israelites, he says, had now contracted all the fashionable habits of Egypt. We are assured that it was till then peculiar to the Egyptian superstition for every city of that empire to have its own tutelary god, besides those which were worshipped in common. But Jeremiah tells us the people of Judah bore a large part with them in this extravagance. *Where are thy gods that thou hast made thee ? let them arise if they can save thee in the time of thy trouble ; for according to the number of thy cities, are thy gods, O Judah.* JER. ii. 28. And by the time the sins of this besotted people were ripe for the vengeance of their approaching captivity, they had polluted them- selves with all kinds of Egyptian abominations, as appears from that famous vision of Ezekiel, where their three capital idolatries are so graphically described. The first is delivered in this manner. *And he brought me to the door of the court, and when I looked, behold a hole in the wall. Then said he unto me, Son of man, dig now in the wall. And when I had digged in the wall, behold a door. And he said unto me, Go in, and behold the wicked abomi nations that they do here. So I went in and saw, and be- held every form of creeping things, and abominable beasts, and all the idols of the House of Israel portrayed upon the*

Q 3

wall round about. And there stood before them Seventy men of the ancients of the House of Israel; and in the midst of them stood Jaazaniah, the son of Shaphan, with every man his censer in his hand, and a thick cloud of incense went up. Then said he unto me, Son of man hast thou seen what the ancients of the House of Israel do in the dark, every man in the chambers of his imagery? EZEK viii. 6. The first conclusion I draw from these words is, that the superstition here described was Egyptian; this appears from its objects being gods peculiar to Egypt: every form of creeping things and abominable beasts, which in another place the same prophet calls with great propriety and elegance, the abominations of the eyes of the Israelites. The second, that they contain a very lively and circumstantial description of the so celebrated mysteries of Isis and Osiris. For the rites are represented as performed in a secret subterraneous place; *And when I looked, behold a hole in the wall. Then said he unto me, Son of man, dig now in the wall; and when I had digged in the wall behold a door; and he said unto me, Go in. Hast thou seen what the ancients of Israel do in the dark?* This secret place was, as the prophet tells us, in the Temple, and such kind of places for this use, the Egyptians had in their Temples, as we learn from a similitude of Plutarch's. Like the disposition, says he, and ordinance of their Temples, which in one place enlarge and extend themselves into long wings, and fair and open aisles, in another sink into dark and secret subterranean vestries, like the adyta of the Thebans. These rites are celebrated by the Sanhedrims, or the Elders of Israel. *And there stood before them Seventy men of the ancients of the House of Israel.* Now, we have shewn in

our account of the Mysteries, that none but princes
rulers, and the wisest of the people, were admitted to their
more secret celebrations; the paintings and imagery on
the walls of this subterraneous apartment answer exactly
to the descriptions the ancients have given us of the mystic cells of the Egyptians. *Behold every form of creeping
things and abominable beasts, and all the idols of the
House of Israel, portrayed upon the wall round about.*
There is a famous antique monument, once a consecrated
utensil in the rites of Isis and Osiris, and now well known
to the curious by the name of the Isiac or Bembine table,
on which, as appears by the order of the several compartments, is portrayed all the imagery that adorned the
walls of the mystic cell.   Now, if one were to describe
the engravings on that table, one could not find juster or
more emphatic terms than what the prophet has employed in his description.   The third conclusion I draw
from this vision is, that the Egyptian superstition was
that to which the Israelites were more particularly ad-
dicted; and thus much I gather from the following words.
*Behold every form of creeping things and abominable beasts,
and all the idols of the House of Israel, portrayed upon
the wall round about.*   I have shewn this to be a description of an Egyptian mystic cell, which certainly was
adorned only with Egyptian gods, consequently those
gods are here called by way of eminence, *all the idols of
the House of Israel.*   But the words, *House of Israel,*
being used in a vision describing the idolatries of the
House of Judah, I take it for granted that in this indefinite number *of all the idols of the House of Israel* were
particularly intimated those two prime idols of the House
of Israel, the calves of Dan and Bethel; and the rather,

for that I find the original calves held a distinguished
status in the paintings of the mystic cell, as the reader
may see by casting his eye on the Bembine table; and this
by the way, will lead us to the reasons of Jeroboam's
erecting two calves, for they were, we see, worshipped in
couples by the Egyptians, as representing Isis and Osiris.
Now the Egyptian gods being, as we said, called by way of
eminence *the idols of the House of Israel*, we must needs
conclude the Israelites to be more particularly devoted to
their service; for other idols they had besides Egyptian,
and of those good store, as we now see. For we are to
understand that this prophetic vision is employed in describing the three master superstitions of this unhappy
people: the Egyptian, the Phœnician, and the Persian. The
Egyptian we have seen; the Phœnician follows in these
words. *He said also unto me, turn thee yet again, and
thou shalt see greater abominations that they do. Then he
brought me to the gate of the Lord's house, which was towards the north, and behold there sat women weeping for
Tammuz.* Ezek. viii., 13. The Persian superstition is
next described, in this manner. *Then he said unto me,
hast thou seen this, O son of man; and thou shalt see
greater abominations than these. And he brought me into
the inner court of the Lord's house, and behold at the door
of the Temple of the Lord, between the porch and the altar,
were about five and twenty men with their backs towards
the Temple of the Lord, and their faces towards the east,
and they worshipped the sun towards the east*, viii., 15.
It is to be observed that when the prophet is bid to turn
from the Egyptian to the Phœnician rites, he is then said
to look towards the north, the situation of Phœnicia with
regard to Jerusalem, consequently he before stood south-

ward, the situation of Egypt, with regard to the same place: and when from thence he is bid to turn into the inner court of the Lord's house to see the Persian rites, this was east, the situation of Persia; with so exact decorum is the whole vision represented. Again as the mysterious rites of Egypt are said, agreeably to their usage, to be performed in secret, by their elders and rulers only, so the Phœnician rites for the same reason are shewn as celebrated by the people in open day: and the Persian to the sun, which were performed by the Magi, are here said to be celebrated by the priests alone: *five and twenty men with their faces towards the east.* These three capital superstitions the prophet again distinctly objects to them in a following chapter. *Thou hast also committed fornication with the Egyptians thy neighbours, great of flesh, and hast increased thy whoredoms to provoke me to anger: thou hast played the whore also with the Assyrians, because thou wast insatiable; yea, thou hast played the harlot with them, and yet couldst not be satisfied. Thou hast moreover multiplied thy fornication in the land of Canaan unto Chaldæa, and yet thou wast not satisfied herewith.* Ezek. xvi., 26. And when that miserable remnant, who, on the taking of Jerusalem, had escaped the fate of their enslaved countrymen, were promised safety and security if they would stay in Judæa, they said: *No, but we will go into the land of Egypt, where we shall see no war, nor hear the sound of the trumpet, nor have hunger of bread, and there will we dwell.* Jer. xlii. 14. Thus we see what a surprising fondness had seized and possessed this infatuated people for Egyptian superstitions.— *Div. Leg.*, iv., 6. He cites also, the following passage to prove that the Jews paid religious honour to the twelve monoliths, or twelve Messenger-idols which Joshua pitched in Gilgal; worshipped Priapic or garden images, and offered up their own children as blood atonements for sin. *But draw near hither, ye sons of the sorceress, the seed of the adulterer and the whore. Against whom do ye sport yourselves, against whom make ye a wide mouth, and draw out the tongue? are ye not children of transgression, a seed of falsehood, enflaming yourselves with idols under every green tree, slaying the children in the valleys under the clifts of the rocks? Among the smooth stones of the stream is thy portion: they, they are thy lot: even to them hast thou poured a drink offering, thou hast offered a meat offering. Should I receive comfort in these?* ISAIAH lvii., 3. (3.) Nor is it only, adds the Bishop, on the negative silence of the sacred writers, or of the speakers they introduce, that we support our conclusion, but from their positive declarations in which they plainly discover there was no popular expectation of a future state or resurrection. Thus the woman of Tekoah to David; *For we must needs die, and are as water spilled on the ground which cannot be gathered up again.* 2 SAM. xiv., 14. The psalmist says: *In death there is no remembrance of Thee; in the grave who shall give Thee thanks?* And again: *What profit is there in my blood when I go down to the pit? Shall the dust praise Thee: shall it declare thy truth?* And again, *Wilt thou shew wonders to the dead? shall the dead arise and praise Thee? shall thy loving kindness be declared in the grave, or thy faithfulness in destruction? shall thy wonders be known in the dark, and thy righteousness in the land of forgetfulness?* Ps. vi., 5, xxx. 9, lxxxviii., 10—12. The writer of the Book of Ecclesiastes is still more express. *For the living know that they shall die, but the dead know not anything : neither have they any more a reward ; for the memory of them is forgotten,* ix. 5. Hezekiah in his song of thanksgiving for his miraculous recovery, speaks in the very same strain. *For the grave cannot praise Thee : death cannot celebrate Thee ; they that go down into the pit cannot hope for thy truth ; the living, the living, he shall praise Thee, as I do this day : the father to the children shall make known thy truth.* Is. xxxviii., 18—19. Lastly Jeremiah in his Lamentations and complaints of the people says : *Our fathers have sinned and are not ; and we have borne their iniquities,* v. 7 ; which implies that the fathers being dead bore no part of the punishment of their sins, but that all was thrown upon the children. But could this have been supposed had the people been instructed in the doctrine of future rewards and punishments? Could this language have been used by a people instructed in the doctrine of life or immortality ?—*Div. Leg.,* v. 5.

10. Nor was this tendency to idolatry a modern fashion : it began in early days. The conduct of Rachel, says Lord Kingsborough, *Mexican Antiquities,* vi., 354, in secretly carrying away her fathers' gods, must appear very strange ; and idolatry in her, who, as well as her elder sister Leah had been for so many years the wife of a patriarch, was much more scandalous than in her father Laban. But throughout the Jewish history the same inconsistences are met with, in the characters even of persons of the greatest reputed sanctity, whom the Jews would hold forth as models for example to all succeeding ages : and it is very unaccountable how such persons in whom faith was the evidence of things seen, should on so many trying occasions have exhibited in their conduct a total

want of it. Of Moses himself it is said that in the wil=
derness his faith was staggered. If David's conduct in
taking the wife of Uriah did not argue a want of faith,
he at least openly displayed the greatest presumption in
so openly defying God and the prophet Nathan. But it
is most strange of all that Solomon's faith in the existence
of only One God, should have become so completely
shaken in the latter years of his reign; and that the
Jews in a body, immediately after emerging from the Red
Sea, ere well the fiery bolt that destroyed Pharaoh had
returned to the hand that launched it, should have called
upon Aaron to make them a golden calf, and have ex-
claimed on beholding the finish which that master's hand
had given to the image : *These be thy Gods, O Israel, which
brought thee out of the land of Egypt.* The faith of Abraham however in paying such ready obedience to the commands of God as to be prepared to shed the blood of his
own son upon his altar, is after all the high example of
faith which the Jews propose for the admiration of all
succeeding ages—may it ever remain inimitable ! Under
the Judges, under the Kings, during the captivity, and
after the captivity until the period of the destruction of
Jerusalem by the Romans, the Jews abandoned themselves
to all kinds of idolatry. They built high places (or taocallis) they planted groves, they worshipped idols under
every green tree, they adored the Sun and the Moon, and
all the Host of Heaven, they burned incense to the
famous brazen serpent called Nehushtan, which in this
manner damned more souls through idolatry than it had
ever cured bodies of diseases ; they worshipped other serpents : the Kings of Israel made new molten images of
calves probably in recollection of the Egyptian Apis, for

certainly they must have forgotten the calf of Aaron, which had brought down plagues and not blessings upon the house of Israel; and the inhabitants of Jerusalem offered up their homage to the Queen of Heaven who was perhaps the same as the Mexican Goddess Chal-chi-uitlicue. The practise of all these idolatries and of far greater abominations, did not last for a day or for a year only, but from the reign of Rehoboam the son of Solomon, from whom the ten tribes revolted, to that of Zedekiah the last king of Judah, who was carried away captive to Babylon; and from the reign of Jeroboam the first king of Israel to that of Hosea the last, who was also carried into captivity by Salmanezer king of Assyria. It is true that in the reigns of the very few Jewish kings whose names are mentioned in terms of approbation in the two Books of Kings, and in the second Book of Chronicles, such as Hezekiah and Josiah, the people influenced by their example became less corrupt; but it must not be forgotten that the time existed when there was only one true prophet in all Israel, as Elijah feelingly declares in the 22nd verse of the 18th chapter of the first Book of Kings. *Thus said Elijah unto the people, I even I only remain a prophet of the Lord, but Baal's true prophets are four hundred and fifty men;* and the followers of Moses did not amount to more than a few thousand persons. This state of things amongst those who boasted that they were the chosen and the sole people of God, can more easily be imagined than described. How they could ever have arrived at it may be a matter of wonder; but it should at the same time be a lesson to their descendants to moderate their pretensions to an honour to which it is clear their merits never entitled them. * * * The custom of worshipping serpents, was however far more innocent than another kind of worship, which that extravagantly idolatrous people are said to have paid to devils. *And he ordained him priests for the high places and for the Devils, and for the calves which he had made.* 2 CHRON. xi. 15. Jeroboam is here signified, to whom the ten tribes revolted from Rehoboam, and who like all usurpers studied in the first acts of his reign to gratify the inclinations of the people—but over what sort of people must he have reigned, when this was the line of state policy which he thought it advisable to pursue? This single verse is sufficient, by justifying an appeal from argument to facts, to confute volumes of laboured apology which have been written in the defence of the Jews, by those who are their mistaken friends, rather than real well-wishers to the great family of mankind, from whom the Hebrew nation was so early separated; and whose professed hatred to idolatry, was, as the ancient philosophers alleged, rather a hatred to the rest of the human race, and to institutions which differed from their own, than any real aversion to idols. (4.) It may be supposed that Warburton and Kingsborough, in thus speaking of those who called themselves a chosen people, have put before us *all* their iniquities. In truth, they have not done so. There are crimes too hideous even to be alluded to, and to these crimes the Jews seem to have adhered with that inflexible obstinacy which is in their nature. I need only refer to Exodus, xxii. 19, to Leviticus, xviii. 23, xx, 15, 16, and Deuteronomy, xxvii. 21, to shew the indescribable horrors in which they indulged; horrors peculiar to themselves; for we read nowhere in ancient history of similar prohibitions, or similar practices, except only on the most rare occasions in a part of Egypt where the worship of the Mendesian goat prevailed. But the Jews made that which was only a ceremony of abomination invented by priests, a part of their daily enjoyments; and even in the Mendesian district, where it once found favour with the hierarchy, it had so grown into disuse, that Herodotus speaks of it as "a prodigy," ii. 46. It certainly never was the ordinary crime of any people but the Jews; and it required no less than four distinct enactments of their legislators to check its universal practise. But all laws appear to have been thrown away upon the Hebrews.

11. So utterly degraded, idiotic, and superstitious, did they become, that they at length venerated an Ass-head, as if Nemesis itself had interfered to bring to scorn the self-styled sons of God. Apion, in the days of Josephus, publicly accused them of placing an Ass's head in their Holy Place, and he affirmed that this was discovered when Antiochus Epiphanes spoiled their Temple, and found the Ass's head there made of gold and worth a great deal of money. Josephus gives a sort of denial to this; but in a way that is hardly satisfactory—although even if it were explicit, he is one of those writers who never scruples to tell a lie for his creed, and his works teem with the most palpable falsehoods. But Apion was not singular in this accusation; and the cock and man and goat sacrificers would be capable of any madness. Tacitus, one of the most cautious of historians, says of the Jews: Whatever is held sacred by the Romans, with the Jews is profane: and what in other nations is unlawful and impure, with them is permitted. The figure of the animal through whose guidance they slaked their thirst, and were enabled to

terminate their wanderings is consecrated in the sanctuary of their Temple. *Hist. Lib.* v., *Chap.* 4. We read also that one Zabidus, having got secretly into the Temple, carried off the Ass's head, and conveyed it to Dora. Suidas says that Democritus the historian, averred that the Jews not only adored this head, but that they sacrificed a man to it every three or every seven years, after having cut him in pieces. Plutarch repeats the same, *Sympos, lib.* iv., *cap.* 5. The Paulite Epiphanius sought to turn the tables upon those writers by declaring that the Gnostics worshipped their god Sabaoth in the shape of an Ass. But as the Gnostics had the most exalted ideas of the Supreme Being and His attributes that it is possible for man to have, this may fairly be reckoned among the other pious frauds (whose name is Legion) of those early fathers of the church. The modern doctors have been wholly puzzled by this Jew idol. Tertullian admits that in his time the Hebrew-born Jesus was ridiculed in a picture with the inscription the "Ass-borne god of the Christians;" and the story of the Ass-head worship had now become an established fact. No wonder that the Paulite converts from this frenzy were ready to believe that God himself had come down from heaven to die the death of a malefactor on the cross, for the express purpose of opening heaven to such brilliant specimens of humanity as they presented to the earth. Nor was their beastly superstition without allusion to Asinine symbols. The Ass of Balaam was regarded as a Prophet: their hero-god Samson had achieved his victories with the jaw of an Ass; and a stream of fresh water flowed from the same, as it was subsequently fabled to do from Oreb. Their prophet Zacharias had said: *Behold thy king cometh unto thee;*

lowly and riding upon an Ass; and it was said that this was imaged in their sanctuary by the stone statue of a Man sitting upon an Ass, and holding a book in his hand. To such a depth of infamy had they sunk who had arrogantly declared themselves to be the chosen of God, and the destined masters of mankind. But this, their worship of the Ass, was probably only a propitiation of the Devil, as Christians hope to compound with God for their sins by subscribing to Bible Societies. The Jews, like their illegitimate sons, the Paulites, were Manichees, who believed in the Two Powers of Good and Evil : and they sacrificed to both, but to the latter most frequently, as Goodness was easily appeased. *I am the Lord, and there is none else,* says one of the Jew priests who compiled the forgeries that pass under the name of Isaiah. *I form the Light, and I create Darkness : I make peace and create Evil. I, the Lord, do all these things,* xlv. 7. Hence their worship of the Evil Power, whom they regarded, as our Paulites do Satan, as the very son of God, who was admitted into his presence [See the forged prologue to Job] ; and whom he employed as one of his agents to tempt them into every species of crime. See *ante,* page 104, the Jews' sacrifice to Az-azel. Nor in this notion are they without modern imitators. The Rev. Mr. Herbert, in *Nimrod,* calls the Devil *one of the Messengers of Heaven,* iv. 207 : and he cites for it Job i. 6. I may add, for the benefit of the many, that this gentleman, like Faber, was one of our most orthodox believers—a Paulite Christian of the most approved fashion, and a stout believer in all that Jews and Protestants believe. The wretched Mosheim, who does all that he can to mislead the minds of his readers, is constrained to write as follows of this degenerate tribe. The leaders of the people, he says, and the chief priests were, according to the account of Josephus, profligate wretches who had purchased their places by bribes, or by acts of iniquity, and who maintained their ill-acquired authority by the most flagitious and abominable crimes. The subordinate and inferior members were infected with the corruption of the head; the priests and those who possessed any shadow of authority, were become dissolute and abandoned to the highest degree; while the multitude, set on by these corrupt examples, ran headlong into every sort of iniquity, and by their endless seditions, robberies, and extortions, armed against them both the justice of God and the vengeance of men. * * * They were all horribly unanimous in excluding from the hopes of everlasting life all the other nations of the world; and, as a consequence of this odious system, they treated them with the utmost rigour and inhumanity when any occasion was offered them. * * * While then such darkness, such errors and dissensions prevailed among those who assumed the character and authority of persons distinguished by their superior sanctity and wisdom, it will not be difficult to imagine how totally corrupt the religion and morals of the multitude must have been. They were accordingly sunk in the most deplorable ignorance of God and of divine things : and had no notion of any other way of rendering themselves acceptable to the Supreme Being than by sacrifices, washings, and the other external rites and ceremonies of the Mosaic law. Hence proceeded that dissoluteness of manners, and that profligate wickedness, which prevailed among the Jews, &c., &c. *Ecclesiastical History*, cap. ii.

12. In the course of these calamities, backslidings, &c., this unhappy savage people wholly lost all knowledge of Hebrew, their own peculiar language; and even if they had had, or cared to use, their sacred books, they would have been of no use to them. But it appears that they did not even have them; their captors having destroyed every copy that could be procured. And they did so for this substantial reason. The Jews for centuries had been looked upon by all nations as the general enemies of the human race; as a horde of murderers, ravishers, and marauders, who declared that they had a divine mission from God to kill and conquer all other people, and take possession of their virgins, their wives, and their lands; and who supported this extraordinary claim by reference to a command or a promise which they said they had received from heaven, and which was contained in their scriptures. *When thou comest nigh unto a city to fight against it* (says DEUTERONOMY, xx., 10), *then proclaim peace unto it. And it shall be if it make thee answer of peace and open unto thee; then it shall be that all the people found therein shall be tributaries and shall serve thee. And if it make no peace with thee, but will make war against thee, then thou shalt besiege it. And when the Lord thy God hath delivered it into thy hands, thou shalt smite every male thereof with the edge of the sword. But the women and the little ones, and the cattle, and all that is in the city, even all the spoil thereof, shalt thou take unto thyself, and thou shalt eat the spoil of thine enemies which the Lord thy God hath given thee. Thus shalt thou do to all the cities, &c., &c.* Such was the doctrine and the practice of Joshua, than whom a more ruthless villain never breathed our air. That he received it from Amosis may indeed be said by the ortho-

dox; but in the first place it is not true that he so received it; and in the second, Amosis *could* not transmit his judicial right to any. Assuming to the fullest that Moses acted like Mohammed, still the Messenger and no other is the Judge: those who come after him are mere men; and have no authority, or right, or pretension, to walk in his footsteps: nor does it follow that the course of conduct which in the eyes of the heaven-sent Cabir of God, is justifiable at one period, is fitting for all other times, and men, and circumstances. This was what the Jews imagined: they held that what Amosis did must be right, for all men of their own creed, and for all future ages; but a more grievous wicked error was never made. Accordingly, it became the very vitals of their religion to extirpate and plunder universally. They declared that a true Israelite ought for ever to hate and destroy heretics and strangers; and where their other scriptures did not aid them, they quoted the authority of David, who had himself written, or caused to be written, by one of his laureates in the Psalms: *Do not I hate them, O Lord, who hate thee?* cxxxix. 21. And Maimonides himself does not hesitate to adopt and defend this doctrine. (*Port. Mos.,* p. 178.) *I will declare the decree,* says another of those hired writers, who wrote in the employ of that flagitious tyrant; and who speaking in the name of the Hebrew people, according to Hebrew idiom, called them the Son of God: *I will declare the decree; the Lord hath said unto me, Thou art my Son; this day have I begotten thee. Ask of me, and I shall give thee the heathen for thine inheritance, and the uttermost parts of the earth for thy possession. Thou shalt break them with a rod of iron thou shalt dash them in pieces like a potter's vessel. Be wise now therefore, O ye kings : be instructed, ye judges of the earth. Serve the Lord with fear, and rejoice with trembling. Kiss the Son, lest he be angry, and ye perish from the way, when his wrath is kindled but a little.* And so widely did the notion of their infamous character, modelled upon these doctrines, prevail, that Tacitus (*Hist.* v. 8) calls the Jews *teterrimam gentem,* which but embodies the universal opinion of all nations ; and was not hastily applied to them by this most grave and careful writer.

13. The sacred duty of assassination when life stood in their way, was inculcated so persistently, that it is not to be wondered that kings and princes should do all they could to exterminate the blood-breathing volume of this truculent tribe. Let the reader turn to *Judges* iii., 14, where he will read as follows :—*So the children of Israel served Eglon the king of Moab eighteen years. But when the children of Israel cried unto the Lord, the Lord raised them up a deliverer, Ehud the son of Gera, a Benjamite, a man left-handed : and by him the children of Israel sent a present unto Eglon the king of Moab. But Ehud made him a dagger which had two edges, of a cubit length : and he did gird it under his raiment upon his right thigh. And he brought the present unto Eglon king of Moab : and Eglon was a very fat man. And when he had made an end to offer the present, he sent away the people that bare the present. But he himself turned again from the quarries that were by Gilgal, and said, I have a secret errand unto thee, O king: who said, Keep silence. And all that stood by him went out from him. And Ehud came unto him ; and he was sitting in a summer parlour, which he had for himself alone. And Ehud said, I have a message*

R

*from God unto thee.   And he arose out of his seat.   And Ehud put forth his left hand, and took the dagger from his right thigh, and thrust it into his belly: And the haft also went in after the blade; and the fat closed upon th blade, so that he could not draw the dagger out of his belly · and the dirt came out.   Then Ehud went forth through the porch, and shut the doors of the parlour upon him, and locked them.   When he was gone out, his servants came; and when they saw that, behold, the doors of the parlour were locked, they said, Surely he covereth his feet in his summer chamber.   And they tarried till they were ashamed: and, behold, he opened not the doors of the parlour; therefore they took a key, and opened them: and, behold, their lord was fallen down dead on the earth.   But Ehud escaped while they tarried, and passed beyond the quarries, and escaped unto Seirath.   And again (*Judges* iv., 17), Howbeit Sisera fled away on his feet to the tent of Jael the wife of Heber the Kenite: for there was peace between Jabin the king of Hazor and the house of Heber the Kenite.   And Jael went out to meet Sisera, and said unto him, Turn in, my Lord, turn in to me; fear not.   And when he had turned in unto her into the tent, she covered him with a mantle.   And he said unto her, Give me, I pray, thee, a little water to drink: for I am thirsty.   And she opened a bottle of milk, and gave him drink and covered him. Again he said unto her, Stand in the door of the tent, and it shall be, when any man doth come and enquire of thee, and say, Is there any man here? that thou shalt say, No. Then Jael, Heber's wife, took a nail of the tent, and took a hammer in her hand, and went softly unto him, and smote the nail into his temples, and fastened it into the ground: for he was fast asleep and weary. · So he died.   And behold,* *as Barak pursued Sisera, Jael came out to meet him, and said unto him, Come, and I will shew thee the man whom thou seekest. And when he came into her tent, behold Sisera lay dead, and the nail was in his temples. So God subdued on that day Jabin the king of Canaan before the children of Israel. And the hand of the children of Israel prospered, and prevailed against Jabin the king of Canaan, until they had destroyed Jabin king of Canaan.* And that none among the people might entertain the least doubt of the glory of such a murder, and its acceptable nature in the sight of the Lord, it is introduced in the next chapter, in the triumphant song of Deborah and Barak. *Curse ye Meroz, said the angel of the Lord, curse ye bitterly the inhabitants thereof; because they came not to the help of the Lord, to the help of the Lord against the mighty. Blessed above women shall Jael the wife of Heber the Kenite be, blessed shall she be above women in the tent. He asked water, and she gave him milk; she brought forth butter in a lordly dish. She put her hand to the nail, and her right hand to the workman's hammer; and with the hammer she smote Sisera, she smote off his head, when she had pierced and stricken through his temples. At her feet he bowed, he fell, he lay down: at her feet he bowed, he fell: where he bowed, there he fell down dead.* (5.)

14. All these circumstances naturally account for the loss by themselves, or the extermination by their masters of a work, which, as interpreted by its possessors, seemed to be the greatest curse that ever came upon the earth. It was accordingly sought out wherever it could be found; and when found it was ruthlessly destroyed; so that its disappearance can create no surprise; the wonder, on the

2 R

contrary, would be that even a single copy should remain. It is related, however, that *one copy* did survive, and and we have the following story of its discovery on the return of the Jews from Captivity. Upon its mythical character I will not say one word; but leave the narrative to the reader's judgment. *And it came to pass in the eighteenth year of king Josiah, that the king sent Shaphan the son of Azaliah, the son of Meshullam, the scribe, to the house of the Lord, saying, Go up to Hilkiah the high priest, that he may sum the silver which is brought into the house of the Lord, which the keepers of the door have gathered of the people: and let them deliver it into the hand of the doers of the work that have the oversight of the house of the Lord: and let them give it to the doers of the work which is in the house of the Lord, to repair the breaches of the house, unto carpenters, and builders, and masons, and to buy timber and hewn stone to repair the house. Howbeit there was no reckoning made with them of the money that was delivered into their hand, because they dealt faithfully.* 2 Kings xxii. *And when they brought out the money that was brought into the house of the Lord, Hilkiah the priest found a book of the law of the Lord given by Moses.* 2 Chron. xxxiv. *And Hilkiah the high priest said unto Shaphan the scribe, I have found the book of the law in the house of the Lord. And Hilkiah gave the book to Shaphan, and he read it. And Shaphan the scribe came to the king, and brought the king word again, and said, Thy servants have gathered the money that was found in the house, and have delivered it into the hand of them that do the work, that have the oversight of the house of the Lord. And Shaphan the scribe shewed the king, saying, Hilkiah the priest hath delivered me a book. And Shaphan read it before the king. And it came to pass, when the king had heard the words of the book of the law, that he rent his clothes. And the king commanded Hilkiah the priest, and Ahikam the son of Shaphan, and Achbor the son of Michaiah, and Shaphan the scribe, and Asahiah a servant of the king's, saying, Go ye, enquire of the Lord for me, and for the people, and for all Judah, concerning the word of this book that is found: for great is the wrath of the Lord that is kindled against us, because our fathers have not hearkened unto the words of this book, to do according unto all that which is written concerning us. So Hilkiah the priest, and Ahikam, and Achbor, and Shaphan and Asahiah, went unto Huldah the prophetess, the wife of Shallum the son of Tikvah, the son of Harhas, keeper of the wardrobe; (now she dwelt in Jerusalem in the college;) and they communed with her. And she said unto them, Thus saith the Lord God of Israel, Tell the man that sent you to me, Thus saith the Lord, Behold, I will bring evil upon this place, and upon the inhabitants thereof, even all the words of the book which the king of Judah hath read: Because they have forsaken me, and have burned incense unto other gods, that they might provoke me to anger with all the works of their hands; therefore my wrath shall be kindled against this place, and shall not be quenched. 2 Kings xxii. (6).*

15. If we met with the above narrative, says Bishop Colenso, in any other Book than the Bible, it would be natural to wish to examine more closely into the statement, and see what this occurrence really means, by which the young king was influenced to take in hand so strenuously the reformation of religion throughout the

land. The high-priest *finds* this Book of the Law in the Temple. If it really had been written by Moses, where, we might ask, had it been lying all this while, *during more than eight centuries?* Part iii, s. 547. It may be said that this, however, is not *quite* accurate; that the law had not been lost for so many centuries, but that it appears to have been used about 300 years before. For we read in 2 Chron. xvii. *Also in the third year of his reign he sent to his princes, even to Ben-hail, and to Obadiah, and Zechariah, and to Nethaneel, and to Michaiah, to teach in the cities of Judah. And with them he sent Levites, even Shemaiah, and Nethaniah, and Zebadiah, and Asahel, and Shemiramoth, and Jehonathan, and Adonijah, and Tobijah, and Tobadonijah, Levites; and with them Elishama and Jehoram, priests. And they taught in Judah, and had the book of the law of the Lord with them, and went about throughout all the cities of Judah, and taught the people.* It cannot be denied that this is recorded, but it is recorded by the same writer, who says that this king Jehoshaphat had *one million six hundred thousand men of valour,* who waited on him, besides those whom the king put in the fenced cities throughout all Judah; and as the population of the whole little kingdom probably did not amount to so many as are said to have been armed soldiers, the authority of this royal panegyrist does not go for much. He is besides the same scribe who records this blasphemous vision, of God sending forth from heaven *a lying Spirit* to deceive a man! *Again he said: I saw the Lord sitting upon his throne, and all the host of heaven standing on his right hand and his left. And he Lord said, Who shall entice Ahab king of Israel,*

*that he may go up and fall at Ramoth-gilead ? And one
spake saying after this manner, and another saying after
that manner. Then there came out a Spirit, and stood
before the Lord, and said, I will entice him. And the
Lord said unto him, Wherewith ? And he said, I will
go out, and be a lying Spirit in the mouth of all his
prophets. And the Lord said, Thou shalt entice him
and thou shalt also prevail; go out, and do even so.
Now therefore, behold, the Lord hath put a Lying Spirit
in the mouth of these thy prophets, and the Lord hath
spoken evil against thee.* It is true a similar story, and
almost in the same words, is given by the writer of
1 Kings xxii., and if one be unreliable the other also
is. But as we are bound to reject them, when they make
God a Father of lies, as in these passages, we may if
we choose, receive their testimony as to the historical
events where it is not their plain interest to deceive ;
and their narrative here is perhaps true. Any person, however, who chooses to believe this tale about
Jehoshaphat may do so : it can make very little difference as to the matter now under discussion, and it leaves
untouched the fact that it is the first mention of such a
Book for a period of more than 400 years since the death of
Moses, and that it undoubtedly appears to have been wholly
lost for several centuries afterwards, when it was found in
the Temple as related above.

16. This story of its being *accidentally* found in the
temple, says Norton, p. 430, may be thought to have been
what was considered a *justifiable artifice,* to account for
the appearance of a book *hitherto unknown.* Not a few
of the German critics have in like manner traced *the origin of the Pentateuch* to the transaction in question. If

the Pentateuch were before in existence, it was impossible, they allege that Josiah and the high priest should have been ignorant of it, or destitute of it (Stuart, *Old Testament*, p. 68). This is an observation which it is not easy to answer. The transaction recorded is of such a nature as for ever to destroy anything like *certainty* regarding the authenticity of the Hebrew books. Yet, if they be not authentic, in what plight are the believers? and how do the everlasting interests of their immortal natures stand? Terrific questions!—and not to be disposed of by the flippancy of schoolmen. I place them before the world in the fullest earnestness, and with the most profound conviction of their solemnity. I implore my readers with all energy and seriousness to apply their minds to the duty of investigating these important matters. The questions of the day, on which so many waste the mighty energies which God has given, are petty and evanescent: but the issues raised by this Volume are entwined with the everlasting condition of the human race.

17. In the historical passages above cited, it will be observed that there is no mention of any other book than the Law, that is, what is now called the Pentateuch, or five books of Amosis. Supposing that the copy which this priest produced was a genuine copy, it was nevertheless of little or no use to the people. If an original copy, it was probably in the old Hebrew, a language of which, as a people, they at that period knew absolutely nothing. The only language which they knew and spoke was the Chaldee: none but the very learned rabbis, as we may suppose, knew Hebrew—though even of this there is no evidence. When, therefore, the people assembled for prayer, it became the custom to read three verses out of the book

that had been found, and certain persons called Interpreters, who were specially appointed for that purpose, then stood up and explained and paraphrased in Chaldee the meaning of what, to the community at large, was nothing but an unknown tongue (7). It must be obvious at a glance to what innumerable opportunities for fraud, for forgery, for interpolations and excision such a practice would open the way. We cannot but perceive, says the reverend author of *Nimrod,* what immense power the prophet, or those *who employed him,* must have enjoyed : he had abundant opportunities to suppress, interpolate, or forge (ii. 75). An artful or evil-minded teacher in a synagogue, under the influence of a wicked king, or his own ambition, might preach what he pleased, or interpret as he deemed fit, or forge as he thought convenient, and give to the most odious notions the sanction of what was regarded as a holy book, while detection from his hearers would be absolutely impossible. The Book of Judith, which like those already cited, justifies *assassination* for political purposes is an instance of this. And this mode of reading continued for some hundred years until the days of Esdras, when there was a general revision of the Jewish writings, under supernatural influence, as already described by that historian (*ante,* p. 78); but of what the 204 chapters consisted, and whether they included what are called the historical, or prophetical, or didactic writings, Esdras supplies no information whatever, nor does any other annalist of the time give us any (8).

18. In the face of this utter disappearance of the Book for so long a period, and of these admitted and universal idolatries of the nation, one of the most noted biblical commentators, dares thus to write :

How could an alteration or forgery of the Pentateuch succeed? Let it be considered that these books were sacred; that the Jews revered them as containing the divine law; that all the tribes considered them as the only rule of their religion and government; and that in all ages the whole nation shewed a respect for these books which bordered even upon superstition. Let it be remembered with what care the Pentateuch solemnly deposited in the ark of the covenant, was there preserved till the time of King Josiah: let it be considered that under pain of the divine malediction, it was forbidden to add to, or take anything from it; let it be considered that if ever work was made public, dispersed and known, it is this; not only the great men, *the priests and people were bound to read it every day of their lives,* not only had they scribes or writers whose profession it was to multiply the copies of it; not only was it enjoined by an express law that they should have it publicly read every seven years, but besides all this, *it is certain that from all antiquity, that is to say from the commencement of the Mosaic dispensation, there were persons who read and who preached the Pentateuch every Sunday.* Therefore the books of Moses must be as well known among the Jews, as the gospels have been since among Christians. I was about to ask can the force of dishonesty farther go? but remembering that there is no limit to the frauds of these writers, I hesitate to put the question. So far from it being true, that the Jews revered them, or regarded them as their rule: that they were made public, or dispersed, and known; that they were read every day, or read publicly every seven years, and preached every Sunday, *the direct contrary* is the truth, as this writer very well knew. The

Jews, as we have seen were living in the grossest idolatry for centuries, they utterly trampled on the Laws of Moses ; and the fact that only *one* copy of their legislator's writings existed throughout all Jewry, is perhaps the most damning and conclusive proof of their paganism, that can be cited. But what are we to say of a class of writers, who like this Paulite, deliberately falsify the records of the Past, and publish to the world what they know to be untrue ? (9.)

19. Josephus, who as an historian of his own people may be credited in matters where he can have no object in deceiving, in his Tract against Apion, says that in his day the Jews acknowledged 22 Books, which are justly believed to be divine. Five of them, he says, belong to Moses, which contain his Laws, and the traditions of the origin of mankind till his death. From the death of Moses till the reign of Artaxerxes King of Persia who reigned after Xerxes, the prophets who were after Moses wrote down *what was done* in their times in thirteen books. This is the king who was surnamed Longimanus, and who reigned about 490 years B.C., according to common chronology. Now the thirteen *historical* books, (for Josephus expressly says they related only what was done), are Joshua, Judges, Ruth, 1 Samuel, 2 Samuel, 1 Chronicles, 1 Kings, 2 Chronicles, 2 Kings, Jeremiah (the historical chapters), Esther, Ezra, and Nehemiah. The remaining four books, he says, contain hymns to God, and precepts for the conduct of human life. There are the Psalms, the Songs of Solomon, Proverbs, and Ecclesiastes—so that the whole of what are now called Prophets, with the exception of Jeremiah, were utterly repudiated or ignored by the historian of the Jews. I

myself, however, believe that in place of Jeremiah, we should put the Book of Judith, now called apocryphal; but only called so when the detestable doctrine which it advocated had excited the abhorrence of the whole world. It was in the reign of this Artaxerxes that Esdras made his compilation of the Jewish Scriptures : and Josephus evidently had this in view, for he excluded everything that was not comprised in that. What we now call the prophetical books, were some of them, or rather their fragments, laid up in secret crypts together with the Apocalypse, on which they were a species of commentary ; and they were never published to any but the most trusted priests; by whom their contents were used as occasion required among the populace. From these broken fragments various compilers have stitched them into their present form. Josephus himself, it may be observed, was so ashamed of the precepts of Judith, that he does not name in his history, either her, or the general whom she assassinated, but the Romish Church acknowledges its canonicity, for the pious purpose of putting kings like Henry IV., and others out of the way, whenever they become inconvenient: Grotius, as may be surmised from his character, endeavours to avoid the difficulties of this book, by surmising that it is a parable ; but it does not matter much whether it is so or not ; for if the Jews as a nation recommend assassination in parables, it is just as bad, as if they did so in any other way.

20. The present version of the Hebrew-Chaldee Pentateuch, if we possess that which was then made, depends absolutely, therefore, on the veracity of two men ; Hilkiah and Shaphan, for it is traced exclusively into their sole

possession ; and it appears to have existed no where else, if the Old Testament itself can be relied on. Where Isaiah, Jeremiah, Daniel, Ezekiel, and the others who are called Minor Prophets, or Minor Poets, come from, nobody knows ; it is perfectly certain that they are not traced to either of the two who alone had possession of the acknowledged Hebrew Scriptures or the Law, in those remote days. But can we safely rely, either upon the men, or upon their successors? What warranty have we, or what decent semblance of warranty, that the Hebrew Scriptures have not been corrupted over and over again, until only a fragment of the original remains. There are 800,000 various readings in the MSS. of the Old Testament, says Stuart, p. 192. Spinosa, I think, has proved from the following passage in *Joshua* viii., that the Book of the Law, or the Book of the Covenant which Moses wrote, was much less than the present Pentateuch. As there are one or two curious differences between our authorized version from the Hebrew, and the Septuagint, I insert both.

PROTESTANT	ROMAN.
Then Joshua built an altar unto the Lord God of Israel in mount Ebal, as Moses the servant of the Lord commanded the children of Israel, as it is written in the book of the law of Moses, an altar of whole stones, over which no man hath lift up any iron . and they offered thereon burnt offerings unto the Lord, and sacrificed peace offerings. And he wrote there upon the stones a copy of the law of Moses, which he wrote in the presence of	*Then Joshua built an altar to the Lord, the God of Israel in mount Ebal ; as Moses the servant of the Lord had commanded the children of Israel, and it is written in the Book of the Law of Moses, an altar of unhewed stones which iron had not touched, and he offered upon it, holocausts to the Lord, and immolated victims of peace offerings. And he wrote upon stones the Deuteronomy of the Law of Moses, which he had ordered be-*

PROTESTANT. ROMAN.

the children of Isreal. And all Israel, and their elders, and officers, and their judges, stood on this side the ark and on that side before the priests the Levites, which bare the ark of the cove-nant of the Lord as well the stranger, as he that was born among them; half of them over against mount Gerizim, and half of them over against mount Ebal; as Moses the servant of the Lord had commanded before that they should bless the people of Israel. And afterwards he read all the words of the law, the blessings and cursings, ac-cording to all that is written in the book of the law. There was not a word of all that Moses commanded, which Joshua read not before all the congregation of Israel, with the women, and the little ones, and the strangers that were conversant among them.

fore the children of Israel, and all the people and the ancients and the princes and the judges stood on both sides of the ark, before the priests that carried the ark of the covenant of the Lord, both the stranger and he that was born among them; half of them by Mount Gerizim, and half by mount Ebal, as Moses the servant of the Lord had com-manded. And first he blessed the people of Israel, after this he read all the words of the blessing and the cursing, and all things that were written in the Book of the Law. He left out nothing of those things which Moses had commanded, but he repeated all before all the people of Israel with the women and children and strangers that dwelt among them.

If therefore the Pentateuch is to be regarded as embrac-ing the Laws of Moses, it must have been *all* transcribed on these stones.

21. The event here recorded, as having been done in the days of Joshua, was in the fulfilment of the command of Moses himself, as detailed in the fictitious *Deuteronomy,* xxvii. *And it shall be on the day when ye shall pass over Jordan unto the land which the Lord thy God giveth thee, that thou shalt set thee up great stones, and plaister them with plaister : and thou shalt write upon them all the words of this law, when thou art passed over, that thou mayest go in unto the land which the Lord thy God giveth thee, a land that floweth with milk and honey ; as the Lord God of*

*thy fathers hath promised thee.   Therefore it shall be when
ye be gone over Jordan that ye shall set up these stones,
which I command you this day, in mount Ebal, and thou
shalt plaister them with plaister.   And there shalt thou
build an altar unto the Lord thy God, an altar of stones :
thou shalt not lift up any iron tool upon them.   Thou shalt
build the altar of the Lord thy God of whole stones : and
thou shalt offer burnt offerings thereon unto the Lord thy
God : and thou shalt offer peace offerings, and shalt eat there,
and rejoice before the Lord thy God.   And thou shalt write
upon the stones all the words of this law very plainly.*
From this extract it would appear that it was *only*
Deuteronomy, which was to be graven on stones, and so
indeed the Seventy translate it, as is shewn above.   If
this be so, it militates greatly against the value of the
other books, for the plain inference is, that the Jews regarded Deuteronomy alone as the true Law-Book, and
the others of no consideration; for as the people were to
abide by that which was written and by that only, the
others may be looked on as repealed or superseded. However the matter may be viewed, it is full of difficulty for
the orthodox believer.   If the whole Pentateuch were
graven it seems an impossibility—if only one book, the
value of the rest as statute books of God seems nearly
worthless.

22. The Talmudists, however, maintain that not only
were the whole five Books of Moses graven on these
stones, but they further affirm that they were written
in seventy languages.   Rabbi Moses, of Náhman, who
tells this legend, testifies that he had found in a book
which treats of the Crowns of the Law, that all the
words of the five books of the Law were engraven upon

these pillars with all the crowns. By these crowns the
Jews understand little strokes or points, which they write
in fashion of a horn or crown upon certain letters for
ornament sake. These crowns are not to be found but in
the Hebrew copies reserved for the use of the synagogues,
and not in those which belong to particular persons;
and, if we are to credit the fancies of these Rabbis,
Moses received these crowns on Mount Sinai, at the
same time as he received the Law, and God taught
him during the 40 days he staid there how to make them.
It may be asked here, how is it, if these stones were thus
graven with the Law, that the Jews in the days of Josiah
should have no knowledge whatever of them, and should
have been in the most complete ignorance of what Moses
had commanded, until Hilkiah found a Book of the Law
in the accidental way described in 2 *Kings* xxii., and 2
Chron. xxxiv. ? but this is a question more easily asked
than answered.

23. It is not difficult, says father Simon, to bring other
proofs to shew that Moses is not the only author of
the whole Pentateuch after the manner in which we
now have it. S. Jerome, as before remarked, durst not
ascribe it wholly to him; and Massius, who is one of
the most learned and judicious interpreters of the Scripture
we have had in these last ages, has not hesitated to
say that several things have been added to the books
of Moses; he acknowledges those public writers of whom
we have before spoken; and Pererius, the Jesuit, is of
the same opinion as Massius, because it seemed to him
that nothing could be more reasonable. This Jesuit,
indeed, believes that *some of the works of those public
writers have been culled out, and inserted into the holy*

scriptures which we have at present. He does not likewise reject the reason which Massius brings to prove that the books of Moses are not now in the same condition they were when Moses writ them, but his reasons consist chiefly in that we see in the Pentateuch, other books, proverbs, and verses or sentences quoted, which none can doubt but were after Moses. The authors of those verses or sentences are called *Moscelim,* that is to say, elegant and subtile writers, who writ books in verse, or rather in a short and sententious style : Bonfrerius, the Jesuit, attributes to other writings than Moses, many things which this legislator could not have writ but by the spirit of prophecy. Shall we say for example that Moses is the author of the last chapter of Deuteronomy, where his death and burial is described ? I know Josephus and Philo upon this occasion *have recourse to prophecy,* but we ought not to believe them more than other Jews who ascribe the whole Law to Moses to render it more authentic. We have already observed that Joshua added something to the Law ; and, moreover, if Moses was the author of the Pentateuch, after the manner in which it is at present writ, would he have used this way of speaking : *The Canaanite was then in the land.* Gen. xii. 6, xiii. 7. It is known that the Canaanites continued in possession of the country here spoken of all the time of Moses [and were not expelled until long after his death], so that this could not have been writ but after they had been driven out. The names of Hebron and Dan, and some others which are in the Pentateuch, were not in being in the time of Moses ; it is likewise probable that he could not have writ these words : *And these are the kings that reign'd in the land of Edom before there*

reigned any king over the children of Israel. Gen. xxxvi.
31. This manner of speaking supposes the establishment
of kings among the Hebrews, and Bonfrerius, the Jesuit,
in expounding some Interpreters on this passage, adds
these words: I had rather say that another writer has
added to the book of Moses than make him pass continually for a Prophet! F. SIMON, *lib.* 1, *cap.* 5.

24. We find in the Book of Joshua the same additions
and changes as in the Books of Moses. Theodoret affirms
that this volume was collected long after Joshua, and that
it was but an abstract of an ancient commentary named
the *Book of Just Men.* Massius, who has writ a learned
commentary upon this history, explaining the 10th chapter of Joshua, shews at full that what is related in that
Book could not be his, and he confirms at the same time
by very good reasons, what we have said touching the
manner of making the collection of the Holy Scriptures.
Don Isaac Abravanel wholly rejects the opinion of his
ancient doctors, who have in the Talmud attributed to
Joshua the book that bears his name, and he proves the
contrary by many actions and ways of speech which
could not proceed from him. As when it is said: (*chap.*
iv. 9) *And Joshua set up twelve stones in the midst of Jordan, and they are there unto this day.* And again (*chap.*
v. 9), *Wherefore the name of the place is called Gilgal
unto this day.* And again (*cap.* x. 27), *Joshua laid great
stones in the cave's mouth, which remain until this day:*
from whence it is easy to conclude that one part of the
Book was written some time after these things happened.
Moreover, the history of the division of the sons of Dan,
who took the city of Lescem (*chap.* xix. 47), happened
not likewise till after the death of Joshua. Massius be-

lieves that it has been inserted into the collection of
Joshua, that the place where the Danites were fixed
might be known.   So likewise we find that the same
story is related more at large in the Book of Judges,
which is its proper place (*chap.* xviii, 29, more than 300
years after the days of Joshua, according to Bible Chronology).   As to the history of the Judges, as it bears no
name of any particular author, some, with the doctors of
the Talmud, have ascribed it to Samuel and others to
Esdras.   It may be that Samuel may have composed it,
and that Esdras, or he who made the last collection of the
Holy Scripture, has added many things.   However it is,
it is certain that this history, or at least some part of it,
was not composed till long after the deeds there spoken
of had happened.   There were not yet kings who governed
the Hebrews, and yet there is mention of them, as
where it is said (*chap.* xvii. 6, xviii. 1) : *In those days
there was no king in Israel :* which plainly supposes that
the Israelites were then under the government of Kings.
One may farther observe that the genealogies of this
history are sometimes only set down in short ; whether
that proceeds from negligence of transcribers, or the design of the author of the collection, or rather from both
together.   The books which we have under the name of
Samuel cannot likewise be wholly his, by reason of certain
ways of speaking which were not in his time : besides,
they contain histories which happened not till after his
death.   When he speaks of the Ark, which was taken by
the Philistines, he says (1 *Sam.* v. 5) : *Therefore neither
the priests of Dagon, nor any that come into Dagon's
house, tread on the threshold of Dagon in Ashdod until this
day :* and in another place he adds (1 *Sam.* vi. 18),

which stone remaineth unto this day in the field of Joshua, the Bethemite: Samuel could not report after this manner deeds which he was witness of. He could not have said in speaking of himself (*chap.* ix. 9) : *Before-time in Israel, when a man went to enquire of God thus he spake : Come and let us go to the Seer : for he that is now called a Prophet was before time called a Seer;* and it is moreover related in the same book (*chap.* vii. 2). *And it came to pass, while the ark abode in Kirjath-jerim, that the time was long, for it was twenty years.* How, says Abravanel, could that be, since the ark remained but thirteen years in that place in the life of Samuel, and that seven years after his death, David brought it from thence ? It is certain that in Samuel's time there were yet no kings of Judah, and nevertheless we read in this book (*chap.* vii. 6), *Wherefore Ziklag pertaineth unto the kings of Judah unto this day.* There are also several other such like examples in the second book, from whence Abravanel, upon the same reasons, concludes that this history cannot be ascribed to Gad and Nathan, because they lived at the same time as Samuel. Bonfrerius, the Jesuit, acknowledges that Samuel could not write all the history that goes under his name, and he ascribes to him only the first 24 chapters of the first book, which nevertheless cannot be wholly true. As to the other chapters of this same book, and the history of the Kings, he judiciously observes, that we cannot assert that one and the same person is the author, but that several prophets or priests have had a hand in it, every one writing what happened in his own time, although what they had writ was not so soon published. Sixtus of Sienna, and several others, have ascribed these books part to Samuel, and part to the prophets Nathan and Gad, because it is said in the Chronicles, the actions of David have been writ in the books of Samuel, Nathan, and Gad. (1 *Chron.* xxix. 29, 2 *Chron.* ix. 29). But, although that agrees with the principles we have already set down concerning the Prophets who collected every one the acts of their times, there are nevertheless in these books several ways of speaking which c'early demonstrate that the last collection was not made till long time after most of these prophets, and by authors who could not possibly be cotemporary with them. It would be unnecessary to relate the opinion of several other authors upon a subject upon which we can affirm nothing certain : *and it is not certainly known even whether Esdras was the undoubted author of the last collection* of the canonical scriptures, as is commonly believed : it is probable that the Jews at their return from captivity made a collection out of the records which they had, part of which they gave to the people, and the other part they kept in their registeries. They called this part which they made public canonical scripture. As there are many records joined together, and that they are not of a chain, we ought not to regard so much the order and time as the things, for there are some things which are related in the same place, although they happened in different times : for this reason likewise it is that several histories have been inserted into the Prophecies, *which were not writ by the Prophets whose names they bear.* We find, for example, in the prophecy of Jeremiah, the history of the destruction of Jerusalem, which is writ in the second of Chronicles.

25. There are several omissions, adds Simon, both in

the Prophecies and other books, which I dare not attribute to the authors of the collection, being persuaded that they proceed from the negligence of the Jews, who have not preserved the text of the Bible with sufficient care. There are, for example, in the text of Jeremiah many phrases so curtailed that the sense of them cannot be found out but by supplying many words, or reversing the order of periods, and placing them in their proper station, which may nevertheless in some measure proceed from the particular style of the writers. For there is a great deal of difference between the style of Isaiah and Jeremiah. This last puts indifferently one preposition for another, the feminine for the masculine, the plural for the singular, and the singular for the plural; the præterperfect tense for the future, and the future for the præterperfect tense, etc. And in this way this deeply learned priest manfully discusses the whole subject with a depth and acuteness very far above that of many who have obtained greater notoriety. I may add here that the Rev. Joseph Wolf (*Journal*, 200) mentions the following conversation which he had with a learned Samaritan named Israel. *W.* Are you in the possession of the Prophets and the Psalms of David? *Is.* We do not acknowledge any other Prophet beside Moses; we do neither acknowledge Isaiah, nor Jeremiah, nor Ezekiel, nor the Psalms of David; nothing, nothing, nothing, but the Books of Moses. We also despise the Talmud and the Mishna. There is much to be found in the Books of Moses; not every one is able to understand them, or enter into the depth of them. *W.* Why do you not believe in the Prophets? *Is. Ye shall not add unto the word which I command you, neither shall ye diminish aught from it, that ye may keep the commandments of the Lord your God, which I command you.*—Deut. iv. 2.

26. The great majority of people, that is, people who know nothing at all, think when they see a Hebrew Bible, that they are looking at an exact copy of the very words and characters that the ancient Hebrew writers used; but this is not so. The Hebrew Bible is precisely as if Homer were printed not in Greek but in English letters; or as if Shakspeare's works were phonographed in Burmese. The letters are not Hebrew letters at all, they are modern Chaldee, between which and Hebrew there is no more analogy than between the Greek and English alphabets; so that instead of knowing or reading what the Hebrew writers wrote, there is only a Chaldee phonograph of their words; as one might print in English type what he supposed to be the sounds of Shanscreet or Chinese. To what imperfections, errors, and absurd mistakes such a course would lead, even in the present days when printing is universal, may easily be imagined; but what it would produce in the days of manuscripts can hardly be surmised. Yet it is on a work of this nature, a phonograph of a dead and almost unknown language, as abstruse as the cuneiform letters on the mountains of Assyria, that both Jew and Paulite rely implicitly, as if it alone were the sole, perfect, and infallible production on the whole earth.

27. The great oriental scholar, Klaproth, does not admit any antiquity in these mysterious characters. It is very likely, he says, that the square Hebrew characters, in which the Biblical manuscripts are written, and which we use in printing, were derived from the Palmyrenian writing, or 'some other Semitic alphabet similar to it.

Attempts have been made, it is true, to carry back the antiquity of the square Hebrew character to the time of the prophet Esdras (B.C. 458), and it is asserted that the Jews adopted it from the Babylonians, at the period of their captivity amongst them. But these assertions are unsupported except by hypotheses, or the vague traditions of the rabbis; they are entitled to no regard, and we may assume, almost with certainty, that *the existing Hebrew writing is no older than the fourth century of our era.* A mere inspection of this alphabet demonstrates that it has been shaped and made regular, in doing which the characteristic marks of some of the letters have been retrenched, in order to render them more square and uniform.—*Asiatic Journal, N. S.,* vii. 275. Higgins, who is one of the most candid and deeply read of writers, speaks thus of the imperfectness of this dialect, on whose authenticity and understanding so many millions of people unhesitatingly build all their future. In the Hebrew language, he says, some words have no vowels, and in almost every word consonants come together without them. The cause of this cannot at this day be *certainly* known; but it may have arisen either from a wish in the priests to conceal or render difficult the art of reading, or merely from a habit of abbreviating words for the sake of expedition, or of reducing works to as small a size as possible. This was similar to a practice which took place in the Latin language some centuries ago, by which it would have been brought to the same situation as the Hebrew if it had been continued. Thus for *manum* they wrote *mnm.* In this state the Hebrew was found when the Jews began to recover after the ruin of their country; and to obviate the inconveniences of it, points, as vowels, vere invented instead of the vowels being restored, as they ought to have been. But nothing simple or plain was likely to suit the followers of the *modern* cabala, the most childish foolery that ever men of common sense permitted themselves to be deluded with.—*Celtic Druids.* (10) In this language, indeed, punctuation is almost everything, and by a judicious placing of the points, a Hebrew scholar might make whatever he pleased out of the Old Testament. A couple of instances will suffice. In *Gen.* xlix. 21, we read, *Napthali is a hind let loose : he giveth goodly words* by only a slight alteration of the points Bochart changes this into : *Nap'hali is a spreading tree, shooting forth beautiful branches ! !* So, again, in *Ps.* xxix. 9, instead of, The voice of the Lord *maketh the hind to calve,* and discovereth the forests ; Bishop Lowth gives, The voice of the Lord *striketh the oak,* and discovereth the forests. The same word in Hebrew signifies God and Nothing, so wonderful is the adaptability of this dialect !

28. As to what has been said, says Bishop Walton, *Prolegomena,* iii 13, by some persons who will have it that the Hebrew is the same as the Syriac or Chaldaic, I will only put forward this single answer, from *Jeremiah* v 15, where the Chaldæans or Assyrians, whom God, by his prophet, threatens that he will bring against Judea, are called *an ancient nation, and a strong, a nation whose language the people of Israel knoweth not, neither do they understand their speech :* What can be brought forward to prove more clearly that these languages were different, when the vernacular of one could not be understood by the other ? . . But during the captivity of seventy years, a great change succeeded, so that the Jews, wholly for-

S

getting their own language, brought back into their own land the language of Chaldæa, with a slight tincture only of Hebrew, from which period Hebrew ceased to be their spoken language, according to the unanimous consent of almost all their doctors. Wherefore we read in *Nehemiah* viii. 7, 8, (11,) that Esdras and the Levites, when they read the Law to the people, expounded the same and explained the meaning (to wit, in the vulgar tongue), so that the people should understand it. And hence arose their Paraphrases, when, after they had read the Law and prophets in their synagogues, they gave an explanation in the vulgar tongue. For the Hebrew, therefore, the Chaldaic thenceforth became the vernacular language of the Jews; and it was at first pure, but afterwards it grew corrupted and vitiated with various dialects and idioms, according to the diversity of nations by whom they were enslaved.

29. This corruption of the language is thus alluded to by a very erudite priest. The most recent researches, says Donaldson, incline to the conclusion that the view of Elias Levita, that *the Massorah was committed to writing in 506 after Christ*, is correct. Jolowictz has undertaken to show that the Talmudists and the later Rabbis, as well as the Chaldee paraphrast, Jonathan Ben Uzziel, not only knew *various readings most strikingly different from our canonical text*, but also determined by the interpretations of the same, the most important usages of life. And in his postcript (p. 15) he gives special proofs that the Talmudists had copies of the Pentateuch containing different readings, and that they sometimes used one MS. roll to correct many others. If then we take into consideration the variations of the He-

brew MSS., none of which can boast any great antiquity, the discrepancies between the Hebrew text and that of the Samaritan and Greek versions, the evidences of different readings furnished by the Talmud, Targumim, and other Rabbinical authorities, the change of the Hebrew character from the older Phœnician form to the square letters borrowed from the Syrians after the Captivity, the late introduction of points, and the distinctions between medial and final letters, the probability that the Jewish editors may have accommodated the Hebrew text to the Septuagint, and the evidence furnished by the very remarkable fact that *some of the Jewish computations of time in the text of the Old Testament, involve the date of the destruction of Jerusalem,* and therefore presume a tampering with the text subsequent to this date—all this and a great deal more that might be alleged, shows that we cannot place implicit reliance on the Masoretic text, and that if conjectural emendation is allowable in the case of the classical authors, it is a still more legitimate instrument in the case of *these compiled, revised, and perpetually re-edited remains* of the ancient Jewish literature.—*Chr. Orth.* (12.)

30. The reverend Dr. Prideaux, Dean of Norwich, does not disguise, but admits, and appears rather to justify taking liberties with the Sacred Volume. Speaking of Ezra, he says, He added in several places throughout the books of this edition what appeared necessary for the illustrating, connecting or completing of them; wherein he was assisted by the same Spirit, by which they were at first wrote: of this sort we may reckon the last chapter of Deuteronomy, which giving an account of the death and burial of Moses and of the succession of Joshua

after him, could not be written by Moses himself, who
undoubtedly was the penman of all the rest of that book.
It seems most probable that it was added by Ezra at this
time.   And such also may we reckon the several interpolations which occur in many places of the holy scriptures, *for that there are such interpolations is undeniable :*
there being many passages through the whole sacred writs
which create difficulties that can never be solved without
the allowing of them.   *   *   *   Of which interpolations
undoubtedly Ezra was the author, in all the books which
passed his examination, and Simon the priest, in all the
rest, which were added afterwards.—*Sacred Connect. Part
I., Book 5*, s. 4.

31. These falsehoods, interpolations, additions, corruptions, corrections, or transcriptions from others, to which
I have above alluded, and which Prideaux defends, are
thus spoken of by Horne, in his *Introduction*, (10th ed.,
vol. ii., p. 33,) which seems to convey the idea that when
a Hebrew writer found a writing *of anybody else*, he was
entitled if he thought fit, being "conscious of the aid of
the Holy Spirit," to do exactly as he pleased with it, to
cut it up, or copy it, or use as much of it as he deemed
right, and so incorporate it with his own compositions.
This, though not an entirely new, is a very startling view
of the authenticity of Holy Scripture ; it appears also to
be a most important admission from this writer, from
whom indeed, it is almost impossible to get any admission
at all that makes against his church, so remarkably
guarded is he in his phraseology, and so wonderfully discreet in the use of words.   His language like a diplomatic
letter, perpetually suggests to the mind ideas other than
those which he really means ; I defy any unlearned per-

son to read his chapter on "Hebrew characters," and to derive *any knowledge* from it whatever of the subject on which he professes to treat, namely the present form of the Chaldee-Hebrew biblical text, and how it came to be used. The passage which I cite is as follows. We are persuaded, he says, that the things to which reference is made, proceeded from the original writers or *compilers* of the books. Sometimes they took other writings, annals, genealogies, and such like, with which they *incorporated additional matter*, or which they put together with greater or less condensation. The Old Testament authors used the sources they employed (that is the writings of other people) with freedom and independence. Conscious of the aid of the Divine Spirit, *they adapted* their own productions, or the productions of others, to the wants of the times. But in these respects they cannot be said to have corrupted the text of Scripture. *They made the text* But of what did they make it? Why from the writings of other persons. And this is Horne's notion of what the Old Testament is—a cento from the writings of unknown persons, collected and put together by those, who, he says, were divinely inspired. No infidel that I know of, has ever made so damaging a charge as this against the authenticity of the Old Testament; yet it is the confession of a clergyman of the most approved Church of England pattern, who made the work the study of his whole life, who never makes an admission until it seems absolutely wrung from him, and whose Introduction to Scripture has become almost a standard work. I do not go so far as he does; but it will be seen that his admission exactly supports my view, as to the use which the priests made of the primeval Apocalypse.

32. Horne, having thus begun, is forced to confess, that the Pentateuch has been so constructed. What is called the supplement hypothesis, he says, is now the most approved one in Germany respecting the Pentateuch. According to it, an ancient document forms the essential basis of the work, which received very considerable insertions and supplements. *The Pentateuch arose out of the primitive or older document, by means of a supplementary one.* In consequence of this twofold material of which the work consists, critics have attempted to trace the groundwork document and the supplementary matter, distinguishing throughout the one from the other. The two principal documents are usually called the Elohim and Jehovah documents. (13). The former is closely connected in its parts, and forms a whole, while the latter is thought to be complementary, supplying details at the points where the former is abrupt and defective. *They were subsequently combined by the hands of an editor,* so skilfully as to render their separation very difficult, indeed almost impossible in some instances. * * * How different the language of Deuteronomy is from that of the other four books every critical scholar perceives, . which is an evidence that the whole Pentateuch could not have been written by Moses. * * How the writer of all in the present Pentateuch that was not composed by Moses himself, proceeded, is a question which can be answered very imperfectly at this distance of time. Assuming at present what will be discussed and adopted hereafter, that the time when the Pentateuch appeared as a whole, was in the reign of the early kings, we believe that *two easily recognised authors* appear in the first four books, the Elohist and Jehovist, so called from the names

they severally give to the Supreme Being. The one
terms the Almighty, Elohim; the other, Jehovah, or Jehovah Elohim. After the origin and import of Jehovah
is described in the sixth chapter of Exodus, the Elohist
also employs the name Jehovah, and so the external
characteristic ceases. But though the outward mark disappears, there are internal characteristics which separate
both. The manner, style, and phraseology differ. The
Elohist employs a style, simple and unpolished : he is
distinguished by breadth, circumstantiality, repetitions,
verbosity. He belonged *to the priestly order,* (14), was
familiar with primitive history, genealogical, and ethno-
graphical registers, and the laws immediately affecting
religion or religious worship. There is also a uniform and
consistent plan in what he composed. His work is pervaded by unity of purpose. On the other hand the
Jehovist writes in a more compact, regular, connected
manner, and though shorter is clearer and smoother in
style and diction. He evinces more reflectiveness and
skill in composition ; *and probably belonged to the prophetic order.* The Elohist document forms the groundwork
of the Pentateuch, and is evidently older than the Jehovist one. Whether the author of the latter had the other
document before him, which he merely supplemented and
interpolated, is not agreed. We believe that the one
writer had not the other's document before him, and that
he did not write with a view towards it. The sources
from which *both* drew were old documents, registers and
tradition, (not the law of Moses.) It is very difficult to
determine the time or times when the two respectively
wrote. Nothing but conjecture has been advanced upon
the point. Thus Ewald and Von Lengerke place the

Elohist in the time of Solomon, (500 years after Moses, according to Bible chronology) the Jehovist under Hezekiah, (800 years after Moses). After mentioning other dates, which are merely conjectural, he resumes. Probably the interval between the two was greater than that assumed. Neither was the Pentateuch completed by the Jehovist, or so early as his day. After him the substance of it had appeared in writing, but it existed in two pieces separately composed. *Some one* must have subsequently put them together, digesting and arranging them as they now are. The final editor, if we may use the word, lived some time after the Elohist and Jehovist. This will appear from an examination of the time when the Pentateuch as it now is, was composed. The passage in 2 KINGS xxii., 8, which speaks of Hilkiah, *finding the Book of the Law in the house of the Lord,* has been already referred to. Notwithstanding the opinion of some that the Book of the Law, there means the present Pentateuch, we cannot think it reasonable or probable, (*vol.* ii., cap. 2. And with an apparent candour which certainly is not imitated by his reverend readers, for they never teach, or allude to these things from the pulpit, he immediately after, scatters to the winds all notions of the authenticity of Isaiah, Jeremiah or Daniel, while Dr. Adam Clarke does the same kind office for some others of the prophets. If there be any truth in these remarks, says Horne, the collecting and arrangement of the various pieces (of Isaiah) *were the works of a later hand.* The collection was begun by the prophet himself and completed after his death—how long after it is impossible to tell. Perhaps a considerable time elapsed, affording occasion for the insertion of a piece, (xxxvi—xxxix) which did not originate with Isaiah himself, in its present form. So also he writes of Jeremiah's Prophecies. The arrangement as it now exists is different in some places from what it originally was. The pieces against foreign nations have been thrown to the end of the book. *Various interpolations have also been made* (15). Some person or persons put their hands to the prophecies and made *different alterations in them,* after the decease of the prophet. The final redactor was not Baruch, as Keil thinks. We must look for him at a later time : *how long after we cannot tell.* And again : A question now remains whether Daniel himself put the book he wrote into its present form. *It is probable he did not.* Some of his countrymen put the prophecies together and prefixed introductory notices respecting the author's person. What leads to this conclusion is the existence of various ·particulars here and there *indicating another hand* &c., &c. Of Hosea, Dr. A. Clarke, says : We read in the introduction to this prophecy that he prophesied under the Kings of Judah, Uzziah, Jotham, Ahaz and Hezekiah, and under Jeroboam II., king of Israel. If he prophesied in the reigns of all these princes *he must have lived a very long time, for there are* 112 *years from the beginning of Uzziah's reign to the end of Hezekiah's.* In the whole collection of Hosea's prophecies we find nothing which proves that he prophesied so long : and besides, why should his prophecies be dated in the title of the reigns of the Kings of Judah when he did not live under their name ? Why indeed ? But he accounts for it by that imaginary transcriber, who is always called in to account for every mistake that is pointed out in these writings, and who is a mythical personage of entirely modern invention. Nobody ever heard

of him, until the mistakes were shewn. The part which
this suppositious scapegoat plays in all biblical commentaries strikes laymen with surprise. He is perpetually
brought on the stage to account for everything. Of Obadiah, Dr. Clarke says : *Who* was this prophet ? *where*
born ? of *what* country ? at what time did he prophesy ?
who were his parents ? when and where did he die ? are
questions which have been asked from the remotest antiquity, and which to this day have received no answer.
Of Habakuk, he says : We know little of this prophet :
for what we find in the *ancients* concerning him is evidently fabulous. Of Malachi, he says : Several have supposed that Malachi is no other than Ezra under *the feigned
name* of angel of the Lord. Thus it appears that all
that we know, is that we know nothing ; yet these imaginary characters are alluded to every day as *historical*
persons, about whom there is or can be, no doubt at all.
Of Zechariah (Chapters ix. to xiv. inclusive) he says :
Most learned men are of opinion that this and the succeeding chapters are *not* the work of Zechariah, but
rather of Jeremiah, Hosea, or *some one* before the Captivity. It is certain that chap. xi. 12, 13, is quoted
Matt. xxvii., 9, 10, as the language of Jeremiah the prophet : the six last chapters are not expressly assigned to
Zechariah, and are unconnected with those that precede :
the three first of them are unsuitable in many parts to the
time when Zechariah lived : all of them have a more
adorned and poetical turn of composition than the eight
first chapters. He concludes that part was written by
Jeremiah, part by Hosea, and the rest by some unknown
person or *thirteenth* prophet!

33. Horne and Dr. Clarke, it may be here added, de-

serve no credit for candour in the admissions that they make—nor could any candour be expected from so dishonest a writer, as any unprejudiced reader will find the first named of these two to be. There is nothing in the above extracts from his Introduction which was not known and confessed before, and published to the world; though the world—with few exceptions—takes good care to remain in ignorance of that which most vitally affects its dearest interests, and prefers its money to its immortal soul. Father Simon, one of the most learned priests of Rome, in his *Critical History of the Old Testament*, published so long ago as the 17th Century, had already put before the world in that erudite work, the conclusions at which some of the most profound commentators on Scripture, Hebrew as well as Christian, had already been forced to arrive. I make no apology for the length of these extracts in consequence of their relevancy to the present matter. Having established, says Father Simon, in the Hebrew Commonwealth, the Prophets or public writers who took care of collecting faithfully the acts of what passed of most importance in the state, we need not too curiously enquire, as usually men do, *who were the authors of each particular book of the Bible,* because it is certain (?) that they were all writ by Prophets, which the Hebrew commonwealth never wanted as long as it lasted. Besides, as these same prophets, which may be called public writers, for the distinguishing of them from other private writers, had the liberty of collecting out of the ancient acts which were kept in the registers of the republic, and of giving a new form to these same acts by adding or diminishing, what they thought fit, we may hereby give a very good reason for the additions and alte-

c 3

rations in the Holy Scriptures without lessening of their authority, *since the authors of these additions or alterations were real Prophets directed by the Spirit of God.* Wherefore their alterations in the ancient acts are of as great authority as the rest of the text of the Bible. St. Jerom, Theodoret, and several other Fathers who were of this opinion, thought not that they hereby lessened the authority of the Holy Scriptures, *supposing at the same time that the authors of these corrections were inspired by God!* By this principle we may also easily answer several objections which are usually made to show that Moses is not the only author of the books which we have under his name, for they prove only that something has been added in series of time, which destroys not the authority of the ancient acts which were writ in Moses's time.—(*Preface.*) And in his first chapter this excellent priest coolly writes : Wherefore we ought not to search with too much curiosity who have been the particular authors of every book of the Bible ; it sufficeth, according to the maxim of Gregory the Great, that these Books were written by the Prophets—which indeed takes for granted every thing really in dispute.

34. It is, moreover, *certain,* he adds, that the books of the Bible that are come to our hands, *are but abridgments of the ancient records* which were more full and copious before the last abridgment was made for the public use of the people : this opinion, which is Origen's and some other Fathers', is conformable to the Scripture, which very often refers the reader to the ancient acts more at large recited, which the Jews no doubt did for some time preserve in their registeries. *Even Tertullian thought that the Jews have suppressed many books of the Bible for par-*

ticular reasons. However, it is, none can doubt, but that we want at present whole histories and prophecies which the Scripture makes mention of. The Jew who composed the Book entitled *Cozri*, is of the same opinion with Origen, that those who made the collection of the Holy Scriptures, put down nothing but what they thought necessary for the instruction of the people, and that the rest remained in their registeries. * * * St. Jerom writes that the Book of Esther, as it was read in the Church, was full of errors, and he affirms that there were wanted near 700 or 800 verses in the Book of Job. Their collections for all this, continues our learned priest, had never the less authority, as Theodoret has judiciously observed on the 10th of Joshua, where he assures us that the History that we have under the name of Joshua is not his, but that it was extracted from ancient records, which the author cites that we might give credit to his collections. Massius, who wrote a learned commentary on the same history, shows that Joshua could not have written all that is recorded in his Book, because facts are mentioned which did not happen till long after his time; *and it is the same thing with most part of the other books of the Bible,* so that it is not absolutely necessary that all the passages which we find in the Bible should be entirely written by Authors of the same age, and who were witnesses of the things which they report, otherwise we shall give no credit to what is written in Genesis. [*Book* i., c. 1] (16)

35. The common opinion of the Fathers who believe that the collection of the Old Testament as now extant *was composed* by Esdras, confirms what I have been saying. For Esdras could not re-establish those Books

which according to them had been corrupted in time of captivity, but in quality of Prophet or public writer, so is he termed in Scripture the Scribe, or Writer, by way of eminency : most of the Jews agree that the records which Esdras made use of in his collection, *were corrupted by reason of the confusion* which happened to their Books in the time of their captivity. It is *probable* that there were from Moses's time these sorts of Prophets, which were necessary in the State to collect the acts which passed in the republick. This being *supposed*, we shall distinguish in the five Books of the Law, what has been writ by Moses, from what has been writ by those prophets or public writers. We may attribute to Moses the commandments and ordinances which he gave to the people, and allow these same public writers to be the authors of the greatest part of the History. Moses, in quality of Legislator, writ all which relates to the Statutes, and left to the scribes or prophets the care of collecting the acts of the most material transactions. * * * Whence it is that Isaac Abravanel, a learned Spanish Jew, strongly maintains the principle which we have mentioned touching these prophets or public writers ; and he pretends moreover that they did not only write the history of their times, but that they took the liberty of *adding or diminishing what they thought fit from the records of the other prophets who went before them.* This is likewise the sentiment of Procopius, Theodoret, and some other Fathers. Procopius observes in his Scholias upon the Books of the Kings, that the authors of these books and those of the Chronicles have taken their history from more ancient acts, from whence they have composed their works. Theodoret, who explains himself more at large upon this subject, assures us that the history of Kings, as it is now, has been drawn from many other prophetic writings, so that it is nothing but a collection of the acts which had been compiled by the prophets or public writers, who had gone before, and who were charged to put into writing what happened in their times. These sorts of collections are called in the Scripture *Dibri Hasamin*, or Day-Books, and it is in this sense we ought to understand the words of the first Book of Kings—*The rest of the Acts of Solomon, are they not written in the Book of the Acts of Solomon ?* There is nothing more ordinary in the Book of Kings and Chronicles than this last expression, whence it evidently appears that the most part of the Holy Scriptures that are come to us are but abridgments and as summaries of ancient acts which were kept in the registeries of the Hebrews. Abravanel is so far persuaded of the truth of his principle that he does not scruple to deny, contrary to the sentiment of certain doctors in the Talmud, that Joshua and Samuel are the authors of the books which bear their names ; and he assures us that notwithstanding the testimony of his fathers, Samuel is the author of the Book of Joshua and that of Judges : he ascribes moreover the Book of Samuel and Kings to the Prophet Jeremiah, who, according to him, did compile them out of the records of Samuel, Nathan, Gad, and other prophets or public writers who lived before him. However, this is most certain, that Joshua and Samuel could never put down in their books acts and expressions which manifestly suppose them to be dead ; and consequently, if they composed those histories which we have under those names it is absolutely necessary that something has been added, and we cannot, methinks, justify these additions but by establishing the prophets or public writers of whom we have already treated.—[FATHER SIMON, *lib.* i., *chap.* 2.]

36. The variety of the style, he adds, which we meet with in the Books of Moses, seems to be a convincing argument that one and the same man was not the author. Sometimes we find a very curt style, and sometimes a very copious one, although the variety of the matter does not require it : we ought, nevertheless, to acknowledge that the Hebrews very often speak but by halves, and that they sometimes begin a matter without ending it, and that they are not exact in the placing of their words. * * * Nevertheless, it would be very difficult to justify the Books of Moses, and the rest of the Bible where this happens, otherwise than by having recourse *to those who have new modelled the Hebrew copies,* and to transcribers who through negligence have omitted whole words and periods. The authors of the Mazoret seem to agree to this, since they have left certain void spaces, as if they would give notice that in those places the Hebrew text is defective : moreover, the Rabbins are so much persuaded of this truth, that they make insertions in some places where there seems no necessity to require it, and what no doubt they never would have done, if they thought the Hebrew text was complete. Thus where the Rabbis interpret what the Serpent said to Eve in *Gen.* iii. 5, they pretend that in the text there is only part related of the discourse between the Serpent and Eve, because there are several particulars in the Hebrew which, according to them, signify much more, whence they infer that the discourse is wholly imperfect, and that what went before has been passed over in silence. Rabbi Moses Cotsi, a

learned Jew, that he might solve those difficulties, has had recourse to a second Law, which he calls the oral law, or the interpretation of the written Law which God gave to Moses, according to their opinion upon Mount Sinai : he believes that the written Law has errors which can be rectified only by the oral, and this last the Jews pretend has been entirely preserved down even unto them : and he gives for an example, *Exod.* xii. 40, where it is said, *Now the sojourning of the children of Israel who dwelt in Egypt, was four hundred and thirty years.* How can one explain that, says this author, without the help of oral law, since it is certain that Kohath, son of Levi, who was one of those that went into Egypt lived but 133 years ; that Amram, lived only 137 years, and that Moses was but 80 years old when God spake to him, which makes in all only 350 ? The second example which he gives is taken from *Genesis* xlvi. 27. *And the sons of Joseph which were born to him in Egypt were two souls, all the souls of the house of Jacob which came into Egypt where three score and ten* : and nevertheless in counting the number there related they are found to be but 69. Moreover, it is observed in *Numbers* iii. 39, that there are reckoned 2200, but if we join all the the numbers together, there remain 300 above that account. This Rabbin brings many other examples to shew that the text of scripture alone cannot be understood without the help of oral law or tradition, and the Fathers seems to agree with him in this opinion (17). And thus far it seems sufficient to cite from Father Simon, whose entire work is well worthy of perusal.

37. Returned from Babylon as a Persian colony, says a learned writer, and authorized by a royal edict, the

priesthood replaced the ancient kings. A priest of the
Sun and Fire-God Azaia (Ezra) replaces or restores the
ancient Sacred Books, and is the Satrap. Here began
the temptation for priestly persons to grasp the power
and to reform the Scriptures with this aim perpetually
before them—to found a government of priests in which
a priest should be Ethnarch. Their hand may be traced
in every provision, every statute, and almost every narrative contained in their Scriptures: everything, even
the accounts of the prophets, is turned in favour of the
priests and *prophets*, the highest order of sacerdos. But
the chief object was to extend the power of Jerusalem
beyond the city and the province of Judæa. The aim
was to exercise authority over the other cities and tribes
of Palestine. The whole Old Testament agrees with this
view. Their jealousy of the Baal or Bacchus worship as
celebrated on the hills of Palestine, and under every
green tree is abundantly evidenced in their writings.
Their prophetical books are loud in their denunciations of
all shrines except that in Jerusalem, and prophecies of
the coming greatness of the Jewish State are thickly
strewn upon the record. Their scriptures claim the
country over the Jordan, the land of the Sabæans (18).
And lest their scriptures themselves should not suffice
they supplemented them by *traditions*. But the traditions themselves are hardly more vague and mysterious
than the allegories which they are fabled to conceal : and
it is impossible not to feel the fine mockery with which
Erasmus treats not only the body of the corrupted Jewish
writings, but also the " wisdom" which he sarcastically declares that they conceal. In Veteri Testamento, he says,
si præter *Historiam* nihil spectes, et audias, Adam è limo

conditum, uxorculam e dormientis latere furtim subtrac-
tam, serpentem illecebrâ pomi solicitantem mulierculam ;
Deum ad auram inambulantem, Romphæam foribus præ-
sidentem, nonne putes ex Homeri officinâ profectam fabu-
lam ? At sub his involucris *quam splendida latet Sapien-
tia ! !* Erasmus, *Chiliad* iii. But he has nowhere unveiled that "splendid wisdom" in the allegories or fables
of which he thus sarcastically speaks. (19.)

38. Sir Isaac Newton, the greatest of astronomers, but
the shallowest of theologians, did not fail to perceive,
even in his time, the way in which these books were
hashed up. The race of kings of Edom, he says (*Observations on Daniel*, p. 4), before there reigned any
king over Israel, is set down in the Book of Genesis
(xxxvi. 3), *and therefore that book was not written entirely in the form now extant before the reign of Saul.*
The writer set down the race of those kings, till his own
time, *and therefore wrote before David conquered Edom.*
The Pentateuch is composed of the Law and the history
of God's people together : *and the history hath been collected
from several books*, such as were the history of the creation composed by Moses (*Gen.* ii. 4) ; the book of the
generations of Adam (*Gen.* v. 1) ; and the book of the
Wars of the Lord (*Num.* xxi. 14). The book of wars
contained what was done at the Red Sea, and in the jour-
neying of Israel through the wilderness, and therefore
was begun by Moses. And Joshua *might* carry it on to
the conquest of Canaan. For Joshua wrote some things
in the book of the Law of God (*Josh* xxiv. 26), and therefore *might* write his own wars in the book of wars,
these being *the principal wars of God ! ! !* And Samuel
had leisure in the reign of Saul to put them in the

form of the books of Moses and Joshua now extant, inserting into the book of Genesis, the race of the kings of Edom, &c. The first chapter of Daniel, adds Sir Isaac, as if the thing were a trifle, and of no religious moment whatever, *was written after his death ! !* This Daniel, who is said to have been prime minister of the King of Babylonia, and especially accomplished in the writing and speaking of Chaldæan (*Dan.* i. 4), is supposed to have written a book which is not Chaldee at all, but a vulgar *lingua franca* of Hebrew and Aramaic. Eichhorn and Bertholdt suppose the work, which we now have, to be written by different persons, and cite i. 21, as contradicting x. 1 : and i. 5—18, as contradicting ii. 1. Porphyry, Bleek, Michaelis, De Wette, Lengerke, and a variety of others, dispute the authenticity of the book. The Greek words recurring (iii. 5, 7, 10), betray that part of it to have been written in a later age, when Greek words began to be introduced into Asia. A variety of other circumstances might be added to prove that it is a forgery.

39. In the version of the Seventy, and of Theodotion, are found some considerable additions to the Book of Daniel, which are wanting in the present Hebrew. These are the prayer of Azarias (*Dan.* iii. 24—25), the Song of the Three Children (iii. 52—90), the History of Susannah (*Dan.* xiii.), the narrative of Bel and the Dragon (xiv.) The question arises where did the heaven-inspired seventy-two translators find the original of those myths which they translated into Greek? They are not to be found in Hebrew now—but will it be denied that they existed in Hebrew then? De Wette adduces several proofs from the style to show that certain parts of it had

a Chaldee original. Bel and the Dragon is read in the Roman office on Ash Wednesday, and in the Church of England on the 23rd of November ; Susannah is read in the Anglican Church on the 22nd of November, and in the Roman on the vigil of the fourth Sunday in Lent. The Book of Esther, says Luther, I toss into the Elbe : I am so an enemy to the Book of Esther that I would it did not exist : for it Judaises too much, and hath in it a great deal of heathenish naughtiness : and in his work, *De Serv. Arb.*, addressed to Erasmus, after saying, In regard to Ecclesiasticus, although I might justly refuse it, yet I receive it in order not to lose time in involving myself in a dispute concerning the books received into the canon of the Hebrews, he adds : Which canon you do not a little reproach when you compare the Proverbs and the Love Song (as you sneeringly call it), with the two books of Esdras and Judith, Susannah, the Dragon and the Book of Esther ; but, though they have this last in their canon, it is, in my judgment, more worthy than all of being excluded from the canon.

40 But even upon these unsatisfactory versions, compilations, centoes, or whatever they were, doubts are thrown. The days of persecution did not end with the return from captivity. As if to destroy every vestige of a book, which was supposed by the nations to have stirred up the Jews to every species of animosity, malignity, and unrighteousness against all other people, Antiochus Epiphanes disgusted with his discoveries in the Temple, of the atoning victim and the ass-head, resolved utterly to destroy every copy of the Law that could be found ; and to compel by violence, a total abandonment by the Hebrews of their rites, their customs, and their very

creed. Nor were many of the Jews themselves unwilling to conform. Their money was their God, and paganism was an abundant source of gold. (20). I cite from the writer of the first of Maccabees, who is more to be depended on than Josephus; though the latter does not contradict but rather abridges the account, which the former has left us. *In those days,* he says, *went there out of Israel wicked men, who persuaded many, saying; let us go and make a covenant with the heathen, that are round about us, for since we departed from them, we have had much sorrow. So this device pleased them well. Then certain of the Jews were so forward herein that they went to the king, who gave them license to do after the statutes of the heathens. Whereupon they built a school at Jerusalem, according to the customs of the heathens, and made themselves uncircumcised and forsook the holy covenant, and joined themselves to the heathen and were sold to do mischief. And after that Antiochus had smitten Egypt, he returned again in the hundred and forty third year, and went up against Israel and Jerusalem with a great multitude; and entered haughtily into the sanctuary and took away the golden altar and the candlestick of light and all the vessels thereof: and the table of the shew bread and the pouring vessels, and the vials, and the censers of gold and the veil; and the crowns and the golden ornaments that were before the temple, all which he pulled off. He took also the silver and the gold, and the precious vessels; also he took the hidden treasures which he found: and when he had carried all away, he went into his own land, having made a great massacre and spoken very proudly. And after two years fully expired, the king sent his chief collector of taxes into the cities of Juda, who came also to*

Jerusalem with a great multitude ; and spoke peaceable words unto them, but all was deceit; for when they had given him credence, he fell suddenly upon the city, and smote it very sore, and destroyed much people of Israel, and when he had taken the spoils of the city he set it on fire, and pulled down the houses and walls thereof on every side, but the women and children took they captive and possessed themselves of their cattle. Thus they shed innocent blood on every side of the sanctuary and defiled it; insomuch that the inhabitants of Jerusalem fled because of them ; whereupon the city was made an habitation of strangers and became strange to those that were born in her, and her own children left her, her sanctuary was laid waste like a wilderness, her feasts were turned into mourning ; her sabbaths into reproach ; her honour into contempt. As had been her glory, so was her dishonour encreased ; and her excellency was turned into mourning. Moreover King Antiochus wrote to his whole kingdom, that all should be one people: and that every one should leave his laws ; so all the heathens agreed, according to the commandment of the King : yea many also of the Israelites consented to his religion and sacrificed unto idols, and profaned the sabbath. For the King had sent letters by messengers into Jerusalem and the cities of Juda, that they should follow the strange laws of the land ; and did forbid burnt offerings and sacrifice and drink offerings in the temple ; and that they should profane the sabbaths and festival days . and pollute the sanctuary and holy people, set up altars and groves and chapels of idols and sacrifice swine's flesh and unclean beasts : that they should also leave their children uncircumcised, and make their souls abominable with all manner of uncleanness and profanation :—to the end that they might

*forget the Law, and change all their statutes : and whoso-
ever would not do according to the commandments of the
king, he said, he should die. In the self-same manner
wrote he to the whole kingdom, and appointed overseers
over all the people, commanding the cities of Juda to sacrifice city by city. Then many of the Jews were gathered
unto them, to wit, every one who forsook the Law, and so
they committed evils in the land ; and drove the Israelites
into hiding places, even wheresoever they could flee for
succour. Now on the fifteenth day of the month Cas-
leu, in the hundred and forty fifth year, they set up the
abomination of desolation upon the altar and builded idol
altars throughout the cities of Juda on every side · and
burnt incense at the doors of their houses and in the streets
And when they had rent in pieces the Books of the Law
which they found, they burnt them in fire : and wheresoever
was found with any the Book of the Covenant* (the Pentateuch) or if any consented to the Law, the king's commandment was that they should put him to death : thus
did they by their authority to the Israelites every month.*
So utter a destruction as this, must well nigh have
annihilated every copy of the Jewish sacred writings.
Assuming that the copies or rather phonographs, which
had been made by Hilkiah and Esdras, and the various
other anonymous editors, were really true and genuine,
they must have been wholly exterminated by Antiochus ,
and the version of the Old Testament which now subsists, must have been made by Judas, or by some unknown
compilers, probably from the Greek of the Seventy, long
after the appearance and death of Jesus. (21). In this,
or in the preceding proscriptions of their sacred books,
perished the following Jewish volumes which were per-

haps of the same character as those which we now possess—realizing that creed of hate which Philo the Jew
tells us was the genuine Hebrew faith. The Sacred
Writings, he says, prescribe what we ought to do, and
what will contribute to our advantage; *commanding us
to hate the heathens and their laws and institutions.*

1. Book of the Wars of the Lord, Numbers xxi. 14, xxvii. 30.
2. Book of Jasher the Upright, Joshua x. 13, 2 Sam. i., 18.
3. Book of the Constitution of the Kingdom, 1 Sam., x. 15.
4. Solomon's Three Thousand Proverbs, his Thousand and five Songs, and his Works on Natural History, 2 Kings, iv. 32, 33.
5. Book of the Acts of Solomon, 1 Kings, xi. 41, 2 Chron. ix. 5.
6. Chronicles of the Kings of Israel, 1 Kings, xiv. 19 xvi. 5, xx. 27, xxii. 39, Micah, vi. 16.
7. Chronicles of the Kings of Judah, 1 Kings, xv. 7.
8. Book of Samuel the Seer, 1 Chron. xxix. 29.
9. Book of Nathan the Prophet, 1 Chron. xxix. 2, 2 Chron. ix. 29.
10. Book of Gad the Seer, 1 Chron. xxix. 29.
11. Nathan the Prophet's Life of Solomon, 2 Chron. ix. 29.
12. Prophecy of Ahijal the Shilonite, 2 Chron. ix. 29.
13. Visions of Iddo the Seer, 2 Chron. ix. 29.
14. Book of Shemaiah the Prophet, 2 Chron. xii. 15.
15. Iddo the Seer on Genealogies, 2 Chron xii. 15.
16. Isaiah's Acts of Uzziah, 2 Chron. xxvi. 22.

T

17. Book of the Kings of Israel and Judah, 1 Chron. ix. 1, 2 Chron. xvi. 11, xxviii. 26, xxxiii. 18, xxxv. 27, xxxvi. 8.

18. Book of Jehu, 2 Chron. xx. 34, 1 Kings, xvi. 17.

19. Isaiah the Prophet's Life of Hezekiah, 2 Chron., xxxii. 32.

20. Lamentations of Jeremiah over Joshua, 2 Chron. xxxv. 25.

21. A Book, Exod. xvii. 14, xxiv. 7.

22. A Book of the Lord, Isaiah xxxiv. 16.

23. Story of the Prophet Iddo, 2 Chron. xiii. 21.

24. Sayings of the Seers, 2 Chron. xxxiii. 19.

25. Book of the Covenant, Exod. xxiv. 7.

26. The Book of Enoch, Jude 14.

27. Songs of Praise, Nehemiah, xii. 46.

28. A Book of Remembrance, Malachi iii. 16.

29. Chronicles of King David, 1 Chron. xxvii. 24

30. Books of Jason, 2 Maccab. ii. 23.

41. It may not be inappropriate to cite here what the Jews themselves say of the composition of their scriptures. It will be seen that *they*, who ought to know better than Christians, who were the *real* writers, of the works that now pass under prophetic names, differ in many particulars from Horne and the critical divines, but do not pretend, and never did profess that they had the genuine and original writings, but only *recollections* as it were, of them : or at all events only such fragmentary materials as enabled recent compilers to put them into one. I quote from the *Babylonian Talmud, Megil. fo* 10, c. 2. And who wrote them ? Moses wrote his books and the section of Balaam and Job, (this it has

been shewn cannot possibly be true.) Joshua wrote his book, and eight verses in the Law. Samuel wrote his book, Judges and Ruth. David wrote the book of Psalms, with the assistance of ten of the elders; by the aid of Adam, the first man, of Melchizedeck, of Abraham, of Moses, of Heman, of Jeduthun, of Asaph, of the three sons of Korah. Jeremiah wrote his book, and the Book of Kings, and Lamentations. *Hezekiah and his assistants* wrote *Isaiah*, Proverbs, Canticles, and Cohelcth (Ecclesiastes.) The men of the great Synagogue wrote Ezekiel and the Twelve, Daniel and the volume of Esther, Ezra wrote his book, and the genealogy of the book of Chronicles down to himself. Whether, therefore, we go upon the statements of Hilkiah and Esdras, and the author of Maccabees: or upon the authority of the Talmud, or upon the almost unanimous agreement of all the most learned critics and divines of the present day, one thing is clear, that upon neither of them can any argument be based for the authenticity of the present Hebrew-Chaldee scriptures; but that on the contrary, if they (who are unquestionably, the only reliable authorities) are to be trusted, there are very few remains of ancient composition, which are more justly open to doubt or disbelief. (22.)

42. And here I may as well advert to an argument, which is constantly put forward by the advocates for the unquestionable authenticity of every part of the Old and New Testament; and put forward too, with a pertinacity of purpose against all objections, whether derived from history or philology, that shews the reliance which those who use it, place upon its apparent strength. But the truth is, there is no force in it at all, though I have no

doubt many persons are deceived by its fallacious aspect.
The argument is this. You have the same reasons for
believing Homer to be genuine, that you have for the
authenticity of Scripture: both are ancient works: the
original manuscript of neither exists: why then should
you accept the one as an undoubted original, while you
require proof of the other? Is not this against all reason? and does it not shew that there must be some concealed or dishonest motive lurking in your mind, that
causes you at once to receive the profane writer's production, without any question of its being genuine, while you
demand from us, proof, step by step, of the genuineness
of those writings which we on equally good grounds
believe to be the inspirations of God. This is not consistent; neither is it fair or just. I think I have herein
stated the argument in all its force. I meet it in this
way. What possible *interest* can any man have in forging
a splendid epic like the Iliad or the Odyssey, and then
assigning it, with all the glory which must for ever accompany it, to another man who is a stranger to its production? The supposition is incredible and absurd. The
man who can compose a poem like that, will never suffer
it to go forth in a false name, but will only be too glad to
demand and await all the laurels which the world is ever
ready to bestow on those who either delight or teach it. It
is therefore unlikely that the poems of Homer can be the
work of any other man than him whose name they bear.
But is this so with a work that purports to be a divine
inspiration given to Ezekiel or Daniel. Why should any
man forge it? say the believers. There is no reason
why he should forge a new prophecy if the original
exists; and is known to the world. But if the original

has been lost or destroyed in the course of ages, and if the interests of a mighty hierarchy depend upon the supposed existence of that original, and if they derive their authority from it, and enormous gains, and all powerful influence, I can see abundant reason why a close body corporate composed of men of learning like the priests, should agree together to put forth as genuine to the world, by a species of "pious fraud," as good an imitation of that original as they can invent; and indeed if they did not do so, they would be fools to their own interest, which I never yet heard that any sacred congregation was. There is, therefore, no analogy between the two cases; and the argument relied on is dissipated into air. Now that the greater number of the sacred writings of the Hebrews were destroyed, must I think be apparent to all who have read these pages. (23). It was the direction of Amosis that every ruler should himself transcribe a copy of the Law with his own hand · he set apart also a tribe of Levites who were to multiply copies and thus preserve it for all time. But if we believe the historical extracts which I have copied from the Old Testament itself, this duty was grossly neglected, and the sole memorial of their illustrious founder was that single most suspicious copy which Hilkiah said he met with in the Temple, and which appears (if genuine) not only to have been the only copy in existence of the writings of Amosis, but also to have been a new light dawning upon the priests, and amazing them, as if not only the Book itself, but the very memory of it had died away out of their minds. And if this could happen to the Law of their great legislator, the very corner stone on which all their power, ecclesiastical and political, was founded,

what must it not have been with the minor writers, their
priests or prophets, nearly every one of whom, while he
lived, was treated as a madman, or a malefactor, and
punished as such (24), and whose productions could consequently have never been deemed sacred until hundreds
of years had passed away, when the writings themselves
were utterly lost, and no means existed of restoring
them ?   The priests would then come forward with their
fiction, and say, We have found the prophecies that Daniel
wrote, or Isaiah gave ; and the *people*, who knew absolutely nothing, would be deceived with the greatest ease.
These facts being premised, it is obvious that no person
can, with any certain assurance, say the writings in the
Old Testament are the genuine writings of the persons
whose names they bear. When, therefore, I find passages
in Isaiah and Ezekiel, and Daniel, which, by internal evidence, show clearly that they have been interpolated by
compilers, whether by Hilkiah, or by Esdras, and his
inspired subordinates, or by the various unknown persons
who meddled with these matters, I care not, I at once
lay hold of them, and transfer them to their proper place
in that work with which it is obvious that they have a
clear connection, and from which I entertain no doubt
that they were cited, either by the original priest or prophet (for the Hebrew priest and prophet were synonymous), or else interpolated by the copying compilers of
the text, as it now stands.   With the latter part of the
four prophecies of Daniel, says Faber, the Revelation of
St John is immediately connected, being, in fact, only a
more minute and comprehensive prediction of the same
events.   As Sir Isaac Newton justly observes, it is
written in the same style and language with the prophe-

cies of Daniel, and hath the same relation to them which
they have to one another, so that *all of them together make
but one complete prophecy.* When, again, I find such
passages as those in Zecharias, chap. i. 8—11, chap. iii.
1—10, chap. iv. 1—5, and 11—14, chap. vi. 1—7 (25),
which have no connection whatever, nor any harmony
with the place in which they are found, nor any uniformity with the writer's tone of mind, but which have a
manifest connection with certain portions of the common
Apocalypse, I have no difficulty in assigning them their
place in it, and restoring them to that situation from
which they have been removed. This is all that I think
it necessary to say at present, as to the principle on which
this edition of the Apocalypse is framed. Those who
look deeper, will probably discover other and more convincing reasons than any that I think it fitting to put
forth at this time or in this place.

43. The account which we have received from Josephus and Philo, of the Septuagint version is nearly as
unsatisfactory as that which we have of the Hebrew
Chaldee; and Butler, in his *Horæ Biblicæ* treats it as an
exploded fable. Josephus is the only ancient historian
of name who gives it, Philo follows him, and seems to
add to the legend: the whole may be summarized thus.
Ptolemy Philadelphus, King of Egypt, hearing from his
librarian an account of the Hebrew Law which moved
his curiosity, wrote to Eleazar, the high priest of the
Jews, to send him six men from each of the twelve tribes,
who should translate the Law for him into Greek. Ten
of the tribes had wholly disappeared for ages before, and no
traces of them had ever been found: the high priest, however, sent six out of each of the twelve tribes to the king,

and by these seventy-two the Greek version was made. Inspired with a species of prophetic enthusiam, they were shut up in an island : Aristeas relates some miraculous legends of these holy men, for which Whiston vouches, but Josephus wisely declined to be responsible · the result of their labours, which were completed in exactly seventy-two days, remains in one of two Greek translations of the Pentateuch, to which Jesus and his followers, and the first Christian Fathers, referred, but where, when, how, or by whom, the *other* books were translated, is involved in mystery and never can be cleared up The Greek is somewhat superior to New Testament Greek, which does not say much for it ; but indifferent as it is, few scholars, who are not paid priests, will deny that it is more authentic, as far as it is genuine, than the Hebrew-Chaldee phonograph. The plain truth, however, is, that not one single sacred volume of the Past is free from corruption , but all are disfigured by figments, which tend only to degrade the true idea of God to a level which the truly wise are grieved to contemplate.

44. Nor are the fables connected · with the finding, transcription, and translation of the Pentateuch less absurd than many of the narratives which those pretended revelations from God, themselves contain : narratives which to all honest minds are instantly repugnant , and which to not a few that are dishonest, are corrupting in the extreme. The Rev. David Jennings, D.D., a strictly orthodox writer, in his chapter on the Prophets. (*Jewish Antiquities*, page 250) has the following suggestive section : That Isaiah should walk naked and barefooted three years together, summer and winter, even if you understand by his being naked, merely being without his

upper garment; that Jeremiah should send yokes to the King of Edom and to the King of Moab, and to the King of the Ammonites, and to the King of Tyrus, and to the King of Sidon (*Jerem.* xxvii. 3), and that he should take so long a journey as from Jerusalem to the Euphrates, which is about 500 miles, to hide his girdle in a rock, and that after it was rotted he should take the same long journey to fetch it back again (*Jerem.* xiii. 4, 6, 7), and that he should take a wine cup from God and carry it up and down to all nations, far and near, even all the kingdoms which are upon the face of the earth, and make them drink it, is more than improbable. (*Jerem.* xxv. 15—29) So likewise that Ezekiel should actually eat a roll which God gave him (*Ezek.* iii. 1—3), and that he should lie upon his left side three hundred and ninety days together, and after that forty days together on his right side, with bands upon him, that he could not turn from one side to the other (*Ezek.* iv.) is not only extremely improbable upon several accounts, but hardly possible to be done in the time allotted to this whole affair; for it all passed betwixt the prophet seeing his first vision at the river Chebar, which was on the fifth day of the fourth month, in the fifth year of King Jehoiachin's captivity (*Ezek.* i. 1—2) and his sitting in his house with the elders of Judah on the fifth day of the sixth month, of the sixth year (*Ezek.* viii. 1), that is, within a year and two months. Now, the Jewish year being lunar, consisted of three hundred and fifty-four days, and their month of twenty-nine days and thirty days alternately; therefore a year and two months (three hundred, fifty-four, twenty-nine, and thirty) added together, would amount to no more than four hundred and thirteen days, which falls short of the number of days during which the prophet is said to lie on his side—(namely, 430 days)—by 17 days. And if you deduct also from the 413 days, the 7 days which he sat among the captives at Telabib (*Ezek.* iii. 15) there remain but 406 days, which are 24 days short of 430. * * To this head of impossibles we may refer God's bringing Abraham abroad into the field, and showing him the stars (*Genesis* xv.) since it appears that it was not yet sunset, "when the sun was going down," it is said, a great sleep fell upon Abraham (v. 12). * * The prophet Hosea is said at the command of God to take a wife of whoredom, that is, a whore, and to have three children by her, which are called the children of whoredom, that is, bastards. (*Hosea* i. 12) Those who will have this to be the real fact, alledge that she is called a wife of whoredom, which intimates, they say, that though she had been a lewd person, yet the prophet was legally married to her ; but they forget that the children which she bore him are called " children of whoredom ; " besides, he is ordered to love another woman, an adulteress (*Hosea* iii. 1), and is said to have bought or hired her for fifteen pieces of silver, and a homer and a-half of barley, to abide with him many days (verses 2 and 3), circumstances which evidently point out a lewd mistress not a lawful wife. Now, can it be supposed that the prophet Hosea, the chief scope of whose prophecy is to discover sin, and to denounce the judgments of God upon a people that would not be reformed, would himself be guilty of such an immoral and scandalous practice, as to cohabit with one harlot after another; much less can it be thought that God would have commanded him so to do ?

45. Such is, in brief, *one* important section of the difficulties with which a student of the Hebrew bible is met : those that beset an English reader of the authorized version are not less formidable, when it is remembered that his very faith, or that opinion on which he bases his *all* for the future, is founded upon them. The authorized version is made, not in accordance with Hebrew, or the literal meaning, or the spirit of the original, but simply and solely in accordance with the thirty-nine articles, and the general notions of religion which pervade protestants, or worshippers of Paul. Never indeed was there a book which in *essential particulars* more thoroughly misrepresents, and even falsifies its original, than the authorized version. Horne, who is the most orthodox of writers, and whom therefore I cite in preference to other and greater scholars, and far deeper thinkers, on whom a shade of a suspicion of heterodoxy may fall, gives for an example one important falsification of the many hundreds that exist. The preceding account of the principal topics, he says, connected with the book of Job, would be thought imperfect without some notice of the remarkable passage in xix., 25—29, a passage which has been much contested among critics. As every attempt at a true explanation of it must be based on a faithful version, and as the English translation is very incorrect in this instance, we shall preface our remarks with a faithful version of the original words :—

But I know my vindicator lives,
And will stand at last upon the earth,
And though after my skin this [body] *be destroyed,*
Even without flesh shall I see God.
Yea, I shall see him for myself.

Mine eyes shall behold him : none other [*shall do so*].

My reins pine away [with longing] *within me.*

The term translated " Redeemer," means Vindicator, Avenger, and applies to God.   Job expresses a confident expectation that God would yet appear and vindicate the justice of his cause, as well as his integrity, which is done accordingly.   (Vol. ii., p. 733.)   He adds that *it cannot with any truth be said to apply to a Messiah,* yet it is to him it ever has been applied by all orthodox writers ; and I have heard the passage repeatedly cited by priests and bishops in the pulpit, as a positive prediction by Job of the coming of Jesus.   When therefore the English translators have not hesitated to corrupt a passage of this description, and to make it read in accordance with Paulite views, namely, an atoner for human sin, and a *bodily* resurrection of the dead (than which nothing can be conceived more gross for a celestial paradise), the text itself expressly *negativing* a body, those who hold that upon their belief in this life depends their future with the Divine, may well pause in solemn terror, and ask themselves this question : If I am thus misled by my teachers upon a vital article of belief, and if I base all my conduct upon earth on that article, how awful will be my condition when after death I find myself to have been in error , and what answer shall I make, when God asks me, *why* I sought not knowledge of the truth, for myself, without depending upon others for its teaching ?   This is a question indeed of the most fearful magnitude.   I leave it to be answered by those whose everlasting welfare it involves.

46. The orthodox version of this famous passage, which indeed people seem to have off by heart, is as follows : *I*

know that my Redeemer liveth, and that he shall stand at the latter day upon the earth, and though after my skin, worms destroy this body, yet in my flesh I shall see God. The literal translation of the Hebrew is, *I know that my avenger* (or kinsman גאל, *Gal; he whose right it was, and still is, among the Orientals to vindicate the honour, or avenge the death of a relative) liveth and shall stand at last over the dust* (the dead) *and after my skin destroy this yet without my flesh I shall see God, whom I shall see myself* (without a mediator), *and mine eyes shall behold him, and no other* (he is the One Sole God—there is no other : the Arabic faith). Horne, it will be observed, is wrong in his interpretation of "no other," by adding [shall do so]. Job was a pure monotheist, and so expresses himself. He never could have intended to say that he alone of all other human or angelic creatures should see God. Such a notion would be manifestly absurd. This word is used also in Gen. xlviii. 16. "The angel who redeemed me (גאל *gal*) that is, recovered me, vindicated me from, avenged me or, delivered me) from all evil, bless the lads :—"meaning, say the commentators, the preserving, protecting, guiding providence of God, which I have experienced during my life." Was this Redeemer Jesus? No one ever pretended that it was—by what reasoning therefore is the passage in Job referred to him; and why should not one interpretation serve for the first as well as for the second? Take again the following hymn as an instance : the composition either of Adam himself, or of Enoch : *Give thanks unto the Lord, call upon his name, make known his deeds among the people. Sing unto him, sing psalms unto him, talk ye of all his wondrous works. Glory ye in his holy name : let the heart of them rejoice*

*that seek the Lord. Seek the Lord and his strength, seek
his face continually Remember his marvellous works
that he hath done, his wonders, and the judgment of
his mouth · He is the Lord, our God; his judgments are
in all the earth. Be ye mindful always of his covenant; the word which he commanded to a thousand
generations: Saying, Touch not* MINE ANOINTED ONES, *
and do my prophets no harm. And when they went from
nation do nation, and from one kingdom to another
people: He suffered no man to do them wrong: yea, he
reproved kings for their sakes. Sing unto the Lord, all
the earth; shew forth from day to day his salvation.
Declare his glory among the heathen; his marvellous
works among all nations. For great is the Lord, and
greatly to be praised: he also is to be feared above all
gods. Glory and honour are in his presence; strength
and gladness are in his place. Give unto the Lord, ye
kindreds of the people, give unto the Lord glory and strength.
Give unto the Lord the glory due unto his name: bring an
offering, and come before him: worship the Lord in the
beauty of holiness. Fear before him, all the earth · the world
also shall be stable, that it be not moved. Let the heavens
be glad, and let the earth rejoice: and let men say among
the nations, The Lord reigneth. Let the sea roar, and the
fulness thereof: let the fields rejoice, and all that is therein.
Then shall the trees of the wood sing out at the presence of
the Lord, because he cometh to judge the earth O give
thanks unto the Lord; for he is good , for his mercy
endureth for ever.* 1 Chron. xvi., 22 Ps. cx. 15. The
word which, in the common version, has been translated *mine anointed,* as if it referred to only one, is in the
plural במשיחי *Bemeshiai;* but as usual it is fraudulently

rendered in the common bibles as if it-were in the singular. Yet even the miserable Eusebius had not so much boldness as our reverend changers into English ; for *he* translates it, *Touch not my anointed ones (my Messiahs), and do my prophets no harm.* And it is in this false and felonious style that the Old and New Testaments have been translated, and in this deceitful manner they have been circulated over the earth : the object, as the reader sees, being in this place to conceal from men that there are other Messiahs and other Messengers from God to earth, than the one whom the Paulites pretend to be the sole Angel after the days of Amosis. How will the men who are parties to these frauds answer for them before God ? or do they indeed believe in God at all ?

47 Nor less awful has been the crime of them who have in other respects, and for other reasons, interpolated and interpreted the Old Testament according to their own base notions. For hundreds and hundreds of years Christians and Jews have alike treated the negro races with the most fiend-like cruelties on the ground that they are the accursed progeny of the accursed Ham, and that God himself has pronounced upon them his malediction. They have been shot, stabbed, flogged, crucified, tortured, drowned, and their wives and daughters torn from them and ravished before their eyes, by reason of this execrable creed : and Paulites have thought that they were but ministers of their Maker's vengeance, in inflicting barbarities upon this fated race. Yet see how Faber disposes of this monstrous faith. An opinion, he says, has I know not how, very generally prevailed, that a curse was pronounced upon Ham, which, devoted his posterity to servitude ; hence the epithet "accursed" has been liberally

bestowed upon that patriarch, as his stated and appropriate designation. Nor has this notion been taken up merely by ordinary and superficial theologists : even such writers as Bochart and Mede are to be found among its advocates. Bochart in one place styles Ham accursed : and in another he represents Noah as *execrating* him, and as foretelling that *his children should be slaves*, while Mede, not content with calling upon us *to tremble at the horrible curse of impious Ham*, and with intimating that he was *destined to be a servant of servants to all his brethren*, roundly asserts that there hath never yet been a son of Ham that hath shaken a sceptre over the head of Japhet ; that Shem hath subdued Japhet, and Japhet hath subdued Shem, but Ham never subdued either ! Yet notwithstanding this general persuasion, Scripture contains not a single syllable respecting either any curse pronounced upon Ham, or any prediction of the general servitude of his posterity ! Canaan, indeed the youngest of the four sons of Ham, is the subject of an imprecatory denunciation ; but Ham himself was never cursed ; consequently neither the curse nor the prophecy can affect any of his descendants except the Canaanites. Those writers, who have been most zealous in applying the curse and the prediction to Ham, were sensible that Scripture, as it stands at present, directly opposed their opinion : but so fully were their minds pre-occupied with the common idea, that rather than relinquish it, they have with mischievous ingenuity attempted to make the Bible speak the language which they had concluded it ought to speak. Hence, because the Arabic version reads, *cursed be the father of Canaan*, and because some copies of the 70, substitute Ham in the place of Canaan, they would, throughout the prophecy, wherever the word Canaan occurs, correct it to Ham, the father of Canaan. With respect to this supposed improvement of the text, it not only runs directly counter both to the Hebrew and the Samaritan copies of the Pentateuch, which perfectly agree in their reading of the prediction, to say nothing of the common reading of the 70 : but it seems to me to bear also the strongest internal marks of spuriousness. Why should Ham throughout the whole prophecy be called the *father of Canaan*, rather than the father of Cush, or of Mizir, or of Phut? Why should this long unmeaning title be thrice repeated? Why should Ham be particularized as the father of Canaan, rather than Japhet as the father of Gomer, or Shem as the father of Elam? When I compare the projected emendation with the commonly received reading, and when I consider the joint high authority of the Hebrew and Samaritan Pentateuchs, I cannot hesitate long in determining where to fix my choice. But I have yet an additional reason in protesting most strongly against any correction or rather alteration of the text. I have termed such critical ingenuity *mischievous;* nor was the epithet applied lightly and without cause. If the prophecy had *really* been penned in the form which has been recommended instead of its present form, its falsehood would have been clearly evinced by the testimony of history. So far from Ham never having shaken a sceptre over the head either of Japhet or Shem, as Mr. Mede most incautiously asserts, it may be clearly proved that his posterity in the line of Cush have been at the head, not only of the Babylonian empire of Nimrod, but of the Persian, the Grecian, and the Roman empires. Nor did their sway cease with the downfall of the last mighty power . the Goths or Scuths, penetrating into the west from their original settlements in Touran and Cashgar, have established and retained their sway over the fairest provinces of Europe ; and thus to the intrepid and freeborn children of the Hammonian Cush or Cusha, are committed the destinies of the world. *Pag. Idol.* i. 90.

(26.) We cannot be surprised to find among our American cousins, who, with our wicked and blasphemous forms of belief have inherited all our vices, and have even outdone us in many modes of crime, a remnant of this old Paulite-Jewish notion, that the whites alone are the people of God ; and that all other peoples may be exterminated as ruthlessly, as we of England massacre the New Zealanders of the present day for the sake of their lands. I read in the *Times* newspaper of April 23, 1866, the following extract, which is appropriately headed " A Community of Monsters," but which is only the old spirit of Judaism and Paulism, and perverted Biblicism, under a new aspect. We find, it says, the following horrid paragraph in an American exchange. A town meeting at Owyhu, Idaho, recently resolved that three men be appointed to select 25 men to go Indian hunting, and all those who fit themselves out shall receive a nominal sum for all scalps they may bring in , and all who cannot fit themselves out shall be fitted out by this committee ; and when they bring in a scalp it shall be deducted out. That for every buck scalp shall be paid 100 dollars, and for every squaw scalp 50 dollars, and 25 for everything in the shape of an Indian under ten years of age. That each scalp shall have the curl of the head, and each man shall make oath that the scalp was taken by the company. The worst Indians of Idaho, says the *Toronto*

Globe, commenting on this fiend-like community, must be civilized when compared with the white savages who held the " town meeting" at which such barbarous resolutions were adopted. Yet, if we could go among them, we should no doubt find them very pious believers in Paul, the redemption, and the Thirty-Nine Articles.

48. In the 2nd Kings (xxiii. 5,) it is said that Josiah put down *them that burnt incense unto Baal, to the Sun, and to the Moon, and* מזלות *Mazaloth.* This word signifies literally, the *flowings,* or *distillations,* that is the incarnate Messiahs, who emanated from the Spirit of Waters. The Rabbins suppose that it means the zodiacal signs : in reality it means the Twelve Messengers who were associated with their parents the Sun and Moon, and who were thus adored by the ancient Jews. *Jos. iv. Isaiah* lvii. 3—6. This word is the same as *Mazaroth,* which also means the Crowns, for the Twelve are as crowned kings. [See *ante,* p. 58.] Again in Isaiah lxv. 11, we read : *but ye are they that prepare a table for that troop, and that furnish a drink offering for that number.* This is a curious specimen of translation, the real version is : *Ye are they that prepare a table for God, and that furnish a drink offering for Meni,* מני ; that is the Holy Spirit of the Heavens, called plurally the Dispensers or Distributors of the מן mannah, or bread from heaven. She was adored by the Arabians under the name of Ma-Nah : and the English word Moon, and month, and many, come from her. She was the Mona, and Mon (Welsh) or Sacred Mountain of Paradise ; and the Mens, or Everlasting Mind, or Logos of the Gentiles And in order to conceal all this, the parsons who translated the Bible for King James, gave the above absurd and false

interpretation. Another instance is to be found in *Psalm* ii. 7, thus translated *Thou art my son: this day have I begotten thee*, which is triumphantly quoted by all Biblical controversialists as conclusive evidence of the Trinity, and of an exclusive Messiahship of Jesus. But the word, translated *begotten*, really means *to appoint to an office*, or in a figurative sense *to bring forth;* [See Parkhurst ילד *yalad*], so that the real version is,

    I will declare the decree,

    The Lord hath said unto me, Thou art my Son,

    This day have I appointed thee to thine office,

an allusion either to the Jews collectively, or a compliment paid to King David by one of his bards. By the Arabian doctors it is rendered " I have educated thee."

49. And here I may premise that in my Introduction to the True Testament of Jesus, I shall shew how the gospels and writings of those who are called apostles have been interpolated and corrupted : at present I need only refer to that well known passage of the three witnesses in *John* v. 7, than which a more impudent forgery was never committed ; and which is now given up (when it is no longer tenable), by all divines—though of course the Bible Society still publish it, without note or comment, as if it were really part of the Testament, and well meaning persons leave them large fortunes little knowing that they are to be disbursed in the diffusion of falsehoods. The Hebrew gospel of Matthew, says Olshausen remained in Phrygia and in Palestine with all sorts of heterogeneous additions on the part of the Jew-Christians. *His disciples coming by night stole him while we (the guard) were asleep. And this story has circulated among the Jews down to the present day. Matt.* xxviii. 13. This expres-

sion *down to the present day*, indicates rather a late date for the *Greek* Matthew. Olshausen himself, much against his will is constrained to confess that Matthew after the Hebrew Evangel, made a free translation of it into Greek. There is a well-known passage in the writings, which are vulgarly or fraudulently assigned to Isaiah, which furnishes another instance of the matchless audacity with which the Old Testament translators presumed on the ignorance of their readers. It is in vii. 14. The Lord himself shall give you a sign; lo *the* Virgin shall conceive and bear a son. What Virgin? The word in the Hebrew is emphatic העלמה *Ha-Almah*. The answer is evident: it meant some particular young person *then* in the mind of the speaker. The vulgate translation a virgin, is as usual deceptive: such a word might apply to Mary, if used by a writer who lived nearly a thousand years before her; but could *not* apply with the definite article prefixed; hence the artfulness of so rendering it in the English. Upon this falsification Rammohun Roy makes the following remark: As to the word "a virgin," found in the English translation, I request my readers to advert to the original Hebrew העלמה "the Virgin," as well as to the Greek both of the Septuagint and the gospel of Matthew, ἡ παρθενος, the Virgin, leaving it to them to judge whether a translation which so entirely perverts the meaning preserved throughout, by men whom we cannot suspect of ignorance of the original language, must not have proceeded from a previous determination to apply the term "virgin," as found in the Prophet to the mother of Christ, in order that the high titles applied to Hezekiah might in the most unqualified manner be understood of Jesus (p. 283). The Jews in *their* Hellenistic version of this passage, in order to spite the Christians, translated it νεανίς, a young woman The whole passage however it will be seen is misconstrued, or misrepresented, for " the child" at the end of it, does not mean Jesus, but the child Shear-Jashub. *Then said the Lord unto Isaiah, Go forth now to meet Ahaz, thou, and Shear-jashub thy son, at the end of the conduit of the upper pool in the highway of the fuller's field; and say unto him, Take heed, and be quiet; fear not, neither be fainthearted for the two tails of these smoking firebrands, for the fierce anger of Rezin with Syria, and of the son of Remaliah. Moreover the Lord spake again unto Ahaz, saying, Ask thee a sign of the Lord thy God, ask it either in the depth, or in the height above. But Ahaz said, I will not ask, neither will I tempt the Lord. And he said, Hear ye now, O house of David; Is it a small thing for you to weary men, but will ye weary my God also? Therefore the Lord himself shall give you a sign; Behold, the virgin shall conceive, and bear a son and shall call his name Immanuel. Butter and honey shall he eat, that he may know to refuse the evil, and choose the good. For before this child* (that is Shear-jashub) *shall know to refuse the evil, and choose the good, the land that thou abhorrest shall be forsaken of both her kings.* Yet this is one of the prophecies which are perpetually cited to prove that Jesus was foreseen by the Jews; though such an interpretation is absolutely false, as any one who reads it all with even ordinary attention can see.

50. For these, or a large majority of these interpolations, the Church of Rome stands guilty; the Jewish sanhedrim are alike flagitious; and the Church of England, which knowingly adopts and circulates over the earth,

the fraudulent forgeries and glosses of both is equally
criminal before the judgment seat of God. The first of
those hierarchies having unlimited power, destroyed
almost all vestiges of the true religion which Jesus
taught, and which was only a renovation of the first and
oldest creed that God gave to man. For Jesus himself
left Judæa at an early age; he quitted the workshop of
his reputed father, and abided in Egypt, where he was
initiated into the Mysteries, and brought with him to
Jerusalem many of the Apocalyptic volumes of the eight
Sacred Messengers who had preceded him. He commenced preaching in his 49th year—(7 X 7, a mystic
number)—(*John* viii. 57), and was put to death in about
3 years after; and as there has been an error of 5 years
in the computation of the Christian Chronology (*Whiston's Sacred History*, vol. v. 10), and Jesus was born
about the middle of June (not on the 25th of December,
as the easy-going public is taught to believe), these five
years added to the true period of his life—namely, 52,
give the date of his death, Anno J. C. 57. That he be-
queathed to his Apostles his foreign books seems certain ;
and this is what is really meant by *Acts* ii. 8, 9, 10 11,
where men of all nations are reported to have heard their
own tongue, that is, the truths of their own religious
volumes, from the assembled Twelve. And this absence
of the Sacred Messenger in Egypt, and his journey
farther eastward, is the true mode of accounting for that
singular disappearance, which is mentioned in the gospels of him who at twelve years of age astonished the
Rabbis by his knowledge, yet who, we are told, continued
for the fol'owing thirty one, working as a common carpenter, mending chairs and tables, while he was during

all that period, as Bishop Pearson says, the Supreme, Almighty, and Eternal God ! But why he came to waste so many years on earth in utter idleness and abandonment of his celestial mission, the priests of error do not say. The truth is, Jesus did not do so : he travelled as a pilgrim in search of knowledge, and acquired all the Oriental sciences. But when Paul, the old enemy of Christianity (*Acts* viii. 1, 3 ; ix. 1 ; xxii. 4, 20), wearied of his persecutions, imprisonments, and slaughters of the meek disciples of Jesus, determined by other, though not less criminal means to destroy his divine religion, and to change it into mongrel Judaism under a new mask, he gradually brought back his less energetic brethren, whom the Messenger had enlightened and converted, to their own original narrow notions ; and thus the broad and splendid views of the Ninth Messiah gradually disappeared from the faith. Yet Peter retained some ; and we have seen that he unquestionably borrowed from the Indian Bhaga-Vad-Geeta (*Ante*, page 163.) But when the accursed Church of Rome and Satan arose, the real creed of Jesus stood in its way ; and so it brought all things back to ancient Paganism, and altered all the books which it did not care to destroy. Thus may be explained the disappearance from the Hebrew and Christian volumes of allusions to the Holy Spirit, of which we nevertheless find vestiges, and of which once universal faith traces are to be found all over the earth (27). Yet the passage which I have cited from Genesis (*ante* page 189), is so conclusive as to be worth a thousand ordinary allusions ; and if the reader will examine it, he will find it to be so. And this was part of that theology, which, as we know, was guarded so closely in the Mysteries ; which the Ninth Messenger dared not publish openly, but which he felt himself at liberty to expound to the disciples when they were alone. (*Mark* iv. 34.) Nor does this assertion stand without record : Jesus himself once said : *My Mother, the Holy Spirit, took me just now by one of the hairs of my head, and carried me up into the Great Mountain, Thabor.* This is quoted by Origen. (*Hom.* xv., *in Jerem.*, p. 148, and Tom. ii., *Comment in Johannem*, p. 58.) And it is twice quoted by Jerom also. (Whiston.˙ *Sacred History of the New Testament,* v. 127.) It is only one of many passages which the half Pagan, half Jewish church of the early ages, dared to expunge from the authentic sayings of the Ninth Messenger ; and of which "the faithful" at the present day are kept in entire ignorance. Yet even Mosheim admits that there was "a secret doctrine ;" and what could it be but this ? Clement, of Alexandria, has these words : For it was not out of envy that our Master [Jesus] said in a certain Gospel : *My secret is to me, and to the children of my family. (Strom.* v. 578.) But what this Gospel was, Clement does not inform us. It was one of those which the Paulites have destroyed , and, acting on the same accursed example that had been set them by Paul himself (*Acts* xix. 19), they burned most of the Sacred Volumes of the Messengers, impudently excusing themselves by calling them *magical.* The wonder only is, that in the prosecution of their unhallowed conspiracy they spared the Apocalypse ; but not comprehending it, they took it in its castrated form, nor fancied that it would ever again be restored to its pristine shape, and arise, as if from the dead, to blast their pretensions to sole and universal sway. Thus, while in the Old Testament we find every crime applauded or forgiven, we find

U

in the New, apologies for adulteresses and the canoniza-
tion of harlots (28); the exaltation of the ignorant, and
the beatification of the lowest cheats and wretches, the
publicans, who gathered the taxes for the Roman Government. For the Church has never, heeded of what its
members consisted, so long as it could swell its numbers,
and thus by the mere force of mobs, overawe the rest of
the community, and seduce the weak and wealthy to endow
it with gold. And it has ever pursued that satanic
policy; preaching that the poor and ignorant are the
assured favourites of heaven, and will inherit its everlasting glories; while there can be no truth more certain
than that the voluntary ignorance of the many is not
only one of the greatest crimes, but is also their heaviest
calamity. (29.)   The writings of Paul himself afford
proof of the character of the first proselytes; and I cite
an extract here for the purpose of showing by unanswerable testimony the truth of what I have just stated; and
also because it is another of the many passages with which
the forgers have been at work. In 1 Corinthians we read
as follows: *Be not deceived; neither fornicators, nor
idolators, nor adulterers, nor effeminate, nor sodomites,
nor thieves, nor covetous, nor drunkards, nor revellers, nor
extortioners, shall inherit the kingdom of God; and of
these things brethren ye are not ignorant, for ye also were
such* (vi. 9, 10, 11). And out of these reeking horrors
were the early followers of Paulism raked, and these are the
wretches who are called martyrs, and saints, and fathers
of the church. In our present version it is translated:
And such were some of you; and even the original Greek
has been altered from what it originally was. In the
fragments preserved by Cyril, Bishop of Alexandria, (one

of the Papal saints), of the Emperor Julian's treatise upon the Christians, the original passage is cited thus: καὶ ὑμεῖς τοιουτοι ἦτε, i. e., *ye also were such*: but in our modern New Testament, this has been altered καὶ ταυτα τινες 'ητε, i e., *and such were some of you*. We have it, however, as a certain fact, that it stood in its first shape in the days of Julian and Cyril : the latter does not question the authenticity of the extract ; and the Emperor adds : ὁρας ὁτι καὶ τουτους γενεσθαι φησι τοιουτους. *You see that he* [Paul] *says they were such characters as these.* (See *Cyril contra Julian*, lib. vii., p. 245.) Infamous, however, as they were, they were of course assured by Paul, that they were thenceforth the children of heaven. *But ye are washed*, he tells them ; *but ye are become holy, but ye are made righteous by the name of the Master Jesus, and by the spirit of our God.* This is what the murderers and villains of the present day are told ; and it is assuredly Satan's creed, not God's. No wonder that Paul follows it up by remarking, *All things are lawful unto me, but all things are not expedient*, that is, I may lie, rob, ravish, and slay ; it is perfectly lawful for me, who am saved by the scapegoat Jesus ; the only thing I shall have to consider is whether it is *expedient ;* whether I shall be found out, and so be punished ! And the whole spirit of this teaching has entered into what is called Christianity ; and fathers defend themselves for cohabiting with their daughters, and brothers for the same crime with their sisters, on the ground that it has been sanctioned by the Old Testament ; or if not, that every crime is atoned for in the New. *They are bought with a price*, as Paul frequently assures them ; and God is bound by the bargain: He dare not, and He cannot recede from it, whatever they may commit.

51. Yet it is not without a grim satisfaction that one may see even in the writings of Paul, that there were times when he felt the weight of his own past actions; when their hideous horrors rose up against him; when the accusing phantom of Stephen stalked all bruised and bloody before his eyes, and pointed to this inflamed and pauper fanatic as one of those who stoned him to his death; when his various persecutions and murders of other unhappy and unresisting followers of the gentle Jesus tortured his waking thoughts, and even *he* felt that for the work of undermining and destroying the stately plan of Christianity as propounded by the Master, and poisoning all its beautiful doctrines with the odious venom of degenerated Judaism, he was "accursed of Christ," although, indeed, labouring in the service of his brethren. *I speak the truth*, he says, *in Christ* [*the Anointed One*], *I lie not in the Holy Spirit, and in this my conscience beareth me witness; that I have great sorrow and pain without intermission in my heart; For I myself have prayed to be* [or boasted that I was], *accursed by Christ* [the Anointed], *because of my brethren, my kinsmen according to the flesh.* Romans ix. 1, 2, 3. And the employment to which he had addressed himself, must indeed have appeared accursed in what remained of conscience to this professing believer in Jesus. Bribed in all probability by Caiaphas and the other members of the priesthood, to abandon his trade of tent-making and become a common informer, he, when he was now satiated with persecution and its attendant blows, perjuries, imprisonments, and bloodshed, devised another

and more desperate policy—that of sapping by poison under the aspect of an ally, that sacred life which he had failed to extinguish by his assaults as a foe. He assumed therefore the *name* of Christian; and step by step infusing his malignant venom into the blood of Truth, he at last succeeded in utterly destroying the doctrine of the heaven-sent Man. So that of true Christianity there now remains little but the ghost; and its spirit may be said to have disappeared for centuries. For though it has, indeed, existed in the hearts of a few, yet from the great mass of Christendom, it has been altogether absent; nor will it again appear lovely and renewed, until Paulism is dead for ever, and has sunk with shrieks into the horrible Abyss.

52. The only apology that can be offered for this man, if he can at all be thought to be sincere, is, that he was insane; and to this affliction the natural violence and ferocity of his character may have reduced him. The story of his vision (*Acts* ix.), if it be not all a falsehood, was probably the first indication of his madness; the passages cited, *ante*, page 238, seem wild in the extreme; and he appears eventually to have brought himself to the notion that in all he did he was only a blind instrument in the hand of the Jewish Lar or God; and that as he sinned only with his body, while he dissented from sin in his mind, he was totally guiltless in the eyes of heaven. This is the clear meaning of his words: although I confess that there is an incoherency about them highly indicative of a disordered brain. *We know*, he says, *that the law is spiritual: but I am carnal, sold under sin. For that which I do, I allow not: for what I would, that I do not; but what I hate, that do I. If then I do that which*

*I would not, I consent unto the law that it is good. Now
then it is no more I that do it, but sin that dwelleth in me.
For I know that in me (that is, in my flesh,) dwelleth no
good thing: for to will is present with me: but how to
perform that which is good I find not. For the good that
I would I do not: but the evil which I would not, that I
do. Now if I do that I would not, it is no more I that
do it, but sin that dwelleth in me. I find then a law, that,
when I would do good, evil is present with me. For I delight in the law of God after the inward man: But I see
another law in my members, warring against the law of
my mind, and bringing me into captivity to the law of sin
which is in my members. O wretched man that I am! who
shall deliver me from the body of this death? I thank God,
through Jesus Christ our Lord. So then with the mind I
myself serve the law of God, but with the flesh the law of sin.*
Romans vii. And this same frantic doctrine is held by
considerable sects, who maintain on this authority, that
it is of no consequence what crimes are perpetrated by
the body, for that the body is a perishable thing; and
that the soul being a spirit, is in no way defiled by that
which its carnal vehicle commits. Murder and robbery are
therefore perfectly innocent amusements This appears
to have been the salve for his accusing conscience which
Saul or Paul professed to have ; and by this doubtless, if
he were not in reality, a bribed emissary, he justified to
himself, like all madmen, the career of hypocritical pretence, and moral assassination of Jesus, in which his
latter days were spent As to the story of his martyrdom,
it must, of course, be set down with the other figments
of the Romish Church ; there is no proof of it, though
plenty of conjecture , it is impossible to believe it, or in-

deed any of the tales which this congregation of Satan has handed down.

53. The foregoing observations would probably appear incomplete if I did not allude to the fell and awful forms of superstition and disbelief, which a blind adherence to works which are now confessed by the learned to be the compilation of designing, ignorant, or wicked men, has produced among mankind. To what what can we attribute the innumerable opposing creeds which fill Europe, America, and Australia, with religious rancour, and convert the divine revelations of religion into conduits of the most bitter hatred and malignity that the human heart can possibly contain?—to what indeed, but to the vague and fallible and wicked notions of God which these congregated priests of old dared to put forth under a divine sanction? To what but this can we attribute the debasing ideas of God and his Government which pollute the earth, and reduce to the lowest level the Divine Master of the Universe, the Infinite, the One, the All-Beautiful? To what can we attribute wars, robberies, and villainy of every kind, but to the horrid examples which these wretched imposters have preserved in history, and rendered holy by the express permission or command of God himself? There is scarcely a crime that cannot find its excuse or palliation in these strange centos from the writings of dead and unknown men I should be sorry to say that *that* is the reason why they have been always hugged to the hearts of the profane as a hallowed treasure ; but we know well that mortal men will even die in defence of what delights their evil passions, and will wage war for it to the cannon's mouth ; thinking only of the present, and heedless of the solemn future. Can we won-

der, therefore, that they have been always doubted by the wise ; or that we should find the Old Testament thus mentioned by writers, far more capable of a true un- biassed and reliable opinion, than any of the hireling sol- diers of the church ? The subject itself, the credulity of mankind, says Lord Kingsborough, in the *Mexican Anti- quities*, vi. 116, is calculated to excite our sorrow rather than our mirth, at beholding reason so fallen from her throne ; and the great, the good, the wise of ancient days, deemed nought in comparison with an outcast race of jugglers, who still pretend that they have "*have an oath in heaven*," for ever constituting them the favourite people of God, and ratifying for ever the articles of the Old Covenants which comprises all the items of the old law which Christians assert has been long since abolished, and which even if Christianity had never been esta- blished, or the old superseded by the new covenant, it might be argued on the grounds of fitness ought to have been abolished, since those laws were certainly not fit to be everlasting, some of which we are told in the Old Tes- tament itself, were not good. And also on the ground of expediency, because many of the Mosaic laws would have been quite unsuitable to the present age ; and one which the Jews were strictly commanded to obey, enjoins an act which we find registered in our statute books as a crime to which both legal penalties and infamy are equally attached. Idolatry, he continues, has existed in many countries in many forms, and it must be confessed that, if the fine arts have greatly contributed by the splendour of architecture, the perfection of statuary, and inimitable paintings, to elevate the religious feelings of the soul, their proper use has not unfrequently been perverted. But there is a great deal of difference between what are called the idolatries of heathen nations : the Egyptian interests the mind by its mysteries ; that of the Brahmins by the sacred solitude of their contemplative life ; and the images in the Grecian temples by the more than mortal beauty with which the sculptor sought to invest them. But it is idolatry accompanied with living sacrifices, altars reeking with gore, Jewish and Mexican idolatry that excite our feelings of abhorrence and disgust. If the Jews were forbidden to make graven images, it was probably on account of their moral debasement, and because Moses could not tell under what figures they might have represented Jehovah himself—a reason which has been assigned by Lyra, a celebrated commentator on Scripture, for God's having chosen to appear to them in the burning bush rather than in any other manner ; and lastly, because he knew they were a nation utterly destitute of taste for the fine arts. Of this we may be sure, judging from the Talmud (that deformed web of sacred history and traditions which the Jews assert to be the *mirror* of God), that if once they had been permitted to consign the allegories of Scripture, and the miraculous events of their own history to painting and sculpture, the most monstrous productions would have emanated from their school, and devils rather than angels would have been the offspring of the imaginations of a people disordered with visions, and ever prying into futurity through dreams. *Mexican Antiquities,* vi. 358.

54. Upon the history and sale of Joseph by his brethren, he remarks : It is evident from this account, that ten out of the twelve patriarchs of the twelve tribes of Israel were implicated in the same degree of guilt ; and

U 3

in vain do we seek for arguments to urge in palliation of their conduct: they were all grown up men, and had long before arrived at years of discretion: nor can it even be said that some of them from fear might have followed the multitude to do evil, since their two elder brothers, (and primogeniture carried·with it great weight amongst the Jews) felt some sentiments of commiseration for their younger brother, and for the affliction into which they knew that their father would be thrown on receiving the intelligence of his death ; and they differed in opinion, from the others *who proposed to murder him, and to throw him into a pit.* Reuben indeed seems to have acted a proper part on the occasion : and his exclamation on not finding his brother in the pit: *The child is not, and I— whither shall I go ?* proves that he was not devoid of every feeling of humanity. But what a scene of hypoc⁻risy was afterwards acted by them all, when all his sons and daughters rose up to comfort their sorrowing father after having shewn him the coat dipped in the blood which he believed to be his son's ! How, after reading this history can we feel or pretend to feel any reverence for the Jewish patriarchs ? Their moral characters were not only bad, but infamous ; and to praise them would be to insult virtue. The Bible records many other crimes which at a subsequent period they committed, and the *evil report*—true it cannot be doubted—which before this time Joseph had brought to his father about them, was the cause of their originally hating him. Reuben alone is presented to us under favourable colours, but how great must be the enormity of which he afterwards became guilty, to have been deprived by his father of his birthright, and to have been cursed by him on his death bed as is recorded in the fourth verse of the forty-ninth chapter of Genesis.—*Mex. Ant.*, vi. 324.

55. I think myself at liberty to observe, says Sir William Drummond, that profound and splendid scholar, in the Preface to his *Œdipus Judaicus*, that the manner in which Christian readers of the Old Testament generally choose to understand it, appears to me to be a little singular. While the Deity is represented with human passions, and those none of the best, while he is described as a quarrelsome, jealous, and vindictive being, while he is shewn to be continually changing his plans for the moral government of the world, and while he is depicted as a material and local god who dwelt in a box made of shittim wood in the temple of Jerusalem—they abide by the literal interpretation. They see no allegory in the first chapters of Genesis; nor doubt that far the greater portion of the human race is doomed to suffer eternal torments, because our first parents ate an apple, after having been tempted by a talking serpent. They find it quite simple, that the triune Jehovah should dine on veal cutlets at Abraham's table; nor are they at all surprised that the God of the Universe should pay a visit to Ezekiel in order to settle with the Prophet, whether he should bake his bread with human dung, or with cow's dung. In these examples the Christian readers of the Hebrew Scriptures understand no allegory. They believe the facts to have happened literally as they are stated; and neither suspect nor allow, that the language of the sacred writers upon such occasions may be entirely figurative. Very different is their mode of interpreting these same scriptures when they think there is any allusion made to the kingdom of Christ: Then they abandon the literal sense without scruple, and

sometimes it may be thought without consideration. The Rabbins learn with astonishment that the Song of Solomon for example is a mere allegory, which represents the love of Jesus for his church; that the lady whose navel was like a round goblet not wanting liquor—whose belly was like a heap of wheat set about with lilies, whose nose was as the tower of Lebanon which looketh towards Damascus, and who promised to her well-beloved that he should lie all night betwixt her breasts—was not Solomon's mistress, but the Church, the spiritual spouse of Christ. But since the Christians do admit allegory—since they even contend that the Old Testament abounds with figurative and symbolical language descriptive of the advent of the Messiah; why will they so strenuously insist upon the strict interpretation of the text in other examples? Be their decision what it may, the Theist is bound to vindicate the majesty of the Deity. Cicero has said that it is easier to tell what God is not than what he is. Now every Theist is surely prepared to say that the Deity is neither unjust, nor cruel, nor liable in any manner to the frailties of human nature. Is it possible for the *literal* interpreter of the Hebrew scriptures to aver this of Jehovah? *The Lord hardened the heart of Pharaoh*—was it just then to afflict Egypt with so many calamities on account of Pharaoh's obstinacy? The destruction of the seven nations ordained in the ninth chapter of Deuteronomy, appears to be utterly irreconcileable either to justice or to mercy. Their crime was idolatry—but this was the crime of all mankind with the exception of the Hebrews: and the seven nations seem to have merited their fate less than the Egyptians, who beheld all the miracles performed by Jehovah, and who yet continued to worship the gods of their country. But we cannot wonder at these things, since the passions of anger and jealousy, and the feeling of repentance or regret which are human infirmities, are frequently attributed to the God of the Hebrews. Is there a mind capable of forming just notions of the Deity, that can believe any testimony which records that the Divine, Infinite, and Eternal Being is affected by accident, or is subject to passion? It is impossible for the Theist to admit that anything is more powerful than God; and therefore he cannot allow that God can ever be in a state of passion; for passion must always be the effect of action, and of action which cannot be resisted. Passion is sufferance, and no being suffers of its own accord. If anything could put the Divine Mind into a state of passion, that thing would act independently and in spite of God. From this view of the subject then I am not afraid to state, that if the writers of the Old Testament were really inspired, they must be supposed to have spoken figuratively on all those occasions, when they have ascribed human passions to the Supreme Being. It may be objected to me, that as the Hebrew scriptures contain little else than the histories of squabblings and bickerings between Jehovah and his people, we might come in this way to allegorize the greater part, if not the whole of the Old Testament. I confess for my own part I would rather believe the whole to be an allegory, than think for a moment that Infinite Wisdom could ever waver in its judgments; could ever be disturbed by anger; or could at any time repent of what it had ordained, (*pp.* vi—xii). There are, however, some yet graver objections which I have to make against them. I cannot reconcile to my notions of the perfectly Wise and

Good Being, the literal interpretation of the verse in Exodus, *And the Lord repented of the evil which he thought to do unto his people.* Perfect wisdom cannot repent of its intentions, any more than perfect goodness can think of doing evil. When it is stated in Genesis that it repented the Lord that he had made man on the earth, and that it grieved him at his heart, we can scarcely suppose that this was literally meant. The prescient God cannot be imagined to do anything which he foreknows he will afterward be grieved at his heart for having done. I have no doubt that the Jewish Rabbins firmly believe that the Deity conversed with their ancestors, upon the very various, but not always very important topics, which the Infinite God is said to have discussed with his priests and his prophets. It is difficult, however, not to observe that some of the divine discourses are dictated by an extraordinary spirit of vindictive jealousy, while others are marked by a prolixity, a garrulity and a familiarity of style, not altogether characteristic of the wisdom and majesty of the Supreme Being. The Platos, the Ciceros, and the Senecas of the Pagan world would probably have been astonished, if they had been assured, that the following sentences had proceeded from the Highest Intelligence. *For I, the Lord thy God, am a jealous God.* (*Exod.* xx.) *I will bring evil upon this place.* (2 *Kings* xxii.) *Behold my anger and my fury shall be poured out upon this place, upon man, upon beast, upon the trees of the field,* &c. (*Jer.* vii.) *It repenteth me that I have set up Saul to be King.* (1 *Sam.* xv.) The sages of antiquity would have thought the tongue to be impious, which had pronounced that the God of the Universe could be in a state either of fury, or of repentance. These are opinions, he adds, which I have no wish of promulgating to the mob : but I call upon the Theist who has contemplated the Universe as the work of intelligence to consider whether the Old Testament if literally interpreted, present him with such exalted notions of the Deity as natural religion itself is capable of inspiring, I must acknowledge that the Jewish scriptures thus understood appear to me to be contrary to all true theology. It is monstrous to be told if the sense be taken literally, that the infinite Mind showed its *back parts* to Moses. I read with pain, if there be no allegory, that the God of Nature revealed himself to Jacob in order that that Hebrew shepherd should make a journey to Bethel—that this same keeper of kine and sheep after having wrestled with a man all night, boasted in the morning that he had seen God. Am I really to believe in the existence of such singular conversations as are said in the Book of Job to have taken place between God and the Devil? "Skin for skin," said Satan to Jehovah. The expression is not very elegant, and it does not sound very spiritual. The story of Jonah in the fish's belly if it be not allegorical is a most surprising one, and the whole must be a little puzzling to the natural historian. I shall leave the literal interpreters to explain these things as they can : and the literal interpreters do so by a series of explanations more absurd and stupid than the juggleries of Mumbo-Jumbo. (30).

NOTES TO BOOK V.

Note 1 (page 332).—They were as ready to *destroy*, as to forge: in this resembling the early Paulite writers, who seem to me to have been as wicked and unscrupulous a crew as the Mormons themselves. It will be here also fit to observe, says that most honest of all theologians, Whiston, a farther greater instance of the wickedness of the Jewish rabbins, in that fatal period after Jerusalem was destroyed, which has not yet been taken notice of by any that I know of ; and that is, *the suppression of such of their ancient Hebrew records* as contained the history of that nation, from the conclusion of their 22 books till the days of Josephus. 'Tis evident those were all extant in the days of Josephus ; for he not only, as we have seen, speaks of them as extant, but all along makes use of them in his history. *On the Old Testament, Ap* 46. The forgery by the Paulites of the following passage, (which they absurdly represent to have been written by the most bigoted of Jews, Josephus), is as good as any other example which I could select. "About the same time there was a certain Jesus, a wise man, if indeed it is proper *to call him a man.* For he was *a performer of extraordinary deeds ;* a teacher of men that received his doctrine with delight ; and he attached to himself many of the Jews, many also of the Greeks. *This was the Christ.* Pilate having inflicted the punishment of the cross upon him, on the accusation of unprincipled men, those who had been attached to him before, did not however afterwards cease to love him : *for he appeared to them alive again on the third day, according to the holy prophets,* who had declared these and innumerable other wonderful things respecting him." The great alterations, says Father Simon, which have happened to the copies of the Bible since the first originals have been lost, utterly destroy the Protestants' and Socinian's principle, who consult only these same copies of the Bible as we at present have them. If the truth of religion remained not in the Church, it would be unsafe to search for it at present in Books which have been subject to so many alterations, and have in many things depended on the pleasure of transcribers: it is certain that the Jews who have writ out these Books have taken the liberty of adding and leaving out certain letters according as they thought fit and yet the sense of the text often depends upon these letters.

Note 2 (page 335).—One argument against the present form of the Mosaic books ought to be by all believers in the immortal nature of man, regarded as conclusive—that these books give no intimation of the immortality of the soul. Can it be for one moment imagined that a Messenger divinely accredited by God, would be ignorant of, or would not promulgate this sublime ennobling doctrine; and in an age too when as in the present, the multitude were but the blind cattle of priests, who had enslaved them under every form of sacerdotal despotism? Such an idea cannot be entertained. If Moses were the Messenger of God, as I believe he was, he taught the immortality of the soul. But the books which now pass under his name do not teach this immortality, *Ergo* · They are not the books of Moses. I see no escape from this dilemma. Warburton's Theory cannot of course, and I should suppose *is not*, now believed in by any churchman: he wrote it for a bishopric and he got one, but scholars from the first rejected it. The logical consequence therefore is irresistible— that Moses was *not* the Author of the books that bear his name— though undoubtedly they contain much that he revealed. Some of the priests who have been confounded by the omission of all allusion to a future life in the so-called writings of Amosis, pretend that the legislator for motives of policy and for the better government of a particular people, had made public a system which he himself was too wise to believe: and they fortify themselves by the authority of Ezekiel, who introduces God as saying: *I gave them* (the Jews), *statutes that were not good, and judgments whereby they should not live:* to such miserable subterfuges have these forged volumes driven even pious men. It is almost painful to see the straits into which some of the early Christian fathers were forced, by some of the questionable matters which were incorporated with the text. Thus St. Ambrose can find no better excuse for Abraham taking a concubine, than this, that he lived before Moses had declared adultery to be a breach of law, and consequently this holy patriarch committed no sin! The truth is that Joshua the accursed, and the abominable hierarchy which he founded, did all they could to destroy the true Mosaic Law, as Paul and the Papists did the Gospel, and the fierce warriors who succeeded Mohammed did the Korân. One might argue from Longinus, to support the view, that in his day, the Hebrew version was different from the present one. So likewise, he says, the Jewish lawgiver, who was no ordinary man, having conceived a just idea of the divine power, he expressed it in a dignified manner, for at the beginning of his Laws, he thus speaks, God said—what? "Let there be light and there was light. *Let there be earth and there was earth.*" (sect. ix.) The latter clause it will be seen has disappeared. Usher, Archbishop of Armagh, not knowing how to escape from all the wretched difficulties and doubts that are suggested by the matters to which I have adverted, declares that there were *two* Septuagint translations, one (the best) of which has perished, but that the other, has survived: a conjecture said to be utterly absurd and groundless by M. Vallois in a letter to Usher on this subject: but which Whiston felt himself compelled to adopt. (*On the Old Testament, passim.*) And the very *rational* supposition, says poor old Keightley in his Mythology, of some learned and pious divines that *it did not suit the scheme of Providence* to give the Israelites more correct ideas on natural subjects than other nations, relieves Scripture from many difficulties ! ! ! He alludes probably to the Jewish notion that their heaven might be made of brass, and their earth of iron. *Deut.* xxviii 23.

Note 3 (page 350).—Many persons are misled by the scriptural names given by the ignorant Arabs or the fraudulent monks, to various places in the East. Are they not all of equal value with the grave of Abel near the river Bassada, which is 30 yards long, corresponding with his stature! Quaresmius, *Elucid. Terrœ Sanctœ,* vii, 7, 1, Maundrell under May 4th. The same remark applies to Abraham's tomb ; and a host of similar names given to places in the East, originally by artful priests, and perpetuated by the simple children of the desert. There is in the church of St. Dominic at Bononia, says Prideaux, a copy of the Hebrew Scriptures kept with a great deal of care which they pretend to be the original copy written by Ezra himself · and therefore it is there valued at so high a rate that great sums of money have been borrowed by the Bononians upon the pawn of it, and again repaid for its redemption. It is written in a very fair character upon a sort of leather, and made up in a roll according to the ancient manner; but it having the vowel points annexed, and the writing being fresh and fair without any decay, both these particulars prove the novelty of that copy. But such forgeries are no uncommon things among the papistical sect. (*Connect* ii. 519.) Prideaux might have added among all sects; and a very singular instance of it occurs to me at this moment. That the Jews meant by the word *Son of God,* a ·

member of the Hebrew faith is shewn by John xi, 52, where we read. *And not for that nation only, but that also he should gather together in one, the Sons of God that were scattered abroad ;* meaning the rest of the ten tribes. The translators of the Testament for the purpose of disguising this from their readers, artfully translate it " Children of God," as if it applied to all the world. The reader should observe that it was in this strictly Jewish sense, and perhaps in this only, that Jesus is said on a few occasions to have alluded to himself as son of God · his most usual title for himself was Son of Man.

Note 4 (page 354).—The priests and scribes, says Donaldson (*Chr. Orth.*), who were the literary men of the nation reduced to a complete and elaborate system the ritual observances which had gradually come into vogue. It would be a waste of words to show that the priestly caste who took it upon themselves to say what books should be regarded as sacred, and what excluded from the Canon, did not during the period from 400. B.C. to 150 B.C abstain from *remodelling, perhaps re-writing* some of the older books ! !

Note 5 (page 363).—The Christians copied the Jews in this, as in other abominations It never was known, says the learned Jortin, by whom the Emperor Julian was killed. Possibly it was a Christian, says Sozomen, who was animated by considering how the destroyers of tyrants had been celebrated in ancient times. *Scarcely can any one blame him, if for the sake of God and of religion, he performed so heroic an action,* (vii. 2). An odd sort of doctrine this that a Christian subject and a soldier might assassinate his Emperor and his general. *Six Dissertations.* p. 283. If any unprejudiced person, says Higgins (*Anacalypsis*, ii. 105) would read the accounts of the plagues of Egypt, the passage of the Angel over the houses of the Israelites, when the first-born of the Egyptians was slain, the hardness of Pharaoh's heart, &c. &c., and give an honest opinion, he certainly must admit that they are absolutely incredible. One of the biblical commentators says that the reason why the Jews were directed to feed on lambs, sheep, doves, &c., was, because these animals were emblems of gentleness, and it was thought that those who fed on them would grow gentle also. As the Jews were among the most blood-thirsty people of whom we have any record, this explanation seems inappropriate : though it is one of these far-fetched subtleties on which pious Paulites lay great stress.

Note 6 (page 365).—The Samaritans acknowledge and possess no other book than the Pentateuch. The hatred between the Jews and Samaritans was just as rancorous, as that which prevails among Christians of different sects. The former called the Samaritan temple the Dunghill Temple, and שֶׁקָר *Sichar* (instead of *Schechem*) a lie. And the Samaritans in return called the Temple of Jerusalem, the *House of Dung;* and after its destruction the House of Misfortune.

Note 7 (page 369).—How rapidly the learning of a people may be destroyed is noticed by Niebuhr; When the higher classes of the Mexicans he says, had been extirpated, the few survivors being either allowed to attach themselves to the conquerors, or sinking into contempt, *the science and learning of this remarkable people were lost in less than a century.*

Note 8 (page 369).—The following discrepancy would convince any reasonable person that the same person was not the author of Exodus, and of Leviticus. In *Exod.* xxi. 16. it is said ; *If any one steal a man he shall be put to death.* Onkelos in his Targum translates it : If any one steal an Israelite; an interpretation which considerably limits the sense of the law. But this paraphrase is confirmed by *Deut.* xxiv. 7, where the narrow-minded Jew, who hated all mankind but his own clan, is apparent. *If any man be found stealing any of his brethren of the children of Israel he shall die.* Maimonides in his decisions on Questions relating to the Hebrew laws, denies that a Jew would be justified by the written law of God in killing an idolator simply because he was an idolator, admitting at the same time that if he saw such a person drowning, it might be a question in their law whether he would have a right to save him if he refused to become a proselyte ! A *new* commandment I give unto you, says Jesus, that ye love one another—implying that in his day they did nothing but hate.

Note 9 (page 371).—When the advocates for the accuracy of the Hebrew text, speak of the great care which the Jews always took in transcribing their sacred books, they should also add that this care was confined exclusively to synagogue manuscripts (which would be the very first that would necessarily be destroyed in days of persecution) but not to those which were for the use of private individuals. These were and are still full of inaccuracies There is no Hebrew manuscript now known that professes to be older than the eleventh century, though I very much question whether there is any so old : those that are used in the synagogue are without vowel points, which are of modern invention. Joseph Scaliger in his notes upon the *Chronicon* of Eusebius, thinks it so evident that the sacred books were originally written in the Samaritan character, at least those of them written before the captivity, that he saith it is *luce clarius* (clearer than light), and calls those of the contrary opinion, *semi-docti, semi theologi, semi-homines,* and *asini.* Note that among the great numbers of inscriptions of different kinds found in the ruins of Chaldæa, one in the Hebrew Chaldee letter and language *has never been found* nor has a single authentic medal or gem in this new-fangled character been ever discovered, which could carry it even to the days of Jesus.

Note 10 (page 385).—Take the following as an example of the evils to which this leads In the beginning God created (*bara* in Kal) the heaven and the earth. The introduction of another *vowel* completely alters the sense. In the beginning God *was* created (*bora* in Pual) with the heaven and the earth. In the text the word is *bra,* so that no one really knows what was meant. Yet upon this we read as follows, in Hutchinson : We may justly say, as John Nierenberg does, that Moses has given us more philosophy in one single chapter, the first of Genesis suppose, than *all the philosophers and explainers of nature put together.—Principia.* Such nonsense will Theologians dare to write · and such extravagancies will their disciples believe. And I might swell the catalogue of great names who have believed in the wildest follies, until the list extended almost to infinity. Much speculation, says *Nimrod,* has been raised because the earth has not been found as full of dead men's bones, as of dead beasts and fishes (iv. 341.) That learned priest, however, soon disposes of the objection, telling us that the earth was visited during the deluge by a number of *ferocious sea-monsters,* who were not intended to form a part of the post-diluvian inhabitants of the sea. Having been reared in the oceanian caverns below, and having disported themselves above only under the thick clouds of darkness, they were killed by the re-appearance of the Sun. Their business was to devour the bodies of the drowned, so that no trace should be found of them !! Poor Faber who saw in every thing that the world contains, a symbol of Noah in his Ark ! winds up by declaring in the supreme degree of lunacy, as follows: *In short the Man in the Moon, is really no other than Noah concealed in the preserving Ark !!* (i. 275.) There is something wonderful, but humiliating also, in the madness of two such highly accomplished men and scholars as Faber and Herbert. That both were thoroughly sincere in all they wrote, I fully believe ; but it was the sincerity of the Bedlamite, who fancies that his rags are robes, and his straw a sceptre of royalty.

Note 11 (page 386).—*And Ezra opened the book in the sight of all the people, and when he opened it all the people stood up . and Ezra blessed the Lord, the great God ; and all the people answered Amen,*

Amen, with lifting up their hands · and they turned their heads and worshipped the Lord, with their faces to the ground. Also Jeshua and Bani and Sherebiah, Jamin, Akkub Shabbethai, Hodijah, Maasiah, Kelita Azariah, Jozabad, Hanan, Pelaiah and the Levites, caused the people to understand the Law, and the people stood in their place. So they read in the book, in the law of God distinctly, and gave the sense and caused them to understand the reading Walton, it will be seen, though he cites this passage, adds to the word law "prophets," in the extract which I have translated from him without the slightest ground from the text. This is a common practice with those writers, who usually assume a great deal, and gravely publish it, without a shadow of authority. The "prophets" do not appear to have been read at all : nor did their writings exist, as I have shewn. That the priests have ever stuck at no falsehood to maintain their systems of imposture, is exemplified by one of their historians, who relates the following incredible fiction The Oracle at Delphi, having become dumb at the birth of Jesus, Augustus Cæsar, who was a great votary of Apollo, desired to know the reason of its silence—the Oracle answered as follows :—

> Me puer Hebræus, divos deus ipse gubernans,
> Cedere sede jubet, tristemque redire sub orcum,
> Aris ergo dehinc nostris abscedito Cæsar.

> An Hebrew child a god, whom Gods adore,
>   Has bid me leave these shrines and go to hell,
> So that my oracles you'll hear no more ;
> ˙   Away, then, from my altar and farewell.

Note 12 (page 387) —In the same fraudulent spirit, the wretched Dr. Dodd, in his preface to the Bible, boldly says : "These books have constantly been acknowledged as authentic : and no one, whether Christian, Jew, Mahometan, or Pagan, ever doubted *of it till the twelfth century ! '* It is a pity this man was hanged for forgery : he had every qualification to be a bishop. The number of years from the division of the Promised Land in the 47th year, or 46th complete from the Exodus to the beginning of the First Servitude under Cushad Rishathaim, is not to be found in the present text of the Scriptures, although from the words of Clemens in the *Stromata,* ὡς δε το βιβλιον του Ιησου περιεχει διεδεξατο τον Μωυσεα ὁ προειρημενος ανηρ ετη κζ (according to the Book of Joshua he succeeded Moses for 27 years), *lib.* i. xxi., it cannot be doubted that it was the Book of Joshua which he used.

There is another chasm, of which we have no record either—namely, from the end of the captivity of the Ark at Kirjath jearim [1 *Sam.* vii. 1. 2] to the accession of David.

Note 13 (page 390).—This question has for the first time in England been honestly brought before the public, and fairly discussed by Bishop Colenso in his second Tract, entitled *Elohistic and Jehovistic Writers.* The critical theological student will not find anything new in the Bishop's pamphlet : but the general reader may peruse it with advantage . and may be assured that the facts stated in it cannot be contradicted.

Note 14 (page 391)—In the *Jewish Antiquities* of the Rev. D. Jennings, D.D., occurs the following passage : " It should seem that the word רָאָה *roeh*, was the more ancient denomination of a prophet ; but, in the days of Samuel, the word נָבִיא *nabhi*, was grown into more common use, as appears from the following passage : " *He that is now a Prophet* נָבִיא *nabhi was before time called a Seer,* רָאָה *roeh.*" 1 Sam. ix. 9. Here a considerable difficulty ariseth, for we do not anywhere meet with the word רָאָה *roeh* in the Scripture history before this time, whereas the word נָבִיא *nabhi* is common in the writings of Moses—*who is therefore by some supposed not to have been the author of the Pentateuch, a word commonly occuring therein, which it seems was not used till long after his days* (page 235). Whether you choose to say, says Jerom, that Moses was the author of the Pentateuch, or Esdras, the renewer of that work, I have no objection. (*Hebr.* c. iii.) Clement, of Alexandria, says · When the Scriptures had been destroyed in the Captivity of Nebuchadnezzar, in the times of Artaxerxes, the king of the Persians, Esdras, the Levite, the priest, *having become inspired* renewed again, and produced prophetically *all* the ancient Scriptures (*Strom.* xxii. 149). The Catholic doctors, conscious that the inspiration of the *whole* Bible can no longer be maintained, and that the binding authority of the book is gone, have invented the subtile notion that as the Church of God was antecedent to the Old and New Testament, it is of higher authority than either ; and therefore that the teaching of the Church of Rome!! (which they thus confound with the Church of God), is to be considered as superior to these Books, and that if they no longer existed, their loss would consequently be of no account

Note 15 (page 393).—*Then was fulfilled that which was spoken by Jeremy the Prophet, saying : And they took thirty pieces of silver, the price of him that was valued, whom they of the children of*

Israel did value, and gave them for the potter's field, as the Lord appointed me. MATT. xxvii. 9. This passage is not in any part of Jeremiah now extant. Was it expunged by the Rabbis after the publication of Matthew ? or was it found in some copy of Jeremiah which is no longer extant ! Another prophecy has disappeared which is cited by the same writer (ii. 23). And he came and dwelt in a city called Nazareth, that it might be fulfilled which was spoken by the prophets : *He shall be called a Nazarene.* It may be added here, that whosoever will fairly and critically study Isaiah, will come to the conviction that it is the work of at least a dozen different writers, and that in its present form it is a mere unconnected rhapsody. There is no continued stream of thought or narrative in it : the style of the various parts is singularly contrasted ; the language is not uniform ; the doctrines are not in harmony : to assign it to one man is a figment worthy only of Jews : to believe it to be one man's work belongs only to Christians, the most ignorant of theology of nearly all other sects. The so-called Book of Daniel, and its prophecies, which come down to the period of Antiochus Epiphanes, is a modern figment, compounded of parts of the true Apocalypse, and of *predictions* written hundreds of years after the things predicted had happened. St. Jerom says the prophecies relate to Antiochus typically, and ultimately to Antichrist !!* The Jews wholly reject the Book. There are 200 verses in Daniel which are in Chaldee—the rest is Greek. After these things, says Newton, Antiochus Epiphanes spoiled the temple, and commanded the Jews to forsake the Law upon pain of death, and caused the sacred books to be burnt wherever they could be found, and in these troubles the bulk of the Chronicles of the Kings of Israel was entirely lost. But upon recovering from this oppression, Judas Maccabæus gathered together all their writings that were to be met with (2 *Maccab.* ii. 14), and in reducing them into order part of the prophecies of Isaiah, *or some other prophet,* have been added to the end of the prophecies of Zechariah, and the book of Ezra has been separated from the Book of Chronicles, and set together in two different orders ; in one order in the book of Ezra received into the canon; and in another order in the first book of Esdras. The authenticity therefore of the present canon depends absolutely on the infallibility of Judas Maccabæus as an honest or inspired compiler of what he supposed to be sacred writings, while his *own chronicles* are ignored as being neither inspired nor canonical.

Note 16 (p. 397)—I have declared truly, says Grotius, that all the books which are in the Hebrew Canon, are *not* dictated by the

Holy Spirit · that they were written with a pious motive I do not deny. But there is no necessity that history should be dictated by the Holy Spirit (why is there not?), it was enough that the writer sufficiently remembered what he had himself seen, or used due diligence in compiling the commentaries of the ancients. If Luke wrote his gospel by the dictation of the Divine Spirit, he would have preferred that authority, as the old prophets did, to that of the witnesses whose account he followed. So in writing those things which he saw Paul doing, there was no need of a divine inspiration.

Note 17 (page 401).—If written history cannot be relied on, how can tradition; yet it is on tradition that most of the mysteries of what is called Christianity exist. The Jews seem to be equally blinded by this folly The Rev. Joseph Wolf, in his *Journal*, 74, details a conversation which he had with Rabbi Gaby (whom the Jews called "the wise man"), to the following effect: *W*. Has Targum Jonathan the same authority among the Jews here as the Targum Onkelos?—*G* Yes, for Targum Jonathan is written by *inspiration of the Holy Ghost. W.* How may this be proved?— *G.* By tradition. *W.* By what tradition?—*G.* Of the Rabbis. *W.* How do you prove the truth of this tradition of the Rabbis? Gabay here broke off, and turned the conversation to another subject!!!

Note 18 (page 402).—Where is the empire of Solomon the Magnificent? It is not noticed by Herodotus, Plato, or Diodorus Siculus. It is a most extraordinary fact that the Jewish nation, over whom but a few years before the mighty Solomon had reigned in all his glory with a magnificence scarcely equalled by the greatest monarchs, spending nearly *eight thousand millions of gold* on a temple, was overlooked by the historian Herodotus writing of Egypt on one side and of Babylon on the other—visiting both places, and of course almost necessarily passing within a few miles of the splendid capital of the national Jerusalem? How can this be accounted for? Suleymân was a Persian title equivalent to the Greek Aiolos, and meant universal emperor. Like Pharaoh, it was not a name, but a designation of rank. The Jews aiming at universal empire, feigned that one of their kings bare this name; and it is with this petty pilfered thane (for in a little place like Judæa, he could be no other), that the mighty Suleymâns of the Orient are confounded alike by the civilized European and the ignorant Bedoween.

Note 19 (p. 403).—It was once a tradition or a custom when those miserable analogies or resemblances between the Jews and Gentiles were pointed out, to say that the *the Devil had done it all :* for the purpose of bringing true religion into contempt ; or that the Gentiles themselves had travestied the faith, which Amosis received from God. This has been well disposed of by Faber. Some, he says, have imagined that the Gentiles were servile copyists of the Israelites, and that each point of similitude was immediately borrowed from the Mosiacal Institutes. But this theory will by no means solve the problem · both, because we find the very same resemblance in the ceremonies of nations far different from Palestine, as we do, in the rites of those who are in its more immediate vicinity : and because it seems incredible that all should have borrowed from one *which was universally disliked and despised.* Others have fancied that the Devil was the copyist, and that various nations in different parts of the globe pervertedly though unwarily adopted certain parts of the Levitical ceremonies in consequence of his infernal suggestion or inspiration. Such, at one period, was deemed no contemptible theory, particularly as some of the early fathers seem inclined to favour it ; or at least to favour the notion of the imitative propensity of the Evil Spirit , but since it appears to have died a natural death, I shall only say may it rest in peace (*Pag. Idol.* 1. 104).

Note 20 (page 406).—Aben Esra, one of the ablest interpreters of the Scriptures among the Jews, has made no question but that there have been many additions to the Books of Moses, but he dared not publicly declare it, although he has sufficiently shewn his opinion on this point. When these sort of difficulties occur, he says, *it is a mystery which those who understand do not divulge.* —*Aben Esra. sup.* 12, *cap. Gen.*

Note 21 (page 408).—Tiberius, says De Pauw, succeeded so completely in destroying the annals of Cremutius Cordus, through the whole extent of the Roman empire, that whatever Tacitus and Dionysius may say to the contrary, not a single copy has been preserved. The classical reader need not be reminded that his works were sentenced to be burned by the senate. (*Tacit. Annal.* iv. 35.) The Biblicals, who have been utterly confounded by these statements of the Talmud, are obliged to say that the word *wrote,* means *copied,* though nothing can be farther from the exact truth.

Note 22 (page 411).—Stuart, it should be noted, argues with great want of candour, when he cites certain ancient fathers, in support of the present volume of Sacred writings ; for *their* testimony is confined to the genuineness of the Septuagint or Greek version ; while he leaves it to be inferred that they mean the

Hebrew. How saddening then it is to find a respectable compilation like *Kitto's Cyclopædia*, speaking thus of the present Old
Testament, with its innumerable errors. We believe with Haver-
nick, it says, that Ezra in unison with other distinguished men of
his time completed the collection of the sacred writings. He revised
the various books, corrected inaccurracies that had crept into
them, and rendered the Old Testament text *perfectly free from
error*. Thus a correct and genuine copy was finished *under the
sanction of Heaven!* Ezra, Nehemiah, and those with whom he
was associated, were *infallibly* guided in the work of completing
the canon. It may be asked, were they infallible, when they declared, according to the computation of Villapandus, that Solomon's
temple cost at least *six thousand nine hundred millions of pounds
sterling?* This argument, for the authenticity of the Jewish and
New Testament scriptures is equally valid it will be seen, when
used in favouring all other notoriously false and forged scriptures
of all the idolators in the world : who have books and miraculous
legends as well attested and authenticated by witnesses,
martyrs, and ancient documents, as the most devout believer of
the transmigration of devils into swine could desire, or could himself produce in support of that strange narrative.

Note 23 (page 413).—Baron Bunsen finds himself compelled to
adopt the alternative of gradual growth of the Pentateuch under
various hands. He makes the Pentateuch Mosaic, as indicating
the mind and embodying the developed system of Moses, *rather
than as written by the great lawgiver's hand.* Numerous fragments
of genealogy, of chronicle, and of spiritual song go up to a high
antiquity, but are *embedded in a crust of later narrative the allusions of which betray at least a time when Kings were established in
Israel.* Hence the idea of composition out of older materials must
be admitted ; and it may in some cases be conceived that the compiler's point of view differed from that of the older pieces. "*That
there was a Bible before our bible, and that some of our present books,
as certainly Genesis and Joshua, and perhaps Job, Jonah, Daniel,
are expanded from simpler elements is indicated in the book before
us, rather than proved as it might be.* * * He rightly rejects the
perversions which make the cursing psalms evangelically inspired."
Essays and Reviews, page 60. A more thoroughly orthodox
churchman than Baron Bunsen never lived ; and it may be taken
as perfectly certain that nothing but *conviction* and *proof* of the
most decided and irresistible nature, could ever have brought *him*
to the conclusion, that the present Pentateuch was a orgery.
Yet we see that such was his view : and that with true German
honesty he did not hesitate to publish it.

Note 24 (page 414).—Thus the Rabbis tell us that Isaiah was sawn to death; Jeremiah was stoned to death; Ezekiel (according to Epiphanius), was condemned and murdered also; Zachariah was slain by the very people between the temple and the altar; Amos was slaughtered by Uzziah, son of Amaziah. How unlikely therefore is it that the Jews who hated and punished them as impostors, rebels and disturbers of the community, should immediately after they had killed them, elevate them to the rank of Prophets, and deposit their writings in the temple!

Note 25 (page 415).—The last six chapters of Zechariah have been denied to be his composition, because they differ from the opening chapters, which I assert not to be the work of Zechariah at all, but copied from this Apocalypse. Those who have *proved* this dissimilarity, are Dr. Mede, Hammond, Kidder, Whiston, Bridge, Secker, and Newcome in this country; Flugge, Doderlein, Michaelis, Seiler, Eichorn, and indeed a host of others, most learned and orthodox scholars and divines on the Continent. will be seen that the dissimilarity is at once accounted for, if we admit that the person who transcribed them under the name of Zechariah transcribed them out of the Apocalypse · if it be not accounted for in this way, the only answer is, that there were several who wrote in the name of Zechariah at different eras, and that some one dovetailed the tracts together: an answer which does not do much for the orthodox   See Dr Henderson's *Minor Prophets*, p. 362. The truth is no part of them was written by Zechariah. So in Daniel, one considerable part is in the Hebrew phonograph and the rest in Chaldee, an entirely different language.

Note 26 (page 426)—If I covered my transgressions as Adam, says Job, *by hiding mine iniquity in my bosom.* No such passage is now to be found in any part of Genesis, or the Old Testament; as the writer of Job evidently had before him when he penned this. Josephus, in the first chapter of his History, relates that God deprived the serpent of speech, out of indignation at his malicious disposition towards Adam; besides this he inserted poison under his tongue and made him an enemy to man; and suggested to them that they should direct their strokes against his head, that being the place wherein lay his mischievious designs towards men and it being easiest to take vengeance on him that way · and when he had deprived him of the use of his feet, he made him to go rolling all along and dragging himself upon the ground. Here it may be asked did Josephus find all this in a Hebrew scripture of his day? and if so, what has become of it? It is however more likely to be talmudical foolishness. *The Holy Ghost,* says Hutchinson (vi. 313.) *choosed to write the New Testament in Greek, a*

heathen language, for many reasons· perhaps one, because all the
other languages which the apostates had used, were so poisoned
by them that they could not be used ; and if any one of them had
been used, we should have been at their mercy for the construction of it. The titles to the Psalms, the preface to Jeremiah, and
Ecclesiasticus, the additions to Esther, Isaiah, and Daniel, and
the prologue to Job, are all well known to be spurious. The
Samaritans do not seem to be better off than Jews or Christians
in respect of *their* Sacred Scriptures. M. Dulaure (*Des Divinites
Génératrices*, p. 29), speaks of a Samaritan Bible which commenced
thus : *In the beginning the Goat Azima created the Heaven and the
Earth* · but this is said to have been a forgery of one of the Jewish
Rabbis to spite the Samaritans. In a manuscript of the 12th century the Apocalypse was entitled, Ἀποκάλυψις του ἁγίου καὶ
ἐνδοξατατου Ἀποστολου καὶ Ἐυαγγελίστου, Παρθένου ἠγα-
πημένου επιστηθίου Ιωαννου θεολογου· The Apocalypse of the
holy and most glorious Messenger, and Herald of good tidings, of
the *Virgin beloved*, who lay in the bosom of Ioannes, the Word
of God. Was this the ancient and genuine heading ? and does
the Virgin mean the Holy Spirit ? That the common Ioannes
is an entirely mythical personage, may be proved from the following outline of his life taken from Cave's *Lives of the Apostles
and Fathers*. He was of noble birth, but brought up to the trade
of a *fisherman*. He lay on the bosom of the Messenger of God.
He confined his teaching to Asia : and had penetrated as far as
Bassora in India· he was cast alive into a caldron of boiling oil,
which did him no harm. He lived to the age of 120 years ; a
mystical number. Ephrem and Saint Cyril say he *never died*, but
is on earth still, because Jesus said of him : *If I will that he tarry
till I come what is that to thee ?* (John xxi 22), and again : *Verily I
say unto you, there be some standing here, which shall not taste of
death, till they see the Son of Man coming in his kingdom.* (Matt.
xvi. 38), a prophecy which was used freely to terrify the cotemporaries of the apostles into conversion by the threat of the world's
approaching end, but which in the following age was pretended
to mean only the destruction of Jerusalem. Augustine reports
of Ioannes as follows. He was not dead, but rested like a man
asleep in his grave at Ephesus, as plainly appeared from the dust
sensibly boiling and bubbling up, which they accounted to be
nothing else, but the continual motion of his breath. This report,
Augustine says, that he had received *from very credible hands.*
He further adds, what was generally known and reported, that,
when S. Ioannes, then in health, had caused his grave to be dug

and prepared, he laid himself down in it, as in a bed, and, as they thought, only fell asleep. By another writer it is related more at large. St. John, foreseeing his translation into heaven, took the presbyters and ministers of the Church of Ephesus, and several of the faithful, along with him out of the city, carried them unto a cemetery near at hand, whither he himself was wont to retire to prayer, and very earnestly recommended the state of the churches to God in prayer. Which being done, he commanded a grave to be immediately dug; and, having instructed them in the more recondite mysteries of theology, the most excellent precepts of a good life, and, solemnly taking his leave of them, he signed himself with the sign of the cross, and before them all went down into the grave; strictly charging them to put on the grave stone, and to make it fast, and the next day to come and open it, and take a view of it. They did so, and having opened the sepulchre, found nothing there but the grave clothes which he had left behind him. Ephrem, adds Cave, relates that from this grave wherein he rested for so short a time, a kind of sacred oil or unguent was wont to be gathered. Gregory, of Tours, says, 'Twas manna which even in his time, like flour, was cast up from the sepulchre, and was carried up and down the world for the curing of diseases. (*Life of St. John*)

Note 27 (page 432).—How far and wide this divine creed of the existence of the Holy Spirit in Heaven, has spread, is exemplified in an anecdote by the missionary Brainerd, which almost startled me when I read it. Far away in the wildest forests, that intrepid and pureminded enthusiast went and sojourned that he might teach what he believed to be the truth. Here amid the wildernesses he relates that he once met a wild Indian enchanter who gave him the following strange narrative. The manner in which he says, he got the spirit of divination was this: He was admitted into the presence of a Great One, who was clothed with the day of many years, yea, of everlasting continuance. This whole world, he says, was drawn upon him, so that in him the earth and all things upon it, rocks, mountains, and seas might be seen. By the side of this Great One, stood a Shadow or Spirit. The Shadow was lovely and filled all places. After this he saw that Being no more; but the Spirit or Shadow appeared to him often in dreams and other ways. If from the savannah and the prairie we pass to the centre of civilization, Athens, we find this creed still prevalent. You inform me, says Plato, writing to Dionysius, that the nature of *The First* has not been sufficiently revealed to you. I must write to you in riddles; in order that if my letter should

miscarry either by sea or land, the reader may not understand it.
All things are round about The King of All Things : and all
things exist for his sake, and that is the Cause of all excellent
things ; and around the SECOND are the things secondary ; and
around the Third are the third class of things. The human soul
endeavours to learn the nature of these, looking for what is ho-
mogeneous with itself, and consequently imperfect; but in the
King, and in these others whom I mentioned, there is nothing
such. * * * The greatest precaution is not to write but to
learn by word of mouth, for it is hardly possible for what is
written not to come abroad. For which reason I have written
nothing upon these topics,—no such book of mine exists or ever
shall. (*Epist.* 2.) If we go from Greece into the forests of Hindostan, we find the same belief in the Brahmin's teaching :
wherein he calls his Hindu Paradise Ila Vratta, or the Circle of
Ila; and Ida-Vratta, or the Circle of Ida. But this Ila, is Ala or
God, and Ida is Ad, the Father, and Ada the Beautiful. So that
Paradise is the *Circle* of God, the Father and the Beautiful, which
is in harmony with the Sanctuary or Tabernacle mentioned in the
Apocalypse. The name Eden seems preserved in Ida : and Ely-
sion in Ila. When we proceed to China, we find that the name
of one of their Scriptures is Y-KING, which word signifies the
Book of Y: and the Book received its name from the mystery of
which it treats ; for the mystery in question was hieroglyphically
represented by a figure representing the Greek Y, or the Roman
Y : that is the Two Powers and Essences; and the Third which
proceeds from them. So also the Rainbow round the Throne in
the Apocalypse, has given rise to the nimbus of glory, which
from the first ages has been attached to the heads of the blessed.
In Didron's Christian Iconography, published by Bohn, Jesus is
seen in a miniature of the 14th century, surrounded by an oval
nimbus of glory supported by *six* angels which represent the
Naros. The oval () I need hardly say is a mystical allusion to
the Holy Spirit, (i. 24) In the same work we learn that
in a stained glass window of the 12th century, the Blessed
Virgin [Holy Spirit] and a Man, whom it calls John the
Baptist, but who is really God, stand beside Jesus on the
cross. Both figures wear the nimbus, and from the top of
each nimbus rise two *sun-flowers* (emblems of the sun), crossing
each other They are therefore crowned with the sun; just as on
the heads of the Egyptian divinities two *lotus flowers* rise in a
similar manner, (i. 29.) The nimbus is sometimes a circle, sometimes a *triangle.* See *ante,* pp. 14, 38. Montfaucon gives an out-

line, copied into Didron, from an engraved gem called Abraxas, used as an amulet by the Gnostics. It is shewn to be celestial by the sun and moon introduced into the field on which he is engraved; terrestrial by the lion's head; aquatic by the serpent-like tail; divine by the nimbus of twice seven luminous rays. (*Ant. Exp.* iv., 363.) It was a primitive type of the Messenger. So in the coins of the Antonine period, we see the Phœnix, with its head encircled by a nimbus. On the coins of Faustina, Eternity, [the Eternal] is represented with a peacock wearing a similar nimbus This peacock has puzzled the christian antiquaries, who do not recollect that Juno the Queen of Heaven was always symbolized by this bird, and that in these coins it represents the Holy Spirit, the beloved of the Eternal. Those among the natives, says Krantz, who are more struck with the beauty and majesty of the heavenly bodies seek for the happy residences of the dead in the highest heavens, *above the Rainbow.* This is a singular allusion. (*Hist. of Greenland,* i., 187.) Didron also gives a sketch of the Hindu Holy Spirit or Maya, pressing her breasts from which flow those copious streams of milk by which all living creatures are nourished and supported. A veil of Ideas, the prototypes of creation surrounds her richly-attired figure. Maya is represented in a semi-aureole, or large nimbus, the circumference of which is indented with zigzags, and the field striated with luminous sparks, parallel with the temples and forehead, and stretching beyond the circumference, three clusters of rays dash forth, corresponding exactly with the *cross* lines in the nimbus of Christian archæology, (i. 40). In the same work, Oannes as a type of the Messenger, is represented in a sitting posture, with a roll in the left hand, and his right arm extended as if he were teaching, his head is surrounded with a globular nimbus bearing the inscription, Ωον, which is his name, the Mundane Egg, and also ὁ ὤν, the I am that I am, of the Apocalypse and the Mosaic book. (i. 46). Figure 18, in the same work represents the Messiah supported on the *rainbow-like* veil of a Beautiful Woman, and this is said to be taken from one of the sarcophagi in the Vatican, belonging to the first ages of Christianity. The allusion is here apparent—the Holy Spirit or Shekinah is as clearly manifested, as she is in the Hina of the Polynesians, *ante* p. 169. In a fresco in the church at Montorio, Jesus is represented bearing on his head a sort of sphere or Egyptian disk, divided into circles like those on the globe of the world. The Egyptian Harpocrates, is constantly figured with a nimbus. In the paintings found at Herculaneum, Circe appearing to Ulysses, is depicted wearing a nimbus, precisely as the Virgin Mary and saints of the Romish church are usually represented. Virgil referred to the nimbus when he spoke of the flame descending from heaven upon the head of the little Iulus, as if to caress and kiss his hair. The passage explains the nature of the aureole, and recalls to mind the two luminous horns which Moses had upon his brow, and that resplendent countenance by which the Hebrews were dazzled and alarmed when their lawgiver descended from Mount Sinai after his long conference with the Deity. *Exod.* xxxiv., 35.

> Ecce levis summo de vertice visus Iuli
> Fundere lumen apex, tactuque innoxia molli
> Lambere flamma comas, et circum tempora pasci.
> Nos pavidi trepidare metu, crinemque flagrantem
> Excutere, et sanctos restinguere fontibus ignes, (*lib.* ii).

The aged Anchises, who was versed in Egyptian lore and oriental symbolism, far from being alarmed at the sight, like the other persons who were present, was filled with great joy. He raises his eyes and hands to heaven, imploring Jupiter to grant that the happy fortune presaged by this augury may be realised. Anchises well knew that that aureole of light, or terrestrial apotheosis, announced that his grandson should be the future sovereign of a great kingdom. The famous Umbrella which was part of the Peacock Throne of the Great Mogul, and which was a blaze of diamonds, emeralds and rubies, was a symbol of the Rainbow in the Apocalypse, and is another proof that the Volume was known in the East. It signified that the Monarch was under the Holy Spirit, and that She was round his Throne, while the golden and jewelled peacock which was the Bird of the Queen of Heaven, standing at either side disclosed the meaning of the whole to the Initiated. The Umbrella, was not only arched like the Rainbow, but it was also an inverted patera, and in this also a type of the Holy Spirit. In Abyssinia there is still an officer named *Kal Hatze*, the "Word of the King," who stands upon the steps of the throne at the side of a lattice window, where there is a hole covered on the inside with a curtain of green taffeta. Behind this curtain the king sits unseen, and speaks through the aperture to the *Kal Hatze*, who communicates his commands to the officers, judges and attendants. We cannot traverse any portion of either this vast continent, or of the East or West, without discovering proofs like the above of the distinction always recognised by the ancients between God and the Word of God, his Holy Spirit, and the Messenger. She, as well as He, is a Spirit of Tongues: and from their mouths all excellence proceeds. So in the analogous Hindu mythos, when Chrishna (the Incarnation) opened his mouth, his foster-mother (the Earth) saw within the cavity, the boundless Universe in all its plenitude of magnificence. That is, when the Messenger speaks, he developes the whole sys-tem of the Creator; or the Apocalypse : it is beheld in his mouth. In our cathedrals, says Didron, the western porch is fre-quently pierced by an immense *circular opening*, to which is given the name of Rose window. The bay of the window is filled with coloured glass, arranged in four, five, or six concentric circles, diminishing in extent in proportion to their proximity to the centre. God seated on his throne, or the Virgin holding in her arms the infant Saviour, shines resplendent in the central circle A cordon of angels surrounds the central group : then the patri-archs ; after them apostles, martyrs and confessors, each in sepa-rate rings or cordons; lastly, the external cordon or outer edge of the circumference is filled by virgins. All these persons are framed in medallions of glass, as transparent and luminous as the saints themselves, and resembling circles of rubies, emeralds, or sapphires, studded with diamonds. These rose windows are *glories*, embracing an entire world, encircling a multitude instead of girdling a single individual. They are symbols thus of the Holy Spirit. Dante has himself given the name of Rose to those circular expansions of light, in which the saints are represented ranged in a divine effulgence emanating from the Centre, which is filled by the splendour and brilliancy of God himself. I close this paragraph with an extract from the Paradise of Dante, which will suffice to prove that the nimbus, aureole, and glory are images of light, reduced to form by the pencil, and that they are all types of the Sacred Spirit, the Queen of Heaven, in whom all existence finally centres.

> I looked,
> And in the likeness of a River, I saw
> Light flowing, from whose amber-seeming wave
> Flashed up effulgence, as they glided on
> 'Twixt banks on either side, painted with spring,
> Incredible how fair · and from the tide
> There ever and anon outstarting flew
> Sparkles instinct with life : and in the flowers
> Did set them like to rubies chased in gold ;   ·
> Then, as if drunk with odours, plunged again
> Into the wondrous Flood, from which as one
> Re-entered, still another rose.   *   *   *

In fashion as a snow-white Rose lay then

Before my view the saintly multitude,
Which in his own blood Christ espoused.   Meanwhile
That other host that soar aloft to gaze
And celebrate His glory whom they love,
Hovered around, and like a troop of bees
Amid the vernal sweets alighting now,
Now clustering where their fragrant labour glows,
Flew downward to the mighty Flower ; a rose
From the redundant petals streaming back
Unto the stedfast dwelling of their joy.
Faces had they of flame, and wings of gold :
The rest was whiter than the driven snow.
And as they flitted down into the flower,
From range to range fanning their plumy loins
Whispered the peace and ardour which they won
From that soft winnowing.   Shadow none, the vast
Interposition of such numerous flights
Cast from above, upon the Flower, or view
Obstructed aught.   For through the Universe
Wherever merited, Celestial Light
Glides freely, and no obstacle prevents.

Cary's Dante Paradiso, xxxi.

And as the Holy Spirit was this Central Rose, or blaze of glory,
and Lotus, so also whenever the Moon is mentioned by the old
theosophists, we are always to understand the Sacred Spirit of
Heaven, the fountain and receiver back of all life. Lucian says that
some placed Elysium in the Moon ; and in his Dream he cites the
mystic proverb, Αρχη ἡμισυ παντος. *Archa is half of the All.*
Psellus commenting on the old Chaldæan Oracles, teaches us that
the abode of souls after death was a region about the Moon, resplendent with marvellous light, while all beneath was gloom and
darkness. Macrobius describes it as being an essential part of
the mysticizing philosophy of the Platonists, to consider the
Moon as the abode of human souls ; and he adds that souls passed
from the Moon to the Earth when they were born in fleshy bodies,
and returned from the Earth to the Moon, when they were delivered from their carnal prisons. So Porphyry tells us that the
Moon was to be esteemed as presiding over generation, because the
souls of men were born from it : and that there was a constant
migration of those souls, ascending and descending through the
two astronomical gates. The Paulite and biblical commentators
have been much puzzled by all this, and have made it not unfrequently

a ground of ridicule; but when we remember that the Holy Spirit was the Fountain which diffused Life throughout the Universe, and that she was as universally symbolized as the Moon, all cause of laughter is at an end. The Paulite notion that the Holy Ghost [Spirit], whom they call a Man, should be symbolized by a *Dove* however is more ludicrous than any other; a Dove being from the beginning a Female emblem of the Beautiful, and Divine.

Note 28 (page 434).—These harlots, the favourites of the Churches, are not so fortunate in Siam. There is a certain day in the year, in which the Siamese practise a ceremony somewhat resembling that of the Scape-Goat. They single out a woman broken down by debauchery, and carry her on a litter through all the streets to the sound of drums and hautboys. The mob insult her and pelt her with dirt: after having sufficiently exposed her through the whole city, they threw her on a dunghill, and sometimes on a hedge of thorns without the ramparts, forbidding her ever to enter them again. This inhuman and superstitious ceremony is founded on the belief that this woman thus draws upon her all the malign influences of the air and of evil spirits —Pinkerton's *Voyages*, ix., 579.

Note 29 (page 434).—Hence it was that so many of the Pagans objected that the impurities, impieties, absurdities, inexplicable doctrines and incomprehensible mysteries contained in the books of the Old and New Testament, rendered Christianity so incredible, that they thought it ridiculous to embrace it, and renounce their own creeds and doctrines which were in their opinions, more rational and intelligible The doctrine of a *dying God* was rejected by their philosophers with disdain and contempt This and many other of the mysteries of Christianity gave to the Gentile philosophers, and to so great a number of Pagans such an aversion to Christianity that Mons. Claude, a French Protestant refugee teacher avers, that had it not been for the severe edicts of Constantine and his son against Paganism, or the old Gentile religion, three parts in four of all Europe would have been at this day Pagans No wonder this should be the case when one of the Fathers observes, that if the doctrines of the Old Testament were to be taken literally, he should blush to own it: the laws contained in it being far inferior to heathen institutions.—*The Morality of the New Testament*, xvii.

Note 30 (page 447).—I close these notes by referring to a Pamphlet, which has just reached me, *Adam not the First Man, by a Believer in the Bible;* and from which the following extracts seem pertinent to the matter in' hand. The reader may refer to the pamphlet itself for further information: it is a valuable one, and it is published by May, 30, Spencer Street, Goswell Road:—

In the portion of the Word of God from the 26th verse of the first to the 3rd verse of the second chapter of Genesis, the prophet is undoubtedly continuing his relation of the general creation of the universe, and of all the worlds contained therein. It is indisputable that the expression, "Let us make man," is used in the generical sense, meaning *mankind*, and it is, throughout the whole of this recital, or history, accompanied by the pronoun "*them*," which gives evidence that it must be received in the plural number, except, indeed, in one particular instance; the intention of the change, in that instance, is most obvious; the alteration is important and impressive , and it tends to give additional force and value to all the other portions, in all of which the plural number prevails without exception. God said, "Let us make mankind in our own image, after our likeness, and let them have dominion over the fish of the sea, and over the fowl of the air, and over the cattle, and over all the earth, and over everything that creepeth upon the earth. So God created mankind, in his own image created he him (the male of all mankind) ; male and female created he *them* (both sexes of all mankind) ; and God blessed them; and God said unto them, 'Be fruitful and multiply and replenish the earth ; and subdue it, and have dominion over the fish of the sea, and over the fowl, and over every living thing that moveth upon the earth.' And God said, 'Behold I have given you every herb bearing seed, which is upon the face of all the earth, and every tree in which is the fruit of a tree yielding seed; to you it shall be for meat.' And God saw every thing that he had made, and behold it was very good, and the evening and the morning were the sixth day. Thus the heavens and the earth were finished, and all the host of them." It must be perfectly apparent that the whole of the first chapter of Genesis, and the three first verses of the second chapter, contained one complete history, the statement of the creation of the universe, including all the hosts of the earth, and the general creation of mankind thereupon ; that in our version the three last verses have been most injudiciously separated from the preceding portion of the recital, tending materially to interfere with, and to break up the meaning of this portion of Scripture, and (as we shall hereafter see) to carry the summing up of this magnificent work to another individual creation, with which it has decidedly not the slightest connexion. If the whole of that portion of the word of God last quoted, be read with a mind uninfluenced by any preconceptions, and by any persons unswayed by impressions which might have been the effect of general and powerfully inculcated doctrines, hostile thereto, every idea conveyed by the expressions therein used, must and will be of a general and widely extended character ; there cannot arise any consistent conception that this recital could possibly be intended to represent the creation of one individual, upon one particular portion of the globe ; there is not one single expression that can have a sense of limitation properly attached thereto ; there are no means employed beyond the mandate of Almighty God. He says "Let us make mankind,"—he speaks alone—and it is done :—and where?—not upon this earth alone, but upon "all the hosts of worlds," at one and the same period of time ; and in one and the same manner ; the Prophet says, "thus the heavens and the earth were finished, and all the host of them ;" the "thus" declares distinctly that the whole of the preceding portion of the recital, both as to time and as to similarity of means, was the history of the creation of the universe, including the general population of this earth ; that the general history of the world is there commenced, and that it is there terminated ; it is so full and so complete that it does not require the aid of any additional statement or recapitulation, and it will not permit of a dissimilar or of a contradictory explanation of any of its parts which have therein been so positively defined, and which have been therein laid down with such peculiar, and with such dignified emphasis. Every lesser or every contracting thought must be considered to be a misconception of, and a degradation from, this bright and glorious portion of the Word of God ; and verse after verse, and word upon word, come thunder-tongued, rolling upon the ear (and thence displaying before the eye), in wonderful and most sublime rapidity, the great and mighty acts whereby Jehovah made his millions of worlds, and gave thereto millions of millions of souls, for whom they were designed, and for whom they were brought, as we have seen, to their appropriate states of perfection ; he who conceives this scene in anywise aright, will have the majestic vision, and the most magnificent array presented to his imagination, of the eternal and the omnific God, seated upon his throne (the circuit of the heavens, (declaring thus the fiat of his will—"Let us make mankind ;" and, without any other process, as soon as that omnific voice goes forth into infinitude, he will as instantly behold a simultaneous burst of thousands upon thousands of human beings, not only upon this world, but upon thousands of thousands of other worlds, and upon "all the host of them," throughout God's vast immensity, thus, and by this mandate alone, furnished with all their varieties of mankind, having immortal souls, with destinies as great and as important as our own ; he will behold the Infinite Lord God, "making of one blood all nations of men, for to dwell on all the face of the earth, determining the times before appointed, and the bounds of their habitations ;" he will see that the "times of their appearance" have been well, and wisely, and mercifully appointed ; that the "bounds of their habitations" had already been determined by the separation of the various lands by the seas, by the intervention of other minor waters, and by the impassable mountains, originated in the more early processes of the creative works ; he will be brought to the admission that the language of Scripture is too wide for any lesser thought ; that the whole recital gives the substance of a scene as grand, as glorious, and as universal, too, as must have been the simultaneous population of all the host of worlds, the mode of which the prophet has thus described as being an instantaneous respondence to the voice of Deity ; and that there is a breadth, a grandeur, and a simplicity in such divine truths, which men's minds should struggle to conceive, which they should be encouraged to admire as worthy of, and as appropriate to, the last recorded act and the most important work of Heaven's eternal God.   *   *   *   *

All who examine carefully the evidences adduced in the various races of mankind, which even yet populate the different portions of the surface of the globe, not with the desire to establish former prejudices, nor to confirm long-imbibed opinions (although such may be considered devout and reverential), but with a desire to learn the truth, will issue from such study with the conviction fastened upon their minds that there are even yet to be found in the features and in the physical conformations of the human races who inhabit the various portions of the globe certain positive and arbitrary distinctions ; that such are clearly indicative of a variety of origins, exhibiting a fitness for those peculiar climates wherein their tribes yet dwell as portions of distinct early races, to which all of similar feature and confirmation are most clearly traceable, of which they are justly termed the natives, or the aborigines, and where many of them yet exist in their unmixed features, as perfect evidences of their peculiar descent. The diligent inquirer after truth will be enabled to discover that it is an invariable *effect*, showing the presence of a positive law of Nature, that all removals of original races to other climates (whether the change

be from temperate or inclement latitudes, or from those which
men would consider hostile to health and longevity, to others
which would be considered more congenial), have ever been manifestly injurious to their individual systems, and that such trans·
portations are in many instances absolutely destructive of life ;
that their physical peculiarities are an evidence that the varieties
of men were undoubtedly designed for continued existence in such
various portions of the earth as formed their first abodes ; and
that the observable impairment and destruction of vital powers,
by removal to other climates, discountenances the probability
that the Almighty ever did originally design to produce, or that,
the earth, in her long series of centuries, ever has been capable
of producing, a healthful and uniform race of beings (different in
complexion and stature from those from whom they emanated),
simply by the operation of a change of station, or by the influence
of climate, however much such change may be held to have been
aided by a lapse of time of any conceivable duration. I believe
that every sincere examiner will be ready to admit, that there is
an absolute impossibility (according to any laws of Nature yet
exhibited to man's comprehension), of producing a conformation
involving such mental and physical powers, and such a complexion
as the European displays, from the Ethiopian stock, or from African parents, wherever such might have been located , or of culti-
vating the features of the Tartaric or of the Northern tribes from
the Esquimaux of the Arctic Regions, or from the Red Indians of
North America, wherever, or however long they may have been
removed ; but I believe he will be ready to admit that the *inverse
consequence*, that of a blending of original characteristics, is not
only perfectly conceivable, as a possible event, but that he will
assent to the fact, that it has also been continually and exten-
tensively in operation ; that man *can* break down original distinctions by amalgamations, but that he never can rebuild nor restore
original classes, when such have been invaded by admixture, operating as a taint; that the admission will be, that the former not
only *can be done*, but that such *has been done ;* and that such
means are now in extensive operation, amalgamating, and thus
breaking down the original distinctions of mankind, by intercourse ; that the *effects* of such intercourse are clearly traceable
to such an extent as to have already caused the original and distinct features of mankind to slide into each other by almost imperceptible degrees ; such mixed and intermediate races now forming the greater portion of the inhabitants of the earth, and being
more and more blended by coming daily into nearer and more ordinary intercourse with each other.   *   *   *   *

We will now proceed to follow up the chain of evidence presented by the recital of the prophet, in the shape of actual historical events occurring in the race of Adam, to convince us that Adam positively was not the first man of all the earth, but that he was absolutely placed, at the time of his creation, in a populated globe, that such world was old, in matters appertaining to man's skill and knowledge, at that very period; and that Adam and his descendants knew that they were surrounded by, and that they were dwelling nigh to, human beings of a different and of a prior origin. We are informed that, immediately after the fall, there were born to Adam and Eve two male children; that at an early period of the lives of these two sons of Adam and Eve, the elder-born, Cain, slew his brother Abel; that the punishments denounced by God for this offence, were such a curse upon the ground as would withhold from Cain the mode of existence to which he had been accustomed by its cultivation, and such a banishment from the land of his birth as would make him a fugitive and a vagabond. It is evident that this sentence was understood by Cain to be a banishment into a populated region; such is evidenced by his reply—"My punishment is greater than I can bear; thou hast driven me out from the face of the earth, and I shall be a fugitive and a vagabond, and it shall come to pass that every one that findeth shall slay me." It must be here admitted that this is a positive record that Cain, at least, fully imagined that there were neighbouring tribes living around him, that, from such, he imagined he would be subjected to acts of violence; that he therefore supposed, or knew, that they were men of strength, perhaps of gigantic stature, and indulging in blood shedding; that the dread of such violence being exerted against him, (such being recorded as being greater than the gloomy prospect of the difficulty of his sustaining life under the curse upon the ground affecting his daily subsistence,) would have been groundless and inconsistent, had not Cain then possessed a vivid conception of the tenancy, by mankind, of the surrounding regions of the earth; that we have, in fact, the culprit Cain suggesting the probability of his being destroyed by the neighbouring tribes, into contact with whom a banishment from the land of his parents would inevitably bring him, but we have infinitely more than this, we have a far more important being giving his testimony to the fact, and joining in the correctness of the assumption contained in this declaration; in the following verse, and in immediate reply to such expressed fear, we have the Great Lord God, who is not the author of confusion, and who does not inculcate error by vague expressions of admission of matters, and of things, and of persons,

the which and the who have never been in existence ;—we have
the Almighty God, admitting the reasonableness of such dread,
and assenting to the consistency of Cain's fears,—"therefore,"
he says, "will I set a mark upon thee, lest any, finding, shall slay
thee;"—and then we find him denouncing vengeance, in a seven-
fold degree, upon any who should slay Cain. Now, I believe that
no possibility exists of giving other than a literal conception to
these words—than of making them supply other than an absolute
marking of the murderer, for the object then expressed, such constituting his protection from those beings then in existence, who
otherwise could or would have slain the fratricide ;—I believe that
to attempt to withdraw from this portion of God's Word, any one
atom of its literal force and meaning, as a relation made of
solemn and important facts, as a veritable history of the first
assize held upon earth, in the presence of the Eternal Judge, who
there gives sentence on the prisoner, must have the effect of
attempting to lessen down, and to degrade, a most awful scene,
and a denouncement made, and a visitation shewn by God, for and
against the greatest sin that man's hand could commit, into a
most unmeaning and into a most unnecessary farce ; and that
such breaking down of a plain declaration of Scripture, because
we will not set our minds to the task of diving deeply, to find
indeed that it truly had the accompanying personages which its
words declare to have necessarily involved in such contemplated
catastrophe, far exceeds all I know of wilful blindness, and of
bold temerity, in an unwillingness to admit that God knew, and that
God intended it to be known by all to whom such language was then
addressed—by him especially who then received his protective
mark—and also that it should known by all for whose instruction
such history is recorded, that there were persons, then in existence, by whom Cain would indeed be liable to be put to death as
an alien and as a vagabond, in the land of Nod, or in any other
neighbouring land, whereunto the erratic life to which he was
then doomed might lead his steps, were he found without the protective mark by which God made him mysteriously, and I have no
doubt, awfully distinguished, as a living spectacle, and as an example of his wrath against the sin of murder to all the then surrounding tribes, and, I believe, to subsequent generations through
many of the earth's succeeding times   *   *   *   *
Other very brief, but very important statements of facts soon
follow, all tending to establish the same point ; and if such statements be duly weighed in all that they most positively declare,
they must lead the mind of every diligent examiner, to the
assumption of the mode of life adopted by Cain, whereby he ob-

tained such power over the labours of others, as to enable him
build a city, and whereby men should be taught to withdraw their
attention from the only natural occupation then known (the
chase), to cause them to congregate in large communities ; to devote themselves to the erection of such structures as we find that
city did certainly contain ; and to concentrate such an abundant
population, as should tend to constitute such a city's occupants ;
such city or cities being undoubtedly the habitations of the
heathen demi-gods, whose myths yet crowd, with hieroglyphic
characters, the fragments of the bygone world ; and of giant races,
admitted by the Word of God, but described not in the history
of the race of Adam, because beyond its intended range. The
Word of God undoubtedly points either to Cain or to some of
those people who preceded him as the discoverers of mineral
wealth ; the unerring authority telling us that Jubal, an early de-
scendant of Cain, was so far advanced in the acquisition and in
the appropriation of mineral property, "that he was skilful both
in the harp and on the organ ;" and that Tubal Cain was " an instructor of every artificer in brass and in iron." These statements, being introduced with wondrous brevity, have not obtained
the weighty consideration which their characteristics for the conveyance of truthful ideas so justly deserve ; and which, if looked
at steadily, in connection with all other matters, which are here
produced for the reader's attention : viz the building of "a
city,"—the finding of inhabitants to occupy that city,—the erecting therein of an organ or organs,—the making of harps,—the raising of minerals,—the appropriating of such minerals to various
purposes,—the teaching of the use of all these to other persons
then existing around and with them,—must, upon mature reflec-
tion, lead to the admission that these statements are inserted for
no other purpose than to lead our minds to the conception of the
fact of an older and surrounding population ; that at any rate,
the Word of God declares that whilst Adam and his first descendants, in the line of Seth, were existing in a most primitive state,
considerable advancement was made in arts and sciences by the
races with whom Cain came in contact at the time of his banishment ; that it is not likely that he could be the sole originator or
the possessor of properties which are spoken of in such wide
terms ; that, as an individual, or as surrounded by persons to
whom they would become desirable, such minerals would have
been valueless as the dust of the earth ; that it is evident that
such substances were miraculously placed within his reach, and
that they at that time did obtain, or had perhaps even previously
obtained, a value in the eyes of mankind ; that it is evident that

either prior to Cain, or else assisted by him, and subsequently perfected by his family, the attention of mankind, in the land of
Nod, was so turned to the conversion of minerals into delicate
uses and to artificial enjoyments, that instruments of music were
constructed of vast magnitude, and such as would only have been
erected in, or would only have been suited to buildings or to
chambers of much architectural importance; or, at any rate, as
would be incompatible with the dwelling in tents, or in other rude
habitations, such as it has been usual to assign to the inhabitants
of the earth at this time, and such as Adam, and his descendants
in the line of Seth, did most certainly only enjoy for many centuries beyond the time during which they are recorded in the few
verses which are devoted to the history of Cain—the disinherited
—the murderer—the henceforth heathen-blended man. Moreover,
the Word of God multiplies its facts, tending to prove upon us,
whether we be willing to receive such truths or not—that there
were other races of men upon the earth at this time than the descendants of Adam; and it is a fallacy to presume that the Bible
does not lead us so to assume, that it does not wish us (connecting such work with the intention of its Divine Author) to be convinced thereof, and that it does not require us to make such truths
a portion of our harmonious worshipping of him as "the God of
the souls of flesh;"—it tells us—"there were giants on the earth
in those days," it is quite evident that these beings (here most
pointedly named and admitted in Scripture as then existing) did
not proceed from the race of Adam; they are here most clearly
mentioned in such a manner as positively manifests the intention
of setting them up most conspicuously in contradistinction to the
race of Adam; the object of God in giving such statement,
through his prophet, is clearly for the alone purpose of denoting
a peculiar and different race, as one of the many varieties of mankind by which Adam was then surrounded, the recital is plainly
introduced for the purpose of showing that such beings were not
accidental productions from parents of ordinary stature, but that
they were a race of men abundant in those days, but now extinct;
the Word of God proceeds to tell us that "the Sons of God" (or
the males of the race of Adam, who acknowledged the true God)
came in unto the daughters of these giants, that they bare children unto them and that such became mighty men of renown, it
says further, that "the sons of God (still the males of the tribe
of Adam) saw the daughters of men (other races not gigantic)
that they were fair, and that they took them wives of all whom
they chose"   *   *   *   *   *   *   *
It is said, immediately after the banishment of Cain, that "Adam

knew his wife again, and she bare a son, and called his name Seth,
'for God,' she said, 'hath appointed me another seed instead of
Abel, whom Cain slew;' and to Seth also there was a son born,
and he called his name Enos; then began men to call upon the
name of the Lord." This statement of the prophet has been
generally explained, as though it was not to be received in its
literal sense, but as though it were there declared that " then began
men to call themselves after or by the name of the Lord," signifying that the men of the earth in their distinguishing appellations
then began to assume the titles or the names of Jehovah   Such
alteration has been made to endeavour to evade the difficulty of
attaching such a statement of "beginning to call on the name of
the Lord" to Adam, to Seth, or to Enos, who were then the only
men upon the earth, (if Adam's race be considered the only original one,) and who had certainly been always taught to call upon
the name of the Lord; that is, to worship the true God, this
text therefore stood in most perplexing opposition to the solitary
family of Adam, then numbering but the three individuals I have
named; therefore, modern commentators felt that there was an
absolute necessity of supplying to the prophet a more suitable
mode of expressing the truths which he intended to declare, than
that which he had adopted; the text, therefore, became amended
in the margin to suit the modern views; but no better effect followed; because we do not find that men did then generally name
themselves after God; that such appellations were either assumed,
or were given to them by their parents; the facts of the bible,
therefore, continued to stand in opposition to the more modern
translation; then, I am obliged to return to my former conception of the word of God, as to the pre-existence of heathen
nations, provided in the general creation; I can then and without
mutilation, I find a perfect harmony in all these points of supposed discrepancies; I perceive clearly that the men here intended
are the vast heathen tribes then contemporaneous with the small
family of Adam; I can perceive, by Seth having then had a son
born to him, that he, and doubtless Adam too, as well as Cain,
had evidently even then obtained an intercourse with the families
of these men; that Seth thence took his wife, from whom he
begat Enos, that Adam and Seth had, in great probability,
already spoken to these races of men and giants then around
them, of Jehovah as the true God; and that, already, the probability is (as here recorded in fact) that some of these men had
received the light of the truth, conveyed by such teaching, and
had " begun," in prayerful mind, " to call upon the name of the
Lord "   *   *   *   *   *   *   *

The prophet having made this demarking period, between the first general and the second and individual creation, immediately proceeds to enter upon the history of the first Adam, or the first man of the important race now about to be created; in introducing such history he makes use of two expressions, or he makes two statements, both of which have had a considerable influence upon the minds of commentators, and also upon the minds of persons in general; and have caused them to arrive at conclusions which are not consistent with the truth of God. The prophet, in the fourth verse of the second chapter of Genesis, begins his new relation of circumstances, by briefly referring to the former periods of creation, and by informing the reader that his past recital "is the history of the heavens and of the earth when they were created;" he then proceeds to state that "the Lord God had not caused it to rain upon the earth, and there was not a man to till the ground, but there went up a mist from the earth, and watered the whole face of the ground. Upon the two points here named, much misconception has arisen, the expression "that there was no man to till the ground," being presumed to mean that "there was no man existing on the whole face of the earth," has appeared to give a sufficient authority for transferring the whole of this statement, through the intervening Sabbath, into the former series of incidents, and for making the whole of the circumstances connected with Adam's creation, to be a recapitulation of works performed upon the latter of the creative days. I hesitate not to say, that to my mind, the authority for such transposition ought to be of the most clear and of the most satisfactory character, to permit of such a liberty being taken with the word of God, as to shift a whole volume of circumstances out of the position in which they are evidently placed, into any other recital. Now when these two recitals are minutely dissected and examined, it will be admitted that it will scarcely be possible to find any two statements having more numerous points of dissimilarity and disagreement, save in the one point—that they both treat of a creative act of Almighty God. The explanation often given to this passage, that there was not "a man upon the whole face of the earth," appears perfectly contradictory to the whole intention of the Scriptures; it is in perfect opposition to the recital in the former chapter, of the creation of mankind, which general creation had as undoubtedly taken place before the Sabbath as this approaching creation of Adam undoubtedly succeeds that demarking period of time. The alteration of the simple words of the prophet, or the removing of either portion out of its assigned a position, is taking most unwarrantable liberty with the word of

God; the true intention of Scripture is to be found in the literal interpretation of the recital; the whole scope and meaning of the statement is to show a coming change in God's economy, as between the natures of the former human beings whom God had created, and the nature of a new human being whom he is now about to create. God, who bestowed the gift of speech and the powers of conception on man, and who made each word to become sufficiently significant for the conveyance of distinct ideas to the human mind, did, by this announcement, as surely purpose to induce the very thought the letter of his language should convey, and it does require that we should take God at his word, and that we should acknowledge that he knows how rightly to pronounce the sum and the substance of his facts; we have no right to warp the word of God, to any views, however they may claim the authority of antiquity; the mind must try and try again, until it arrives at the knowledge of all truth, until it becomes enabled to receive each part and portion of Scriptural evidence in its manifest sense, and the literal sense of the bible must ever be considered to be its true sense, unless we have (clearly and fully defined within that book itself) the authority which distinctly shows that such mode of speech was a figurative passage, or that it certainly was an idiom of Eastern phraseology God (as we have seen) had, prior to this time, created the numerous varieties of mankind upon the earth; he had commanded them (as before observed) to feed upon its uncultivated fruits; they had remained fully obedient to God's command in this respect, therefore, the prophet truly speaks when he declares "there was not a man to till the ground," therefore, we are told that God is now about to introduce another man who should be commanded and instructed by him to perform—who should therefore do—and who should teach others of mankind to continue to fulfil—the very act for which God's word declares that there was the want of a human being to effect before; for this purpose, we shall shortly see, a man was created, and was placed in a garden, previously prepared to dress it and to keep it, who also we shall find (when expelled thence for disobedience) is again brought out into the uncultivated wilderness, and commanded "to till the ground from whence he was taken," such clearly-expressed deficiency, combined with all the consequences which we shall shortly see defined in the history of this individual (as we proceed to trace it in its minor features), the correcting of this declared want of an industrial being by the creating of another man, who should have those habits naturally implanted within him by the command of

God rather than by changing the former habits (which were equally permanently implanted in all mankind originally,) do tend materially to the easy and to the consistent reception of the truth of the record of the absolute existence of each preceding work, and of each stedfast law which was then attached thereto , such announcement in the word of God, as giving cause for a new creation, seems to declare, fully, that the habit of the cultivation of the soil does not proceed from any natural desire residing in the breast of all the races of mankind, but that it is, in truth, a law proceeding solely from God, and therefore a habit implanted, and a beneficial occupation taught by him, originally to one peculiar being; and it is evident that the word of God, which declared to Adam that "in the sweat of his face he should eat his bread," did make "the tilling of the soil" to commence with that peculiar man, and that in Eden it was an easy and a pleasurable occupation, but that on his being thrust thence, it became laborious and less productive ; the research into the history of all mankind does positively show us that the cultivation of the soil proceeds from the spot of Adam's residence ; that it has been thence disseminated amongst other races of mankind who did not previously practice it ; that we do find that in this race were the first "keepers of sheep" and the first "tillers of the ground ;" and that such natural and such historical evidences do tend to convince us of God's eternal truth, in the most minute word, and in the most brief expression found within the book, which is a transcript of his most almighty will; and that these evidences do thus make his meaning and his intent to be both audible and visible to man, when engaged in running his thought and his most diligent research through all the lengthened stages of earth's olden times unto the abiding testimonials of the present day.

The Book of God.

—⚬—

BOOK VI.

1. One word before I conclude on the commonly received Chronology, respecting which the greatest ignorance prevails in all European countries, and in which
indeed they seem to possess only the intellects of children. It of course, differs materially from the true chronology which the Apocalypse developes; but that will not
be wondered at by those who know how all the chronologers from Bede downwards have differed among themselves.
The chronology of the Hebrew Text, says the learned
Whiston, has been grossly altered, especially in the interval next after the deluge (*Old Test.* p. 20). The Chronology of Scripture, says Malcolm (*Hist. of Persia*, i. 233), is
unsatisfactory from the scantiness of facts, the confusion
of dates, the errors arising from the writing of proper
names in different languages, and the variety of appellations, often used to designate the same person. Bryant

shews how some of the best chronologers have differed with respect to the age of a most important character in history, Semiramis; Syncellus placing her before the æra of Jesus, 2177 years; Petavius, 2060; Helvicus, 2248; Eusebius, 1984; Jackson, 1964; Usher, 1215; Philo-Byblius, 1200; and Herodotus, 713. What credit, asks he, can be given to the history of a person, the time of whose life cannot be ascertained within 1535 years? So Newton places Shishak about the middle of the 10th century before our æra; Usher fixes him at B.C. 1489. One chronologer determines the epoch of Menes, first king of Egypt, at about B.C. 2231. Champollion *deduces from the same authorities* that he lived 6000 years before Mohammed. Horner's researches, says a late writer, have rendered it in some degree probable that man sufficiently civilized to have manufactured pottery, existed in the valley of the Nile *thirteen or fourteen thousand years ago*: and who will pretend to say how long before those ancient periods savages like those of Terra del Fuego, or Australia, who possess a semi-domestic dog, may not have existed in Egypt? (DARWIN, *Origin of Species*, p. 18.)

2 Sir William Drummond, in his Essay on the Zodiacs of Esnè and Dendera, thus alludes to the uncertainty on this subject. The world, he says, as I have just stated, has been created 5824 years according to the received chronology; it has been created 6065 years according to the Samaritan text; 7210 years according to the Septuagint; and 7508 years according to the testimony of Josephus. The received chronology is founded on a literal, but as I conceive, a mistaken interpretation of the Hebrew text. * * It appears, both from the version of the

Seventy and from Josephus, that some error has crept into the Hebrew text in fixing the number of years between the creation and the deluge, and that a similar error has occurred in reckoning the number of years from the deluge to the birth of Abraham, is still more apparent. * * The Masters in Israel are not agreed among themselves about the chronology of the Bible, the age of the world being now [A.D. 1820], 5571 years according to the Seder Olam Sutha ; 5878 according to Maimonides ; 5574 years according to Gersom ; about 6000 years according to the Asiatic Jews. * * Those, then, who adhere to the present Hebrew text, but who read it, as I think it ought to be read, will reckon not less than 6562 years from the creation to the present time. For my own part; however, I do not scruple to adopt the chronology of the Seventy, and to assign a period of 7210 years from the creation to the year 1820 of the Christian æra. Had Sir William lived to our own time, he would probably have been constrained to own the true chronology of the age, not of the earth, but since the advent of man upon the earth, to be very different from that which he surmised. What Dr. Ferguson writes of the Great Sewers of Rome, is not inappropriate here. These works, he says, were in the midst of the Roman greatness, and still are reckoned among the wonders of the world. And yet they are said to have been works of the elder Tarquin, a prince whose territory did not extend in any direction above sixteen miles : and on this supposition they must have been made to accommodate a city that was calculated chiefly for the reception of cattle, herdsmen, and banditti. Rude nations sometimes execute works of great magnitude, as fortresses and

v 2

temples for the purposes of war and superstition, but seldom palaces ; and still more seldom works of mere convenience and cleanliness, in which, for the most part, they are long defective. It is not unreasonable therefore to question the authority of tradition in respect to this singular monument of antiquity, which so greatly exceeds what the best accommodated city of Europe could undertake for its own conveniency. And as these works are still entire, and may continue so for thousands of years, it may be suspected that they were even prior to the settlement of Romulus, and may have been *the remains of a more ancient city, on the ruins of which the followers of Romulus settled,* as the Arabs now hut or encamp on the ruins of Palmyra and Baalbec. Livy owns that the common sewers were not accommodated to the plan of Rome as laid out in his time : they were carried across the streets and passed under buildings of the greatest antiquity. This derangement he imputes to the hasty rebuilding of the city after its destruction by the Gauls. But haste, it is probable, would have determined the people to build on the old foundations, or at least not to change them so much as to cross the directions of former streets. Dr. Ferguson, adds Nimrod, from whom I cite this passage, has omitted to notice one remarkable passage of Lactantius, which shows that the sewers were in existence before the time of Romulus, and were an object of ignorant veneration to that founder and his colleague. *Cloacinæ simulacrum in cloacâ maximâ repertum Tatius consecravit, et quia cujus effigies esset ignorabat, ex loco illi nomen imposuit.* Yet we are asked to believe that they were made by the fourth king after Romulus ! (iii 75). The reader is referred back to Book

II, for many curious historical facts that corroborate the view of the vast antiquity of those wonderful remains which exist in almost all the old world. Thus Chitor, the supposed capital of Pourava, the Porus of the Greeks, was seen in ruins by Terry in 1615, crowded with stately pagodas and beautiful palaces, statues, and columns, exquisitely wrought, magnificent gates and vast reservoirs then mouldering in decay, with 100,000 *stone houses* totally uninhabited except by storks and owls, and enclosed with a strong wall ten miles in circumference. *Maurice Hist. of Hindostan*, i. 19.

3. And what was this image of Clo-ac-Ina, found in this subterraneous ancient city? Clo, we have already seen, was 600—the Naros; A, Ag, and Ac, was a name for God, and the Spirit; and Kina, or Ina, is the Hina, or the Holy Spirit of the Polynesians, which is a part of the compound word Shekinah. The image, therefore, that was found, was an image of the Tri-Une All, which probably belonged to the primeval inhabitants of Hesperia, or Latium, where Saturn, Sat-Ur-Nous, the Pure Fire-Mind, the Messenger, lay *concealed*. And the Romans having read the inscription, supposed it to be an image of the Goddess, to whom the disentombed city was consecrated; and called their Sewers after the name inscribed upon it. To such base uses may even the most holy things descend. The world, says Celsus, according to Moses, was created at a certain time, and has from its commencement existed for a period far short of *ten thousand years*. There is no such system of chronology as this in the present Hebrew scriptures. Celsus wrote 1700 years ago; and assuming at the farthest, that in the Mosaic books of that period, the age of the race of

man was said to be 7500, this would bring it very nearly to that which I assert to be about the true period of man's advent on the earth. Did Celsus use a different copy of Genesis from that which we have? It seems clear enough from the above passage. (See *Arguments of Celsus, &c.*, by *T. Taylor*, p. 3.)

4. There is a tradition, says *Mitchell*, in his *Exposition of St. John*, mentioned by one of the Jewish rabbis, that the world is to last 6000 years, and be under the dominion of the wicked; but that the seven thousandth year is to be the beginning of a grand jubilee, wherein God will restore all things to their original beauty, and men shall enjoy peace and happiness. The Scriptures know nothing of this tradition; it seems to have arisen from the mode of commenting on the sacred writings, which was so much in vogue among the ancient rabbis; and although it may be adopted as a truth, yet there is no advantage to be gained from it, in knowing when the seven thousandth year would commence, for the age of the world cannot be told with any certainty. The chronology of the Seventy, or Greek translation of the Bible which was in use at the Apostles' time, differs from the original Hebrew, and makes the world at the birth of Abraham older by more than 1400 years than the Hebrew does. Those who contend for the truth of the Hebrew chronology say that the Seventy translators added these years that they might surpass in antiquity the traditions of the Egyptians, and that this error in chronology arose from a pious fraud in the Seventy. This allegation against the Seventy might be of some weight, did the Samaritan Pentateuch, or Five Books of Moses agree in the main with the Hebrew; the Pentateuch was sup-

posed to be written in the time of Shalmanazer, 700 years
before Christ, some hundred years before the Seventy:
the Pentateuch, notwithstanding, does not agree with the
Hebrew; but for the most part, especially after the Flood,
with the chronology of the Seventy. *From this, and
many other considerations, it may be safely said that the
age of the world, at this present time cannot be known by
some hundred years;* and that our usual reckoning is no
more than the most likely conjecture. (p. 73)

5. Little or no dependence can in truth be placed on
any of their systems: the compilers of the Old Testament
have been guity of wilful fabrications to support their
particular views. The chronology of the Alexandrine
text of the Mosaic Scriptures differs from the Masoretical
Hebrew text by 1376 years. Klaproth (*Asie Polyglotte*)
quotes a passage from Kennicott, in which that profound
Hebraist avows a reluctant conviction that of the three
oldest versions of the Old Testament, the Jewish, the Septuagint, and the Samaritan *the former has been designedly
falsified.* (*Bjornsterna on the Hindoos*, page 133.) It is
certain, says Father Simon, that the ancient Jews not
finding in their histories genealogies enough to fill up the
time, *made one single person to live during many ages;*
wherefore there is nothing more common in their histories than these long-lived men. We ought therefore to
reflect upon this principle, that we may not so easily give
belief to the Jewish histories which make their doctors
survive, till such time as they can find another to join
them. I speak here only of those Jewish doctors who
lived at the captivity of Babylon, and not of the ancient
patriarchs, although it appears that some Jews have also
called in question the great number of years, which are

given them in the Books of Moses. Thus Rabbi Gedalia in the beginning of his history, where he makes mention of several opinions touching this matter, avers that there were some who believed that one of our years contained ten of those other years, which St. Augustine was not unacquainted with, as may be seen in his Books of the City of God. (*Lib.* ii. c. 4.) How unlike is English to Welsh, and Greek to Sanskrit, says a well-known writer, yet all indubitably are of one family of languages. What years were required to create the existing divergence of members of this family. How many more for other families, separated by a wide gulf from this, yet retaining traces of primeval aboriginal affinity, to have developed themselves either in priority or collaterally ! The same consonantal roots, appearing either as verbs inflected with great variety of grammatical form, or as nouns with case-endings in some languages, and with none in others, plead as convincingly as the succession of strata in geology *for enormous lapses of time.* When again we have traced our Gaelic and our Sanskrit to their inferential pre-Hellenic stem, and when reason has convinced us that the Semitic languages which had as distinct an individuality four thousand years ago, as they have now, require *a cradle of longer dimensions than Archbishop Usher's chronology,* what farther effort is not forced upon our imagination, if we would guess the measure of the dim background in which the Mongolian and Egyptian languages, older probably than the Hebrew, became fixed, growing early with the type which they retain ? Do we see an historical area of nations and languages *extending itself over nearly ten* thousand years , and can we imagine less than *another ten thousand,* during which the possibilities of these

things took body and form? (*Essays and Reviews*, p. 55.)
By astronomical calculations found in the Pyramid of
Gizeh, it appears to have been built 4950 years before
Jesus lived.

6. Care must be taken, says Butler, to distinguish between the Pentateuch in the Hebrew language, but in
the letters of the Samaritan alphabet, and the version of
the Pentateuch in the Samaritan language. One of the
most important differences between the Samaritan and
the Hebrew text, respects the duration of the period between the deluge and the birth of Abraham. The Samaritan text makes it longer by some centuries than the
Hebrew text; and the Septuagint makes it longer by
some centuries than the Samaritan. It is observable that
in her authentic translation of the Latin vulgate, the
Roman Catholic Church follows the computation expressed in the Hebrew text; and in her Martyrology
follows that of the Seventy. (*Horæ Biblicæ.*) This is
certainly accommodating. Father Simon in his Critical
History, mentions the same fact.

7. The learned and candid Du-Halde has the following
observation on the astounding discrepancy between the
chronology of the Vulgate and the Septuagint versions of
the Old Testament. Thus, says he, we see the points of
chronology that are, or ought to be, most certain, are contested every day by the ablest men : and this difference of
opinion, together with the liberty that is allowed of saying
what one will, within certain bounds, has sometimes embar-
rassed the missionaries in answering questions put to them
on this subject. The late Emperor Kang-hi, perceiving this
diversity, in reading the religious books written by different missionaries, some of whom followed the Septua-

gint, others the Vulgate : How comes it, said he, that your *King* (Sacred Books), are not clear ? Don't you affirm that they contain nothing, but what is sure and indubitable ? They did not want solid answers to satisfy an European ; but what effect could such have on a Prince who was but little acquainted with our religion, and could not conceive how its doctrines could be true and its chronology false ? (*Hist. of China.*)

8. With these observations I send into the world, this great Revelation from God : satisfied that there is no Book in the whole world better calculated to give it light, or to fill mankind universally with a true idea of the Benign Father, and a vivid sense of the confraternity of all His creatures ; convinced also that there is no other Book on earth, which tends more to enlarge the understanding with those grand ennobling views of God's providence, which it seems to be the object of all mere sects to pare down to the meanest and most miserable standard. Contemplated as a whole I believe it to be a Divine and Perfect Poem, worthy of the Soul that inspired it, and utterly beyond the invention of any mere man, whose faith was partial ; whose religion was confined. Every sentence, yea sometimes every word carries in it a world of divine mysteries, reminding one of that golden saying : There is not the least letter in the Law, on which great mountains of doctrines depend not. The mystic hallowed song that baffled Luther, and has been a stumbling block to millions, reduced into its plain and natural order, appears as simple and as beautiful as every work of God is ; and fills the mind with those consolatory reflections, that as from the very first, the Father regarded man and human affairs with a consideration worthy of His provi-

dence, so will He ever continue so to regard them, until
the fulfilment of all things; that there is a future life of
glory and of happiness, exceeding in transcendency all
that the most imaginative can fancy; and that this life is
positively assured herein to the virtuous and wise; and
that if we study for ourselves the writings of the Holy
Messengers of Heaven, we shall be more certain of attaining that Paradise, which God reserves for those who seek
Him, than if we were assured by all the hierarchies on
earth, that ignorance alone is perfect bliss, and that the
road to heaven is open only to those who are in that condition of slavish blindness, which the good and wise
deplore, but which the priests of darkness have called
faith.

9. The vast, magnificent and sublime notions which
our Apocalypse gives of the Divine Economy, are indeed
unequalled by any Book ever written, and would alone
prove by internal testimony, if others were wanting,
its superiority to all other works on earth. Contrasted
with the rhapsodical mixture, which has so long usurped its
name, and which might well have puzzled its thousand
commentators to unfold its meaning, it must flash conviction upon all who are not wilfully blind. Regard it
as a Poem, and it transcends the highest flights of Homer
or Æschylus, of Dante or Valmiki; contemplate it as a
Prophecy, and its predictions so literally fulfilled, must
strike the reader with astonishment and awe: view it as
a Picture of the Supreme Government, and it is impossible not to be convinced by its grandeur, its stupendous
images, and above all by its universality. All other
revelations purport to be given to certain peoples who
are supposed to be the exclusive favourites of heaven:

and the All-Father is wickedly represented as confining a knowledge of His celestial laws to a few, while He leaves the rest of His children in the abyss of utter darkness; a pretence, which even a Pagan Poet holds up to merited scorn. God he says, has not chosen the parched sands of Libya to bury truth in those deserts, *that it might be known only by a small number.* He makes himself known to all the world: He fills all places, the earth, the sea, the air, the heavens. He makes his abode in the soul of the just: why then should we seek him elsewhere? *Pharsalia* ix. 566. Such narrow notions find no place in this all-embracing Revelation; they are worthy only of such as are alluded to by Socrates in his sublime discourse. The Universe is immense, he says; we know and we inhabit only a small corner of it. The ethereal Sphere the antient abode of Souls, is placed in the pure regions of heaven, where the fixed stars are seated. We that live in this low abyss are apt enough to fancy that we are in a high place, and we call the air, the Heavens: just like a man that from the bottom of the sea, should view the Sun and Stars through the water, and fancy the ocean to be the firmament itself. But if we had wings to mount on high, we should see that *there* is the true heaven, the true light, and the true earth; and as in the sea everything is changed and disfigured by the salts that abound in in it, so in our present earth every thing is deformed, corrupted, and in a ruinous condition.

10. In the Apocalypse, says Herder, everything is in rapid motion: everything hastens and urges on towards a goal: it is a messenger of the swiftly-coming Lord, of lightning, of the Judge; at one time the image is that

of the sharp sword of the spirit; at another the snow-white locks on the head of the conqueror: here a fiery look of Jehovah , there the rushing of his approaching feet; a cry, a breath, a voice of the Spirit. In the whole book is rapidity, presence, arrival; a seal to be broken, the sound of flying trumpets, signs and messengers, and visions passing through the air, which hasten on and almost present themselves at one and the same time. Were it possible that the Four living Creatures should cry out together and the four seals be broken in rapid succession, and the four first trumpets root up the elements at once, and could I put all these visions together, so that seven churches should flame up around one Son of man, so that the Lamb on the loftiest heights of the blessed should appear at the same time with the beast from the pit of destruction below, and great Babylon impress itself at once on the mind, as harlot, as city, as beast, and as monster, all this and unspeakably more, were it possible, and possible for me, then might I count upon one entire impression of the meaning and explanation of this Book. But it is beyond my reach. The meaning soars on wings, but words can merely creep. I can conceive, says Stuart, of no more magnificent and ennobling view of the Creator and Lord of all things, than that which regards him as delighting to multiply even to an almost boundless extent, beings made in his own image, and therefore, rational and moral, and immortal like himself. How different from representing him as the Master of a magnificent puppet show, all of which he manages by merely pulling the wires with his own hands. To make him the only real agent in the Universe, and all else as mere passive recipients of his influence, is to take

from him the glory that results from the creation of num-
berless beings in his own image : beings which reflect the
brightness of their great Original. It is this intelligent
and rational creation in which the Prophet of the Apocalypse lives, moves, thinks, and speaks. The universe as
viewed by him is filled with ministers swift to do
Jehovah's will. They stand before his throne : they pre-
side over nations ; they guide the sun in his shining
course ; the moon and stars send forth radiance at their
bidding ; the very elements are watched over by them :
even infants are committed to the guidance of presence
angels : and the Angel of the Lord encompasseth round
about all that fear him. Such is the Universe which the
God who is, and was, and is to come, has created and
governs : and amid the contemplation of productions and
arrangements such as these, were the glowing pages of
the Apocalypse written.

INVOCATION OF THE SUPREME.

O GOD! thou glorious and divine One, grant that the day may now dawn, when all thy children shall be embraced in the one fold of Truth; when knowledge and reason shall take the place of prejudice and ignorance, and THINE UNIVERSAL CHURCH shall be established on the ruins of sects, denominations and creeds. Great indeed and strong is their power! They are mailed in wealth and helmetted in bigotry, and shielded most of all by that fearful ignorance of Thee and of Thy Nature, of the past and of the present, in which the large majority of human kind allow themselves to be; for interest of self is their ruling passion, and following it, they lose the sight of thine immortal splendours that beam on them from heaven, and becken them to Thee. Yet even amid the mass are there many who are fair, and pure, and snow white: who would fain emerge from the surrounding slime, in which they know and feel that their virgin loveliness is dimmed; men, in whose ethereal souls all beauty is not deadened by the lust of gold, or the fear of their fellows; women in whose starry spirits burn those fires which are akin to the celestial lights of Paradise, and are as flashing mirrors of their purity. On these O HOLY ONE, may the rays of truth descend, that they may now come forth, and in sublime faith confess Thee; on these O HOLY ONE, may thy beam of loveliness fall, that their minds may open like the flowers to the sunray, and the immortal essence which they derive from Thee, may be led into that One True and Splendid Path, which like the constellated sphere enfolds the globe within its grasp; which like thine own Sun, and thine own Rainbow, shines over all alike; the lowly and the great, the slave and the sovereign; a symbol of beauty, a herald of happiness, an emblem of love. And unto Thee also, O thou Bright and Holy SPIRIT of GOD, may it be permitted unto me, to raise my prayer. Thou art the Queen—the splendid Virgin of the Heavens, everlasting in divine loveliness and purity; the ever-producing Mother of all ethereal natures. Upon me may thy benign blessing fall, while labouring thus to bring back the children of men to the One Faith, which was revealed of old, and in which God, and Thou were the bright prevailing Stars of Glory, by whose light the world was directed. Ages have passed on ages, since this most blessed Creed prevailed; and Thou hast long been ignored, or hast yielded up thy place to earth-born idols, whom it were profane to name. May it be that this infidelity shall now give way to Truth, and that the Holy Religion which is developed in this Work, may be substituted for the irreverent superstitions which universally prevail, and which have led the footsteps of the world into that practical rejection of God, which is the source of all evil. Amen! Amen!

SUMMARY.

1. The prologue to the Sacred Vision.
2. The splendid symbol of the Messiah of God, whose light was to shine forth in heavenly Messengers.
3. The initiation of the Prophet.
4. Vision of the Four Living Creatures.
5. The Prophet is uplifted into the Glory of God.
6. Heaven opens—the Throne and the 24 Ancients.
7. The Book of Heaven opened by the Lamb.
8. The Holy Spirit of God, and the Red Dragon.
9. The Sacred Hymn of Victory.
10. Explication of the Red Dragon.
11. The four races of mankind.
12. ADAM, the First Messenger of God, A.M. 3000.
13. ENOCH, the second Messenger of God, A.M. 3600.
14. Fo-HI, the third Messenger of God, A.M. 4200.
15. The submersion of Atlantis foreshewn.
16. BRIGOO, the fourth Messenger of God, A M. 4800
17. Vision of an Universal Church which followed this Avatara.
18. Vision of the flying sickle.
19. Rise, growth, and condemnation of Serpent-worship.
20. ZARATUSHT, the fifth Messenger of God, A.M. 5400.

21. The vision of the archangel Michael.

22. THOTH, the sixth Messenger of God, A.M. 6000.

23. Symbolic vision of this great Messenger's teaching.

24. AMOSIS, the seventh Messenger of God, A.M. 6600.

25. Symbolic vision of the glory that was to follow.

26. The first four great monarchies of the Earth : the Indo-Ethiopic, the Scythian, the Hindu, the Chinese

27. The Medo-Persian, and the Greek-Macedonian monarchies.

28. LAO-TSEU and JESUS, the eighth and ninth Messengers of God, A.M. 7200 and 7800.

29. The coronation of these two Messengers in Heaven.

30. Their teaching shewn to be identical with that of their predecessors.

31. MO'AHMED, the tenth Messenger, A.M. 8400.

32. The monotheistic hymn of praise in Heaven.

33. CHENGIZ-KHAN, the eleventh Messenger of God, A.M. 9000.

34. The Seven trumpet-bearing Angels.

35. The French Empire and Napoleon.

36. The Angels with the Seven last Plagues.

37. The great hierarchic Capitals of the world described, and their fate predicted.

38. The lamentation of the wicked over their downfall.

39. The dirge of the Destroying Angel.

40. The symbolic vision of the British empire.

41. The symbolic vision of the American empire.

42. The final overthrow of all evil dominion by the monotheistic power.

43. The twelfth MESSENGER of God, A.M. 9600.

44. A vision of his followers.

45. The Voice of Heaven proclaiming his epiphany.

46. The glorious congregation of believers.

47. A vision of Angels who follow after the Twelfth.

48. The command given to the sixth trumpet-bearing Angel.

49. The sounding of the Seventh Trumpet.

50. Prologue to the dissolution of the Kalpa.

51. Another vision of Angels who succeed the Twelfth Messenger.

52. The opening of the Fifth Seal.

53. The commandment to the Seven Angels.

54. The Seven Angels pour out their vials.

55. The opening of the Sixth Seal.

56. The vision of the Martyrs for Truth.

57. The opening of the Seventh Seal: and the end of the Kalpa.

58. The Majesty of the Lord God is seen.

59. The day of the Great Judgment.

60. The day of transmigrations into various life.

61. The renovation into new beauty.

62. Vision of the Holy Spirit.

63. The Messengers claim their followers from God.

64. The promises of the Holy Spirit to the good.

65. The vision of the New Paradise.

66. The same vision continued.

67. The River and the Tree of Life.

68. The glorification of the Holy City.

69. The ambrosial Waters, and the Trees of Heaven.

70. The great and final Commandment.

ΑΠΟΚΑΛΥΨΙΣ

ΩΑΝΝΟΥ, ΤΟΥ ΘΕΟΥ ΛΟΓΟΥ.

Ἐπιγραφὴ.

Ἐν Ἀρχῇ ἦν ὁ Λόγος, καὶ ὁ Λόγος ἦν πρὸς τὸν Θεὸν, καὶ θεὸς ἦν ὁ Λόγος· οὗτος ἦν ἐν ἀρχῃ πρὸς τὸν Θεόν· Πάντα δί Αὐτοῦ ἐγένετο καὶ χωρὶς Αὐτοῦ ἐγένετο οὐδὲ ἓν ὁ γέγονεν. Ἐν Αὐτῷ ζωὴ ἦν, καὶ ἡ ζωὴ ἦν τὸ φῶς τῶν ἀνθρώπων· καὶ τὸ φῶς ἐν τῇ σκοτίᾳ φαίνει, καὶ ἡ σκοτία αὐτὸ οὐ κατέλαβεν· Ἐγένετο ἄνθρωπος ἀπεσταλμένος παρὰ Θεοῦ, ὄνομα αὐτῷ Ὠάννης· οὗτος ἦλθεν εἰς μαρτυρίαν, ἵνα μαρτυρήσῃ περὶ τοῦ Φωτὸς, ἵνα πάντες πιστεύσωσι δί αὐτοῦ. Οὐκ ἦν ἐκεῖνος τὸ Φῶς, ἀλλ' ἵνα μαρτυρήσῃ περὶ τοῦ Φωτός : τὸ Φῶς τὸ ἀληθινὸν, ὁ φωτίζει πάντα ἄνθρωπον ἐρχόμενον εἰς τὸν κόσμον· Ἐν τῷ κόσμῳ ἦν, καὶ ὁ κόσμος δί αὐτοῦ ἐφωτισθη, καὶ ὁ κόσμος αὐτὸν οὐκ ἔγνω. Εἰς τὰ ἴδια ἦλθε, καὶ οἱ ἴδιοι αὐτὸν οὐ παρέλαβον. Ὅσοι δὲ ἔλαβον αὐτὸν, ἔδωκεν αὐτοῖς ἐξουσίαν τέκνα Θεοῦ γενέσθαι· οἱ οὐκ ἐξ αἱμάτων, οὐδὲ ἐκ θελήματος σαρκὸς, οὐδὲ ἐκ θελήματος ἀνδρός, αλλ' ἐκ Θεοῦ ἐγγενήθησαν. Καὶ ὁ Λόγος σὰρξ ἐγένετο καὶ ἐσκήνωσεν ἐν ἡμιν, πλήρης χαριτος καὶ ἀληθείας Ἀμὴν.

.

.

ΚΕΦ. 1.

ΑΠΟΚΑΛΥΨΙΣ Ἰσσης, καὶ του Χριστοῦ, ἣν ἔδωκεν ὁ Θεὸς, δεῖξαι τοῖς δούλοις αὐτοῦ ἃ δεῖ γενέσθαι, καὶ ἐσήμανεν

THE APOCALYPSE
OF OANNES, THE WORD OF GOD.

In Archa was the Word, and the Word was in the presence of God, and the Word was a god. This was in the beginning with God. All things were made by Him, and without Him was not anything made that is made. In Him was Life, and the Life was the light of men. And the Light shineth in darkness, and the darkness comprehendeth it not. There was a man sent from God whose name was Oannes. The same came for a Witness to bear witness of the Light, that all men through him might believe. He was not *the* Light, but was sent to bear witness of the Light : the true light which enlightens every man that cometh into the world. He was in the world, and the world was enlightened by him, and the world knew him not. He came unto his own, and his own received him not. But as many as received him to them gave he power to become the Children of God ; which were born not by bloods, nor of the will of the flesh, nor of the will of man, but of God : And the Word became flesh, and dwelt among us full of grace and truth. Amen.

1.

A Revelation of Issa, and the Anointed One, which God gave to make manifest to his Servants, those things

άντα ἀποστείλας διὰ τοῦ Ἀγγέλου αὐτοῦ τῷ δούλῳ αὐτοῦ
Ἰωάννῃ· Ὃς ἐμαρτύρησε τὸν Λόγον τοῦ Θεοῦ, καὶ τὴν
φανέρωσιν Ἰσσης, καὶ τοῦ Χριστοῦ, ὅσα εἶδε. Μακάριος ὁ
ἀναγινώσκων, καὶ οἱ ἀκούοντες τοὺς λόγους τῆς Προφητείας,
καὶ τηροῦντες τὰ ἐν αὐτῇ γεγραμμένα.

ΚΕΦ. 2.

Ἰωάννης ταῖς ἑπτὰ ἐκκλησίαις ταῖς ἐν τῇ Ἀσίᾳ· Χάρις
ὑμῖν καὶ εἰρήνη ἀπὸ ὁ ὢν καὶ ὁ ἦν καὶ ὁ ἐρχόμενος· καὶ ἀπὸ
τῶν ἑπτὰ Πνευμάτων ἅ ἐστιν ἐνώπιον τοῦ θρόνου αὐτοῦ·
Ἀμήν· Ἰδού, ἔρχεται μετὰ τῶν νεφελῶν, καὶ ὄψεται Ἀυτὸν
πᾶς ὀφθαλμός. Ἀμήν. Ἐγώ εἰμι ΑΩ, λέγει Κύριος ὁ
Θεὸς, ὁ ὢν, καὶ ὁ ἦν, καὶ ὁ ἐρχόμενος, ὁ παντοκράτωρ. Ἐγὼ
Ἰωάννης, ὁ ἀδελφὸς ὑμῶν, ἐγενόμην ἐν Πνεύματι ἐν τῇ κυριακῇ
ἡμέρᾳ· καὶ ἤκουσα ὀπίσω μου φωνὴν μεγάλην ὡς σάλπιγγος,
λεγούσης· Ἐγώ εἰμι ΑΩ, ὁ πρῶτος καὶ ὁ ἔσχατος· καὶ ὁ
βλέπεις γράψον εἰς βιβλίον, καὶ πέμψον ταῖς ἑπτὰ ἐκκλησίαις. Καὶ ἐπέστρεψα βλέπειν τὴν φωνὴν ἥτις ἐλάλησε
μετ' ἐμοῦ· καὶ ἐπιστρέψας εἶδον ἑπτὰ λυχνίας χρυσᾶς· Καὶ
ἐν μέσῳ τῶν ἑπτὰ λυχνιῶν ὅμοιον Υἱῷ ἀνθρώπου, ἐνδεδυμένον
ποδήρη, καὶ περιεζωσμένον πρὸς τοῖς μαστοῖς ζώνην χρυσῆν·
Ἡ δὲ κεφαλὴ αὐτοῦ καὶ αἱ τρίχες λευκαὶ ὡς ἔριον λευκὸν, ὡς
χιών· καὶ οἱ ὀφθαλμοί αὐτοῦ ὡς φλὸξ πυρός· και οἱ πόδες
αὐτοῦ ὅμοιοι χαλκολιβάνῳ, ὡς ἐν καμίνῳ πεπυρωμένοι· καὶ
ἡ φωνὴ αὐτοῦ ὡς φωνὴ ὑδάτων πολλῶν. Καὶ ἔχων ἐν τῇ
δεξιᾷ αὐτοῦ χειρὶ Ἀστέρας Ἑπτά· καὶ ἐκ τοῦ στόματος αὐτοῦ
ρομφαία δίστομος ὀξεῖα ἐκπορευομένη· καὶ ἡ ὄψις αὐτοῦ, ὡς ὁ
ἥλιος φαίνει ἐν τῇ δυνάμει ἀυτοῦ. Καὶ ὅτε εἶδον αὐτὸν, ἔπεσα
πρὸς τοὺς πόδας αὐτοῦ ὡς νεκρός· καὶ ἔθηκε τὴν δεξιὰν αὐτοῦ
ἐπ' ἐμὲ λέγων· Μὴ φοβοῦ· ἐγώ εἰμι ὁ πρῶτος καὶ ὁ ἔσχατος,

which shall come to pass; and He hath signified them by
the sending of his Messenger; his Servant Oannes, who
hath declared the Word of God, and the manifestation
of Issa and the Anointed One; which he beheld also.
Blessed is he who knoweth—blessed also shall they be
who hear the words of this Prophecy, and shall keep the
things that are therein written.

2.

Oannes to the Seven Churches which are in Asia;
Grace be with you, and Peace from Him, who is, and
was, and is to come; and from the Seven Spirits that
are before his Throne. Amen! Behold he cometh with
the clouds, and every eye shall see Him. Amen! I am
AO. saith the Lord God, who is, and who was, and
who will be : (1)—the Almighty. I, Oannes, your brother, was in the Spirit, in the day of the Lord; and
lo! behind me I heard a great Voice as of a trumpet,
saying: I am AO: (2) the First and the Last: and
what thou seest write into a Book, and send it to the
Seven Churches. And I turned to see what the Voice
was that spake with me; and, turning, I beheld Seven
Golden Lamp-bearers; and in the midst of the Seven
Lamp-bearers, I saw one like unto a Son of Man, He was
clothed to the foot with a flowing garment; and was girt
about the paps with a golden girdle. His head and his
hair were pure white like wool; like snow itself: and
his eyes were as a flashing flame; his feet were like smelting brass, when it burneth brightly in a furnace of fire,
and his voice was as the voice of many waters. And in his
right hand he held Seven Stars; and out of his mouth
there went a sharp double-edged sword; and his appear-

καὶ ὁ ζῶν· καὶ ἐγενόμην νεκρὸς, καὶ ἰδοὺ ζῶν εἰμι εἰς τοὺς
αἰῶνας τῶν αἰώνων· καὶ ἔχω τὰς κλεῖς τοῦ θανάτου καὶ τοῦ
Ἄδου. Γράψον οὖν ἃ εἶδες, καὶ ἅ εἰσι, καὶ ἃ μέλλει γίνεσθαι
μετὰ ταῦτα· τὸ μυστήριον τῶν Ἑπτὰ Ἀστέρων ὧν εἶδες ἐπὶ
τῆς δεξιᾶς μου, καὶ τὰς ἑπτα λυχνίας τὰς χρυσᾶς. Οἱ Ἑπτὰ
Ἀστέρες, ἄγγελοι τῶν ἑπτὰ ἐκκλησιῶν εἰσι· καὶ αἱ λυχνίαι αἱ
ἑπτὰ, ἑπτὰ ἐκκλησίαι εἰσί.

ΚΕΦ. 3.

ΚΑΙ ἔιδον, καὶ ἰδοῦ χεὶρ ἐκτεταμενη πρός με, καὶ ἐν ἀυτῃ,
κεφαλις βιβλίου· Καὶ ἀνείλησεν αὐτὴν ἐνωπίον μου, καὶ ἐν
ἀυτῇ γεγραμμένα τὰ ἔμπροσθεν καὶ τὰ ὀπισω· καὶ ἐγέγραπτο
θρῆνος, καὶ μέλος, καὶ ὀναὶ· Καὶ ἔιπε πρός με, Ὑιὲ ἀνθρωπου,
στῆθι ἐπι τοῦς πόδας σου, καὶ λαλῆσω πρός σε καὶ κατάφαγε
τὴν κεφαλὶδα ταύτην· Καὶ ἦλθεν ἐπ᾽ ἐμὲ Πνεῦμα, καὶ ἀνέ-
λαβέ με, καὶ ἐξῆρέ με, καὶ ἔστησέ με ἐπὶ τοῦς πόδας μοῦ,
καὶ ἤκουον ἀυτοῦ λαλοῦντος πρός με· Καὶ διήνοιξε τὸ στόμα
μου καὶ ἐψώμισέ με τὴν κεφαλὶδα· καὶ ἔιπε πρός με, Ὑιὲ
ἀνθρώπου, τὸ στόμα σου φάγεται, καὶ ἡ κοιλία σοῦ πληθή-
σεται της κεφαλίδος ταύτης της δεδομένης εἰς σέ· καὶ ἔφαγον
ἀυτὴν, καὶ ἐγενετο ἐν τῳ στοματὶ μου, ὡς μέλι γλυκάζον.

ΚΕΦ. 4.

ΚΑΙ ἔιδον, καὶ ἰδοὺ ζάλη ἤρχετο ἀπό βορρᾶ, καὶ
νεφέλη μεγάλη ἐν αὐτῷ, καὶ φέγγος κύκλῳ αὐτοῦ, καὶ πῦρ.

ance was like the sun when he glitters in his full splendour. And when I saw him I fell before his feet, even as though I were a dead man : but he laid his right hand on me, saying : Fear thou not ! I am the First and the Last . I am he who lives and dies, yet am I Life unto the ages of ages . and I hold the keys of Death and the Invisible. Write then the things which thou hast seen ; the things that are, and those that are to be hereafter : the sacred mystery of the Seven Stars, which thou didst see upon my right hand ; and of the Seven Golden Lamp-bearers. The Seven Stars are the Messengers of the Seven Churches ; and the Seven Lamp-bearers are those Seven Churches.

3.

And I looked, and lo, a hand was extended unto me, and behold in it a chapter of a Book, and he spread it out before me, and in it were written the things that are before, and the things that are past : and lamentation, and mourning and woe was written ; and he said to me : Son of Man stand upon thy feet, and I will speak with thee ; and eat thou this roll. And the Spirit came upon me, and uplifted me, and raised me, and set me upon my feet ; and I heard him that spake unto me : and he opened my mouth and caused me to eat that roll, and he said to me, Son of Man, let thy mouth eat and thy stomach be filled with this the roll that I have given : and I did eat, and it was in my mouth as honey for sweetness.

4.

And I looked, and lo ! a whirlwind out of the North ; and in the whirlwind there was a great Cloud ; and a daz-

z

ἐξαστράπτον· καὶ ἐν τῷ μέσῳ αὐτοῦ ὡς ὅρασις ἠλέκτρου ἐν μέσῳ τοῦ πυρὸς, καὶ φέγγος ἐν αὐτῷ· Καὶ ἐν τῷ μέσῳ ὡς ὁμοίωμα τεσσάρων Ζώων· καὶ αὕτη ἡ ὅρασις αὐτῶν· ὁμοίωμα ἀνθρώπου ἐπ᾽ αὐτοῖς· καὶ τέσσαρα πρόσωπα τῷ ἑνὶ, καὶ τέσσαρες πτέρυγες τῷ ἑνὶ· Καὶ τὰ σκέλη αὐτῶν ὀρθα, καὶ πτερωτοὶ οἱ πόδες αὐτῶν, καὶ σπινθῆρες ὡς ἐξαστράπτων χαλχος, καὶ ἐλαφραὶ αἱ πτέρυγες αὐτῶν· Καὶ χεὶρ Ἀνθρώπου ὑποκάτωθεν τῶν πτερύγων αὐτῶν ἐπὶ τὰ τέσσαρα μέρη αὐτῶν· Καὶ τὰ πρόσωπα αὐτῶν τῶν τεσσάρων οὐκ ἐπεστρέφοντο ἐν τῷ βαδίζειν αὐτά· ἕκαστοι ἀπεναντι τοῦ προσώπου αὐτῶν ἐπορεύοντο· Καὶ ὁμοίωσις τῶν προσωπων αὐτῶν, πρόσωπον Ἀνθρώπου, καὶ πρόσωπον Λέοντος ἐκ δεξιῶν τοῖς τέσσαρσιν, κιὶ πρόσωπον Μόσχου ἐξ ἀριστερῶν τοις τέσσαρσιν, καὶ πρόσωπον Ἀετου τοις τέσσαρσιν. Καὶ αἱ πτέρυγες αὐτῶν ἐκτεταμέναι ἄνωθεν τοῖς τέσσαρσιν, ἑκατέρῳ δύο συνεζευγμέναι πρὸς ἀλλήλας, καὶ δύο ἐπεκάλυπτον ἐπάνω τοῦ σώματος ἀυτῶν· Καὶ ἑκάτερον κατὰ πρόσωπον αὐτοῦ ἐπορεύετο· οὗ ἂν ἦν το πνεῦμα πορευόμενον ἐπορεύοντο, καὶ οὐκ επεστρεφον· Καὶ ἐν μέσῳ τῶν Ζώων ὅρασις ὡς ἀνθράκων πυρος καιομένων, ὡς ὄψις λαμπάδων συστρεφομένων ἀνὰ μέσον τῶν Ζώων· καὶ φέγγος τοῦ πυρός, καὶ εκ τοῦ πυρός εξεπορευέτο ἀστραπή. Καὶ εἶδον, καὶ ἰδοὺ τροχὸς εἷς ἐπὶ τῆς γῆς ἐχόμενος τῶν Ζώων τοις τέσσαρσιν· καὶ τὸ εἶδος τῶν τροχῶν ὡς εἶδος θαρσεὶς, καὶ ὁμοίωμα ἕν τοῖς τέσσαρσιν, καὶ τὸ ἔργον αὐτῶν ἦν, καθὼς ἂν εἴη τροχὸς ἐν τροχῷ· και ἐπὶ τα τέσσαρα μέρη ἀυτῶν ἐπορευοντο· οὐκ ἐπέστρεφον ἐν τῷ πορευεσθαι αὐτὰ, καὶ ὕψος ἦν ἀυτοῖς· καὶ εἶδον ἀυτα, καὶ οἱ νῶτοι ἀυτῶν πλήρεις ὀφθαλμων κυκλοθεν τοῖς τέσσαρσιν· Καὶ ἐν τῷ πορεύεσθαι τὰ Ζῶα, ἐπορεύοντο οἱ τροχοὶ ἐχόμενοι αὐτῶν· καὶ ἐν τῷ ἐξαίρειν τὰ Ζῶα ἀπὸ τῆς γῆς ἐξήροντο οἱ τροχοί· Οὗ ἂν ἦν ἡ νεφέλη, ἐκεῖ τὸ πνεῦμα τοῦ πορεύεσθαι, πορεύοντο οἱ τροχοὶ, καὶ ἐξήροντο σὺν ἀυτοῖς διότι πνευμα

zling splendour in the cycle thereof; and a fire flashing
lightnings. And in the centre thereof was the appearance of a diamond, in the centre of the very fire : and a
blinding brightness was in the midst. And out of the
central flame appeared the likeness of four Living Beings,
and this was the appearance which they showed : the
likeness of a Man was over them, and there were four
faces in each one ; and there were four wings to every one ;
and their legs were straight; and their feet were plumed
with wings ; and their sparklings were like brass emitting
flashes of light ; and light as air were their feathered
pinions ; and the hand of a Man was under their wings ;
a hand upon each of their four sides. And the faces of
the four turned not in their goings, but they went every
one straightforward ; and this was the likeness of their
faces : the face of a Man and the face of a Lion out of
the right of the Four, and the face of a young Bull out
of the left of the Four, and the face of an Eagle in the
Four. And their wings were opened out above the Four ;
two wings of each one were entwined with the others ;
and two covered their bodies from above ; and they went
every one straightforward ; whither the Spirit willed that
they should go they went, and they turned not when they
went. And in the midst of these Living Splendours I
saw as it were the appearance of burning coals of fire
and as the likeness of lamps rapidly whirled, through
the mid centre of these Living Beings ; and the clear
glittering brightness of flame, and lightning flashed out
of that flame. And I looked, and lo ! one wheel was on
the earth, and it proceeded from the Living Creatures in
the Four ; and the likeness of the wheels was as the
brightness of beryl ; and in the Four there was but one

ζωῆς εν τοῖς τροχοῖς. Καὶ ὁμοίωμα ὑπὲρ κεφαλῆς αὐτῶν τῶν Ζώων ὡσεὶ στερέωμα ὡς ὅρασις κρυστάλλου ἐκτεταμένων ἐπὶ τῶν πτερύγων αὐτῶν ἐπάνωθεν· Καὶ ὑποκάτωθεν τοῦ στερεώματος ἅι πτέρυγες αὐτῶν ἐκτεταμέναι, πτερυσσόμεναι ἑτέρα τῇ ἑτέρᾳ. ἑκάστῳ δύο ἐπικαλύπτουσαι τὰ σώματα αὐτῶν· Καὶ ἤκουον τὴν φωνὴν τῶν πτερύγων αὐτῶν ἐν τῷ πορεύεσθαι αυτὰ, ὡς φωνὴν ὑδάτων πολλῶν καὶ ἐν τῷ ἱστάναι αὐτὰ, κατέπαυον αἱ πτέρυγες αὐτῶν.

ΚΕΦ. 5.

Καὶ ἰδοὺ φωνη ὑπεράνωθεν τοῦ στερεώματος τοῦ ὄντος ὑπὲρ κεφαλῆς αὐτων· ὡς ὅρασις λίθου σαπφείρου ὁμοίωμα Θρόνου ἐπ᾽ αὐτοῦ, καὶ ἐπὶ τοῦ ὁμοιώματος τοῦ Θρόνου ὁμοίωμα ὡς εἶδος Ἀνθρώπου ἄνωθεν· Καὶ ἀνέλαβέν με Πνεῦμα, καὶ ἤκουσα κατόπισθέν μου φωνὴν σεισμοῦ μεγάλου, εὐλογομενη ἡ δόξα Κυρίου ἐκ τοῦ τόπου αὐτοῦ· Καὶ εἶδον φωνὴν πτερύγων τῶν Ζώων πτερυσσομένων ἑτέρα πρός τήν ἑτέραν, καὶ φωνὴ τῶν τροχῶν ἐχομένη αὐτῶν, καὶ φωνὴ τοῦ

radiant brightness: and the form of the wheels and their construction was in this wise; a wheel within a wheel; and when they went, they went by their four parts; and they turned not when they went. The wheels had also a sublimity of greatness; and I viewed them, and their bodies were full of eyes, (3) round about the Four. And when these Living Splendours moved, the wheels proceeding from them moved also; and when these Living Splendours lifted themselves from earth, the wheels were also lifted up with them. And wheresoever was the Cloud, thither did the spirit will them to go; and thither also went the wheels; and they were lifted with them on high: for in these wheels there was a living spirit. And the likeness over the heads of the Living Splendours was as the shining starry firmament, and as the radiancy of crystal arched, over their waving wings from heaven. And under the star-canopy were their wings extended, fluttering, waving, one towards the other, but each one used two, to veil their shining bodies. And I heard the sound of their wings when they went, as the deep voice of many waters; and when they rested they folded their wings.

5.

And behold a Voice came from above; from the firmament of stars arching over their heads; and I saw as it were the splendour of a sapphire stone: and the apparition of a Throne was over it: and over the apparition of this royal Throne, an apparition as it were of a human being from heaven. And the Divine Spirit lifted me on high; and I heard behind me the voice of a great rushing; and the Glory of the Lord in blessing from its place. And

σεισμοῦ· καὶ τὸ Πνεῦμα ἀνέλαβέν με, καὶ εἶδον ὡς ὄψιν
ἠλέκτρου, ἀπὸ ὁράσεως ὀσφύος καὶ ἐπάνω, καὶ ἀπὸ ὁρασέως
ὀσφυός καὶ ἕ½ς κάτω εἶδον ὅρασιν πυρός, καὶ τό φέγγος
αὐτοῖ κύκλῳ. Ὡς ὅρασις τόξου, ὅταν ᾖ ἐν τῇ νεφελῇ ἐν
ἡμέραις ὑετοῦ, οὕτως ἡ στάσις τοῦ φέγγους κυκλόθεν· Αὕτη
ἡ ὅρασις ὁμοιώματος δόξης Κυρίου· καὶ εἶδον, καὶ πίπτω ἐπὶ
πρόσωπόν μου, και ἤκουσα φωνὴν λαλοῦντος· καὶ ἐξέτεινεν
ὁμοίωμα χειρός, καὶ ἀνέλαβεν με τῆς κορυφῆς μου, καὶ ανε-
λαβεν με Πνευμα ἀνὰ μέσον τῆς γῆς καὶ ἀνὰ μέσον του
οὐρανοῦ, και ἤγαγέν με εἰς ὅράσιν Θεοῦ, καὶ δόξαν Κυρίου
Θεοῦ·

ΚΕΦ. 6.

Καὶ μετὰ ταῦτα εἶδον, καὶ θύρα ἀνεῳγμενη ἐν τῷ οὐρανῷ,
καὶ ἡ φωνὴ ἡ πρώτη ἣν ἤκουσα, ὡς σάλπιγγος λαλούσης
μετ᾽ ἐμοῦ, λέγων· Ἀνάβα ὧδε, καὶ δείξω σοι ἃ δεῖ γενέσθαι
μετὰ ταῦτα. Καὶ εὐθέως ἐγενόμην ἐν Πνεύματι· καὶ ἰδοὺ,
θρόνος ἔκειτο ἐν τῷ οὐρανῷ, καὶ ἐπὶ τοῦ θρόνου καθήμενος·
Καὶ ὁ καθήμενος ὅμοιος ὁράσει λίθῳ ἰάσπιδι καὶ σαρδίῳ·
καὶ ἶρις κυκλόθεν τοῦ θρόνου ὅμοιος ὁράσει σμαραγδίνῳ. Καὶ
κυκλόθεν τοῦ θρόνου θρόνοι εἴκοσι τέσσαρες· καὶ ἐπὶ τοὺς
θρόνους εἴκοσι τέσσαρας πρεσβυτέρους καθημένους περιβεβλημένους ἐν ἱματίοις λευκοῖς· καὶ ἐπὶ τὰς κεφαλὰς αὐτῶν
στεφάνους χρυσοῦς Καὶ ἐκ τοῦ θρόνου ἐκπορεύονται ἀστραπαὶ καὶ φωναὶ καὶ βρονταί καὶ ἑπτὰ λαμπάδες πυρὸς καιό-

I perceived the sound of the wings of the Living Ones; waving, fluttering one amid the others : and the sound of the wheels proceeding from them ; and the sound of a rushing host. And the Divine Spirit raised me on high ; and lo, a likeness as the appearance of diamond, from the appearance of the loins upward ; and from the appearance of the loins downwards I saw the appearance as of fire, with a dazzling splendour of light in the midst. As the appearance of the *Rainbow* in the cloud, when the rain falls in the day time ; so was the permanence of that dazzling Splendour ; breaking out of the inmost centre. This was the manifestation of the likeness of the Lord's Glory. And I beheld, and lo ! I fell upon my face ; and I heard the Voice of one who spake ; and he put forth the apparition of a hand ; and took me up by a lock of mine head ; and the Divine Spirit lifted me on high between the earth and heaven ; and brought me into the Vision of God ; and before the Glory of the Lord God.

6.

And after this I looked and saw ; and behold, a Gate was opened in Heaven , and the heavenly Voice which first I heard, speaking with me as in trumpet tones, spake again : Ascend thou by this path ; and I will shew thee future times and things. And in a moment I was before the Spirit of God , and behold a Throne was set in heaven : and One sat upon the Throne ; like a diamond and fiery sard beautiful to see. And over and about the Throne was a RAINBOW, in sight like unto an emerald. And circled round the Throne were four and twenty Thrones, and on these four and twenty Thrones, Ancients sat : (4) they were clothed in robes of glittering white, and on their

μεναι ἐνώπιον τοῦ θρόνου, ἅι εἰσι τὰ ἑπτὰ πνεύματα τοῦ
Θεοῦ· Καὶ ἐνώπιον τοῦ θρόνου θάλασσα ὑαλίνη, ὁμοία κρυ-
στάλλῳ· καὶ ἐν μέσῳ τοῦ θρόνου καὶ κύκλῳ τοῦ θρόνου
τέσσαρα Ζῶα γέμοντα ὀφθαλμῶν ἔμπροσθεν καὶ ὄπισθεν.
Καὶ τὸ Ζῶον τὸ πρῶτον ὅμοιον λέοντι, καὶ τὸ δεύτερον Ζῶον
ὅμοιον μόσχῳ, καὶ τὸ τρίτον Ζῶον ἔχον τὸ πρόσωπον ἀνθρώπου, καὶ τὸ τέταρτον Ζῶον ὅμοιον ἀετῷ πετομένῳ. Καὶ
τὰ τέσσαρα Ζῶα, ἓν καθ᾽ ἓν αὐτῶν ἔχον ἀνὰ πτέρυγας ἓξ,
κυκλόθεν καὶ ἔσωθεν γέμουσιν ὀφθαλμῶν· καὶ ἀνάπαυσιν οὐκ
ἔχουσιν ἡμέρας καὶ νυκτὸς, λέγοντες· Ἅγιος, ἅγιος, ἅγιος
Κύριος ὁ Θεὸς ὁ παντοκράτωρ· ἅγιος, ἅγιος, ἅγιος Κύριος,
ὁ ἦν, καὶ ὁ ὢν, καὶ ὁ ἐρχόμενος. Καὶ ὅταν δώσουσι τὰ Ζῶα
δόξαν καὶ τιμὴν καὶ εὐχαριστίαν τῷ καθημένῳ ἐπὶ τοῦ θρόνου,
τῷ ζῶντι εἰς τοὺς αἰῶνας τῶν αἰώνων, πεσοῦνται οἱ εἴκοσι
τέσσαρες πρεσβύτεροι ἐνώπιον τοῦ καθημένου ἐπὶ τοῦ θρόνου,
καὶ προσκυνήσουσι τῷ ζῶντι εἰς τοὺς αἰῶνας τῶν αἰώνων, καὶ
βαλοῦσι τοὺς στεφάνους αὐτῶν ἐνώπιον τοῦ θρόνου, λέγοντες·
Ἄξιος εἶ, Κύριε, λαβεῖν τὴν δόξαν καὶ τὴν τιμὴν καὶ τὴν
δύναμιν· ὅτι σὺ ἔκτισας τὰ πάντα, καὶ διὰ τὸ θέλημά συο
εἰσὶ, καὶ ἐκτίσθησαν.

ΚΕΦ. 7.

ΚΑΙ εἶδον ἐπὶ τὴν δεξιὰν τοῦ καθημένου ἐπὶ τοῦ θρονου
βιβλίον γεγραμμένον ἔσωθεν καὶ ὄπισθεν, κατεσφραγισ-
μένον σφραγῖσιν ἑπτά. καὶ εἶδον ἄγγελον ἰσχυρὸν κηρύσ-

heads were golden diadems. And out of the Throne lightnings leaped ; and thunders also, and deep Voices rolled ; and Seven Lamps of Fire blazed before the Throne ;— these are the Seven Spirits of God. And before the Throne there was a sea of hyaline, bright and clear as pure crystal : and in the midst of the Throne and the Cycle of the Throne, were four Living Splendours : and they were full of eyes before and behind. And the first living One was like a Lion ; and the second living One was like a Bull ; and the third living One had the face of a Man ; and the fourth living One was like an Eagle when flying. And the four Living Ones each had six wings ; and they were full of eyes all round and within ; and they have no rest either in the day or in the night ; saying, Holy ! Holy ! Holy ! is the Lord ; the Lord God who is Almighty. Holy ! Holy ! Holy ! is the Lord ; who was, and is, and is to come. And when these Living Ones give praise and glory, and language of thanksgiving to the Sitter on the Throne, who lives throughout the ages of ages , then the four and twenty Ancients fall down before the Sitter on the Throne ; and worship the Life that lives throughout the ages of ages ; and cast their diadems before the foot of the throne, saying, Thou art worthy, O Sovereign, to receive honour, glory, and dominion : for thou didst form all these things, and by thy will they are and they were formed.

7.

And I saw in the right had of the Sitter upon the Throne, a Book, written within and without ; sealed with seven seals : and I saw a strong Angel proclaiming in a

σοντα φωνῇ μεγάλῃ· Τίς ἐστιν ἄξιος ἀνοῖξαι τὸ βιβλίον, καὶ λῦσαι τὰς σφραγῖδας αὐτοῦ; καὶ οὐδεὶς ἠδύνατο ἐν τῷ οὐρανῷ, οὐδὲ ἐπὶ τῆς γῆς, οὐδὲ ὑποκάτω τῆς γῆς, ἀνοῖξαι τὸ βιβλίον, οὐδὲ βλέπειν αὐτό. Καὶ ἐγὼ ἔκλαιον πολλά, ὅτι οὐδεὶς ἄξιος εὑρέθη ἀνοῖξαι τὸ βιβλίον, οὔτε βλέπειν αὐτό. Καὶ εἷς ἐκ τῶν πρεσβυτέρων λέγει μοι· Μὴ κλαῖε· ἰδοὺ, ἐνίκησεν ὁ Λέων ὁ ἐκ τῆς φυλῆς Ἰδ, ἀνοῖξαι τὸ βιβλίον καὶ τάς ἑπτὰ σφραγῖδας αὐτοῦ. Καὶ εἶδον ἐν μέσῳ τοῦ θρόνου καὶ τῶν τεσσάρων Ζώων, καὶ ἐν μέσῳ τῶν πρεσβυτέρων Ἀρ-νίον ἔχον κέρατα δώδεκα, καὶ ὀφθαλμοὺς δώδεκα, οἵ εἰσι τὰ πνεύματα δώδεκα τοῦ Θεοῦ, τὰ ἀπεσταλμένα εἰς πᾶσαν τὴν γῆν. Καὶ τὸ Ἀρνίον ἦλθε καὶ εἴληφε τὸ βιβλίον ἐκ τῆς δεξιᾶς τοῦ καθημένου ἐπὶ τοῦ θρόνου. Καὶ ὅτε ἔλαβε τὸ βι-βλίον, τὰ τέσσαρα Ζῶα καὶ οἱ εἰκοσιτέσσαρες πρεσβύτεροι ἔπεσον ἐνώπιον τοῦ Ἀρνίου, ἔχοντες ἕκαστος κιθάρας, καὶ φιάλας χρυσᾶς γεμούσας θυμιαμάτων. Καὶ ᾄδουσιν ᾠδὴν καινήν, λέγοντες· Ἄξιος εἶ λαβεῖν τὸ βιβλίον, καὶ ἀνοῖξαι τὰς σφραγῖδας αὐτοῦ· ὅτι σφαγήσῃ καὶ ἀγοράσεις θνητοὺς τῷ Θεῷ ἐν τῷ αἵματί σου ἐκ πάσης φυλῆς καὶ γλώσσης καὶ λαοῦ καὶ ἔθνους, καὶ ποιήσεις αὐτοὺς τῷ Θεῷ ἡμῶν βασι-λεῖς καὶ ἱερεῖς, καὶ βασιλεύσουσιν ἐπὶ τῆς γῆς. Καὶ εἶδον, καὶ ἤκουσα φωνὴν ἀγγέλων πολλῶν κύκλῳ τοῦ θρονου καὶ τῶν Ζώων καὶ τῶν πρεσβυτέρων· καὶ ἦν ὁ ἀριθμὸς αὐτῶν μυριάδες μυριάδων, καὶ χιλιάδες χιλιάδων, λέγοντες φωνῇ μεγάλῃ· Ἄξιόν ἐστι τὸ Ἀρνίον λαβεῖν τὴν δύναμιν καὶ πλοῦτον καὶ σοφίαν καὶ ἰσχὺν καὶ τιμὴν καὶ δόξαν καὶ εὐλο-γίαν. Καὶ πᾶν κτίσμα ὅ ἐστιν ἐν τῷ οὐρανῷ, καὶ ἐπὶ τῆς γῆς, καὶ ὑποκάτω τῆς γῆς, καὶ ἐπὶ τῆς θαλάσσης ἅ ἐστι, καὶ τὰ ἐν αὐτοῖς πάντα, ἤκουσα λέγοντας· Τῷ καθημένῳ ἐπὶ τοῦ θρονου καὶ τῷ Ἀρνίῳ ἡ εὐλογία, καὶ ἡ τιμὴ, καὶ ἡ δοξα, καὶ τὸ κράτος εἰς τοὺς αἰῶνας τῶν αἰώνων· Ἀμήν, Ἀμήν· καὶ τὰ τεσσαρα Ζῶα ἔλεγον, Ἀμήν, Ἀμήν· καὶ οἱ εἰκοσι-

great voice : Who is worthy to open the Book, and to loose the seals that be upon it? and there was no one able in the heaven above; nor upon the earth, nor under the earth, to open the Book, nor even to look upon it. And I wept much because no one was found worthy to open the book nor even to look upon it. And one of the Ancients spoke unto me, saying : Weep not! Weep thou not! Behold! the Lion of the tribe of Jid ;—he hath conquered and shall open the Book ; and the seven seals that are thereon. And I beheld and saw in the middle of the Throne, and of the four Living Ones and the sacred Ancients, a young Lamb, with twelve horns and twelve eyes, which are the twelve sent unto the whole earth. And the Lamb advanced and took the Book out of the right hand of the Sitter upon the throne ; and when he took the Book, the four Living Ones, and the four-and-twenty Ancients fell before the Lamb : holding each harps and golden vials, filled with sweet and sacred perfumes. And they chanted a new song, saying, Thou art worthy to take the Book, and to unseal the seals thereof ; because thou shalt be sacrificed, and thou shall redeem unto God mortal creatures in thy blood out of every tribe and tongue, and people and nation ; and thou shalt make them kings and priests unto our God, and they shall rule over the whole earth. And I beheld, and heard the voice of many Angels, round about the Throne : and of the Living Creatures, and of the Ancients also ; and their number was ten thousand times ten thousand : and they were thousands of thousands : Saying, with a loud voice, Worthy is the Lamb to receive power and wealth and wisdom, and strength and honour, and glory and blessing. And every creature that is in

τέσσαρες πρεσβύτεροι ἔπεσαν, καὶ προσκύνησαν ζῶντι
ἐις τοὺς αἰῶνας τῶν αἰώνων· Καὶ ἤκουσα ἀγγελους ἄδοντας,
καὶ αὕτη ἦν ἡ ᾠδὴ· Ἐξελεύσεται ῥάβδος ἐκ τῆς ῥίζης Ἰσσα,
καὶ ἄνθος ἐκ τῆς ῥίζης ἀναβήσεται, καὶ ἀναπαύσεται ἐπ'
αὐτὸν Πνεῦμα τοῦ Θεοῦ, Πνεῦμα σοφίας καὶ συνέσεως,
Πνεῦμα βουλῆς καὶ ἰσχύος, Πνεῦμα γνώσεως καὶ εὐσεβείας·
Ἐμπλήσει αὐτὸν Πνεῦμα φόβου Θεοῦ. οὐ κατὰ τὴν δόξαν
κρινεῖ, οὐδέ κατὰ τὴν λαλιὰν ελέγξει, ἀλλὰ κρινεῖ ταπεινῷ
κρίσιν. καὶ ἐλέγξει τοὺς ταπεινοὺς τῆς γῆς, καὶ πατάξει γῆν
τῷ λογῳ τοῦ στοματος αὐτοῦ, καὶ ἐν πνεύματι δια χειλέων
ἀνελεῖ ἀσεβῆ. Καὶ ἔσται δικαιοσύνη ἐζωσμένος τὴν ὀσφὺν
αὐτοῦ, καὶ ἀληθείᾳ εἰλημένος τάς πλευράς· Καὶ συνβοσ-
κηθήσεται λύκος μετὰ ἀρνὶς, καὶ πάρδαλις συναναπ-
αύσεται ἐρίφῳ, καὶ μοσχάριον καὶ ταῦρος καὶ λέων ἅμα
βοσκηθήσονται, καὶ παιδίον μεικρὸν ἄξει αὐτούς· Καὶ
βοῦς καὶ ἄρκος ἅμα βοσκηθήσονται, καὶ ἅμα τὰ παιδία
αὐτῶν ἔσονται, καὶ λέων ὡς βοῦς φάγεται ἄχυρα· καὶ
παιδίον νήπιον ἐπὶ τρογλῶν ἀσπιδων καὶ ἐπὶ κοίτην ἐκγο-
νων ἀσπίδων τὴν χείρα ἐπιβαλεῖ, καὶ οὐ μὴ κακοποιή-
σουσιν, οὐδὲ μὴ δύνωνται ἀπολέσαι οὐδένα ἐπὶ τὸ ὅρος
τὸ ἅγιον μου, ὅτι ἐνεπλήσθη ἡ σύμπασα τοῦ γνῶναι τον
κύριον, ὡς ὕδωρ πολὺ κατακαλύψαι θαλάσσας· Καὶ ἔσται
ἐν τῇ ἡμέρα ἐκείνη ἡ ἄνθος Ἰσσα, καὶ ὁ ἀνιστάμενος ἄρχειν
ἐθνῶν, ἐπ' αὐτῷ ἔθνη ἐλπιοῦσιν, καὶ ἔσται ἡ ἀνάπαυσις
αὐτοῦ τιμὴ.

the heavens; and over the earth and under the earth, and in the sea; and all those that are in them, and all together, heard I saying : Blessing, honour, unto the sacred Sitter upon the Throne; and to the Lamb, praise, and honour, and glory, and power throughout ages of ages. Amen! Amen! And the Four Living Ones answered and said, Amen! Amen! and the Ancients fell down and worshipped Him who lives throughout ages of ages. And I heard angels singing, and this was the song they sang. There shall come forth a shoot of the stem of ISSA, and a Flower shall grow out of the root, and the Spirit of God shall rest upon him; the Spirit of wisdom and understanding: the Spirit of counsel and strength; the Spirit of knowledge and holiness; the Spirit of the fear of God shall fill him; and he shall not judge according to vain opinion, nor shall he administer justice according to idle talk, but with righteousness shall he judge the lowly, and decide with equity unto the meek of the earth; and he shall smite the earth with the blast of his mouth, and in the breath of his lips shall he cut off the wicked. And righteousness shall be the girdle of his loins, and truth shall gird up his reins. The wolf also shall feed with the lamb, and the leopard shall lie down with the kid, and the calf and the bull and the lion shall pasture together, and a little child shall lead them. And the cow and the she-bear shall feed together, and their young ones shall be with them: and the lion shall eat straw like the ox: and the sucking child shall play over the hole of the asp: and the weaned child shall put his hand on the den of the basilisk, and they shall not be molested. They shall not destroy any on my Holy Mountain; for the whole thereof shall be filled with the know-

.

ΚΕΦ. 8.

ΚΑΙ᾽ σημεῖον μέγα ὤφθη ἐν τῷ οὐρανῷ· γυνὴ περιβεβλημένη τὸν ἥλιον, καὶ ἡ σελήνη ὑποκάτω τῶν ποδῶν αὐτῆς, καὶ
ἐπὶ τῆς κεφαλῆς αὐτῆς στέφανος ἀστέρων δώδεκα· καὶ ἐν
γαστρὶ ἔχουσα κράζει ὠδίνουσα, καὶ βασανιζομένη τεκεῖν·
Καὶ ὤφθη ἄλλο σημεῖον ἐν τῷ οὐρανῷ, καὶ ἰδοὺ δράκων μέγας
πυῤῥος, ἔχων κεφαλὰς ἑπτὰ καὶ κέρατα δέκα, καὶ ἐπὶ τάς κεφα-
λάς αὐτοῦ ἑπτὰ διαδήματα· καὶ ἡ οὐρα αὐτοῦ σύρει τὸ τρίτον
τῶν ἀστέρων τοῦ οὐρανοῦ, καὶ ἔβαλεν αὐτοὺς εἰς τὴν γῆν·
Καὶ ὁ δράκων ἔστηκεν ἐνώπιον τῆς γυναικὸς τῆς μελλούσης
τεκεῖν, ἵνα, ὅτ᾽ ἂν τέκῃ, τὸ τέκνον αὐτῆς καταφάγῃ· καὶ ἔτεκεν υἱὸν ἄῤῥενα, ος μέλλει ποιμαίνειν πάντα τὰ ἔθνη ἐν
ῥάβδῳ σιδηρᾷ· καὶ ἡρπάσθη τὸ τέκνον αὐτῆς πρὸς τὸν Θεὸν
καὶ πρὸς τὸν θρόνον αὐτοῦ· καὶ ἡ γυνὴ ἔφυγεν εἰς Ἑρμον
ὅπου ἔχει τόπον ἡτοιμασμένον ὑπὸ τοῦ Θεοῦ, ἵνα ἐκεῖ τρέ-
φωσιν αὐτὴν ἡμέρας χιλίας διακοσίας ἑξήκοντα· Καὶ ἐγένετο πόλεμος ἐν τῷ οὐρανῷ· ὁ Μιχαὴλ καὶ οἱ ἄγγελοι αὐτοῦ
τοῦ πολεμῆσαι μετὰ τοῦ δράκοντος, καὶ ὁ δράκων ἐπολέμησεν
καὶ οἱ ἄγγελοί αὐτοῦ· καὶ οὐκ ἴσχυσεν, οὐδὲ τόπος εὑρέθη
αὐτῶν ἔτι ἐν τῷ οὐρανῷ· Καὶ ἐβλήθη ὁ δράκων ὁ μέγας, ὁ
ὄφις ὁ ἀρχαῖος, ὁ καλούμενος διάβολος, καὶ σατανᾶς, ὁ πλανῶν τὴν οἰκουμένην ὅλην, ἐβλήθη εἰς τὴν γῆν, καὶ οἱ ἄγγελοι
αὐτοῦ μετ᾽ αὐτοῦ ἐβλήθησαν· Καὶ ὅτε εἶδεν ὁ δράκων, ὅτι
ἐβλήθη εἰς τὴν γῆν, ἐδίωξεν τὴν γυναῖκα ἥτις ἔτεκεν τὸν
ἄῤῥενα· καὶ ἐδόθησαν τῇ γυναικὶ δύο πτέρυγες τοῦ ἀετοῦ τοῦ
μεγάλου, ἵνα πέτηται εἰς Ἑρμον, εἰς τὸν τόπον αὐτῆς, ὅπου
τρέφηται ἐκεῖ καιρὸν καὶ καιροὺς καὶ ἥμισυ καιροῦ, ἀπό προ-

ledge of the Lord, as the waters cover the sea. And in
that day shall be the Flower of Issa, which shall arise to
govern the nations, and in him shall the nations put their
hope, and his rest shall be glorious.

8.

And there appeared a great sign in the Heaven; a
Woman clothed around with the sun : and the moon was
underneath her feet, and on her head a crown of Twelve
Stars : and she, being with child, cried out, travailing in
birth, as though she pained to be delivered. And there
appeared another portent in the heavens, and behold a
fiery red Dragon ;—vast, with seven heads and ten horns,
and upon his heads seven diadems : and his tail drew
away the third of the stars of heaven, and flung them
down upon the earth. And the Dragon stood before the
Woman who was with child, to devour her child as soon
as it should be born : and she brought forth a Man child,
who was to rule all nations as a shepherd, but with a rod
of iron : and her child was caught up unto God, and
before his very Throne : and the Woman was borne away
into Hermon, where she hath a place prepared under the
Most High : that they should minister to her needs in
that place, one thousand two hundred and sixty days.
And there arose war in heaven; Michael and his angels
fought against the Dragon : and the Dragon fought and
his angels with him ; but they prevailed not, neither was
a place found for them any more in the heaven. And
the great Dragon was cast out ; that ancient Serpent,
who is called Accuser and Satanas ; he who wandereth
over the whole Universe, was cast out headlong unto the
earth, and his angels headlong were cast out with him.

σώπου τοῦ ὄφεως. Καὶ ἔβαλεν ὁ ὄφις ἐκ τοῦ στόματος αὐτου ὀπίσω τῆς γυναικὸς ὕδωρ ὡς ποταμὸν, ἵνα αὐτὴν ποταμοφόρητον ποιήσῃ· καὶ ἐβοήθησεν ἡ γῆ τῇ γυναικι, καὶ ἤνοιξεν ἡ γῆ τὸ στόμα αὐτῆς, καὶ κατέπιεν τὸν ποταμὸν, ὃν ἔβαλεν ὁ δράκων ἐκ τοῦ στόματος αὐτοῦ· Καὶ ὠργίσθη ὁ δράκων ἐπὶ τῇ γυναικὶ, καὶ ἀπῆλθεν ποιῆσαι πόλεμον μετὰ τῶν λοιπῶν τοῦ σπέρματος αὐτῆς, των τηρούντων τὰς ἐντολάς τοῦ Θεου, και ἐχόντων τὴν μαρτυρίαν Ισσα·

ΚΕΦ. 9.

ΚΑΙ' ἤκουσα φωνὴν μεγάλην ἐν τῷ οὐρανῷ, λέγουσαν· ἄρτι ἐγενέτο ἡ σωτηρία καὶ ἡ δύναμις, καὶ ἡ βασιλεία τοῦ Θεοῦ ἡμῶν, καὶ ἡ ἐξουσία τοῦ χριστοῦ αὐτοῦ· ὅτι κατεβλήθη ὁ κατήγορος τῶν ἀδελφῶν ἡμῶν, ὁ κατηγορῶν αὐτῶν ἐνώπιον τοῦ Θεοῦ ἥμων ἥμερας καὶ νυκτός· Καὶ αὐτοὶ ἐνίκησαν αὐτὸν διά τὸν Ἀρνίον, καὶ διὰ τὸν λόγον τῆς μαρτυρίας αὐτῶν· καὶ οὐκ ἠγάπησαν τὴν ψυχὴν αὐτῶν ἄχρι θανάτου· Διὰ τοῦτο εὐφραίνεσθε οἱ οὐρανοὶ, καὶ οἱ ἐν αὐτοῖς σκηνοῦντες οὐαὶ τῇ γῇ, καὶ τῇ θαλάσσῃ, ὅτι κατέβη ὁ διάβολος πρὸς ὑμᾶς· ἔχων θυμὸν μέγαν, εἰδὼς ὅτι ὀλίγον καιρὸν ἔχει· Καὶ ἰδου φωνὴ βοῶντος ἐν τῇ ἐρήμῳ, ἑτοιμάσατε τήν ὁδόν Κυρίου, ἐυθείας ποιεῖτε τὰς τρίβους τοῦ Θεοῦ ἡμῶν· πᾶσα φάραγξ πληρωθήσεται, καὶ πᾶν ὄρος καὶ βουνὸς ταπεινωθήσεται, καὶ ἔσται πάντα τὰ σκολιὰ εἰς ἐνθείαν, καὶ ἡ τραχεῖα εἰς πεδία· καὶ ὀφθήσεται ἡ δόξα Κυρίου, καὶ ὄψεται πᾶσα σὰρξ τὸ σωτήριον του Θεοῦ, ὅτι Κυριος αὐτος ἐλάλησεν·

And when the Dragon saw that he was cast unto the earth; he persecuted the Woman who brought forth the Man-child; but they gave to her the two wings of an Eagle to flee into Hermon, where was her place: there should she be nourished a time and times, and half a time from the presence of the Serpent. And the Serpent cast out of his mouth water, like a flood, after the Woman that he might cause her to be carried away: but the earth gave assistance to the Woman, and the earth opened its mouth and swallowed down the flood, which the Dragon cast out of his mouth. And the Dragon was violently enraged against the Woman, and departed to make war with the remainder of her seed, who executed the commandments of God, and have the witnessing of ISSA.

9.

And I heard a great Voice in heaven, saying, Now is come the kingdom of God, salvation, strength, and the reign of the Anointed; because the Tempter of our brethren is cast out: He who tempts them before our God night and day And they have triumphed over him through the Lamb, and through the wisdom of their martyrdom; and they loved not their lives unto death. Therefore rejoice ye, O ye heavens! and all ye who do abide in the heavens: but weep ye, who are on lands and waters, for now hath the Accuser gone down among you. And he hath great rage, because he knoweth that his time is but short. And behold the Voice of one crying in the wilderness; prepare ye the way of the Lord: make ye straight the path of our God · every abyss shall be filled up, and every mountain and hill shall be made low: and all the crooked shall be

Ἰδού καὶ Κύριος ὡς πῦρ ἥξει, καὶ ὡς καταιγὶς τὰ ἅρματα αὐτοῦ, ἀποδοῦναι ἐν θυμῷ ἐκδίκησιν αὐτοῦ, καὶ ἀποσκορα- κισμὸν αὐτοῦ ἐν φλογὶ πυρός, ἐν γὰρ τῷ πυρὶ Κυρίου κριθή- σεται πᾶσα ἡ γῆ, καὶ ἐν τῇ ῥομφαίᾳ αὐτοῦ πᾶσα σάρξ.,

ΚΕΦ. 10.

ΚΑΓ φωνη ελεγεν· Αἱ ἑπτὰ κεφαλαὶ τοῦ δράκοντος, ἑπτὰ ὄρη εἰσιν, καὶ βασιλεῖς ἑπτὰ εἰσιν· καὶ τὰ δέκα κέρατα ἃ εἶδες δέκα βασιλεῖς εἰσιν· οἵτινες βασιλείαν οὔπω ἔλαβον, ἀλλ' ἐξουσίαν ὡς βασιλεῖς μίαν ὥραν λαμβάνουσι μετὰ τοῦ δράκοντος· οὗτοι μίαν ἔχουσι γνώμην, καὶ τὴν δύναμιν καὶ τὴν ἐξουσίαν ἑαυτῶν τῷ δράκοντῳ διαδιδώσουσιν· Οὗτοι μετὰ τοῦ Ἀρνίου πολεμήσουσιν, καὶ τὸ Ἀρνίον νικήσει αὐτους, ὅτι κύριος κυρίων ἐστὶ, καὶ βασιλεὺς βασιλέων, καὶ οἱ μετ' αὐτοῦ, κλητοὶ καὶ ἐκλεκτοὶ καὶ πιστοί.

ΚΕΦ. 11.

ΚΑΓ ἐπέστρεψα, καὶ ἦρα τοὺς ὀφθαλμούς μου, καὶ εἶδον, καὶ ἰδοὺ τέσσαρα ἅρματα ἐκπορευόμενα ἐκ μέσου δύο ὀρέων, καὶ τὰ ὄρη ἦν ὄρη χαλκα· ἐν τῷ ἅρματι τῶ πρώτῳ ἵπποι μέ- λανες, καὶ ἐν τῷ ἅρματι τῳ δευτέρῳ ἵπποι πυῤῥοὶ· καὶ ἐν τῷ ἅρματι τῷ τρίτῳ ἵπποι λευκοὶ, καὶ ἐν τῷ ἅρματι τῷ τετάρτῳ ἵπποι ποικίλοι ψαροί· Καὶ εἶπα πρὸς τὸν ἄγγελον τὸν λα- λοῦντα ἐν ἐμοί· τί ἐστι ταῦτὰ κύριε; καὶ ἀπεκρίθεν ὁ ἄγγε- λος ὁ λαλῶν ἐν ἐμοί, καὶ εἶπεν· ταῦτά ἐστιν οἱ τέσσαρες πνεύματα τοῦ οὐρανου, ἐκπορεύονται παραστῆναι τῷ κυρίῳ πάσῃς τῆς γῆς· καὶ οἱ ἵπποι οἱ μέλανες, ἐξεπορευοντο ἐπὶ

made into the straight ; the rough places smooth : and
the Glory of the Lord shall be revealed ; and all flesh
shall see the Saviour sent of God, because the Lord himself hath spoken it. Behold also the Lord will come as
fire, and as a whirlwind shall his chariot roll ; to render
justice with a strong will, and his rebuke in flames of fire :
for in the fire of the Lord, and by his fiery sword, shall
all the earth and all flesh be judged.

10.

And a Voice said : The seven Dragon heads are seven
mountains and seven monarchs ; and the ten horns which
thou sawest are ten kings, and they have received no
kingdom as yet, but receive power as kings one hour with
the Dragon. These have but one mind, and they shall
give their strength and power to the Dragon ; these shall
wage war against the Lamb ; and the Lamb shall overcome them in war ; because he is lord of lords and king
of kings, and those that are with him are called, and
chosen, and faithful.

11.

And I turned and lifted up mine eyes, and looked,
and behold there came four chariots; they came out
from between two mountains ; and the mountains were
mountains of brass. In the first chariot were black
horses; and in the second chariot fire-red horses, and in
the third chariot white horses ; and in the fourth chariot speckled and bay horses. And I said unto the Angel
speaking in me : What are these my lord ? and the Angel
speaking in me answered and said : These are the four
Spirits of the Heaven ; they go forth from standing be-

γῆν βορρᾷ, καὶ οἱ πυρροὶ ἐξεπορεύοντο κατόπισθεν αυτῶν, ἐπὶ γῆν νότου· καὶ οἱ λευκοὶ ἐξεπορευοντο εἰς τὴν ανατολην ηλιου· καὶ οἱ ποικίλοι καὶ οἱ ψαροὶ ἐξεπορευοντο πρὸς ζόφον. καὶ Θεος εἶπεν· πορεύεσθε, καὶ περιοδεύσατε τὴν γῆν· αὐξάνεσθε καὶ πληθύνεσθε καί πλήρώσατε τὴν γῆν· Καὶ ἐξεπορευοντο, καὶ περιωδεῦσαν τὴν γῆν·

ΚΕΦ. 12.

ΚΑΓ εἶδον ὅτε ἤνοιξεν τὸ Ἀρνίον μίαν ἐκ τῶν ἑπτα σφραγίδων, καὶ ἤκουσα ἑνὸς ἐκ τῶν τεσσάρων Ζώων λέγοντος, ὡς φωνὴ βροντῆς· Ἔρχου καὶ ἴδε. Καὶ εἶδον, καὶ ἰδοὺ ἵππος μέλας καὶ ὁ καθήμενος ἐπ᾽ αὐτὸν ἔχων τόξον· καὶ ἐδόθη αὐτῷ (5) στέφανος, καὶ ἐξῆλθε νικῶν, καὶ ἵνα νικήσῃ.

ΚΕΦ. 13.

ΚΑΓ ὅτε τὸ Ἀρνίον ἤνοιξεν τὴν δευτέραν σφραγῖδα ἤκουσα τοῦ δευτέρου Ζώου λέγοντος· Ἔρχου καὶ ἴδε· Καὶ ἐξῆλθεν ἄλλος ἵππος πυρρός· καὶ τῷ καθημένῳ ἐπ᾽ αὐτὸν ἐδόθη αὐτῷ λαβεῖν τὴν εἰρήνην ἐκ τῆς γῆς, καὶ ἐδόθη αὐτῷ μάχαιρα μεγάλη. καὶ νὺξ ἐγένετο, καὶ ἰδου ὁ ἀνὴρ ἐπιβεβηκὼς ἐπί ἵππον πυρρόν, εἱστήκει ἀνὰ μέσον τῶν ὀρέων τῶν κατασκίων, καὶ ὀπίσω αὐτοῦ ἵπποι πυρροὶ, καὶ ψαροὶ, καὶ ποικίλοι, καὶ λευκοὶ. Καὶ εἶπα· τὶ οὗτοι κύριε; καὶ εἶπεν πρός με ὁ ἄγγελος ὁ λαλῶν ἐν ἐμοί· ἐγὼ δείξω σοι τί ἐστι ταῦτα· Καὶ ἀπεκρίθη ὁ ἀνὴρ ὁ ἐφεστηκὼς ἀνά μέσον τῶν ὀρεῶν, καὶ εἶπε πρός με· οὗτοι εἰσιν οὓς ἐξαπεστειλεν Κύριος, περιοδεῦσαι τὴν γῆν· Καὶ ἀπεκρίθησαν τῷ ᾽ΑΓΓΕΛΩ Κυρίου τῷ ἐφεστῳτι ἀνὰ μέσον τῶν ὀρεῶν, καὶ ε῾πον· περιωδεύσαμεν πᾶσαν τὴν γῆν, καὶ ἰδοὺ πᾶσα ἡ γῆ κατοικεῖται, καὶ ἡσυχαζει·

fore the Lord ; they go forth over all the earth. And the black horses issued forth unto the North; and the fire-red followed after them to the South; and the white horses went unto the East; and the speckled and bay went unto the West. And God said, Go ye forth and traverse the earth; be fruitful and multiply and fill ye up the earth ; and they went and traversed the earth.

12.

And when the Lamb opened one of the seven seals, I looked and heard one of the four Living Ones saying, as in a voice of thunders, Come and see ! And I looked, and behold, a black horse ; and HE who sat on him held a bow (5) ; and there was given unto him a royal crown ; and he went forth conquering and to conquer.

13.

And when the Lamb opened the second seal, I heard the second Living One say : Come and see ! and there went out another horse fiery-red ; and HE who sat on him took away peace from the earth ; and there was given to him a mighty sword. And it was night, and the Man who rode the fiery-red horse stood in the middle of shady mountains. And after him were other fiery-red horses, and speckled and bay and white. Then said I, O my lord, what are these ? And the Angel who spake within me, made answer ; I will shew thee what these things are. And the Man who stood in the midst of the mountains, made answer and spake unto me : These are they whom the Lord hath sent to traverse the whole earth. And they made answer to the MESSENGER of the Lord, who stood still in the middle of the mountains, and

ΚΕΦ. 14.

ΚΑΓ ὅτε ἤνοιξεν τὸ Ἀρνίον τὴν σφραγῖδα τὴν τρίτην, ἤκουσα τοῦ τρίτου Ζώου λέγοντος· Ἔρχου καὶ ἴδε. Καὶ εἶδον, καὶ ἰδοὺ ἵππος λευκὸς, καὶ ὁ καθήμενος ἐπ᾽ αὐτὸν ἔχων ζυγὸν ἐν τῇ χειρὶ αὐτοῦ Καὶ ἤκουσα φωνὴν ἐν μέσῳ τῶν τεσσάρων Ζώων λέγουσαν· Χοῖνιξ σίτου δηναρίου, καὶ τρεῖς χοίνικες κριθῶν δηναρίου· καὶ τὸ ἔλαιον καὶ τὸν οἶνον μὴ αδικήσῃς.

ΚΕΦ. 15.

ΚΑΓ ὅτε ἤνοιξεν τὸ Ἀρνίον τὴν σφραγῖδα τὴν τετάρτην, ἤκουσα τοῦ τετάρτου Ζώου λέγοντος Ἔρχου καί ἴδε. Καὶ ε῀δον, καὶ ἰδοὺ ἵππος χλωρὸς, καὶ ὁ καθήμενος ἐπάνω αὐτοῦ, ὄνομα αὐτῷ ὁ Θάνατος· καὶ ὁ ᾅδης ἠκολούθει μετ᾽ αὐτοῦ· καὶ ἐδόθη αὐτῳ ἐξουσία ἐπὶ τὸ τέταρτον τῆς γῆς, ἀποκτεῖναι ἐν ῥομφαίᾳ, καὶ ἐν λιμῷ, καὶ ἐν θανάτῳ, καὶ ἱπὸ τῶν θηρίων τῆς γῆς. Καὶ μετὰ ταῦτα εἶδον τέσσαρας μεγαλους ἑστῶτας ἐπὶ τὰς τέσσαρας γωνίας τῆς γῆς, κρατοῦντας τοὺς τέσσαρας ἀνέμους τῆς γῆς, ἵνα μὴ πνέῃ ἄνεμος ἐπὶ τῆς γῆς, μήτε ἐπὶ τῆς θαλάσσης, μήτε ἐπι τὶ δένδρον.

ΚΕΦ. 16.

ΚΑΓ εἶδον ἄλλον ΑΓΓΕΛΟΝ, ἀναβαίνοντα ἀπὸ ἀνατολῆς ἡλίου, ἔχοντα σφραγῖδα Θεοῦ ζῶντος· καὶ ἔκραξε φωνῇ μεγάλῃ τοῖς τέσσαρσιν μεγαλοις, οἷς ἐδόθη αὐτοῖς δύναμις ἐπὶ τὴν γῆν καὶ τὴν θάλασσαν, λέγων· Μὴ ἀδικήσητε τὴν γῆν, μήτε τὴν θάλασσαν, μήτε τὰ δένδρα, ἄχρι σφραγίσωμεν τοὺς δούλους τοῦ Θεοῦ ἡμῶν ἐπὶ τῶν μετώπων αὐτῶν. Καὶ

said, We have gone to and fro on the whole earth, and behold, the whole earth rests, and is at peace.

14.

And when the Lamb opened the third seal, I heard the third Living Creature say: Come and see! and I looked, and lo! a white horse (7); and HE that sat on him had a pair of balances in his hand; and I heard a Voice in the midst of the four Living Ones saying; A measure of wheat for a deenâr; and three measures of barley for a deenâr: and see that thou defraud not in oil or wine.

15.

And when the Lamb opened the fourth seal, I heard the fourth Living One say, Come and see! and I looked, and lo! a grassy-green horse; and he that rode upon him was named Death; and Hades followed after him; and to him was permitted sway over the fourth part of the earth, (8) and to kill by the sword and famine and ruin; and by the wild creatures of the earth. And after these things I saw four Mighty Ones, standing on the four corners of the earth; and they held the four winds of the earth; so that not a single blast should blow over the earth, nor upon the sea, nor upon any tree.

16.

And I saw another MESSENGER (9) ascending from the rising of the sun, holding the seal of the living God; and he cried with a loud voice to the four Mighty Ones, to whom was given power over the earth and sea; saying: Hurt ye not the earth, nor the sea, nor the trees, until we shall have sealed the servants of our God upon their

ἤκουσα τὸν ἀριθμὸν τῶν ἐσφραγισμένων· ἑκατὸν τεσσαράκοντα τέσσαρες χιλιάδες ἐσφραγισμένων ἐκ πάσης φυλῆς,
καὶ ἐκ πασεῶν ἐθνῶν·

ΚΕΦ. 17.

ΚΑΙ μετὰ ταῦτα εἶδον, καὶ ἰδοὺ ὄχλος πολὺς, ὃν ἀριθμῆ-
σαι αὐτὸν οὐδεὶς ἠδύνατο, ἐκ παντὸς ἔθνους καὶ φυλῶν καὶ
λαῶν καὶ γλωσσῶν, ἑστῶτες ἐνώπιον τοῦ θρόνου καὶ ἐνώπιον τοῦ Ἀρνίου, περιβεβλημένους στολὰς λευκὰς, καὶ φοί-
νικες ἐν ταῖς χερσὶν αὐτῶν· Καὶ κράζουσιν φωνῇ μεγάλῃ,
λέγοντες· Ἡ σωτηρία τῷ Θεῷ ἡμῶν, καὶ τῷ καθημένῳ ἐπὶ
τοῦ θρόνου, καὶ τῷ Ἀρνίῳ, τῷ ἀγγελῳ· Καὶ πάντες οἱ ἀγγε-
λοι εἱστήκεισαν κύκλῳ τοῦ θρόνου καὶ τῶν πρεσβυτέρων καὶ
τῶν τεσσάρων Ζώων, καὶ ἔπεσαν ἐνώπιον τοῦ θρόνου ἐπὶ τὰ
πρώσωπα αὐτῶν, καὶ προσεκύνησαν τῷ Θεῷ, λέγοντες·
Ἀμήν· ἡ εὐλογία καὶ ἡ δόξα καὶ ἡ σοφία καὶ ἡ εὐχαριστία
καὶ ἡ τιμὴ καὶ ἡ δύναμις καὶ ἡ ἰσχὺς τῷ Θεῷ ἡμῶν εἰς τοὺς
αἰῶνας τῶν αἰώνων· Ἀμήν. Ἀμήν.

ΚΕΦ. 18.

ΚΑΙ ἐπέστρεψα, καὶ ἦρα τοὺς ὀφθαλμους μου, καὶ εἶδον,
καὶ ἰδου δρέπανον πετόμενον· καὶ εἶπεν προς με· τὶ σὺ βλέπεις; καὶ εἶπα ἐγὼ, ὁρῶ δρέπανον πετόμενον, μήκους πήχεων
εἴκοσι, καὶ πλάτους πήχεων δέκα· καὶ εἶπεν πρός με· αὑτη
ἡ ἀρὰ ἡ ἐκπορευομένη ἐπὶ πρόσωπον πάσης τῆς γῆς διότι
πᾶς ὁ κλέπτης ἐκ τουτου ἕως θανάτου ἐκδικηθήσεται, καὶ πᾶς
ὁ ἐπίορκος ἐκ τούτου ἐκδικηθήσεται· Καὶ ἐξοίσω αὐτὸ, λέγει
Κύριος παντοκράτωρ, καὶ εἰσελεύσεται εἰς τόν οἶκον τοῦ
κλέπτου, καὶ εἰς τον οἶκον τοῦ ὀμνυόντος τῷ ὀνόματι μου
ἐπὶ ψεύδει, καὶ καταλυσέι ἐν μέσῳ τοῦ οἴκου αὐτοῦ, καὶ συν-
τελέσει αὐτὸν, καὶ τὰ ξύλα αὐτου, καὶ τοὺς λίθους αὐτοῦ.

foreheads. And I heard the number of those that were sealed, a hundred and forty-four thousand sealed, out of every tribe and out of all nations.

17.

And after these things I looked, and lo ! a great multitude, which no one could number : out of all nations and tribes and peoples and tongues, standing before the Throne and before the Lamb : clothed in pure white garments ; and palm branches in their hands. And they cried out with a loud voice, saying, Our salvation is from our God, and from the Sitter on the Throne, and from the Lamb, the Messenger. And all the angels standing in the cycle of the Throne, and of the Ancients, and the four Living Ones, fell before the Throne upon their faces ; and began to worship the Divine One · saying, Amen ! blessing and glory ! and wisdom and grace and honour and power ! and strength unto our God throughout ages of ages ! Amen ! Amen ;

18.

And I turned and raised mine eyes aloft, and I looked, and lo, a flying sickle : and he said to me, What seest thou ? and I said, I see a flying sickle : the length thereof is twenty cubits, and the breadth is ten cubits. And he said to me, This is the divine Judgment, that goeth over the face of the whole earth : for all who steal shall be adjudged unto death on this side ; all who swear falsely shall be adjudged on that. Behold, I bring it forth, saith the Lord Almighty, and it shall enter into the house of him who steals, and into the house of him who sweareth falsely by my name ; and it shall bring ruin in the midst

A A

ΚΕΦ. 19.

ΚΑΙ' ἐξῆλθεν ὁ ἄγγελος ὁ λαλῶν ἐν ἐμοὶ, καὶ εἶπεν πρός με· ἀνάβλεψον τοῖς ὀφθαλμοῖς σου, καὶ ἴδε τὸ ἐκπορευόμενον τοῦτο· καὶ εἶπα τὶ ἐστιν ; καὶ εἶπεν τοῦτο τὸ ὤβι τὸ ἐκπορευόμενον· καὶ εἶπεν αὕτη ἡ ἀδικία ἀυτῶν ἐν πάσῃ τῇ γῇ· Καὶ ἰδοὺ τάλαντον μολίβδου ἐξαιρόμενον, καὶ ἰδοὺ μία γυνὴ ἐκάθητο ἐν μέσῳ τοῦ ὤβι· καὶ εἶπεν· αὕτη ἐστὶν ἡ ἀνομία. καὶ ἐῤῥιψεν αὐτὴν ἐν μέσῳ τοῦ ὤβι, καὶ ἔῤῥιψεν τὸν λίθον τοῦ μολίβδου εἰς τὸ στόμα αὐτῆς· καὶ ἦρα τοὺς ὀφθαλμούς μου, καὶ εἶδον, καὶ ἰδοὺ δύο γυναῖκες ἐκπορευόμεναι, καὶ πνεῦμα ἐν ταῖς πτέρυξιν ἀυτῶν, καὶ αὗται εἶχον πτέρυγας ἔποπος, καὶ ἀνέλαβον τὸ ὤβι ἀνὰ μέσον τῆς γῆς, καὶ ἀνὰ μέσον τοῦ οὐρανοῦ· Καὶ εἶπα πρὸς τὸν ἄγγελον τὸν λαλοῦντα ἐν ἐμοί· ποῦ αὗται ἀποθέρουσι τὸ ὤβι ; καὶ εἶπεν πρός με· οἰκοδομῆσαι αὐτῶ οἰκίαν ἐν γῇ, καὶ ἑτοιμάσαι, καὶ θήσουσιν ἀυτὸ ἐκεῖ ἐπὶ τὴν ἑτοιμασίαν ἀυτοῦ.

ΚΕΦ. 20.

ΚΑΙ' ἄλλος ΑΓΓΕΛΟΣ ἦλθε, καὶ ἐστάθη ἐπὶ τὸ θυσιαστήριον, ἔχων λιβανωτὸν χρυσοῦν· καὶ ἐδόθη αὐτῷ θυμιάματα πολλὰ, ἵνα δώσῃ ταῖς προσευχαῖς τῶν ἁγίων πάντων ἐπὶ τὸ θυσιαστήριον τὸ χρυσοῦν τὸ ἐνώπιον τοῦ θρόνου. Καὶ ἀνέβη ὁ καπνὸς τῶν θυμιαμάτων ταῖς προσευχαῖς τῶν ἁγίων ἐκ χειρὸς τοῦ ἀγγέλου, ἐνώπιον τοῦ Θεοῦ. Καὶ ἔλεγεν· ἀκούσατέ μου νῆσοι καὶ προσέχετε ἔθνη, διὰ χρόνου πολλοῦ στήσεται λέγει Κύριος· ἐκ κοιλίας μητρός μου ἐκάλεσε τὸ ὄνομὰ μου· καὶ ἔθηκε τὸ στόμα μου ὡς μάχαιραν ὀξεῖαν, καὶ ὑπὸ τὴν σκέπην τῆς χειρὸς αὐτοῦ ἔκρυψέ με· ἔθηκέ με ὡς

of his house, and shall destroy him with the wood and stone work thereof.

19.

And again the Angel speaking in me came and said: Lift up thine eyes, and see what cometh forth · and I said, What is it? and he said : This is the Obi that comes forth ; and he said : This is their impiety in all the land. And behold, a mighty weight of lead uplifted ; and I saw a lone woman sitting in the centre of the Obi : and he said : This is indeed a defiance of the law ; and he hurled it down on the heart of the Obi : and he threw the mountain of lead into her mouth. And I lifted up mine eyes and looked, and behold, there were two Women who came forth ; and there was a wind in their wings; and they had the wings of a Stork ; and they caught up the Obi between earth and heaven ; and I said unto the Angel speaking in me : whither do they carry the Obi? and he said to me : To build for it a home on earth ; and there they shall establish it upon its stablishment.

20.

And another MESSENGER came, and stood at the altar, having a golden censer : and there were given unto him many fragrant treasures, that he might offer them with the prayers of all the holy, upon the golden incense altar in front of the Throne. And the cloud of the perfumes ascended on high, with the prayers of the holy before God, out of the hand of the divine Messenger. And he said : Hearken unto me ye islands ! and hearken unto me ye people from afar ! After a long time and it shall come to pass, saith the Lord ; from the womb of my mother

A A 2

βέλος ἐκλεκτὸν, καὶ ἐν τῇ φαρέτρᾳ αὐτοῦ ἔκρυψέ με· Καὶ εἶπε μοι· δοῦλος μου εἶ σὺ, καὶ ἐν σοὶ ἐν σοὶ ἐνδοξασθήσομαι. Καὶ εἴληφεν ὁ ἄγγελος τὸν λιβανωτὸν, καὶ ἐγέμισεν αὐτὸν ἐκ τοῦ πυρὸς τοῦ θυσιαστηρίου, καὶ ἔβαλεν εἰς τὴν γῆν, ὥσει ην τὸν ἀστέρα τὸν πρωϊνόν· καὶ ἐγένοντο φωναὶ καὶ βρονταὶ καὶ ἀστραπαὶ καὶ σεισμός.

ΚΕΦ. 21.

ΚΑΙ` μετα ταυτα ἐιδον ἄγγελον μεγαν, ἐφεστῶτα ἐπι του θυσιαστηρίου, καί εἶπε· πάταξον ἐπὶ τὸ ἱλαστήριον, καὶ σεισθήσεται τὰ πρόπυλα, καὶ διάκοψον εἰς κεφαλὰς πάντων· καὶ τοὺς καταλοίπους αὐτῶν ἐν ῥομφαίᾳ ἀποκτενῶ· οὐ μὴ διαφύγῃ ἐξ αὐτῶν φεύγων, καὶ οὐ μὴ διασωθῇ ἐξ αὐτῶν ἀνασωζόμενος· Ἐάν κατακρυβῶσιν εἰς ᾅδου ἐκεῖθεν ἡ χείρ μου ἀνασπάσει αὐτούς, καὶ ἐὰν ἀναβῶσιν εἰς τὸν οὐρανὸν, ἐκεῖθεν κατάξω αὐτούς· καὶ ἐὰν καταδύσωσιν ἐξ ὀφθαλμῶν μου εἰς τὰ βάθη τῆς θαλάσσης ἐκεῖ ἐντελοῦμαι τῷ δράκοντι, καὶ δήξεται αἰτούς.

ΚΕΦ. 22.

ΚΑΙ` ἰδοὺ ἕξ ἄνδρες ἤρχοντο ἀπὸ τῆς ὁδοῦ τῆς πύλης τῆς ὑψηλῆς τῆς βλεπούσης πρὸς βορρᾶν, καὶ ἑκάστου πελυξ ἐν τῇ χειρὶ αὐτοῦ· καὶ εἷς ἀνὴρ ἐν μέσῳ αὐτῶν ενδεδυκὼς ποδήρη, καὶ ζώνη σαπφείρου ἐπὶ τῆς ὀσφύος αὐτοῦ, καὶ εἰσήλθοσαν καὶ ἔστησαν ἐχόμενοι τοῦ θυσιαστηρίου τοῦ χρυσοῦ· Καὶ δόξα Θεοῦ ἀνέβη ἀπὸ τῶν Χερουβεὶν εἰς τόν αἴθερον, καὶ ἐκάλεσε τὸν ἄνδρα τὸν ἐνδεδυκοτα τὸν ποδήρη,

hath he called my name. He hath made my mouth like a sharp sword : and under the shadow of his hand hath he hid me. He hath placed me as a choice shaft : in his quiver hath he concealed me. And He hath said unto me, Thou art my servant in whom I shall be glorified. And the divine Messenger took the censer, and filled it with fire from the incense altar, and he cast it out upon the earth, as if it were the morning star : and there arose voices and thunders, and lightnings also, and an earthquake.

21.

And after these things I saw a great Angel (11) standing upon the incense altar ; and he said : Smite upon the mercy seat ; and the gate shall be shaken ; and cut through into the heads of all : and I will slay the remnant of them with the sword. No one of them fleeing shall escape ; and no one of them striving to deliver himself shall be delivered : though they hide themselves in Hades, thence shall my hand drag them forth : and though they should mount up to heaven, thence also will I bring them down : and if they should go down from my presence into the depths of the sea, there will I command the Serpent, and he shall bite them.

22.

And behold ! Six Men came from the way of the higher gate that looks towards the North ; and an axe was in the hand of every man ; and there was one Man in the midst of them clothed in a flowing robe down to the feet ; and a sapphire girdle was over his loins. And they came in and stood holding the golden incense altar, and the Glory of God ascended from the Cherubim into the æther, and

ὃς εἶχεν ἐπὶ τῆς ὀσφύος αὐτοῦ τὴν ζώνην· καὶ εἶπε πρὸς
αὐτόν· δίελθε μέσην γῆν, καὶ δὸς σημειον **T** (Ταυ) ἐπὶ τα
μέτωπα τῶν ἀνδρων τῶν καταστεναξόντων καὶ τῶν κατωδυ-
νωμένων ἐπὶ πάσαις ταῖς ἀνομίαις ταῖς γινομέναις ἐν μέσω
αὐτῶν· Καὶ τούτοις εἶπεν ἀκούοντος μου, πορεύεσθε ὀπίσω
αὐτοῦ εἰς τὴν γῆν, καὶ κόπτετε, καὶ μὴ φείδεσθε τοῖς ὀφθαλμοῖς ὑμῶν, καὶ μὴ ἐλεήσητε ἐπὶ δὲ πάντας ἐφ' οὓς ἐστιν τὸ
σημεῖον, μὴ ἐγγίσητε· Καὶ ἰδοὺ ὁ ἀνηρ ὁ ενδεδυκὼς τὸν
ποδήρη, καὶ ἐζωσμένος τῇ ζώῃ τὴν ὀσφύν αὐτοῦ, ἀπεκρίνατο
λέγων· πεποίηκα καθὼς ἐνετείλω μοι· Καὶ εἶδον, καὶ ἰδοὺ
ἐπάνω τοῦ στερεώματος τοῦ ὑπερ κεφαλῆς τοῦ Χερουβειν ὡς
λίθος σαπφείρου ὁμοίωμα θρόνου ἐπ' αὐτῶν.

ΚΕΦ. 23.

ΚΑΙ' φωνὴ ἔλεγεν πρὸς ἄνδρα τον ἐνδεδυκότα τὴν στολήν·
εἴσελθε εἰς τὸ μέσον τῶν τροχῶν, τῶν ὑποκάτω τῶν Χερουβεὶν, καὶ πλῆσον τὰς δράκας σου ἀνθράκων πυρὸς ἐκ μέσου
τῶν Χερουβεὶν, καὶ διασκόρπισον ἐπὶ τὴν γῆν· καὶ εἰσῆλθεν
ἐνώπιον ἐμοῦ. Καὶ τὰ Χερουβεὶν εἰστήκει εκ δεξιῶν τοῦ
θρόνου ἐν τῷ εἰσπορεύεσθαι τὸν ἄνδρα, καὶ ἡ νεφέλη ἔπλησεν
τήν αὐλὴν τὴν ἐσωτεραν· καὶ ἀπῆρεν ἡ δόξα Κυρίου ἀπὸ
τῶν Χερουβεὶν εἰς τὸ αἴθριον τοῦ θρόνου, καὶ ἐνέπλησεν τόν
θρόνον ἡ νεφέλη, καὶ ἡ αὐλὴ ἐπλήσθη τοῦ φέγγους τῆς
δόξης Κυρίου· Καὶ φωνὴ τῶν πτερύγων τῶν Χερουβεὶν
ἠκούετο ἕως τῆς αὐλῆς τῆς ἐξωτέρας, ὡς φωνὴ Θεοῦ Σαδδαῒ
λαλοῦντος, ἐν οὐρανοῖς· καὶ ἐγένετο ἐν τῷ ἐντέλλεσθαι
αὐτὸν τῷ ἀνδρὶ τῷ ἐνδεδυκότι τὴν στολὴν τὴν ἁγίαν, λέγων,
λάβε πῦρ ἐκ μεσου τῶν τροχῶν εκ μέσου τῶν Χερουβεὶν,
καὶ εἰσῆλθε καὶ ἔστη ἐχόμενος τῶν τροχῶν· Καὶ ἐξέτεινεν

it called the Man clothed in the flowing robe, who had
the girdle round his loins; and it said unto him : Go
thou over the mid earth, and mark the sign T (*Tau*) upon
the forehead of every man, who groans and grieves for all
the iniquities that are committed in the midst of mortals.
And to the others it said in mine hearing, Go ye after
him throughout the length and breadth of the land ; and
smite, and spare not with your eyes and pity not : but
approach not against any on whom is the sign. And lo !
the Man clothed in the flowing robe, and girt around the
loins with the sapphire girdle, answered saying, I have
done as thou didst command. Then I looked, and lo, in
the firmament, that was above the head of the Cherubim,
there appeared over them, as it were, a sapphire stone,
the appearance of a royal seat.

23.

And the Voice spake unto the Man clothed in linen ;
Enter thou into the middle of the circles, even under the
cherubic choirs · and fill thine hands with fire from between the Cherubim, and scatter the fire on the earth :
and he went in before my face. Now the Cherubim stood
on the right side of the throne when the Man went in,
and a cloud filled the inner court, and the Glory of the
Lord went up from the Cherubim, and stood over the
threshold of the throne, and the cloud filled the throne
and the court also was filled with the dazzling splendour
of the Lord's Glory. And the sound of the Cherubim's
wings was heard even unto the court that was outside,
as the Voice of God the All-powerful, when he speaketh
high amid his heavens. And when he had commanded the
Man clothed in sacred robe saying, Take fire from between

εἰς τῶν Χερουβεὶν τὴν χεῖρα αὐτοῦ εἰς μέσον τοῦ πυρὸς τοῦ ὄντος ἐ.ς μέσον τῶν Χερουβεὶν, καὶ ἔλαβεν, καὶ ἔδωκεν εἰς τὰς χεῖρας τοῦ ἐνδεδυκότος τὴν στολὴν τὴν ἁγίαν, καὶ ἔλαβεν, καὶ ἐξῆλθεν· Καὶ ἐξῆραν τὰ Χερουβεὶν τὰς πτέρυγας αὐτῶν, καὶ οἱ τροχοὶ ἐχόμενοι αὐτῶν, καὶ ἡ δόξα Θεοῦ ἐπ' αὐτὰ ὑπεράνω αὐτῶν· Τοῦτο τὸ Ζῶόν ἐστιν ὃ εἶδον ὑποκάτω τῆς δόξης τοῦ Θεοῦ, καὶ ἔγνων ὅτι Χερουβεὶν ἐστι· τέσσαρα πρόσωπα τῷ ἑνὶ, καὶ ὀκτω πτέρυγες τῷ ἑνὶ, καὶ ὁμοιωμα χειρῶν ανθρώπων ὑποκάτωθεν τῶν πτερύγων αὐτων·

ΚΕΦ. 24.

ΚΑΓ εἶδον ἄλλον ΑΓΓΕΛΟΝ ἰσχυρὸν καταβαίνοντα ἐκ τοῦ οὐρανοῦ, περιβεβλημένον νεφέλην, καὶ ἡ ἶρις ἐπὶ τῆς κεφαλῆς αὐτου, καὶ τὸ πρόσωπον αὐτοῦ ὡς ὁ ἥλιος, καὶ οἱ πόδες αὐτοῦ ὡς στύλοι πιρός· καὶ ἔχων ἐν τῇ χειρὶ αὐτοῦ βιβλαρίδιον ἀνεῳγμένον καὶ ἔχοντα σφραγίδα του Θεου ζωντος· καὶ ἔθηκε τὸν πόδα αὐτοῦ τὸν δεξιὸν ἐπὶ τῆς θαλάσσης, τὸν δὲ εὐώνυμον ἐπὶ τῆς γῆς· Καὶ ἔκραξεν φωνῇ μεγάλῃ ὥσπερ λέων μυκᾶται· καὶ ὅτε ἔκραξεν, ἐλάλησαν αἱ ἑπτὰ βρονταὶ τὰς ἑαυτῶν φωνάς. καὶ ὅτε ἐλάλησαν αἱ ἑπτὰ βρονταὶ, ἔμελλον γράφειν· καὶ ἤκουσα φωνὴν ἐκ τοῦ οὐρανοῦ λέγουσαν· Σφράγισον ἃ ἐλάλησαν αἱ ἑπτὰ βρονταὶ, καὶ μὴ ταῦτα γράψῃς· Καὶ ὁ ἄγγελος, ὃν εἶδον ἑστῶτα ἐπὶ τῆς θαλάσσης καὶ ἐπὶ τῆς γῆς, ἦρεν τὴν χεῖρα αὐτοῦ τὴν δεξιὰν εἰς τὸν οὐρανὸν, καὶ ὤμοσεν ἐν τῷ Ζῶντι ἐ.ς τοὺς αἰῶνας τῶν αἰώνων, ὃς ἔκτισε τὸν οὐρανὸν καὶ τὰ ἐν αὐτῷ, καὶ τὴν γῆν καὶ τὰ ἐν αὐτῇ, καὶ τὴν θάλασσαν καὶ τὰ ἐν αὐτῇ, ὅτι ψευδοσοφία οὐκέτι ἔσται·

the wheels, and from between the midst of the Cherubim ;
the Man went in, and stood holding the wheels.   And
one of the Cherubim stretched forth his hand from between the Cherubim unto the centre fire ; and took fire
and gave it unto the Man, who was clothed in the
sacred garment ; and he received it and went forth.
Then did the Cherubim lift up their wings, and the
wheels proceeding from them ; and the Glory of God
was over and upon them.   This was the Living Splendour which I saw under the Glory of God ; and I knew
it to be the Cherubim : and each one had four faces,
and each one had eight (12) wings ; and the likeness of
the hands of men under their wings.

24.

And I saw another strong MESSENGER (13) coming.
down upon the earth from heaven : he was wrapped
around in a cloud : and a *Rainbow* arched above his
head.   His face was like the sun : and his feet were·
pillars of fire : and he had in his hand a little Book
open, which bare the seal of the living God ; and he
set his right foot upon the sea, and his left foot he set upon
the earth.   And he cried out with a mighty voice, as a
lion roaring was his cry.   And when he cried, the Seven
Thunders muttered deep Voices among themselves ; and
when the Seven Thunders had spoken, I was about to
write, but I heard a Voice from Heaven saying unto
me, Seal thou up the words which the Seven Thunders
have spoken ; and write them not at all.   And the Messenger whom I saw standing upon the sea, and upon the
land, raised his right hand to heaven ; and sware in the
Living One through ages of ages, who made the heaven,

A A 3

ΚΕΦ. 25.

ΚΑΓ ἰδοῦ δόξα Θεοῦ ἤρχετο κατα τὴν ὁδον τὴν πρὸς ἀνατολάς, καὶ φωνη τῆς παρεμβολῆς, ὡς φωνὴ διπλασιαζόντων πολλων· καὶ ἡ γῆ ἐξελαμπεν ὡς φέγγος ἀπὸ τῆς δόξης κυκλόθεν· Καὶ δόξα Κυρίου ἐισῆλθεν ἐις τόν οἶκον, κατα την ὁδον της πύλης τῆς βλεπούσης κατ᾽ ἀνατολας.

ΚΕΦ. 26.

ΚΑΓ ἰδοὺ οἱ τέσσαρες ἄνεμοι τοῦ οὐρανοῦ προσέβαλλον ἐις τὴν θάλασσην τὴν μεγάλην· καὶ τέσσερα θηρία μεγάλα ἀνέβεβαινεν ἐκ τῆς θαλάσσης, διαφέροντα ἀλλήλων. Τὸ πρῶτον ὡσεὶ λέαινα, καὶ πτερὰ αὐτῇ ὡς ἀετου; ἐθεώρουν ἕως οὗ ἐξετίλη τὰ πτερὰ αὐτῆς· καὶ ἐξήρθη ἀπὸ τῆς γῆς, καὶ ἐπὶ ποδῶν ἀνθρώπου ἐστάθη, καὶ καρδία ἀνθρώπου ἐδόθη αὐτῇ· Καὶ ἰδοὺ θηρίον δεύτερον ὅμοιον ἄρκτῳ, καὶ ἐις μέρος ἓν ἐστάθη, καὶ τρεῖς πλευραὶ ἐν τῷ στόματι αὐτῆς, ἀνάμεσον τῶν ὀδόντων αὐτῆς· καὶ οὕτως ἔλεγον αὐτῇ· ἀνάστηθι, φάγε σάρκας πολλάς· Ὀπίσω τουτο ἐθεώρουν· καὶ ἰδοὺ ἕτερον θηρίον ὡσεὶ πάρδαλις· καὶ αὐτῇ πτερα τέσσερα πετεινου ἱπεράνω αὐτῆς, καὶ τέσσαρες κεφαλαὶ τῷ θηρίῳ, καὶ ἐξουσία ἐδόθη αὐτῇ· Ὀπίσω τουτο ἐθεώρουν· καὶ ἰδοὺ θηρίον τέταρτον φοβερὸν καὶ ἔκθαμβον, καὶ ἰσχυρὸν περισσῶς, καὶ οἱ ὀδόντες αὐτοῦ σιδηροῖ, ἐσθίον καὶ λεπτύνον, καὶ τὰ ἐπίλοιπα τοῖς ποσὶν αὐτοῦ συνεπάτει, καὶ αὐτὸ διάφορον περισσῶς παρὰ πάντα τὰ θηρία τὰ ἐμπροσθεν αὐτοῦ· καὶ κέρατα δέκα αὐτῷ· Προσενοιουν τοῖς κέρασιν αὐτοῦ, καὶ ἰδοὺ κέρας ἕτερον μικρὸν ἀνέβη ἐν μέσῳ αὐτῶν, καὶ τρία κέρατα τῶν ἔμπροσθεν

and those that are therein, and the earth also, and those that are therein; and the sea also, and those that are therein, that the False shall be no more.

25.

And behold the Glory of God came from the way of the East, the voice of its march was as the voice of many, doubled and redoubled into a sound of might, and the earth shone out, as splendour came from the cycle of the Glory, and the Glory of the Lord entered into the House, by the way of the Gate that looks unto the East.

26.

And behold! the four winds of the heaven, struggled hard upon the Great Sea; and four great Wild Beasts came up from the sea; different all, each one from the other. The first was like a Lioness and had eagle's wings; and I looked until her wings were plucked away: nevertheless she was lifted up from the earth, and upon the feet of a man she stood: and the heart of a Man was given to her. And behold a second Wild Beast like unto a Bear, raised itself up on one side; and three ribs were in the mouth of it, in the very middle of the Wild Beast's teeth. And thus they said to it: Arise, devour much flesh! And after this I looked again, and behold another Wild Beast like unto a Leopard; and she had upon her, four wings like a bird; and this Wild Beast also had four heads, and great sway was given unto her. And after this I looked, and beheld a fourth Wild Beast; dreadful and terrible and amazing, and strong exceedingly with teeth of iron, devouring and grinding in pieces, and treading down the residue beneath its feet; and it was entirely

αἰτοῦ ἐξερρίζωθη, ἀπὸ προσώπου αἰτοῦ· καὶ ἰδοὺ ὀφθαλμοὶ, ὡσεὶ ὀφθαλμοὶ ἀνθρώπου, ἐν τῷ κέρατι τούτῳ, καὶ στόμα λαλοῦν μεγάλα.

ΚΕΦ. 27.

ΚΑΙ͑ ἀναβλέψας, εἶδον κριὸν ἕνα μέγαν ἐστῶτα ἀπέναντι τῆς πύλης· καὶ εἶχε κέρατα καὶ τὰ κέρατα ὑψηλά, καὶ τὸ ἕν ὑψηλότερον τοῦ ἐτέρου, καὶ τὸ ὑψηλότερον ἀνέβαινε· Μετὰ δὲ ταῦτα εἶδον τὸν κριὸν κερατίζοντα πρὸς ἀνατολὰς, καὶ πρὸς βορρᾶν, καὶ πρὸς δυσμὰς, καὶ πρὸς μεσημβρίαν· καὶ πάντα τὰ θηρία οὐκ ἔστησαν ὀπίσω αὐτοῦ, καὶ οὐκ ῖν ὁ ῥυόμενος ἐκ τῶν χειρῶν αὐτοῦ, καὶ ἐποίει ὡς ἤθελε, καὶ ὑψώθη· Καὶ ἐγὼ διενοούμην, καὶ ἰδοὺ τράγος αἰγῶν ἤρχετο ἀπὸ δυσμῶν ἐπὶ προσώπου τῆς γῆς· καὶ ῖν τοῦ τράγου κέρας ἕν θεωρητὸν, ἀνὰ μέσον τῶν ὀφθαλμῶν αἰτῶν· Καὶ ῖλθεν ἐπὶ τὸν κριὸν τὸν τὰ κέρατα ἔχοντα, ὃν εἶδον ἐστῶτα πρὸς τῇ πυλῇ, καὶ ἔδραμε πρὸς αὐτὸν ἐν θυμῷ ὀργῆς· καὶ εἶδον αἰτὸν προσάγοντα πρός τὸν κριὸν, καὶ ἐθυμώθη ἐπ᾿ αἰτὸν, καὶ ἐπάταξε τὸν κριὸν· καὶ σύνετριψε τὰ δύο κέρατα αὐτοῦ, καὶ οὐκ ἔτι ῖν ἰσχὺς ἐν τῷ κριῷ στῆναι κατέναντι τοῦ τράγου, καὶ ἐσπάραξεν αὐτὸν ἐπὶ τὴν γῆѵ, καὶ συνέτριψεν αὐτὸν, καὶ οὐκ ῖν ὁ ῥυόμενος τὸν κριὸν ἀπο τοῦ τράγου· Καὶ ὁ τράγος τῶν αἰγῶν κατίσχυσε σφόδρα, καὶ ὅτε κατίσχυσε, συνετρίβη αἰτοῦ τὸ κέρας τὸ μέγα, καὶ ἀνέβη ἔτερα τέσσαρα κέρατα κατόπισθεν αἰτοῦ εἰς τοὺς τέσσαρας ἀνέμους τοῦ οἰρανοῦ· Καὶ ἐξ ἑνὸς αὐτῶν ἀνεφύη κέρας ἰσχυρὸν ἕν, καὶ κατίσχυσε, καὶ ἐπάταξεν ἐπὶ μεσημβρίαν, ἐπὶ νότον, καὶ ἐπ᾿ ἀνατολὰς, καὶ ἐπὶ βορρᾶν· καὶ ὑψώθη ἕως τῶν ἀστέρων τοῦ οὐρανοῦ·

different from all the other Beasts which I had seen pass
before it: and it had ten horns. And behold, as I closely
watched these horns, there came up amid them another
little horn, before which three of the first horns were
plucked out, and behold, in this horn were bright eyes,
like unto the eyes of a Man, and it had a mouth speaking
great things.

27.

And lifting up mine eyes, I saw a single mighty Ram,
standing before the gate and he had horns; and his horns
were lofty, and one more lofty than the other; and the
loftier of the two was ascending. And after these things
I saw the Ram butting, towards the East and the North
and the West and the South: and not one of all the Wild
Beasts stood after he went; nor was there one delivered
out of his hand: and he did as he thought fit and was
exalted. And I looked carefully, and beheld, a he-Goat,
began to arise out of the West, over the face of the whole
earth: and he had one observable horn, in the middle
between his two eyes. And he came upon the Ram that
had two horns, which I saw standing before the gate:
and he ran at him in the fury of his heart: and I saw
him bearing down against the Ram; and he was filled
with rage against him. And he smote the Ram, and
brake up his two horns: and there was no longer any
strength in the Ram, so that he could stand against the
he-Goat. And he flung the Ram upon the earth; and
he stamped and trampled upon him; and there was none
who could deliver the Ram from the Goat. And the he-
Goat prevailed wonderfully over the goats: but in his
mightiest strength, his great horn was broken; and there

καὶ ἐῤῥάχθη ἐπὶ τὴν γῆν ἀπὸ τῶν ἀστέρων, καὶ ἀπὸ αὐτῶν κατεπατήθη.

ΚΕΦ. 28.

ΚΑΙ᾿ ἐπέστρεψεν ὁ ἄγγελος ὁ λαλῶν ἐν ἐμοὶ, καὶ ἐξῆρεν με ὃν τρόπον, ὅταν ἐξεγερθῇ ἄνθρωπος ἐξ ὕπνου αὐτοῦ· καὶ εἶπεν πρός με· τί σὺ βλέπεις; καὶ εἶπα· ἑώρακα· καὶ ἰδοὺ λυχνία χρυσῆ ὅλη· καὶ τὸ λαμπάδιον ἐπάνω αὐτῆς, καὶ ἑπτὰ λύχνοι ἐπάνω αὐτῆς, καὶ ἑπτὰ ἐπαρυστρίδες τοῖς λύχνοις τοῖς ἐπάνω αὐτῆς· Καὶ δύο ἐλαῖαι ἐπάνω αὐτῆς, μία ἐκ δεξιῶν τοῦ λαμπαδίου αὐτῆς, καὶ μία ἐξ εὐωνύμων· καὶ ἐπηρώτησα, καὶ εἶπον πρὸς τὸν ἄγγελον τὸν λαλοῦντα ἐν ἐμοὶ λέγων· τί ἐστιν ταῦτα κύριε; καὶ ἀπεκρίθη ὁ ἄγγελος ὁ λαλῶν ἐν ἐμοὶ καὶ εἶπεν πρός με, λέγων· οὐ γινώσκεις τί ἐστι ταῦτα; καὶ εἶπα· οὐχὶ κύριε. Καὶ ἀπεκρίθη, καὶ εἶπε πρός με, λέγων· ἕπτα οὗτοι ὀφθαλμοί Θεοῦ εἰσιν οἱ ἐπιβλέποντες ἐπὶ πᾶσαν τὴν γῆν· καὶ ἀπεκρίθην καὶ εἶπα πρὸς αὐτόν· τί αἱ δύο ἐλαῖαι αὗται αἱ ἐκ δεξιῶν τῆς λυχνίας, καὶ ἐξ εὐωνύμων αὐτῆς; Καὶ ἐπηρώτησα ἐκ δευτέρου, καὶ εἶπα πρὸς αὐτόν· τί οἱ δύο κλάδοι τῶν ἐλαιῶν οἱ ἐν ταῖς χερσὶν τῶν δύο μυξωτήρων τῶν χρυσῶν τῶν ἐπιχεόντων, καὶ ἐπαναγόντων τὰς ἐπαρυστρίδας τὰς χρυσᾶς; καὶ εἶπε πρός με· οὐκ οἶδας τί ἐστι ταῦτα; καὶ εἶπα, οὐχὶ κύριε. Καὶ εἶπεν, οὗτοι οἱ δύο υἱοὶ τῆς πιότητος παρεστήκασιν κυρίῳ πάσης τῆς γῆς· οὗτοι εἰσιν αἱ δύο ἐλαῖαι, καὶ αἱ δύο λυχνίαι αἱ ἐνώπιον τοῦ Κυριου τῆς γῆς ἑστῶτες· καὶ δώσω τοις δυσὶ μάρτυσί μου, καὶ προφητεύσουσιν ἡμέρας χιλίας διακοσίας ἑξήκοντα, περι-

arose up four other horns after it, towards the four winds
of heaven : and out of one of them arose one strong horn,
which waxed great and extended towards the South ; and
to the South-west, and to the East also, and to the North ;
and it was uplifted even to the stars of heaven ; and it
brought down to earth some even of the stars, and over
them it walked.

28.

And the Angel that spake in me, turned towards me ;
and he wakened me as one wakens a man from sleep :
and he said unto me : What seest thou ? And I said, I
have looked ; and behold a candlestick all golden : and a
glittering light (14) is on the top of it : and there are Seven
Lamps depending therefrom ; and there are seven pipes
to the Seven Lamps. And there were two OLIVE TREES
near it : one was upon the right side of the glittering
Light, and the other upon the left side. And I asked and
said unto the Angel that spake in me ; What are these
my lord ? and the Angel speaking in me answered and
said : Knowest thou not what these are ? And I made
answer. No my Lord. And he answered me and spake,
saying : These are Seven Eyes of God that look over the
whole earth. And I made answer and said to him, What
be those two Olive Trees, on the right hand and on the
left of the Light ? and I enquired again and said to him,
What be those two Branches of the Olive Trees, which
through the two golden pipes empty the golden oil out of
themselves ? And he said to me : Knowest thou not
what these be ? I said : No my lord. And he said :
These are the two Anointed Ones, (15) who stand before
the Lord of the whole earth : these are the two Olive

βεβλημένοι σάκκους. Καὶ εἴ τις αὐτοὺς θέλει ἀδικῆσαι, πῦρ ἐκπορεύεται ἐκ τοῦ στόματος αὐτῶν, καὶ κατεσθίει τοὺς ἐχθροὺς αὐτῶν· καὶ εἴ τις αὐτοὺς θέλει ἀδικῆσαι οὕτως δεῖ αἰτὸν ἀποκτανθῆναι· Οὗτοι ἔχουσιν ἐξουσίαν κλεῖσαι τον οὐρανὸν ἵνα μὴ ὑετὸς βρέχῃ τάς ἡμέρας τῆς προφητείας αὐτῶν· καὶ ἐξουσίαν ἔχουσιν ἐπὶ τῶν ὑδατῶν, στρέφειν αὐτὰ εἰς αἷμα, καὶ πατάξαι τὴν γῆν, ὁσάκις ἐὰν θελήσωσιν, ἐν πάσῃ πληγῇ· Καὶ ὅταν τελέσωσι τὴν μαρτυρίαν αὐτων τὸ θηρίον τὸ ἀναβαῖνον ἐκ τῆς ἀβύσσου ποιήσει μετ᾽ αὐτῶν πόλεμον, καὶ νικήσει αὐτοὺς, καὶ ἀποκτενεῖ αὐτοὺς· καὶ τὸ πτῶμα αὐτων ἐπί τῆς πλατείας τῆς πολεως τῆς μεγάλης, ἥτις καλεῖται πνευματικῶς Σόδωμα. καὶ βλέπουσιν ἐκ τῶν λαῶν καὶ φυλῶν καὶ γλωσσῶν καὶ ἐθνων τὸ πτῶμα αὐτῶν ἡμέρας τρεῖς καὶ ἥμισυ, καὶ τα πτῶμα αὐτῶν οὐκ ἀφήσουσι τεθῆναι εἰς μνῆμα. Καὶ οἱ κατοικοῦντες ἐπὶ τῆς γῆς χαίρουσιν ἐπ᾽ αὐτοῖς, καὶ εὐφρανθήσονται, καὶ δῶρα πέμψουσιν ἀλλήλοις, ὅτι οὗτοι οἱ δύο προφῆται ἐβασάνισαν τοὺς κατοικοῦντας ἐπί τῆς γῆς· Καὶ μετά τὰς τρεῖς ἡμέρας καὶ ἥμισυ, Πνεῦμα ζωῆς ἐκ τοῦ Θεου εἰσῆλθεν ἐν αὐτοῖς, καὶ ἔστησαν ἐπὶ τοὺς πόδας αὐτῶν, καὶ φόβος μέγας ἔπεσεν ἐπὶ τοὺς θεωροῦντας αὐτούς. Καὶ ἤκουσα φωνὴν μεγάλην ἐκ τοῦ οὐρανοῦ, λέγουσαν αὐτοῖς· Ἀνάβητε ὧδε. Καὶ ἀνέβησαν εἰς τὸν οὐρανὸν ἐν τῇ νεφέλῃ· καὶ ἐθεώρησαν αὐτοὺς οἱ ἐχθροὶ αὐτῶν.

Trees; and these are the Two shining Lamp-bearers before the Lord. And I will give power to these two Witnesses of me; and they shall prophecy twelve hundred and sixty days, (16) clothed in garments of sackcloth. (17) And if any man willeth to do them hurt, behold! fire cometh out of their mouths: (18) and it shall devour their enemies: and if any man willeth to do them wrong, it is meet that in this manner he shall perish. These have power to shut up the heaven, (19) so that even a shower of rain fall not to earth, during the days of their prophecy. And they have power also over the waters, so as to change them into blood; and to smite the earth if they think fit. (20) And when they shall be finishing their testimony, the Wild Beast that riseth out of the Abyss, shall make war upon them, and shall overcome them and slay them. And the dead body of one of them (21) shall lie in the streets, of the great city, which is mystically called Sodom: and men from peoples and tribes and tongues and nations, shall see the body three days and a-half; and shall not suffer the wreck to be put in a grave. And they whose whole lives are in the earth, shall rejoice over them and shall make merry, and shall send gifts to one another, because those two Prophets tormented the dwellers on the earth. But after three days and a-half, (22) the Spirit of Life from God shall enter into them: and they stood upon their feet, (23) and great fear fell upon those who saw them. And I heard a mighty Voice from Heaven, saying unto them. Come up hither; and they ascended into Heaven in the Cloud; and they who hated them beheld it. (24)

ΚΕΦ. 29.

ΚΑΓ ἔδειξέν μοι Ἰάσων τὸν ἱερέα τὸν μέγαν, ἑστῶτα πρὸ προσώπου ἀγγέλου Κυρίου, καὶ ὁ διάβολος εἱστήκει ἐκ δεξιῶν αὐτοῦ, τοῦ ἀντικεῖσθαι αὐτῷ· καὶ εἶπεν Κύριος πρὸς τὸν διάβολον· ἐπιτιμήσαι Κύριος ἐν σοὶ διάβολε, οὐκ ἰδοὺ τοῦτο ὡς δαλὸς ἐξεσπασμένος ἐκ πυρός; Καὶ Ἰάσων ἦν ἐνδεδυμένος ἱμάτια ῥυπαρὰ καὶ εἱστήκει πρὸ προσώπου τοῦ ἀγγέλου καὶ ὁ ἄγγελος εἶπεν πρός τοὺς ἑστηκότας πρὸ προσώπου, λέγων· ἀφέλετε τὰ ἱμάτια τὰ ῥυπαρὰ ἀπ᾽ αὐτοῦ· καὶ εἶπεν πρός αὐτον ἰδοὺ ἀφήρηκα τὰς ἀνομίας σου, καὶ ἐνδύσατε αὐτόν ποδήρη· καὶ ἐπίθετε κίδαριν καθαρὰν ἐπὶ τὴν κεφαλὴν αὐτοῦ· καὶ ἐπέθηκαν κίδαριν καθαράν ἐπὶ τὴν κεφαλήν αὐτοῦ, καὶ περιέβαλον αὐτὸν ἱμάτια, καὶ ὁ ἄγγελος Κυρίου εἱστήκει· Καὶ διεμαρτύρατο ὁ ἄγγελος Κυρίου πρός Ἰάσων, λέγων. Τάδε λέγει Κύριος παντοκράτωρ· ἐὰν ταῖς ὁδοῖς μου πορεύε, καὶ ἐν τοῖς προστάγμασίν μου φυλάξῃ, καὶ σὺ διακρινεῖς τὸν οἶκον μου· καὶ ἐὰν διαφυλάσσῃς τὴν αὐλήν μου, καὶ δώσω σοι ἀναστρεφομένους ἐν μέσῳ τῶν ἑστηκότων τούτων· Ἄκουε δὴ Ἰάσων ὁ ἱερεὺς ὁ μέγας, σὺ καὶ οἱ πλησίον σου οἱ καθήμενοι πρὸ προσώπου, διότι ανδρες τερατοσκόποι ἐισι· διότι ἰδοὺ ἐγὼ ἄγω τὸν δοῦλον μου ἀνατολήν· διότι ὁ λίθος, ὅν ἔδωκα προ προσώπου Ἰάσων, ἐπὶ τὸν λίθον τὸν ἕνα ἑπτα ὀφθαλμοὶ εἰσιν· ἰδοὺ ἐγὼ ὀρύσσω βόθρον, λέγει Κύριος Θεός παντοκράτωρ, καὶ ψηλαφήσω πᾶσαν τὴν ἀδικίαν τῆς γῆς ἐν ἡμέρα μιᾷ· Ἐν τῇ ἡμέρᾳ ἐκείνῃ, λέγει Κύριος Θεός παντοκράτωρ· συνκαλέσετε ἕκαστος τὸν πλησίον αυτοῦ ὑποκάτω ἀμπέλου καὶ ὑποκάτω συκῆς·

29.

And he shewed me Jah-son the great Priest, standing before the face of the Lord's Angel; and the Accuser stood at his right hand, ready to resist him. And the Lord said to the Accuser: The Lord rebuke thee, O Accuser! seest thou not this one as a brand plucked out of the fire? Now Jah-son was clothed in wretched garments, as he stood before the face of the Minister :- and the Minister spake to those that were about: Take away these wretched garments from him: and the Minister said to him: Behold! I have taken away thy wretchedness; and clothe ye him from head to foot, and put ye a fair mitre on his head; so they set a fair mitre on his head, and clothed him with bright garments, and the Minister of the Lord stood by. And the Minister of the Lord said unto Jah-son: These things, saith the Lord, who is Almighty; if thou wilt walk in my ways, and if thou wilt keep my charges, then thou also shalt judge mine house, and thou shalt keep my courts . and I will give thee some of those who are now present, who shall walk also with thee. Hearken then Jah-son! thou great Priest; thou and those who sit near before thy face; for they indeed are wonder seeing men: Behold, I bring my servant the Awakener; and the stone which I have placed before the face of Jah-son, upon that one stone there are seven eyes: behold I will engrave its graving, saith the Lord God Almighty; and I will remove all the iniquity of earth in one day. In that very day saith the Lord God Almighty, shall ye summon every man his own neighbour, under the vine and under the fig tree.

ΚΕΦ. 30.

ΚΑΙ ἡ φωνὴ ἣν ἤκουσα ἐκ τοῦ οὐρανοῦ, ἔλεγεν αὐτοῖς· Ὕπαγε, λάβε τὸ βιβλαρίδιον τὸ ἀνεῳγμένον ἐν τῇ χειρὶ τοῦ ἀγγέλου τοῦ ἑστῶτος ἐπὶ τῆς θαλάσσης καὶ ἐπὶ τῆς γῆς. Καὶ ἀπῆλθεν πρὸς τὸν ἄγγελον, λέγων αὐτῷ, δοῦναί τὸ βιβλαρίδιον. Καὶ λέγει αὐτῷ· Λάβε καὶ κατάφαγε αὐτό· καὶ πικρανεῖ σου τὴν κοιλίαν, ἀλλ᾽ ἐν τῷ στόματί σου ἔσται γλυκὺ ὡς μέλι. Καὶ ἔλαβεν τὸ βιβλαρίδιον ἐκ τῆς χειρὸς τοῦ ἀγγέλου, καὶ κατέφαγεν αὐτό· καὶ ἦν ἐν τῷ στόματί αὐτοῦ ὡς μέλι γλυκύ· καὶ ὅτε ἔφαγεν αὐτὸ, ἐπικράνθη ἡ κοιλία αυτοῦ· Καὶ λέγει αυτῳ· Δεῖ σε πάλιν προφητεῦσαι ἐπὶ λαοῖς καὶ ἔθνεσι· καὶ γλώσσαις καὶ βασιλεῦσι πολλοῖς.

ΚΕΦ. 31.

ΚΑΙ μετὰ ταῦτα εἶδον ΑΓΓΕΛΟΝ καταβαίνοντα ἐκ τοῦ οὐρανου, ἔχοντα ἐξουσίαν μεγάλην· καὶ ἡ γῆ ἐφωτίσθη ἐκ τῆς δόξης αὐτου. Καὶ εγένετο λόγος Κυρίου πρός με, λέγων· Τάδε λέγει Κύριος παντοκράτωρ· Ἰδοῦ ἀνὴρ, Ἀνατολὴ ὄνομα αὐτῳ, καὶ ὑποκάτωθεν αὐτου ἀνατελεῖ, καὶ οἰκοδομήσει τον οἶκον Κυρίου. καὶ αὐτος λήψεται ἀρετην, καὶ καθιεῖται, καὶ κατάρξει ἐπὶ τοῦ θρόνου αὐτου· καὶ ἔσται ἱερεὺς ἐκ δεξιῶν αὐτου· Καὶ ἐλέγε Κύριος ὁ παντοκράτωρ· ἔτι ἅπαξ ἐγὼ σείσω τὸν οὐρανὸν, καὶ τὴν γῆν, καὶ τὴν θάλασσαν, καὶ τὴν ξηραν, καὶ συνσείσω πάντα τὰ ἔθνη, καὶ ἥξει τὰ ἐκλεκτὰ πάντων τῶν ἐθνῶν, καὶ πλήσω τὸν οἶκον τοῦτον δόξης, λέγει Κύριος παντοκράτωρ· Ἐμὸν τὸ ἀργύριον, καὶ ἐμὸν τὸ χρυσίον, λέγει Κύριος παντοκράτωρ· διότι μεγάλη ἔσται ἡ δοξα τοῦ οἴκου αὐτοῦ, ἡ ἐσχάτη ὑπὲρ τὴν πρωτήν, λέγει Κύριος παντοκράτωρ, καὶ ἐν τῷ τόπῳ τούτῳ δώσω εἰρήνην, λέγει Κύριος παντοκράτωρ, καὶ εἰρήνην ψυχῆς εἰς περιποίησιν παντὶ τῷ κτίζοντι, τοῦ ἀναστῆσαι τόν ναὸν

30.

And the Voice which I heard from Heaven said unto them : Up, and take the little Book, which is open in the hand of the MESSENGER who stands on the sea and over the land. And he went unto the Messenger saying unto him : Give me the little Book : he said ; Take it and eat it up : and it shall make thy belly bitter ; but in thy mouth it shall be sweet as honey. And he took the little Book out of the hand of the MESSENGER and ate it ; and it was in his mouth sweet as honey ; but when he had eaten it his belly was bitter. And he said to him ; Now it becomes thee to utter prophecies to many peoples ; and before nations and tongues and kings.

31.

And after these things I saw a MESSENGER, (25) coming down from the high heaven ; and having great power and strength : and the earth was lightened with his glory. And the Word of the Lord came to me saying, Thus saith the Lord of hosts—*Behold a Man, the Orient is his name.* and under him shall he spring up, and shall build a Temple to the Lord : yea, he shall build a Temple to the Lord, and he shall bear the glory, and shall sit and rule upon his throne ; and he shall be a priest upon his throne. And the Lord, the All-Ruler proclaimed : Yet again will I shake the heaven and the earth ; and the sea and the dry land ; and I will shake all nations ; and the Desire of all nations shall come. And I will fill this his house with glory, says the Lord Almighty : mine is the silver and mine is the gold, says the Lord Almighty— for the glory of his house shall be great ; the latter more than the former, says the Lord Almighty. And in this

Θεοῦ· Ἐν τῷ οὐρανῷ ἡ μάχαιρα αὐτοῦ ἐμεθύσθη· ἰδοὺ καταβήσεται ἐπὶ τοὺς βασιλεῖς καὶ λαους τῆς απωλειας μετα
κρίσεως· Σαλπίσατε σάλπιγγι ἐν Ζειὼν, κηρύξατε ἐν ὄρει
ἁγίῳ μου, καὶ συγχυθήτωσαν πάντες οἱ κατοικοῦντες τὴν
γῆν, διότι πάρεστιν ἡμερα Κυρίου, ὅτι ἐγγύς ἡμέρα σκότους
καὶ γνόφου, ἡμέρα νεφέλης καὶ ὁμίχλης· Ὡς ὄρθρος χυθή-
σεται ἐπὶ τὰ ὄρη λαὸς πολὺς καὶ ἰσχυρὸς, ὅμοιος αὐτῷ οὐ
γέγονεν ἀπὸ τοῦ αἰῶνος, καὶ μετ᾽ αὐτὸν οὐ προστεθήσεται
ἕως ἐτῶν εἰς γενεὰς γενεῶν· Τὰ ἔμπροσθεν αὐτοῦ πῦρ ἀνα-
λισκον, καὶ τὰ ὀπίσω αὐτοῦ ἀναπτομένη φλόξ· ὡς παρά-
δεισος τρυφῆς ἡ γῆ πρὸ πρόσώπου αὐτοῦ, καὶ τὰ ὄπισθεν
αὐτοῦ πεδίον ἀφανισμοῦ, καὶ ἀνασωζόμενος οὐκ ἔσται αὐτῷ·
Ὡς ὄρασις ἵππων ἡ ὄρασις αὐτῶν, καὶ ὡς ἱππεῖς οὕτως κατα-
διώξονται· ὡς φωνὴ ἁρμάτων ἐπὶ τὰς κορυφὰς τῶν ὀρέων
ἐξαλοῦνται, καὶ ὡς φωνὴ φλογὸς πυρὸς κατεσθιούσης καλά-
μην, καὶ ὡς λαὸς πολὺς καὶ ἰσχυρὸς παρατασσόμενος εἰς πό-
λεμον· Ἀπὸ προσώπου αὐτοῦ συντριβήσονται λαοὶ, πᾶν
πρόσωπον ὡς πρόσκαυμα χύτρας· ὡς μαχηταὶ δραμοῦνται,
καὶ ὡς ἄνδρες πολεμισταί ἀναβήσονται ἐπὶ τὰ τειχη, καὶ
ἕκαστος ἐν τῇ ὁδῷ αὐτοῦ πορεύσεται, καὶ οὐ μὴ ἐκκλείνωσιν
τάς τρίβους αὐτῶν. Καὶ ἕκαστος ἀπο τοῦ ἀδελφοῦ αὐτοῦ
οὐκ ἀφέξεται· καταβαρυνόμενοι ἐν τοῖς ὅπλοις αὐτῶν πορεύ-
σονται, καὶ ἐν τοῖς βέλεσιν αὐτῶν πεσοῦνται, καὶ οὐ μὴ
συντελεσθῶσιν· Τῆς πόλεως επιλήμψονται, καὶ ἐπὶ τῶν
τειχέων δραμοῦνται, καὶ ἐπὶ ταῖς οἰκίαις ἀναβήσονται, καὶ
διὰ θυρίδων εισελεύσονται ὡς κλέπται· Πρὸ προσώπου αὐτοῦ
συγχυθήσεται ἡ γῆ, καὶ σεισθήσεται ὁ οὐρανός· ὁ ἥλιος καὶ
ἡ σελήνη συσκοτάσουσιν, καὶ ἄστρα δύσουσιν τὸ φέγγος
αὐτῶν· καὶ Κύριος δώσει φωνὴν αὐτοῦ πρὸ προσώπου δυνάμεως αὐτοῦ, ὅτι πολλή ἐστιν σφόδρα ἡ παρεμβολὴ αὐτοῦ,
ὅτι ἰσχυρὰ ἔργα λόγων αὐτοῦ, διότι μεγάλη ἡμέρα Κυρίου
μεγάλη καὶ επιφανὴς σφόδρα, καὶ τίς ἔσται ἵκανος αὐτῇ;

place will I give peace, says the Lord Almighty ; even peace of soul for a possession, to every one that builds to raise up a temple to God. In the heaven is his sword baptised ;—behold! it shall descend with heavy judgment upon the kings and peoples of perdition. Sound ye, sound ye the trumpet in Zion ; and sound an alarm on my holy mountain; let all the inhabitants of the land be confounded, for the Day of the Lord is near. A day of darkness and of gloominess, a day of clouds, and of thick darkness. As the morning spread upon the mountains, a great people and a strong ; there hath not been ever the like ; neither shall there be any more after it, even unto the years of many generations. A fire devoureth before them, and behind them a flame burneth ; the land before their face is as a Paradise, and behind them a desolate wilderness ; yea, and there shall nothing escape them. As the appearance of horses is their appearance, and as horsemen even so shall they run. Like the noise of chariots on the tops of mountains shall they leap, like the noise of a flame of fire that devoureth the stubble ; as a strong people set in battle array. Before their face the people shall be afflicted ; all faces shall gather blackness. They shall run like mighty men : they shall climb the wall like men of war, and they shall march every one on his ways, and they shall not break their ranks : and not one shall stand aloof from his brother. They shall go on weighed down with their arms ; and even though they fall upon their weapons, yet shall they be in no wise destroyed. They shall seize upon the city and run upon the walls ; they shall climb up upon the houses ; they shall enter the windows as thieves. Before them the earth shall be confounded, and the sky shall be shaken :

Ἀλλ' ὁ φοβερὸς καὶ ἐπιφανής ἐστιν, ἐξ αὐτοῦ τὸ κρίμα
αὐτοῦ εσται, καὶ τὸ λῆμμα αὐτοῦ ἐξ αὐτοῦ ἐξελεύσεται· καὶ
ἐξαλοῦνται ὑπὲρ παρδάλεις οἱ ἵπποι αὐτοῦ, καὶ ὀξύτεροι
ὑπὲρ τοὺς λύχους τῆς Ἀραβίας, καὶ ἐξιππάσονται οἱ ἱππεῖς
αἰτοῦ, καὶ ὁρμήσουσιν μακρόθεν, καὶ πετασθήσονται ὡς
ἀετὸς πρόθυμος εἰς τὸ φαγεῖν· Συντέλεια εἰς ἀσεβεῖς ἥξει,
ἀνθεστηκότας προσώποις αὐτῶν ἐξεναντίας, καὶ συνάξει ὡς
ἄμμον αἰχμαλωσίαν· καὶ αὐτὸς ἐν βασιλεῦσιν ἐντρυφήσει,
καὶ τύραννοι παίγνια αὐτοῦ, καὶ αὐτὸς εἰς πᾶν ὀχύρωμα ἐμ-
παίξεται, καὶ βαλεῖ χῶμα καὶ κρατήσει αὐτοῦ. Τότε μετα-
βαλεῖ τὸ πνεῦμα, καὶ διελεύσεται καὶ ἐξειλάσεται αὕτη ἡ
ἰσχὺς τῷ Θεῷ μου.

ΚΕΦ. 32.

ΤΑΔΕ λέγει ὁ Ἀμὴν, ὁ μάρτυς ὁ πιστὸς καὶ ἀληθινὸς, ἡ
Ἀρχη τῆς κρίσεως τοῦ Θεοῦ· Καὶ μετὰ ταῦτα ἤκουσα ὡς
φωνὴν μεγάλην ὄχλου πολλοῦ ἐν τῷ οὐρανῷ, λεγόντων·
Ἀλλαλούϊα, Ἀλλαλούϊα, Ἀλλαλούϊα, ἡ σωτηρία καὶ ἡ
δόξα, καὶ ἡ δύναμις τοῦ Θεοῦ ἡμῶν· Ὅτι ἀληθιναὶ καὶ
δίκαιαι αἱ κρίσεις αὐτοῦ· ὅτι ἔκρινε τὴν πόρνην τὴν μεγάλην,
ἥτις ἔφθειρεν τὴν γῆν ἐν τῇ πορνείᾳ αὐτῆς, καὶ ἐξεδίκησε τὸ
αἷμα τῶν δούλων αὐτοῦ ἐκ χειρὸς αὐτῆς· Καὶ δεύτερον εἴρηκαν·
Ἀλλαλούϊα, Αλλαλούϊα, Αλλαλούϊα, καὶ ὁ ὕμνος αὐτῶν
ἀναβαίνει εἰς τοὺς αἰῶιας τῶν αἰώνων. Καὶ ἔπεσαν οἱ πρεσβύτεροι οἱ εἴκοσι τέσσαρες, καὶ τὰ τέσσαρα Ζῶα, καὶ προ-

the sun and the moon shall be darkened; and
the stars shall veil their brightness; and the Lord
shall utter his voice before his host, for his camp is very
great: for the execution of his words is mighty. Yea,
the Day of the Lord is great—very glorious; who shall
be able to resist it? But he—HE is terrible and famous:
his judgment shall proceed of himself, and his dignity
shall come out of himself, and his horses shall bound over
leopards; they are more fierce than Arabian wolves, (26)
and his horsemen shall ride and rush from afar; and they
shall fly as an Eagle hasting to eat. Destruction shall
come upon ungodly men, resisting with an adverse front;
and he shall gather captives as the sand; and he shall
treat kings with derision, and tyrant princes shall be his
toys: and he shall mock at every stronghold, and shall
raise a mound, and take possession of it. Then shall
he change his spirit and he shall make an atonement
saying; All this strength belongeth to my God.

32.

These things saith the Amen, the Witness; the faithful
and the true, the Sovereign of the Judgment of God. And
after them I heard, as it were, a great voice, as of a vast
multitude in heaven; saying, Allalouia! Allalouia! Allalouia! Salvation, glory and honour of our God with us;
true and righteous are his judgments. For he hath con-
démned the Great Harlot who did corrupt the earth with
her impureness, and he hath taken vengeance for his
servants' blood, who suffered wrong at her hands. (27.)
And again they said, Allalouia! Allalouia! Allalouia!
and their hymn ascendeth through ages of ages. And
the four and twenty Ancients; and the Four living

B B

σεκύνησαν τῷ Θεῷ τῷ καθημένῳ ἐπὶ τοῦ θρόνου, λεγοντες·
'Αμὴν· Ἀλλαλούια, Ἀλλαλούϊα, Ἀλλαλούια. Καὶ φωνὴ ἐκ
τοῦ θρόνου ἐξῆλθε, λέγουσα· Αἰνεῖτε τὸν Θεὸν ἡμῶν πάντες
οἱ δοῦλοι αὐτοῦ, καὶ οἱ φοβούμενοι αὐτὸν οἱ μικροὶ καὶ οἱ
μεγάλοι.   Καὶ ἤκουσα ὡς φωνὴν ὄχλου πολλοῦ, καὶ ὡς
φωνὴν ὑδάτων πολλῶν, καὶ ὡς φωνὴν βροντῶν ἰσχυρῶν,
λέγοντες. Ἀλλαλούϊα, Ἀλλαλούϊα, Ἀλλαλούϊα· ὅτι ἐβασί-
λευσεν Κύριος ὁ Θεὸς ἡμῶν, ὁ παντοκράτωρ. Χαίρωμεν καὶ
ἀγαλλιώμεθα, καὶ δῶμεν τὴν δόξαν αυτῷ· ὅτι ἦλθεν ὁ γάμος
τοῦ 'Αρνίου, καὶ ἡ γυνὴ αὐτοῦ ἡτοίμασεν ἑαυτήν· Καὶ ἐδόθη
αὐτῇ ἵνα περιβάληται βύσσινον λαμπρὸν καὶ καθαρόν· Τὸ
γὰρ βύσσινον τὰ δικαιώματά ἐστι τῶν ἁγίων. Καὶ λέγει
μοι· Γράψον· Μακάριοι οἱ εἰς τὸ δεῖπνον τοῦ γάμου τοῦ
'Αρνίου κεκλημένοι· Καὶ λέγει μοι· Οὗτοι οἱ λόγοι ἀληθινοί
εἰσι τοῦ Θεοῦ.   Καὶ ἔπεσον ἔμπροσθεν τῶν ποδῶν αὐτοῦ
προσκυνῆσαι αὐτῷ· καὶ λέγει μοι· Ὅρα μή· σύνδουλός σου
εἰμὶ, καὶ τῶν ἀδελφῶν σου τῶν ἐχόντων τὴν μαρτυρίαν
Ἴσσα, τὸ Πνευμα τῆς προφητείας· τῷ Οεῷ μονῳ προσ-
κύνησον·

ΚΕΦ. 33.

ΚΑΙ' εἶδον τὸν οὐρανὸν ἀνεῳγμένον, καὶ ἰδοὺ ἵππος λευκὸς,
καὶ ὁ καθήμενος ἐπ' αὐτὸν, καλούμενος πιστὸς καὶ ἀληθινὸς,
καὶ ἐν δικαιοσύνῃ κρίνει καὶ πολεμεῖ. Οἱ δε ὀφθαλμοὶ αὐτοῦ
ὡς φλὸξ πυρὸς, καὶ ἐπὶ τὴν κεφαλὴν αὐτοῦ διαδήματα
πολλά· ἔχων ονοματα χεγραμμενα, και ὄνομα γεγραμμένον
ὃ οὐδεὶς οἶδεν, εἰ μὴ αὐτός· Καὶ περιβεβλημένος ἱμάτιον
βεβαμμένον αἵματι· και καλεῖται τὸ ὄνομα αὐτοῦ· Ὁ
λόγος τοῦ Θεοῦ. Καὶ τὰ στρατεύματα τὰ ἐν τῷ οὐρανῷ ἠκολούθει αὐτῷ ἐφ' ἵπποις λευκοῖς, ἐνδεδυμένοι βύσσινον λευκὸν
καθαρόν.   Καὶ ἐκ τοῦ στόματος αὐτοῦ ἐκπορεύεται ῥομφαία

Creatures fell down and adored God, who sitteth upon his throne; saying, Amen, Allalouia ! Allalouia ; Allalouia ! And a Voice came out of the Throne, saying; Praise our God, all ye his servants; and ye who fear him both small and great. And I heard the voice as of a vast multitude; and as it were the voice of many waters; and as the voice of strong thunders, saying; Allalouia ! Allalouia ! Allalouia ! the Lord our God the Almighty reigneth. Let us be glad and rejoice; and let us give glory unto Him : for the bridal of the Lamb hath come, and his bride hath made herself ready. And to her was granted that she should be arrayed in fine linen, pure and shining : for this fine linen is the righteousness of the holy. And he said unto me, Write ! Blessed are the called to the marriage supper of the Lamb. And he said to me : These are the true words of God. And I fell before his feet to worship him; and he said unto me : See thou do it not; I am thy fellow servant, and the servant also of thy brethren, who have the testimony of Issa, the divine Spirit of Prophecy ! Worship God alone.

33.

And I saw Heaven opened, and behold a white horse and He that sat on him was called Faithful and True (28); and in righteousness did he judge and make war. And his eyes were as a flame of fire; and on his head were many diadems, having names written upon them, and he had a name (29) written, which no man knew but himself. And he was clothed in a vesture dipped in blood; and his name is called the Messiah of God; and heavenly armies followed him on white horses, clothed in fine linen, white and pure. And out of his mouth there

δίστομος ὀξεῖα ἵνα ἐν αὐτῇ πατάξῃ τὰ ἔθνη· καὶ αὐτὸς
ποιμανεῖ αὐτοὺς ἐν ῥάβδῳ σιδηρᾷ· καὶ αὐτὸς πατεῖ τὴν
ληνὸν τοῦ οἴνου τοῦ θυμοῦ τῆς ὀργῆς τοῦ Θεοῦ τοῦ παντοκράτορος. Καὶ ἔχει ἐπὶ τὸ ἱμάτιον καὶ ἐπὶ τὸν μηρὸν
αὐτοῦ ὄνομα γεγραμμένον· Βασιλεὺς βασιλέων καὶ Κύριος
κυρίων. Καὶ εἶδον ἕνα ἄγγελον ἑστῶτα ἐν τῷ ἡλίῳ· καὶ
ἔκραξε φωνῇ μεγάλῃ, λέγων πᾶσι τοῖς ὀρνέοις τοῖς πετομέ-
νοις ἐν μεσουρανήματι· Δεῦτε, συνάχθητε εἰς τὸ δεῖπνον
τοῦ μεγάλου τοῦ ἀνάκτος. Ἵνα φάγητε σάρκας βασιλέων,
καὶ σάρκας χιλιάρχων καὶ σάρκας ἰσχυρῶν, καὶ σάρκας ἵππων καὶ τῶν καθημένων ἐπ᾽ αὐτῶν, καὶ σάρκας πάντων ἐλευ-
θέρων τε καὶ δούλων, καὶ μικρῶν καὶ μεγάλων·

ΚΕΦ. 34.

ΚΑΙ᾽ εἶδον ἑπτὰ ἀγγέλους, οἳ ἐνώπιον τοῦ Θεοῦ ἑστή-
κασιν· καὶ ἐδόθησαν αὐτοῖς ἑπτὰ σάλπιγγες· Καὶ οἱ ἑπτὰ
ἄγγελοι οἱ ἔχοντες τὰς ἑπτὰ σάλπιγγας, ἡτοίμασαν ἑαυτοὺς
ἵνα σαλπίσωσι· Καὶ ὁ πρῶτος ἐσάλπισεν, καὶ ἐγένετο
χάλαζα καὶ πῦρ μεμιγμένα ἐν αἵματι, καὶ ἐβλήθη εἰς τὴν γῆν.
καὶ τὸ τρίτον τῆς γῆς κατεκάη, καὶ τὸ τρίτον τῶν δένδρων
κατεκάη, καὶ πᾶς χόρτος χλωρὸς κατεκάη Καὶ ὁ δεύτερος
ἄγγελος ἐσάλπισεν, καὶ ὡς ὄρος μέγα πυρὶ καιόμενον ἐβλήθη εἰς τὴν θάλασσαν· καὶ ἐγένετο τὸ τρίτον τῆς θαλάσσης
αἷμα· καὶ ἀπέθανε τὸ τρίτον τῶν κτισμάτων τῶν ἐν τῇ θαλασ-
σῃ, τὰ ἔχοντα ψυχάς· καὶ τὸ τρίτον τῶν πλοίων διεφθάρη.
Καὶ ὁ τρίτος ἄγγελος ἐσάλπισεν, καὶ ἔπεσεν ἐκ τοῦ οὐρανοῦ
ἀστὴρ μέγας καιόμενος ὡς λαμπάς, καὶ ἔπεσεν ἐπὶ τὸ τρίτον
τῶν ποταμῶν, καὶ ἐπὶ τὰς πηγὰς τῶν ὑδάτων. καὶ τὸ ὄνομα
τοῦ ἀστέρος λέγεται ὁ ἄψινθος, καὶ ἐγένετο τὸ τρίτον τῶν
ὑδάτων εἰς ἄψινθον. καὶ πολλοὶ τῶν ἀνθρώπων ἀπέθανον ἐκ
τῶν ὑδάτων, ὅτι ἐπικράνθησαν. Καὶ ὁ τέταρτος ἄγγελος

went a sharp two edged sword, that with it he should strike the nations; and he ruleth them like a shepherd, with an iron rod; and he treadeth the wine press of wine, of the just judgment of God, the All-Ruling. And on his vesture and on his thigh, he hath written, this name: King of kings and Lord of lords. And I saw a single Angel standing in the sun, and he cried out with a loud voice; saying unto all the fowls that fly in mid-heaven; Come and flock to the supper of the great King. That ye may eat the flesh of kings and princes, and the flesh of mighty men and horses; and of them that sate on the horses; and the flesh of all, both free and slave; and of the mean and of the mighty.

34.

And I saw Seven Angels stand before God; and to them were given seven trumpets; and the Seven Angels who had the seven trumpets prepared themselves to sound. And the first Angel sounded, and straight there followed hail and fire mingled with blood: and they were hurled down upon the earth: and the third part of the land was burnt up; and the third part of trees was burnt up; every green garden was destroyed in fire. And the second Angel sounded; and as a great mountain burning with fire (30), it was hurled down into the sea; and the third part of the sea became blood; and the third part of the inhabitants of the sea, having living souls, were killed; and the third part of ships was destroyed. And the third Angel sounded (31), and there fell from heaven a mighty star, blazing like a bright lamp; and it fell upon the third part of the rivers; and upon the fountains of waters;

ἐσάλπισεν καὶ ἐπλήγη τὸ τρίτον τοῦ ἡλίου καὶ τὸ τρίτον τῆς σελήνης καὶ τὸ τρίτον τῶν ἀστέρων, ἵνα σκοτισθῇ τὸ τρίτον αὐτῶν, καὶ ἡ ἡμέρα μὴ φανῃ τὸ τρίτον αὐτῆς, καὶ ἡ νὺξ ὁμοίως. Καὶ εἶδον, καὶ ἤκουσα ἑνὸς ἀετοῦ πετομένου ἐν μεσουρανήματι, λέγοντος φωνῇ μεγάλῃ· Οὐαὶ, οὐαὶ, οὐαὶ τοῖς κατοικοῦσιν ἐπὶ τῆς γῆς, ἐκ τῶν λοιπῶν φωνῶν τῆς σάλπιγγος τῶν τριῶν ἀγγέλων τῶν μελλόντων σαλπίζειν.

ΚΕΦ. 35.

ΚΑΙ ὁ πέμπτος ἄγγελος ἐσάλπισεν, καὶ εἶδον ἀστέρα ἐκ τοῦ οὐρανοῦ πεπτωκότα εἰς τὴν γῆν, καὶ ἐδόθη αὐτῷ ἡ κλεὶς τοῦ φρέατος τῆς ἀβύσσου· Καὶ ἤνοιξεν τὸ φρέαρ τῆς ἀβύσσου, καὶ ἀνέβη καπνὸς ἐκ τοῦ φρέατος ὡς καπνὸς καμίνου μεγάλης καιομενης, καὶ ἐσκοτίσθη ὁ ἥλιος καὶ ὁ ἀὴρ ἐκ τοῦ καπνοῦ τοῦ φρέατος. Καὶ ἐκ τοῦ καπνοῦ ἐξῆλθον ἀκρίδες εἰς τὴν γῆν, καὶ ἐδόθη αὐταῖς ἐξουσία ὡς ἔχουσιν ἐξουσίαν οἱ σκορπίοι τῆς γῆς· Καὶ ἐρρέθη αὐταῖς, ἵνα μὴ ἀδικήσωσιν τὸν χόρτον τῆς γῆς, οὐδὲ πᾶν χλωρὸν, οὐδὲ πᾶν δένδρον, εἰ μὴ τοὺς ἀνθρώπους οἵτινες οὐκ ἔχουσὶ τὴν σφραγῖδα τοῦ Θεοῦ ἐπὶ τῶν μετώπων αὐτῶν. Καὶ ὁ βασανισμὸς αὐτῶν ὡς βασανισμὸς σκορπίου, ὅταν παίσῃ ἄνθρωπον. Καὶ ἐν ταῖς ἡμέραις ἐκείναις ζητήσουσιν οἱ ἄνθρωποι τὸν θάνατον, καὶ οὐ μὴ εὑρήσουσιν αὐτόν· καὶ ἐπιθυμήσουσιν ἀποθανεῖν, καὶ φεύξεται ἀπ᾽ αὐτῶν ὁ θάνατος. Καὶ τὰ ὁμοιώματα τῶν ἀκρίδων ὅμοια ἵπποις ἡτοιμασμένοις εἰς πόλεμον· καὶ ἐπὶ τὰς κεφαλὰς αὐτῶν ὡς στέφανοι ὅμοιοι χρυσῷ, καὶ τὰ πρόσωπα αὐτῶν ὡς πρόσωπα ἀνθρώπων, καὶ εἶχον τρίχας ὡς τρίχας γυναικῶν, καὶ οἱ ὀδόντες αὐτῶν ὡς λεόντων ἦσαν,

and the name of the star is called Wormwood; and the third part of the waters became wormwood; and many men died of the waters, because they were changed to poison. And the fourth Angel sounded, and the third part of the sun was smitten; and the third of the moon and stars was made dark; and the day shone not for a third part, and the night likewise. And I beheld, and I heard an Eagle flying through the mid-heaven, proclaiming aloud in mighty voice, Woe! Woe! Woe! to the dwellers on the earth; for the voices of the trumpets of the three Angels which are destined yet to sound.

35.

And the fifth Angel sounded, and I saw a Star fall from heaven to earth; and to him was given the key of the bottomless pit. And he opened the pit of the bottomless deep. And there arose a smoke out of the pit, as the smoke of a great blazing furnace; and the sun and the firmament were made dark, by reason of the smoke of the pit. And there came out of the smoke locusts over the earth; and they had power like scorpions of the earth; and it was commanded them to do no harm, to the gardens of the earth, or any green thing; nor to any tree, but to those men only, who had not the seal of God upon their foreheads: and their sting was as the sting of a scorpion, when he strikes a man. And in those days men shall seek death, and they shall not find it; and they shall desire to die, and death shall flee away from them. And the appearance of these locusts was that of war-horses prepared for battle; and on their heads were like, as it were, crowns of gold; and their faces were as the faces of men; and they had hair as the hair of

καί είχον θώρακας ὡς θώρακας σιδηροῦς, καὶ ἡ φωνὴ τῶν πτερύγων αὐτῶν ὡς φωνὴ ἀρμάτων ἵππων πολλῶν τρεχόντων εἰς πόλεμον. Καὶ ἔχουσιν οὐρὰς ὁμοίας σκορπίοις, καὶ κέντρα· καὶ ἐν ταῖς οὐραῖς αὐτῶν ἡ ἐξουσια αὐτῶν ἀδικῆσαι τοὺς ἀνθρώπους μῆνας πέντε. Ἔχουσιν ἐφ᾽ αὐτῶν βασιλέα ἄγγελον τῆς ἀβύσσου· ὄνομα αὐτῷ, Ἀβαδδὼν, καὶ ὄνομα ἔχει Ἀπολλύων. Ἡ οὐαὶ ἡ μία ἀπῆλθεν· ἰδοὺ ἔρχονται ἔτι δύο οὐαὶ μετὰ ταῦτα.

ΚΕΦ. 36.

ΚΑΙ᾽ εἶδον ἄλλο σημεῖον ἐν τῷ οὐρανῷ μέγα καὶ θαυμαστὸν, ἀγγέλους ἑπτὰ ἔχοντας πληγὰς ἑπτὰ τὰς ἐσχάτας, ὅτι ἐν αὐταῖς ἐτελέσθη ὁ θυμὸς τοῦ Θεοῦ. Καὶ μετὰ ταῦτα εἶδον, καὶ ἠνοίγη ὁ ναὸς τῆς σκηνῆς τοῦ μαρτυρίου ἐν τῷ᾽ οὐρανῷ. Καὶ ἐξῆλθον οἱ ἑπτὰ ἄγγελοι οἱ ἔχοντες τὰς ἑπτὰ πληγὰς ἐκ τοῦ ναοῦ, ἐνδεδυμένοι λιθον καθαρὸν λαμπρὸν, καὶ περιεζωσμένοι περὶ τὰ στήθη ζώνας χρυσᾶς. Καὶ ἓν ἐκ τῶν τεσσάρων Ζώων ἔδωκεν τοῖς ἑπτὰ ἀγγέλοις ἑπτὰ φιάλας χρυσᾶς, γεμούσας τοῦ θυμοῦ τοῦ Θεοῦ του ζῶντος εἰς τοὺς αἰῶνας τῶν αἰώνων. Καὶ ἐγεμίσθη ὁ ναὸς καπιοῦ ἐκ τῆς δόξης τοῦ Θεοῦ, καὶ ἐκ τῆς δυνάμεως αὐτοῦ καὶ οὐδεὶς ἠδύιατο εἰσελθεῖν εἰς τὸν ναὸν, ἄχρι τελεσθῶσιν αἱ ἑπτὰ πληγαὶ τῶν ἑπτὰ ἀγγέλων.

ΚΕΦ. 37.

ΚΑΙ᾽ ἦλθεν εἷς ἐκ τῶν ἑπτὰ ἀγγέλων τῶν ἐχόντων τὰς ἑπτὰ φιάλας, καὶ ἐλάλησεν μετ᾽ ἐμοῦ, λέγων· Δεῦρο, δείξω σοι τὸ κρίμα τῆς πόρνης τῆς μεγάλης, τῆς καθημέιης ἐπὶ τῶν ὑδάτων τῶν πολλῶν· μεθ᾽ ἧς ἐπόρνευσαν οἱ

women; and their teeth were as the teeth of lions. And
they had breastplates, as breastplates of iron; and the
sound of their wings was as the sound of chariots, of
many horses charging to battle. And they had tails like
scorpions, and sharp stings, and in their tails was their
power to hurt men during five moons. And they had
a king set over them, an angel out of the abyss; whose
names are Abaddon and Apollyon. One woe is past, and
behold there come two more hereafter!

36.

And I saw another sign in heaven; great and wonderful it was: Seven Angels, having the seven last
plagues, that in them might be perfected the justice of
God. And after these things I looked, and behold the
Temple of the tabernacle of the testimony was opened in
Heaven and the Seven Angels came out of the temple,
having the seven plagues: they were clothed in stone
pure and shining, and their breasts were girt around
with golden girdles. And one of the Four living Ones,
presented unto the Seven Angels, seven golden vials,
filled with the justice of God, the Eternal Life through
ages of ages; and the Temple was filled with a cloud
from the Glory of God and from His power; and no one
was able to enter into the Temple, till the seven plagues
of the Seven Angels were fulfilled.

37

And there came one of the Seven Angels, who bare
the seven golden vials; and he talked with me, saying
Come hither, and I will shew unto thee the judgment of
the Mighty Harlot that sitteth upon many waters: with

βασιλεῖς τῆς γῆς, καὶ ἐμεθύσθησαν οἱ κατοικοῦντες τὴν γῆν ἐκ τοῦ οἴνου τῆς πορνείας αὐτῆς. Καὶ ἀπήνεγκε με εἰς ἔρημον ἐν πνεύματι· καὶ εἶδον γυναῖκα καθημένην ἐπὶ θηρίον κόκκινον, γέμον ὀνομάτων βλασφημίας, ἔχον κεφαλὰς ἑπτὰ καὶ κερατα δέκα. Καὶ ἡ γυνὴ ἦν περιβεβλημένη πορφυροῦν καὶ κόκκινον, καὶ κεχρυσωμένη χρυσίῳ καὶ λίθῳ τιμίῳ καὶ μαργαρίταις, ἔχουσα ποτήριον χρυσοῦν ἐν τῇ χειρὶ αὐτῆς γέμον βδελυγμάτων, καὶ τὰ ἀκάθαρτα τῆς πορνείας αὐτῆς, καὶ ἐπὶ τὸ μέτωπον αὐτῆς ὄνομα γεγραμμένον· Μυστήριον· Βα-Βελ-Ον ἡ μεγάλη μήτηρ τῶν πορνῶν καὶ τῶν βδελυγμάτων τῆς γῆς. Καὶ εἶδον τὴν γυναῖκα μεθύουσαν ἐκ τοῦ αἵματος τῶν ἁγίων, καὶ ἐκ τοῦ αἵματος τῶν μαρτύρων Ἰσσα· Καὶ ἐθαύμασα, ἰδὼν αὐτὴν, θαῦμα μέγα. Καὶ εἶπέ μοι ὁ ἄγγελος. Διατί ἐθαύμασας; ἐγώ σοι ἐρῶ τὸ μυστήριον τῆς γυναικὸς, καὶ τοῦ θηρίου τοῦ βαστάζοντος αὐτὴν, τοῦ ἔχοντος τὰς ἑπτὰ κεφαλὰς καὶ τὰ δέκα κέρατα. τὸ θηρίον ὃ εἶδες, ἦν, καὶ οὐκ ἔστιν καὶ μέλλει ἀναβαίνειν ἐκ τῆς ἀβύσσου, καὶ εἰς ἀπώλειαν ὑπάγειν· καὶ θαυμάσονται οἱ κατοικοῦντες ἐπὶ τῆς γῆς, ὧν οὐ γέγραπται τὰ ὀνόματα ἐπὶ τὸ βιβλίον τῆς ζωῆς, βλεπόντων τὸ θηρίον ὅτι ἦν, καὶ οὐκ ἔστι, καὶ πάρεσται. Καὶ λέγει μοι· τὰ ὕδατα ἃ εἶδες οὗ ἡ πόρνη κάθηται, λαοὶ καὶ ὄχλοι εἰσὶν, καὶ ἔθνη καὶ γλῶσσαι· καὶ ἡ γυνὴ ἣν εἶδες ἔστιν πόλις μεγάλη ἔχουσα βασιλείαν ἐπί τῶν βασιλέων τῆς γῆς· Καὶ ἔκραξεν ἐν ἰσχυρᾷ φωνῇ, λέγων· Ἔπεσεν, ἔπεσεν πολις ἡ μεγάλη, καὶ ἐγένετο κατοικητήριον δαιμόνων, καὶ φυλακὴ παντὸς πνεύματος ἀκαθάρτου, και φυλακὴ παντὸς ὀρνέου ἀκαθάρτου καὶ μεμισημένου· ὅτι ἐκ τοῦ οἴνου·τοῦ θυμοῦ τῆς πορνείας αὐτῆς πέπωκασιν πάντα τὰ ἔθνη, καὶ οἱ βασιλεῖς τῆς γῆς μετ' αὐτῆς ἐπόρνευσαν, καὶ οἱ ἔμποροι τῆς γῆς ἐκ τῆς δυνάμεως τοῦ στρήνους αὐτῆς ἐπλούτησαν.

whom the kings of the earth have harlotted; and the inhabitants of the earth have made themselves drunken with the wine of her evil wantonness. And he carried me away in the spirit into a desert place, and I saw a Woman sitting on a scarlet-coloured Wild Beast, full of the names of blasphemy; having seven heads and ten horns. And the Woman was arrayed in purple and scarlet, and gilded with gold and precious stones and pearls; having a golden chalice in her hand, full of the abominations and corruptions of her filthiness. And on her front was this name written. A Mystery! Ba-Bel-On, the great Mother of the filthiness, and of the foul abominations of the whole earth. And I saw the Woman, and she was drunken with the blood of the holy and with the blood of the witnesses of ISSA: and I wondered, seeing her, a great wonder. And the Angel said unto me: Wherefore dost thou marvel? I will reveal to thee the Mystery of this Woman; and of the Wild Beast on which she rides; which hath the seven heads and ten horns: the Wild Beast which thou seest, was and is not; and shall ascend out of the bottomless pit: and shall pass away into utter ruin. And they who dwell upon the earth shall wonder, they whose names are not enrolled in the Book of Life, when they see the Wild Beast that was and is not, and yet is (34). And he saith unto me: The waters which thou lookest upon, wherein this odious Harlot sitteth, are peoples and multitudes and nations and tongues: and the Woman which thou sawest is a mighty city, having dominion over the rulers of the earth. And he cried mightily with a strong voice, saying: She is fallen! She is fallen! the mighty city is fallen! She is become the habitation of demons, and the hold of every unclean spirit;

ΚΕΦ. 38.

ΚΑΙ ἤκουσα ἄλλην φωνὴν ἐκ τοῦ οὐρανοῦ, λέγουσαν. Ἐξέλθετε ἐξ αὐτῆς, ὁ λαός μου, ἵνα μὴ συγκοινωνήσητε ταῖς ἁμαρτίαις αὐτῆς, καὶ ἐκ τῶν πληγῶν αὐτῆς ἵνα μὴ λάβητε· ὅτι ἐκολλήθησαν αὐτῆς αἱ ἁμαρτίαι ἄχρι τοῦ οὐρανοῦ, καὶ ἐμνημόνευσεν ὁ Θεὸς τὰ ἀδικήματα αὐτῆς. Ἀπόδοτε αὐτῇ, ὡς καὶ αὐτὴ ἀπέδωκεν, καὶ διπλώσατε αὐτῇ διπλᾶ, κατὰ τὰ ἔργα αὐτης. ἐν τῷ ποτηρίῳ αὐτῆς ᾧ εκερασεν, κεράσατε αὐτῇ διπλουν. Ὅσα εδοξασεν ἑαυτην καὶ ἐστρηνίασεν τοσουτον. δότε αὐτῇ βασανισμὸν καὶ πένθος. Ὅτι ἐν τῇ καρδίᾳ αὐτῆς. λέγει· Κάθημαι βασίλισσα, καὶ χήρα οὐκ εἰμὶ, καὶ πένθος οὐ μὴ ἴδω. Διὰ τοῦτο ἐν μιᾷ ἡμέρᾳ ἥξουσιν αἱ πληγαὶ αὐτῆς, θάνατος καὶ πένθος καὶ λιμός· καὶ ἐν πυρὶ κατακαυθήσεται· ὅτι ἰσχυρὸς Κύριος ὁ Θεὸς ὁ κρίνας αὐτήν. Καὶ κλαύσουσιν καὶ κόψονται ἐπ' αὐτῆν οἱ βασιλεῖς τῆς γῆς, οἱ μετ' αὐτῆς πορνεύσαντες καὶ στρηνιάσαντες, ὅταν βλέπωσιν τὸν καπνὸν τῆς πυρώσεως αὐτῆς. ἀπὸ μακρόθεν ἑστηκότες διὰ τὸν φόβον τοῦ βασανισμοῦ αὐτῆς, λέγοντες· Οὐαὶ, οὐαὶ, ἡ πόλις ἡ μεγάλη, ἡ πόλις ἡ ἰσχυρὰ, ὅτι μιᾷ ὥρᾳ ἦλθεν ἡ κρίσις σου. Καὶ οἱ ἔμποροι τῆς γῆς κλαίουσιν καὶ πενθοῦσιν ἐπ' αὐτῇ ὅτι τὸν γόμον αὐτων οὐδεὶς ἀγοράζει οὐκ ἔτι· γόμον χρυσοῦ καὶ ἀργύρου, καὶ λίθου τιμίου καὶ μαργαρίτου, καὶ βυσσίνου καὶ πορφύρας, καὶ σηρικοῦ καὶ κοκκίνου· καὶ πᾶν ξύλον θύινον, καὶ πᾶν σκεῦος ἐλεφάντινον, καὶ πᾶν σκεῦος ἐκ ξύλου τιμιωτάτου καὶ χαλκοῦ

and the retreat of every impure and hateful bird : for
of the wine of the passion of her foul impurity, have
all the nations drunk . and the kings of the earth have
harlotted with her ; and the traffickers of the earth have
been enriched through the abundance of her odious
things.

38.

And I heard another Voice from Heaven, saying : Come
out of her, O my people, that ye be not made partakers
of her sins : that ye receive not of the plagues that come
upon her ; for her iniquities have reached to heaven ; and
God hath borne in mind her evil doings. Give ye unto
her, even as she gave unto you ; and double unto her
double, according to her works : in the cup which she hath
mixed mix ye up a double portion. By so much as she
hath glorified herself, and lived sumptuously, repay ye
her with sorrows and affliction. For she said in her
heart : I am a throned queen ; I am no widow and shall
see no sorrow. Therefore shall her plagues come in one
day : death and mourning and famine : and she shall
be utterly burned with fire ; for strong is the Lord God
who judgeth her. And they shall lament, and they shall
be aggrieved ; those kings of the earth who have harlotted with her : who have feasted with her in her luxuries ; when they shall see the smoke of her burning, and
shall stand afar off for the terror of her torment. They
shall cry out, Alas ! alas ! thou great city, thou mighty
city ; in one hour is thy judgment come. And the traffickers of the earth mourn and wail over her, for no man
shall buy her merchandize any more : merchandize of gold
and silver and precious stones and pearls, and fine linen and

καὶ σιδήρου καὶ μαρμάρου. Καὶ κινάμωμον, καὶ ἄμωμον, καὶ θυμιάματα, καὶ μύρον, καὶ λίβανον, καὶ οἶνον, καὶ ἔλαιον, καὶ σεμίδαλιν, καὶ σῖτον, καὶ κτήνη, καὶ πρόβατα, καὶ ἵππων, καὶ ῥεδῶν, καὶ σωμάτων· καὶ ψυχὰς ἀνθρώπων. Καὶ ἡ ὀπώρα τῆς ἐπιθυμίας τῆς ψυχῆς σου ἀπῆλθεν ἀπὸ σοῦ, καὶ πάντα τὰ λιπαρὰ καὶ τὰ λαμπρὰ ἀπώλετο ἀπὸ σοῦ, καὶ οὐκέτι αὐτὰ οὐ μὴ εὑρήσῃς. Οἱ ἔμποροι τούτων, οἱ πλουτήσαντες ἀπ᾽ αὐτῆς, ἀπὸ μακρόθεν στήσονται, διὰ τὸν φόβον τοῦ βασανισμοῦ αὐτῆς, κλαίοντες καὶ πενθοῦντες, λέγοντες· Οὐαὶ, οὐαί· ἡ πόλις ἡ μεγάλη, ἡ περιβεβλημένη βύσσινον καὶ πορφυροῦν καὶ κόκκινον, καὶ κεχρυσωμένη ἐν χρυσίῳ καὶ λίθῳ τιμίῳ καὶ μαργαρίταις· ὅτι μιᾷ ὥρᾳ ἠρημώθη ὁ τοσοῦτος πλοῦτος. Καὶ πᾶς κυβερνήτης, καὶ πᾶς ὁ ἐπὶ τόπον πλέων, καὶ ναῦται, καὶ ὅσοι τὴν θάλασσαν ἐργάζονται, ἀπὸ μακρόθεν ἔστησαν, καὶ ἀπὸ μακρόθεν· καὶ ἔκραζον βλέποντες τὸν καπνὸν τῆς πυρώσεως αὐτῆς, λέγοντες· Τίς ὁμοία τῇ πόλει τῇ μεγάλῃ; Καὶ ἔβαλον χοῦν ἐπὶ τὰς κεφαλὰς αὐτῶν, καὶ ἔκραζον κλαίοντες καὶ πενθοῦντες, λέγοντες· Οὐαὶ, οὐαί· ἡ πόλις ἡ μεγάλη, ἐν ᾗ ἐπλούτησαν πάντες οἱ ἔχοντες τὰ πλοῖα ἐν τῇ θαλάσσῃ ἐκ τῆς τιμιότητος αὐτῆς, ὅτι μιᾷ ὥρᾳ ἠρημώθη. Εὐφραίνου ἐπ᾽ αὐτῇ, οὐρανὲ, καὶ οἱ ἅγιοι καὶ οἱ ἀπόστολοι καὶ οἱ προφῆται, ὅτι ἔκρινεν ὁ Θεὸς τὸ κρίμα ὑμῶν ἐξ αὐτῆς.

ΚΕΦ. 39.

ΚΑΙ᾽ ἦρεν εἷς ἄγγελος ἰσχυρὸς λίθον ὡς μύλον μέγαν, καὶ ἔβαλεν εἰς τὴν θάλασσαν, λέγων· Οὕτως ὁρμήματι

purple and silk and scarlet, and all thyine wood, and every ivory vessel; and every ornament of the most precious material; of fine wood and brass and iron and marble; (35) and cinnamon and amomum and perfumes and ointment; and frankincense and wine and oil and fine flour; and wheat and cattle and sheep; horses and chariots and bodies; yea, and even the very souls of men. And the autumn fruits of the lust of thy soul,—these also have departed from thee; and all thy priceless and thy shining treasures;—these also have departed from thee: and thou shalt find them never again. The traffickers of those things, who were made rich by her, shall stand afar off, for the fear of her torment; weeping and wailing, and saying pitifully, Woe! Woe! that glorious city, that was clothed in fine linen and purple and scarlet; and gilded with gold and jewels and pearls; in one hour her riches are come to nought. And every shipmaster, and all who were sailing to that place, and mariners, and all who work by sea, stood afar off, and afar off; and cried out when they saw the smoke of her burning, saying: What city was like unto this great city? and they cast dust upon their heads; and cried aloud, weeping and wailing, saying: Woe! woe! the city that was so great; wherein were enriched all who had ships upon the sea, by reason of her costly luxuries;—that in one hour she should be made desolate! Rejoice over her, O thou heaven! and ye O holy ones! the Apostles and the Prophets; for God hath judged your judgment upon her.

39.

And a strong Angel took up a stone, like a great millstone, and cast it into the sea, saying: Thus with vio-

βληθήσεται ἡ μεγάλη πόλις, καὶ οὐ μὴ εὑρεθῇ ἔτι. Καὶ φωνὴ κιθαρῳδῶν καὶ μουσικῶν καὶ αὐλητῶν καὶ σαλπιστῶν οὐ μὴ ἀκουσθῇ ἐν σοὶ ἔτι, καὶ πᾶς τεχνίτης πάσης τέχνης οὐ μὴ εὑρεθῇ ἐν σοὶ ἔτι, καὶ φωνὴ μύλου οὐ μὴ ἀκουσθῇ ἐν σοὶ ἔτι, καὶ φῶς λύχνου οὐ μὴ φανῇ ἐν σοὶ ἔτι, καὶ φωνὴ νυμφίου καὶ νύμφης οὐ μὴ ἀκουσθῇ ἐν σοὶ ἔτι. οἱ ἔμποροί σου ἦσαν οἱ μεγιστᾶνες τῆς γῆς, ἀλλ᾽ ἐν τῇ φαρμακείᾳ σου ἐπλανήθησαν πάντα τὰ ἔθνη. Καὶ ἐν αὐτῇ αἵματα προφητῶν καὶ ἁγίων εὑρέθη, καὶ πάντων τῶν ἐσφαγμένων ἐπὶ τῆς γῆς· Οὐ κατοικηθήσεται εἰς τὸν αἰῶνα χρόνον, οὐδὲ μὴ εἰσέλθωσιν εἰς αυτὴν διὰ πολλῶν γενεῶν οὐδὲ ποιμένες οὐ μὴ ἀναπαύσονται ἐν αὐτῇ. καὶ ἀναπαύσονται ἐκεῖ θηρία, καὶ ἐμπλησθήσονται αἱ οἰχίαι ἤχου καὶ ἀναπαύσονται ἐκεῖ σειρῆνες, καὶ δαιμόνια ἐκεῖ ὀρχησόνται· καὶ ὀνοκένταυροι ἐκεῖ κατοικήσουσιν καὶ νοσσοποιήσουσιν ἐχεῖνοι ἐν τοῖς οἴκοις ἀυτῶν· Καὶ ἐν ἐκείνῃ τῇ ὥρᾳ ἐγένετο σεισμὸς μέγας, καὶ τὸ δέκατον τῆς πόλεως ἔπεσε, καὶ ἀπεκτάνθησαν ἐν τῷ σεισμῷ ὀνόματα ἀνθρώπων χιλιάδες ἑπτά· καὶ οἱ λοιποὶ ἔμφοβοι ἐγένοντο, καὶ ἔδωκαν δόξαν τῷ Θεῷ τοῦ ὀυρανοῦ. Ἡ ὀυαὶ ἡ δευτέρα ἀπῆλθεν· ἰδοῦ, ἡ ὀυαὶ ἡ τρίτη ἔρχεται ταχύ.

ΚΕΦ. 40.

ΚΑΙ᾽ ἐστάθην· ὥσει ἐπὶ· τήν ἄμμον τῆς θαλάσσης, καὶ εἶδον ἐκ τῆς θαλάσσης θηρίον ἀναβαῖνον ἔχον κέρατα δέκα καὶ κεφαλὰς ἑπτά· καὶ ἐπὶ τῶν κεράτων ἀυτοῦ δέκα διαδηματα, καὶ ἐπὶ τὰς κεφαλὰς ἀυτοῦ ὀνόματα βλασφημίας. Καὶ τὸ θηρίον ὃ εἶδον, ἦν ὅμοιον παρδάλει, καὶ οἱ πόδες ἀυτοῦ ὡς ἄρτκου, καὶ τὸ στόμα ἀυτοῦ ὡς στόμα λέοντος. Καὶ ἔδωκεν

lence shall this great city be cast, and shall no more be found at all. And the voice of harpers and musicians and pipers, and trumpeters, shall never more be heard in thee; and no craftsman of whatsoever craft shall ever again be found within thy walls; and the sound of the millstone shall not be heard within thee ever again; and the light of a lamp shall not be seen within thee ever again; and the voice of the bridegroom and of his young bride, shall never more be heard within thy dwelling: thy traffickers were princes on the earth, but by thy sorceries were all nations deceived. And in her was found the blood of prophets, and of holy ones, and of all who were slain on earth. She shall not be inhabited for an everlasting time; neither shall any enter her for many generations: nor shall any shepherds pasture in her: but wild beasts shall rest there; and doleful creatures shall abide there; and devils shall dance there; and tailless apes shall dwell there; and hedge hogs shall make nests in thine houses. And in that same hour there was a great earthquake, and the tenth part of the city fell: and there were slain in the earthquake names of men, seven thousand: and the remnant became afraid, and gave glory to the God of Heaven. The second woe is past: and behold the third woe cometh quickly.

40.

And I stood as it were upon the sand of the sea; and I raw out of the sea a Wild Beast (36) ascending, having ten horns and seven heads; and upon his horns ten diadems; and upon his heads the names of blasphemy. And the Wild Beast which I saw was like a Leopard; and his feet were as the feet of a Bear; and his mouth was as the

αὐτῷ ὁ δράκων τὴν δύναμιν αὐτοῦ, καὶ τὸν θρόνον αὐτοῦ, καὶ ἐξουσίαν μεγάλην, καὶ μίαν ἐκ τῶν κεφαλῶν αὐτοῦ ὡς ἐσφαγμένην εἰς θάνατον· καὶ ἡ πληγὴ τοῦ θανάτου αὐτοῦ ἐθεραπεύθη, καὶ ἐθαύμασεν ὅλη ἡ γῆ ὀπίσω τοῦ θηρίου, καὶ προσεκύνησαν τῷ δράκοντι, ὅτι ἔδωκε τὴν ἐξουσίαν τῷ θηρίῳ, καὶ προσεκύνησαν τῷ θηρίῳ, λέγοντες· Τίς ὅμοιος τῷ θηρίῳ; καὶ τίς δυνατὸς πολεμῆσαι μετ᾽ αὐτοῦ; καὶ ἐδόθη αὐτῷ στόμα λαλοῦν μεγάλα καὶ βλασφημίας πρὸς Θεὸν μόνον· Καὶ ἐδόθη αὐτῷ ἐξουσία πόλεμον ποιῆσαι μῆνας τεσσαράκοντα δύο. Καὶ ἤνοιξε τὸ στόμα αὐτοῦ εἰς βλασφημίαν πρὸς τὸν Θεὸν μόνον, βλασφημῆσαι τὸ ὄνομα αὐτοῦ, καὶ τὴν σκηνὴν αὐτοῦ, καὶ τοὺς ἐν τῷ οὐρανῷ σκηνοῦντας. Καὶ ἐδόθη αὐτῷ πόλεμον ποιῆσαι μετὰ τῶν ἁγίων, καὶ νικῆσαι αὐτούς· καὶ ἐδόθη αὐτῷ ἐξουσία ἐπὶ πᾶσαν φυλὴν καὶ λαὸν καὶ γλῶσσαν καὶ ἔθνος. Καὶ προσκυνήσουσιν αὐτὸν πάντες οἱ κατοικοῦντες ἐπὶ τῆς γῆς, ὧν οὐ γέγραπται τὸ ὄνομα ἐν τῷ βιβλίῳ τῆς ζωῆς· τοῦ Ἀρνίου τοῦ ἐσφαγμένου, ἀπὸ καταβολῆς κόσμου. Εἴ τις ἔχει οὖς, ἀκουσάτω. Εἴ τις εἰς αἰχμαλωσίαν ὑπάγῃ εἰς αἰχμαλωσίαν ὑπάγει· εἴ τις ἐν μαχαίρᾳ ἀποκτενεῖ, δεῖ αὐτὸν ἐν μαχαίρᾳ ἀποκτανθῆναι. Ὧδέ ἐστιν ἡ ὑπομονὴ καὶ ἡ πίστις τῶν ἁγίων.

ΚΕΦ. 41.

ΚΑΙ᾽ εἶδον ἄλλο θηρίον ἀναβαῖνον ἐκ τῆς γῆς, καὶ εἶχε κέρατα δύο ὅμοια ἀρνίῳ, καὶ ἐλάλει ὡς δράκων. Καὶ τὴν ἐξουσίαν τοῦ πρώτου θηρίου πᾶσαν ποιεῖ. καὶ ποιεῖ τὴν γῆν καὶ τοὺς ἐν αὐτῇ κατοικοῦντας, ἵνα προσκυνήσωσι τὸ θηρίον τὸ πρῶτον, οὗ ἐθεραπεύθη ἡ πληγὴ τοῦ θανάτου αὐτοῦ. Καὶ

mouth of a Lion. And to him the Dragon gave his power, his throne, and his great dominion. And I saw one of his heads as it were wounded to death; yet was this wound of death healed; and the whole earth won‐dered in the train of the Beast; and they adored the Dragon which gave power to the Beast (37), and they adored the Beast also, saying : Who is like unto this Beast? and who is able to make war against him? And there was given to him a mouth speaking great things and blasphemies against the One God; and there was given to him power to make war for the space of forty and two months (38). And he opened his mouth in blas‐phemy against the One God; to blaspheme His name and his Tabernacle; and those also who dwell with Him in heaven. And it was permitted him to make war against the holy; and even to overcome them in war : and he had sway over every tribe and tongue and people and nation. And all who dwelled on earth adored him; those whose names are not enrolled in the Book of Life : and of the Lamb who was sacrificed from the foundation of the world. He that hath an ear let him hear! If any man leadeth into captivity, he also shall be led into captivity : if any man killeth with the sword, he also shall be slain by the sword :—this is the endurance and the faith of the holy.

41.

And I saw another Wild Beast ascending out of the earth (39), and he had two horns like a Lamb; but he spake as a Dragon. And he exercised all the power of the first Beast (40), and made the earth and all who dwelled upon the earth, that they should adore the first Wild

ποιεῖ σημεῖα μεγάλα, ἵνα καὶ πῦρ ποιῇ καταβαίνειν ἐκ τοῦ οὐρανοῦ εἰς τὴν γῆν ἐνώπιον τῶν ἀνθρώπων. Καὶ πλανᾷ τοὺς κατοικοῦντας ἐπὶ τῆς γῆς, διὰ τὰ σημεῖα ἃ ἐδόθη αὐτῷ ποιῆσαι· λέγων τοῖς κατοικοῦσιν ἐπὶ τῆς γῆς, ποιῆσαι εἰκόνα τῷ θηρίῳ, ὃ ἔχει τὴν πληγὴν, καὶ ἔζησεν ἀπὸ τῆς μαχαίρας· Καὶ ἐδόθη αὐτῷ δοῦναι πνεῦμα τῇ εἰκόνι τοῦ θηρίου, ἵνα καὶ λαλήσῃ ἡ εἰκὼν τοῦ θηρίου, καὶ ποιήσῃ, ἵνα ὅσοι ἂν μὴ προσκυνήσωσιν τῇ εἰκόνι τοῦ θηρίου, ἀποκτανθῶσιν· Καὶ ποιεῖ πάντας, τοὺς μικροὺς καὶ τοὺς μεγάλους, καὶ τοὺς πλουσίους καὶ τοὺς πτωχοὺς, καὶ τοὺς ἐλευθέρους καὶ τοὺς δούλους, ἵνα δῶσιν αὐτοῖς χάραγμα ἢ ἐπὶ τῆς χειρὸς αὐτῶν τῆς δεξιᾶς, ἢ 'πὶ τὸ μέτωπον αὐτῶν· Καὶ ἵνα μή τις δύνηται ἀγοράσαι ἢ πωλῆσαι, εἰ μὴ ὁ ἔχων τὸ χάραγμα, ἢ τὸ ὄνομα τοῦ θηρίου, ἢ τὸν ἀριθμὸν τοῦ θηρίου, ἢ τον ἀριθμὸν ονοματος αυτου. Ὧδε ἡ σοφία ἐστίν· ὁ ἔχων νοῦν ψηφισάτω τον ἀριθμὸν τοῦ θηρίου ἀριθμὸς γάρ ἀνθρώπου ἐστὶ, καὶ ὁ ἀριθμός αὐτοῦ χξς.

ΚΕΦ. 42.

ΚΑΙ' εἶδον τὸ θηρίον, καὶ τοὺς βασιλεῖς τῆς γῆς, καὶ τὰ στρατεύματα αὐτῶν συνηγμένα, ποιῆσαι πόλεμον μετὰ τοῦ καθημένου ἐπὶ τοῦ ἵππου λέυκου καὶ μετὰ τοῦ στρατεύματος αὐτοῦ. Καὶ ἐπιάσθη τὸ θηρίον, καὶ οἱ μετ' αὐτοῦ ψευδοπροφῆται οἱ ποιήσαντες τὰ σημεῖα ἐνώπιον αὐτοῦ, ἐν οἷς επλάνησε τοὺς λαβόντας τὸ χάραγμα τοῦ θηρίου, καὶ τοῖς προσκυνοῦντας τῇ εἰκόνι αὐτοῦ, ζῶντες ἐβλήθησαν οἱ εἰς τὴν λίμνην τοῦ πυρὸς τὴν καιομένην ἐν θείῳ. Καὶ οἱ λοιποὶ ἀπεκτάνθησαν ἐν τῇ ῥομφαίᾳ τοῦ καθημένου ἐπὶ τοῦ ἵππου

Beast, whose wound of death was healed. And he produced great signs (41), and that even fire should come
down from heaven, unto the earth, in the sight of men.
And he deceived those who dwelled upon the earth by
the signs which it was permitted him to do : command.
ing those who dwelled upon the earth to make an image
to that Wild Beast, which had the wound and lived by
the sword (42). And it was permitted to him to give
life to the image of the Wild Beast, so that the image of
the Beast should both speak and do ; that as many as
adored not the image of the Wild Beast should (43)
suffer death. And he caused all, both small and great,
and the rich and the poor, and the free and the bond,
that they should receive a mark either on the right hand
or upon the foreheads of them (44) · and that no man
should buy or sell unless he possessed that mark : either
the name of the Wild Beast or his number, or the number of the Wild Beast's name. Herein is wisdom to be
shewn ! let him who is wise calculate the number of the
Beast ; for it is the number of a man ; and his number is
Chi-xi-bau. (45.)

42.

And I saw the Wild Beast, and the rulers of the earth ;
and their armies gathered together to make war against
him who rode upon the white horse ; and against the
armies that were with him. And the Beast was taken,
and with him his false priests, who wrought their jugglery
before him, wherein they deceived those who wore his
brand, and who adored the image of the Wild Beast.
They were cast alive into the Lake of Fire, the lake that
. burns with brimstone : the rest were slain by the sword

λεύκου, τῇ ἐξελθούσῃ ἐκ τοῦ στόματος αὐτοῦ, καὶ πάντα τὰ ὄρνεα ἐχορτάσθησαν ἐκ τῶν σαρκῶν αὐτῶν.

ΚΕΦ. 43.

ΚΑΙ εἶδον ᾿ΑΓΓΕΛΟΝ καταβαίνοντα ἐκ τοῦ οὐρᾶνοῦ, ἔχοντα τὴν κλεῖν τῆς ἀβύσσου, καὶ ἅλυσιν μεγάλην ἐπὶ τὴν χεῖρα αὐτοῦ. Καὶ ἐκράτησε τὸν δράκοντα, τὸν ὄφιν τὸν ἀρχαῖον, ὅς ἐστι διάβολος καὶ σατανᾶς, καὶ ἔδησεν αὐτὸν χίλια ἔτη· Καὶ ἔβαλεν αὐτὸν εἰς τὴν ἄβυσσον, καὶ ἔκλεισε καὶ ἐσφράγισεν επάνω αὐτοῦ, ἵνα μὴ πλανᾷ ἔτι τὰ ἔθνη, ἄχρι τελεσθῇ τὰ χίλια ἔτη·

ΚΕΦ. 44.

ΚΑΙ εἶδον, καὶ ἰδοὺ τὸ ᾿Αρνίον ἑστηκὸς ἐπὶ τὸ ὄρος Ζειών, καὶ μετ᾿ αὐτοῦ ἑκατὸν τεσσαράκοντα τέσσαρες χιλιάδες, ἔχουσαι τὸ ὄνομα αὐτοῦ, καὶ τὸ ὄνομα τοῦ Πατρὸς γεγραμμένον ἐπὶ τῶν μετώπων αὐτῶν. Καὶ ἤκουσα φωνὴν ἐκ τοῦ οὐρανοῦ ὡς φωνὴν ὑδάτων πολλῶν, καὶ ὡς φωνὴν βροντῆς μεγάλης· καὶ ἡ φωνὴ ἣν ἤκουσα ὡς κιθαρῳδῶν κιθαριζόντων ἐν ταῖς κιθάραις αὐτῶν· καὶ ᾄδουσιν ᾠδὴν καινὴν ἐνώπιον τοῦ θρόνου, καὶ ἐνώπιον τῶν τεσσάρων Ζώων, καὶ τῶν πρεσβυτέρων. καὶ οὐδεὶς ἠδύνατο μαθεῖν τὴν ᾠδὴν, εἰ μὴ αἱ ἑκατὸν τεσσαράκοντα τέσσαρες χιλιάδες, οἱ ἠγορασμένοι ἀπὸ τῆς γῆς. Οὗτοί εἰσιν οἳ μετὰ γυναικῶν οὐκ ἐμολύνθησαν· παρθένοι γάρ εἰσιν· οὗτοί εἰσιν οἱ ἀκολουθοῦντες τῷ ᾿Αρνίῳ ὅπου ἂν ὑπάγῃ. Καὶ ἐν τῷ στόματι αὐτῶν οὐχ εὑρέθη ψεῦδος· ἄμωμοι γάρ εἰσιν.

of him, who sat upon the white horse; by the sword that came out of his mouth : and all the fowls were filled with their flesh.

43.

And I saw a MESSENGER come down from Heaven having the key of the bottomless pit; and a great chain was in his hand. And he grasped the Dragon, that old Serpent, who is the Accuser, and Satanas; and he bound him for a thousand years ; and cast him into the bottomless pit ; and shut him up, and set a seal on him, that he might not wander any more among the nations, until the thousand years should be completed.

44.

And I looked, and behold the Lamb stood upon Mount Zion ; and with him a hundred and forty-four thousand, having his name, and the name of the Father (47) written full upon their foreheads. And I heard a Voice out of Heaven, as the voice of many waters ; and as the voice of pealing thunder. And the voice which I heard was as the voice of harpers, harping sweetly on their harps ; and they sang a new song (48) before the Throne, and before the Four Living Ones ; and the Ancients ; and none could learn that song, but the hundred and forty and four thousand, who had been purchased from the earth. These are they who are undefiled with women, for they are as pure virgins (49). These are they who follow the Lamb, whithersoever he goeth ; and in their mouths was found no lie, for they are without fault.

576 ΑΠΟΚΑΛΥΨΙΣ.

ΚΕΦ. 45.

ΚΑΙ᾽ ἤκουσα φωνὴν ἐκ τοῦ οὐρανοῦ· Οὗτος ὁ παῖς μου, ἀντιλήψομαι αὐτοῦ· οὗτος ὁ ἐκλεκτός μου προσεδέξατο αὐτὸν ἡ ψυχή μου, ἔδωκα τὸ Πνεῦμά μου ἐπ᾽ αὐτὸν, κρίσιν τοῖς ἔθνεσιν ἐξοίσει· Οὐ κεκράξεται, οὐδὲ ἀνήσει, οὐδέ ἀκουσθήσεται ἔξω ἡ φωνὴ αὐτοῦ· κάλαμον τεθλασμένον οὐ συντρίψει, καὶ λίνον καπνιζόμενον οὐ σβέσει ἀλλὰ εἰς ἀλήθειαν ἐξοίσει κρίσιν· Ἀναλάμψει, καὶ οὐ θραυσθήσεται, ἕως ἂν θῇ ἐπί τῆς γῆς κρίσιν, καὶ ἐπί τῷ ὀνόματι αὐτοῦ ἔθνη ἐλπιοῦσιν.

ΚΕΦ. 46.

ΚΑΙ᾽ ἤκουσα φωνῆς ἀλλῆς ἐκ τοῦ οὐρανοῦ, λεγούσης Γράψον· Μακάριοι οἱ νεκροὶ οἱ ἐν Κυρίῳ ἀποθνήσκοντες ἀπ᾽ ἄρτι. Ναὶ, λέγει τὸ Πνεῦμα, ἵνα ἀναπαύσωνται ἐκ τῶν κόπων αὐτῶν· τὰ δὲ ἔργα αὐτῶν ἀκολουθεῖ μετ᾽ αὐτῶν. Καὶ εἶδον ὥς θάλασσαν ὑαλίνην μεμιγμένην πυρὶ, καὶ τοὺς νικῶντας ἐκ τοῦ θηρίου καὶ ἐκ τῆς εἰκόνος αὐτοῦ, καὶ ἐκ τοῦ ἀριθμοῦ τοῦ ὀνόματος αὐτοῦ, ἐστῶτας ἐπὶ τὴν θάλασσαν τὴν ὑαλίνην, ἔχοντες κιθάρας τοῦ Θεοῦ. Καὶ ἄδουσι τὴν ᾠδὴν δούλου τοῦ Θεοῦ, καὶ τὴν ᾠδὴν τοῦ Ἀρνίου, λέγοντες· Μεγάλα καὶ θαυμαστὰ τὰ ἔργα σου, Κύριε ὁ Θεὸς ὁ παντοκράτωρ· δίκαιαι καὶ ἀληθιναί αἱ ὁδοί σου, ὁ βασιλεὺς τῶν ἐθνῶν. Τίς οὐ μὴ φοβηθῇ σε, Κύριε, καὶ δοξάσῃ τὸ ὄνομά σου; ὅτι μόνος ὅσιος· ὅτι πάντα τὰ ἔθνη ἥξουσι καὶ προσκυνήσουσιν ἐνώπιόν σου· ὅτι τὰ δικαιώματά σου ἐφανερώθησαν.

ΚΕΦ. 47.

ΚΑΙ᾽ εἶδον ἄλλον ἄγγελον πετόμενον ἐν μεσουρανήματι, ἔχοντα εὐαγγέλιον αἰώνιον εὐαγγελίσαι τοὺς καθημενους

45.

And I heard a Voice from Heaven; This is my son: I will help him; this is my chosen one; my soul has accepted him; I have put my spirit upon him; he shall bring forth judgment to the nations. He shall not cry, nor lift up his voice; nor shall his voice be heard without; a bruised reed he shall not break: and smoking flax he shall not quench; but he shall bring forth judgment unto truth. He shall shine out and shall not be discouraged; until he shall have set judgment upon the earth; and in his name shall the nations trust.

46.

And I heard another Voice from Heaven, saying unto me, Write: blessed are the dead who die in the Lord henceforth. Yea, said the Spirit (50), that they may rest from their labours; but their good works do follow them. And I saw as it were a sea of hyaline mingled with fire; and those who had conquered the Wild Beast and his image; and had abjured his mark, and the number of his name, standing upon that fiery sea of glass, holding the harps of God. And they sang the song of the servant of God; and the song of the Lamb, saying: Great and wonderful are thy works, O Lord God Almighty; just and true are thy ways, thou King of all nations. Who shall not revere thee, O Lord; and glorify thy name, thou only Divine One? All nations shall come and adore Thee; for now thine ordinances are made manifest.

47.

And I saw another Angel (51) flying in mid-heaven, having the everlasting evangel to (52) evangelize those

c c

ἐπὶ τῆς γῆς, καὶ πᾶν ἔθνος καὶ φυλὴν καὶ γλῶσσαν καὶ λαόν·
Λέγων ἐν φωνῇ μεγάλῃ· Φοβήθητε τὸν Θεὸν καὶ δότε
αὐτῷ δόξαν, ὅτι ἦλθεν ἡ ὥρα τῆς κρίσεως αὐτοῦ· καὶ
προσκυνήσατε τῷ ποιήσαντι τὸν οὐρανὸν καὶ τὴν γῆν καὶ
τὴν θάλασσαν καὶ πηγὰς ὑδάτων. Καὶ ἄλλος ἄγγελος
δεύτερος ἠκολούθησε, λέγων· Ἔπεσεν, ἔπεσε Βα-Βελ-Ον ἡ
μεγάλη· ἣ ἐκ τοῦ οἴνου τοῦ θυμοῦ τῆς πορνείας αὐτῆς
πεπότικε πάντα ἔθνη. Καὶ ἄλλος ἄγγελος τρίτος ἠκολού-
θησεν αὐτοῖς, λέγων ἐν φωνῇ μεγάλῃ· Εἴ τις προσκυνεῖ τὸ
θηρίον καὶ τὴν εἰκόνα αὐτοῦ, καὶ λαμβάνει χάραγμα ἐπὶ τοῦ
μετώπου αὐτοῦ, ἢ ἐπὶ τὴν χεῖρα αὐτοῦ, καὶ αὐτὸς πίεται
ἐκ τοῦ οἴνου τοῦ θυμοῦ τοῦ Θεοῦ, τοῦ κεκερασμένου ἀκράτου
ἐν τῷ ποτηρίῳ τῆς ὀργῆς αὐτοῦ, καὶ βασανισθήσεται ἐν
πυρὶ καὶ θείῳ ἐνώπιον τῶν ἁγίων ἀγγέλων καὶ ἐνώπιον τοῦ
Ἀρνίου. Καὶ εἰς τὴν γῆν κάτω ἐμβλέψονται, καὶ ἰδοὺ
ἀπορία στενή, καὶ σκότος θλίψις καὶ στενοχωρία, καὶ σκότος
ὥστε μὴ βλέπειν· Καὶ ὁ καπνος τοῦ βασανισμοῦ αὐτῶν
εἰς αἰῶνας αἰώνων ἀναβαίνει· καὶ οὐκ ἔχουσιν ἀνάπαυσιν
ἡμέρας καὶ νυκτὸς οἱ προσκυνοῦντες τὸ θηρίον καὶ τὴν
εἰκόνα αὐτοῦ, καὶ εἴ τις λαμβάνει τὸ χάραγμα τοῦ ὀνόματος
αὐτοῦ. Ὧδε ὑπομονὴ τῶν ἁγίων ἐστίν· οἱ τηροῦντες τὰς
ἐντολὰς τοῦ Θεοῦ καὶ τὴν πίστιν Ἰσσα·

ΚΕΦ. 48.

ΚΑΙ῾ ἤκουσα φωνὴν μίαν ἐκ τῶν τεσσάρων κεράτων τοῦ
θυσιαστηρίου τοῦ χρυσοῦ τοῦ ἐνώπιον τοῦ Θεοῦ, λέγουσαν
τῷ ἕκτῳ ἀγγέλῳ ὁ ἔχων τὴν σάλπιγγα· Λῦσον τοὺς
τέσσαρας ἀγγέλους τοὺς δεδεμένους ἐπὶ τῷ ποταμῷ τῷ μεγά-
λῳ Εφρ· Καὶ ὁ ἕκτος ἄγγελος ἐσάλπισε καὶ ἐλύθησαν οἱ

who rested upon the earth, and every nation and tribe, and tongue, and people; saying in a loud voice: Fear ye God, and give Him glory, because the hour of his judgment is near: and adore ye Him who made the Heaven and the earth, and the sea, and the fountains of waters. And another Angel (a second) followed, saying: She is fallen Ba-Bel-On is fallen: the great city has fallen, has fallen: because of the wine of the passion of her impurity, did she make all nations drink. And another Angel (a third) followed them, saying in a loud voice: If any worship the Wild Beast and his image, and receive his mark upon his forehead, or upon his hand; he also shall drink of the wine of the justice of God, which is poured out unmixed into the cup of his fierce wrath; he shall be tormented in fire and brimstone before the face of the Holy Messengers of the Lamb. And they shall look to the earth, and behold trouble and darkness, weakness and distress and a mist following them, and they cannot fly away from their distress. And the smoke of their torment ascends upward throughout ages of ages: and they have no rest, in the day nor in the night who do adore the Wild Beast and his image: and who have received the brand of his name. This is the endurance of the holy, who keep the commandments of God and the faith of ISSA.

48.

And I heard a voice from the four horns of the golden incense altar before God; saying to the sixth Angel who held the trumpet: Loose the four angels that are bound in the great river Ephr. (53.) And the sixth Angel sounded; and the four angels were let loose, who were reserved,

τέσσαρες ἄγγελοι οἱ ἡτοιμασμένοι εἰς τὴν ὥραν καὶ ἡμέραν
καὶ μῆνα καὶ ἐνιαυτὸν, ἵνα ἀποκτείνωσιν το τρίτον τῶν
ἀνθρώπων. Καὶ ὁ ἀριθμος τῶν στρατευμάτων τόυ ἱππικου
δυό μυριάδες μυριάδων· ἤκουσα τὸν ἀριθμον ἀυτῶν· καὶ
ὅυτως εἶδον τόυς ἵππους ἐν τῇ ὁράσει, καὶ τόυς καθημένους
ἐπ᾿ ἀυτῶν, ἔχοντας θώρακας πυρίνους καὶ ὑακινθίνους καὶ
θειωδεις· καὶ αἱ κεφαλαὶ τῶν ἵππων ὡς κεφαλαὶ λεόντων,
καὶ ἐκ τῶν στομάτων ἀυτῶν ἐκπορεύεται πῦρ καὶ καπνὸς καὶ
θεῖον. Ἀπὸ τῶν τριῶν πληγῶν τούτων ἀπεκτάνθησαν τὸ
τρίτον τῶν ἀνθρώπων, ἐκ τοῦ πυρὸς καί τοῦ καπνοῦ καὶ τοῦ
θείου τοῦ ἐκπορευομένου ἐκ τῶν στομάτων ἀυτῶν. Ἡ γὰρ
ἐξουσία τῶν ἵππων ἐν τῷ στόματι ἀυτῶν ἐστιν καί ἐν ταῖς
ὀυραις ἀυτῶν· αἱ γὰρ ὀυραὶ ἀυτῶν ὅμοιαι ὄφεσιν, ἔχουσαι
κεφαλὰς, καὶ ἐν ἀυταῖς ἀδικοῦσιν. Καὶ οἱ λοιποὶ τῶν ἀνθρώπων, οἱ ὀυκ ἀπεκτάνθησαν ἐν ταῖς πληγαῖς ταύταις, ὀυ μετενόησαν ἐκ τῶν ἔργων τῶν χειρῶν ἀυτῶν, ἵνα μὴ προσκυνήσωσιν τά δαιμόνια, καὶ τα εἴδωλα τὰ χρυσᾶ καὶ τὰ ἀργυρᾶ
καὶ τὰ χαλκᾶ καὶ τὰ λίθινα καὶ τὰ ξύλινα, ἃ ὀύτε βλέπειν
δύνανται, ὀύτε ἀκούειν, ὀύτε περιπατειν· Καὶ ὀυ μετενόησαν
ἐκ τῶν φόνων ἀυτῶν, ὀύτε ἐκ τῶν φαρμακειῶν ἀυτῶν, ὀύτε
ἐκ τῆς πορνείας ἀυτῶν, ὀύτε ἐκ τῶν κλεμμάτων ἀυτῶν.

ΚΕΦ. 49.

ΚΑΙ᾿ ὁ ἔβδομος ἄγγελος ἐσάλπισεν· καὶ ἐγένοντο φωναὶ
μεγάλαι ἐν τῷ ὀυρανῷ, λέγοντες· Ἐγένετο ἡ βασιλεία τοῦ
κόσμου, τοῦ Κυρίου ἡμῶν καὶ τοῦ χριστοῦ ἀυτοῦ, καὶ
βασιλεύσει εἰς τοὺς αἰῶνας τῶν αἰώνων. Καὶ οἱ εἴκοσι
τέσσαρες πρεσβύτεροι οἱ ἐνώπιον τοῦ Θεοῦ καθήμενοι ἐπὶ
τοὺς θρόνους ἀυτῶν, ἔπεσαν ἐπὶ τὰ πρόσωπα ἀυτῶν, καὶ
προσεκύνησαν τῷ Θεῷ, λέγοντες· Ἐυχαριστοῦμέν σοι,
Κύριε ὁ Θεὸς ὁ παντοκράτωρ, ὁ ὤν, καὶ ὁ ἦν, καὶ ὁ ἐρχόμενος·
ὅτι εἴληφας τὴν δύναμίν σου τὴν μεγάλην καὶ ἐβασίλευσας.

unto that hour and day, and month and year, to slay the third of men. And the number of the army of the horsemen was two myriads of myriads; and I heard their number. And thus I saw the horses in the apparition, and those who rode upon the horses: they had corslets of fire and jacinth and brimstone; and the heads of the horses were as the heads of lions; and out of their mouths came fire and smoke and sulphur. By these three plagues was the third of men destroyed; by the fire and the smoke and the brimstone that issued forth out of their mouths. For their powers were in their mouths and tails; and their tails were like unto headed serpents with stings; and with these they worked iniquity. And the rest of men who sank not under these blows, nevertheless repented them not of the works of their hands; nor turned them away from the adoration of demons; nor from their images of gold and silver; nor from their idols of brass and wood and stone: which see and hear not, neither can they walk. Neither did they repent them of their murders, nor of their sorceries, nor impurities, nor thievings.

49.

And the seventh Angel sounded; and there were great Voices in the Heaven; and they said: The kingdom of the world of men is become the kingdom of our God and his Anointed, and He shall rule them unto ages of ages. And the four and twenty Ancients, who sat on thrones before the face of God, fell down upon their faces before Him, and adored the God of Heaven: saying, We give thee thanks, O Lord God Almighty, which art and wert and art to come; because thou hast assumed thy great

Καὶ τὰ ἔθνη ὠργίσθησαν, καὶ ἦλθέν ἡ ὥρα σου, καὶ ὁ καιρὸς τῶν νεκρῶν κριθῆναι, καὶ δοῦναι τὸν μισθὸν τοῖς δούλοις
σου τοῖς προφήταις καὶ τοῖς ἁγίοις καὶ τοῖς φοβουμένοις τὸ
ὄνομά σου τοῖς μικροῖς καὶ τοῖς μεγάλοις, καὶ διαφθεῖραι
τοὺς διαφθείροντας τὴν γῆν. Καὶ ἠνοίχθη ὁ ναὸς τοῦ Θεοῦ ὁ
ἐν τῷ οὐρανῷ, καὶ ὤφθη ἡ κιβωτὸς τῆς διαθήκης τοῦ Κυρίου ἐν τῷ ναῷ αὐτοῦ· καὶ ἐγένοντο ἀστραπαὶ καὶ φωναὶ καὶ
βρονταὶ καὶ σεισμὸς καὶ χάλαζα μεγάλη.

ΚΕΦ. 50.

ΚΑΙ' ἐδόθη αὐτῷ κάλαμος ὅμοιος ῥάβδῳ, καὶ ὁ αγγελος
εἱστήκει λέγων. Ἔγειραι καὶ μέτρησον τὸν ναὸν τοῦ Θεοῦ,
καὶ τὸ θυσιαστήριον, καὶ τοὺς προσκυνοῦντας ἐν αὐτῷ· Καὶ
τὴν αὐλὴν τὴν ἔξωθεν τοῦ ναοῦ ἔκβαλε ἔξω, καὶ μὴ αὐτὴν
μετρήσῃς, ὅτι ἐδόθη τοῖς ἔθνεσι· Καὶ εἶδον, καὶ ἰδοὺ νεφέλη
λευκὴ, καὶ ἐπὶ τὴν νεφέλην καθήμενον ὅμοιον υἱῷ ἀνθρωπου,
ἔχων ἐπὶ τῆς κεφαλῆς αὐτοῦ στέφανον χρυσοῦν, καὶ ἐν τῇ
χειρὶ αὐτοῦ δρέπανον ὀξύ. Καὶ λέγει, ἐξαποστείλατε δρέπανα,
ὅτι παρέστηκεν τρυγητός· εἰσοπορεύεσθε, πατεῖτε, διότι
πλήρης ἡ ληνὸς. ἠχοι ἐξήχησαν ἐν τῇ κοιλάδι τῆς δίκης,
ὅτι ἐγγὺς ἡμέρα Κυρίου· Ὁ ἥλιος καὶ ἡ σελήνη συσκοτάσουσιν, καὶ οἱ ἀστέρες δύσουσιν φέγγος αὐτῶν· ὁ δε Κύριος
ἐκ Ζειὼν ἀνακεκράξεται, καὶ σεισθήσεται ὁ οὐρανὸς καὶ
ἡ γῆ.

ΚΕΦ. 51.

ΚΑΙ' ἄλλος ἄγγελος ἐξῆλθεν ἐκ τοῦ ναοῦ, κράζων ἐν
φωνῇ μεγάλῃ τῷ καθημένῳ ἐπὶ τῆς νεφέλης· Πέμψον τὸ
δρέπανόν σου, καὶ θέρισον, ὅτι ἦλθεν ἡ ὥρα τοῦ θερίσαι·

power and hast reigned. And the nations were enraged,
but thine hour is come; and the time of the dead that
they should be judged: and that thou shouldst give thy
reward to thy servants the Prophets, and to the holy and
to those who revered thy name: and to the little and to
the great; and shouldst cut off the corrupters of the
earth. And the Temple of God was opened in the
heaven; and there was seen the *Ark of his Covenant* in
the Temple: there were lightnings and voices and peals
of thunder; and an earthquake and great hail.

50.

And there was given to him a reed like unto a rod;
and an Angel stood saying; Rise and measure the Temple
of God; and the incense altar and those who worship on
it: but the court, which is without the Temple, leave
out (54); measure it not, for it belongeth to the nations.
And I looked, and behold a white Cloud; and on the
Cloud, One sitting like a Son of Man; having on his
head a golden crown; and in his hand a sharp sickle.
And he said: Bring forth the sickles for the vintage is
come, go in; tread the grapes, for the press is full; noises
have resounded in the Valley of Judgment, for the Day
of the Lord is close at hand. The sun and the moon
shall be darkened: and the stars shall withdraw their
light; and the Lord shall cry out of Zion; and the
heaven and the earth shall be shaken.

51.

And another Angel came out of the Temple; crying
out with a loud voice, to him who sat upon the Cloud:
Thrust in thy sickle and reap; for the time is come for

ὅτι ἐξηράνθη ὁ θερισμὸς τῆς γῆς. Καὶ ἔβαλεν ὁ καθήμενος ἐπὶ τὴν νεφέλην τὸ δρέπανον αὐτοῦ ἐπὶ τὴν γὴν· καὶ ἐθερίσθη ἡ γῆ. Καὶ ἄλλος ἄγγελος ἐξῆλθεν ἐκ τοῦ ναοῦ τοῦ ἐν τῷ οὐρανῷ, ἔχων καὶ αὐτὸς δρέπανον ὀξύ. Καὶ ἄλλος ἄγγελος ἐξῆλθεν ἐκ τοῦ θυσιαστηρίου, ἔχων ἐξουσίαν ἐπὶ τοῦ πυρός· καὶ ἐφώνησε κραυγῇ μεγάλῃ τῷ ἔχοντι τὸ δρέπανον τὸ ὀξύ, λέγων· Πέμψον σου τὸ δρέπανον τὸ ὀξύ, καὶ τρύγησον τοὺς βότρυας τῆς ἀμπέλου τῆς γῆς, ὅτι ἤκμασαν αἱ σταφυλαὶ αὐτῆς. Καὶ ἔβαλεν ὁ ἄγγελος τὸ δρέπανον αὐτοῦ εἰς τὴν γῆν, καὶ ἐτρύγησε τὴν ἄμπελον τῆς γῆς, καὶ ἔβαλεν εἰς τὴν ληνὸν τοῦ θυμοῦ τοῦ Θεοῦ τὸν μέγαν. Καὶ ἐπατήθη ἡ ληνὸς ἔξωθεν τῆς πόλεως, καὶ ἐξῆλθεν αἷμα ἐκ τῆς ληνοῦ ἄχρι τῶν χαλινῶν τῶν ἵππων ἀπὸ σταδίων χιλίων ἑξακοσίων.

ΚΕΦ. 52.

ΚΑΙ´ ἤνοιξε τὸ Ἀρνίον τὴν πέμπτην σφραγῖδα, καὶ εἶδον ὑποκάτω τοῦ θυσιαστηρίου τὰς ψυχὰς τῶν ἐσφαγμένων διὰ τὸν λόγον τοῦ Θεοῦ, καὶ διὰ τὴν μαρτυρίαν ἣν εἶχον· Καὶ ἔκραξαν φωνῇ μεγάλῃ, λέγοντες· Ἕως πότε, ὁ Δεσπότης ὁ ἅγιος καὶ ἀληθινός, οὐ κρίνεις καὶ ἐκδικεῖς τὸ αἷμα ἡμῶν ἐκ τῶν κοτοικούντων ἐπὶ τῆς γῆς; καὶ ἐδόθη αὐτοῖς στολὴ λευκὴ, καὶ ἐῤῥέθη αὐτοῖς, ἵνα ἀναπαύσωνται ἔτι χρόνον. Καὶ ἀπεκρίθη εἷς ἐκ τῶν πρεσβυτέρων, λέγων μοι. Οὗτοι οἱ περιβεβλημένοι τὰς στολὰς τὰς λευκὰς, τίνες εἰσὶ, καὶ πόθεν ἦλθον; καὶ εἴρηκα αὐτῷ· Κύριέ μου, σὺ οἶδας. Καί εἰπέ μοι· Οὗτοί εἰσιν οἱ ἐρχόμενοι ἐκ τῆς θλίψεως τῆς μεγάλης, καὶ ἔπλυναν τὰς στολὰς αὐτῶν, καὶ ἐλεύκαναν στολὰς αὐτῶν ἐν τῷ αἵματι τοῦ Ἀρνίου, τοῦ ἅγιον. Διὰ τοῦτό εἰσιν ἐνώπιον τοῦ θρόνου τοῦ Θεοῦ, καὶ λατρεύουσιν αὐτῷ ἡμέρας καὶ νυκτὸς ἐν τῷ ναῷ αὐτοῦ· καὶ ὁ καθήμενος ἐπὶ τοῦ θρόνου σκηνώσει ἐπ᾽ αὐτούς. Οὐ πεινάσουσιν ἔτι, οὐδὲ διψήσουσιν

thee to reap : the harvest of the earth is ripe. And he that sat upon the Cloud, cast his sickle upon the earth ; and behold, the earth, it was reaped. And another Angel came out of the Temple in Heaven ; and he also had a sharp sickle : and another Angel came out of the incense altar, having power over fire. And he cried with a loud voice to him who held the sharp sickle, saying : Thrust in thy sharp sickle, and gather the clusters of the vine of the earth ; for her grapes are fully ripe. And the Angel thrust in his sickle into the earth, and gathered the vine of the earth : and cast it into the great wine-press of God's Justice : and the wine-press was trodden outside the city, and blood came out of the wine-press, even unto the horse-bridles, for the space of sixteen hundred furlongs.

52.

And the Lamb opened the fifth seal, and I saw under the incense altar the souls of those who had been sacrificed for the Word of God, (55) and for the testimony of Him which they bare. And they cried out with a loud voice saying : How long, O Lord, thou Holy and True, dost thou not judge and avenge our blood upon those who dwell over the earth ? And white robes were given to them, and it was said to them, that they should rest yet a little while. And one of the Ancients spake unto me, saying : Who are these clothed in white robes ? and whence also have they come ? and I said to him, My lord, thou knowest. And he said to me : These are they who have come forth out of the depth of great tribulation : and they have washed their robes and made them white in the blood of the Holy Lamb. Therefore are they now before the Throne of God ; and they serve Him day and

ἔτι, οὐδὲ μὴ πέσῃ ἐπ' αὐτοὺς ὁ ἥλιος, οὐδὲ πᾶν καῦμα· Ὅτι
τὸ Ἀρνίον τὸ ἀνὰ μέσον τοῦ θρόνου ποιμανεῖ αὐτοὺς, καὶ
ὁδηγήσει αὐτοὺς ἐπὶ ζωῆς πηγὰς ὑδάτων· καὶ ἐξαλείψει ὁ
Θεὸς αὐτὸς πᾶν δάκρυον ἐκ τῶν ὀφθαλμῶν αὐτῶν.

ΚΕΦ. 53.

ΚΑΙ ἤκουσα φωνῆς μεγάλης ἐκ τοῦ ναοῦ, λεγούσης
τοῖς ἑπτὰ ἀγγέλοις. Ἰδοὺ Κύριος καταφθείρει τὴν οἰκουμένην, καὶ ἐρημώσει αὐτὴν, καὶ ανακαλύψει τὸ πρόσωπον
αὐτῆς, καὶ διασπερεῖ τοὺς ενοικοῦντας ἐν αὐτῇ· καὶ ἔσται ὁ
λαὸς ὡς ὁ ἱερευς, καὶ ὁ παῖς ὡς ὁ κυρίος, καὶ ἡ θεράπαινα ὡς
ἡ κυρία· εσται ὁ ἀγοράζων ὡς ὁ πωλῶν, ὁ δανείζων ὡς ὁ
δανειζόμενος, καὶ ὁ ὀφείλων ὡς ᾧ ὀφείλει. Φθορᾷ φθαρήσεται
ἡ γῆ, καὶ προνομῇ προνομευθήσεται ἡ γῆ, τὸ γὰρ στόμα
Κυρίου ἐλάλησε ταῦτα. Επένθησεν ἡ γῆ καὶ ἐφθάρη ἡ
οἰκουμενη, επένθησαν οἱ ὑψηλοὶ τῆς γης, ἡ δε γῆ ἠνόμησεν διὰ
τοὺς κατοικοῦντας αὐτὴν, διότι παρήλθοσαν τὸν νόμον, καὶ
ἤλλαξαν τα προστάγματα. Ὑπάγετε τοιγαροῦν καὶ ἐκχέατε
τὰς ἑπτα φιάλας τοῦ θυμοῦ τοῦ Θεοῦ εἰς τὴν γῆν.

ΚΕΦ. 54.

ΚΑΙ ἀπῆλθεν ὁ πρῶτος, καὶ ἐξέχεε τὴν φιάλην αὐτοῦ,
ἐπὶ τὴν γῆν· καὶ ἐγένετο ἕλκος κακὸν καὶ πονηρὸν εἰς τοὺς
ανθρώπους τοὺς ἔχοντας τὸ χάραγμα τοῦ θηρίου, καὶ τοὺς
προσκυνοῦντας τῇ εἰκόνι αὐτοῦ. Καὶ ὁ δεύτερος ἄγγελος

night in his Temple; and the Sitter on the Throne shall dwell among them. They shall not hunger or thirst any more; neither shall the sun burn them, nor any heat; for the Lamb who is in the midst of the Throne feeds them; and leads them unto living fountains of waters; and God himself shall wipe away every tear out of their eyes.

53.

And I heard a great Voice out of the Temple, giving a command to the Seven Angels: Behold the Lord lays waste the world, and He will change it into a wilderness; and He will lay bare the face thereof; and He will disperse the dwellers therein; and the people shall be as the priest; and the boy shall be as the master; and the maidservant shall be as the mistress. The buyer also shall be as the seller; and the lender as the borrower, and the debtor as his creditor. The earth shall be utterly laid waste, and the earth shall be utterly made desolate: for the mouth of the Lord hath spoken these things. The land mourns and the earth is ruined: the lofty ones of the land mourn; for the land has sinned by the dwellers thereon; because they transgressed the Law; and have broken the Ordinances. Go ye forth therefore and pour out the Seven Vials of the justice of God upon the earth.

54.

And the first went and poured out his vial on the land; and there fell a sore, evil and dreadful upon those men, who bare the brand of the Wild Beast; and upon all those who did adore his image. And the second Angel poured his vial on the sea; and it became as the blood of a dead

ἐξέχεε τὴν φιάλην αὐτοῦ εἰς τὴν θάλασσαν. καὶ ἐγένετο
αἷμα ὡς νεκροῦ, καὶ πᾶσα ψυχὴ ζωῆς ἀπέθανεν ἐν τῇ
θαλάσσῃ. Καὶ ὁ τρίτος ἄγγελος ἐξέχεε τὴν φιάλην αὐτοῦ εἰς
τοὺς ποταμοὺς καὶ εἰς τὰς πηγὰς τῶν ὑδάτων· καὶ ἐγένετο
αἷμα. Καὶ ἤκουσα τοῦ ἀγγέλου τῶν ὑδάτων λέγοντος·
Δίκαιος εἶ, ὁ ὢν καὶ ὁ ἦν, ὁ ὅσιος, ὅτι ταῦτα ἔκρινας· ὅτι
αἷμα ἁγίων καὶ προφητῶν ἐξέχεαν, καὶ αἷμα αὐτοῖς ἔδωκας
πιεῖν· ἄξιοί εἰσιν· Καὶ ἤκουσα ἄλλου ἐκ τοῦ θυσιαστηρίου
λέγοντος· Ναὶ, Κύριε ὁ Θεὸς ὁ παντοκράτωρ, ἀληθιναὶ καὶ
δίκαιαι αἱ κρίσεις σου. Καὶ ὁ τέταρτος ἄγγελος ἐξέχεεν
τὴν φιάλην αὐτοῦ ἐπὶ τὸν ἥλιον· καὶ ἐδόθη αὐτῷ καυματίσαι
ἐν πυρὶ τοὺς ἀνθρώπους· Καὶ ἐκαυματίσθησαν οἱ ἄνθρωποι
καῦμα μέγα, καὶ ἐβλασφήμησαν οἱ ἄνθρωποι τὸ ὄνομα τοῦ
Θεοῦ τοῦ ἔχοντος ἐξουσίαν ἐπὶ τὰς πληγὰς ταύτας· καὶ οὐ
μετενόησαν δοῦναι αὐτῷ δόξαν. Καὶ ὁ πέμπτος ἄγγελος
ἐξέχεε τὴν φιάλην αὐτοῦ ἐπὶ τὸν θρόνον τοῦ θηρίου· καὶ
ἐγένετο ἡ βασιλεία αὐτοῦ ἐσκοτωμένη· καὶ ἐμασσῶντο τὰς
γλώσσας αὐτῶν ἐκ τοῦ πόνου, καὶ ἐβλασφήμησαν τὸν
Θεὸν τοῦ οὐρανοῦ ἐκ τῶν πόνων αὐτῶν καὶ ἐκ τῶν ἑλκῶν
αὐτῶν· καὶ οὐ μετενόησαν ἐκ τῶν ἔργων αὐτῶν. Καὶ ὁ
ἕκτος ἄγγελος ἐξέχεε αὐτοῦ τὴν φιάλην ἐπὶ τὸν πελαγὸν
τὸν μέγαν Εφρ· καὶ ἐξηράνθη τὸ ὕδωρ αὐτοῦ, ἵνα ἑτοιμασθῇ
ἡ ὁδὸς τῶν βασιλέων τῶν ἀπὸ ἀνατολῶν ἡλίου. Καὶ εἶδον
ἐκ τοῦ στόματος τοῦ δράκοντος, καὶ ἐκ τοῦ στόματος τοῦ
θηρίου καὶ ἐκ τοῦ στόματος τῶν ψευδοπροφήτων αὐτῶν,
πνεύματα ἀκάθαρτα τρία ὡς βάτραχοι· εἰσὶ καὶ πνεύματα
δαιμόνων ποιοῦντα σημεῖα· ἃ ἐκπορεύεται ἐπὶ τοὺς βασιλεῖς
τῆς οἰκουμένης ὅλης, συναγαγεῖν αὐτοὺς εἰς τὸν πόλεμον τῆς
ἡμέρας ἐκείνης τῆς μεγάλης τοῦ Θεοῦ τοῦ παντοκράτορος.
Καὶ συνήγαγεν αὐτοὺς εἰς τὸν τόπον τὸν καλούμενον Ἀρμα-
γεδών. Καὶ ὁ ἕβδομος ἄγγελος ἐξέχεε τὴν φιάλην αὐτοῦ
ἐπὶ τὸν ἀέρα· Καὶ ἐγένοντο ἀστραπαὶ καὶ φωναὶ καὶ βρον-

man; and every living soul died in the sea. And the third Angel poured out his vial upon the rivers and upon the fountains of waters; and they all became blood. And I heard the Angel of the Waters saying: Thou art just, O Holy One, who art and wert, because thou hast judged thus : for they have shed the blood of saints and prophets; and blood thou hast given them to drink; worthy are they thereof. And I heard One say, from the incense altar : Yea, O Lord God, who art the Almighty, just and true are all thy judgments! And the fourth Angel poured out his vial on the sun; and power was given to it to scorch men with fire : and men were scorched with great heat; and these men blasphemed the name of God, who had power over these plagues; yet they repented not, to give him honour. And the fifth Angel poured out his vial upon the throne of the Wild Beast: and his kingdom was wrapped in darkness ; and they gnawed their tongues in agony ; and they blasphemed the God of Heaven, because of their agonies and their grievous sores ; yet did they not repent them of their evil works. And the sixth Angel poured out his vial upon the vast ocean Ephr : and the water thereof was dried up; that the way of the kings of the sunrise might be ready. And I saw out of the mouth of the Dragon, and out of the mouth of the Wild Beast, and out of the mouth of their false priests, three unclean spirits like frogs : and they are the spirits of demons working signs ; which go forth over the rulers of the whole earth ; to bring them together unto the battle of the great day of the Lord Almighty: and He gathered them into the place called Armagedon ! And the seventh Angel poured out his vial on the air, and there were lightnings and voices, and thunders ; and there was

ται, καὶ σεισμὸς ἐγένετο μέγας, οἷος οὐκ ἐγένετο ἀφ' οὗ οἱ ἄνθρωποι ἐγένοντο ἐπὶ τῆς γῆς, τηλικοῦτος σεισμὸς οὕτω μέγας. Καὶ χάλαζα μεγάλη ὡς ταλαντιαία καταβαίνει ἐκ τοῦ οὐρανοῦ ἐπὶ τοὺς ἀνθρώπους· καὶ ἐβλασφήμησαν οἱ ἄνθρωποι τὸν Θεὸν ἐκ τῆς πληγῆς τῆς χαλάζης, ὅτι μεγάλη ἐστὶν ἡ πληγὴ αὐτῆς.

ΚΕΦ. 55.

ΚΑΙ εἶδον ὅτε τὸ Ἀρνίον ἤνοιξε τὴν σφραγῖδα τὴν ἕκτην, καὶ σεισμὸς μέγας ἐγένετο, καὶ ὁ ἥλιος μέλας ἐγένετο ὡς σάκκος τρίχινος, καὶ ἡ σελήνη ὅλη ἐγένετο ὡς αἷμα· Καὶ οἱ ἀστέρες τοῦ οὐρανοῦ ἔπεσαν εἰς τὴν γῆν, ὡς συκῆ βάλλει τοὺς ὀλύνθους αὐτῆς ὑπὸ ἀνέμου μεγάλου σειομένη· Καὶ οἱ βασιλεῖς τῆς γῆς καὶ οἱ μεγιστᾶνες καὶ οἱ χιλίαρχοι καὶ οἱ πλούσιοι καὶ οἱ ἰσχυροί, καὶ πᾶς δοῦλος καὶ πᾶς ἐλεύθερος ἔκρυψαν ἑαυτοὺς εἰς τὰ σπήλαια καὶ εἰς τὰς πέτρας τῶν ὀρέων· Καὶ λέγουσι τοῖς ὄρεσι καὶ ταῖς πέτραις· Πέσετε ἐφ' ἡμᾶς, καὶ κρύψατε ἡμᾶς ἀπὸ προσώπου τοῦ καθημένου ἐπὶ τοῦ θρόνου, καὶ ἀπὸ τῆς ὀργῆς τοῦ Ἀρνίου· Ὅτι ἦλθεν ἡ ἡμέρα ἡ μεγάλη τῆς ὀργῆς αὐτοῦ· καὶ τίς δύναται σταθῆναι;

ΚΕΦ. 56.

ΚΑΙ εἶδον θρόνους, καὶ ἐκάθισαν ἐπ' αὐτούς, καὶ κρίμα ἐδόθη αὐτοῖς καὶ τὰς ψυχὰς τῶν πεπελεκισμένων διὰ τὴν μαρτυρίαν Ἴσσα, καὶ διὰ τὸν Λόγον τοῦ Θεοῦ καὶ οἵτινες οὐ προσεκύνησαν τὸ θηρίον, οὔτε τὴν εἰκόνα αὐτοῦ, καὶ οὐκ ἔλαβον τὸ χάραγμα ἐπὶ τὸ μέτωπον καὶ ἐπὶ τὴν χεῖρα αὐτῶν· καὶ ἔζησαν, καὶ ἐβασίλευσαν μετὰ τοῦ χριστοῦ τὰ χίλια ἔτη· Οἱ δὲ λοιποὶ τῶν νεκρῶν οὐκ ἔζησαν ἄχρι τελεσθῇ τὰ χίλια ἔτη. Αὕτη ἡ ἀνάστασις ἡ πρώτη. Μακάριος καὶ

, a mighty earthquake such as was not seen since men began to live upon the earth; so terrible was that mighty earthquake. And there fell upon men a great hail out of Heaven; each stone weighed a talent: and men blasphemed God because of the plague of the hail, for the plague thereof was exceeding heavy.

55.

And I looked, when the Lamb opened the sixth seal, and the mighty earthquake continued; and the sun became black as hair sackcloth; and the entire moon became as blood : and the stars of heaven fell unto the earth, even as a fig tree casts her untimely fruit, when she is shaken by a mighty wind : and the kings of the earth and the chief princes, and the commanders of thousands, and the rich men, and the valiant men and the slave and the free, hid themselves into dens ; and into the caverns of the mountains. And they said to the mountains and the caverns : Fall ye upon us, and hide us from the face of Him who sitteth upon the Throne, and from the indignation of the Lamb, for the great day of his anger is come ; and who shall be able to stand.

56.

And I saw thrones, and those who sat upon them ; and a judgment was pronounced unto them ; and I saw the souls of these who had been cut with an axe, through the witnessing of Issa, and the Messiah of God : and who had not bent themselves to the wild Beast; nor adored his image, nor taken his mark upon their front, nor into their hand : and they lived and reigned with the Anointed One, a thousand years. But the rest of the dead lived

ἅγιος ὁ ἔχων μέρος ἐν τῇ ἀναστάσει τῇ πρώτῃ· ἐπὶ τούτων ὁ δεύτερος θάνατος οὐκ ἔχει ἐξουσίαν, ἀλλ' ἔσονται ἱερεῖς τοῦ Θεοῦ καὶ τοῦ χριστοῦ, καὶ βασιλεύσουσι μετ' αὐτοῦ χίλια ἔτη· Καὶ ὅταν τελεσθῇ τὰ χίλια ἔτη, λυθήσεται ὁ σατανᾶς ἐκ τῆς φυλακῆς αὐτοῦ· καὶ ἐξελεύσεται πλανῆσαι τὰ ἔθνη τὰ ἐν ταῖς τέσσαρσιν γωνίαις τῆς γῆς, τὸν Γὼγ καὶ τὸν Μαγὼγ, συναγαγεῖν αὐτοὺς εἰς πόλεμον, ὧν ὁ ἀριθμὸς αὐτῶν ὡς ἡ ἄμμος τῆς θαλάσσης. Καὶ ἀνέβησαν ἐπὶ τὸ πλάτος τῆς γῆς, καὶ ἐκύκλωσαν τὴν παρεμβολὴν τῶν ἁγίων, καὶ τὴν πόλιν τὴν ἠγαπημένην· καὶ κατέβη πῦρ ἐκ τοῦ οὐρανοῦ ἀπὸ τοῦ Θεοῦ καὶ κατέφαγεν αὐτούς. Καὶ ὁ διάβολος ὁ πλανῶν αὐτοὺς, ἐβλήθη εἰς τὴν λίμνην τοῦ πυρὸς καὶ θείου, ὅπου καὶ τὸ θηρίον καὶ οἱ ψευδοπροφῆται· καὶ βασανισθήσονται ἡμέρας καὶ νυκτὸς εἰς τοὺς αἰῶνας τῶν αἰώνων.

ΚΕΦ. 57.

ΚΑΙ' ὅτε ἤνοιξε τὸ Ἀρνίον τὴν σφραγῖδα τὴν ἑβδόμην ἐγένετο σιγὴ ἐν τῷ οὐρανῷ ὡς ἡμιώριον· Καὶ ἐξῆλθε φωνὴ μεγάλη ἀπο τοῦ ναοῦ τοῦ οὐρανοῦ, ἀπο τοῦ θρόνου λεγουσα. Γέγονε· Καὶ πᾶσα νῆσος εφυγε, καὶ ὄρη οὐχ εὑρέθησαν· Καὶ ὁ οὐρανὸς ἀπεχωρίσθη ὡς βιβλίον εἱλισσόμενον, καὶ πᾶν ὄρος καὶ νῆσος ἐκ τῶν τόπων αὐτῶν ἐκινήθησαν· Ἐπέβλεψα ἐπὶ τὴν γῆν, καὶ ἰδοὺ οὐθέν, καὶ εἰς τόν οὐρανόν, καὶ οὐκ ἦν τὰ φῶτα αὐτοῦ. εἶδον τὰ ὄρη, καὶ ἦν τρέμοντα, καὶ πάντας τοὺς βουνοὺς ταρασσομένους· Ἐπέβλεψα, καὶ ἰδοὺ οὐκ ἦν ἄνθρωπος, καὶ πάντα τὰ πετεινὰ τοῦ οὐρανοῦ επτοεῖτο.

not again, until the thousand years had been fulfilled; this is the first ascension. Blessed and holy is he who hath a part in the first ascension unto God: over them the second death hath no power; but they shall be priests of God and his Anointed; and shall reign with him a thousand years. And when the thousand years are expired, Satanas shall be loosed out of his prison; and shall go out to deceive the nations, that are in the four quarters of the earth, Gog and Magog; and shall collect them to battle, and their number shall be as the sands of the sea. And they ascended up on the breadth of the earth, and compassed the camp of the holy ones, and the beloved city; and fire came down from heaven from God; in this fire were they consumed. And the Accuser who had deceived them, was cast into the Lake of fire and brimstone, where were the Wild Beast and his false priests; and there shall they be racked day and night, even unto ages of ages.

57.

And when the Lamb opened the seventh seal, there was silence in Heaven for the space of half an hour (56), and a great Voice came out of the Temple of Heaven from the Throne, saying: It is done. And every island fled away; and the mountains were not found: and the heaven departed, as a scroll when it is rolled together; and every mountain and every island was removed out of its own place. I looked upon the earth and it was void; and upon the heaven, and it had no lights; I beheld the mountains, and they were trembling; and all the hills were disturbed and shaken. I looked, and behold, there was no man; and all the birds of the heaven were fled.

ΚΕΦ. 58.

ΚΑΙ᾽ εἶδον θρόνον μέγαν λευκὸν καὶ πλήρης ὁ οὐρανος τῆς δόξης αὐτοῦ· και Σεραφεὶμ εἰστήκεισαν κύκλῳ αὐτοῦ, ἐξ πτέρυγες τῷ ἑνί, καὶ ταῖς μὲν δυσὶν κατεκάλυπτον τὸ πρόσωπον, ταῖς δὲ δυσὶν κατεκάλυπτον τούς πόδας, καὶ ταῖς δυσὶν επεταντο· Καὶ ἐκέκραγεν ἕτερος πρὸς τὸν ἕτερον, καὶ ἔλεγον : ἅγιος, ἅγιος, ἅγιος Κύριος Ζαβαὼθ, πλήρης πᾶσα ἡ γῆ τῆς δόξης αὐτοῦ· Καὶ εἶπον ὦ τάλας ἐγώ, ὅτι κατανένυμαι, ὅτι ἄνθρωπος ων, καὶ ἀκάθαρτα χείλη ἔχων ἐν μέσω λαοῦ ἀκάθαρτα χείλη ἔχοντος ἐγὼ οἰκῶ, καὶ τὸν βασιλέα Κύριον Ζαβαὼθ εἶδον τοῖς ὀφθαλμοῖς μου· καὶ ἀπεστάλη πρός με ἓν τῶν Σεραφεὶμ, καὶ ἐν τῇ χειρὶ εἶχεν ἄνθρακα, ὅν τῇ λαβίδι ἔλαβεν ἀπὸ τοῦ θυσιαστηρίου· καὶ ἥψατο τοῦ στόματος μου, καὶ εἶπεν : ἰδου ἥψατο τοῦτο τῶν χειλέων σου, και ἀφελεῖ τὰς ἀνομίας σου, καὶ τας ἁμαρτίας σου περικαθαριεῖ.

ΚΕΦ. 59.

ΚΑΙ᾽ εἶδον τὸν καθήμενον ἐπὶ θρόνῳ, οὐ ἀπὸ προσώπου ἔφυγεν ἡ γῆ καὶ ὁ οὐρανος, καὶ τόπος οὐχ εὑρέθη αὐτοῖς. Ἐθεωρουν ἕως ὅτου δι θρόνοι ἐτέθησαν, καὶ παλαιὸς ἡμερῶν ἐκάθητο, καὶ τὸ ἔνδυμα αὐτοῦ ὡσει χιὼν λευκὸν, καὶ ἡ θρὶξ τῆς κεφαλῆς αὐτοῦ ὡσει ἔριον καθαρον, ὁ θρόνος αὐτοῦ φλὸξ πυρὸς, οἱ τροχοὶ αὐτοῦ πῦρ φλέγον· ποταμὸς πυρὸς εἷλκεν ἔμπροσθεν αὐτοῦ χίλιαι χιλιάδες ἐλειτούργουν αὐτῷ, καὶ μύριαι μυριάδες περιεστήκεισαν ἀυτῷ· κριτήριον ἐκάθισεν, καὶ βιβλοι ἠνεῴχθησαν· Καὶ εἶδον τοὺς νεκροὺς, τοὺς μικροὺς καὶ τοὺς μεγάλους, ἑστῶτας ἐνώπιον τοῦ θρόνου, καὶ βιβλία ἠνοίχθησαν· καὶ βιβλίον ἄλλο ἠνεῴχθη, ὅ ἐστι τῆς ζωῆς· καὶ ἐκρίθησαν οἱ νεκροὶ ἐκ τῶν γεγραμμένων ἐν τοῖς βιβλίοις, κατὰ τὰ ἔργα αὐτῶν. Καὶ ἔδωκεν ἡ θάλασσα

58.

And I saw a great Throne, white and splendid; and
heaven was filled with the glory of it; above it stood the
Seraphim in a circle; and each one had six wings: with
two they covered the face; with two they covered the
feet; and with two they did fly. And they cried one to
the other: Holy, Holy, Holy is the Lord Zabaoth: the
whole earth is full of his Glory. And I said: Woe is me,
for now I am undone; for I am a man and have unclean
lips; in the midst of a people with unclean lips I dwell;
and I have seen the majesty of the Lord Zabaoth with
mine eyes. And one of the Seraphim came near me, and
in his hand he held a coal of fire, which he had taken
with a pincers from the incense altar; and he touched
my mouth, and touching said: Behold, this has touched
thy lips; and it takes away thine iniquities from thee,
and cleanses all thy faults.

59.

And I saw One sitting upon the Throne, from whose
face had fled the earth and heavens; and there was no
place found for them. I beheld till the thrones were set
in order; and the Ancient of Days did sit; and his robe
was white like snow; and the hair of his head as pure
wool: his throne was a flame of fire; his wheels were
burning fire: a river of fire flowed forth before him;
thousand thousands ministered unto him; and ten thousand times ten thousand stood in his presence: the judgment was set: the Books were opened. And I saw the
dead, small and great, standing full in front of the throne:
and lo! the Books were opened: and one Book was
opened, which is the Book of Life, and the dead were

τοὺς νεκροὺς τοὺς ἐν αὐτῇ, καὶ ὁ θάνατος καὶ ὁ ᾳδης ἔδωκαν τοὺς νεκροὺς τοὺς ἐν αὐτοῖς, καὶ ἐκρίθησαν ἕκαστος κατὰ τὰ ἔργα αὐτῶν· Καὶ ὁ θάνατος καὶ ὁ ἅδης ἐβλήθησαν ἐις τὴν λίμνην τοῦ πυρός· οὗτος ὁ θάνατος ὁ δεύτερος ἐστί, ἡ λίμνη τοῦ πυρος.

ΚΕΦ. 60.

ΚΑΙ᾽ ἐν τῷ καιρῷ ἐκείνω ἀναστήσεται ὁ Μιχαὴλ, ὁ αρχων ὁ μέγας, καὶ ἔσται καιρὸς θλίψεως, θλίψις ὅια οὐ γέγονεν ἀφ᾽ ἧς γεγένηταί ἔθνος ἐν τῇ γῇ, ἕως τοῦ καιροῦ ἐκείνου. Ἐν τῷ καιρῷ ἐκείνω σωθήσεται ὁ λαός πᾶς ὁ γεγραμμένος ἐν τῇ βίβλῳ, καὶ πολλοὶ τῶν καθευδόντων ἐν γῆς χώματι ἐξεγερθήσονται, οὗτοι ἐις ζωήν αἰώνιον, καὶ οὗτοι ἐις ὀνειδισμον καὶ ἐις αἰσχύνην αἰώνιον· καὶ οἱ συνίεντες λάμψουσιν ὡς ἡ λαμπρότης τοῦ στερεώματος, καὶ ἀπὸ τῶν δικαίων τῶν πολλῶν ὡς οἱ ἀστέρες ἐις τοὺς αἰῶνας καὶ ἔτι· Καὶ ἔι τις οὐχ εὑρέθη ἐν τῇ βίβλῳ τῆς ζωῆς γεγραμμένος ἐβλήθη ἐις τὴν λίμνην τοῦ πυρός.

ΚΕΦ. 61.

ΚΑΙ᾽ εἶδον οὐρανόν καινόν καὶ γῆν καινήν· ὁ γὰρ πρῶτος οὐρανὸς καὶ ἡ πρώτη γῆ ἀπῆλθον, καὶ ἡ θάλασσα οὐκ ἔστιν ἔτι. Καὶ τὴν πόλιν τὴν ἁγίαν καινὴν εἶδον καταβαίνουσαν ἐκ τοῦ οὐρανοῦ, ἀπὸ τοῦ Θεοῦ, ἡτοιμασμένην ὡς νύμφην κεκοσμημένην τῷ ἀνδρὶ αὐτῆς. Καὶ ἤκουσα φωνῆς μεγάλης ἐκ τοῦ οὐρανοῦ, λεγούσης· Ἰδοὺ, ἡ σκηνὴ τοῦ Θεοῦ μετὰ τῶν ἀνθρώπων, καὶ σκηνώσει μετ᾽ αὐτῶν, καὶ αὐτοὶ λαὸς αὐτου ἔσονται, καὶ αὐτὸς ὁ Θεὸς μετ᾽ αὐτῶν ἔσται, Θεὸς αὐτῶν· καὶ ἐξαλείψει πᾶν δάκρυον ἀπὸ τῶν ὀφθαλμῶν αὐτῶν, καὶ ὁ θάνατος οὐκ ἔσται ἔτι, οὔτε πένθος οὔτε κραυγὴ

judged by the writings in the Books; according to their own works. And the sea gave up the dead which were in it; and Death and Hades delivered up their dead; and they were each judged according to their works. And Death and Hades were thrown headlong down into the Lake of Fire : this is the second death—the Lake of Fire.

60.

And at that time shall Michael stand up, that prince of might among princes; and it shall be a time of tribulation, such as never was, since there was a nation on the earth up to that time. And at that very time there shall be salvation for all whose names are written in the Book ; and many of those who sleep in the dust of earth shall awake and shall arise again; some to everlasting life, and some to everlasting pain and shame; and the wise shall shine as the brightness of the firmament; and the just as the stars of ages ; and if there be any found, who is not in the Book of Life, the same shall be flung into the Lake of Fire.

61.

And I saw a new heaven and a new earth ; for the first heaven and the first earth were past away ; and there was no longer any sea. And I saw the Holy City, the new City, descending down from the God of Heaven ; ready as a young bride adorned for her husband. And I heard a great Voice from Heaven, saying : Behold the Tabernacle of God is with men : and he shall abide among them : and they shall be his people ; and God himself shall be with them ; and he shall be their God : and God shall wipe away all tears from their eyes ; and there shall be no more death: neither sorrow,

οὔτε πόνος οὐκ ἔσται ἔτι· ὅτι τὰ πρῶτα ἀπῆλθον. Καὶ εἶπεν ὁ καθήμενος ἐπὶ τῷ θρόνῳ· Ἰδοὺ, καινὰ πάντα ποιῶ. Καὶ λέγει μοι· Γράψον· ὅτι. οὗτοι οἱ λόγοι πιστοὶ καὶ ἀληθινοί εἰσι.

ΚΕΦ. 62.

ΚΑΙ' εἶπέ μοι· Γέγοναν· Ἐγώ εἰμι ΑΩ, ἡ Ἀρχὴ καὶ τὸ Τέλος. Ἐγὼ τῷ διψῶντι δώσω αὐτῷ, ἐκ τῆς πηγῆς τοῦ ὕδατος τῆς ζωῆς δωρεάν. Ὁ νικῶν κληρονομήσει ταῦτα, καὶ ἔσομαι αὐτῷ Θεὸς, καὶ αὐτὸς ἔσται μοι ὁ υἱός. Τοῖς δὲ δειλοῖς καὶ ἀπίστοις, καὶ ἐβδελυγμένοις, καὶ φονεῦσι καὶ πόρνοις, καὶ φαρμακοῖς καὶ ἁμαρτωλοῖς καὶ εἰδωλολάτριαις, καὶ πᾶσι τοῖς ψευδέσι, τὸ μέρος αὐτῶν ἐν τῇ λίμνῃ τῇ καιομένῃ πυρὶ καὶ θείῳ, ὅ ἐστιν ὁ θάνατος ὁ δεύτερος.

ΚΕΦ. 63.

- ΚΑΙ' ἰδοὺ μετὰ τῶν νεφελῶν τοῦ οὐρανοῦ, ὡς υἱὸς ἀνθρώπου ἐρχόμενος, καὶ ἕως τοῦ παλαιοῦ τῶν ἡμερῶν ἔφθασεν, καὶ προσήχθη αὐτῷ· καὶ αὐτῷ ἐδόθη ἡ ἀρχὴ καὶ ἡ τιμὴ καὶ ἡ βασιλεια, καὶ παντες οἱ λαοὶ, φυλαὶ καὶ γλωσσαι δουλεύουσιν αὐτῷ· ἡ ἐξουσία αὐτοῦ ἐξουσία αἰώνιος, ἥτις οὐ παρελεύσεται, καὶ ἡ βασιλεία αὐτοῦ οὐ διαφθαρήσεται· Καὶ τὸ σῶμα αὐτοῦ ὡσεὶ θαρσὶς, καὶ τὸ πρόσωπον αὐτοῦ ὡς ἡ ὅρασις ἀστραπῆς, καὶ οἱ ὀφθαλμοὶ αὐτοῦ ὡσεὶ λαμπάδες πυρὸς, καὶ οἱ βραχίονες αὐτοῦ καὶ τὰ σκέλη ὡς ὅρασις χαλκοῦ στίλβοντος, καὶ ἡ φωνὴ τῶν λόγων αὐτοῦ ὡς φωνὴ ὄχλου.

ΚΕΦ. 64.

. ΚΑΙ' φωνῃ μεγαλη εκραξε· Ὁ ἔχων οὖς ἀκουσάτω τί το

nor crying, nor pain any more ; for the former things are passed away. And the Sitter upon the Throne said Behold, I make all things new ; and he said unto me : Write—for these words are true and faithful.

62.

And one said to me : It is done ; I am AO—the beginning and the end (58). I will give to him that is athirst, of the Fountain of the Water of Life freely ; he who overcometh shall inherit all things : I will be his God, and he shall be my son. But the cowardly and faithless and the abominable of soul, and murderers, and the impure and sorcerers, and idol-worshippers and all the false, shall have their part in the Lake that burns with fire and brimstone, which is the second death.

63.

And behold one like the Son of Man came with the clouds of heaven (59) ; and stood before the Ancient of Days ; and they brought him near before him. And to him was given rule and honour and a kingdom ; and all peoples, tribes, and tongues, serve him : his dominion is an everlasting dominion, which shall never pass away ; and his kingdom shall not be destroyed. And his body was like the beryl ; and his face as the appearance of lightning ; and his eyes as lamps of fire ; and his arms and his feet like glittering brass ; and the voice of his words like the voice of a multitude.

64.

· And a great Voice cried out : Let him who hath an

Πνεῦμα λέγει· τῷ νικῶντι δώσω αὐτῷ φαγεῖν ἐκ τοῦ ξύλου τῆς ζωῆς, ὅ ἐστιν ἐν τῷ παραδείσῳ τοῦ Θεοῦ μου· Γίνου πιστὸς ἄχρι θανάτου. Καὶ τῷ νικῶντι δώσω αὐτῷ φαγεῖν ἀπὸ τοῦ μάννα τοῦ κεκρυμένου, καὶ δώσω αὐτῷ ψῆφον λευκὴν, καὶ ἐπὶ τὴν ψῆφον ὄνομα καινὸν γεγραμμένον, ὃ οὐδεὶς ἔγνω εἰ μὴ ὁ λαμβάνων· Καὶ ὁ νικῶν, ποιήσω αὐτὸν στύλον ἐν τῷ ναῷ τοῦ Θεοῦ μου, καὶ ἔξω οὐ μὴ ἐξέλθῃ ἔτι· καὶ γράψω ἐπ᾽ αὐτὸν τὸ ὄνομα τοῦ Θεοῦ μου, καὶ τὸ ὄνομα τῆς πόλεως τοῦ Θεοῦ μου, πόλεως τῆς καινῆς ἡ καταβαίνουσα ἐκ τοῦ οὐρανοῦ ἀπὸ τοῦ Θεοῦ μου, καὶ τὸ ὄνομά μου τὸ καινὸν. Καὶ ὁ νικῶν, οὗτος περιβαλεῖται ἐν ἱματίοις λευκοῖς· καὶ οὐ μὴ ἐξαλείψω τὸ ὄνομα αὐτοῦ ἐκ τῆς βίβλου τῆς ζωῆς, καὶ ὁμολογήσω τὸ ὄνομα αὐτοῦ ἐνώπιον τοῦ Πατρός μου, καὶ ἐνώπιον τῶν ἀγγέλων αὐτοῦ. Καὶ ὁ νικῶν, καὶ ὁ τηρῶν ἄχρι τέλους τὰ ἔργα μου, δώσω αὐτῷ ἐξουσίαν ἐπὶ τῶν ἐθνῶν· Καὶ ποιμανεῖ αὐτοὺς ἐν ῥάβδῳ σιδηρᾷ· ὡς τὰ σκεύη τὰ κεραμικά ὁ πονηρὸς συντρίβεται, ὡς καγὼ εἴληφα παρὰ τοῦ Πατρός μου· Καὶ δώσω αὐτῷ τὸν ἀστέρα τὸν πρωϊνόν. Ἰδοὺ, ἕστηκα ἐπὶ τὴν θύραν, καὶ κρούω· ἐάν τις ἀκούσῃ τῆς φωνῆς μου, καὶ ἀνοίξῃ τὴν θύραν, εἰσελεύσομαι πρὸς αὐτὸν, καὶ δειπνήσω μετ᾽ αὐτοῦ, καὶ αὐτὸς μετ᾽ ἐμοῦ. Καὶ ὁ νικῶν, δώσω αὐτῷ καθίσαι μετ᾽ ἐμοῦ ἐν τῷ θρόνῳ μου, ὡς καγὼ ἐνίκησα, καὶ ἐκάθισα νυν μετὰ τοῦ Πατρός μου ἐν τῷ θρόνῳ αὐτοῦ. Τάδε λέγει ὁ κρατῶν τοὺς ἕπτα ἀστέρας ἐν τῇ δεξιᾷ αὐτοῦ, ὁ περιπατῶν ἐν μέσῳ τῶν ἕπτα λυχνιῶν τῶν χρυσῶν. Ἰδου ἔπεμψα τὸν ἄγγελον μου μαρτυρῆσαι ὑμῖν ταῦτα ἐπὶ ταῖς ἐκκλησίαις. Ἐγὼ εἰμι ἡ ῥίζα καὶ τό γένος τόν Ἰδ, ὁ ἀστὴρ ὁ λαμπρὸς καὶ ὀρθινός· Καὶ τὸ πνεῦμα καὶ ἡ νυμφη λέγουσιν, Ἐλθέ· καὶ ὁ ἀκούων ἐιπατω, Ἐλθὲ· καὶ ὁ διψῶν ἐλθετο, καὶ ὁ θέλων λαμβανέτω τὸ ὕδωρ ζωῆς δωρεάν· ὁ ἔχων οὖς ἀκουσάτω τὶ τὸ Πνεῦμα λέγει ταῖς ἐκκλησίαις· Μακάριοι οἱ ποιοῦντες τας ἐντολὰς αὐτοῦ, ἵνα

ear hear what the Spirit saith. To him who conquers I will give to eat of the beauteous Tree of Life, that stands in the midst of the Paradise of God ; be thou faithful unto death. To him who conquers will I give to eat of the manna that is laid up in secret ; and I will give to him a white stone, and on that stone a new name written, which none shall know but the receiver. And he who conquers I will make of him a pillar in the glorious Temple of my God ; and outside he shall never go ; and I will write upon him the name of my God (60) ; and the name of the City of God, the new City which descends from the heaven, wherein my God dwells : and the new name that is mine. And he who conquers—the same shall be enrobed in white and glittering garments : and I will not blot his name from the Book of Life . and I will confess his name before my Father's face ; and before all his angels. And he who conquers, fulfilling my works unto the end, shall have power over nations : and he shall rule them as a shepherd with an iron sceptre ; as the vessels of a potter shall the wicked be broken ; as I also have received from my Father. And I will give to him the Morning Star. Behold! I have stood at the door and knock ; if any shall hear my voice and open his door, I shall enter in unto him ; and I will feast with him and he with me. And he who conquers—to him will I give to sit down with me on my throne ; as I have conquered and now sit down with my Father upon his Throne. These things saith he, who holds the seven Stars in his right hand ; who walketh in the midst of the seven golden Lamp-bearers. Behold, I have sent mine Angel unto thee, to testify to you these things in the Churches : I am the root and the offspring of Jid : and

ἔσται ἡ ἐξουσια αὐτῶν ἐπὶ τὸ ξύλον τῆς ζωῆς, καὶ τοῖς
πυλῶσιν εἰσέλθωσιν εἰς τὴν πόλιν· Ἔξω δε οἱ κύνες, καὶ οἱ
φαρμακοὶ, καὶ οἱ πόρνοι, καὶ οἱ φονεῖς, καὶ οἱ εἰδωλολατραι,
καὶ πᾶς ὁ φιλῶν καὶ ποιῶν ψεῦδος· Καὶ λέγει μοὶ. Μὴ
σφραγίσῃς τοὺς λόγους τῆς προφητείας τοῦ βιβλίου τούτου·
Ὁ ἀδικῶν ἀδικησάτω ἔτι. καὶ ὁ ῥυπαρὸς ῥυπαρευθήτω ἔτι·
καὶ ὁ δίκαιος δικαιοσύνην ποιησάτω ἔτι· καὶ ὁ ἅγιος
ἁγιασθήτω ἔτι· Ἰδου ἔρχομαι ταχὺ, καὶ ὁ μισθός μου μετ'
ἐμοῦ ἀποδοῦναι ἑκάστῳ ὡς τὸ ἔργον αὐτοῦ ἔσται· Εγώ εἰμι
ΑΩ. Αρχὴ καὶ Τέλος, ὁ πρῶτος καὶ ὁ ἔσχατος.

ΚΕΦ. 65.

ΚΑΙ ἦλθεν εἷς ἐκ τῶν ἑπτὰ ἀγγέλων τῶν ἐχόντων τὰς
ἑπτὰ φιάλας τὰς γεμούσας τῶν ἑπτὰ πληγῶν τῶν ἐσχάτων,
καὶ ἐλάλησε μετ' ἐμοῦ, λέγων· Δεῦρο, δείξω σοι τὴν νύμφην
τοῦ Ἀρνίου τὴν γυναῖκα· καὶ ἀπήνεγκέ με ἐν πνεύματι ἐπ'
ὄρος μέγα καὶ ὑψηλὸν, καὶ ἔδειξέ μοι τὴν πόλιν τὴν ἁγίαν
καταβαίνουσαν ἐκ τοῦ οὐρανοῦ ἀπὸ τοῦ Θεοῦ, ἔχουσαν τὴν
δόξαν τοῦ Θεοῦ· ὁ φωστὴρ αὐτῆς ὅμοιος λίθῳ τιμιωτάτῳ,
ὡς λίθῳ ἰάσπιδι κρυσταλλίζοντι· ἔχουσα τεῖχος μέγα καὶ
ὑψηλὸν, ἔχουσα πυλῶνας δώδεκα, καὶ ἐπὶ τοῖς πυλῶσιν
ἀγγέλους δώδεκα, καὶ ὀνόματα ἐπιγεγραμμένα, ἅ ἐστι τῶν
δώδεκα υἵων τοῦ Θεοῦ· Ἀπὸ ἀνατολῶν, πυλῶνες τρεῖς· καὶ
ἀπὸ βορρᾶ, πυλῶνες τρεῖς· καὶ ἀπὸ νότου, πυλῶνες τρεῖς·

the bright and Morning Star. And the Spirit and the bride say : Come ! and let him who heareth say : Come ! and let him who is athirst come ; and whosoever will shall have the Water of Life. He that hath ears let him hear what the Spirit saith unto the Churches. Blessed are they who do his commands ; that they may have a right to the Tree of Life ; and may enter in through the gates into the City : for outside are dogs and sorcerers and the impure ; and idol worshippers and murderers ; and all who love and make a lie. And he said unto me · Thou mayest not seal the words of the prophecy of this Book. He that is unjust let him be unjust still : and he that is defiled let him be defiled still ; and he that is righteous let him work righteousness still ; and he that is holy let him be holy still. Behold, I come soon : and my reward is with me ; to give to every man according as his work shall be. I am AO. the Beginning and the Ending, the First and the Last.

65.

And there came unto me one of the Seven Angels, who held the seven golden vials, filled with the seven last plagues. And he spake with me, saying : Come hither ; and I will shew thee the Bride, the spouse of the Lamb ; and he raised me in the spirit to a Mountain, great and lofty, and shewed me the Holy City, descending down from the Heaven of God ; gloriously beautiful with the splendour of God. And her light was like the most precious jewel ; like a diamond stone, flashing brightness ; and it had a wall vast and lofty ; and it had twelve gates ; and at the gates the Twelve Messengers ; and their names were written on the gates ; the names of

καὶ ἀπὸ δυσμῶν, πυλῶνες τρεῖς. Καὶ τὸ τεῖχος τῆς πόλεως ἔχον θεμελίους δώδεκα, καὶ ἐπ᾽ αὐτῶν δώδεκα ὀνόματα τῶν δώδεκα ἀποστόλων τοῦ Ἀρνίου. Καὶ εἰσήγαγεν με ἐκεῖ, καὶ ἰδοὺ ἀνὴρ, καὶ ἡ ὅρασις αὐτοῦ ἦν ὡσεὶ ὅρασις χαλκοῦ στίλβοντος, κι ἐν τῇ χειρὶ αὐτοῦ ἦν σπαρτίον οἰκοδόμων καὶ κάλαμος μέτρον, καὶ αὐτὸς εἰστήκει ἐπί τῆς πύλης Καὶ εἶπεν πρός με ὁ ἀνήρ· ὁ ἑώρακας υἱέ ἀνθρώπου ἐν τοῖς ὀφθαλμοῖς σου ἴδε, καὶ ἐν τοῖς ὠσὶν σου ἄκουε, καὶ τάξον εἰς τὴν καρδίαν σου πάντα ὅσα ἐγὼ δεικνύω σοι, διότι ἕνεκα τοῦ δεῖξαι σοι εἰσελήλυθας ὧδε, καὶ δείξεις πάντα ὅσα σὺ ὁρᾳς τῷ οἴκῳ τῆς Ἴσσα.

ΚΕΦ. 66.

ΚΑΙ᾽ ἰδοὺ περίβολος ἔξωθεν τῆς πολεως· Καὶ ὁ λαλῶν μετ᾽ ἐμοῦ εἶχε κάλαμον χρυσοῦν, ἵνα μετρήσῃ τὴν πόλιν, καὶ τοὺς πυλῶνας αὐτῆς, καὶ τὸ τεῖχος αὐτῆς. Καὶ ἡ πόλις τετράγωνος κεῖται, καὶ τὸ μῆκος αὐτῆς, ὅσον καὶ τὸ πλάτος. Καὶ ἐμέτρησε τὴν πόλιν τῷ καλάμῳ· ἐπὶ σταδίους δώδεκα χιλιάδων· τὸ μῆκος καὶ τὸ πλάτος καὶ τὸ ὕψος αὐτῆς ἴσα ἐστί. Καὶ ἐμέτρησε τὸ τεῖχος αὐτῆς ἑκατὸν τεσσαράκοντα τεσσάρων πηχῶν, μέτρον ἀνθρώπου, ὅ ἐστιν ἀγγέλου. Καὶ ἦν ἡ ἐνδόμησις τοῦ τείχους αὐτῆς, ἴασπις· καὶ ἡ πόλις χρυσίον καθαρὸν ὁμοία ὑάλῳ καθαρῷ, καὶ οἱ θεμέλιοι τοῦ τείχους τῆς πόλεως παντὶ λίθῳ τιμίῳ κεκοσμημένοι· ὁ θεμέλιος ὁ πρῶτος, ἴασπις· ὁ δεύτερος, σάπφειρος· ὁ τρίτος, χαλκηδών· ὁ τέταρτος, σμάραγδος· ὁ πέμπτος, σαρδόνυξ· ὁ ἕκτος, σάρδιος· ὁ ἕβδομος, χρυσόλιθος· ὁ ὄγδοος, βήρυλλος· ὁ ἔννατος, τοπάζιον· ὁ δέκατος, χρυσόπρασος· ὁ ἑνδέκατος, ὑάκινθος· ὁ δωδέκατος, ἀμέθυστος.

the Twelve Sons of God. On the East, three gates; on the North, three gates; on the South, three gates; on the West, three gates. And the wall of the City had twelve foundations; and in them the names of the Twelve Apostles of the Lamb. And he brought me thither, and behold a Man; and his likeness was the likeness of glittering brass. And in his hand he held a builder's line, and a measuring rod, and he stood at the gate. And the Man said to me, Son of man! what thou hast seen with thine eyes, behold: and what thou hast heard with thine ears, hear; and grave upon thine heart all these things, which I shall now shew thee; for unto this end hast thou come hither, and that thou shouldst also shew all that thou beholdest to the House of Issa.

66.

And lo, an enclosure outside the City. And he who spake had a golden reed, that he might measure the City, and the gates and walls. And the City lieth foursquare; and the length is as large as the breadth; and he measured the City with the reed, for twelve stadia of chiliads; the length and the breadth and the height are equal. And he measured the wall thereof; one hundred and forty and four cubits; the measure of the Man, who was an Angel. And the building of the wall of it was diamond; and the City was pure gold, like bright glass; and the foundation stones of the wall of the City were adorned with all precious jewellery. The first foundation was diamond; the second, sapphire; the third, chalcedony; the fourth, an emerald; the fifth, sardonyx; the sixth, fiery sard; the seventh, chrysolite; the eighth, beryl; the ninth, topaz; the tenth, chrysophrasus; the eleventh,

Καὶ οἱ δώδεκα πυλῶνες, δώδεκα μαργαρίται· ἀνὰ εἷς ἕκαστος τῶν πυλώνων ἦν ἐξ ἑνὸς μαργαρίτου, καὶ ἡ πλατεῖα τῆς πόλεως, χρυσίον καθαρὸν ὡς ὕαλος διαυγής. Καὶ ναὸν οὐκ εἶδον ἐν αὐτῇ· ὁ γὰρ Κύριος ὁ Θεὸς ὁ παντοκράτωρ ναὸς αὐτῆς ἐστιν· Καὶ ἡ πόλις οὐ χρείαν ἔχει τοῦ ἡλίου οὐδὲ τῆς σελήνης, ἵνα φαίνωσιν ἐν αὐτῇ· ἡ γὰρ δόξα τοῦ Θεοῦ ἐφώτισεν αὐτήν, καὶ ὁ λύχνος αὐτῆς τὸ Ἀρνίον. Καὶ περιπατήσουσι τά ἔθνη διὰ τοῦ φωτὸς αὐτῆς. Καὶ οἱ βασιλεῖς τῆς γῆς φέρουσιν τὴν δόξαν καὶ τὴν τιμὴν αὐτῶν εἰς αὐτήν, καὶ οἱ πυλῶνες αὐτῆς οὐ μὴ κλεισθῶσιν ἡμέρας· νὺξ γὰρ οὐκ ἔσται ἐκεῖ. Καὶ οἴσουσι τὴν δόξαν καὶ τὴν τιμὴν πάντων τῶν ἐθνῶν εἰς αὐτήν, ἵνα εἰσέλθωσιν· Καὶ οὐ μὴ εἰσέλθῃ εἰς αὐτὴν πᾶν κοινὸν, καὶ ποιοῦν βδέλυγμα καὶ ψεῦδος· εἰ μὴ οἱ γεγραμμένοι ἐν τῷ βιβλίῳ τῆς ζωῆς.

ΚΕΦ. 67.

ΚΑΙ' ἔδειξέ μοι ποταμὸν ὕδατος ζωῆς, λαμπρὸν ὡς κρύσταλλον, ἐκπορευόμενον ἐκ τοῦ θρόνου τοῦ Θεοῦ· Ἐν μέσῳ τῆς πλατείας αὐτῆς καὶ τοῦ ποταμοῦ ἐντεῦθεν καὶ ἐν- τεῦθεν ξύλον ζωῆς, ποιοῦν καρποὺς δώδεκα, κατὰ μῆνα ἕκαστον ἀποδιδοῦν τὸν καρπόν αὐτοῦ· καὶ τὰ φύλλα τοῦ ξύλου εἰς θεραπείαν τῶν ἐθνῶν, καὶ πᾶν κατάθεμα οὐκ ἔσται ἔτι· καὶ ὁ θρόνος τοῦ Θεοῦ καὶ τοῦ Ἀρνίου ἐν αὐτῇ ἔσται, καὶ οἱ δοῦλοι αὐτοῦ λατρεύσουσιν αὐτῷ· Καὶ ὄψονται τὸ πρόσωπον αὐτοῦ, καὶ τὸ ὄνομα αὐτοῦ ἐπὶ τῶν μετώπων αὐτῶν. Καὶ νὺξ οὐκ ἔσται· καὶ οὐ χρεία λύχνου καὶ φωτὸς ἡλίου, ὅτι Κύριος ὁ Θεὸς φωτιεῖ ἐπ' αὐτούς· καὶ βασιλεύσουσιν εἰς τοὺς αἰῶνας τῶν αἰώνων. Καὶ εἶπέ μοι· Οὗτοι οἱ λόγοι πιστοὶ καὶ ἀληθινοί· καὶ Κύριος ὁ Θεὸς τῶν πνευμάτων τῶν προφητῶν ἀπέστειλεν τὸν ἄγγελον αὐτοῦ δεῖξαι τοῖς δούλοις αυτοῦ ἅ δεῖ γενεσθαι.

jacinth ; the twelfth, amethyst. And the Twelve Gates were twelve pearls; each one of the Gates was but one pearl ; and the street of the City pure gold like transparent glass. And I saw no Temple in it; for the Lord God, the Almighty, He is its Temple. And the City hath no need of the sun, nor of the moon that they should shine in it ; for the Glory of God enlightens it ; and the Lamp thereof is the Lamb. And the nations shall walk in the light of it. And the kings of the earth bring their glory and honour into it ; and the gates thereof are not closed by day ; for there is no night there. And they shall bring the glory and honour of all nations into it, so that they may enter : and there shall not enter it aught that is defiled, or practising abomination or falsehood ; but they only who are written in the Book of Life.

67.

And he showed me a River of Water of Life, bright as crystal, flowing out of the Throne of God : and in the midst of the street of the City, and on either side of the River was the Tree of Life, which bare Twelve blooming fruits ; and yielded her fruit every moon. And the leaves of the Trees were for the healing of nations ; and there shall be no more affliction ; but the Throne of God and the Lamb shall be in it ; and his servants shall serve Him. And they shall behold his face : and his name shall be upon their foreheads. And there shall be no night there ; and they need no lamp or sunshine, for the Lord God shines upon them ; and they shall be kings to ages of ages. And he said to me : These words are faithful and true, and the Lord God of the Spirits of the Prophets hath sent his Messenger to show unto his servants things which shall come to pass.

ΚΕΦ. 68.

ΚΑΓ εξηραν τα Χερουβειν τάς πτέρυγας αὐτῶν, καὶ οἱ τροχοὶ ἐχόμενοι αὐτῶν, καὶ ἡ δοξα Θεου ἐπ' αὐτὰ ὑπεράνω αὐτῶν· καὶ ἀνέβη ἡ δοξα Κυριόυ ἐκ μέσης τῆς πόλεως, καὶ ἔστη ἐπὶ τοῦ ὄρου ὁ ἦν ἀπέναντι τῆς πόλεως.

ΚΕΦ. 69.

ΚΑΓ εἰσήγαγέν με ἐπὶ τὰ πρόθυρα τῆς πολεῶς, καὶ ἰδοὺ ὕδωρ ἐξεπορεύετο ὑποκάτωθεν τοῦ αἰθερος κατ' ἀνατολὰς ὑτι τὸ πρόσωπον τῆς πολεως ἔβλεπεν κατ' ἀνατολὰς, καὶ τὸ ὕδωρ κατέβαινεν ἀπὸ τοῦ κλίτους τοῦ δεξιου ἀπὸ νότου ἐπὶ τὸ θυσιαστήριον χρυσοῦν· Καὶ ἐξήγαγεν με κατὰ τὴν ὁδὸν τῆς πύλης τῆς πρὸς βορρᾶν, καὶ περιήγαγέν με τὴν ὁδὸν πρὸς τὴν πύλην τῆς αὐλῆς τῆς βλεπούσης κατ' ἀνατολάς καὶ ἰδοὺ τὸ ὕδωρ κατεφέρετο ἀπὸ τοῦ κλίτους τοῦ δεξιοῦ· Καὶ μέτρον ἐν τῇ χειρι αὐτοῦ, καὶ διεμέτρησεν χειλίους ἐν τῷ μέτρω, καὶ διῆλθεν ἐν τῷ ὕδατι, ὕδωρ αφεσεως· καὶ διεμέτρησεν χιλίους, καὶ διῆλθεν ἐν τῷ ὕδατι, ὕδωρ ἕως τῶν μηρῶν· καὶ διεμέτρησεν χιλίους, καὶ διῆλθεν ὕδωρ ἑώς ὀσφύος· Καὶ διεμέτρησεν χιλίους, καὶ ὀυκ ἠδύνατο διελθεῖν, ὅτι ἐξύβριζεν ὡς χειμάρρου ὂν ὀυ διαβήσονται· καὶ εἶπεν πρός με, ἑώρακας υἱὲ ἀνθρώπου; καὶ ἤγαγεν με ἐπὶ το χεῖλος τοῦ ποταμοῦ ἐν τῇ ἐπιστροφῇ μου· Καὶ ἰδοὺ ἐπὶ τοῦ χείλοις τοῦ ποταμοῦ δένδρα πολλά σφόδρα ἔνθεν καὶ ἔνθεν· καὶ εἶπεν πρός με· τὸ ὕδωρ τουτο ἐστι ἀμβροτον, ὕδωρ τῆς ζωῆς· καὶ ἔσται πᾶσα ψυχὴ τῶν ζωῶν τῶν ἐκζεόντων ἐπὶ πάντα ἐφ' ἃ ἂν ἐπέλθῃ ἐκεῖ ὁ ποταμὸς ζήσεται· Καὶ ἐν τῇ διεκηβολῇ αὐτοῦ, καὶ ἐν τῃ ἐπίστροφῃ αὐτοῦ, καὶ ἐν τῃ ὑπεράρσει αὐτοῦ, ὂν μὴ ὑγιάσωσιν· καὶ πᾶν ξύλον ἀμβροσιον ὂν μὴ παλαιωθῇ ἐπ' αὐτοῦ, ὀυδέ μὴ ἐκλίπῃ ὁ καρπὸς αὐτοῦ, τῆς καινότητος αὐτου πρωτοβολήσει εἰς αιωνας των αιωνιων,

68.

Then did the Cherubim lift up their wings, and the wheels that were attached to them: and the Glory of God was over them above; and the Glory of the Lord rose from amid the City, and rested on the mountain which is opposite to the City.

69.

And he brought me to the entrances of the City, and behold Water flowed down from the æther above, towards the East, which the front of the City faced. And the Water descended from the right side, from the South unto the golden incense altar. Then he brought me out of the way of the Gate which lieth towards the North; and he led me round by the way to the gate of the court that looketh towards the East; and behold, Waters ran down also from the right side. And he had a measure in his hand, and with it he measured the banks; and he went into the Water—Water of Liberation, and he measured a thousand; and passed into the Water, until the Water reached to his thighs; and he measured a thousand; and passed through Water to the loins; and he measured a thousand; and could not pass, for it rose as a torrent which could not be crossed. And he said to me, Son of Man, hast thou seen this? And he brought me to the river bank as I returned; and behold upon the bank of the River were Trees, very numerous on this side and on that. And he said to me : This Water is Ambrosial Water, Water of Life; and it shall be that every soul of the living upon whom this Water cometh shall exist. But in the outlet of the Water and its turning, and in its overflowing they shall not have help. And every

ὅτι τὰ ὕδατα αὐτῶν ἐκ τῶν ἁγιων ταῦτα ἐκπορεύεται, καὶ
ἔσται ὁ καρπὸς αὐτῶν εἰς βρῶσιν, καὶ ἀνάβασις αὐτῶν εἰς
ὑγίειαν· Καὶ ἰδου δύο ἕτεροι εἰστήκεισαν, εἷς ἐντεῦθεν τοῦ
χείλεος τοῦ ποταμοῦ, καὶ εἷς ἐντεῦθεν τοῦ χείλεος τοῦ
ποταμοῦ· καὶ εἶπεν τῷ ὅς ἦν ἐπάνω τοῦ ὕδατος τοῦ ποταμοῦ
ἕως πότε τὸ πέρας, ὧν εἴρηκας τῶν θαυμασίων; καὶ ἤκουσα
τοῦ ἀνδρὸς ὅς ἦν ἐπάνω τοῦ ὕδατος τοῦ ποταμοῦ· καὶ ὕψωσεν
τήν δεξιὰν αὐτοῦ καὶ τὴν ἀριστεράν αὐτοῦ εἰς τὸν οὐρανὸν,
καὶ ὅμωσεν ἐν τῷ ζῶντι τὸν αἰῶνα, ὅτι εἰς καιρὸν καιρῶν, καὶ
ἥμισυ καιροῦ, γνώσονται πάντα ταῦτα.

ΚΕΦ. 70.

ΚΑΙ ἐγὼ Ωάννης ὁ βλέπων ταῦτα καὶ ἀκουων· καὶ ὅτε
ἤκουσα καὶ ἔβλεψα, ἔπεσον προσκυνῆσαι ἔμπροσθεν τῶν
ποδῶν του ἀγγέλου του δεικνύοντός μοι ταῦτα. Καὶ λέγει
μοι· Ὅρα μή· σύνδουλός σου γάρ εἰμι, καὶ τῶν ἀδελφῶν σου
τῶν προφητῶν, καὶ τῶν τηρουντων τους λόγους του βιβλιου
τουτου· τῷ Θεῷ μόνῳ προσκυνησον.

ambrosial tree shall bloom without old age ; neither shall its fruit ever fail ; its freshness shall put forth into ages of ages ; for these their waters, flow out of the Holy ; and their fruit shall be for food ; and their spreading for an enjoyment. And behold ! there stood two others, the one on this side of the bank of the River ; the other on that side of the bank of the River. And one said to the Man above the waters of the River : How long to the end of these wonders ? And I heard the Man above the waters of the River, when he held up his right hand, and his left also unto Heaven : and sware by him who liveth for ever, that it shall be a time and times and half a time, when all these things shall be accomplished.

70.

And I, Oannes, saw and heard these things ; and when I heard and saw them I fell on my face ; before the feet of the Angel who shewed them, and he said to me : Do it not, for I am thy fellow servant ; and the servant of thy brothers, the Prophets : those who do the words of this Book. WORSHIP ONLY GOD.

ΑΙ ΕΠΤΑ ΒΡΟΝΤΑΙ.

1.

ΟΥΑΙ` οναὶ πλῆθος ἐθιῶν πολλῶν· ὡς θάλασσα κυμαίνουσα, οὕτω ταραχθήσεσθε, καὶ νῶτος ἐθνῶν πολλῶν, ὡς ὕδωρ ἠχήσει· Ὡς ὕδωρ πολὺ ἔθνη πολλὰ, ὡς ὕδατος πολλοῦ βίᾳ φερομενοῦ· καὶ ἀποσκορακιεῖ ἀυτα, καὶ πόῤῥω ἀυτα διώξεται, ὡς χνοῦν ἀχυρου λικμώντων ἀπέναντι ἀνέμου, καὶ ὥς κονιορτὸν τροχου καταιγὶς φέρουσαν· Πρὸς ἑσπέραν καὶ ἔσται πένθος, πρινὴ πρῶι, καὶ οὐκ ἔσται ἔτι· Φοβος καὶ βόθυνος καὶ παγὶς ἐφ᾽ ὑμᾶς τους ἐνοικοῦντας ἐπὶ τῆς γῆς· καὶ ἔσται ὁ φεύγων τόν φόβον ἐμπεσεῖται εἰς τὸν βόθυνον, καὶ ὁ ἐκβαινων ἐκ τοῦ βοθύνου ἁλώσεται ὑπὸ τῆς παγίδος· ὅτι θυρίδες ἐκ τοῦ οὐρανου ανεώχθησαν, καὶ σεισθήσεται τὰ θεμέλια τῆς γῆς· Ταραχῇ ταραχθήσεται ἡ γῆ, καὶ ἀπορίᾳ ἀπορηθήσεται ἡ γῆ· ἔκλεινεν ὡς ὁ μεθύων καὶ κραιπαλῶν, καὶ σεισθήσεται ὡς ὀπωροφυλάκιον ἡ γῆ, κατισχυσεν γὰρ ἐπ᾽ ἀυτῆς ἡ ἀνομία, καὶ πεσεῖται, καὶ οὐ μὴ δύνηται ἀναστῆναι· καὶ ἐπάξει ὁ Θεος ἐπὶ τον κόσμον τοῦ ὀυρανοῦ τὴν χεῖρα, καὶ ἐπὶ τοὺς βασιλεῖς τῆς γῆς· Ὁ δε ποταμος εκλειψει, καὶ ξηρανθησεται, καὶ ἐκλείψουσιν οἱ ποταμοί, καὶ αἱ διώρυχες τοῦ ποταμοῦ, καὶ ξηρανθήσεται πᾶσα συναγωγὴ ὕδατος, καὶ ἐν παντὶ ἕλει καλάμου καὶ παπύρου· καὶ τὸ ἄχι τὸ χλωρὸν πᾶν τὸ κύκλῳ τοῦ ποταμοῦ, καὶ πᾶν τὸ σπειρόμενον διὰ τοῦ ποταμοῦ ξηρανθήσεται ἀνεμόφθορον. Καὶ στενάξουσιν οἱ ἁλιεῖς, καὶ στενάξουσι πάντες οἱ βάλλοντες ἄγκιστρον εἰς τὸν ποταμὸν, καὶ οἱ βάλλοντες σαγήνας, καὶ οἱ ἀμφιβολεῖς πενθήσουσι· Ἰδοὺ ἡμέρα Κυρίου ἔρχεται, ἀνείατος θυμοῦ καὶ ὀργῆς, θεῖναι τὴν ὀικουμένην ἔρημον, καὶ τοὺς ἁμαρτωλοὺς ἀπολέσαι ἐξ ἀυτῆς. Οἱ γάρ ἀστέρες τοῦ ὀυρανοῖ, καὶ Ὠρείων, καὶ πᾶς ὁ κόσμος τοῦ ὀυρανοῦ, τὸ φῶς ὀυ δώσουσιν· καὶ σκοτισθήσεται τοῦ ἡλίου ἀνατέλλοντος, καὶ ἡ σελήνη ὀυ δώσει τὸ φῶς ἀυτῆς·

THE SEVEN THUNDERS. (61)

1. The Destruction of Atlantis.—Woe! woe! to the multitude of many people; as the rolling waves of the sea, even so shall they be in confusion, and the back of many peoples shall make a tumult like the ocean. As the great billows are many nations; as of a body of waters borne on with violence: but He shall rebuke them, and shall put them to flight afar off, as the dust of chaff when men winnow before the wind, and as a storm whirling the dust of the wheel. In the evening time, and there was sorrow; and early in the morning, behold it was not any more. Fear and the pit, and the snare are upon ye, O inhabitants of the land; and it shall come to pass that he who flees from the fear, shall fall into the pit; and he that shall rid himself out of the pit, shall be taken in the snare; for the windows of the heaven are opened, and the foundations of the earth shall be shaken. With desolation shall the earth be desolated, with breaking shall the earth be broken. As a drunken man, and giddy with strong drink it staggereth: the earth shall be shaken as the hut of a harvest watcher; for its lawlessness shall be heavy upon it, and it shall sink, and it shall not be able to rise again. And God shall lay his hand upon the order of the heaven, and upon the rulers of the earth. And the river shall be wasted and dry; and the rivers and their canals shall fail: and every reservoir of water shall be dried up: in every marsh also of reed and papyrus. And all the green herbage round about the river and every thing sown by the side of the river shall be blasted with the wind and dried up. The fishers also shall mourn and all that cast a hook into the river shall lament; and they that spread nets

Καὶ ἔσονται οἱ καταλελειμμένοι ἔντειμοι μᾶλλον ἤ τὸ χρυσίον τὸ ἄπυρον· καὶ ἄνθρωπος μᾶλλον ἔντιμος ἔσται ἤ ὁ λίθος ὁ ἐν Σουφειρ· Ὁ γάρ οὐρανὸς θυμωθήσεται, καὶ ἡ γῆ σεισθήσεται ἐκ τῶν θεμελίων ἀυτῆς· καὶ ἔσονται οἱ κατα- λελειμένοι ὡς δορκάδιον φεῦγον, καὶ ὡς πρόβατον πλανώμενον, καὶ ὀυκ ἔσται ὁ συνάγων, ὥστε ἄνθρωπον ἐις τόν λαὸν ἀυτοῦ ἀποστραφῆναι, καὶ ἄνθρωπος ἐις τὴν χώραν ἑαυτοῦ διώξεται· Ὁυ κατοικηθήσεται ἐις τον αἰῶνα χρόνον, ὀυδὲ μὴ ἐισελθωσιν ἐις ἀυτὴν διὰ πολλῶν γενεῶν, ὀυδὲ μὴ διέλθωσιν ἀυτὴν Ἄραβες, ὀυδὲ ποιμένες ὀυ μὴ ἀναπαυσονται ἐν ἀυτῇ. Καὶ ἀναπαύσονται ἐκεῖ θηρία, καί ἐμπλήσθήσονται ἀῖ ὀικιαι ἠχου, καὶ ἀναπαύσονται ἐκεῖ σειρῆνες, καὶ δαιμόνια ἐκεῖ ὀρχήσονται, καὶ ὀνοκένταυροι ἐκεῖ κατοικήσουσι, καὶ νοσσοποιήσουσιν ἐχῖνοι ἐν τοῖς ὀίκοις ἀυτῶν· ταχὺ ἔρχεται καὶ ὀυ χρονιεῖ.

2.

ΠΡΟΣΑΓΑΓΕΤΕ ἔθνη, καὶ ἀκούσατε ἄρχοντες· ἀκουσατω ἡ γῆ, καὶ ὀι ἐν ἀυτῇ, ἡ ὀικουμενή, καὶ ὁ λαὸς ὁ ἐν ἀυτῇ. Διότι θυμὸς Κυρίου ἐπὶ πάντα τὰ ἔθνη, καὶ ὀργὴ ἐπὶ τον ἀριθμὸν ἀυτων, του ἀπολέσαι αυτους, καὶ παραδουναι ἀυτους ἐις σφαγὴν. Ὁι δε τραυματίαι ἀυτων ῥιφήσονται, καὶ ὀι νεκροι, καὶ ἀναβήσεται ἀυτων ἡ ὀσμὴ, καὶ βραχήσεται τὰ ὄρη ἀπο του ἅιματος ἀυτων. Καὶ τακήσονται πᾶσαι ἀι

and snares upon the waters shall languish away. Behold the day of the Lord shall come ; a cruel day and full of wrath and fury, to lay the earth desolate ; and to destroy the sinners thereof even from its face. For the stars of heaven, and Orion, and all the brightness of heaven shall not give their light ; the sun shall be darkened in his rising, and the moon shall not shine with her lustre. And they who are left shall be more precious than fine gold ; yea, a man shall be more in honour even than the stone wedge of Syphir. For the heavens shall be filled with fury, and the earth shall be shaken out of her place, and they who shall have escaped, shall be as a chased roe, and as a sheep that wandereth away : and there shall be none to gather them together. Every man shall turn to his own people : and every one shall flee to his own land. It shall no more be inhabited for ever, neither shall it be dwelt in from generation to generation : neither shall the Arab pass through it, nor shall shepherds rest there. But wild creatures shall abide there, and the houses shall be filled with howling, and sirens shall cry there, and devils shall dance there. And monstrous creatures shall live therein ; and sea-urchins shall make their nests in their desolate houses ; and the time is near, and shall not be deferred.

2. The Judgment on evil doers.—Come near, ye nations, and ye O princes, hear : let the earth hear, and all that are therein ; the whole world and the people that be in it ; for the justice of the Lord is upon every nation, and his wrath is upon their multitudes, to destroy them, and to give them over to the sword. Their wounded shall be cast forth, and their slain ones ; and there shall arise out of them a stink ; and the mountains shall be

δυνάμεις των ουρανών, και ελιγήσεται ο ουρανος ως βιβλίον, και πάντα τα άστρα πεσεῖται ως φύλλα εξ αμπέλου, και ως πίπτει φύλλα απο συκῆς. Ἐμεθύσθη ἡ μάχαιρά μου ἐν τῷ ουρανῷ· ἰδου καταβήσεται ἐπι τον λαον τῆς ἀπωλείας μετα κρίσεως. Ἡ μαχαιρα του Κυρίου ἐνεπλήσθη αἵματος, επαχύνθη απο στέατος, απο αἵματος τράγων και ἀμνῶν, και απο στεατος τράγων και κριῶν. Ἡμέρα γαρ κρίσεως Κυρίου, και ἐνιαυτος ἀνταποδόσεως κρισεως Σιὼν. Και στραφῆσονται αἱ φάραγγες ἀυτῆς εἰς πίσσαν, και ἡ γῆ ἀυτῆς εἰς θεῖον. και ἔσται ἡ γῆ ἀυτῆς ὡς πίσσα καιομένη, νυκτος και ἡμέρας, και ου σβεσθήσεται εἰς τον αἰῶνα χρόνον, και αναβησεται ὁ καπνος ἀυτῆς ἄνω· εἰς γενεὰς αυτῆς ἐρημωθήσεται, και εἰς χρονον πολὺν· Ὄρνεα και ἐχῖνοι, και ἵβεις και κόρακες κατοικησουσιν ἐν ἀυτῇ. και επιβληθησεται ἐπ᾽ ἀυτην σπαρτιον γεωμετριας ερημου, και ονοκενταυροι οἰκησουσιν ἐν αυτῇ. Ὅι ἀρχοντες ἀυτης ουκ ἔσονται, ὁι γαρ βασιλεῖς, και ὁι μεγιστανες ἀυτης ἐσονται εἰς ἀπωλειαν. Και αναφυησει εἰς τας πολεις αυτων ακανθινα ξυλα, και εἰς τὰ ὀχυρωματα ἀυτης· και ἔσται επαυλεις σειρηνων, και αυλὴ στρουθῶν. Και συναντησουσι δαιμονια ονοκενταὺροις, και βοησονται ἔτερος προς τον ἔτερον, ἐκει ἀναπαυσονται ὀνοκενταυροι, ἔυροντες ἀυτοις ἀναπαυσιν. Ἐκει ἐνοσσευσεν ἐχῖνος, και ἔσωσεν ἡ γῆ τα παιδια ἀυτης μετα ἀσφαλείας· εκει συνηντησαν ἐλαφοι και ἔιδον τα πρόσωπα ἀλληλων. Ἀριθμῳ παρηλθον, και μια ἀυτων ουκ ἀπωλετο ἑτερα τῆν ἑτεραν ουκ ἐζήτησαν, ὅτι Κὺριος ἀυτοῖς ἐνετειλατο, και το Πνευμα ἀυτου συνηγαγεν ἀυτά. Και αυτος ἐπιβαλει ἀυτοις κλήρους, και ἡ χειρ ἀυτου διεμερισε βόσκεσθαι ἐις τόν ἀιῶνα χρόνον κληρονομησετε, γενεας γενεῶν ἀναπαυσονται επ᾽ ἀυτης.

made wet with their blood. And all the powers of the
heavens shall waste away, and the heavens shall be rolled
together as a scroll; and all the stars shall fall as the
leaves from the grape vine, and as the leaves that fall
from the fig tree. My sword hath been made drunk in
the heavens : behold it shall descend with judgment upon
the people of destruction. The sword of the Lord is
filled with blood; it is fattened with fatness from the
blood of goats and he-lambs, and from the fatness of he-
goats and rams. For it is the day of the judgment of
the Lord, the year of recompenses of the justice of Sion.
And the streams thereof shall be turned into pitch; and
the ground thereof into brimstone : and the soil thereof
shall be burning pitch night and day, and it shall never
be quenched; but the smoke thereof shall ascend for ever;
it shall be made desolate throughout her generations,
and for a long time. Birds and sea-urchins, the
ibis and the raven shall make their homes therein . and
the measuring line of desolation shall be stretched out
upon it · and wild monsters shall have their habitation in
its recesses. Its princes shall not be; its kings shall
cease : and its mighty men shall pass into destruction :
and thorns and nettles shall grow up in its cities and in
its strong fortresses : and there shall be the dwelling of
sirens, and the court of ostriches And demons shall
consort with monsters, and they shall howl one to another; there shall savage creatures live, and in it shall they
find a resting place. There shall the sea-urchin make her
hole, and the earth has safely preserved its young ones.
There the wild deer meet, and look upon each others'
faces. In their herds they pass along : and not one of
them shall perish they seek not after each other : for

3.

Ὁ ΘΕΟΣ ἐκ Θαιμὰν ἥξει, καὶ ὁ Ἅγιος ἐξ ὄρους Φαραν κατασκίου δασεος· διάψαλμα· ἐκάλυψεν οὐρανους ἡ ἀρετὴ αὐτοῦ, καὶ αἰνεσεως αὐτοῦ πλήρης ἡ γῆ. Καὶ φεγγος αὐτοῦ ὡς φῶς ἐσται· κερατα εκ χερσιν αὐτοῦ, καὶ ἔθετο ἀγάπησιν κραταιὰν ἰσχυος αὐτοῦ. Πρὸ προσώπου αὐτοῦ πορευσεται Λόγος, καὶ ἐξελευσεται εἰς πεδία κατα πόδας αὐτοῦ· Ἔστη, καὶ ἐσαλευθη ἡ γῆ, επέβλεψε καὶ διετάκη ἔθνη, διεθρυβη τὰ ὄρη βία, ἐτακησαν βουνοὶ αἰώνιοι πορείας αἰωνιας αὐτου· Αντὶ κόπων εἶδον σκηνώματα Ἀιθιόπων, πτοηθήσονται καὶ ἁι σκηναὶ γῆς Μαδιάμ· Μὴ ἐν ποταμοις ὠργίσθης Κύριε; ἤ ἐν ποταμοις ὁ θυμός σου; ἤ ἐν θαλάσσῃ τὸ ὁρμημα σου; ὅτι ἔπιβήσῃ ἐπὶ τους ἵππους σου, καὶ ἡ ἱππασια σου σωτηρία· Ἐντείνων ἐνέτεινας τόξον σοῦ ἐπι σκῆπτρα, λεγει Κυριος· διαψαλμα· ποταμων ραγησεται γῆ. Ὄψονται σε καὶ ὠδινησουσιλαοι. σκορπιζοντα ὑδατα πορείας, ἔδωκεν ἡ ἄβυσσος φωνὴν αὐτῆς ὕψος φαντασιας αὐτῆς· Ἐπήρθη ὁ ἥλιος, καὶ ἡ σεληνή ἔστη ἐν τῃ ταξει αὐτῆς· εἰς φῶς βολίδες σου πορευσονται, εἰς φέγγος ἀστραπῆς ὁπλων σου· Ἐν ἀπειλῃ ὀλιγώσεις γῆν, καὶ ἐν θυμῳ κάταξεις ἔθνη. Ἐξῆλθες εἰς σωτηρίαν λαοῦ σου, του σῶσαι τους ἔδωκας τὸν χριστὸν σου· βαλεῖς εἰς κεφαλας ἀνομων θάνατον, ἐξήγειρας δεσμους ἕως τραχηλου· διάψαλμα· Καὶ ἐπιβὰς εἰς θάλασσαν τους ἵππους σου, ταρασσοντας ὕδωρ πολυ.

the Lord hath given them a command, and his Spirit hath brought them together. And he himself casteth their lots for them, and his hand hath divided for them their pastures; inherit ye it for an everlasting time; it shall be theirs from generation to generation. (62.)

3. THE ADVENT OF THE FIRST CABIR PREDICTED.—God shall come from Thæman, and the Holy One from the dark shady Mount Pharan, Selah. His glory covered the heavens, and the earth was full of his praise. And his brightness was as the light; he had horns coming out of his hand; and he caused a mighty love of his strength. Before Him went the Word and it shall go forth in the plains on foot. The earth stood at his feet and trembled: he beheld, and drove asunder the nations; and the mountains were crushed to pieces; the perpetual hills were bowed down by the journies of his eternity. I saw the tents of Cushan in affliction; and the curtains of the land of Midian did tremble. Wert thou displeased against the rivers, O Lord? was thine anger against the rivers? was thy wrath against the sea, that thou didst ride upon thine horses, and thy chariots of salvation? Straining, thou didst stretch thy bow over sceptres, says the Lord. Pause! The land of rivers shall be torn asunder. The people shall see Thee, and they shall tremble; they shall see Thee scattering the waters of the way; the deep put forth its voice; the sublimity of her madness. The sun and the moon stood still in their habitation; into the light shall thine arrows go; into the brightness of the splendour of thine arms. Thou wilt bring low the land with threatening; and in wrath Thou wilt break down the nations. Thou didst go forth unto the salvation of thy people; for their salvation thou hast

4.

'ΕΠ' ὄρους πεδινοῦ ἄρατε σημεῖον, ὑψώσατε τὴν φωνὴν αὐτοῖς, παρακαλεῖτε τῇ χειρὶ, ἀνοίξατε οἱ ἄρχοντες· Ἐγὼ συντάσσω, καὶ ἐγὼ ἄγω αὐτοὺς· ἡγιασμένοι εἰσὶ, καὶ ἐγὼ ἄγω αὐτους· γίγαντες ἔρχονται πληρῶσαι τὸν θυμόν μου χαίροντες ἅμα καὶ ὑβρίζοντες· Φωνὴ ἐθνῶν πολλῶν ἐπὶ τῶν ὀρέων, ὁμοία ἐθνῶν πολλῶν, φωνὴ βασιλεων καὶ ἐθνῶν συνηγμενων. Κύριος Σαβαὼθ ἐντεταλται ἔθνει ὁπλομάχῳ ἔρχεσθαι ἐκ γῆς πόῤῥωθεν ἀπ' ἄκρου θεμελίου τοῦ οὐρανοῦ, Κύριος καὶ οἱ ὁπλομάχοι αὐτοῦ, καταφθεῖραι πᾶσαν τὴν οἰκουμενην· Ὀλολύζετε ἐγγὺς γαρ ἡμέρα Κυρίου, καὶ συντριβὴ παρὰ τοῦ Θεοῦ ἥξει· Δια τοῦτο πᾶσα χεὶρ ἐκλυθησεται, καὶ πᾶσα ψυχὴ ἀνθρώπου δειλιάσει· Ταραχθή-σονται οἱ πρέσβεις, καί ὠδῖνες αὐτους ἕξουσιν ὡς γυναικὸς τικτούσης, καὶ συμφορασουσιν ἕτερος πρὸς τον ἕτερον καὶ ἐκστήσονται, καὶ τὸ πρόσωπον αὐτων ὡς φλόξ μεταβαλοῦσιν· Ὃς γὰρ ἄν ἁλῷ ἡττηθήσεται, καὶ ὅιτινες συνηγμένοι εἰσὶ μαχαίρᾳ πεσοῦνται· καὶ τὰ τέκνα αὐτων ῥαξουσιν ἐνώπιον αὐτων, καὶ τὰς οἰκίας αὐτων προνομευσουσι· καὶ τὰς γυναῖκας αὐτων ἕξουσιν.

5.

ΠΩΣ; ἀναπεπαυται ὁ ἀπαιτων, καὶ ἀναπέπαυται ὁ ἐπισ-πουδαστὴς; Συνέτριψε Κύριος τόν ζυγὸν τῶν ἁμαρτωλῶν, τόν ζυγὸν τῶν ἀρχοντων· Πατάξας ἔθνος θύμῳ πληγῇ ἀνιάτῳ παίων ἔθνους πληγὴν θυμοῦ, ᾗ ὀυκ εφείσατο, ἀνεπαύ-σατο πεποιθώς. Πᾶσα ἡ γῆ βοᾷ μετ' εὐφροσύνης. Ὁ ᾅδης

given thine Anointed One. Thou didst strike death upon the heads of the lawless ; thou didst enchain them even to the neck. Thou didst make a way for thine horses over the sea, amid the boiling and disturbed waters. (63).

4. THE THREE CABIRI OF GOD.—Upon the mountains of the plain lift ye up a banner, exalt the voice to them ; beckon ye with the hand, and open ye, your gates, O Princes I give command, and I bring them ; they are my sanctified ones, and I lead them ; giants are coming to fulfil my wrath, rejoicing at the same time and insulting. The voice of many nations in the mountains, even as that of many nations ; a voice of kings and nations gathered together. The Lord of hosts hath given charge to the troops of war, to come from a land afar off, from the utmost foundation of the heaven ; the Lord and his warriors are coming to destroy all the world. Howl ye, for the day of the Lord is near ; and destruction from God shall arrive. Therefore shall all hands be faint; and every man's heart shall melt. The elders shall be troubled, and pangs shall seize them, as of a woman in labour ; and they shall mourn one to another, and shall be amazed, and shall change their countenance as a flame. Every one that shall be found shall be slain ; and they that are gathered together shall fall by the sword ; and they shall dash their children before their eyes ; and they shall spoil their houses, and take their wives (64.)

5. THE JUDGMENT UPON THE GREAT EARTH CONQUERORS. —How? hath the oppressor come to nothing? and hath the driver ceased? The Lord hath broken the yoke of the wicked, the yoke of the rulers. Having smitten a nation in wrath with an incurable wound, smiting a

κάτωθεν ἐπικράνθη συναντήσας σοι· συνηγέρθησάν ἀυτῳ
πάντες ὁι γίγαντες ὁι ἄρξαντες τῆς γῆς, ὁι ἐγείραντες ἐκ τῶν
θρόνων ἀυτῶν πάντας βασιλέῖς ἐθνῶν· πάντες ἀποκριθήσονται
καὶ ἐροῦσιν σοι· καὶ σὺ ἑαλως ὥσπερ καὶ ἡμεῖς, ἐν ἡμῖν δε
κατελογίσθης; Κατέβη εἰς ἅδου ἡ δόξα σου, ἡ πολλὴ
ἐυφροσυνη σου· ὑποκάτω σόυ στρώσουσιν σῆψιν, καὶ το
κατακάλυμμα σου σκωληξ. Πῶς; ἐξέπεσεν ἐκ τοῦ ὀυρανου
ὁ ἑωσφορος ὁ πρῶι ἀνατέλλων; συνετρίβη εἰς τὴν γῆν ὁ
ἀποστέλλων πρὸς πάντα τὰ ἔθνη· Σὺ δὲ εἶπας τῇ δίανοίᾳ
σου, εἰς τὸν ὀυρανον ἀναβήσομαι, ἐπάνω τῶν ἀστερων του
ὀυρανου θήσω τὸν θρόνον μου· Καθιῶ ἐν ὄρει ὑψηλῷ, ἐπί τὰ
ὄρη τὰ ὑψηλὰ τὰ πρὸς βορρᾶν, ἀναβήσομαι ἐπάνω τῶν νεφῶν,
ἔσομαι ὅμοιος τῷ ὑψίστῳ. Νῦν δε εἰς ᾅδην καταβήσῃ, καὶ
εἰς τὰ θεμέλια τῆς γῆς· Οἱ ἰδόντες σε θλυμάσονται ἐπί σοὶ,
καὶ ἐροῦσιν· ὁυτος ὁ ανθρωπος ὁ παροξύνων τήν γῆν, σείων
βασιλεῖς; ὁ θεὶς τὴν ὀικουμένην ὅλην ἔρημον, καὶ τὰς πόλεις
ἀυτου καθειλεν, τοὺς ἐν ἐπαγωγῇ ὀυκ ἔλυσεν. Πάντες ὁι
βασιλεῖς τῶν ἐθνῶν ἐκοιμήθησαν ἐν τιμῇ, ἄνθρωπος ἐν τῷ
ὀίκῳ ἀυτου· Σὺ δε ῥιφήσῃ ἐν τοῖς ὄρεσιν, ὡς νεκρος ἐβδελυγ-
μένος μετὰ πολλῶν τεθνηκότων ἐκκεκεντημένων μαχαίραις
καταβαινόντων εἰς ᾅδου· ὃν τρόπον ἱμάτιον ἐν ἅιματι
πεφυρμένον ὀυκ ἔσται καθαρὸν ὁύτως ὀυδε σὺ ἔσῃ καθαρός.
Διότι τήν γῆν μου ἀπώλεσας, καὶ τὸν λαόν μου ἀπέκτεινας,
ὀυ μὴ μείνῃς, εἰς τὸν ἀιῶνα χρόνον σπέρμα πονηρον·
Ἑτοίμασον τὰ τέκνα σου σφαγῆναι ταις ἁμαρτίαις του
πατρὸς ἀυτων, ἵνα μὴ ἀναστῶσι, καὶ κληρονομήσωσι τήν
γῆν, καὶ εμπλήσωσι τὴν γῆν πολέμων.

nation with a wrathful plague, which spared not, He
rested in quiet. All the earth cries aloud with joy.
Hades from beneath was in an uproar to meet thee at
thy coming. All the giants who have ruled over the
earth, have risen up together to thee; they who have
lifted up from their thrones all the kings of the nations.
All shall answer and say unto thee : Thou also hast been
taken even as we; thou art numbered amongst us. Thy
pride is brought down to Hades, and thy great mirth;
under thee they shall spread corruption, and the worm shall
be thy covering. How ? has *he* fallen from heaven, Lucifer
that rose in the morning ? He who did send forth unto
all the nations is crushed to the earth. For thou saidst
in thine heart, I will ascend to heaven : I will set my
throne above the stars of heaven. I will sit in the
exalted mountain, in the lofty mountains that be towards
the north. I will ascend above the clouds : I will be like
the Most High. But now thou shalt go down to Hades
and even unto the foundations of the earth. They that
see thee shall wonder at thee, and say, Is this the man
that troubled the earth ? that made kings to shake?
that made the world a wilderness, and destroyed its cities ?
that loosed not those who were in captivity ? All the
kings of the nations lie in honour, every one in his own
house. But thou shalt be cast forth on the mountains
as an abominable corpse, among many of the dead who
have been pierced with the sword, and have gone down
into Hades. In the same manner as a garment polluted
with gore is mere filthiness, even so art thou all unclean ;
because thou hast destroyed my land, and hast slain my
people, thou shalt not stand for ever, thou evil seed.
Prepare thy children to be slain for the sins of their

6.

ΟΥΑΓ 'Αριηλ· ἐκθλίψω γάρ 'Αριήλ· καὶ ἔσται αἰτῆς
ἡ ἰσχὺς καὶ ὁ πλοῦτος ἐμοί· καὶ κυκλώσω σὲ, καὶ βαλῶ
περὶ σὲ χάρακα, καὶ θήσω περὶ σὲ πύργους, καὶ ταπεινω-
θησονται ἐ᾽ς τὴν γῆν οἱ λόγοι σου, καὶ εἰς τὴν γῆν οἱ
λόγοι σου δύσονται καὶ ἔσονται ὡς οἱ φωνοῦντες ἐκ
τῆς γῆς ἡ φωνή σου, καὶ πρὸς τὸ ἔδαφος ἡ φωνή σου
ἀσθενήσει· Καὶ ἔσται ὡς κονιορτὸς ἀπὸ τροχοῦ ὁ
πλοῦτος τῶν ἀσεβῶν, καὶ ὡς χνοῦς φερόμενος τὸ πλῆθος
τῶν καταδυναστευόντων σε, καὶ ἔσται ὡς στιγμὴ παρα-
χρῆμα παρὰ Κυρίον Σαβαωθ· ἐπισκοπὴ γὰρ ἔσται
μέτα βροντῆς καὶ σεισμοῦ, καὶ φωνῆς μεγάλης καταιγίς
φερομένη, καὶ φλὶξ πυρὸς κατεσθίουσα· Καὶ ἔσται ὡς
ἐνυπνιαζόμενος καθ᾽ ὕπνους νυκτὸς, ὁ πλοῦτος ἁπαντων τῶν
ἐθνῶν, ὅσοι ἐπεστράτευσαν ἐπὶ 'Αριηλ, καὶ πάντες οἱ
συνηγμένοι ἐπ᾽ αἰτὴν, καὶ οἱ θλίβοντες ἀυτην. Καὶ ὡς οἱ
ἐν τῳ ὕπνῳ πίνοντες καὶ ἔσθοντες, καὶ ἐξαναστάντων μάταιον
τὸ ἐνύπνιον· καὶ ὃν τρόπον ἐνυπνιάζεται ὁ διψῶν ὡς πίνων,
καὶ ἐξαναστὰς ἔτι διψᾷ, ἡ δὲ ψυχὴ ἀυτου εἰς κενὸν ἤλπισεν·
ὅυτως ἔσται ὁ πλοῦτος τῶν ἔθνῶν πὰντων ὅσοι ἐπεστράτευσαν
ἐπὶ 'Αριηλ. Ἐκλύθητε καὶ ἔκστητε, καὶ κραιπαλήσατε οἱκ
ἀπὸ σίκερα ὁυδὲ ἀπὸ ὅινου, ὅτι πεπότικεν ὑμᾶς Κύριος πνεύματι κατανύξεως, και καμμύσει τοὺς ὀφθαλμοὺς ἀυτων, καὶ
τῶν προφητῶν ἀυτων, καὶ τῶν ἀρχοντων ἀυτων οἱ ὁρῶντες
τὰ κρυπτα· Καὶ ἔσται ὑμῖν τὰ ῥήματα πάντα ταῦτα, ὡς οἱ
λόγοι τὸυ βιβλίου τὸυ ἐσφραγισμένου τούτου, ὁ ἐὰν δῶσιν
ἀυτὸ ἀνθρωπῳ ἐπισταμένῳ γράμματα, λέγοντες. 'Αι άγνωθι
ταῦτα· καὶ ἐρεῖ, 'Ου δύναμαι ἀναγνῶναι, ἐσφράγισται γάρ.
Καὶ δοθήσεται τὸ βιβλίον τούτο εἰς χε῀ρας ἀνθρώπου μὴ
ἐπισταμένου γράμματα, καὶ ἐρεῖ ἀυτῳ· 'Ανάγνωθι τοῦτο· καὶ
ἐρεῖ· 'Ουκ ἐπίσταμαι γράμματα. Καὶ εἶπε Κύριος· 'Εγγίζει

father, that they arise not, and inherit the earth, nor fill
the earth with wars. (65.)

6. THE OVERTHROW OF THE CHINESE EMPIRE.—Woe
to Ariel: for I will distress Ariel, and its strength and
treasure shall be mine; and I will enclose thee in a
circle, and I will cast a trench round thee, and I will
raise towers about thee; and thy vauntings shall be
humbled to the dust, and unto the earth thy words shall
sink; and they shall be as the words of one who speaketh
out of the earth, and thy voice shall be lowered to the
ground. But the wealth of the ungodly shall be as dust
from a wheel; and the multitude of them who oppress
thee as flying chaff; and it shall be suddenly as a moment
from the Lord of Hosts; for there shall be a visitation
with thunder, and earthquake, and great outcries; a
tempest hurrying on, and the all-devouring flame of fire.
And the multitude of all the nations together who shall
pitch their tents against Ariel, and all who are leagued
together against it, and who join themselves so as to bring
affliction upon it, shall be as the dream of one who
dreameth in the night. And as they who in their sleep
drink and eat, and when they have arisen, their dream is
vain; and in the same way as a thirsty man dreams
as if he drank, but when he hath awakened he still thirsts,
and his soul hath hoped in vain; so shall be the multitude
of all the nations who have pitched their tents against
Ariel. Stay yourselves and wonder: stagger ye, but not
from strong drink, nor from wine; for the Lord hath
mingled for you the spirit of a profound sleep, and he will
shut up the eyes of them, and of their prophets, and of
their princes who see the hidden things. And all these
things shall be to you as the words of this Sealed Book;

E E

μοὶ ὁ λαὸς οὗτος ἐν τῳ στόματι ἀυτου, καὶ ἐν τοῖς χείλεσιν
ἀυτων τιμῶσι με, ἡ δὲ καρδία ἀυτων πόῤῥω ἀπέχει ἀπ᾽ ἐμοῦ·
μάτην δὲ σέβονταί με, διδάσκοντες ἐντάλματα ἀνθρωπων
καὶ διδασκαλίας. Διὰ τοῦτο ἰδοὺ προσθήσω τοῦ μεταθεῖναι
τόν λαὸν τοῦτον, καὶ μεταθήσω ἀυτους, καὶ ἀπολῶ τὴν σοφίαν
τῶν σοφῶν, καὶ τὴν σύνεσιν τῶν συνετων κρύψω· Ὀυαὶ ὁι
βαθέως βουλὴν ποιοῦντες, καὶ ου διὰ Κυρίου· ὀυαὶ ὁι ἐν
κρυφῇ βουλὴν ποιοῦντες, καὶ ἔσται ἐν σκότει τά ἔργα ἀυτων·
καὶ ἐροῦσι· Τίς ἑώρακεν ἡμᾶς; καὶ τίς ἡμᾶς γνώσεται ἤ ἅ
ἡμεῖς ποιουμεν ; Ὀυχ ὡς πηλὸς του κεραμέως λογισθησεσθε ;
μὴ ἐρεῖ τὸ πλάσμα τῳ πλάσαντι ἀυτό· Ὀυ σύ με ἐμπλασας ;
ἤ τὸ ποίημα τῳ ποιήσαντι, Ὀυ συνετῶς με ἐποίησας, Καὶ
ἀκουσονται ἐν τῇ ἡμέρα ἐκείνῃ κωφοὶ λόγους βιβλίου, καὶ
ὁι ἐν τῳ σκότει, καὶ ὁι ἐν τῇ ὁμίχλῃ· ὀφθαλμοὶ τυφλῶν
ὄψονται· καὶ ἀγλιασονται πτωχοὶ διὰ Κύριον ἐν ἐυφροσύ ͵η,
καὶ ὁι ἀπηλπισμένοι τῶν ἀνθρώπων ἐμπλησθήσονται
ἐυφροσύνης.

7.

ΟΥΤΩΣ λέγει Κύριος, ἰδοῦ τῳ ἐλεγμῳ μου ἐξερημώσω
την θάλασσαν, καὶ θησω ποταμοὺς ἐρήμους, καὶ ξηρανθή-
σονται ὁι ἰχθύες ἀυτων ἀπο του μὴ εἶναι ὕδωρ, καὶ
ἀποθανοῦνται ἐν δὶψει. Ἐνδύσω τον οὐρανὸν σκότος, καὶ ὡς
σάκκον θήσω τὸ περιβόλαιον αὐτου. Τις ἐν ὑμῖν ὁ
φοβουμενος τον Κύριον ; ὑπακουσάτω τὴς φωνῆς του,
παιδὸς αὐτου· ὁι πορευόμενοι ἐν σκότει, καὶ ὀυκ ἔστιν αὐτοῖς

which, if they shall give to a learned man, saying, Read this; he then shall say, I cannot read it, for it is sealed. And this same Book shall be delivered into the hands of a man who is not learned, and they shall say to him ; Read this : and he shall answer, I know not letters. Wherefore the Lord has said ; This people draw near to me with their mouth, and with their lips do give me praise, but their heart is far from me, and their worship is as nought, being founded on the commandments and teachings of men ; therefore will I proceed to remove this people, and I will remove them ; and I will destroy the wisdom of their sophists, and I will wrap up the understanding of their prudent men. Woe to them who devise deep counsels without the Lord ; woe to them who work their plots in secret ; and whose deeds are done in darkness. And they say, Who hath seen us, and who shall know us, or what we do ? Is it not as if the clay should cry out against the potter ? and the work exclaim against the maker thereof, Thou didst not make me ? or the thing framed should say to him who fashioned it, Thou hast not made me wisely ? And in that day the deaf shall hear the words of this Book ; and out of the darkness and out of obscurity the eyes of the blind shall see : and the meek shall increase their joy in the Lord ; and the hopeless among men shall be filled with gladness. (66.)

7. Before the Final Apocastasis of the Earth.—Thus saith the Lord : Behold at my rebuke, I will make the sea a desert; and I will change the rivers into a wilderness, and the fishes shall rot for want of water, and they shall perish in their thirst. I will cloathe the heaven with darkness, and I will make its covering like sackcloth. Who is there among you that feareth the

φῶς, πεποίθατε ἐπι τῳ ὀνόματι Κυρίου, καὶ ἀντιστηρίσασθε
ἐπὶ τῳ θεῳ. Ἰδου πάντες ὑμεῖς πῦρ καίετε, καὶ κατισχύετε
φλόγα· πορευεσθε τῳ φωτι τοῦ πυρὸς ὑμῶν, καὶ τῇ φλογὶ ᾗ
ἐξεκαύσατε δι ἐμὲ εγενετο ταῦτα ὑμῖν, ἐν λύπῃ κοιμαθησεσθε.
Ἐγγιζει ταχὺ ἡ δικαιοσυνη μου, καὶ ἐξελευσεται ὡς φῶς τὸ
σωτηριον μου, καὶ εἰς τον βραχείονα μου ἔθνη ἐλπιόυσιν·
ἐμὲ νῆσοι ὑπομενοῦσιν, καί εἰς τον βραχείονα μου ἐλπιοῦσιν.
Ἄρατε εἰς τον οιρανον τους ὀφθαλμοῦς ὑμῶν, καὶ ἐμβλέψατε
ἐις τήν γῆν κάτω. ὅτι ὁ ὀυράνὸς ὡς καπνος ἐστερεωθη, ἡ δε
γῆ ὡς ἱμάτιον παλαιωθήσεται, οἱ δε κατοικουντες ὥσπερ
ταῦτα ἀποθανουνται, το δέ σωτήριόν μου ἐ᾽ς τον αἰωνα
ἔσται, ἡ δε δικαιοσύνη μου ὀυ μὴ ἐκλείπῃ. Πορεύετε ἄγγελοι
κοῦφοι πρὸς ἔθνος μετέωρον, καὶ ξένον λαὸν καὶ χαλεπόν·
τίς ἀυτοῦ ἐπέκεινα; ἔθνος ἀνέλπιστον καὶ καταπεπατημενον
νυν ὁι ποταμοὶ τῆς γῆς. Πάντες, ὡς χώρα κατοικουμενη,
κατοικηθήσεται ἡ χώρα ἄυτων ὡσεὶ σημείον ἀπὸ ὅρους ἀρθῇ,
ὡς σάλπιγγος φωνὴ ἀκουστὸν ἔσται. Διότι ὅυτως εἶπε
Κύριός μοι. Ἀσφάλεια ἔσται ἐν τῇ ἐμῇ πόλει, ὡς φῶς
καῦματος μεσημβρίας, καὶ ὡς νεφέλη δρόσου ἡμέρας ἀμητοῦ
ἔσται πρὸ τοῦ θερισμοῦ ὅταν συντελεσθῇ ἄνθος, καὶ ὄμφαξ
ἐξανθήσῃ ἄνθος ομφακίζουσα· καὶ ἀφελει τὰ βοτρυδια τὰ
μικρὰ τοῖς δρεπάνοις, καὶ τὰς κληματίδας ἀφελει, καὶ
ἀποκόψει.

Lord ? let him hearken to the voice of his Son : ye who walk in darkness, and unto whom there is no light; trust ye in the name of the Lord, and turn yourselves unto God. Behold all ye who kindle a fire, and prevail with flame; walk ye in the light of your fire, and in the flame which ye have kindled : this ye shall have of me, that ye shall lie down in sorrow. My righteousness is near at hand, and as light my salvation shall go forth, and in mine arm shall the nations hope ; the islands shall wait upon me, and in my arm shall their trust be placed. Lift up your eyes to heaven, and cast them down upon the earth beneath, for the heaven shall fade away like smoke, and the earth shall wax old as a garment, and they that dwell therein shall die in like manner, but my salvation shall be for ever, and my justice shall not fail. Go ye swift messengers to a nation rent and torn in pieces, to a strange and harsh people. For thus saith the Lord to me. For there shall be security in my city, even as the noon-light is clear, and it shall be as a cloud of dew in the day of harvest. Before the reaping-time, when the flower has been completely formed, and the unripe grape has put forth its flower and blossomed, then shall he take away the little clusters with pruning hooks, and shall take away the small branches and cut them off. (67)

PSALM OF ADAM.

It is a good thing to give thanks unto Ya-voh,*

And to sing praises unto thy name, O Eli-oun,†

To proclaim thine abundant mercy in the morning,

And thy faithful loving-kindness in the night.

Upon the aser, upon the nebel,

Upon the higgayon, and sweet kinnōr.

For thou, O Lord, hast made me glad through thy creations;

I rejoice in the works of thine hands.

How mighty are thy works, O Lord!

And thy thoughts—they are very deep.

A brutish man will not know,

And a senseless man will not understand this:

When the wicked spring as the grass,

And when all the workers of iniquity do flourish,

It is that they shall be destroyed for ever.

But thou, O Lord! art most high for evermore:

For, behold! thine enemies shall perish

All the workers of iniquity shall be scattered

But my horn shalt thou exalt like the reeym:

I shall be anointed with fresh oil;

The righteous shall flourish as the phœnix.

Those that be planted in the House of the Lord

Shall blossom in the courts of our God.

They shall bring forth fruit in a fine old age,

They shall prosper and flourish,

To show that the Lord is just.

He is my rock,

And there is no unrighteousness in Him. (68)

* Ieue, the Lord A O.　　　　† The Most High.

THE PSALM OF ADAM AND EVA.

He.

O Lord my God, Adonai,
Have mercy on me, in thy great mercifulness,
Because thy love and pity are abounding.
Hearken unto me, all ye heavens,
And ye, O children of heaven, hear my voice—
Let the Angels report all I think and say;
Let the Celestial Powers repeat them;
Let God himself open out his ears,
To this, my prayer.
O my God, thou art very bright,
True light, and splendour the most glorious;
All other things are mixed with darkness;
Thou art as a Sun which sets not;
Inhabiting light inaccessible;
Thou art the goal and end of all;
Thou art the only happiness of the Blessed.

She.

O Lord, my God, Adonai,
Have mercy on me in thine abounding mercy;
Great indeed is thy mercifulness,
And thy compassion hath no limit.
Before all other things thou didst form the heavens,
Thy pure, sublime, immoveable habitation,
Thou didst beautify it with Angel-Spirits;
Thou didst make manifest all that thou didst make.
In it were the Morning Stars,
Which praised thee for so many ages,
Thou didst make the moveable heavens also,
And didst name the waters that be above the heavens.

All things obey thine ordinance,
And by their own motion are other heavens moved ;
And the waters that be under the immoveable heaven.
But above all other things that are moved,
Thou didst create the Light—the Sun :
Thou didst form the Moon and fine planets ;
And didst set the firmament around them ;
In which thou didst collect the constellations,
And the beauty of the powerful stars.
Thou didst give forth the four elements,
And thou didst animate all things from them by thy
      wisdom.

Both.

The Lord is my shepherd ; I shall not want,
He maketh me to lie down in green pastures ;
He leadeth me beside the still waters ;
He restoreth, he makes strong my soul :
He goeth with me in the way of righteousness,
Yea, though I walk through the valley of the shadow of
      death,
I will fear no evil,
For thou art with me ;
Thy rod and thy staff do comfort me ;
Thy mercy shall follow me all my days :
I will abide in thine house for ever.

NOTES TO APOCALYPSE.

Note 1 (page 503).—This is the sentiment, though not the actual form of the ancient Greek oracle, quoted by Pausanias, *lib.* x, c. 12. Ζεὺς ἦν, Ζεὺς ἔστι, Ζεὺς ἔσσεται. ὦ μεγάλε Ζεν. Zeus was, Zeus is, Zeus will be. O mighty Zeus! In commemoration of this Revelation to the Seven Churches, a most majestic temple was built at Maha-Bali-poor-aum, or the City of the Great God Bel, about 38 miles south of Madras. This was called the Seven Pagodas. It was destroyed in the great Atlantean Deluge. *As. Res* v.

Note 2 (page 503)—All Greek words ending in these two vowels have a mystic reference to the Holy Spirit, Β-αω, I proceed from : Γ-αω, I am born, I come forth ; I bring forth ; Ζ-αω, I live : Κ-αω, I kindle : Ν-σω, I flow : Τ-αω, I extend : Φ-αω, I shine fo th ; I declare, &c. To this word also may be referred αει, always ; and A-IO, I say. In the missionary accounts of the South Sea Islands, Tao means the dearest and most intimate friend, analogous to the AO. of the Etruscans, *ante* page 199. In Mexico Tao-Calli, is the House of God. The word שׁדַי [Shadai] in the title page to this Volume, is a noun, plural in regimen, and has also a dual termination. It means the Two Powers—God and the Holy Spirit ; but it more particularly alludes to the latter ; its roots having an affinity to words that mean wine pouring or wine-bestowing ; a productive field that yields abundant nutriment, symbolically the All-Bountiful , a breast that pours forth milk (hence Mamma) ; the Genial Powers of Nature, the *Multimammiæ*, or many bosomed, like Egyptian Isis and Ephesian Diana ; on which Montfaucon observes, " all the learned agree that all these (*i.e.*, the various symbols which accompany the goddess) signify nature, or the Kosmos with all its productions"—in other words, the Holy Spirit. The English word to *shed* comes from this root She is the Power who sheds fruitfulness and beauty over all things.

Note 3 (page 509)—In the ancient Egyptian theology, Osiris, as we are told by Diodorus, and Horus-Apollo, meant πολυοφ-θαλμος, or *many eyed*. Jablonski's Lexicon gives a derivation of the word Osiris, which he deduces from Osh-Iri, that is, He who makes time. Osiris holds in one hand a key with a circular handle; this is the *crux ansata*. On the obelisk at San the *crux ansata*, or sacred T, with the circle attached to the top, is suspended from the middle part of the Serpent. The same key mystically alludes to the key with which the Twelfth Messenger opens and reveals all the secrets hitherto undisclosed.

Note 4 (page 511).—Those were the 24 Boodhoos, or Patri-Archas (images of the All), who preached in succession the religion of Boodh (Wisdom), anterior to the coming of the First Messiah. They are called in the East, Maha Bads and Solymi.

Note 5 (page 525).—This was Adim Oannes, the First of the Twelve Holy Messengers or Messiahs of God.

Note 6 (page 525).—Enoch, Enosh, or Anûsh, the Second Messiah. The ancient Irish had a god whom they called Aonach, Eoghna, and Ao-Anu, or the second Ith . this was Enoch: it is interpreted *Fire from AO:* God and the Spirit.

Note 7 (page 527).—Fo-hi, the Third Messiah.

Note 8 (page 527).—The submersion of the vast continent Atlantis, which is predicted in the first of the Seven Thunders.

Note 9 (page 527).—Brigoo, the Fourth Messiah.

Note 10 (page 531).—Zaratusht, the Fifth Messiah.

Note 11 (page 533).—Thoth, the Sixth Messiah.

Note 12 (page 537).—So, in the best MSS.

Note 13 (page 537).—Amosis, the Seventh Messiah.

Note 14 (page 543).—Jesus, knowing that this prophecy applied to him, said · *I am the Light of the World.*

Note 15 (page 543).—Lao-Tseu and Jesus.

Note 16 (page 545).—This means an indefinite period. It *may* allude to the double Naros in which they would appear.

Note 17 (page 545).—Their humble condition is indicated.

Note 18 (page 545).—Jesus, again alluding to this prophecy, said : *I am come to send fire on the earth*, LUKE xii 49 The same allusion is in JER. v. 14 : *Because ye speak this word, Behold I will make my words in thy mouth fire, and this people wood, and it shall devour them.*

Note 19 (page 545).—*And I will give unto thee 'the keys of the kingdom of heaven ; and whatsoever thou shalt bind on earth shall be bound in heaven , and whatsoever thou shalt loose on earth shall be loosed in heaven,* MATT. xvi. 19. The key is always an indication of Messiahship : so the Twelfth Messenger brings the key that opens all secrets. The Hand of Might and the Key of '

Knowledge are carved in the Alhambra; but none of the explorers ever knew that both alluded to the Apocalyptic mysteries.

Note 20 (page 545).—*Think not that I am come to send peace on earth: I came not to send peace, but a sword*, MATT. x. 34. The Messengers may if they think it necessary, change even water into blood, that is, use the sword, and baptize in it, in place of peace and gentleness.

Note 21 (page 545).—This is the true translation. it is an astonishing prediction of the death of Jesus. The peculiar language of the Greek text intimates that Lao-Tseu and Jesus were really one and the same order of spirit.

Note 22 (page 545).—After death the animating principle is in torpor for three days, when it arises again into full existence. This interval is called by the Arabs *al Bezzakh.* It is alluded to by the Jewish priest, *Hosea* vi 2 *After two days will He revive us · in the third day He will raise us up, and we shall live in his sight.* Like all the other sublime but subtle mysteries of the heavenly ordinances as connected with man, it is wholly unknown in Western theology, as administered by the priests; and it is connected by them with the fable of the resurrection of Jesus with which it has nothing to do If Jesus were God, it is clear he could not die: if he were a man, it is equally certain he could not live as a man after death. Another of those legends, the flight into Egypt, is thus alluded to by an ancient anti Paulite. What occasion, says Celsus, was there, while you [Jesus] were yet an infant, that you should be brought to Egypt in order that you might not be slain? For it was not fit that a god should be afraid of death. But an angel came from heaven, ordering you and your associates to fly, lest being taken you should be put to death. For the Great God (it seems) could not preserve you, his own son, in your own country, but sent two angels on your account. Here, it may be asked: In what gospel did Celsus find this story of the two angels?

Note 23 (page 545).—The change of tense here vividly images the sudden rising again of these Divine Ones. It is an oriental idiom

Note 24 (page 545).—In this originated the legend of a bodily ascension into heaven, which all but Paulites know to be impossible. The splendid-shining Cloud that enwrapped their ascending spirits was the Spirit of God

Note 25 (page 549)—Ahmed, or Mo'Ahmed, *i e.*, the *Illustrious*, the Desired of all nations, the Tenth Messiah.

Note 26 (page 553).—A wolf was a sacred symbol, and meant Light, *ante*, page 107. Isis, appears in ancient carvings with a wolf's head—that is, crowned with the Sun, for the Wolf was emblematic thereof. Romulus was divinely fed by a Wolf. There is a mystic meaning therefore in the text.

Note 27 (page 553).—The Great Harlot is a personification of idolatry, which Mo-Ahmed did more to destroy than any other of the Messengers.

Note 28 (page 555).—Chengiz-Khan, the Eleventh Messiah.

Note 29 (page 555).—This is the Naros, which no one but the Messiah, and his initiated ones, ever knew in its mystic meaning until now.

Note 30 (page 557).—Timûr.

. Note 31 (page 557).—This preludes the discovery of the great American Continent, and the consequent butchery of its peoples.

Note 32 (page 559).—Nadir Shah is here symbolized.

Note 33 (page 559).—The French Empire.

Note 34 (page 563).—Alludes to the transitory nature of all sin and the pleasure which it affords—it was, yet is not.

Note 35 (page 567).—The fine artistic manufactures of Ba-Bel-On, and of Saturnian Hesperia, or Italy at a later period, are here distinctly alluded to.

Note 36 (page 569).—England.

Note 37 (page 571).—The Paulites in effect worship the Dragon. Every *word* of this prophecy applies with singular felicity to England and her characteristics.

Note 38 (page 571).—1260 days—an indefinite period.

Note 39 (page 571).—The American empire, whose beginning was very humble: the two horns are North and South. It professes to be religious, but is in reality the servant of Evil, its bragging insolence is well shown by the text, *He spake as a dragon.*

Note 40 (page 571).—It will eventually succeed to the influence which England now has. In the exhaustion of her minerals, England's weakness will be shown.

Note 41 (page 573).—Spirit-rapping and other blasphemous wonders

Note 42 (page 573)—The American empire will in every way imitate the mother from which she sprang; and after it is dead she will re-vivify, as it were, its image on the earth, in cruelty, spoliation, selfishness, and superstition.

Note 43 (page 573).—Those who did not in all respects conform to her crimes she slew, or persecuted, or proscribed.

Note 44 (page 573).—She used the right hand (force) and the forehead (intellect) to uphold her wicked power; and in those two bare the unmistakeable mark of the mother from which she sprang. Observe the Beast always leaves its mark upon its followers. To buy and sell, that is to make money by any and every kind of traffic, seemed the main object of her existence. Money was her God. She worshipped the dollar, and called it the Almighty. If this be not the indubitable mark of the Beast, I know not what is.

Note 45 (page 573).—This is the primeval name of the Americas.

Note 46 (page 575).—The Twelfth Messiah.

Note 47 (page 575).—Not the name of Jesus, or any of the Messengers. but the name of the One God, the Father, who alone is to be adored.

Note 48 (page 575).—A new Revelation, that of the Twelfth Messenger.

Note 49 (page 575).—The word in the text is πορθενοι— the masculine form. The word signifies male-virgins, and is deeply mystic. It has puzzled all the commentators, particularly the married ones, who think that if the words are literally taken, *they* must be excluded from heaven.

Note 50 (page 577).—Here is a positive declaration that God and his Sacred Spirit are distinct existences.

Note 51 (page 577).—This is a Messenger of Truth, who shall preach the Word revealed by the Twelfth Messiah.

Note 52 (page 577).—The Book of God, collected into one Volume, and free from all human corruptions. the sacred revelations of the Twelve.

Note 53 (page 579).—These are four Conquerors, who are yet to come.

Note 54 (page 583).—There are in all Seven Messianic Angels from the appearance of the day of the Twelfth Messenger, not including him who sate upon the Cloud. A long interval of time necessarily elapses in the intervals of the appearances of these Angels.

Note 55 (page 585).—This does not mean absolutely killed, but all who sacrifice their worldly prospects for the sake of God and his Holy Truth, are likened to martyrs who are slain.

Note 56 (page 593).—This indicates another long interval before the dissolution of the Kalpa.

Note 57 (page 597).—The Children of Heaven who are on the earth, must expect to meet with trials, persecutions, and afflictions ; but in the end they shall overcome, their enemies and be crowned in Paradise by their Lord and Father.

Note 58 (page 599).—This is the same Holy Spirit who appeared at first. I have shown that She is the same as Isis, the tutelary Goddess of the Egyptians. This is Io, the Virgin-Spouse of Zeus—the Holy Spirit—the loved One of God. Isis, says Plutarch, is the Feminine part of Nature, and the recipient (or Shekinah) of all generation ; accordingly she is called by Plato the Nurse and Receiver of all things ; and by many others Myrionomos, that is, having an infinity of names. In her is implanted a love of the First and Principal, or God, the Good · him she desires and pursues.

Note 59 (page 599).—Each of the Incarnations comes before the Ancient of Days to demand his own followers, so as to lead them into that Star-Paradise, which he had prepared for them.

Note 60 (page 601).—In commemoration of this the Hebrew priests had written on their foreheads, *Holiness to the Lord.*

Note 61 (page 613).—These Seven Thunders were graven on brass, and kept in brazen caskets—hence they were called the Seven Brazen Pillars of Cham (See *ante*, p. 312.)

Note 62 (page 619)—In this prediction is wonderfully shown the confusion which should prevail after the submersion of Atlantis The sandy deserts which now exist were before that time covered with inland seas or lakes, which all flowed down over that unhappy continent.

Note 63 (page 621).—In this prediction God specially appears with his Holy One (the Sacred Spirit, bearing with her the first Cabir) who came as the Judge to execute judgment upon the evil.

Note 64 (page 621).—The Three Cabiric Messengers are predicted in this prophecy.

Note 65 (page 625)—Cyrus, Cæsar, Attila, Aureng-Zebe, Napoleon, and such odious man-slayers, who for their own selfishness, massacre and pillage the sons of men, are here spoken of.

Note 66 (page 627).—The fall of the Chinese empire, the greatest the world has yet seen, is here predicted. Its magnitude and importance seemed to require a special prediction.

Note 67 (page 629). The transformation of the earth of man is here foreshown. The whole human race will perish ; and there will be a new creation of creatures of a higher order.

Note 68 (page 630).—Rabbi Levi said, *Adam composed this psalm, and they who came after him forgot it. Amosis came and renewed it in the name of Adam.* I have removed a manifest interpolation.

INDEX.

Ab, Abba, a name of God, 18;
Note upon, 95; anagramma-
tically BA and DI, BAD,
BUD, or Holy Father.
Hence Abad.
Abondana Rabbi, cited 72.
Abraham, see Ibrahim.
Acts of the Apostles, cited 63,
99
Actæon, a symbol of Messiah,
99.
Ad-Ad, note upon, 97.
Adah, 97.
Adam, the name in Hindostan,
327; Tract on, cited in Notes,
468
Adam's riddle, 321.
Adam Kadmon, 263.
Adam-Oannes, wrote the Apo-
calypse, 233; tradition of the
Arabs, 240, 242; Books found
in his chest, 243, vestiges of
the name, 262, 265; his Vision
mentioned in Genesis, 269;
Berosus alludes to, 292.
Adamas Gemma, 265.
Ælian on an Apocalyptic Book,
244.
Æsar, a divine name, 44, 114.
Ag, the radical explained, 107.
Ahmed and Mo'Ahmed, 37, 93,
260; predicted by Haggai,
261
Ain, the radical, explained, 98,
188, 190.
Al, the radical, explained, 96.
Alexander the Great why he
destroyed Chehûl Minar, 306

Aleim, absurdly defined by Parkhurst, 96.
Al-Ham Bra, a mystic word,
188.
Allegorical nature of the O T.,
238.
Alm, explained 10, it is akin
to Ailm, i.e, the First.
Almas-Cherk, the Talisman of
Fate, a name for the Apoca-
lypse, 307.
Ambrose, St., his excuse for
concubinage, 449.
American community of murderers, 426; Indian idea of
final dissolution, 153.
Amosis, one of the Twelve, 59;
called Osarsiph, 68, 98; pre-
dicts a successor, 93; legend
of, 274, His law lost, 364.
Ancients, the Twenty-Four, 51.
Anna Perenna, 98.
Antiochus Epiphanes, 106; on-
slaught on the Jews and their
books, 406.
Ao, T'Ao, Io, On Ao, 10, 14; a
Rock, 16, 35, 99.
Aph, the radical, explained,
178.
Apocalypse, the ritual of the
Mysteries, 107; proved to be
primeval by internal evidence,
187; doubted by various
authors to be the work of
John, 216, used by the Gnostics, 241; names by which it
was symbolized, 248, 253,
256, 273, 276, 297, 307, 312;

B. AND J. DRAWN, PRINTERS, 13, PRINCES STREET, LITTLE QUEEN STREET, HOLBORN, W C.